BUILDING MODERN CRIMINOLOGY

PIONEERS IN CONTEMPORARY CRIMINOLOGY

Series Editor: David Nelken

The titles in this series bring together the best published and unpublished work by the leading authorities in contemporary criminological theory. By drawing together articles from a wide range of journals, conference proceedings and books, each title makes readily available the authors' most important writings on specific themes. Each volume in this series includes a lengthy introduction, written by the editor and a significant piece of scholarship in its own right, which outlines the context of the work and comments on its significance and potential. The collected essays complement each other to give a retrospective view of the authors' achievements and a picture of the development of criminology as a whole.

Titles in the series

A Criminological Imagination
Pat Carlen

Working Out of Crime
David Downes

Building Modern Criminology: Forays and Skirmishes
David F. Greenberg

Breaking Criminological Convention: Selected Essays of Richard Ericson
Kevin D. Haggerty, Aaron Doyle and Janet Chan

Victims, Policy-making and Criminological Theory
Paul Rock

Essays on Transnational Crime and Policing
James Sheptycki

Thinking about Punishment
Michael Tonry

Building Modern Criminology

Forays and Skirmishes

DAVID F. GREENBERG
New York University, USA

PIONEERS IN CONTEMPORARY CRIMINOLOGY SERIES

Routledge
Taylor & Francis Group
LONDON AND NEW YORK

First published 2010 by Ashgate Publishing

2 Park Square, Milton Park, Abingdon, Oxfordshire OX14 4RN
711 Third Avenue, New York, NY 10017

Routledge is an imprint of the Taylor & Francis Group, an informa business

First issued in paperback 2018

British Library Cataloguing in Publication Data
Building modern criminology : forays and skirmishes. –
(Pioneers in contemporary criminology)
1. Criminology.
I. Series II. Greenberg, David F.
364-dc22

US Library of Congress Cataloging-in-Publication Data
Greenberg, David F.
Building modern criminology : forays and skirmishes / [written and] edited by David Greenberg.
p. cm. – (Pioneers in contemporary criminology)
Includes index.
ISBN 978-0-7546-2874-3 (hbk.)
1. Criminology. I. Title.
HV6025.G724 2010
364–dc22

2010018682

ISBN 978-0-7546-2874-3 (hbk)
ISBN 978-1-138-37854-4 (pbk)

Contents

Acknowledgements

The chapters in this volume are taken from the sources listed below. The editor and publishers wish to thank the authors, original publishers or other copyright holders for permission to use their material as follows:

Chapter 1: 'Delinquency and the Age Structure of Society', *Contemporary Crises*, **1**, 1977, pp. 189–223. Copyright © 1977 Elsevier Scientific Publishing Company.

Chapter 2: 'The Gendering of Crime in Marxist Theory', in David F. Greenberg (ed.), *Crime and Capitalism: Readings in Marxist Criminology*, Philadelphia: Temple University Press, 1993, pp. 405–42. Copyright © 1993 by Temple University.

Chapter 3: 'Time Series Analysis of Crime Rates', *Journal of Quantitative Criminology*, **17**, 2001, pp. 291–327. Copyright © 2001 Plenum Publishing Corporation.

Chapter 4: 'Long-Term Trends in Crimes of Violence', *Criminology*, **41**, 2003, pp. 1407–18. Copyright © 2003 by the American Society of Criminology.

Chapter 5: 'Modeling Criminal Careers', *Criminology*, **29**, 1991, pp. 17–46. Copyright © 1991 by the American Society of Criminology.

Chapter 6: 'The Effect of Arrests on Crime: A Multivariate Panel Analysis', *Social Forces*, **60**, 1982, pp. 771–90. Copyright © 1982 The University of North Carolina Press.

Chapter 7: 'The Incapacitative Effect of Imprisonment: Some Estimates', *Law and Society Review*, **9**, 1975, pp. 541–80. Copyright © 1975 The Law and Society Association.

Chapter 8: 'The Dialectics of Crime Control', with Drew Humphries in David F. Greenberg (ed.), *Crime and Capitalism: Readings in Marxist Criminology*, Philadelphia: Temple University Press, 1993, pp. 463–508. Copyright © 1993 by Temple University.

Chapter 9: 'The Dynamics of Oscillatory Punishment Processes', *The Journal of Criminal Law and Criminology*, **68**, 1977, pp. 643–51. Copyright © 1977 by Northwestern University School of Law.

Chapter 10: 'The Prison as a Lawless Agency', with Fay Stender, *Buffalo Law Review*, **21**, 1972, pp. 799–838. Copyright © 1972 by Buffalo Law Review.

Chapter 11: 'Punishment, Division of Labor, and Social Solidarity', in William S. Laufer and Freda Adler (eds), *The Criminology of Criminal Law*, New Brunswick and London: Transaction Publishers, 1999, pp. 283–361. Copyright © 1999 by Transaction Publishers , New Brunswick, New Jersey.

Chapter 12: 'State Prison Populations and their Growth, 1971–1991', with Valerie West, *Criminology*, **39**, 2001, pp. 615–54. Copyright © 2001 by the American Society of Criminology.

Chapter 13: 'Siting the Death Penalty Internationally', with Valerie West, *Law and Social Inquiry*, **33**, 2008, pp. 295–343. Copyright © 2008 American Bar Foundation.

Every effort has been made to trace all the copyright holders, but if any have been inadvertently overlooked the publishers will be pleased to make the necessary arrangement at the first opportunity.

"Hoc es corpus meum"

– Jesus of Nazareth, Matthew 26:26, Mark 14:22, Luke 22:19, 1 Cor. 11:24

"Criminological research is not for putting people to sleep; it is for waking them up."

– paraphrase of a quotation from Rabbi Nachman of Bratislava

"I have been a stranger in a strange land."

– Exodus 2:22

Introduction

Of crime and of a man I sing. Here, O Muse, is how the story about a man of many turns began. I grew up in the shadow of Wrigley Field in Chicago, and became a Cubs fan at an early age. It was by no means the last time I was to embrace a losing cause. It was there that I became a pre-adolescent-limited thief[1] who shoplifted candy from the local pharmacy, and quickly escalated to other forms of theft. Somehow the police learned of some of these activities, and came after me. I will never forget the surprised look on my third-grade teacher's face when a messenger came to my class to say that the police were in the principal's office to question me about a burglary.

Fortunately, I had an air-tight alibi for the burglary. However, the short time spent in a holding cell at the police station was enough to scare me straight – for a time. I relapsed during the Vietnam War, when, frustrated by President Lyndon Johnson's failure to stop the American war on Vietnam in the face of widespread opposition, I became a founding member of CADRE (Chicago Area Draft Resisters). Inspired by the French Resistance, the Indian Independence and US civil rights movements, CADRE was devoted to stopping US war crimes in South-East Asia by ending the war through open non-violent refusal of cooperation with military recruitment, including conscription. On October 16, 1967 I was one of more than 1,200 draft-age men throughout the country who handed in their draft cards, giving up all deferments and exemptions and placing themselves in jeopardy of a five-year federal prison sentence for non-possession of a draft card.

This was by no means my first attempt to bring about social change. While in college I was an active member of the University of Chicago chapter of CORE (Congress of Racial Equality), and did civil rights work in the US South, as well as in Chicago. After I became a criminologist, the exposure I had to police and court practices while active in the civil rights and anti-war movements made me receptive to the critical currents roiling the field of criminology in the 1970s. I didn't need to read the radical criminologists who were making an appearance on the criminological scene to learn that law enforcement could be used as a weapon in political conflict, because my associates and I had already experienced or witnessed it.

In anticipation of a prison sentence for refusing to aid and abet the murderers in the Pentagon and State Department, I began reading about courts and prisons so that I would know

1 Terry Moffitt (1993) has proposed that offenders have criminal career trajectories that permit them to be classified as either 'adolescent-limited' or 'life-course persistent' offenders. Offenders in the former category largely restrict their illegal activities to the teen-age years, while those in the latter category do not abandon their illegal activities as they get older. This typology has been the subject of much research. Most of this work finds evidence for more than two classes of criminal careers. My brief career in theft came too early for me to fit into either category.

what to expect. As it happened, I was never prosecuted. The Justice Department prosecuted only cases referred to it by the local draft board, and mine never referred me. I believe I was protected by my high school science and math teachers, both of whom served on the board. I was their pride and joy for getting a PhD in physics from the University of Chicago. Many of my fellow draft resisters, however, were prosecuted. Visiting and corresponding with them while they were serving prison sentences added to my knowledge of, and curiosity about, the penal system. I even co-edited with Beverly Houghton a book of prison writings authored by war resisters – but was unable to get it published. Every publisher we contacted thought the war would end before the book came out, reducing sales. In fact the war was to continue for a number of years.

When my post-doctoral fellowship in the Carnegie-Mellon University Physics Department ended, a collapsing job market in physics, combined with political discrimination, made it impossible for me to find a physics job, even though I'd published a co-authored book and a dozen journal articles in theoretical physics. Leonard Rapping, an economist who studied with Milton Friedman and worked at the Rand Corporation before going to CMU, encouraged me to apply for admission to the CMU PhD program in Economics. I had been team-teaching an undergraduate course in radical social, political and economic theory with Rapping and two historians, Daniel Resnick and Paul Garver. Recognizing that I already knew a good deal of economics, the Department waived all course requirements. I was to take a qualifying exam and write a dissertation while being supported on Rapping's grant. After I was admitted, however, CMU revoked the admission on the grounds that I had applied after the deadline. I had, in fact, applied after the deadline, but that hadn't stopped the University from admitting me in the first place. I was told informally that a wealthy donor had threatened to withhold a very large contribution to the University if I were allowed into the PhD program. I had caught the eye of the donor through my authorship of a pamphlet about the influence the old Pittsburgh wealth had on the university through membership on the Board of Trustees, and my role in organizing a disruption of the Gulf Oil Company's stockholder's meeting.

The radical historian Staughton Lynd – a fellow draft resister – came to my aid by helping me obtain a job teaching in the Social Science Department at Columbia College. While teaching four courses a semester as a part-time adjunct instructor and working with a prisoner-support group I had founded, I wrote the first draft of the book *Struggle for Justice* under the sponsorship of the American Friends Service Committee. With young Quakers going to prison for draft law violations, the AFSC felt called to do more about courts and prisons than opening a new half-way house every five years. In response to this call, it assembled a Working Party to provide guidance for a new AFSC prison initiative. *Struggle for Justice* broke with the dominant liberal treatment ideology and argued that the exercise of unreviewed and unchecked discretion at multiple points in the criminal justice decision-making led to unjustified disparities, including systematic racial differences. Without repudiating programs to help those incarcerated, the book argued that a criminal justice philosophy based primarily on treatment enabled the infliction of profound injustices on those whose freedom was taken away for the ostensible purpose of helping them.

After one year, I lost my job at Columbia College, and for a time was unemployed. Physics jobs were still unavailable, and the social science departments to which I applied told me to go back to graduate school, something I did not want to do. An unexpected telephone call gave me an alternative. The caller, Andrew von Hirsch, explained that when the former Republican Senator from New York, Charles Goodell, lost his re-election bid, his friends in the foundation world set him up with a large grant to study incarceration. Von Hirsch, his former legislative assistant, would actually do the study. As Goodell and von Hirsch lacked any background in the field of penology, they needed a research assistant. Though *Struggle for Justice* had not yet been released, word of it was leaking out, and von Hirsch offered me the job. The book that von Hirsch subsequently published, *Doing Justice* – an articulation of a retributivist approach to sentencing – was the product of several years of deliberation and debate by the members of the Committee for the Study of Incarceration.

When I saw the grant money running out, I applied for academic jobs in sociology with several publications on criminal justice subjects on my vita, and prominent members of the Committee as references. Hiding my sordid past by omitting my physics publications and saying nothing about the field my PhD was in, I had better luck when I applied for jobs this time. After receiving several offers, I came to New York University as a beginning assistant professor of sociology. I have been there now for 37 years.

Tenure provides the freedom and support that enables one to explore diverse subjects. Though most of my work has concerned crime and criminal justice, I have occasionally turned to the sociology of law, human sexuality (primarily gay studies), evolutionary psychology, computational linguistics, mathematical modeling and statistics. This sampling of my work is limited to crime and criminal justice. Its subtitle, *Forays and Skirmishes*, reflects two styles of writing represented in the collection. In some essays I explore new ideas, or take previously formulated theories into new areas to assess their capacity to shed light on patterns not well-understood. In other essays I criticize and debate the work of others, sometimes by finding fault with their theoretical logic, sometimes by showing that it is not consistent with empirical evidence.

Chapter 1 of this collection, 'Delinquency and the Age Structure of Society', grew out of my teaching. Textbooks in criminology all noted that adolescents commit crimes at higher rates than older adults, but offered little in the way of explanation. In teaching my first criminology class I wanted to do more than describe the phenomenon. At that time, Marxist analyses of crime and law were being developed by criminologists influenced by the New Left. My political experiences made me sympathetic to this approach, even though I found some of the writings of this camp to be oversimplified and mechanical. I decided to see what insights this approach might furnish when used to examine a pattern of crime that, on its face, would not seem easy to explain in a Marxist framework. Marxism was created to understand class and its social implications, not age differences, and not crime.

In developing my ideas I drew substantially on my own limited experiences as a juvenile thief and alienated student, but I tried to understand those experiences in terms provided by criminological theory. The essay's effort to integrate macro and micro considerations was an attempt to demonstrate that the study of the master institutions of society did not preclude the study of face-to-face interactions. In my conceptualization, the dominant institutions shape the settings within which interpersonal transactions take place. At the time I was writing, many social theorists were arguing for the incompatibility of macro and micro analyses. The essay also tried to bridge theoretical gaps by drawing on two strands of criminological theory sometimes held to be mutually incompatible – strain theory and control theory. Strain theory considers variability across individuals or groups in the strength of motivation to violate the law as a cause of differential involvement in illegal activity, while control theory considers factors that prevent those who are motivated to violate the law from actually doing so.

Some of the ideas in the paper have a close relationship to subsequent developments in analyses of crime, such as Terry Moffitt's (1993) characterization of the 'adolescence-limited' delinquent whose illegal activities are assumed to grow out of the life circumstances of teenagers, and those of Robert Sampson and John Laub (1993) about crime and the life course. They traced a group of male offenders for decades after their initial involvement in juvenile delinquency. Sampson and Laub's analyses, however, focus exclusively on social control as a factor influencing the shape of a criminal career. My essay considers both strain and control as influences on criminal behavior. I have returned to the age–crime relationship on occasion, and am currently doing research on criminal careers, a subject intimately related to the essay reprinted here.

At the time I worked on the age–crime relationship, I paid very little attention to another striking feature of contemporary crime: it is predominantly male. Differential socialization provided an obvious explanation for this predominance. There didn't seem to be much need to say more than this. Some years later, however, when I began preparing the second edition of my anthology, *Crime and Capitalism*, I realized that sex differences in crime could not be neglected. Feminist criminologists had made clear that gender was important and interesting enough to be worth studying, and I could not ignore it. Knowing little about the subject myself, I asked a leftist criminologist who specialized in gender to write a paper dealing with the gender dimension of crime from a Marxist perspective. She agreed, but after some months, told me that she couldn't write the essay. If the job was to be done, I had to do it myself.

A fortuitous conversation with political scientist Malcolm Feeley helped to shape my approach. Button-holing me at a meeting, Feeley told me that the trial proceedings of London's Old Bailey Court documented remarkably high levels of female criminality in the eighteenth century. Later, reading the trial records with NYU graduate student Annette Sroka, I confirmed what Feeley told me: the ratio of women to men among the defendants peaked in the first half of the 18th century, and then began a slow decline that bottomed out only in the early 20th century. This pattern demonstrated that the sex ratio of crime was not something that could be understood exclusively by reference to genes or hormones; there were clearly powerful social forces at work. Gender socialization could not explain this pattern either, if understood as a trans-historical universal. My essay was an attempt to see what could be said about these trends within a Marxist theoretical framework.

This use of Marxism in several of my pieces – along with my editing of an anthology highlighting Marxist analyses of crime and criminal justice – inevitably raises the question of my relationship to this theoretical tradition. Some people know from a very early age which all-embracing theory best explains the world. For some it is Freud; for others Darwin or Marx, or in the past couple of decades, Foucault. It has never seemed to me that any one theoretical tradition was likely to provide the key that would unlock every criminological door. The great theorists all seem to me to have achieved some important insights, but they also had blind spots and made mistakes. I have always viewed their works as resources for the theorist to use in understanding the world, not as divinely inspired doctrine. Not knowing whether any specific theoretical tools will, in fact, clarify the world, I do not commit myself dogmatically to any of them. Only an ideologue would. For the same reason I do not think it helpful to view the theoretical terrain as a battleground where one sets out to demolish the claims of rival theorists. While it is essential to identify mis-steps in theorizing, I try to avoid putting all of my energies into this enterprise. This openness to all ideas does not, of course, inhibit me from pointing out what I believe to be mistakes in reasoning or in research methods when I see them. When I do so, however, I do so with the recognition that my own ideas may be mistaken. No one is infallible, not even me!

My skepticism about grand theory restrains me from trying to formulate a new grand theory of everything. In principle, ambitious theorizing has the potential for parsimoniously explaining a wide range of phenomena. When successful, such theorizing advances science greatly, and it is not surprising that some criminologists strive for it. As a result we already have a bunch of theories that aim to explain all crime. Yet each of them, it seems to me, falls short when compared with grand theories in the natural sciences, such as natural selection in biology, or quantum mechanics and relativity in physics. Reading the general theories of crime, I find myself thinking of phenomena they don't explain, or that they rely on dubious reasoning. While such efforts nevertheless deserve our admiration for their ambition, for stimulating thought, and for providing topics for PhD dissertations, I limit my own theorizing to more modest and manageable topics. I do not necessarily recommend this strategy for everyone, but for me, a sound middle-range theory is worth more than a more encompassing theory built on sand. When we have a collection of modest theories that seem to be valid, perhaps they can be synthesized into a more far-reaching theoretical structure.

Empirical research to determine whether the patterns expected on the basis of theory conform to the patterns actually present in the world is an essential part of every science. A good deal of my own empirical work on crime causation has grown out of skepticism about overstated theoretical claims made by other theorists, or about empirical claims made on the basis of research that is methodologically flawed.

When I shifted from physics to sociology, I received enormous help and support from the late John Irwin, an ex-convict criminologist who conducted interviews and observations to learn about social life. He argued that the analysis of quantified data was a poor way to study social reality. Quantitative data, he contended, are often of poor quality, and fail to capture the meanings of actions held by those being studied. The patterns revealed by statistical studies of data collected by law enforcement agencies, he insisted, reflect little more than the differential enforcement practices of the agencies, not underlying patterns of criminality.

For a time I was persuaded by these critiques of quantitative methods, and limited myself to qualitative methods. Then one of my colleagues told me that he would be going on sabbatical, and wondered whether I would be willing to teach the year-long graduate course in statistics that he regularly taught. When I told him that I did not know any statistics (as a physicist I did theoretical work, and did not analyze data), he lent me a copy of Hubert Blalock's *Social Statistics*. Reading it over the weekend, I could see that the subject was not difficult, but it also left me frustrated by its 'cook book' approach. I could apply the formulas, but didn't know how they were derived. Then I went to the library, found a book of mathematical statistics, and fell in love with the subject. A good deal of my work since then has been quantitative. I recognize some of the limitations of the data pointed out by the symbolic interactionists, but like most quantitative criminologists, consider them to be overstated. While it is important to keep questions about the validity of the data in mind, my own assessment is that it is possible to do meaningful work using statistical methods.

The next two essays were provoked by discontent with other criminologists' analyses of temporal change in rates of violent crime. Research being done on the effect of unemployment on crime rates was failing to make use of recent developments in the statistical tools available for analyzing time series. Like a great deal of statistical research in criminology, this body of work was too casual in translating ideas about causality into equations. The essay, 'Time Series Analyses of Crime Rates' (Chapter 3) was intended to show what the new tools could teach us. The essay on long-term trends in violent crime (Chapter 4) is concerned not with annual variation but with shifts in levels of crime over the centuries. Much historical criminology strikes me as glib and superficial. Writers commonly postulate major cultural or social-structural change without doing the hard work of digging up evidence that change has actually occurred, and that it was caused by the factors postulated. This essay emphasizes the importance of doing the nitty-gritty work to accomplish this.

'Modeling Criminal Careers' (Chapter 5) was an intervention into a controversy regarding the temporal dimension of criminal offences committed. Two competing characterizations of the patterning of individual offence histories had been proposed, with the rival parties each offering some empirical evidence supporting their views. This essay showed that the aggregate patterns being cited in this debate were inherently incapable of resolving the controversy. Much research on criminal careers using individual data has taken place since my essay was written, but the issues it addresses remain unresolved to this day. Some of them are the subject of my current research.

When I first began studying criminal justice issues empirically, little was known about the effectiveness of the criminal justice system in preventing crime. I set out to establish what its impact was, to the extent that existing data permitted. In a series of essays I examined the effectiveness of rehabilitation programs, the deterrent impact of policing, and the incapacitative effect of imprisonment. In the decades since that work was done the criminal justice system has changed a great deal, so that some of the conclusions reached in those essays would not necessarily apply today. Better statistical methods are now available, but limitations of data remain a vexing problem in this type of research.

Of the two essays from this body of work included in this volume, 'The Effect of Arrests on Crime: A Multivariate Panel Analysis' (Chapter 6), represents an early use of statistical methods for the analysis of panel data to study the criminal justice system. Though newer methods for analyzing panel data are now in vogue, the methods described in this essay represent approaches of potential criminological value. 'The Incapacitative Effect of Imprisonment' (Chapter 7) illustrates my preference for analyzing quantitative problems with simple models rather than elaborate and sophisticated ones, at least when data are lacking or are of poor quality. The concerns this essay raises about selective incapacitation are as relevant today as they were 30 years ago. Though claims about the adoption of actuarial methods in the criminal justice system advanced by Feeley and Simon (1992) are over-statements,[2] there

2 See Greenberg (2008). Some of the most striking developments in American sentencing practices of the past few decades include high statutory minimum sentences, very long sentences for repeat

are a number of places where American courts are making use of statistical predictions of dangerousness, most notably in dealing with sex offenders.

Criminologists seek to understand not only the effects of criminal justice interventions, but the historical development of the criminal justice system. Why does the criminal law prohibit some activities but not others? Why have forms of punishment changed over time? 'The Dialectics of Crime Control' (Chapter 8) attempts to clarify the conceptual tools Marxism offers for answering these questions and uses them for insights into some of the most important developments in criminal law and criminal justice in the past few centuries. At the same time it also notes the limitations of Marxist theory for this purpose.

'The Prison as a Lawless Agency' (Chapter 10) was written when Fay Stender, a California attorney specializing in prisoners' rights litigation, approached me with the idea of publishing a law review article based on letters she received from prison inmates about the conditions of their confinement. The essay tries to analyze their circumstances in light of the political philosophy of power and attempts to restrict it in order to protect individuals from abuses by power-holders.

'The Dynamics of Oscillatory Punishment Processes' (Chapter 9) was provoked by my skepticism about Durkheimian explanations of the operations of the criminal justice system. Alfred Blumstein, Jacqueline Cohen and Daniel Nagin drew creatively on Durkheim's ideas about primitive social control to explain oscillations in prison populations. As much as I admire Durkheim, I have always found his ideas about punishment and social solidarity to be dubious. The notion that short-term oscillations in prison populations could be explained as a consequence of short-term fluctuations in social solidarity seemed especially dubious. In this paper I offered an alternative explanation, consistent with the same data Blumstein et al. used.

Despite this skepticism about some of Durkheim's ideas, his writings also provide theoretical tools that remain useful now, more than a hundred years after he wrote them. 'Punishment, Division of Labor, and Social Solidarity' (Chapter 11), draws on those ideas to illuminate the 'punitive turn' in modern criminal justice policy. Some of the best criminological minds have attempted to understand this development, and have proposed valuable insights into the social and political conditions that have given rise to this turn. However, they have not always attended to differences in the ways different polities have dealt with crime. The essay, 'State Prison Populations and Their Growth, 1971–1991' (Chapter 12), attempts to understand variability among the American states in the growth of prison populations, while 'Siting the Death Penalty Internationally' (Chapter 13), similarly addresses comparative issues by trying to explain why some countries retain the death penalty while others have abolished it. The essay argues against a narrow focus on economic factors, and provides evidence that a country's culture and politics are important determinants of its criminal justice policy. I continue to study capital punishment, both cross-nationally and within the United States.

While engaged in assembling this collection of work reflecting four decades of engagement with crime, I could not help reflecting on the field to which the essays in this collection attempt to contribute. This assessment evokes feelings of both modest satisfaction and

offenders, and sentencing provisions that exclude consideration of characteristics of the defendant that might help to predict future return to crime.

profound unease. As an institutionalized enterprise, criminology is in good shape. Courses in criminology draw large enrollments; schools and departments devoted to criminology and criminal justice proliferate, as do journals. Increasingly, criminology is an international enterprise.

Advances in research methods – particularly quantitative methods – make it possible for researchers to draw conclusions from their data with greater confidence in their answers than was possible in the past. However, limitations in the availability of data and in their reliability limit the uses of these methods. Moreover, many students are not adequately trained in these methods and some practicing criminologists misuse them. Research funding is nowhere near a desirable level, and is often limited to topics and methods of interest to the funders. The field is vulnerable to theoretical and methodological fads. The very justification for the existence of criminology as a distinct specialty within the social sciences is unclear. Still, the number of researchers and journals increases the likelihood that shaky ideas will draw criticism. The field possesses possibilities for correcting its errors.

It is in criminology's potential for informing crime control policy that unease is particularly warranted. Time and again, researchers make policy recommendations on the basis of their research findings. Then others find serious weaknesses or mistakes in the original research. Sometimes better research follows and affirms the original conclusions; sometimes it doesn't. In the years I have been working, criminological research about the effectiveness of correctional rehabilitation programs, gun control, imprisonment, capital punishment, habitual offender legislation and the effect of legalized abortion on crime have all come in for serious question (Greenberg, 2006). This instability of research findings means that criminologists ought to be cautious in formulating policy recommendations on the basis of their research. And policy-makers should treat criminal justice policy recommendations with a healthy dose of skepticism. Chances are high that someone will come along to point out a methodological flaw that raises serious doubts about the conclusions.

Even when policy-relevant research findings are sound, advocacy based on that research commonly fails to take the full range of alternatives into account. That policy A is superior to policy B according to some agreed-upon criterion does not automatically imply that A should be adopted. Perhaps policy C would be even better. Moreover, the criteria relevant for evaluating policies are sometimes open to challenge. Civil libertarians tend not to see eye-to-eye with criminal justice 'hawks' or efficiency-maximizing policy analysts about what the former consider invasions of privacy and loss of personal autonomy that accompany some crime-control policies. There may be political reasons why a policy, even if effective, should not or cannot be adopted.

Typically, authors who make recommendations about policies assume that governments are benign, and are waiting with bated breath for the insights that criminologists can give them. Yet, when major policy initiatives are undertaken, criminologists often go unconsulted. Few criminologists favored the enormous expansion of prison populations the United States has seen in recent decades, but that hasn't slowed down prison construction. In November, 1989, the American Society of Criminology adopted a resolution condemning capital punishment, but there is no evidence that any legislator has changed a vote on the death penalty, or that any judge has decided a case differently, on the basis of this resolution.

On many issues, politicians have little to gain by consulting criminologists, and consequently criminological research, even when sound, and even when it would improve crime control policy, has had limited influence on policy adoption. However, hope springs eternal, even in the hearts of criminologists, and they soldier on, hoping that next time it will be different. My political experiences and observations of the policy formation process leave me pessimistic about what my writings and those of my colleagues can accomplish by enlightening a well-intended benevolent political leadership. In principle these writings can inform a larger public, but this is an audience not easily reached. Where I think my work can inform public policy, I cannot in good conscience hold my tongue, but when I write I do so with little faith that I will make a difference. I would, of course, be delighted were my readers to prove me wrong.

References

Feeley, Malcolm and Jonathan Simon (1992), 'The New Penology: Notes on the Emerging Strategy of Corrections and its Implications', *Criminology*, **30**, pp. 449–74.

Greenberg, David F. (2006), 'Criminological Research and Crime Control Policy: Not a Marriage Made in Heaven', *Criminology and Public Policy*, **5**.2: pp. 203–12.

_____ (2008), 'More Fictions about Predictions', *Criminal Justice Ethics* (Summer/Fall): pp. 64–81.

Sampson, Robert J. and, John H. Laub (1993), *Crime in the Making: Pathways and Turning Points through Life*, Cambridge, MA: Harvard University Press.

Moffitt, Terry E. (1993), 'Adolescent-limited and Life-Course-Persistent Antisocial Behavior: A Developmental Taxonomy', *Psychological Review*, **100**, pp. 674–701.

Taylor, Ian, Paul Walton and Jock Young (1973), *The New Criminology: For a Social Theory of Deviance*, London: Routledge and Kegan Paul.

Part I
Causes of Crime

[1]
Delinquency and the Age Structure of Society

Much attention has been paid in research on the causes of delinquency to the role of such variables as class, sex, and race. By comparison, the relationship between age and criminality or delinquency, though noted in passing in many studies, has received little systematic attention. This paper will present a theoretical analysis of the age distribution of criminal involvement. In particular, I will attempt to show that the increasingly disproportionate involvement of juveniles in major crime categories, though not readily explained by current sociological theories of delinquency, can be understood as a consequence of the historically changing position of juveniles in industrial societies. This changing position, I will argue, has its origin, at least in Europe and the United States, in the long term tendencies of a capitalist economic system. Although the conceptual framework for this analysis is Marxist, the approach taken appropriates Marxian theory for criminology in a way that departs from earlier Marxist writings on crime. The nature of this departure will be spelled out explicitly in the concluding section.

Age and Criminal Involvement

As can be seen from Table 1, crime-specific arrest rates in the United States show substantial variation with age. For 1970, per capita arrest rates for vandalism and property crimes not involving confrontation with a person (burglary, grand larceny, auto theft) peak at age 15–16, fall to half their peak values in two to four years, and continue to decline rapidly. Arrest rates for narcotics violations and offenses involving confrontation with a person (homicide, forcible rape, aggravated assault, robbery) peak at age 19–21 and also decline with age, but less rapidly.

Studies of recidivism show that rearrest rates for those officially labeled as offenders also decline with age [1].

TABLE I

1970 Arrests Per 100,000 Population by Age*

OFFENSE / AGE	13–14	15	16	17	18	19	20	21	22	23	24	25–29	30–34	% under 18	% under 21
Murder and non-negligent manslaughter	3.5	13.2	20.1	25.2	35.8	35.5	35.2	*40.2*	35.3	36.6	37.8	30.7	24.4	10.2	24.5
Forcible rape	12.5	32.5	43.2	54.3	61.8	*64.7*	60.6	60.4	54.3	52.6	50.6	36.1	22.9	20.6	41.6
Robbery	164	274	340	373	393	*394*	358	346	293	250	250	154	82.5	32.2	55.3
Aggravated assault	109	189	243	272	309	317	320	*347*	328	316	*355*	284	240	17.6	30.5
Burglary	979	979	*1463*	1302	1176	968	788	697	585	527	505	320	191	50.9	69.8
Larceny over $50	2178	*2741*	*2740*	2408	2183	1788	1460	1309	1100	953	936	631	463	50.4	66.4
Auto theft	397	898	*965*	759	556	436	344	295	236	197	193	119	69.1	52.9	71.6
Vandalism	570	*613*	514	375	238	191	141	134	111	76.4	97.1	69	50.6	71.6	80.8
Narcotic drug laws	215	665	1169	1585	1971	*2073*	1187	1763	1447	1199	1039	587	312	22.0	52.2

*Arrests are based on F.B.I. statistics for 1970, population is number of males recorded in the 1970 census.
The peak age in each offense category is set in italic type.

The risks in using agency-generated data to draw conclusions about group differences in rates of criminal involvement have been underscored repeatedly [2]. However, field and self-reporting studies of delinquency confirm that delinquents do abandon crime in late adolescence [3,4]. West, for example, found the average career length of his "serious thieves" to be about two years in his field study [5]. Evidence that declining arrest rates cannot be attributed to improved ability to escape apprehension is provided by Wilson [6], who found that self-reported participation in crime declined after age 15, with no relationship between age and probability of apprehension.

There is also evidence from self-reporting studies that recruitment to delinquency declines with age [7].

Already in nineteenth century United States, it had been noted that criminal involvement tended to decline with age [8], but fragmentary evidence suggests that the peak was higher than at present, and the decline gradual [9]. Tabulations of prosecutions, convictions and imprisonments for nineteenth century Europe show higher peak ages in agrarian nations like France, Italy and Austria than in industrialized nations like England [10]. The shift in arrest toward younger age brackets in recent decades in a number of other countries [11] is also suggestive of a relationship between the age distribution of crime and economic development.

In terms of delinquency theory, systematic variation in delinquent involvement with age requires explanation no less than other systematic differences. Indeed, age variation may help to test delinquency theories constructed to explain other sources of variation, such as class or sex. Since these other sources of variation can be explained in many ways, the adequacy with which rival theories explain age variation may help us to distinguish among them.

At a practical level, the rising volume of juvenile crime is creating public clamor for less lenient treatment of juvenile offenders. Intelligent response to this development requires an understanding of the social forces that have led to the increase.

Delinquency Theory and the Age Distribution of Crime

Since neither infants nor the elderly possess the prowess and agility required for some forms of crime, *some* association between age and criminal involvement can be expected on biological grounds alone. It is equally evident that the strong variation with age shown in Table 1 cannot be explained in these terms alone. Biological explanations based on other correlates of age than physical ability are equally weak. The Gluecks' proposal that delinquency may be caused by delayed maturation [12] is inconsistent with the absence of any difference in physical maturity between delinquent and non-delinquent boys of the same age [13]. Moreover, any explanation of age variation in criminality based on psychological reactions to physiological changes accompanying adolescence would be difficult to reconcile with the great variation in delinquent involvement among juveniles as well as the lateness of peak involvement in violence offenses. If age is relevant to criminality, the link should lie primarily in its social significance.

Yet contemporary sociological theories of delinquency shed little light on the relationship between crime and age. If, for example, lower class male gang delinquence is simply a manifestation of a lower class subculture as Miller [14] has maintained, it would be mysterious why 21-year-olds act in conformity with the norms of their subculture so much *less* often than their siblings just a few years younger – unless the norms themselves were age-specific. While age-specific expectations may contribute to desistance from some forms of delinquent play, such as vandalism and throwing snowballs at cars, as Clark and Haurek [15] suggest, there is no social class in which felony, theft and violence receive general *approval* for persons of any age. Moreover, adult residents of high crime areas often live in fear of being attacked by teenagers, suggesting that if delinquency is subcultural, community does not form the basis of the subculture.

The difficulty of accounting for "maturational reform" within the framework of the motivational theories of Cloward and Ohlin [16] and Cohen [17] has already been noted by Matza [18]. In both theories, male delinquents cope with the problems arising from lower class status by entering into and internalizing the norms of a subculture which repudiates conventional rules of conduct and *requires* participation in crime. As with other subcultural theories, it is not at all clear why most subculture carriers abandon activities that are so highly prized within the subculture with such haste.

This desistance is doubly perplexing in anomie or opportunity theories [19] because the problem assumed to cause delinquency, namely the anticipation of failure in achieving socially inculcated success goals through legitimate means, does not disappear at the end of adolescence. At the onset of adulthood, few lower and working class youths are close to conventionally defined "success," and realization that opportunities for upward mobility are drastically limited can only be more acute. Students can perhaps entertain fantasies about their future prospects, but graduates or dropouts must come to terms with their chances. It is true that they can do this by reducing their aspirations and thus lessening anomie, but this seems to happen only slowly. According to Bachman [20], high school drop-outs' aspirations decline by about half a standard deviation over a four-year period, not fast enough to account for the rapid decline in theft involvement with age.

Cloward and Ohlin do note that many delinquents desist, but explain this in *ad hoc* terms unrelated to the main body of their theory. Writing of neighborhoods where violence is common, they assert,

> As adolescents near adulthood, excellence in the manipulation of violence no longer brings status. Quite the contrary, it generally evokes extremely negative sanctions. What was defined as permissible or tolerable behavior during adolescence tends to be sharply proscribed in adulthood. New expectations are imposed, expectations of "growing up," of taking on adult responsibilities in the economic, familial, and community spheres. The effectiveness with which these definitions are imposed is attested by the tendency among fighting gangs to decide that conflict is, in the final analysis, simply "kid stuff." . . . In other words, powerful community expectations emerge which have the consequence of closing off access to previously useful means of overcoming status deprivation [21].

In view of Cloward and Ohlin's characterization of neighborhoods where gang violence is prevalent as so disorganized that no informal social controls limiting violence can be exercised [22], one can only wonder whose age-specific expectations are being described. Cloward and Ohlin do not say. This explanation, for which Cloward and Ohlin produce no supporting evidence, is inconsistent with their own larger theory of delinquent subcultures. In addition, it seems inconsistent with the *slowness* of the decline in the violence offense categories. Since recent panel studies [23] find no support for opportunity theory, the failure of the theory to explain the age distribution of crime is not surprising.

In a departure from the emphasis placed on social class membership in most motivational theories of delinquency, Bloch and Niederhoffer [24] interpret such forms of delinquency as adolescent drinking, sexual experimentation, and "wild automobile rides" as responses to the age status problems of adolescence. Denied the prerogatives of adulthood, but encouraged to aspire to adulthood and told to "act like adults," teenagers find in these activities a symbolic substitute which presumably is abandoned as soon as the genuine article is available. As an explanation for joy-riding and some status offenses, this explanation has manifest plausibility. For other categories it is more problemmatic, since it assumes that delinquents interpret activities behaviorally associated largely with adolescence as evidence of adult stature. When Bloch and Niederhoffer turn to more serious teenage crime, their explanations are vague and difficult to interpret, but in any event seem to depend less on the structural position of the juvenile.

In *Delinquency and Drift*, Matza [25] provides an alternative approach to the explanation of desistance. His assumption that many delinquents fully embrace neither delinquent nor conventional norms and values, but instead allow themselves to be easily influenced without deep commitment, makes desistance possible when the delinquent discovers that his companions are no more committed to delinquency than he is. This discovery is facilitated by a reduction in masculinity anxiety that accompanies the attainment of adulthood. There are valuable insights in this account, but unresolved questions as well. Insofar as the discovery of a shared misunderstanding depends on chance events, as Matza suggests [26], *systematic* differences in desistance remain unexplained (I will cite evidence for such systematic differences below). Why does desistance from violence offenses occur later and more slowly than for theft offenses? Why are some juveniles so much more extensively involved in delinquency than others? Matza's remarkable presentation of the subjective elements in delinquency must be supplemented by an analysis of more "objective," structural elements in causation if such questions are to be answered.

That is the approach I will take. Working within the tradition established by Bloch and Niederhoffer, I will present an analysis of the structural position of juveniles in American society and elaborate the implications of that position for juvenile involvement in crime. Because the focus will be on age differences, no attempt will be made to address unresolved issues in delinquency theory that have no obvious relationship to age differences (e.g. does association with delinquents follow or precede delinquent acts); however, when the theory does predict variations in delinquency *within* an age-cohort, these will be noted and compared with the available empirical data.

The theory to be presented will have two major components. The first, a theory of motivation, locates sources of motivation toward criminal involvement in the structural position of juveniles in American society. The second, derived from a control theory perspective, suggests that the willingness to act on the basis of criminal motivation is distributed unequally among age groups because the costs of apprehension are different for persons of different ages. Although some of the theoretical ideas (e.g. control theory) on which I will be drawing have already appeared in the delinquency literature, each by itself is inadequate as a full theory of delinquence. When put together with some new ideas, however, a very plausible account of age and other systematic sources of variation in delinquent involvement emerges.

Anomie and the Juvenile Labor Market

Robert Merton's discussion of anomie [27] has provided a framework for a large volume of research on the etiology of crime. Although Merton observed that a disjunction between socially inculcated goals and legitimate means available for attaining them would produce a strain toward deviance *whatever the goal* [28], specific application of the perspective to delinquency has been restricted to an assessment of the contribution to delinquency causation of the one cultural goal Merton considered in depth, namely occupational success. Cloward and Ohlin [29], for example, attribute lower class male delinquency to the anticipation of failure in achieving occupational success goals as adults. Their involvement in theft is interpreted as a strategy for gaining admission to professional theft and organized crime circles, that is, a way of obtaining the tutelage and organizational affiliations necessary for the successful pursuit of *career* crime, rather than for immediate financial return. Crime is thus seen as a means toward the attainment of *future* goals rather than *present* goals.

The assumption that delinquency is instrumentally related to the attainment of adult goals is plausible only for limited categories of delinquency, e.g. students who cheat on exams in the face of keen competition for admission to college or graduate school [30], and youths who save what they earn as pimps [31] or drug merchants [32] to capitalize investment in conventional business enterprises.

For other forms of delinquency this assumption is less tenable. Delinquents would have to be stupid indeed to suppose that shoplifting, joy-riding, burglary, robbery or drug use could bring the prestige or pecuniary rewards associated with high status lawful occupations. Nor is there evidence that most delinquents seek careers in professional theft or organized crime. In the face of Cohen's characterization of delinquents as short-run hedonists [33] and the difficulty parents and teachers encounter in attempting to engage delinquent youths in activities which could improve chances of occupational success (like school homework), the future orientation assumed in opportunity theory is especially farfetched.

The potential explanatory power of anomie theory, is, however, not exhausted by Cloward and Ohlin's formulation, because delinquency can be a response to a discrepancy between aspirations and expectations for the attainment of goals other than occupational ones. Most people have a multiplicity of goals, and only some of them are occupational. As the salience of different life goals can vary with stage of the life-cycle, our understanding of delinquency may be advanced more by an examination of those goals given a high priority by adolescents than by considering the importance attached to different goals in American culture generally.

The literature on youth reports a consensus that the transition from childhood to adolescence is marked by a heightened sensitivity to the expectations of peers, and concommitantly, a reduced concern with the fulfillment of parental expectations [34]. High value comes to be attached to popularity with peers, and exclusion from the most popular cliques becomes the occasion for acute psychological distress.

196

Adolescent peer groups and orientation to the expectations of peers are found in many societies [35]. In American society, the natural tendency of those who share common experiences and problems to prefer one another's company is accentuated by the importance parents and school attach to popularity and to the development of the social skills they believe will be necessary for later occupational success [36]. In addition, the exclusion of young people from adult work and leisure activity forces adolescents into virtually exclusive association with one another, cutting them off from alternative sources of validation for the self (as well as reducing the degree of adult supervision). A long run trend toward increased age segregation created by changing patterns of work and education has increased the vulnerability of teenagers to the expectations and evaluations of their peers [37].

This dependence on peers for approval is not itself criminogenic. In many tribal societies, age-homogeneous bands of youths are functionally integrated into the economic and social life of the tribe and are not considered deviant [38]. In America, too, many teenage clubs and cliques are not delinquent. Participation in teenage social life, however, requires resources. In addition to personal assets and skills (having an attractive appearance and "good personality," being a skilled conversationalist, being able to memorize song lyrics and learn dance steps, and in some circles, being able to fight), money is needed to purchase clothing, cosmetics, cigarettes, alcoholic beverages, narcotics, phonograph records, transistor radios, gasoline for cars and motorcycles, tickets to films and concerts, meals in restaurants [39], and for gambling. The progressive detachment of teenage social life from that of the family and the emergence of advertising directed toward a teenage market (this being a creation of postwar affluence for major sections of the population and the "baby boom") have increased the importance of these goods to teenagers and hence have inflated the costs of their social activities.

When parents are unable or unwilling to subsidize their children's social life at the level required by local convention, when children want to prevent their parents from learning of their expenditures, or when they are reluctant to incur the obligations created by taking money from their parents, alternative sources of funds must be sought. Full or part-time employment once constituted such an alternative.

The long-run, persistent decline in teenage employment and labor force participation has progressively eliminated this alternative. During the period from 1870 to 1920, many states passed laws restricting child labor and establishing compulsory education. Despite a quadrupling of the "gainfully employed" population from 1870 to 1930, the number of gainfully employed workers in the 10–15 year-old age bracket *declined*. The Great

Depression resulted in a further contraction of the teenage labor force and increased the school-leaving age [40]. Only in 1940 did the U.S. government stop counting all persons over the age of 10 as part of the labor force [41]. In recent years, teenage labor market deterioration has been experienced mainly by black teenagers. From 1950 to 1973, black teenage labor force participation declined from 67.8% to 34.7%, while white teenage labor force participation remained stable at about 63%. The current recession has increased teenage unemployment in the 16–19 year old age bracket to about 20%, with the rate for black teenagers being twice as high [42].

This process has left teenagers less and less capable of financing an increasingly costly social life whose importance is enhanced as the age segregation of society grows. Adolescent theft then occurs as a response to the disjunction between the desire to participate in social activities with peers and the absence of legitimate sources of funds needed to finance this participation.

Qualitative evidence supporting this explanation of adolescent theft is found in those delinquency studies that describe the social life of delinquent groups. Sherif and Sherif noted in their study of adolescent groups that theft was often instrumentally related to the group's leisure time social activities,

> In several groups. . . , stealing was not the incidental activity that it was in others. It was regarded as an acceptable and necessary means of getting needed possessions, or, more usually, cash. Members of the aforementioned groups frequently engaged in theft when they were broke, usually selling articles other than clothing, and *often using the money for group entertainment and treats* [43].

Carl Werthman reports that among San Francisco delinquents:

> Shoplifting . . . was viewed as a more instrumental activity, as was the practice of stealing coin changers from temporarily evacuated buses parked in a nearby public depot. In the case of shoplifting, most of the boys wanted and wore the various items of clothing they stole; and when buses were robbed, either the money was divided among the boys. or it was used to buy supplies for a party being given by the club [44].

Studies of urban delinquent gangs or individuals in England [45], Israel [46], Sweden [47], Taiwan [48] Holland [49] and Argentina [50] present a uniform picture: unemployed or employed but poorly paid male youths steal to support their leisure-time, group-centered social activities.

198

Joseph Weis' study of middle class delinquency using self-reports [51] is also consistent with the interpretation of adolescent theft presented here. Using key cluster analysis, Weis extracted three distinct factors from the correlation matrix for involvement in different forms of delinquency for the males in the sample. These oblique factors could be characterized as social, property, and aggression. The analysis for girls produced two factors: there was no aggression factor, while the other two factors were very similar to the social and property factors among the boys. For both boys and girls, the correlation between the oblique factor domains for social offenses (drinking, marijuana use, curfew violations, gambling use of false I.D. cards, drag racing, and similar offenses) and for property offenses (theft, burglary, shoplifting, etc.) was positive and moderately strong, as would be predicted if thefts are undertaken to finance peer-related social activities.

On the reasoning presented here, strain should be experienced most acutely by teenagers who are unable to achieve popularity on the basis of personal attributes and who lack alternative sources of self-esteem (e.g. school success or warm relationships with parents). Indeed, teenagers in this position may attempt to win friends by spending money on them [52]. Evidence that unpopular boys are more likely to become delinquent [53], and that delinquents tend to have unsatisfactory relations with peers [54] and parents [55] is consistent with my argument.

Where parents subsidize their children adequately, the incentive to steal is obviously reduced. Because the cost of social life can increase with class position, a strong correlation between social class membership and involvement in theft is not necessarily predicted. Insofar as self-reporting studies suggest that the correlation between participation in nonviolent forms of property acquisition and parental socio-economic status is not very high [56], this may be a strong point for my theory. By contrast the theories of Cohen, Miller, and Cloward and Ohlin all clash with the self-reporting studies.

In view of recent suggestions that increases in female crime and delinquency are linked with changing gender roles (of which the women's liberation movement is taken either as a cause or a manifestation), it is of interest to note that the explanation of adolescent theft presented here is applicable to boys and girls, and in particular, allows for female delinquency in support of *traditional* gender roles related to peer involvement.

Weis' work is consistent with this interpretation, as are differences in the forms of theft boys and girls undertake. Boys, who traditionally have paid girls' expenses on dates and therefore have a greater need for cash, are more likely to rob or to burglarize homes and stores, taking items for resale, while girls more often steal items (such as clothing and cosmetics) for personal use.

Increases in female crime which have occurred largely in those forms of theft in which female involvement has traditionally been high [57] are thus more plausibly attributed to the same deteriorating economic position in the face of escalating costs of social life that males confront, than to changes in gender role.

As teenagers get older, their vulnerability to the expectations of peers is reduced by institutional involvements that provide alternative sources of self-esteem; moreover, opportunities for acquiring money legitimately expand. Both processes reduce the motivation to engage in acquisitive forms of delinquent behavior. Consequently, involvement in theft should fall off rapidly with age, and it does.

Delinquency and the School

My explanation of juvenile theft in terms of structural obstacles to legitimate sources of funds at a time when peer-oriented leisure activities require access to financial resources implicitly characterizes this form of delinquency as instrumentally rational; the theory assumes that money and goods are stolen because they are useful. Acts of vandalism, thefts in which stolen objects are abandoned or destroyed, and interpersonal violence not necessary to accomplish a theft cannot be explained in this way. These are the activities that led Albert Cohen to maintain that much delinquency is "malicious" and "non-utilitarian" [58] and to argue that the content of the delinquent subculture arose in the lower class male's reaction to failure in schools run according to middle class standards.

Although Cohen can be criticized for not indicating the criteria used for assessing rationality – indeed, for failure to find out from delinquents themselves what they perceived the goals of their destructive acts to be – and though details of Cohen's theory (to be noted below) appear to be inaccurate, his observation that delinquency may be a response to school problems need not be abandoned. Indeed, the literature proposing a connection between one or another aspect of school and delinquency is voluminous [59]. I will concentrate on two features of the school experience, its denial of student autonomy and its subjection of some students to the embarrassment of public degradation ceremonies.

In all spheres of life outside the school, and particularly within the family, children more or less steadily acquire larger measures of personal autonomy as they mature. Over time, the "democratization" of the family has reduced the age at which given levels of autonomy are acquired. The gradual extension of freedom that normally takes place in the family (not without struggle!) is not accompanied by parallel deregulation at school. Authoritarian styles of teaching, and rules concerning such matters as smoking, hair styles, manner of dress, going to the bathroom, and attendance, come into conflict with expectations students derive from the relaxation of controls in the family [60]. The delegitimation of hierarchical authority structures accomplished by the radical movements of the 1960s has sharpened student awareness of this contradiction.

The symbolic significance attached to autonomy exacerbates the inherently onerous burden of school restrictions. Parents and other adults invest age-specific rights and expectations with moral significance by disapproving "childish" behavior and by using privileges to reward behavior they label "mature." Because of this association, the deprivation of autonomy is experienced as "being treated like a baby," that is, as a member of a disvalued age-status.

All students are exposed to these restrictions, and to some degree, all probably resent them. For students who are at least moderately successful at their schoolwork, who excel at sports, participate in extra-curricular school activities, or who are members of popular cliques, this resentment is likely to be more than compensated by rewards associated with school attendance. These students tend to conform to school regulations most of the time, rarely collide with school officials, and are unlikely to feel overtly hostile to school or teachers. Students who are unpopular, and whose academic record, whether from inability or disinterest, is poor, receive no comparable compensation. For them, school can only be a frustrating experience: it brings no current gratification and no promise of future pay-off. Why then should they put up with these restrictions? These students often get into trouble, and feel intense hostility to the school.

Social class differences must of course be taken into account. Pre-adolescent and early adolescent middle and upper class children are supervised more closely than their working class counterparts, and thus come to expect and accept adult authority, while working class youths, who enter an unsupervised street life among peers at an early age have more autonomy to protect, and guard their prerogatives jealously [61]. To the extent that they see in the school's denial of their autonomy preparation for a future in occupations that also deny autonomy, and see in their parents' lives the psychic costs of that denial, they may be more prone to rebel than middle-class students, who can generally anticipate entering jobs that allow more discretion and autonomy.

Middle class youths also have more to gain by accepting adult authority than their working class counterparts. Comparatively affluent parents can control their children better because they have more resources they can withhold, and are in a better position to secure advantages for their children. Likewise, children who believe that their future chances depend on school success may conform regardless of whether they reject close regulation intellectually. Where returns on school success are reduced by class or racial discrimination, the school loses this source of social control. It similarly loses control over upper class children, whose inherited class position frees them from the necessity of doing well in school to guarantee their future economic status.

Only a few decades ago, few working class youths – or school failures with middle class family backgrounds – would have been exposed to a contradiction between their expectations of autonomy and the school's attempts to control them because a high proportion of students, especially working class students, left school at an early age. However, compulsory school attendance, low wages and high unemployment rates for teenagers, and increased educational requirements for entry-level jobs have greatly reduced dropout rates. Thus in 1920, 16.8% of the 17 year-old population were high school graduates; and in 1956, 62.3% [62]. In consequence, a greater proportion of students, especially those who benefit least from school, is exposed to this contradiction.

Common psychological responses to the irritation of the school's denial of autonomy range from affective disengagement to the school ("tuning out" the teacher) to smouldering resentment, and at the behavioral level from truancy to self-assertion through the flouting of rules. Such activities as getting drunk, using drugs, joy-riding, truanting, and adopting eccentric styles of dress, apart from any intrinsic gratification these activities may provide, can be seen as forms of what Gouldner has called "conflictual validation of the self" [63]. By helping students establish independence from authority (school, parental, etc.), these activities contribute to self-regard. Their attraction lies in their being forbidden.

As a status system, the school makes further contributions to the causation of delinquency. Almost by definition, status systems embody invidious distinctions. Where standards of evaluation are shared, and position is believed to reflect personal merit, occupants of lower statuses are likely to encounter problems in maintaining self-esteem [64]. The problem is somewhat alleviated by a strong tendency to restrict intimate association to persons of similar status. If one's associates are at roughly the same level as oneself, they provide the standards for self-evaluation [65]. In addition, "democratic" norms of modesty discourage the flaunting of success and boasting of personal merit, thereby insulating the less successful from an implied attribution of their failures to their own deficiencies.

202

These norms are not, however, universal in applicability. In our society, certification as a full-fledged social member is provided those whose commitment to the value of work and family is documented by spouse, home, car and job (for women, children have traditionally substituted for job). Institutional affiliations are thus taken as a mark of virtue, or positive stigma. Those who meet these moral tests are accorded standards of respect in face-to-face interaction not similarly accorded members of unworthy or suspect categories – e.g. prison and psychiatric hospital inmates, skid row bums, the mentally retarded, and unaccompanied women on the streets of New York. In particular, members are permitted to sustain self-presentations as dignified, worthy persons, regardless of what may be thought or said of them in private [66]. Students, however, especially failing students and those with lower class or minority origins, are accorded no comparable degree of respect. As they lack the appropriate institutional affiliations, their moral commitment to dominant institutions of society is suspect. In this sense, they are social strangers; we don't quite know what we can expect from them. They are, moreover, relatively powerless. In consequence, they are exposed to evaluations from which adults are ordinarily shielded.

This is especially true at school, where school personnel continuously communicate their evaluations of students through grades, honor rolls, track positions, privileges, and praise for academic achievement and proper deportment. On occasion, the negative evaluation of students conveyed by the school's ranking systems is supplemented by explicit criticism and denunciation on the part of teachers who act as if the academic performance of failing students could be elevated by telling them they are stupid, or lazy, or both. Only the most extreme failures in the adult world are subjected to degradation ceremonies of this kind.

The feelings of students subjected to this form of status derogation are well captured by a high school student describing a conversation with his school principal,

> I told him that the teacher was always trying to "put me down" in front of the class. I told him that the teacher knew I didn't like math so why did he keep calling on me – just to "put me down," to make me look bad. I'm not as dumb as he thinks so I "turned it around" on him and got the class to laugh at him. See how he likes being the fool. The principal said I was a wise guy, thought I was a "smart alec." He said that what I needed was a good old-fashioned talk behind the wood shed. I told him "Who're you going get to do it: better not try or somebody is going to get hurt, bad!" Man he turned white and started to shake, "You're suspended for threatening a school official." That's good, I said, this school, this school ain't worth a shit anyway [67].

Cohen [68] has argued that working class youths faced with this situation protect their self-esteem by rejecting conventional norms and values. Seeking out one another for mutual support, they create a delinquent subculture of opposition to middle-class norms in which they can achieve status. This subculture is seen as supporting the non-utilitarian acts of destructiveness that alleviate frustration.

There is little difficulty in finding evidence of adolescent destructiveness, however the choice of target may be more rational than Cohen allows. The large and growing volume of school vandalism and assaults on teachers indicate that delinquents often do see the school in antagonistic terms. Other targets, too may be chosen for clear reasons. In his study of gang violence, Miller found that,

> Little of the deliberately inflicted property damage represented a diffuse outpouring of accumulated hostility against arbitrary objects; in most cases the gang members injured the possession of properties of particular persons who had angered them, as a concrete expression of that anger (defacing automobile of mother responsible for having gang member committed to correctional institution; breaking windows of settlement house after eviction therefrom). There was thus little evidence of 'senseless' destruction; most property damage was directed and repressive [69].

Other targets may be chosen because of their symbolic value, e.g. membership in a despised racial group or class stratum, or in the adult world, which represents repressive authority. It is not unlikely that an unanticipated consequence of recent black nationalist movements has been an increase in crimes by minority group members that victimize whites.

Empirical research suggests the need for revision of other components of Cohen's theory as well. Delinquents do not necessarily reject conventional values or career goals except when in the presence of their peers [70]. A modern society contains numerous status systems that are not in competition with one another; acceptance of one need not require repudiation of others. In particular, students who do not reject the value system endorsed by parents and school officials but who do not succeed in its terms can nevertheless accept the value system of a subculture of delinquency (in the sense of Matza [71]) as a "second best" alternative on pragmatic grounds.

Self-reporting studies of delinquency indicate the association between class and most forms of delinquency to be weaker than Cohen supposed. School failure, though class-linked, is not the monopoly of any class, and the self-esteem problems of middle class youths who fail are not necessarily any less than those of working class schoolmates. Since parental expectations for academic achievement may be higher in middle class families, and since school failure may auger downward mobility, these problems could conceivably be worse. If delinquency restores self esteem lost through school failure, it may serve this function for students of all class backgrounds.

The impact of school degradation ceremonies is not limited to their effect on students' self-esteem. When a student is humiliated by a teacher the student's attempt to present a favorable self to schoolmates is undercut. Even students whose prior psychological disengagement from the value system of the school leaves their self-esteem untouched by a teacher's disparagement may react with anger at being embarrassed before peers. The high school student quoted earlier complained of being ridiculed *in front of his class.* It is the situation of being in the company of others whose approval is needed for self-esteem that makes it difficult for teenagers to ignore humiliation that older individuals, with alternative sources of self-esteem, could readily ignore.

Visible displays of independence from, or rejections of authority can be understood as attempts to re-establish moral character in the face of affronts. This can be accomplished by direct attacks on teachers or school, or through daring illegal performances elsewhere. These responses may or may not reflect anger at treatment perceived to be unjust may or may not defend the student against threats to self-esteem, may or may not reflect a repudiation of conventional conduct norms. What is crucial is that these activities *demonstrate* retaliation for injury and the rejection of official values to an audience whose own resentment of constituted authority causes it to be appreciative of rebels whom it would not necessarily dare to imitate. Secret delinquency and acts that entailed no risk would not serve this function.

Field research on the interaction between teachers and delinquent students [72] and responses of delinquent gangs and individuals to challenges to honor [73] support this dramaturgical interpretation of delinquency. Most gang violence seems not to erupt spontaneously out of anger, but is chosen and manipulated for its ability to impress others. Nonutilitarian forms of theft, property destruction and violence may well be understood as quite utilitarian if their purpose is the establishment or preservation of the claim to be a certain sort of person, rather than the acquisition of property.

Goffman [74] has called attention to the common features of activities in which participants establish moral character through risk-taking. Such activities as dueling, bull fighting, sky diving, mountain climbing, big game hunting, and gambling for high stakes are undertaken for the opportunity they provide to carve out a valued social identity by exhibiting courage, daring, pluck and composure.

These qualities are those the industrial system (factory and school) tend to disvalue or ignore: the concept of seeking out risks and "showing off" is antithetical to the traditional ethos of capitalism, where the emphasis has been placed on minimizing risk, using time productively, and suppressing the self to demonstrate moral character. Consequently, participants in action systems based on displays of risk-taking have traditionally been drawn primarily from classes not subject to the discipline and self-denial of industrial production, e.g. the European nobility, bohemian populations, and the unemployed poor.

More recently, as production has come to require less sacrifice and self-denial from large sectors of the work force, and to require the steady expansion of stimulated consumption for its growth, the more affluent sectors of the labor force are increasingly encouraged to seek an escape from the routinicity of daily life through mild forms of risk-taking (e.g. gambling and skiing) as well as through the leisure use of drugs and sex.

The similarity between the subculture of delinquency and that of the leisurely affluent [75] makes sense in view of the position of the delinquent *vis à vis* the school. Like the factory, the school frequently requires monotonous and meaningless work. Regimentation is the rule. Expressions of originality and spontaneity are not only discouraged, but may be punished [76]. Students who reap no present rewards from school work or anticipate only the most limited occupational rewards in return for subordinating themselves to the discipline of the school are free to cultivate the self-expressive traits which the school fails to reward. As Downes [77] has pointed out, they may come to regard adults who work as defeated and lifeless because of their subordination to a routine that necessitates self-suppression, and hence try to avoid work because of the cost in self-alienation.

Traditionally this has been especially true of students with lower class backgrounds; Finestone [78] has described their adaptation and Rainwater [79] has interpreted the expressive features of lower class black male urban culture in these terms. However, when the political and occupational sectors of society lose their legitimacy, students of other classes may find the prospect of entering conventional careers in those sectors so repugnant that they lose the motivation to achieve in school, and also cultivate life styles based on self-expression or politically motivated risk-taking. The bright hippies and radicals from white middle-class backgrounds in the late 1960s are a case in point.

The similarity between delinquent and non-criminal recreational risk-taking warns us that the pursuit of status through risk-taking need not *necessarily* arise from problems in self-esteem. Once a status system rewarding delinquent activity exists, students may act with reference to it in order to *increase* prestige in the group, not only to prevent prestige from falling. Thus teachers may be provoked [80], gang rivals taunted, and daring thefts and assaults perpetrated, even in the absence of humiliation.

When students drop out or graduate from high school, they enter a world that, while sometimes inhospitable, does not restrict their autonomy and assault their dignity in the same way the school does. The need to engage in crime to establish a sense of an autonomous self, and to preserve moral character through risk-taking is thus reduced. In addition, the sympathetic audience of other students of the same age is taken away. Thus school-leaving eliminates major sources of motivation toward delinquency.

In this respect, it is especially ironic that delinquency prevention programs have involved campaigns to extend the duration of schooling. American panel studies indicate that the self-esteem of dropouts rises after leaving school [81] and that dropping out produces an immediate decline in delinquency [82]. In England, when the school-leaving age was raised by one year, the peak age for delinquency also rose simultaneously by one year [83].

Despite this evidence that the school contributes to delinquency, it is hardly necessary. In Cordoba, Argentina, patterns of delinquency are fairly similar to those in the United States even though the school-leaving age for working-class children is 10, and delinquents report generally favorable attitudes toward school [84]. Unsatisfactory school experiences simply add to the economic motivations created by the exclusion of juveniles from the labor market.

Masculine Status Anxiety and Delinquency

Many observers have remarked on the disproportionate involvement of males in delinquent activity and the exaggerated masculine posturing that characterizes much male delinquency. Though sex differences in delinquency are not as pronounced in self-report studies as in arrest reports, and seem to be gradually narrowing, they nevertheless remain considerable, especially in the violence offense categories. Theoretical explanations for these differences not based on innate sex differences have alternatively emphasized differences in the socialization of boys and girls, which lead to differences in gender role [85], and "masculine protest" against maternal domination and identification [86], especially in the female-based households of the lower class [87]. In such households, the argument goes, boys will tend to identify with the mother, and hence will experience uncertainty and anxiety in later years in connection with their identification as a male. To allay this anxiety, they reject the "good" values of the mother and engage in "masculine" forms of delinquency.

Application of the theory to delinquency in the United States has not been entirely successful. Male delinquency does appear to be associated with what has been interpreted as anxiety over masculinity, but is independent of whether the household in which the child is raised lacked an adult male [88].

This finding points to the need for a revision in the argument.

Hannerz [89] has pointed out that children raised in homes without fathers may still have alternative male role models. Indeed, children raised in a community where adult male unemployment rates are high may spend more of their time in the company of adult males who could serve as role models than their middle class peers. I would argue, in addition, that Miller's adherence to the psycho-analytic framework blinds him to important sources of anxiety connected with masculinity that are unrelated to the family configuration in early childhood. Males who are not in doubt about their identity as males may nevertheless feel anxiety in connection with anticipated or actual inability to fulfill traditional sex role expectations concerning work and support of family. This masculine *status* anxiety can be generated by a father who is present but ineffectual, and by living in a neighborhood where, for social-structural reasons, many men are unemployed – regardless of whether one's own father is present in the household.

Men who experience such anxiety because they are prevented from fulfilling conventional male role expectations may attempt to alleviate their anxiety by exaggerating those traditionally male traits that *can* be expressed. Attempts to dominate women (including rape) and patterns of interpersonal violence can be seen in these terms. In other words, crime can be a response to masculine status anxiety no less than to anxiety over male identity; it can provide a sense of potency that is expected and desired but not achieved in other spheres of life.

In this interpretation, a compulsive concern with toughness and masculinity arises not from a hermetically sealed lower-class subculture "with an integrity of its own" nor from the psychodynamics of a female-headed household [90] but as a response to a contradiction between structural constraints on male status attainment imposed by the larger economic and political order, and the cultural expectations for men that permeate American society. The role of the subculture Miller describes is to make available the behavioral adaptations that previous generations have developed in response to this contradiction, and thus to shape those responses. We should therefore expect persons suffering from masculine status anxiety who were members of groups in which the structural sources of masculine status anxiety have been common and long-standing to develop more coherent and stereotyped adaptations than individuals who were not members of such groups, e.g. in lower class blacks as compared with recently unemployed white collar employees [91]. We should also expect those adaptations to attenuate in groups that ceased to encounter such contradictions, either because structural constraints to the fulfillment of traditional role expectations had been eliminated, or because expectations for men in the larger society had changed.

208

If I am correct in assuming that delinquents in the last years of elementary school and early years of high school are not excessively preoccupied with their occupational prospects, but become more concerned with their futures toward the end of high school – and there is some qualitative evidence to support this assumption [92] – then masculine anxiety during these early years must stem from other sources. One plausible source lies in the contradiction between the school's expectations of docility and submission to authority, and more widely communicated social expectations of masculinity. While the school represses both boys and girls, the message that girls get is consistent; the message boys receive is contradictory. This difference would help to explain sex differences in delinquency in early adolescence.

Most of the behavior that can be explained plausibly in this way – smoking, sexual conquests, joy-riding, vandalism, fighting between boys – is fairly trivial, and either becomes legal in mid to late adolescence, or abates rapidly. Anxiety over inability to fulfill traditional male occupational roles would show up late in adolescence. If I am correct in holding that such anxiety is an important source of criminal violations, the ratio of male to female participation should increase with age during adolescence, and there is evidence from self-reports that it does, at least among middle class youths [93].

One would expect masculine status anxiety to appear with greatest intensity and to decline most slowly in those segments of the population in which adult male unemployment is exceptionally high. This conforms to the general pattern of arrests for violence offenses such as homicide, forcible rape and assaults – offenses often unconnected with the pursuit of material gain, and hence most plausibly interpreted as a response to masculine status anxiety. Rates of arrest for these offenses peak in the immediate post-high school age brackets (several years later than for the property offenses) and the decline is slower than for property offenses. Moreover, blacks are over-represented in violence offense arrests to a much greater degree than in arrests for property offenses. Thus in 1973, the ratio of black to white arrests for burglary, larceny and auto theft was 0.45; for non-negligent homicide, forcible rape and aggravated assault, 0.85; for robbery, 1.79 [94]. This relative over-representation of blacks is confirmed in victimization studies [95] and in self-reporting studies of delinquency [96] and thus cannot be explained as a manifestation of racial differences in risk of apprehension.

Costs of Delinquency

So far some possible sources of variation with age in motivation to participate in common forms of criminal activity have been identified, but this is only half the story, for one may wish to engage in some form of behavior but nevertheless decide not to do so because the potential costs of participation are deemed unacceptably high. Costs can be a consequence of delinquency, and must be taken into account. Control theorists have begun to do so [97].

Costs can originate with internal or external sources of control. Superego restraints and favorable self-concepts and ideals exemplify internal sources of control [98]; they threaten the potential delinquent with guilt and shame. External costs can include parental disapproval and loss of privileges, school-imposed sanctions (ranging from teacher's disapproval to suspension or expulsion), loss of job and reduced prospects for future employment, acquisition of a police or juvenile court record, and deprivation of freedom through a reformatory sentence. Although external costs are actually imposed only on those who are caught, fear of incurring costs can inhibit potential delinquents and lead actual delinquents to desist.

To what extent can internal or external costs contribute to the age distribution of criminality? With the exception of those forms of minor delinquency considered far more discrediting to adults than to juveniles [99], it is unlikely that *internal* controls play a major role in generating age *differences* in criminal involvement, for it seems unlikely that moral inhibitions substantially increase from mid to late adolescence. Indeed, we generally expect people to take a more pragmatic view of morality as they get older.

External costs, however, are likely to vary with age. In early adolescence the potential costs of all but the most serious forms of delinquency are relatively slight. Parents and teachers are generally willing to write off a certain amount of misbehavior as "childish mischief," while enormous caseloads have forced juvenile courts in large cities to adopt a policy that comes very close to what Schur [100] has called "radical nonintervention" for all but the most serious cases. Moreover, the confidentiality of juvenile court records reduces the extent to which prospects are jeopardized by an arrest.

Given the slight risk of apprehension for any single delinquent act, the prevalence of motivations to violate the law, and the low costs of lesser violations, we should expect minor infractions to be common among juveniles, and the self-reporting studies generally suggest that they are. Where the risk of incurring costs does procure abstention, we should suppose fear of parental disapproval would be the most salient. Teenagers who have good relationships with parents would presumably be the most concerned with incurring their disapproval, and they do have lower rates of involvement in delinquency [101].

As teenagers get older, the potential costs of apprehension increase: victims may be more prone to file a complaint, and police to make an arrest.

Juvenile court judges are more likely to take a serious view of an older offender, especially one with a prior record. Older offenders risk prosecution in criminal court, where penalties tend to be harsher, and where an official record will have more serious consequences for later job opportunities.

Delinquents are acutely sensitive to these considerations. According to several youthful offenders testifying before the New York State Select Committee at a hearing on assault and robbery against the elderly,

> If you're 15 and under you won't go to jail ... That's why when we do a "Rush and Crib" – which means you rush the victim and push him or her into their apartment, you let the youngest member do any beatings. See, we know if they arrest him, he'll be back on the street in no time [102].

In interviews, former delinquents often attribute their own desistance to their unwillingness to risk the stiffer penalties they would receive if arrested and tried as adults [103]. Thus the leniency of the juvenile court contributes to high levels of juvenile crime.

Just as the costs of crime are escalating, new opportunities in the form of jobs, marriage, or enlistment in the armed forces create stakes in conformity and, as Matza points out [104], may also relieve problems of masculine status anxiety. Toward the end of high school, when student concern about the future increases, the anticipation of new opportunities is manifested in desistance from delinquency and avoidance of those who do not similarly desist. Consistent with this interpretation is the fact that in both England and the United States, the peak year for delinquent involvement is the year *before* school-leaving.

Labeling theorists have tended to emphasize the role that apprehension and official processing of delinquents may play in increasing their subsequent delinquent involvement, either through the effect of labeling on self-concept and attitudes [105] or because prospects for legitimate employment are jeopardized through stigmatization [106]. The evidence available does not suggest that this happens to any great extent [107]. This is not necessarily surprising. As Schur [108] has pointed out, children may develop psychological defenses that serve to neutralize the discrediting imputations of others. When the negative label is applied by adults who are perceived as antagonists (police, judges, jailers) it should not be difficult to avoid being deeply influenced by their evaluations. Moreover, the confidentiality of juvenile court records helps to shield delinquents from later stigma.

Those whose opportunities for lucrative employment are limited by obstacles associated with racial and/or class membership will have far less reason to desist from illegal activity than those whose careers are not similarly blocked. The kinds of jobs available to young members of the lower strata of the working class tend to be tedious and financially unrewarding (when they are available at all). Marriage may appear less appealing to young men whose limited prospects promise inability to fulfill traditional male expectations as breadwinner. Even an army career may be precluded by an arrest record, low intelligence test scores, physical disability, or illiteracy. Thus the legitimate opportunity structure, even if relatively useless for understanding entrance into delinquency, may still be helpful in understanding patterns of desistance.

The same may be said of the illegal opportunity structure. Those few delinquents who are recruited into organized crime or professional theft face larger rewards and less risk of serious penalty than those not so recruited, and their personal relationships with partners may be more satisfying. They should be less likely to desist from crime, but their offense patterns can be expected to change.

This reasoning suggests that the association between criminal involvement on the one hand and race and class on the other should be stronger for adults than for juveniles. If this is so, arrest rates in a given offense category should decline more rapidly for whites and youths with middle class backgrounds than for blacks and youths with working class and lower class backgrounds. In the male birth cohort studied by Wolfgang, Figlio and Sellin, whites were more likely to desist after an offense [109]. F.B.I. crime career data also suggest higher rearrest rates for blacks than for whites [110] and a number of studies of recidivism of released prisoners have found somewhat higher recidivism among black ex-prisoners than among white ex-prisoners. Though based on small samples, Chambliss' field study of delinquency [111] does indicate a much higher desistance rate for middle class delinquents.

If, as is often suggested, crimes of violence involve less reflection and deliberation than crimes of acquisition, violence offenses should respond less elastically to increased external costs than property offenses. For this reason, we should expect violence crime rates to decline less rapidly with age than property crime rates, and this prediction is verified (see Table I).

Delinquency and the Social Construction of the Juvenile

Among the structural sources of adolescent crime identified here, the exclusion of juveniles from the world of adult work plays a crucial role. It is this exclusion that simultaneously exaggerates teenagers' dependence on peers for approval and eliminates the possibility of their obtaining funds to support their intensive, leisure-time social activities. The disrespectful treatment students receive in school depends on their low social status, which in turn reflects their lack of employment. In late adolescence and

212

early adulthood, their fear that this lack of employment will persist into adulthood evokes anxiety over achievement of traditional male gender role expectations, especially among males in the lower levels of the working class, thus contributing to a high level of violence.

Institutionalized leniency to juvenile offenders, which reduces the potential costs of delinquency, stems from the belief that teenagers are not as responsible for their actions as adults [112]. The conception of juveniles as impulsive and irresponsible gained currency around the turn of the century (see for example, Hall [113]) when organized labor and Progressive reformers campaigned for child labor laws to save jobs for adults, a goal given high priority after the Depression of 1893. This conception was, in a sense, self-fulfilling. Freed from ties to conventional institutions, teenagers *have* become more impulsive and irresponsible.

The exclusion of teenagers from serious work is not characteristic of all societies. Peasant and tribal societies could not afford to keep their young idle as long as we do. In such societies, juvenile crime rates were low. Under feudalism, too, children participated in farming and handicraft production as part of the family unit beginning at a very early age.

In depriving masses of serfs and tenant farmers of access to the means of production (land), European capitalism in its early stages of development generated a great deal of crime, but in a manner that cut across age boundaries. Little of the literature on crime in Elizabethan and Tudor England singles out juveniles as a special category.

The industrial revolution in the first half of the nineteenth century similarly brought with it a great deal of misery, but its effect on crime was not restricted to juveniles. Children of the working class in that period held jobs at an early age and in some sectors of the economy were given preference. Only middle and upper class children were exempt from the need to work, and they were supervised much more closely than they are nowadays. As far as can be judged, juvenile crime in that period was a much smaller fraction of the total than at present, and was more confined to the lower classes than it is now [114].

In modern capitalist societies, children of all classes share, for a limited period, a common relationship to the means of production (namely exclusion) which is distinct from that of most adults, and they respond to their common structural position in fairly similar ways. Although there are class differences in the extent and nature of delinquency, especially violent delinquency, these are less pronounced than for adults, for whom occupational differentiation is much sharper.

The deteriorating position of juveniles in the labor market in recent years has been ascribed to a variety of causes, among them the inclusion of juveniles under minimum wage laws, changes in the structure of the economy (less farm employment), teenage preference for part-time work (to permit longer periods of education) which makes teenage labor less attractive to employers, and the explosion in the teenage labor supply created by the baby boom at a time when women were entering the labor market in substantial numbers [115]. Whatever contribution these circumstances may have made to shifting teenage employment patterns in the short-run, the exclusion of juveniles from the labor market has been going on for more than a century, and may more plausibly be explained in terms of the failure of the oligopoly-capitalist economy to generate sufficient demand for labor, than to these recent developments [116].

In both the United States and England, the prolongation of education has historically been associated with the contraction of the labor market [117], casting doubt on the view that more education is something that the general population has wanted for its own sake. Had this been true, the school leaving age would have jumped upward in periods of prosperity, when a larger proportion of the population could afford more education, not during depressions. Moreover, the functionalist argument that increased education is necessary as technology becomes more complex would apply at best to a small minority of students, and rests on the dubious assumption that full-time schooling is pedagogically superior to alternative modes of organizing the education of adolescents.

The present social organization of education, which I have argued contributes to delinquency, has also been plausibly attributed to the functional requirement of a capitalist economy for a docile, disciplined and stratified labor force [118], as well as to the need to keep juveniles out of the labor market.

Thus the high and increasing level of juvenile crime we are seeing in present-day United States and in other Western countries orginates in the structural position of juveniles in an advanced capitalist economy.

Delinquency is not, however, a problem of capitalism alone. Although there are many differences between crime patterns in the United States and the Soviet Union, the limited information available indicates that delinquency in the Soviet Union is often associated with leisure-time consumption activities on the part of youths who are academic failures, and who are either not working or studying, or are working at or preparing for unrewarding jobs [119]. This suggests that some of the processes described here may be at work in the Soviet Union. Since Soviet society is based on hierarchical domination and requires a docile, disciplined and stratified labor force, this parallel is not surprising.

One might, in fact, generalize from this analysis, to conclude that any society that excluded juveniles from the world of adult work for long periods and imposed mandatory attendance at schools organized like ours would have a substantial amount of delinquency.

Criminology and Marxist Theory

For the first time in many decades, criminologists are again drawing on Marxian social theory. The small corpus of literature in this vein has thus far been devoted primarily to the analysis of criminal law and criminal justice administration [120], the criticism of liberal reform proposals [121], and the critique of non-Marxist contributions to the theory of crime causation [122].

Until recently, the only positive contribution this literature made to the theory of crime causation was the assertion that under capitalism crime is not pathological but rational [123]. The limitations of such an approach are manifest. When the mechanisms by which capitalism causes crime are left unspecified, only True Believers are likely to be persuaded of the connection, especially in the face of the persistence of crime in non-capitalist societies. In addition, other important questions about causation (why is there such variability in criminal behavior on the part of those who live in capitalist societies? Why does the amount and nature of crime undergo historical change?) are left unanswered.

However, several developments are leading radical criminologists to a new interest in questions of etiology. The prominence crime has assumed as a political issue has made it difficult for radicals trying to organize working class constituencies to dismiss the continuing rise in street crime by pointing out that crime is merely a "social construction" (feminist agitation over rape has had a similar effect), or by changing the subject to government and corporate crime. Within the discipline, the current reassessment of labeling theory is redirecting theoretical interest from secondary deviation resulting from labeling by law enforcement agencies to social structural sources of primary deviance [124]. Moreover, the recent Marxist critiques of phenomenology, existential sociology and symbolic interactionism as excessively voluntaristic, ahistorical and astructural [125] (paralleling the collapse of a New Left that emphasized voluntarism and subjectivity) has made radical criminologists more receptive to causal explanations of criminal behavior than has been the case in the recent past.

This paper has attempted to develop a Marxian perspective on the causation of crimes commonly committed by juveniles – for other recent Marxian work on causation see [126]. I have assumed throughout that there is no necessary contradiction between such traditional criminological concerns as the causal role of such institutions as family and school or psychological concepts like self-esteem and anxiety on the one hand, and Marxist theory on the other (although I have criticized elements in non-Marxist theories of delinquency, many of the points of criticism concern elements that are not crucial from the point of view of Marxism). Rather, Marxism compliments these traditional concerns by placing them in a larger framework.

Although not so fully developed that it can simply be "applied" to problems at hand, Marxism directs our attention to the manner in which changing modes and relations of production lead to historically changing criminogenic contradictions [127] within or between particular institutions. The analysis of these contradictions can only be carried out concretely, for particular historical epochs and particular forms of criminality. The same approach can be brought to the sociology of criminal law (which from this perspective need not be seen *solely* as an instrument of class rule), and can be of value in studying crime in non-capitalist as well as in capitalist societies. To leave off analysis with the statement that crime is rational and creative under capitalism is to fail to draw on the richness of the Marxist legacy.

From the point of view of theory, Marxism can serve to integrate criminology with questions central to macrosociological theory. The viewpoint I am recommending constitutes an implicit reproach to both consensus and conflict models in criminology. The conflict model, embraced by many radical criminologists in the 1960s in the face of massive social conflicts in American society (major statements of the conflict perspective can be found in [128]) fails to specify the lines along which conflicts appear, and where cooperation can be located. In that any society has elements of both consensus and dissensus, cooperation and conflict, varying historically in degree and form, both points of view distort social reality by omission, and by portraying a uniformity where diversity exists. Historical materialism provides the conceptual tools for investigating the degree of conflict present in a society and the forms it takes.

At the level of practice, the Marxist perspective exposes the limitations of liberal meliorism. For decades, criminologists have proposed such reforms as the elimination of poverty and racial discrimination in order to reduce crime, as if these social problems were mere oversights, little snags in a generally beneficial social order. Marxist theorists tend to see these problems largely as produced by and insoluble within the framework of a class society. My analysis of delinquency suggests that most proposed "solutions" to the delinquency problem would have little impact. A thorough integration of

216

teenagers into the labor force would require a major restructuring of work and education, and this is hardly to be expected in the foreseeable future.

Although I have argued for the general compatibility between Marxist and non-Marxist approaches to crime causation, there are points of tension which must be mentioned. Unlike positivists, Marxists have been concerned with the dynamic interplay between objective conditions and subjective consciousness. Responses to objective conditions – including criminal responses – are contingent on the level of group awareness of the origins of oppressive objective conditions in class dynamics and of the possibilities for engaging in collective action to change these conditions. My analysis of delinquency is implicitly predicated on the low level of such consciousness now present among most American teenagers. That could change, though the prospects of change in the immediate future do not appear especially bright.

Marxists have also approached the question of class differently from non-Marxists. In this essay, I have used the term "class" in the very imprecise manner of non-Marxist criminologists, to refer to position on a ranked scale. In applications to delinquency this usage is ordinarily extended to juveniles by assigning them to the class of their parents. This approach has been relatively unsuccessful in explaining delinquency; class, thus defined, is a poor predictor of delinquency.

Marxian theorists take class to be defined by relationship to the means of production [129], but have conceptualized such relationships too narrowly. Feminist theorists have pointed out the unique relationship to production of the housewife in a capitalist economy (for a summary of the major statements on this question, see Fee [130]) and here I have argued that juveniles in an advanced capitalist economy have a common, if temporary, relationship to the means of production, characterized by exclusion during a period of mandatory training for entry into the labor force. In Marxian terms, this means that juveniles can no more be assigned the class of their parents than housewives can be assigned the class of their husbands. The high rate of juvenile crime is largely a response to the conditions imposed on this class under conditions of weak class consciousness.

In this instance, at least, the Marxian perspective yielded insights into the nature of delinquency that non-Marxian approaches to class have failed to provide. It is not necessarily true, however, that all forms of crime originate *directly* in the problems confronting a particular class, even if class is defined in the flexible manner I propose. The dynamic functioning of a class society leads to social differentiation along many lines other than class, and the resulting differences in experiences, opportunities and costs may have great relevance for criminal involvement. The contribution of Marxism is to view such differentiation as the product of relations of production and reproduction, rather than as an *a priori* given.

Acknowledgements

I am grateful to Ava Baron, Eliot Freidson, Daniel Glaser, Irwin Goffman, Drew Humphreys, Caroline Persell, Edwin Schur and James Q. Wilson for helpful discussions and suggestions.

NOTES

1 Wolfgang, M.E., R.M. Figlio and T. Sellin (1972). *Delinquency in a Birth Cohort*. Chicago: University of Chicago Press; Glueck, S. and E. Glueck (1937). *Later Criminal Careers*. New York: The Commonwealth Fund; Glaser, D. (1964). *The Effectiveness of a Prison and Parole System*. Indianapolis: Bobbs-Merrill, 469–474.

2 Beattie, R.H. (1955). "Problems of Criminal Statistics in the United States," *Journal of Criminal Law, Criminology and Police Science* 55: 359–369; Kitsuse, J.I. and A.V. Cicourel (1963). "A Note on the Uses of Official Statistics." *Social Problems* 11: 131–139; Wolfgang, M.E. (1963). "Uniform Crime Reports: A Critical Appraisal," *University of Pennsylvania Law Review* 111: 708–738; Robinson, S.M. (1966). "A Critical View of Uniform Crime Reports," *Michigan Law Review* 64: 1031–1054; Wheeler, S. (1967). "Criminal Statistics: A Reformulation of the Problem," *Journal of Criminal Law, Criminology and Police Science* 58: 317–324.

3 Baittle, B. (1961). "Psychiatric Aspects of the Development of a Street Corner Group: An Exploratory Study," *American Journal of Orthopsychiatry* 31: 703–712; Miller, W.B. (1966). "Violent Crime in City Gangs," *Annals of the American Academy of Political and Social Science* 364: 96–112; Gold, M. (1970). *Delinquent Behavior in an American City*. Belmont, Cal.: Brooks Cole; Hindelang, M.J. (1971). "Age, Sex, and the Versatility of Delinquent Involvements," *Social Problems* 18: 522–535;

4 Offer, D. (1969). *The Psychological World of the Teenager: A Study of Normal Adolescent Boys*. New York: Basic Books.

5 West W.G. (1976). "Serious Thieves: Lower Class Adolescent Males in a Short-Term Deviant Occupation." Unpublished paper.

6 Wilson, N.K. (1972). *Risk Ratios in Juvenile Delinquency*. Ann Arbor: University Microfilms.

7 Private communication from Patricia Miller.

8 Michigan State Prison (1878). *Annual Report*.

9 Monkkonen, E. (1975). *The Dangerous Class: Crime and Poverty in Columbus Ohio 1860–1884*. Cambridge: Harvard University Press.

10 Neison, F.G.P. (1857). *Contributions to Vital Statistics*. Third Edition. Quoted in J.J. Tobias, *Nineteenth Century Crime: Prevention and Punishment*. Newton Abbott: David and Charles; Quetelet, A.J. (1831). *Recherches sur le Penchant au Crime aux Différents Ages*. Brussels: Académie Royale; Lombroso C. (1968). *Crime: Its Causes and Remedies*. Montclair, N.J.: Patterson Smith 175–177.

11 Normandeau A. (1968). *Trends and Patterns of Robbery*. Unpublished Ph. D. Dissertation University of Pennsylvania; McClintock, F.H., N.H. Avison and G.N.G. Rose (1968). *Crime in England and Wales* London: Heinemann Educational Books 179; Lopez-Rey, M. (1970). *Crime: An Analytical Approach*. New York: Praeger; Schichor, D. and A. Kirschenbaum (1975). "Juvenile Delinquency and New Towns: The Case of Israel." Paper presented to the American Society of Criminology.

12 Glueck, S. and E. Glueck (1968). *Delinquents and Non-delinquents in Perspective*. Cambridge: Harvard University Press 169–171.

13 Ferracuti F., S. Dinitz and A. Esperanza (1975). *Delinquents and Nondelinquents in the Puerto Rican Slum Culture*. Columbus: Ohio State University Press.

14 Miller W B. (1958), "Lower Class Subculture as a Generating Milieu of Gang Delinquency" *Journal of Social Issues* 14: 5–19.

218

15 Clark J.P. and E.W. Haurek (1966). "Age and Sex Roles of Adolescents and their Involvement in Misconduct: A Reappraisal." *Sociology and Social Research* 50: 495–503
16 Cloward, R A. and L.E Ohlin (1960). *Delinquency and Opportunity: A Theory of Delinquent Gangs.* New York: Free Press.
17 Cohen, A.K. (1955). *Delinquent Boys*. New York: Free Press.
18 Matza, D. (1964). *Delinquency and Drift*. New York: Wiley 24–27.
19 Merton, R.K. (1957). *Social Theory and Social Structure*. Revised Edition. New York: Free Press; Cloward R. and L. Ohlin (1960), op cit.
20 Bachman, J.G., S. Green and I. Wirtanen (1972). *Dropping Out – Problem or Symptom*. Ann Arbor: Institute for Social Research.
21 Cloward, R. and L. Ohlin (1960). op. cit.
22 Ibid., 174–175.
23 Elliot, D.S. and H.L. Voss (1974). *Delinquency and Dropout*. Lexington, Mass.: Lexington Books; Quicker, J. (1974). "The Effect of Goal Discrepancy on Delinquency" *Social Problems* 22: 76–86; Lalli, M. and W. Roberts (1974). "The Strain Theory of Delinquency " Unpublished paper University of Pennsylvania.
24 Bloch, H.A. and A. Niederhoffer (1958). *The Gang*. New York: Philosophical Library 29–30.
25 Matza, D. (1964). Op. cit.
26 Ibid. 54–58.
27 Merton, R. (1957). Op. cit., 131 -194
28 Ibid., 166
29 Cloward, R. and L. Ohlin (1960), op. cit.
30 Perlin, L.I., M.R. Yarrow and H.A. Scarr (1967). "Unintended Effects of Parental Aspirations: The Case of Children's Cheating " *American Journal of Sociology* 73: 73–83, Bergman, D. (1974). "The Absence of Guilt in Cheating." Unpublished paper presented to the American Anthropological Association; Barnes, B. (1975). "School's Honor Code Gets an F," *New York Post* (September 24): 18.
31 Milner, R and C. Milner (1972). *Black Players: The Secret World of Black Pimps*. Boston: Little Brown, Ianni, F. (1974). *The Black Mafia.* New York: Simon and Schuster.
32 Woodley, R. (1972). *Dealer: Portrait of a Cocaine Merchant*. New York: Warner Paperback Library.
33 Cohen, A. (1955). Op.cit. 25.
34 Blos, P. (1941). *The Adolescent Personality: A Study of Individual Behavior.* New York: Appleton: Bowerman C.E. and J.W. Kinch (1959). "Changes in Family and Peer Orientation of Children between the Fourth and Tenth Grades," *Social Forces* 37: 206; Tuma, E. and N. Livson (1960). "Family Socioeconomic Status and Attitudes toward Authority," *Child Development* 31: 387; Conger, J.J. (1971). "A World They Never Knew: The Family and Social Change," *Daedalus* 100: 1105–1138; (1973). *Adolescence and Youth*. New York: Harper & Row 286–292.
35 Eisenstadt, S.N. (1956). *From Generation to Generation: Age Groups and Social Structure.* New York: Free Press; Bloch and Niederhoffer (1958), op. cit.
36 Mussen, P H., J.J. Conger and J. Kagan (1969). *Child Development and Personality.* New York: Harper & Row.
37 Panel on Youth of the President's Science Advisory Committee (1974). *Youth: Transition to Adulthood*. Chicago: University of Chicago.
38 Mead, M. (1939). *From the South Seas: Part III. Sex and Temperament in Three Primitive Societies.* New York: Morrow; Eisenstadt, S.N. (1956), op. cit., 56–92; Minturn, L. and W.W. Lambert (1964). *Mothers in Six Cultures: Antecedents of Child Rearing*. New York: Wiley.
39 Insofar as meals are not served regularly in some lower class families, biological and social needs here converge. Mertonian theory implicitly but erroneously assumes that the welfare state functions well enough to meet basic biological needs.
40 Panel on Youth (1974), op. cit., 36–38.
41 Tomson, B. and E.R. Fiedler (1975). "Gangs: A Response to the Urban World (Part II)," in Desmond S. Cartwright, Barbara Tomson and Herschey Schwartz (eds.), *Gang Delinquency.* Monterey, Cal.: Brooks/Cole.

42 Raskin, A.H. (1975). "The Teenage Worker is Hardest Hit," *New York Times* (May 4): F3.

43 Sherif, M. and C.W. Sherif (1964). *Reference Groups: Exploration into Conformity and Deviation of Adolescents.* New York: Harper & Row, 174.

44 Werthman, C. (1967). "The Function of Social Definitions in the Development of Delinquent Careers," in *Task Force Report: Juvenile Delinquency.* Washington, D.C.: Government Printing Office, 157.

45 Fyvel, T.R. (1962). *Troublemakers.* New York: Schocken Books; Parker, H.J. (1974), op. cit.

46 Toby, J. (1967), op. cit., 136–137.

47 Ibid., 137–138.

48 Lin, T. (1959), op. cit., 259.

49 Bauer, E.J. (1964). "The Trend of Juvenile Offenses in the Netherlands and the United States," *Journal of Criminal Law, Criminology and Police Science* 55: 359–369.

50 DeFleur, L. (1970), op. cit.

51 Weis, J. (1976). "Liberation and Crime: The Invention of the New Female Criminal." *Crime and Social Justice* 6: 17–27.

52 Parker, H.H. (1974), op. cit.; Toby (1967), op. cit., 137.

53 Rolf, M. and S.B. Sells (1968). "Juvenile Delinquency in Relation to peer Acceptance-Rejection and Socioeconomic Status." *Psychology in the Schools* 5: 3–18; West, D. (1973). "Are Delinquents Different?" *New Society* 26 (November 22): 456.

54 Rothstein, E. (1962). "Attributes Related to High Social Status: A Comparison of the Perceptions of Delinquents and Non-Delinquent Boys," *Social Problems* 10: 75–83; Short, J.F., Jr. and F.L. Strodtbeck (1965). *Group Process and Gang Delinquency.* Chicago: University of Chicago Press, 243–244; Hirschi, T. (1969). *The Causes of Delinquency.* Berkeley: University of California Press, 145–161.

55 Nye, F.I. (1958). *Family Relationships and Delinquent Behavior.* New York: Wiley, ch. 8; Hirschi, T. (1969), op. cit., 83–109.

56 Short, J.F., Jr. and F.I. Nye (1958). "Extent of Unrecorded Delinquency: Tentative Conclusions." *Journal of Criminal Law, Criminology and Police Science* 49: 296–302; Reiss, A.J., Jr. and A.L. Rhodes (1961). "The Distribution of Juvenile Delinquency in the Social Class Structure," *American Sociological Review* 26: 730–732; Dentler, R. and L.J. Monroe (1961). "Early Adolescent Theft," *American Sociological Review* 26: 733–743; Clark, J.P. and E.P. Wenninger (1962). "Socio-Economic Class and Area as Correlates of Illegal Behavior Among Juveniles," *American Sociological Review* 27: 826–834; Akers, R.L. (1964). "Socio-Economic Status and Delinquent Behavior: A Retest," *Journal of Research in Crime and Delinquency* 1: 38–46; Hirschi, T. (1969), op. cit., pp. 66–82.

57 Simon, R.J. (1975). *Women and Crime.* Lexington, Mass.: Lexington Books.

58 Cohen, A. (1955), op. cit., p. 25.

59 Schafer, W.E. and K. Polk (1967). "Delinquency and the Schools," in *Task Force Report: Juvenile Delinquency and Youth Crime.* Washington, D.C.: Government Printing Office; Polk, K. and W.E. Schafer (1972). *Schools and Delinquency.* Englewood Cliffs, N.J. Prentice-Hall.

60 These expectations are derived from young peoples' knowledge of family arrangements in our society generally, not only from their own family circumstances. When controls in their own family are not relaxed, this can provide an additional source of conflict.

61 Psathas, G. (1957). "Ethnicity, Social Class, and Adolescent Independence from Parental Control," *American Sociological Review* 22: 415–423. Kobrin, S. (1962). "The Impact of Cultural Factors in Selected Problems of Adolescent Development in the Middle and Lower Class," *American Journal of Orthopsychiatry* 33: 387–390; Werthman, C. (1967), op. cit.: Rainwater, L. (1970). *Behind Ghetto Walls.* Chicago: Aldine, 211–234; Ladner, J. (1971). *Tomorrow's Tomorrow: The Black Woman.* Garden City: Doubleday, 61–63; Elder, G. (1974). *Children of the Great Depression: Social Change in Life Experience.* Chicago: University of Chicago Press.

62 Toby, J. (1967), op. cit., 141.

63 Gouldner, A. (1970). *The Coming Crisis in Western Sociology.* New York: Basic Books, 221–222.

64 Cohen, A. (1955), op. cit., 112–113; Sennett, R. and J. Cobb (1972), *The Hidden Injuries of Class.* New York: Alfred A. Knopf.

65 Hyman, H.H. (1968). "The Psychology of Status," in H.H. Hyman and E. Singer (eds.), *Readings in Reference Group Theory and Research.* New York: Free Press, 147–168.

66 Goffman, E. (1955). "On Face-Work: An Analysis of Ritual Elements in Social Interaction," *Psychiatry* 18: 213–231.

67 Ellis, H.G. and S.M. Newman (1972). "The Greaser is a 'Bad Ass'; The Gowster is a 'Muthah'; An Analysis of Two Urban Youth Roles," in Thomas Kochman (ed.), *Rappin' and Stylin' Out: Communication in Black America.* Urbana: University of Illinois Press, 375–376.

68 Cohen, A. (1955), op. cit., 121–137.

69 Miller, W.B. (1966). "Violent Crime in City Gangs," *Annals of the American Academy of Political and Social Science* 364: 96–112.

70 Matza, D. (1964), op. cit., 33–68; Short, J.F., Jr. and F.L. Strodtbeck (1965), op.cit., 47–75.

71 Matza, D. (1964), op. cit., 33.

72 Werthman, C. (1967). op. cit.

73 Short, J.F., Jr. and F.L. Strodtbeck (1965), op. cit., 185–216, Horowitz, R. and G. Schwartz (1974). "Honor, Normative Ambiguity and Gang Violence," *American Sociological Review* 39: 238–251.

74 Goffman, E. (1974). "Where the Action Is," in *Interaction Ritual.* Garden City: Anchor Books, 149–270.

75 Matza, D. and G.M. Sykes (1961), "Juvenile Delinquency and Subterranean Values," *American Sociological Review* 26: 712–719.

76 Dennison, G. (1969). *The Lives of Children: The Story of the First Street School.* New York: Random House; Friedenberg, E.Z. (1964). *The Vanishing Adolescent.* Boston: Beacon Press; (1965). *Coming of Age in America: Growth and Acquiescence.* New York: Random House; Goodman, P. (1964). *Compulsory Miseducation.* New York: Horizon Press; Greene, M.F. and O. Ryan (1965). *The School Children: Growing Up in the Slums.* New York: Pantheon; Hargreaves, D.H. (1972). *Interpersonal Relations and Education.* London: Routledge and Kegan Paul; Hentoff, N. (1966). *Our Children Are Dying.* New York: Viking Press; Herndon, J. (1968). *The Way It Spozed to Be.* New York: Simon and Schuster; Jackson, P.W. (1968). *Life in Classrooms.* New York: Holt Rinehart and Winston; Kohl, H. (1967). *36 Children.* New York: New American Library; Nordstrom, C., E.Z. Friedenberg and H.A. Gold (1967). *Society's Children: A Study of Ressentiment in the Secondary School.* New York: Random House; Roberts, J.I. (1970). *Scene of the Battle: Group Behavior in Urban Classrooms.* Garden City: Doubleday; Webb, J. (1962). "The Sociology of a School," *British Journal of Sociology* 13: 264–272.

77 Downes, D.M. (1966). *The Delinquent Solution: A Study in Subcultural Theory.* New York: Free Press.

78 Finestone, H. (1957). "Cats, Kicks and Color," *Social Problems* 5: 3–13.

79 Rainwater, L. (1970), op. cit.

80 Werthman, C. (1967), op. cit.

81 Bachman, J.G., S. Green and I. Wirtanen (1972). *Dropping Out – Problem or Symptom.* Ann Arbor: Institute for Social Research.

82 Elliot, D.S. and H.L. Voss (1974). *Delinquency and Dropout.* Lexington, Mass.: Lexington Books, 115–122; Mukherjee, S.K. (1971). *A Typological Study of School Status and Delinquency.* Ann Arbor: University Microfilms.

83 McClean, J. D. and J.C. Wood (1969), op. cit.

84 DeFleur (1970), op. cit.

85 Grosser, G. (1952). *Juvenile Delinquency and Contemporary American Sex Roles.* Unpublished Ph.D. Dissertation, Harvard University.

86 Parsons, T. (1947). "Certain Primary Sources and Patterns of Aggression in the Social Structure of the Western World," *Psychiatry* 10: 167–181; Cohen, A. (1955), op. cit., 162–169.

87 Miller, W.B. (1958), op. cit.

88 Tennyson, R.A. (1967). "Family Structure and Delinquent Behavior," in M.W. Klein (ed.), *Juvenile Gangs in Context.* Englewood Cliffs, N.J.: Prentice-Hall; Monahan, T.P. (1957). "Family Status and the Delinquent Child: A Reappraisal and Some New Findings," *Social Forces* 35:

251–258; Rosen, L. (1969). "Matriarchy and Lower Class Negro Male Delinquency," *Social Problems* 17: 175–189.

89 Hannerz, U. (1969). *Soulside: Inquiries into Ghetto Culture.* New York: Columbia University Press.

90 Miller, W.B. (1958) op. cit.

91 A similar perspective on subcultures of violence and their relationship to masculinity has been developed by Curtis, L. (1975). *Violence, Race and Culture.* Lexington, Mass.: Lexington Books.

92 Werthman, C. (1967), op. cit.

93 Weis, J. (1967), op. cit.

94 Federal Bureau of Investigation (1974). *Crime in the United States. Uniform Crime Reports – 1973.* Washington, D.C.: Government Printing Office, 133.

95 Task Force Report (1967). *The Assessment of Crime.* Washington, D.C.: Government Printing Office.

96 Puntil, J.E. (n.d.). "Youth Survey Marginals." Chicago: Institute for Juvenile Research.

97 Briar, S. and I. Piliavin (1965). "Delinquency, Situational Inducements, and Commitment to Conformity," *Social Problems* 13: 35–45; Piliavin, I.M., A.C. Vadum and J.A. Hardyck (1969). "Delinquency, Personal Costs and Parental Treatment: A Test of a Reward-Cost Model of Juvenile Criminality," *Journal of Criminal Law, Criminology and Police Science* 60: 165–172; Hirschi, T. (1969), op. cit.; Ehrlich, I. (1973). "Participation in Illegitimate Activities: A Theoretical and Empirical Investigation," *Journal of Political Economy* 81: 521–565.

98 Reckless, W.C., S. Dinitz and E. Murray (1956). "Self Concept as an Insulator against Delinquency." *American Sociological Review* 21: 744–746.

99 Clark, J.P. and E.W. Haurek (1966), op. cit.

100 Schur, E.M. (1973). *Radical Nonintervention: Rethinking the Delinquency Problem.* Englewood Cliffs, N.J.: Prentice-Hall.

101 Hirschi, T. (1969), op. cit., 81–109.

102 Williams, L. (1976). "Three Youths Call Mugging the Elderly Profitable and Safe," *New York Times* (December 8): B2.

103 I have discussed the question of desistance with male juveniles on probation in Manhattan for theft offenses, and with a number of my students who have been involved in various forms of theft. The latter group includes both apprehended and unapprehended former thieves. No claim is made for the representativeness of this small sample.

104 Matza, D. (1964), op. cit., 55.

105 Tannenbaum, F. (1938). *Crime in the Community.* New York: Columbia University Press, 19–20.

106 Schwartz, R.D. and J.H. Skolnick (1962). "Two Studies of Legal Stigma," *Social Problems* 10: 133–142.

107 Hirschi, T. (1975). "Labelling Theory and Juvenile Delinquency: An Assessment of the Evidence," in Walter R. Gove (ed.), *Labeling of Deviance: Evaluating a Perspective.* New York: Halsted Press; Tittle, C.R. (1975). "Labelling and Crime: An Empirical Evaluation," in Walter R. Gove (ed.), *The Labelling of Deviance: Evaluating a Perspective.* New York: Halsted Press; Mahoney, A.R. (1974). "The Effect of Labeling upon Youths in the Juvenile Justice System: A Review of the Evidence," *Law and Society Review*, 8: 583–614.

108 Schur, E.M. (1973), op. cit., 125.

109 Wolfgang, M.E., R.M. Figlio and T. Sellin (1972), op. cit., 201.

110 Federal Bureau of Investigation (1972). *Crime in the United States. Uniform Crime Reports – 1971.* Washington D.C.: Government Printing Office, 138.

111 Chambliss, W.J. (1973). "The Saints and the Roughnecks," *Society* 11: 24–31.

112 This leniency has increased over the past decade, partly in response to the arguments of labeling theorists such as Schur, E.M. (1973), op. cit., that punishment of delinquents would be counter-rehabilitative, and because of the state's growing fiscal inability to cope with the social problems engendered by a deteriorating capitalist economy and polity, described by O'Connor, J. (1973). *The Fiscal Crisis of the State.* New York: St. Martin's Press. Scull, A. (1977). *Decarceration: Community Treatment and the Deviant – A Radical View.* Englewood Cliffs, N.J.: Prentice Hall, explicitly discusses the community corrections movement in these terms.

113 Hall, G.S. (1904). *Adolescence: Its Psychology and Its Relations to Physiology, Anthropology, Sociology, Sex, Crime, Religion, and Education.* New York: Appleton.

114 In nineteenth century England, juveniles were over-represented in crime statistics by comparison with the continent not because the social position of juveniles was very different, but because the age distribution of the English population was skewed toward the younger age brackets by the rapid growth in the English population during the nineteenth century. In the latter half of the century, juveniles were under-represented by comparison with their numbers in the English population, despite the high percentages of offenders who were juveniles; see, e.g. Lombroso, C. (1968), op. cit., 176; Tobias, J.J. (1972). *Urban Crime in Victorian England.* New York: Schocken Books, 78, 167.

115 Kalacheck, E. (1973). "The Changing Economic Status of the Young," *Journal of Youth and Adolescence* 2: 125–132.

116 Carson, R.B. (1972). "Youthful Labor Surplus in Disaccumulationist Capitalism," *Socialist Revolution* 9: 15–44; Bowers, N. (1975). "Youth and the Crisis of Monopoly Capitalism," in *Radical Perspectives on the Economic Crisis of Monopoly Capitalism.* New York: Union of Radical Political Economy.

117 Musgrove, F. (1965). *Youth and the Social Order.* Bloomington: Indiana University Press.

118 Cohen, D.K. and M. Lazerson (1972). "Education and the Corporate Order," *Socialist Revolution* 8: 47–72; Gorz, A. (1972). "Technologie, Techniker und Klassenkampf," in A. Gorz, *Schule and Fabrik.* Quoted in Gero Lenhardt, "On the Relationship between the Education System and Capitalist Work Organization." *Kapitalistate* 3: 128–146; Bowles S. and H. Gintis (1975). *Schooling in Capitalist America: Educational Reform and the Contradictions of Economic Life.* New York: Basic Books.

118 Connor, W. (1970). *Deviance in Soviet Society.* New York: Columbia University Press; Polk, K. (1972). "Social Class and the Bureaucratic Response to Youthful Deviance." Paper presented to the American Sociological Association.

120 Quinney, R. (1974). *Criminal Justice in America: A Critical Understanding.* Boston: Little, Brown; Quinney (1974). *Critique of Legal Order: Crime Control in Capitalist Society.* Boston: Little, Brown.

121 Platt, T. (1974). "Prospects for a Radical Criminology in the United States," *Crime and Social Justice: A Journal of Radical Criminology* 1: 2–10.

122 Taylor, I., P. Walton and J. Young (1973). *The New Criminology.* London: Routledge, Kegan Paul; Manders, D. (1975). "Labelling Theory and Social Reality: A Marxist Critique," *The Insurgent Sociologist* 6: 53–66.

123 Gordon, D. (1971). "Class and the Economics of Crime," *Review of Radical Political Economics* 3: 51–75; Taylor, I., P. Walton and J. Young (1973), op. cit.

124 Mankoff, M. (1971). "Societal Reaction and Career Deviance: A Critical Analysis." *Sociological Quarterly* 12: 204–218; Taylor, I., P. Walton and J. Young (1973), op. cit.; Manders, D. (1975), op. cit.

125 Lichtman, R. (1970). "Symbolic Interactionism and Social Reality: Some Marxist Queries." *Berkeley Journal of Sociology* 15: 75–94; McNall, S.G. and J.C.M. Johnson (1975). "The New Conservatives: Ethnomethodologists, Phenomenologists, and Symbolic Interactionists," *The Insurgent Sociologist* 5: 49–55; Grabiner, G. (1975). "The Situational Sociologies: A Theoretical Note." *The Insurgent Sociologist* 5: 80–81.

126 Seppilli, T. and G.G. Abbozzo, "The State of Research into Social Control and Deviance in Italy in the Post-War Period (1945–1973)," in Herman Bianchi, Mario Simoni and Ian Taylor (eds.), *Deviance and Control in Europe.* New York: Wiley, Pearce, F. (1975). *Crimes of the Powerful: Marxism, Crime and Deviance.* London: Pluto Press; Schwendinger, H. and J.R. Schwendinger (1976). "Delinquency and the Collective Varieties of Youth," *Crime and Social Justice* 5: 7–25.

127 I use this word, with some reservations, to indicate that steps taken to produce or reproduce social domination may be responded to in ways that interfere with that production or reproduction. Students may not be "cooled out" by low grades; they may rebel. Reservations are necessary because a Marxian contradiction has, at least potentially, the capability of overturning its source, not merely of being somewhat dysfunctional. The conventional sorts of crime

discussed in this paper do not have that capability; if anything, they tend to stabilize existing social arrangements, though in a manner that is disadvantageous for much of the population Only if the nature of the crimes were to change drastically would criminality be a manifestation of contradiction in the strict sense of the word. In that case we would be talking about a revolutionary movement.

128 Chambliss, W.J. (1976). "Functional and Conflict Theories of Crime: The Heritage of Emile Durkheim and Karl Marx," in William J. Chambliss and Milton Mankoff (eds), *Whose Law, What Order*? New York: Wiley; Denisoff, R.S. and C. McCaghy (1973). *Deviance, Conflict and Criminology*. Rand McNally.

129 Stolzman, J. and H. Gamberg (1973–1974). "Marxist Class Analysis versus Stratification Analysis as General Approaches to Social Inequality," *Berkely Journal of Sociology* 18: 105–126.

130 Fee. T. (1976). "Domestic Labor: An Analysis of Housework and Its Relation to the Production Process," *Review of Radical Political Economics* 8: 1–8.

Erratum

In Table 1 on p. 190[4], the entry for arrests for narcotic drug offenses at age 20, 1187, is incorrect.

[2] The Gendering of Crime in Marxist Theory

MARXISM AND THE GENDERING OF CRIME

Imagine, in your mind's eye, a criminal. Chances are high that the person you've imagined is male. When criminologists think of criminals, they too usually think of males, and for reasons that are not just imaginary. So far as we know, in all countries throughout the world, crimes of interpersonal violence and theft are committed very disproportionately by males (Mannheim, 1967:697; Sutherland and Cressey, 1978: 130–36).[1]

With women seriously underrepresented in the annals of crime, criminology until recently gave only occasional and limited attention to female criminality. Even less attention was given to the role culturally defined conceptions of masculinity might play in crimes committed by males. Sparked by the rise of the women's liberation movement and by the belief that women's law violations had gradually been increasing, criminologists of the 1970s and 1980s—many of them feminists—have been been paying more attention to female crime. The study of the etiological significance of masculinity stereotypes is just beginning (Adler, 1975; Simon, 1975; Smart, 1976; Adler and Simon, 1979; A. Harris, 1977; Datesman and Scarpitti, 1980; Leonard, 1982; Carlen, 1985; Heidensohn, 1985; Brown, 1986; Chesney-Lind, 1986; Currie, 1986; Smith and Paternoster, 1987; Daly and Chesney-Lind, 1988; Naffine, 1988; Steffensmeier and Allan, 1991).

Though many suggestions have been offered, we still do not have a good understanding of why men assault and steal more than women, or why the ratio of female to male involvement changes with time. To date, Marxist criminologists have done little to address these questions. They have simply stood aside while others have analyzed the gendering of crime.

I am grateful to Annette Sroka for invaluable research assistance, to Whitney Bagnall for help in using the Columbia Law Library's collection of Old Bailey sessions. Freda Adler, Ava Baron, Harold Benenson, Peter Linebaugh, James Messerschmidt, Antony Simpson, Ross Matsueda, and Carol Smart offered helpful comments and suggestions. My greatest debt, however, is to Malcolm Feeley, from whom I learned of the relevance of the Old Bailey sessions to my problem, and for sharing his thoughts and work with me prior to publication.

Since Marxists have long slighted gender issues of all kinds, their neglect of the gendering of crime is not so surprising. That feminist criminologists have neglected Marx as a possible theoretical resource is also not surprising. Pioneering feminist scholars had to legitimate their focus on gender by arguing that gender relations are autonomous from other dimensions of social life, hence not explained by or reducible to them.[2] The persistence of discrimination against women in the aftermath of revolutions led by Marxists who had made the equality of men and women one of their goals (Stacey, 1983; Croll, 1984) lent plausibility to the feminist claim of autonomy.

Some radical feminists went so far as to propose a new reductionism. To them, class was not the key that unlocked the secrets of society, as Marxists claimed; instead, it was gender that illuminated class relations and the state: "The profoundly radical analysis beginning to emerge from revolutionary feminism [is] that capitalism, imperialism, and racism are symptoms of male supremacy-sexism" (Morgan, 1970:xxiv; see also Redstockings, 1970). That perspective looks to displacing Marxism, not to achieving a synthesis with it.

As appealing as feminists' bold monocausal ambition may have seemed twenty years ago, it is now widely regarded as being just as inadequate as all the other monocausal theories of history. Too much is left out. The realization that this is so stimulated some feminist thinkers to grapple with the theoretical problems of incorporating gender into Marxist theory, but thus far, most of these efforts have been programmatic or at a very abstract level, or in a context largely restricted to contemporary American or English society.[3] Many of these efforts focused on such questions as whether housework produced surplus value and, if so, who appropriated it. Ultimately these efforts reached a dead end, having failed to explain anything. Their criminological relevance remains obscure.

The present essay seeks to explore what resources Marxism might offer for understanding the gendering of crime. At first glance, the answer is not obvious. Gender is not a category in Marxist theory. Thus, Marxism *alone* would seem to have nothing to say about the gendering of crime. If Marxism is to be helpful, it will have to be supplemented by a theory of gender.

Because the gendering of crime is still largely *terre inconnu,* it makes sense to undertake such an exploration without prejudice to the outcome of the inquiry. The goal is not to *demonstrate* that Marxism holds the answers but to find out whether it has any. The possibility of a negative answer must be left open.

The exploration proceeds by developing theoretical models in which changes in gender relations are understood as the consequence of developments in capitalism. I will interpret that task as placing the burden of explanation on class relations. Marxist concern with this part of the causal model dates back to Engel's (1972) claim that the subordination of women occurred as a result of the rise of private property. The models will be restricted to those aspects of gender that appear to be helpful in understanding criminal behavior. Many other aspects of gender also merit exploration, but they cannot be taken up here. The second part of the model states only that gender relations have consequences for involvement in crime. For the time being, I leave open the ways these consequences are produced.

Right from the start, it seems sensible to acknowledge the insight from feminist social science that gender relations (like just about everything else) are not completely determined by class relations. As a purely hypothetical example, if assaultive behavior is influenced by serum testosterone levels, which are in turn influenced by diet, then class position could affect involvement in crimes of violence through its influence on what people eat.[4] That would be true even if class did not fully determine diet and if hormone levels were influenced by other factors as well.

Nor do we expect gender relations to be the only influence on criminal behavior. It would, then, be unrealistic to expect Marxism to explain everything about the gendering of crime. The most sophisticated theories imaginable will fail to do so. I will be satisfied if I can explain something.

The effects of gender on crime

The existing criminological literature leaves us with many possibilities for theorizing the effects of gender on crime. For example, women have fewer opportunities to commit some kinds of crime. Their exclusion from military combat and from high government office deprives them of the opportunity to commit war crimes. Few women are high corporate executives; consequently few commit crimes that can be committed only by top executives, such as antitrust violations. When women do commit white-collar crime, it is largely petty, reflecting the restricted criminal opportunities of lower-level employees (Daly, 1989).

Women have fewer opportunities to learn techniques that are useful for some criminal activities. Where military service is performed primarily by males, women are less likely to learn how to use weapons. Fathers often teach sons, but not daughters, how to fight.

Girls are socialized differently from boys in ways that might be expected to affect involvement in crime. In recent times (without being too precise about dates), girls have by and large been encouraged not to be overly assertive, but rather to be gentle, docile, self-effacing, cautious, cooperative, and nurturing; males, to be rugged, self-assertive, achievement-oriented, and competitive, often to the point of aggressiveness.[5] Boys are expected to fight as a normal part of growing up; girls are not. In studies of the ways American parents interact with children of kindergarten age, one of the strongest findings to emerge was that boys were permitted to act much more aggressively than girls (Sears, Maccoby, and

Levin, 1957).[6] Much more than girls, boys are encouraged, and given opportunities, to develop muscle strength through vigorous sports.

Expectations of earning income for themselves are communicated to boys; until recently, the expectation in most social strata of American society has been that after they marry, women will be supported by their husbands. According to one influential theory, failure to meet this expectation may lead unsuccessful males to try to fulfill male gender role expectations illegally (Merton, 1938).

On average, girls are more closely supervised than boys, and are afforded less freedom—reducing their opportunities for participation in delinquency without their parents' knowledge (Hagan, Simpson, and Gillis, 1979, 1987, 1988; Morash, 1986; Simmons and Blyth, 1987). This is less true for women than for girls, but juvenile delinquency is an important entry route to adult crime. A girl who has been kept from delinquency through close supervision when she is a teenager has, by the time she has become an adult, probably become enmeshed in and committed to a "straight" life-style that is not easily combined with many kinds of criminal activity. Even if she wanted to commit crime, she would lack the skills and personal contacts required for many kinds of crime.

Psychoanalytically oriented sociologists have pointed to the different consequences for boys and girls of being raised primarily by mothers or mother-surrogates. Both boys and girls, it is argued, form their first identification with their mothers. With very few exceptions, boys break this identification at a very young age and identify themselves as male. The process of differentiation from the mother may entail a repudiation of everything the mother stands for, including the moral standards she tries to uphold. In this way, masculinity can come to stand for "badness." Girls do not need to break with a primary identification with their mothers and are less likely to strive to be "bad." Consequently they do not need to differentiate themselves from others as sharply (Parsons, 1947:162–69; Cohen, 1955; Chodorow, 1978).

Gilligan (1982) has profiled differences in the styles of moral reasoning supposedly employed by boys and girls in dealing with moral dilemmas. Girls, she claims, are more likely than boys to seek solutions to personal problems that accommodate the interests of all the affected parties; boys are more likely to reason in absolute terms and opt for solutions with winners and losers. This is the sort of difference one would expect to find if girls' ego boundaries were indeed less sharply defined than those of boys.

Sykes and Matza (1957) have argued that delinquents often victimize others, even though they have internalized moral standards that would seem to preclude such behavior. They do so by mentally constructing justifications and excuses that "neutralize" the prohibition, such as blaming or denying the moral worthiness of the victim. No one has specifically compared the neutralization techniques of boy and girl delinquents, but Gilligan's analysis suggests that there should be differences. Girls' greater tendency to identify empathetically with others and to take their interests into account should make it harder for them to blame prospective victims. This sex-linked capacity to empathize would inhibit thefts and interpersonal violence.[7]

The inevitable frustrations an infant experiences in interaction with its mother, Dinnerstein (1976) argues, lead to infantile rage directed toward its mother. In girls, this rage is moderated by the girl's identification with the mother; in boys it is not. In later years, this rage may lead to rape or assaults against women who are identified with the mother.

No great ingenuity is required to devise explanations of this kind; their conformity with commonsense understandings of gender gives some of them a manifest plausibility. It would be amazing if some of them were not true. Needless to say, much research to test them systematically remains to be done.

For present purposes, explanations of this sort will be taken as valid in the aggregate, in the sense that at least some of them explain at least part of the sex differences in crime rates. Although the empirical evidence I examine may suggest something about the validity of these different explanations, it is far beyond the scope of this essay to distinguish among them empirically.

Explaining gender

My next task is to account for these gender differences. Why are soldiers male? Why is child care performed mainly by females? Why do parents supervise girls more than boys?

It is tempting to observe that humans evolved from primate species in which gender distinctions already existed. This observation pushes the explanation of gender differentiation back into the prehuman stages of evolution. If men differ from women in more ways than the obvious, it can only have been a result of natural selection. The skeletons of early hominids show men to have been taller and larger than women (Leibowitz, 1986). Perhaps other gender differences are equally a part of our primate legacy, built into our genes.

Sociobiologists have found this line of reasoning appealing. Thus, Steven Goldberg contends, "men and women differ in their hormonal systems. . . . every society demonstrates patriarchy, male dominance and male attainment. The thesis put forth here is that the hormonal renders the social inevitable" (1973:93; see also Morris, 1967, and Wilson, 1975:551).

Yet, in some primate groups, including chimpanzees, who are genetically very close to humans, neither gender differentiation nor male domination is pronounced (Gough, 1971). In some human societies, too, gender differentiation is weak, and male domination weak or absent. Though it is possible that the genetic legacy we have inherited from our primate ancestors plays a role in human patterns of gender differentiation, it is clearly far from being the only factor. The whole story must include social phenomena that do not arise directly from genetically transmitted sex differences. The present essay explores Marxist ways of conceptualizing the social aspects of gender.

On the face of it, there is nothing in Marxism, a theory of class society, that would offer an explanation of why males and females should have different opportunities, or be exposed to different levels or kinds of parental control, or should be socialized differently. As I already observed, Marxism is gender-neutral. Not a single one of its fundamental categories—class, state, capital, surplus value, and so forth—has anything to do with sex or gender (Kuhn and Wolpe, 1978; Eisenstein, 1979; Hartmann, 1979). How to introduce gender into Marxism or to achieve a unified theoretical treatment of gender and class is not entirely clear.

Faced with this difficulty, some investigators have decided not to make the attempt. "Dual systems" theorists, for example, characterize modern Western society as having two *independent* systems of subordination—capitalism and patriarchy, offering no explanation for the existence of patriarchy (Mitchell, 1971; Hartmann, 1979).[8] By default, it appears as a transhistorical system of domination that lies outside of and remains unaffected by historical transformation or, at least, by the transformation of class relations.[9] Such independence is not very plausible.

To seek a Marxist explanation for gender is implicitly to take the position that gender does not operate totally independent of class relations. Our model, however, seems to be saying something more. By placing class relations causally (and therefore temporally) prior to gender relations, it seems to imply that gender did not exist until it was created by class relations. This can hardly be true. People living in classless societies are already gendered. The same is true of people who live in class societies. There are no class relations of ungendered people.

For this reason, we must be careful in the way we interpret the model. At least hypothetically, we can imagine that in any given social formation, class relations among gendered people change for reasons that have nothing to do with gender, such as class conflict in which gender issues are irrelevant. The assumption is that the consciousness and actions of capitalists and workers will be the same whether the capitalist or the worker is male or female. That is how Marxists have generally understood social change. This sort of analysis, however, is incapable of explaining why men and women of the same class do not always have the same consciousness and behave differently.

Early Marxist writings on gender issues finessed this issue. Engels (1972), for example, argued that the subordination of women occurred when social evolution reached the point of creating surpluses. Men, wanting to pass surpluses on to their progeny, wrested power away from mothers, who, in earlier matrilineal kinship systems, had the power to bequeath *their* property to their offspring.

Although this reasoning still has its defenders (Reed, 1978; Sayers, Evans, and Redclift, 1987) it is obviously deficient insofar as it assumes much of what needs to be explained. Why should it matter to fathers that their wealth goes to their own children instead of their mother's brothers' children? Why should men have been able to subordinate women? Clearly, a more coherent account is needed.[10] We also need one that can address changes that have taken place since the primordial "worldwide defeat of women." Engels has little to say about changes in gender relations in historical time.

Vogel (1983) has proposed one strategy for introducing gender into Marxism. It is inspired by Engels's (1972:71) observation that a society's persistence entails both the *production* of material goods and the *reproduction* from day to day, year to year, and generation to generation of its population. This observation, which could have been made as easily by a functionalist as by a Marxist, focuses attention on both biological and social processes of reproduction. There must be births and provisions for ensuring the survival of children. There must also be arrangements for channeling individuals into the roles needed to keep the social system functioning, and for ensuring that role occupants are able to perform their roles adequately and are motivated to do so.

A number of contemporary scholars have attempted to clarify the historical processes by which gender differences in human society emerged and led to a gender hierarchy in which women are subordinated. The precise processes at work have been the subject of considerable debate. Vogel suggests that such attempts should focus on women's unique capacity to conceive and bear children. This capacity implicates women in the social reproduction system differently from men. Although this is not the only way a gender difference can be introduced into social theory, it is one I adopt here. It has the convenience of breaking the gender symmetry of social theory by introducing a biological distinction between the sexes from outside the social realm. Yet it severely limits the role of biology. The many gender differences found in modern societies are by no means *direct* consequences of pregnancy and lactation. Therefore, social processes must play an important role. But, if the model is correct, these social processes should be traceable to pregnancy and lactation, even if the causal connections are complex and indirect.

Arguably, under conditions of early human life, pregnancy and lactation had implications for the kinds of food-gathering activities men and women could pursue. Pregnant and nursing women would have been unable to participate in hunting as effectively as men. Had they hunted, their reduced agility would have placed them at higher risk of death from predators and jeopardized their reproductive capacity. If they were carrying small children, the children would also have been at risk. On the other hand, small children left at home by hunting mothers would have been in danger of being orphaned. Moreover, women on long treks would have been unable to nurse them. Where hunting entailed unanticipated chases of wild game, child care would have been difficult to arrange on short notice (Quinn, 1977; Leibowitz, 1986). Bands in which women hunted would have been less likely to survive.[11]

Because the density of early hominid populations was probably very low, warfare between bands was most likely infrequent or nonexistent. For that reason I have developed the argument with reference to hunting. However, it is possible that warfare did occur under special circumstances, such as famine.[12] For present purposes this is irrelevant; similar arguments could as easily be made in reference to warfare. What is important is the development of some differentiation in task performance or division of labor based on sex, as an adaptation to biological differences in males and females connected with reproduction, in the conditions under which early hominids lived.

In itself, differentiation need not imply subordination. The form human sex differention took, however, could have led to subordination. Men's primary responsibility for hunting could have given them the physical capacity—and perhaps the mental and emotional outlook—needed to dominate women. One might speculate that women would have preferred husbands who were taller and stronger, and perhaps more aggressive, as those qualities would make them better at hunting and fighting[13] Sexual selection would then have produced domineering husbands and fathers.

Yet if that did happen, it did not necessarily produce male supremacy. Having the physical capacity to dominate women is not the same as doing so. Many anthropological studies of band societies have found that men do not usually dominate women. Typically, gender stereotypes and constraints are flexible and are not accompanied by the subordination of women (Kaberry, 1939: 142–43, 277; Leacock, 1972; Sacks, 1974, 1976, 1979; Sanday, 1981; Bell, 1983:23; Lerner, 1986). In some regions of the world, however, subsequent developments enabled men to capitalize on the earlier differentiation of the sexes in such a way as to dominate women.

Much effort has been devoted to identifying the points in history at which this shift occurred. Marxist analyses have posited the rise of exploitative classes as the critical point, but their adequacy has been contested (Messerschmidt, 1986:20). Anthropological research has focused on such factors as warfare, herding, residence rules, and the domestication of large animals, with its attendant problems of theft (see, for example, Burstyn, 1983a, 1983b; Coontz and Henderson, 1986b). As interesting as they are, these efforts will not be reviewed here.

Once a given gender division of labor is established, it tends to perpetuate itself. Those who benefit from it will use resources at their disposal—force, material rewards, ideological manipulation—to perpetuate that division.[14] Legitimating ideologies that define the existing arrangement as natural and desirable will be created and communicated to the next generation. Children tend to model their own behavior on the example of adults they see around them. To encourage their children to follow established patterns, parents will apply positive and negative reinforcements to shape their behavior. Once a given division is established, there are costs in abandoning it: habits have to be broken, unfamiliar skills acquired, and new arrangements established. The benefits of change, on the other hand, may be remote or hypothetical.

But of course, conditions can and do change. Climactic shifts can alter the conditions of social reproduction, forcing new adaptations (e.g., the disappearance of big game in the Stone Age). A technological innovation may affect men differently from women. New access to external markets made possible by conquest can bring financial benefits to those who make the products that can be sold in those markets. In some instances these benefits have gone to men, in others to women (Boserup, 1970; Moore, 1988). Changes in resources going to men and to women will tend to shift the balance of power in the group.

In the long run, gender relations will change in response to these exogenous changes in resources and power. However, in the short run, the conserving processes described in the previous paragraph may retard the impact of these changes. Indeed, those who perceive their situation as deteriorating because of these changes may resist them. These intended and unintended conserving processes are a major source of the partial independence of gender from the social or ecological conditions to which gender differences were an initial adaptation. Still, this independence can be only partial. Any set of gender relations is dependent on resources and possibilities made available by the entire complex of social relations. Under these circumstances, neither gender nor anything else can be totally autonomous.

Thus far I have been speaking as if all men and all women of a given social formation were implicated by any particular gender system in more or less the same way. Yet once social cleavages or divisions of other sorts are present in a society (e.g., those of class or occupation), change can affect women (or men) of different categories in different ways. Relations between men and women will, in general, differ depending on whether they are aristocrats, serfs, slaves, capitalists, or workers.

Moreover, changes in the gender system—however they arise—can have implications for the class system. In stateless groups structured on the basis of corporate kinship, gifts of daughters as wives, and surpluses extracted from them, are used to build patron-client relations that form the basis of "big man" political systems. A specific type of gender relation thus appears to have been critical in the development of early stratification systems (Chevillard and Leconte, 1986; Coontz and Henderson, 1986b). In Africa, relations between men and women were of great importance in state formation (Goody, 1976; Meillasoux, 1981). Some of the surplus that helped to finance early industrialization in England may have been produced by the labor of housewives and appropriated by their husbands (Middleton, 1983). This dependence of state and class on gender has largely gone unstudied within Marxist social science, which has implicitly taken them to be unimportant; for that reason they are omitted from the model. Even if the long-term influences of gender on class should prove to be large, in any given short time frame, their omission may be innocuous.

CRIME IN EIGHTEENTH- AND NINETEENTH-CENTURY ENGLAND

To explore the implications of this crude causal model, it is necessary to examine the gendering of crime over an extended period. Enough time must elapse for major changes in the social relations of production to occur and for these changes to influence socialization practices, learning patterns, kinds and degrees of control, and opportunities to commit crimes of different kinds.

I shall examine these changes in England between the early eighteenth and the early twentieth centuries. Crime statistics of a sort are available for this period and have recently been exploited by Feeley and Little (1991), and the development of capitalism and the transformation of gender relations have both been much studied. A "standard model," appearing in synthetic histories addressed to a wide audience of nonspecialists, has women in early modern England participating actively in a wide range of productive and distributive activities. This participation was cut back as industrialization removed production to the factory, leaving women isolated in the home.[15]

My model of gender and crime suggests that as women's roles were restricted to housework and child care, they were less likely to violate the law. Socialized to care for others, they would not have been disposed to steal or assault. Lacking the personality traits of assertiveness and competitiveness, they would have been inhibited in confronting victims. Being out in public less than men, women would have had fewer opportunities to steal small objects from carts and coaches, or laundry from clothes lines, to shoplift or pickpocket, to take pewter pots from public houses, or to pilfer tools, raw materials, or finished products from their employers. These were common forms of theft in eighteenth- and nineteenth-century London.

In principle, this is only half the story. Reconstructions of women are at the same time reconstructions of men. The historical process by which women were removed from the pool of criminals was not a necessary one for the production of high levels of male involvement in crime; as far as we can tell, there was a great deal of it in the eighteenth century. But newer definitions of masculinity may have prevented male rates from dropping along with those of women. A full account of historical trends in the gendering of crime must deal with both aspects of the gendering process; here, however, I can tell only half the story.

The pioneering study of trends in the gendering of crime recently carried out by Feeley and Little (1991), using the trial records of the Old Bailey court in London, examines trial records for every twentieth year between 1715 and 1895 (as well as the years 1687 and 1912). They discovered that female involvement in crime (as measured by their representation in the court records) peaked around 1735 at approximately 42 percent, with a secondary peak in 1795, at about 32 percent. Thereafter female participation fell steadily, relative to male participation, reaching about 9 percent in 1912. For both sexes, the offenses charged overwhelmingly involved theft.

That London was not unique in seeing this type of change is demonstrated by a recent study of crime rates in Toronto, where women's participation also underwent a long-term decline between 1859 and 1955. Apart from year-to-year fluctuations, the percentage of property crime arrestees who were female declined from about 31 percent around 1865 to about 12 percent in the mid–twentieth century. Female involvement in crimes of violence also declined substantially for several decades but then rose somewhat in the twentieth century (Boritch and Hagan, 1990). Women's involvement in diverse forms of crime was also exceptionally high in eighteenth-century Amsterdam and Leiden (Kloeck, 1990).

The common lore about female crime is that there has always been little of it. Thus Barbara Hanawalt, who studied crime in medieval England, concluded "The role of women in crime has remained remarkably consistent from the fourteenth century to the present. In the fourteenth century, with some minor county to county variations, the suspect was female in 10 percent of the cases. . . . In Elizabethan Essex, 250 years later, women still comprised only 10 percent of the cases" (1979:115). This constancy, she notes, could be explained by the stability of women's roles since medieval times, or by biological causes.[16] Yet the analyses of Feeley and Little, and of Boritch and Hagan, showing substantial changes in levels of female criminality over long periods of time, point to substantial historical change. These changes clearly call for a social, not a biological, explanation.

I follow the lead of Feeley and Little by examining the Old Bailey trial transcripts. With only a few exceptions, the Old Bailey had exclusive jurisdiction over felony cases during this period. Peers accused of crime were tried by the House of Lords, and commoners could remove their cases to the Court of King's Bench. But few peers were put on trial, and few criminal defendants could afford the high costs of bringing a case to the Court of King's Bench.

I examined every tenth year from 1730 to 1910, instead of every twentieth year, in the hope of being able to identify the beginnings and ends of trends with greater precision than was possible with Feeley and Little's sampling procedure.[17] In addition, I wanted to examine patterns for individual offenses classified less broadly than in their work, and to examine relations between defendants and accusers. Many of the defendants in this period were employed by the victims of their thefts, raising the possibility that changes in female labor-force participation might account for changes in their involvement in crime.

Table 1 shows the percentage of defendants who were female in each of the years I sampled. Because the volume containing transcripts for 1870 was missing from the Columbia University Law Library—the only library in the New York area holding the Old Bailey proceedings—I substituted the closest period included in the collection, November 1872 to April 1973.

Table 1

Sex Composition of Old Bailey Defendants, 1730–1910

Year	*Percent Female*	*Total Number of Defendants*
1730	34.0	745
1740	41.7	465
1750	n.a.	n.a.
1760	n.a.	n.a.
1770	26.0	682
1780	33.4	674
1790	24.9	587
1800	21.3	1012
1810	19.0	126
1820	24.4	299
1830	22.0	2676
1840	22.1	402
1850	17.7	367
1860	25.9	158
1872/3	11.7	264
1880	13.2	212
1890	15.1	146
1900	4.3	163
1910	7.4	955

The years 1750 and 1760 were also missing. Unfortunately, the volumes for neighboring years were also missing, making a similar substitution impossible. For some years, the Columbia University Law Library collection of Old Bailey sessions was incomplete. For that reason, the figures I cite for 1810 and 1820 are based on court records for just part of those years.

As Feeley and Little found, the percentage of defendants who were female was high in 1730 and 1740. For both sexes, this involvement was primarily in theft; the number of cases involving interpersonal violence is quite small. Moreover, male and female criminals sometimes worked together in small teams to commit burglaries or robberies.

Despite this broad similarity, there were some qualitative differences between male and female patterns of involvement. In 1730, for example, 18.7 percent of the males on trial were charged with robbery, compared with 3.2 percent of the females. Similarly, 10.2 percent of the males were charged with burglary, compared with 3.2 percent of the females; 10.2 percent of the males were being tried for shoplifting, compared with 5 percent of the female defendants. Females, on the other hand, were overrepresented in other kinds of theft. Some women, for example, were prostitutes accused of stealing from their male clients; no men were charged with stealing under comparable circumstances. The offenses of pickpocketing, fraud, larceny, counterfeiting and uttering false currency, and receiving stolen goods accounted for 84.1 percent of the female defendants, 59.8 percent of the male defendants.

These figures suggest that when women stole, they tended to avoid crimes that involved real or potential confrontation with a victim, or the destruction of property. In 1730, only one female defendant was on trial for homicide; twelve of the male defendants were. That lone female was charged with killing her small child; all but one of the victims of the male defendants were adults.

I have no data for the next thirty years, but Feeley and Little's figures show that in 1755, female involvement had declined only moderately, to about 30 percent. After 1780, rates fluctuated in the range of 20 to 25 percent, then dropped again between 1860 and 1872. At the end of the nineteenth century, female involvement fell further, to less than 10 percent.

Trends for individual crimes are more difficult to identify with confidence, because percentages for each year are based on small numbers of cases. Year-to-year fluctuations due to chance can be high under these circumstances. Thus, in 1840, 60 percent of the robbery defendants were female, a higher percentage than in any other year of my data. But there were only 5 robbery cases in that year. Little confidence can be placed on the figure of 60 percent when it is based on just 3 female robbers. More significant, for the years 1860 to 1910, only 2.6 percent of the robbery defendants were female (1 female defendant compared to 37 male defendants). This compares with 13 percent (of 96 defendants) between 1730 and 1810. A similar downward trend is visible for burglaries. Between 1730 and 1810, 10.8 percent of the 434 burglary defendants were female; between 1860 and 1900, just 1.6 percent of 65 defendants.

Robbery and burglary both entail the use or threat of force, but the downward trend is equally visible for thefts not involving force. An examination of trends for other forms of theft is plagued by ambiguities in classifying many thefts on the basis of the limited information provided by the transcripts and by small numbers of cases. I handle this difficulty by aggregating shoplifting, pickpocketing, fraud, embezzlement, larcenies, counterfeiting and uttering false currency, receiving stolen goods, and smuggling. I then find that levels of female involvement in miscellaneous thefts declined more or less steadily from 1730 to 1900 (see Table 2).

These figures must be interpreted with a good deal of caution, as they are not fully representative of all the crime that occurred in London. Business and governmental crime hardly appear. My figures are not for crimes that occurred, or for crimes reported to the police; indeed, with the exception of the Thames River Police, there was no salaried full-time police force in England before 1829. My figures are for prosecutions, which were brought by victims. Then, as now, there must have been many cases that did not come to the courts, because victims thought it pointless to prosecute, did not know the perpetrators, knew them and did not want to prosecute, had been paid by the perpetrator not to prosecute, or because the constables had not been able to apprehend the perpetrators.

Table 2

Sex Composition of Old Bailey Defendants Charged with Stealing, 1730–1910*

Year	*Percent Female*	*Total Number of Defendants*
1730	34.9	602
1740	42.8	439
1750	n.a.	n.a.
1760	n.a.	n.a.
1770	26.2	682
1780	40.6	547
1790	21.5	653
1800	22.0	982
1810	21.8	119
1820	15.5	264
1830	29.7	495
1840	23.4	393
1850	17.1	322
1860	23.8	101
1872/3	9.4	201
1880	13.3	150
1890	12.8	94
1900	2.3	129

*See text for offense categories included.

Feeley and Little note that even trends cannot be taken at face value, because offenses involving minor thefts were downgraded from felonies to misdemeanors during the nineteenth century and were then tried in lesser courts. It was in these offenses that women's involvement was especially high. Nevertheless, their examination of trends within offense categories established that at least for the eighteenth century, the decline in female involvement was not entirely artifactual. Zedner (1991a) notes that English judicial statistics for the period 1857–92 show declines in the ratio of women to men for the lesser offenses. It thus seems unlikely that legal reclassification could fully explain the nineteenth-century trends.

The possibility that contemporary changes in rates of female involvement in crime reflect changes in "chivalry" has been proposed and debated. According to this view, recent rises in female participation in crime seen in arrest records reflect only the greater willingness of victims, police, and prosecutors to arrest, charge, and prosecute them. (Curran, 1983; Krohn, Curry, and Nelson-Kilger, 1983; Rans, 1978; Steffensmeier, 1980). In a period in which feminist demands for gender equality have received much public attention, perhaps victims, police, and prosecutors will prosecute female criminals more readily.

Whether or not an earlier double standard favoring female defendants has been disappearing in recent decades, it is possible that rising standards of chivalry in earlier centuries reduced the willingness of victims to prosecute female defendants. Several students of eighteenth-century English crime have found that juries and judges were more lenient to women (Beattie, 1977; King, 1983; McLynn, 1989:128).

Certainly one encounters many cases in the transcripts in which judges and juries failed to act according to standards we would call chivalrous. In 1777, Mary Jones "was destitute and her children starving. She took a piece of raw linen off a shop counter but put it back when the shopkeeper saw her. For this alone, she was hanged" (McLynn, 1989:125). Among the death sentences in my sample, I find the cases of women shoplifting a linen cloth (1780, p. 675), pickpocketing (December 6, 1780, p. 15), shoplifting (1790, p. 596), and stealing laundry from an employer (1800, p. 447).

Where the defendant was young, as in the case of the sixteen-year-old sentenced to hang for stealing money from her employer's home (1820, p. 14), juries commonly recommended mercy. In the case of the thirty-four-year-old Mary Beckworth, who was convicted of shoplifting £5 worth of calico with her fourteen-year-old daughter, both were sentenced to death, with a recommendation of mercy for the daughter on account of her age (1800, p. 473). But none of the juries recommended mercy on account of sex. Nor did troops hesitate to fire on female rioters (Bohrstedt, 1988).

Perhaps the Victorian age brought greater leniency to women. If this leniency extended to the willingness of victims to prosecute female criminals, they would be underrepresented in the court records in the latter part of the time span under study. If so, my analysis, which assumes that the gender ratio really changed, would be seriously threatened. However, eighteenth-century writings about crime suggest that the ratio of women to men *was* higher then than later. Thus, Joseph Massie, writing in 1758, wrote that it would be necessary to guard charity homes for women to prevent "street robbers etc." from coming to the homes to recruit female accomplices (Beattie, 1975). This would not have been thought necessary a century later. One observer estimated in 1859 that at least one-third of all English criminals were female (Zedner, 1991b:38). Victorian-age discussion of crime focused on female criminality to a far greater degree than has been true in the twentieth century.

Moreover, indirect evidence suggests that in the nineteenth century, the trend was not in the direction of more leniency toward female defendants. Over the period 1857–90, the discharge rate (dismissal rate) for women apprehended for indictable offenses dropped from 38.1 percent to 17.9 percent. The dismissal rate for men dropped almost exactly as much. The decline was probably brought about by better police work, and did not favor either sex (Zedner, 1991b:316). Moreover, with the exception of a few feminist writers, middle-class commentators on crime had little sympathy for female criminals, whom they tended to see as more depraved than their male counterparts. Women, they thought, tended innately toward morality and respectability. Those who turned to crime had fallen farther than had their male counterparts, and thus were more depraved and less susceptible to redemption (Zedner, 1991b:40–46).

A further complication is that the percentages of defendants who were female are not *per capita* rates; they have not been adjusted to take into account possible differences in the numbers of males and females in the London population. The earliest British census was held in 1801, leaving no figures at all for the eighteenth century. With immigrants from the countryside streaming into London, I cannot assume that the sex ratio for adolescents and adults would have equaled 1.[18]

That a substantial fraction of the defendants were female in the eighteenth century has implications for the notion that gender differences in crime stem from differences in styles of moral reasoning. Either differences in styles of moral reasoning have little relation to criminality, or the differences were not very sharp in the eighteenth century. Perhaps children were raised differently 250 years ago, or perhaps the theory itself is flawed.

It seems implausible that people's moral reasoning should fail to affect their involvement in crime. However, women's domestic responsibilities as wives and mothers sometimes led them to steal in order to feed their children, as in the shoplifting cases cited above. Women sometimes led eighteenth-century food riots; according to one contemporary account, they were "foremost in violence and ferocity" (Thompson, 1963:65; Thompson 1971; but see Bohrstedt, 1988). In the early nineteenth century, they gave militant support to strikes, sometimes stoning police and scabs (Taylor, 1979). In these circumstances, caring for others (spouses, children, members of their class and community) did not preclude crime.

Of course, many women's crimes did not stem from altruism. If one wishes to reconcile these illegalities with the work of Gilligan and Chodorow, one might note that in the "standard model" of gender and capitalist development, much production took place in and around the home before the Industrial Revolution. Even though women generally had primary responsibility for small children, men were usually present and to some extent involved in child care merely by their presence. Gender differences in the permeability of ego boundaries, and in styles of moral reasoning, should have been smaller then because child rearing was not so exclusively the task of women (Davidson, 1982:185–88; Bohrstedt, 1988).

On the other hand, one may question how important gender differences in child rearing are for styles of moral reasoning. Empirical research casts doubt on Gilligan's claim that there are major sex differences in moral reasoning. Because children have less extrafamilial experience than adults, parents' child-rearing practices should have the greatest impact on their children while they are young. Yet, when boys and girls below the age of eighteen are compared, very few differences in moral reasoning style are found. Some differences are found among adults, but mostly when the female subjects are housewives. Once controls for educational attainment and job status are introduced, these differences tend to disappear (Kohlberg, Levine, and Hewer, 1983:127–30; Walker, 1984).[19]

It seems likely, then, that where gender differences in styles of moral reasoning are found for adults, they reflect later influences, including socialization connected with different kinds of occupational careers.[20] An orientation toward formal rules is most appropriate in large-scale bureaucratic organizations; an informal, flexible ethic based on individualized "caring" is most appropriate in the family.[21]

These considerations redirect our attention to the kinds of work English women of the eighteenth and nineteenth centuries did, and the work settings in which they found themselves.

WOMEN IN THE ENGLISH LABOR FORCE

Under English common law, women's legal rights were severely restricted. Although an unmarried or widowed woman enjoyed the same rights as a man to operate a business, enter into a contract, and sue, when she married she lost all these rights under the common law doctrine of *coverture* (Lewis, 1984:119–21; Earle, 1989:158).[22] Women were excluded from the civil service, law, medicine, and the clergy; most guilds excluded women except for widows of male members. Cultural stereotypes defining women as "weaker vessels," "the softer sex," and "the gentle sex" must have made these exclusions seem justifiable (Fraser, 1984:1–4; M. Roberts, 1985)

Though many occupations were effectively closed to women, the English economy was too inefficient to permit half its potential labor force to remain idle. The political economist Sir William Petty observed in his 1690 *Political Arithmetic* that "all women and girls over seven years of age are to labour except among the upper tenth" (quoted in Richards, 1974).

The range of their activities was wide. On the farms, women engaged in heavy labor in the fields, and to a limited extent in animal husbandry. Women of the early eighteenth century baked and brewed. They worked as milliners, seamstresses, mantua makers, and stay makers (Hill, 1989:89, 94). As wives of artisans and craftsmen, they helped supervise journeymen and apprentices and sold finished goods from shops that were part of or attached to their homes. Women operated public houses, inns, and lodging houses, sometimes with their husbands. They peddled, took in laundry, and worked as prostitutes. Many of their occupations involved the production and sale of clothing, food, and drink, and drew on skills that were also utilized in the household (Charles, 1985). Yet women also worked in occupations that later became male dominated: there were female blacksmiths, butchers, plumbers, carpenters, tailors, bricklayers, and coopers (Davidoff and Hall, 1987:312–13; Hill, 1989:259).[23]

As guilds in corporate towns such as York and Norwich lost control over entry to the crafts in the period 1690–1770, it became easier for women to become makers of women's garments (Rendall, 1990:28). Even at wages that were usually less than men's, their contributions to the family income were sufficiently important that one man of the 1750s remarked, "None but a fool will take a wife whose bread must be earned solely by his labour and who will contribute nothing towards it herself" (quoted in Chapman and Chambers, 1970:10, and Richards, 1974).

Can women's relatively high rate of involvement in crime be explained, at least in part, by their relatively extensive experience in what later came to be defined as men's jobs? So some nineteenth century writers suggested. Thus, an 1850 newspaper article on the Black Country, a region of England that included Wolverhampton, attributed its exceptionally high female crime rate[24] to women who worked "at rude and unsexing labour at the pit mouth, partly assuming the habiliments and altogether adopting the coarseness of the men" (quoted in Philips, 1977:34).

One could, of course, object to this reasoning by pointing out that working under the close supervision of an employer does not instill independence and assertiveness. Surely employers tried to inculcate subservience and obedience to authority in their servants and employees. However, in many of these occupations, women were not working under close and continual direction, but exercised a reasonable degree of autonomy and judgment. Besides, employers who tried to inculcate subservience did not necessarily succeed. Then, as now, employees sometimes resisted their employers—by demanding higher wages and shorter hours, and, at times, by stealing from their employers. Descriptions of eighteenth- and nineteenth-century work life do not suggest that laborers of either sex were timid or compliant.[25] They rather suggest a vigorous independence. Much of this militancy came from craftsmen and artisans, whose work generally required a large degree of autonomy and independence of judgment. Still, even where workers worked under closer supervision, the experience of working collectively may have bolstered self-confidence, facilitating criminal activity.[26]

In the absence of motivation, there is little reason to think that assertiveness alone would lead anyone to crime. Working women certainly had reason to be motivated to violate the law, because most were poorly paid (Collett, 1889; Cadbury, Matheson, and Shann, 1906; Alexander, 1983; Morris, 1986; Fishman, 1988; Rose, 1988). In many sectors of the economy, employment was irregular for both sexes. The contrast between servants' poverty and their employers' relative affluence must have tempted many to steal.[27] In some instances, employees may have wanted to retaliate against employers who treated them abusively. Where it is possible to draw inferences from the trial transcripts about the social-class backgrounds of female defendants, they are mostly from the laboring classes, like the male defendants. Even when the stringent penalties meted out by the courts were taken into account, it would have been rational for many of the poor to steal.

If high levels of female involvement in crime are predictable in light of women's economic standing and socialization in the early eighteenth century, can their declining involvement be traced to reduced labor force participation? That is what the "standard model" would suggest. A rigorous statistical test of this possibility cannot be carried out, however, because there are no occupational or labor-force statistics for the eighteenth century, and those for the nineteenth century are considered to be of such poor quality as to be virtually unusable (Hall, 1979; Higgs, 1986:29–41). Experts are not even in complete agreement as to the overall trends. Though some historians think the Industrial Revolution expanded job opportunities for women (Pinchbeck, 1930; Hartwell, 1971:343), others think it reduced them (Tilly and Scott, 1978; Richards, 1974). Hunt (1981:17) thinks that in the aggregate it made little difference.

Trends within particular sectors of the economy can be tracked, and they are variable, suggesting that the "standard model" needs to be elaborated (Freifeld, 1986; E. Roberts, 1988). In textile manufacturing, for example, machinery was initially introduced in the context of the putting-out system, in which male and female family members cooperated in producing cloth at home, using raw materials provided by a capitalist entrepreneur. In London, women began displacing men from the tailoring trade, working at very low wages at home or in small workshops (Rendall 1990:29).

When power looms were introduced into the factories in the 1830s and 1840s, they were operated primarily by women and children, who were attractive to employers because they could be paid less than men and might be less militant (Hutchins, 1915:56; Pinchbeck, 1930:187–88; Neff, 1966:30–31). But the number of such jobs was limited. In some instances, women lacked the craft skills needed to operate the machines, and for certain time periods, the physical strength. Later the Factory Acts limiting the employment of children made it difficult for mothers to work (Atkinson, 1914; Smelser, 1959:184–92; Lazonick, 1976; Medick, 1979; Hall, 1982a, 1982b; Freifeld, 1986; Bradley, 1989:45).[28]

In other sectors of the economy, the exclusion or downgrading of women to the least-skilled, worst-paid jobs *preceded* the factory system or the introduction of new machinery (Snell, 1985; Middleton, 1985). On the farms, the introduction of machinery displaced some female workers, but the reasons for this are not altogether clear. In some instances, great strength may have been required to operate heavy machinery. But since women traditionally performed heavy labor, this explanation is doubtful.[29] (Clark, 1919). More likely, women had been performing the least-skilled, highly routinized tasks. It was these tasks that new machines were being designed to perform (Bradley, 1989:80–87).

With the expansion of the scale of production in nonagricultural sectors of the economy during the eighteenth century, some artisan and craft production was being relocated from the home to separate locations preceding the Industrial Revolution, simply because homes were not large enough. Before the separation, wives could learn a trade informally while helping their husbands; afterwards, this was no longer possible (Alexander, 1970; Hall, 1982a).

Beginning in the late eighteenth century, male workers protested the hiring of women, alleging unfair competition: employers were hiring women instead of men because they could pay them less (Taylor, 1979; Walby, 1986; Lown, 1990). This pressure, which was not always successful, was framed in terms of an ideology that originated higher in the social structure and earlier in English history. John Browne, secretary to the Grand Lodge of Operative Tailors, wrote in a union publication in 1834, "Have not women been unfairly driven from their proper sphere in the social scale, unfeelingly torn from the maternal duties of a parent, and unjustly encouraged to compete with men in ruining the money value of labour?" (Taylor, 1979).

The notion that women should be subordinate to men has a long history in Christian thought, dating back to the Pauline injunction that women should submit to their husbands (Colossians 3:18; Ephesians 5:22; 1 Peter 3:1). Upper-class Puritans gave this ancient teaching a particular twist, one that placed great emphasis on the family. As their opposition to the Church of England made it impossible for them to rely on the established church as a social control institution, they turned—especially after the Restoration in 1660—to the male-headed family based on a sharp gender division of labor as a remedy for threatening social upheaval.

In the hands of the evangelical reformers of the eighteenth and nineteenth centuries, the Puritan doctrine developed into an ideology of separate spheres, in which work was considered a distinct—and distinctly male—sphere of life. The ideal upper-class woman was no longer active in her husband's business or a partner with him in the management of his farm; her place was at home, ruled by her husband, caring for him and for their children, and upholding high standards of virtue and morality in the face of the market economy's tendency to undermine them (Hall, 1980; Davidoff and Hall, 1987:149, 155). The Puritan poet John Milton had Adam express this new thinking about the family when he told Eve:

> . . . for nothing lovelier can be found
> In Woman, than to study household good
> And good works in her Husband to promote.
> (*Paradise Lost*, 9:232–34)

It is reflected in the comment of a member of Parliament in 1649 that "it was not for women to Petition, they might stay at home and wash the dishes" (quoted in Fraser, 1984:4).

At first, only wealthy men could afford to relinquish their wives' incomes or contributions to household production and maintenance. It thus became a badge of male achievement to be able to keep a wife idle. In 1726, Daniel Defoe, in *The Complete English Tradesmen*, remarked sarcastically that "the tradesman is foolishly vain of making his wife a gentlewoman, and forsooth he will have her sit above in the parlour, receive visits, drink Tea, and entertain her neighbors" (355; quoted in George, 1988:9). Once a few shopkeepers barred their wives from working in their shops, others went along so as "not to have their trades or shops thought less masculine or less considerable than others" (348; quoted in George, 1988:4–5). Conduct books telling "the new domestic woman" how to behave circulated widely among the nascent middle class (Armstrong, 1987), to great effect. According to Defoe, "Ladies . . . scorn to be seen in the compting house, much less behind the counter, despise the knowledge of their husband's business, and act as if they were ashamed of being tradesmen's wives, and never intended to be tradesmen's widows" (348; quoted in George, 1988:4–5).

For practical reasons, this innovation spread downward through the class structure only slowly. Most eighteenth–century shops were still parts of houses, and women continued to play a large role in running them (Hall, 1980). By mid–nineteenth century, however, the cult of domesticity was well established, at least as an ideal. According to a woman's diary for 1853, a respectable woman of the middle classes,

> must not work for profit . . . the conventional barrier that pronounces it ungenteel to be behind a counter, or serving the public in any mercantile capacity is greatly extended. The same in household economy. . . . [L]adies, dismissed from the dairy, the confectionary, the story room, the still room, the poultry yard, the kitchen garden and the orchard, have hardly yet found themselves a sphere equally useful in the pursuits of trade and art to which to apply their too abundant leisure. (Quoted in Pinchbeck, 1930:315–16, and Hall, 1980)

Even in the middle classes, the ideology of separate spheres was imperfectly realized. Some feminists protested their exclusion from male occupations; many women had to work because they could not marry or did not want to do so. There being more women than men, some women could not be supported by a husband. Their occupational choices were restricted by their limited education and skills and by discrimination on the part of employers (Collett, 1902). When women of the middle class did work, it was mostly in occupations that least threatened gender stereotypes—as governesses or shopkeepers or managers of lodging houses. But the women of the middle class hardly ever appear in the Old Bailey records except as prosecutors or witnesses. Neither the ideology nor the reality of domestic life reduced their involvement in crime substantially, because it was very low right from the start.

Notwithstanding some legal restrictions, women of the laboring classes continued to work in many occupations, often at very low wages and under wretched working conditions. One study of women in London in 1888 found them in two hundred trades (Alexander, 1983; Fishman, 1988:115). Henry Mayhew's (1862) ethnographic study of life among the

London poor confirms what the figures in my tables show: many women participated in a range of criminal activities, even if at a lower level than they had a century earlier.

When male workers like John Browne complained that women were undercutting their wages, they invoked the discourse of separate spheres: a woman's place was at home, not in the factory (Taylor, 1979:268–75). This exclusionary principle had been brought to the working class by middle-class reformers. The evangelical reformers of the eighteenth century had been preoccupied with the reconstitution of gender relations in the more affluent classes. In the nineteenth, they targeted the working class. One reason for working-class crime and radicalism, they thought, was that working mothers were failing to fulfill their domestic responsibilities. Husbands were going to public houses to eat their meals because wives were not at home to cook. Daughters were not learning domestic skills because their mothers were not home to teach them. As part of a broad offensive directed at working-class culture, they established Sunday schools and day schools, preached sermons, and wrote moral tales espousing middle-class values and norms, among them, the ideology of female domesticity (Hewitt, 1958; Hall, 1979, 1980; Purvis, 1989:45).

In the lower classes, the contradiction between what was ideal and what was practical was even larger than in the middle classes. Deaths, desertions, and a man's unemployment could force wives and daughters to take jobs. Thus, in Lancashire during the 1790s, if a man enlisted in the military, his wife might take up weaving; by 1808, "possibly half of all weavers were women and children" (Benenson, 1991a). Single women could not afford to remain idle, and were not expected to do so. Indeed, as far as one can tell from the census data, the percentage of women who were employed hardly changed between 1851 and 1901.

Gender stereotypes had a larger impact on the kinds of jobs women held (Jordan, 1989). Women could, for example, work without violating gender role stereotypes by working as domestic servants in the homes of those who were more fortunate. If a middle- or upper-class woman was to live a life of leisure, she needed servants to perform domestic chores.[30] Rising incomes for the middle classes enabled them to expand the number of household servants they employed. Most of these positions were filled by women (Banks and Banks, 1969:58; Higgs, 1986; Kent, 1989; Purvis, 1989:64–65). In 1881, 36 percent of all employed women were domestic servants (Lewis, 1984:149, Purvis, 1989:30), far more than in any other single occupation.

Increased employment opportunities for women as household servants may have reduced their need to steal, while the long hours and close supervision to which servants living in their masters' homes were subjected kept them away from criminal subcultures (e.g., the local pub, where many criminal enterprises were organized), exposed them to noncriminal influences, and reduced their opportunities to steal.[31]

In one respect, however, those opportunities were enhanced. It was very easy for a servant to steal from her master or mistress, and judging from the court records, quite a few did. In 1730, for example, 18.7 percent of the female larceny defendants were employees of the victim (as were 12 percent of the male larceny defendants).[32] These figures undoubtedly understate the percentages, because the circumstances of a number of the thefts suggest that the defendant had been a domestic servant (or perhaps a lodger), even though the transcript does not say so. These are cases in which the defendant is accused of stealing a single silver teaspoon or a few miscellaneous articles of clothing. On balance, it is unclear that increased employment in domestic service reduced women's representation in the court records, though it very likely did so. The personal ties that often develop between employers and domestic servants must have inhibited prosecution in many instances.

Working-class women usually began their work careers at an early age, before marriage. Once they married or had children, they often left their jobs or worked out of their homes (Collett, 1889).[33] The success of working-class trade unions in winning "a family wage" enabled many working-class women to quit their jobs when they married or had a child. Some women were probably eager to do so; their poorly paid, monotonous jobs offered few rewards; and some were no doubt persuaded by middle-class propaganda that their place was in the home (Humphries, 1977a, 1977b; Lewis, 1984:50).[34] Indeed, women in the labor movement gave high priority to women's domestic and familial responsibilities (Humphries, 1977a; Taylor, 1979; Benenson, 1984; Ross, 1984; Lown, 1990:77; but see Benenson, 1991b).

In other instances women were fired by employers who thought it improper for married women to work. Their husbands, no doubt, welcomed the higher level of domestic labor their unemployed wives could now supply (especially as working hours fell, giving them more time at home), felt assured by their wives' dependence on them, and took pride in being able to support a wife and family. Thus, according to Collett (1889, "no respectable man would willingly let the mother of his children go out to a factory, nor would the 10s a week she could thus earn make up for the loss incurred by her absence if he brought home even so little as 18s" (see also Jones, 1974; Vincent, 1981; Rose, 1988).

The low wages paid to working-class women have generally been attributed to male employers' beliefs—not very well-founded—that female laborers did not need to be paid as well as men because they were merely supplementing a husband's earnings (Rose, 1986). That contention, however, implies that individual employers can set wages as they wish. In a competitive labor market, however, employers do not have that power. Of course, labor markets are not perfectly competitive. Where one or a few plants dominated a town's economy, employers may have been able to fix wages, confident that many workers would not leave.

Employers themselves sometimes said that women were not as productive as men. In some instances that may have been true, though there is no way to verify the claim. In an age of machine production, however, productivity can depend on the design of the machinery as well as the skill of the workers using it (Beechey, 1982; Lewis, 1984:170–71). If women were less skilled—as was often the case—it was because male workers and employers denied them the opportunities to acquire skills (Freifeld, 1986). The failure of the male-dominated trade unions to demand equal opportunities for women on the job, or to insist on equal pay, clearly worked to the detriment of women as well. With women kept out of many jobs by gender stereotyping and restricted to those requiring limited skill, employers faced "an almost unlimited supply of women . . . who were an elastic labor force" for unskilled jobs (Rose, 1986; Lown, 1985; Jordan, 1989; Purvis, 1989:45). It was this that kept wages down in unskilled jobs.

This combination of low pay, unattractive work conditions, hiring discrimination, and ideological pressures to stay at home, drove many married women from the labor market. Between the middle and end of the nineteenth century, the number of married women holding jobs dropped, probably by more than 50 percent (Hewitt, 1958:19; Lewis, 1984:149). Once women left, they were unlikely to return unless forced to do so by widowhood or a husband's unemployment.

CONCLUDING REMARKS

This account has placed the complex history of the gendering of paid labor in the context of the development of capitalism. Although concepts familiar to Marxist theory—ideology, class conflict, profit-maximizing capitalists who prefer docile to militant employees, and workers whose consciousness of common class interests does not extend as far as the Marxist might hope—are evident in that account, they are not organized into a formal theory.

Though the rise of capitalism is one of the most central issues that Marxist theory has addressed, fundamental questions regarding this process, such as the source of the capital that made primitive accumulation possible and the class background of the early capitalists, remain controversial (Williams, 1944; Dobb, 1946; Wallerstein, 1974; Hilton, 1978; Brenner, 1976, 1982; Middleton, 1983, 1985). This is not the place to explore those issues in depth.

For present purposes, I assume that a satisfactory Marxist account can be elaborated, without delivering one. What is important for my purposes is that as industrial capitalism evolved, it transformed gender relations in complex ways. While middle-class women were being restricted from remunerative labor, many working-class women were being pulled out of the household into shops and factories. In the long run, they too were pushed and pulled back into the home by a complex combination of factors—employers who paid women low wages, male-dominated unions that failed to defend the interests of women workers, deprivation of opportunities for appealing jobs, deskilling, pressures from husbands who wanted their wives to do housework, propaganda that gave women primary responsibility for raising small children, the absence of child-care facilities at work, the lack of equal-opportunity legislation. The detailed histories currently available to us are not fully adequate to assess the relative weight or importance of these factors; I have certainly not tried to do so. I have rather tried to depict a context within which English gender relations and ideologies were transformed, indicating some of the causal forces at work without pinning the narrative down to a sharply defined model.

The developments responsible for this transformation are not inherent in capitalism as a mode of production. A capitalist society that does not rely on women to do housework and care for small children is not an impossibility. However, the transformation as it occurred can only be understood in the context of a particular capitalist society with a particular initial sexual division of labor, technology, and ideology differentiating men's and women's tasks and capabilities.

At times alternative understandings of gender were promulgated, for example, by the Owenite movement of the nineteenth century and by some feminists; however, their limited appeal suggests that even if details of this history were contingent, the main trends could hardly have taken place in any other way.

These trends created women who would have had to surmount high barriers to commit serious crimes of theft or violence. Women who were not employed were unlikely to be out at night or at a public house or on the streets. Their conventional routines reduced their opportunities to commit crime and to enlist potential partners. With wages rising for working-class men, marriage kept many women from the extreme poverty that drove women of earlier decades to steal. Rising incomes for men of the working and middle classes also made it possible for a larger number of women to support themselves through prostitution, avoiding the necessity of stealing. Even when working-class women's needs became pressing, the newer notions of femininity may have inhibited theft.

Although there is no way to disentangle the separate effects of each of these processes, together the ideological effect of missionizing work, the raising of working-class living standards, and the confinement of many working-class women to their fathers' or their husband's homes, or to the homes where they worked as domestics, dramatically reduced their involvement in crime. Only in the twentieth century, as women gradually returned to the paid labor force, were women to begin to return to the ranks of crime.

NOTES

1 In the United States in 1988, 82.2 percent of those arrested were male (U.S. Department of Justice, 1989:185). For the so-called crimes of violence the figure was 88.6 percent, for property crimes, 76.0 percent.

2 When Marxists did discuss gender, it was often in crudely reductionist terms. Marx's letter to P. V. Annenkov of December 28, 1846, is typical: "Assume particular stages of development of production, commerce and consumption and you will have a corresponding social constitution, a corresponding organization of the family, of orders and classes, in a word, a corresponding civil society" (quoted in Nicholson, 1986:194).

3 For a fuller discussion of these efforts, see O'Laughlin, (1977), Barett and McIntosh (1979), Hartman (1979), Barrett (1980), Harris and Young (1981), Coward (1983:270–77), Vogel (1983), and Delphy (1984).

4 As it happens, some studies have found a positive correlation between levels of serum testosterone and involvement in crime (e.g., Dabbs and Morris, 1990), but other studies have not (Fausto-Sterling, 1985:126–28).

5 Some of these sex differences appear in many cultures. In a cross-cultural study of sex differences in socialization, 82 percent of the thirty-three cultures in the sample placed greater stress on nurturance in the socialization of girls (Barry, Bacon, and Child, 1957).

6 This is not true in all societies. On the Melanesian island of New Britain, girls "are encouraged to behave aggressively toward males" and do so (Goodale, 1980:135).

7 David Franks's (1985) study of rape is consistent with this analysis. So are survey results showing sex differences in support of war. A New York Times/CBS News telephone survey of 1044 Americans, conducted in the second week of December 1990, found 37 percent of the women and 53 percent of the men saying that military actions should be initiated against Iraq if it did not withdraw from Kuwait by the date of the United Nations deadline (Oreskes, 1990). A British survey conducted in 1991 is also consistent with this gender difference. It found that 11 percent of men and 3 percent of women would commit murder to become millionaires if they could be confident of not being caught (*New York Newsday,* July 1, 1991, 3).

8 By contrast, Marx offered, in *Das Kapital,* a lengthy account of the the origins of capitalism and tried to explain its historical evolution. Because Messerschmidt's (1986) analysis of crime issues draws on feminist as well as Marxist theory, and insists that capitalism and patriarchy are two independent systems of subordination, it is tempting to take his work as an example of dual systems theory. However, Messerschmidt sees these two systems as interacting so extensively that in practice they are far from fully independent.

9 The very vocabulary dual systems theorists (and many other feminist writers) use suggests this. In Weberian sociology, patriarchy means "rule by the father." It designates forms of society in which a patriarch literally rules an extended household, with powers over its members that are close to absolute. Weber had in mind the Biblical Patriarchs, the heads of Albanian *zagorras,* and the Roman *pater familia,* not the modern male "head of household," whose powers over wives and minor children have been seriously eroded by the expansion of legal rights for women and children. Understood in this way, patriarchy is only one form male domination has taken. Modern discrimination against women is predominantly not a manifestation of patriarchy but a bureaucratic form of male domination. The term "patriarchy" has been convenient for those who wish to see gender relations in transhistorical terms precisely because it tends to blur distinctions between different forms of male supremacy. There has been a lively feminist debate over the pros and cons of the term "patriarchy" and its conceptualization (e.g., Edholm, Harris, and Young, 1977; Beechey, 1979; Barrett, 1980:10–19; Coward, 1983:268–77; Walby, 1990).

10 Though undertheorized, some parts of Engels's proposal may be valid empirically. When the conditions underlying matrilineality among the Nayars of India changed (disappearance of the demand for mercenary soldiers), fathers wanted to give their property to their own children instead of their sisters', and the traditional kinship system collapsed (Fuller, 1976; Quale, 1988:260–61).

11 The loss of a fertile or potentially fertile female is more damaging to the reproductive potential of a band than the loss of a male. This is so because pregnancy in humans limits women's reproductive capacity, but not men's. If a man dies, other men can impregnate surviving women. If a woman dies, other women will not be able to replace her to the same degree. This argument is not seriously damaged by the existence of some bands in which women participate effectively in hunting (Dahlberg, 1981; Estroko-Griffin and Griffin, 1985). These bands hunt game of moderate size (wild pigs, deer), not large game, and appear to live in milieux where danger from large predators does not exist. In most cultures, women stay close to home. Men travel farther and take on riskier pursuits (Parker and Parker, 1979).

12 Warfare plays a central role in the kinship theories developed by Ember and Ember (1971) and Divale and Harris (1976), but their arguments and evidence have been criticized by Dow (1983) and Coontz and Henderson (1986a).

13 Since many human males are not aggressive, this argument is questionable. It is just as likely that women would have preferred their husbands to be cooperative and conciliatory. There has also been speculation that early marriage systems favored male domination. If early marriages were exogamous to the band—an arrangement that might have come about to avoid the deleterious genetic consequences of inbreeding, or to create alliances—under certain conditions it would have been favorable to exchange females rather than males. Where warfare occurred, a son who was sent to another band as a husband might return with them and use his fighting skills against his natal band (Lerner, 1986:47–48). In hunting, there may be advantages in keeping together boys who were raised together (Quale, 1988). Such an arrangement facilitates bonding among adult males and makes it difficult for in-marrying females to find allies. But this is speculative, because we know nothing about the marriage arrangements that prevailed as the human species evolved, or even whether there was an institution resembling marriage.

14 Where the gender division of labor is one of domination and exploitation, those who benefit will be members of the dominant gender. Where the division is more equitable, both sexes may perceive themselves as benefiting from it.

15 The seminal works are Schreiner (1911:50–51), Clark (1919), and Pinchbeck (1930). Zaretsky (1976), Hamilton (1978), and Hartmann (1976) draw on these and more recent sources.

16 Hanawalt's data may have been atypical of medieval England; Bennett (1987:38–39) found that about a third of the criminal defendants in her study of Brigstock before the Black Plague (1348) were female. Curtis (1980) found 15.4 percent of the defendants in quarter sessions during the years 1610–19 to be female; the percentage rose to 30.4 percent for the years 1680–84. In Middlesex, 23 percent of the quarter sessions defendants for the years 1613–17 were female.

17 The published version of Feeley and Little's paper contains data for every fifth year; however, their preliminary analysis, presented to the Law and Society Association in 1990, contained data only for every twentieth year.

18 Every indication is that there were more women than men (Wrigley, 1967; Glass, 1968). According to one estimate, the ratio of women to men in the eighteenth century was as high as 1.3 to 1, and the census of 1881 found one million more women than men (Branca, 1975; Hall, 1979).

19 Additional criticisms of Gilligan's work can be found in Brighton (1983), Nails (1983), Greeno and Maccoby (1986), Benhabib (1987), Colby and Damon (1983), and Epstein (1988:76–94).

20 This possibility was, in fact, suggested by Kohlberg and Kramer (1969). Supporting evidence comes from Ember's (1973) study of children in a Kenyan community. In families where the absence of daughters led parents to assign stereotypically girls' tasks to their sons, the boys were less aggressive than in other families where they did not. The difference was greatest when boys' work took place inside the home rather than out-of-doors.

21 This is not to say that a concern for caring is out of place in the policies of the state or large organizations. However, for practical reasons, when policies are to be implemented on a large scale, they must be implemented bureaucratically, on the basis of formal rules.

22 In special circumstances, this restriction could be circumvented, allowing a woman to engage in business as a *feme sole merchant*, independent of her husband.

23 This occupational pattern had persisted since medieval times (Bennett, 1987:5–7, 116). A fifteenth-century source indicates that women could be "Brewers, Bakers, Carders and Spinners, and Workers as well of Wool, as of Linen Cloth, and of Silk, Brawdester, and Breakers of Wool, and all others that do use and work all handy works" (Dale, 1928:27; quoted in Lown, 1990:9). On the manor, flexibility in the gender division of labor prevailed: "Manorial bailiffs sometimes hired women to do work usually assigned to men (even plowing), and men were similarly employed for traditionally female jobs (e.g., dairying, gleaning). Although many tasks were loosely associated with either men or women, few were actually proscribed for one sex" (Bennett, 1987:116–19; see also Bradley, 1989:77–78). More extensive treatment of medieval Englishwomen's tasks and occupations can be found in Abrams (1916), Dale (1932), Thrupp (1948), Power (1975), Middleton (1979, 1981a, 1981b, 1983), and Kowaleski (1986).

24 Between 1835 and 1860, 25.7 percent of the defendants in the criminal court were female (Philips, 1977:148).

25 Large numbers of women workers participated in the Owenite union movement of the 1830s. Certain "female" trades, such as lace making and glove making, had a reputation in the 1830s for militancy, even violence (Taylor, 1979).

26 Female participation in riots in the period 1790 to 1810 was facilitated by their employment in manufacturing jobs (Bohrstedt, 1988).

27 Belief that theft by domestic servants was extremely common and difficult to prevent led to its exemption in 1706 from the ancient rule that those who were literate could not be executed (Beattie, 1975).

28 High production costs blocked the introduction of factory production in London through the nineteenth century. The developments discussed here took place largely outside of London; if they had any effect on crime patterns in the metropolis, it would probably have been through immigration from the countryside. The limited scope of factory production also limited its impact; only in textiles did factories largely replace production at home or in small workshops (Hill, 1989:11). According to Rule (1986:8), as late as 1851, "the majority of those employed in manufacturing . . . still did not work in factories." In the short run, the Industrial Revolution expanded domestic production more than it did factory production.

29 On average, men are capable of attaining greater physical strength than women, but the extent to which potential strength is actually attained depends strongly on exercise and training. In some societies, such as rural Uganda and Albania, women have traditionally performed heavy labor, while men have not (Perlea, 1990; Binder, 1991).

30 Recruitment of domestic servants may have been a secondary goal for the middle-class women who, unable to hold remunerative employment, turned in vast numbers to philanthropy (Prohaska, 1980).

31 Servants in the 1880s were normally not allowed out of the house in the evening unless they had advance permission, and that was given only for a specified purpose (Purvis, 1989:30). Employers tried to prevent servants from associating with "disreputable" people. Servants had to go along with these conditions to keep their jobs and to obtain references when they left.

32 Terminological ambiguities make it difficult to distinguish household servants from business employees. The latter were usually called servants, as well.

33 Thus, in the 1851 census, 42 percent of employed women between the ages of twenty and forty were unmarried (Richards, 1974). In some sectors of the economy, employers were reluctant to hire young women, because they tended to quit when they married (Fishman, 1988:70). Dependent on their husbands for sustenance, they could do little when their husbands beat them (London, 1903:135; quoted in Fishman, 1988).

34 Other women protested their exclusion; they liked the income from their jobs, and did not want to be cooped up inside the house all day (Benenson, 1991b).

REFERENCES

Abrams, Annie (1916). "Women Traders in Medieval London." *Economic Journal* 26:276–85.

Adler, Freda (1975). *Sisters in Crime: The Rise of the New Female Criminal.* New York: McGraw-Hill.

Adler, Freda, and Rita J. Simon, eds. (1979). *The Criminology of Deviant Women.* Boston: Houghton Mifflin.

Alexander, David (1970). *Retailing in England during the Industrial Revolution.* London: Athlone.

Alexander, Sally (1983). *Women's Work in Nineteenth Century London: A Study of the Years 1820–1850.* London: Journeyman's Press.

Armstrong, Nancy (1987). "The Rise of the Domestic Woman." In Nancy Armstrong and Leonard Tennenhouse, eds., *The Ideology of Conduct: Essays in Literature and the History of Sexuality,* 96–141. New York: Methuen.

Atkinson, Mabel (1914). *The Economic Foundations of the Women's Movement.* London: Fabian Society Tract No. 175.

Banks, J. A., and Olive Banks (1969). *Feminism and Family Planning in Victorian England.* Liverpool: University of Liverpool Press.

Barrett, Michèle (1980). *Women's Oppression Today.* London: Verso.

Barrett, Michèle and Mary McIntosh (1979). "Christine Delphy: Towards Materialist Feminism." *Feminist Review* 1:95–105.

Barry, Herbert, III, Margaret K. Bacon, and Irvin L. Child (1957). "A Cross-Cultural Survey of Some Sex Differences in Socialization." *Journal of Abnormal and Social Psychology* 55:327–32.

Beattie, John (1975). "The Criminality of Women in Eighteenth-Century England." *Journal of Social History* 8:80–116.

——— (1977). "Crime and Courts in Surrey, 1736–53." In J. S. Cockburn, ed., *Crime in England, 1500–1800,* 155–86. Princeton, N.J. Princeton University Press.

Beechey, Virginia (1979). "On Patriarchy." *Feminist Review* 3:66–82.

——— (1982). "The Sexual Division of Labour and the Labour Process." In Stephen Wood, ed., *The Degradation of Work? Skilling, Deskilling, and the Labour Process*, 54–73. London: Hutchinson.

Bell, Diane (1983). *Daughters of the Dreaming*. Melbourne: McPhee Gribble.

Benenson, Harold (1984). "Victorian Sexual Ideology." *International Labor and Working Class History* 25:1–23.

——— (1991a). "The 'Family Wage' and Working Women's Consciousness in Britain, 1880–1914." *Politics and Society* 19:71–108.

——— (1991b). "Patriarchal Constraints and Women Workers' Movements—The Lancashire Female Cotton Weavers, 1842–1919." Paper presented to the American Sociological Association.

Benhabib, Seyla (1987). "The Generalized and the Concrete Other." In Drucilla Cornell and Seyla Benhabit, eds., *Feminism as Critique: Essays on the Politics of Gender in Late Capitalist Society*, 77–95. London: Polity.

Bennett, Judith M. (1987). *Women in the Medieval English Countryside: Gender and Household in Brigstock before the Plague*. New York: Oxford University Press.

Binder, David (1991). "The Land of Talkative Men and Toiling Women." *New York Times*, April 23a, A4.

Bohrstedt, John (1988). "Gender, Household, and Community Politics: Women in English Riots, 1790–1810." *Past and Present* 120:88–122.

Boritch, Helen, and John Hagan (1990). "A Century of Crime in Toronto: Gender, Class, and Patterns of Social Control, 1859 to 1955." *Criminology* 28:567–600.

Boserup, Esther (1970). *Women's Role in Economic Development*. London: George Allen and Unwin.

Bradley, Harriet (1989). *Men's Work, Women's Work: A Sociological History of the Sexual Division of Labour in Employment*. Minneapolis: University of Minnesota Press.

Branca, Patricia (1975). *Silent Sisterhood: Middle Class Women in the Victorian Home*. Pittsburgh, Pa.: Carnegie-Mellon University Press.

Brenner, Robert (1976). "Agrarian Class Structure and Economic Development in Europe." *Past and Present* 70:30–75.

——— (1982). "The Agrarian Roots of European Capitalism." *Past and Present* 97:16–123.

Brighton, John M. (1983). "Women's Rationality and Men's Virtues: A Critique of Gender Dualism in Gilligan's Theory of Moral Development." *Social Research* 50:597–642.

Brown, Beverly (1986). "Women and Crime: The Dark Figures of Criminology." *Economy and Society* 15:355–402.

Burstyn, Varda (1983a). "Economy, Sexuality, and Politics: Engels and the Sexual Division of Labour." *Socialist Studies* (July) 19–39.

——— (1983b). "Masculine Dominance and the State." In Ralph Miliband and John Saville, eds., *Socialist Register* 20:45–89. London: Merlin Press.

Cadbury, Edward, M. Cécile Matheson, and George Shann (1906). *Women's Work and Wages: A Phase of Life in an Industrial City*. London: T. Fisher Unwin.

Carlen, Pat (1985). *Criminal Women: Autobiographical Accounts*. New York: Basil Blackwell.

Chapman, Stanley D., and J. D. Chambers (1970). *The Beginnings of Industrial Britain*. London: University Tutorial Program.

Charles, Lindsay (1985). Introduction to Lindsay Charles and Lorna Duffin, eds., *Women and Work in Pre-Industrial England*. London: Croom Helm.

Chesney-Lind, Meda (1986). "Women and Crime: The Female Offender." *Signs* 12:78–96.

Chevillard, Nicole, and Leconte, Sébastien (1986). "The Dawn of Lineage Societies: The Origins of Women's Oppression." In Stefanie Coontz and Peta Henderson, eds., *Women's Work, Men's Property: The Origins of Gender and Class*. 76–107. London: Verso.

Chodorow, Nancy J. (1978). *The Reproduction of Mothering: Psychoanalysis and the Sociology of Gender*. Berkeley: University of California Press.

Clark, Alice (1919). *Working Life of Women in Seventeenth-Century England*. New York: E. P. Dutton.

Cohen, Albert (1955). *Delinquent Boys: The Family of the Gang*. Glencoe, Ill.: Free Press.

Colby, Ann, and William Damon (1983). "Listening to a Different Voice: A Review of Gilligan's *In a Different Voice*." *Merrill-Palmer Quarterly* 29:473–81.

Collett, Clara (1889). "Women's Work." In Charles Booth, ed., *Labour and Life of the People*, vol. 1, *London*, 406–76. London: Williams and Norgate.

——— (1902). *The Economic Position of Women Workers in the Middle Classes*. London: P. S. King.

Coontz, Stephanie, and Peta Henderson (1986a). " 'Explanations' of Male Dominance." In Stefanie Coontz and Peta Henderson, eds., *Women's Work, Men's Property: The Origins of Gender and Class*, 1–42. London: Verso.

——— (1986b). "Property Forms, Political Power, and Female Labour in the Origins of Class and State Societies." In Stefanie Coontz and Peta Henderson, eds., *Women's Work, Men's Property: The Origins of Gender and Class*, 108–56. London: Verso.

Coward, Rosalind (1983). *Patriarchal Precedents: Sexuality and Social Relations*. Boston: Routledge.

Croll, Elizabeth (1984). "The Exchange of Women and Property: Marriage in Post-Revolutionary China." In Renée Hirschon, ed., *Women and Property, Women as Property*, 44–61. London: Croom Helm.

Curran, D. A. (1983). "Judicial Discretion and Defendant's Sex." *Criminology* 21:41–58.

Currie, Dawn (1986). "Female Criminality: A Crisis in Feminist Theory." In Brian D. MacLean, ed., *The Political Economy of Crime*, 232–46. Scarborough, Ont.: Prentice-Hall Canada.

Curtis, Timothy (1980). "Explaining Crime in Early Modern England." *Criminal Justice History: An International Annual* 1:117–37.

Dabbs, James M., Jr., and Robin Morris (1990). "Testosterone, Social Class, and Antisocial Behavior in a Sample of 4,462 Men." *Psychological Science* 1:209–11.

Dahlberg, Frances (1981). *Woman the Gatherer*. New Haven, Conn.: Yale University Press.

Dale, Marion K. (1928). *Women in the Textile Industry and Trade of Fifteenth Century England*. London: n.p.

——— (1932). "The London Silkwomen of the Fifteenth Century." *Economic History Review*, 1st ser. 4:324–25.

Daly, Kathleen (1989). "Gender and Varieties of White-Collar Crime." *Criminology* 27:769–94.

Daly, Kathleen, and Meda Chesney-Lind (1988). "Feminism and Criminology." *Justice Quarterly* 5:101–43.

Datesman, Susan K., and Frank R. Scarpitti, eds. (1980). *Women, Crime, and Justice*. New York: Oxford University Press.

Davidoff, Leonore, and Catherine Hall (1987). *Family Fortunes: Men and Women of the English Middle Class, 1780–1850*. London: Hutchinson.

Davidson, Caroline (1982). *A Woman's Work Is Never Done: A History of Housework in the British Isles, 1650–1950*. London: Chatto and Windus.

Delphy, Christine (1984). *Close to Home: A Materialist Analysis of Women's Oppression*. Amherst: University of Massachusetts Press.

Dinnerstein, Dorothy (1976). *The Mermaid and the Minotaur: Sexual Arrangements and Human Malaise*. New York: Harper Colophon.

Divale, William, and Marvin Harris (1976). "Population, Warfare, and the Male Supremacist Complex." *American Anthropologist* 78:521–38.

Dobb, Maurice (1946). *Studies in the Development of Capitalism*. London: Routledge.

Dow, James (1983). "Woman Capture as a Motivation for Warfare: A Comparative Analysis of Intra-Cultural Variation and a Critique of the 'Male Supremacist Complex.'" In Rada Dyson-Hudson and Michael A. Little, eds., *Rethinking Human Adaptation: Biological and Cultural Models*, 97–115. Boulder, Colo.: Westview.

Earle, Brian (1989). *The Making of the English Middle Class: Business, Society, and Family Life in London, 1660–1730*. Berkeley and Los Angeles: University of California Press.

Edholm, Felicity, Olivia Harris, and Kate Young (1977). "Conceptualizing Women." *Critique of Anthropology* 3:101–30.

Eisenstein, Zillah (1979). *Capitalist Patriarchy and the Case for Socialist Feminism*. New York: Monthly Review Press.

Ember, Caroline (1973). "Feminine Task Assignment and the Social Behavior of Boys." *Ethos* 1:424–39.

Ember, John, and Caroline Ember (1971). "The Conditions Favoring Matrilocal versus Patrilocal Residence." *American Anthropologist* 73:571–94.

Engels, Friedrich (1972). *The Origin of the Family, Private Property, and the State*. New York: Monthly Review Press.

Epstein, Cynthia Fuchs (1988). *Deceptive Distinctions: Sex, Gender, and the Social Order*. New Haven, Conn.: Yale University Press.

Estroko-Griffin, Agnes A., and P. Bion Griffin (1985). "Women Hunters: The Implications for Pleistocene Prehistory and Contemporary Ethnography." In Madeleine J. Goodman, ed., *Women in Asia and the Pacific*, 61–81. Honolulu: University of Hawaii Press.

Fausto-Sterling, Anne (1985). *Myths of Gender: Biological Theories About Women and Men*. New York: Basic.

Feeley, Malcolm M., and Deborah L. Little (1991). "The Vanishing Female: The Decline of Women in the Criminal Process, 1687–1912." *Law and Society Review* 25:719–58.

Fishman, W. J. (1988). *East End 1888: Life in a London Borough among the Laboring Poor*. Philadelphia: Temple University Press.

Franks, David D. (1985). "Role-Taking, Social Power, and Imperceptiveness: The Analysis of Rape." *Studies in Symbolic Interaction* 6:229–59.

Fraser, Antonia (1984). *The Weaker Vessel*. New York: Alfred A. Knopf.

Freifeld, Mary (1986). "Technological Change and the 'Self-Acting' Mule: A Study of Skill and the Sexual Division of Labour." *Social History* 11:321–43.

Fuller, Christopher J. (1976). *The Nayars Today*. New York: Cambridge University Press.

George, Margaret (1988). *Women in the First Capitalist Society: Experiences in Seventeenth-Century England*. Urbana: University of Illinois Press.

Gilligan, Carol (1982). *In a Different Voice: Psychological Theory and Women's Development*. Cambridge, Mass.: Harvard University Press.

Glass, D. V. (1968). "Notes on the Demography of London at the End of the Seventeenth Century." *Daedalus* 97:581–92.

Goldberg, Steven (1973). *The Inevitability of Patriarchy*. New York: Morrow.

Goodale, Jane (1980). "Gender, Sexuality, and Marriage: A Kaulong Model of Nature and Culture." In Carol MacCormack and Marilyn Strathern, eds., *Nature, Culture, and Gender*, 119–42. Cambridge, Eng.: Cambridge University Press.

Goody, Jack (1976). *Production and Reproduction: A Comparative Study of the Domestic Domain*. Cambridge, Eng.: Cambridge University Press.

Gough, Kathleen (1971). "The Origin of the Family." *Journal of Marriage and the Family* 33:760–71.

Greeno, Catherine, and Eleanor Maccoby (1986). "How Different Is the Different Voice." *Signs* 11:310–16.

Hagan, John, John H. Simpson, and A. R. Gillis (1979). "The Sexual Stratification of Social Control: A Gender-Based Perspective on Crime and Delinquency." *British Journal of Sociology* 30:25–38.

——— (1987). "Class in the Household: A Power-Control Theory of Gender and Delinquency." *American Journal of Sociology* 82:788–816.

——— (1988). "Feminist Scholarship, Relational and Instrumental Control, and a Power-Control Theory of Gender and Delinquency." *British Journal of Sociology* 39:301–36.

Hall, Catherine (1979). "The Early Formation of Victorian Domestic Ideology." In Sandra Burman, ed., 15–32. *Fit Work for Women*. New York: St. Martin's.

——— (1980). "The History of the Housewife." In Ellen Melos, ed., *The Politics of Housework*, 44–71. London: Allison and Busby.

——— (1982a). "The Butcher, the Baker, the Candlestick Maker: The Shop and the Family in the Industrial Revolution." In Elizabeth Whitelegg et al., eds., *The Changing Experience of Women*, 2–16. Oxford: Martin Robertson.

——— (1982b). "The Home Turned Upside Down? The Working-Class Family in Cotton Textiles 1780–1850." In Elizabeth Whitelegg et al., eds., *The Changing Experience of Women*, 17–29. Oxford: Martin Robertson.

Hamilton, Roberta (1978). *The Liberation of Women: A Study of Patriarchy and Capitalism*. Boston: Allen and Unwin.

Hanawalt, Barbara (1979). *Crime and Conflict in English Communities, 1300–1348*. Cambridge, Mass.: Harvard University Press.

Harris, Anthony (1977). "Sex and Theories of Deviance: Towards a Functional Theory of Deviant Type-Scripts." *American Sociological Review* 42:3–16.

Harris, Olivia, and Kate Young (1981). "Engendered Structures: Some Problems in the Analysis of Reproduction." In Joel S. Kahn and Josep R. Llobera, eds., *The Anthropology of Pre-Capitalist Societies*. Atlantic Highlands, N.J.: Humanities Press.

Hartmann, Heidi (1976). "Capitalism, Patriarchy, and Job Segregation by Sex." *Signs* 1 (3, pt. 2): 137–70.

——— (1979). "The Unhappy Marriage of Marxism and Feminism: Towards a More Progressive Union." *Capital and Class* 8:1–33.

Hartwell, Ronald Maxwell (1971). *The Industrial Revolution and Economic Growth*. London: Methuen.

Heidensohn, Frances (1985). *Women and Crime: The Life of the Female Offender*. New York: New York University Press.

Hewitt, Margaret (1958). *Wives and Mothers in Victorian Industry*. London: Rockliff.

Higgs, Edward (1986). *Domestic Servants and Households in Rochdale, 1851–1871*. New York: Garland.

Hill, Bridget (1989). *Women, Work, and Sexual Politics in Eighteenth-Century England*. Oxford: Basil Blackwell.

Hilton, Rodney, ed. (1978). *The Transition from Feudalism to Capitalism.* London: Verso.

Humphries, Jane (1977a). "Class Struggle and the Resistance of the Working Class Family." *Cambridge Journal of Economics* 1:241–58.

——— (1977b). "The Working Class Family, Women's Liberation, and Class Struggle: The Case of Nineteenth Century British History." *Review of Radical Political Economics* 9:25–41.

Hunt, E. H. (1981). *British Labour History, 1815–1914.* Vol. 2. London: Weidenfeld and Nicholson.

Hutchins, Elizabeth Leigh (1915). *Women in Modern Industry.* London: Cass.

Jones, Gareth Stedman (1974). "Working-Class Culture and Working-Class Politics in London, 1870–1900: Notes on the Remaking of a Working Class." *Journal of Social History* 7:460–508.

Jordan, Ellen (1989). "The Exclusion of Women from Industry in Nineteenth-Century Britain." *Comparative Studies in Society and History* 31:273–96.

Kaberry, Phyllis (1939). *Aboriginal Woman: Sacred and Profane.* London: Routledge and Kegan Paul.

Kent, D. A. (1989). "Ubiquitous but Invisible: Female Domestic Servants in Mid-Eighteenth Century London." *History Workshop Journal* 28:111–28.

King, Peter (1984). "Decision-Makers and Decision-Making in the English Criminal Law, 1750–1800." *The Historical Journal* 27:25–58.

Kloek, Els (1990). "Criminality and Gender in Leiden's Confessieboeken, 1678–1794." *Criminal Justice History* 11:1–29.

Kohlberg, Lawrence, and R. Kramer (1969). "Continuities and Discontinuities in Childhood and Adult Moral Development." *Human Development* 12:93–120.

Kohlberg, Lawrence, Charles Levine, and Alexandra Hewer (1983). *Moral Stages: A Current Formulation and a Response to Critics.* Basel: S. Karger.

Kowaleski, Maryanne (1986). "Women's Work in a Market Town: Exeter in the Late Fourteenth Century." In Barbara Hanawalt, ed., *Women and Work in Preindustrial Europe,* 145–64. Bloomington: Indiana University Press.

Krohn, Marvin D., James P. Curry, and Shirley Nelson-Kilger (1983). "Is Chivalry Dead? An Analysis of Police Dispositions of Males and Females." *Criminology* 21:417–38.

Kuhn, Annette, and Ann-Marie Wolpe, eds. (1978). *Feminism and Materialism: Women and the Modes of Production.* London: Routledge and Kegan Paul.

Lazonick, William (1976). "The Subjection of Labour to Capital: The Rise of the Capitalist System." *Review of Radical Political Economics* 10 (Spring):1–31.

Leacock, Eleanor Burke (1972). *Myths of Male Dominance.* New York: Monthly Review Press.

Leibowitz, Lila (1986). "In the Beginning . . .: The Origins of the Sexual Division of Labour and the Development of the First Human Societies." In Stephanie Coontz and Peta Henderson, eds., *Women's Work, Men's Property: The Origins of Gender and Class,* 43–75. London: Verso.

Leonard, Eileen B. (1982). *Women, Crime, and Society: A Critique of Theoretical Criminology.* New York: Longman.

Lerner, Gerda (1986). *The Creation of Patriarchy.* London: Oxford University Press.

Lewis, Jane (1984). *Women in England, 1870–1950: Sexual Divisions and Social Change.* Bloomington: Indiana University Press.

London, Jack (1903). *The People of the Abyss.* London: Macmillan.

Lown, Judy (1985). "Not So Much a Factory, More a Form of Patriarchy: Gender and Class during Industrialization." In Eva Garmarnikow, David H. J. Morgan, June Purvis, and Daphne E. Taylorson, eds., *Gender, Class and Work*, 36–43. London: Gower.

——— (1990). *Women and Industrialization: Gender at Work in Nineteenth Century England.* Minneapolis: University of Minnesota Press.

McLynn, Frank J. (1989). *Crime and Punishment in Eighteenth-Century England.* London: Routledge.

Mannheim, Hermann (1967). *Comparative Criminology.* 2d ed. Boston: Houghton Mifflin.

Mayhew, Henry (1862). *London Labour and London Poor.* Vol. 4. London: C. Griffin.

Medick, Hans (1979). "The Proto-Industrial Family Economy: The Structural Function of Household and Family during the Transition from Peasant Society to Industrial Capitalism." *Social History* 3:291–316.

Meillasoux, Claude (1981). *Maidens, Meal, and Money: Capitalism and the Domestic Community.* Cambridge, Eng.: Cambridge University Press.

Merton, Robert K. (1938). "Social Structure and Anomie." *American Sociological Review* 3:672–82.

Messerschmidt, James (1986). *Capitalism, Patriarchy, and Crime: Toward a Socialist-Feminist.* Criminology. Totowa, N.J.: Rowman and Littlefield.

Middleton, Christopher (1979). "The Sexual Division of Labor in Feudal England." *New Left Review* 113–14:147–68.

——— (1981a). "Peasants, Patriarchy, and the Feudal Mode of Production: A Marxist Appraisal; Part 1, Property and Patriarchal Relations within the Peasantry." *Sociological Review* 29:105–35.

——— (1981b). "Peasants, Patriarchy, and the Feudal Mode of Production: A Marxist Appraisal; Part 2, Feudal Lords and the Subordination of Peasant Women." *Sociological Review* 29:137–54.

——— (1983). "Patriarchal Exploitation and the Rise of English Capitalism." In Eva Gamarnikow, David H. J. Morgan, June Purvis, and Daphne E. Taylorson, eds., *Gender, Class, and Work*, 11–45. London: Heinemann.

——— (1985). "Women's Labour and the Transition to Industrial Capitalism." In Lindsey Charles and Lorna Duffin, eds., *Women and Work in Pre-Industrial England*, 181–206. London: Croom Helm.

Mitchell, Juliett (1971). *Women's Estate.* New York: Pantheon.

Moore, Henrietta L. (1988). *Feminism and Anthropology.* Minneapolis: University of Minnesota Press.

Morash, Merry (1986). "Gender, Peer Groups, and Delinquency," *Journal of Research in Crime and Delinquency* 23:43–67.

Morgan, Robin (1970). *Sisterhood Is Beautiful.* New York: Random House.

Morris, Desmond (1967). *The Naked Ape: A Zoologist's Study of the Human Animal.* New York: McGraw-Hill.

Morris, Jenny (1986). "The Characteristics of Sweating: The Late Nineteenth-Century London and Leeds Tailoring Trade." In Angela V. John, ed., *Unequal Opportunities: Women's Employment in England, 1800–1918*, 95–121. Oxford: Basil Blackwell.

Naffine, Mgaore (1988). *Female Crime: The Construction of Women in Criminology.* Boston: Allen and Unwin.

Nails, Deborah (1983). "Social Scientific Sexism: Gilligan's Mismeasure of Man." *Social Research* 50:643–44.

Neff, Wanda Fraiken (1966). *Victorian Working Women: An Historical and Literary Study of Women in British Industries and Professions, 1832–1850.* New York: AMS.

Nicholson, Linda J. (1986). *Gender and History.* New York: Columbia University Press.

O'Laughlin, Brigit (1977). "Production and Reproduction: Meillasoux's 'Femmes, geniers et capitaux.' " *Critique of Anthropology* 2:3–32.

Oreskes, Michael (1990). "Poll Finds Americans Divided on Sanctions or Force in Gulf." *New York Times,* December 14, A1, A14.

Parker, Seymour, and Hilda Parker (1979). "The Myth of Male Superiority: Rise and Demise." *American Anthropologist* 81:289–309.

Parsons, Talcott (1947). "Certain Primary Sources and Patterns of Oppression in the Social Structure of the Western World." *Psychiatry* 10:167–81.

Perlea, Jane (1990). "For the Oppressed Sex, Brave Words to Live By." *New York Times,* June 6, A4.

Philips, David (1977). *Crime and Authority in Victorian England: The Black Country 1835–1860.* London: Croom Helm.

Pinchbeck, Ivy (1930). *Women Workers and the Industrial Revolution, 1750–1850.* London: Routledge.

Power, Eileen E. (1975). *Medieval Women.* New York: Cambridge University Press.

Prohaska, F. K. (1980). *Women and Philanthropy in Nineteenth-Century England.* New York: Oxford University Press.

Purvis, June (1989). *Hard Lessons: The Lives and Education of Working-Class Women in Nineteenth-Century England.* Minneapolis: University of Minnesota Press.

Quale, G. Robin (1988). *A History of Marriage Systems.* New York: Greenwood.

Quinn, Naomi (1977). "Anthropological Studies of Women's Status." *Annual Review of Anthropology* 6:181–225.

Rans, L. L. (1978). "Women's Crime: Much Ado About . . .?" *Federal Probation* 42:45–49.

Redstockings (1970). "Manifesto." In Robin Morgan, ed., *Sisterhood is Powerful: An Anthology of Writings from the Women's Liberation Movement,* 533–36. New York: Random House.

Reed, Evelyn (1978). *Sexism and Science.* New York: Pathfinder.

Rendall, Jane (1990). *Women in an Industrializing Society: England 1750–1880.* Oxford: Basil Blackwell.

Richards, Eric (1974). "Women in the British Economy since About 1700: An Interpretation." *History* 59:337–57.

Roberts, Elizabeth (1988). *Women's Work, 1840–1940.* Houndmills, Eng.: Macmillan.

Roberts, Michael (1985). " 'Words They Are Women, and Deeds They Are Men': Images of Work and Gender in Early Modern England." In Lindsey Charles and Lorna Duffin, eds., *Women and Work in Pre-Industrial England,* 122–80. London: Croom Helm.

Rose, Sonya O. (1986). " 'Gender at Work': Sex, Class, and Industrial Capitalism." *History Workshop* 21:113–31.

——— (1988). "Gender Antagonism and Class Conflict: Exclusionary Strategies of Male Trade Unionists in Nineteenth-Century Britain." *Social History* 13:191–208.

Ross, Ellen (1984). "Response to Harold Beneson's 'Victorian Sexual Ideology.' " *International Labor and Working Class History* 25:30–36.

Rule, John (1986). *The Labouring Classes in Early Industrial England, 1750–1850.* London: Longman.

Sacks, Karen (1974). "Engels Revisited: Women, the Organization of Production, and Private Property." In Michele Rosaldo and Louise Lamphere, eds., *Woman, Culture, and Society*, 207–222. Stanford, Calif.: Stanford University Press.

——— (1976). "State Bias and Women's Status." *American Anthropologist* 78:131–54.

——— (1979). *Sisters and Wives: The Past and Failure of Sexual Equality*. Westport, Conn.: Greenwood.

Sanday, Peggy Reeves (1981). *Female Power and the Male Dominance*. Cambridge, Eng.: Cambridge University Press.

Sayers, Janet, Mary Evans, and Nanneke Redclift (1987). *Engels Revisited: New Feminist Essays*. London: Travistock.

Schreiner,Olive (1911). *Woman and Labour*. London: Fischer Unwin.

Sears, Robert R., Eleanor. E. Maccoby, and Harry Levin (1957). *Patterns of Child Rearing*. Evanston, Ill.: Row, Peterson.

Simmons, Roberta G., and Dale A. Blyth. (1987). *Moving into Adolescence*. New York: Aldine.

Simon, Rita James (1975). *Women and Crime*. Lexington, Mass.: D. C. Heath.

Smart, Carol (1976). *Women, Crime, and Criminology*. London: Routledge and Kegan Paul.

Smelser, Neil J. (1959). *Social Change in the Industrial Revolution: An Application of Theory to the Lancaster Cotton Industry, 1770–1840*. Chicago: University of Chicago Press.

Smith, Douglas A., and Ray Paternoster (1987). "The Gender Gap in Theories of Deviance: Issues and Evidence." *Journal of Research in Crime and Delinquency* 24:140–72.

Snell, Keith D. M. (1985). *Annals of the Labouring Poor: Social Change in Agrarian England, 1600–1900*.

Stacey, Judith (1983). *Patriarchy and Social Revolution*. Berkeley: University of California Press.

Steffensmeier, Darrell (1980). "Assessing the Impact of the Women's Movement on Sex-Based Differences in the Handling of Adult Criminal Defendants." *Crime and Delinquency* 76:344–57.

Steffensmeier, Darrell, and Emilie Allan (1991). "Gender, Age, and Crime." In Joseph F. Sheley, ed., *Criminology: A Contemporary Handbook*, 67–94. Belmont, Calif.: Wadsworth.

Sutherland, Edwin, and Donald R. Cressey (1978). *Criminology*. 10th ed. Philadelphia: Lippincott.

Sykes, Gresham, and David Matza (1957). "Techniques of Neutralization: A Theory of Delinquency." *American Sociological Review* 22:665–66.

Taylor, Barbara (1979). " 'The Men Are as Bad as Their Masters . . .': Socialism, Feminism, and Sexual Antagonism in the London Tailoring Trade in the Early 1830s." *Feminist Studies* 5:7–40.

Thompson, E. P. (1963). *The Making of the English Working Class*. New York: Vintage.

——— (1971). "The Moral Economy of the English Crowd in the Eighteenth Century." *Past and Present* 50:76–136.

Thrupp, Sylvia (1948). *The Merchant Class of Medieval London, 1300–1500*. Chicago: University of Chicago Press.

Tilly, Louise, and Joan Scott (1978). *Women, Work, and Family*. New York: Holt, Rinehart and Winston.

U.S. Department of Justice (1989). *Crime in the United States, 1988*. Washington, D.C.: Government Printing Office.

Vincent, David (1981). *Bread, Knowledge, and Freedom: A Study of Nineteenth-Century Working Class Autobiography*. London: Europa.

Vogel, Lise (1983). *Marxism and the Oppression of Women.* New Brunswick, N.J.: Rutgers University Press.

Walby, Sylvia (1986). *Patriarchy at Work.* Cambridge, Eng.: Polity.

——— (1990). *Theorizing Patriarchy.* Cambridge, Mass.: Basil Blackwell.

Walker, L. J. (1984). "Sex Differences in the Development of Moral Reasoning: A Critical Review." *Child Development* 55:677–91.

Wallerstein, Immanuel (1974). *The Modern World System,* vol. 1: *Capitalist Agriculture and the Origins of the European World Economy in the Sixteenth Century.* New York: Academic Press.

Williams, Eric E. (1944). *Capitalism and Slavery.* Chapel Hill: University of North Carolina Press.

Wilson, Edward O. (1975). *Sociobiology: The New Synthesis.* Cambridge, Mass.: Harvard University Press.

Wrigley, E. A. (1967). "A Simple Model of London's Importance in Changing English Society and Economy." *Past and Present* 37:46–49.

Zaretsky, Eli (1976). *Capitalism, the Family, and Personal Life.* New York: Harper and Row.

Zedner, Lucia (1991a). "Women, Crime, and Penal Responses: A Historical Account." In Michael Tonry, ed., *Crime and Justice: A Review of Research,* 307–62. Chicago: University of Chicago Press.

——— (1991b). *Women, Crime, and Custody in Victorian England.* Oxford: Clarendon Press.

[3] Time Series Analysis of Crime Rates

A methodological critique of Cantor and Land's (1985) approach to the time series analysis of the crime–unemployment relationship is developed. Error correction models for U.S. homicide and robbery rates for the years 1946–1997 are presented to illustrate procedures for analyzing nonstationary time series data. The critique is followed by a discussion of methodological problems in work by Devine *et al.* (1988), Smith *et al.* (1992), and Britt (1994, 1997) that builds on Cantor and Land's approach.

KEY WORDS: time series; crime; unemployment; age; divorce; cointegration.

1. INTRODUCTION

David Cantor and Kenneth Land's (1985) analysis of the relationship between annual unemployment rates and crime rates in the United States has served as a paradigm for subsequent criminological time series analyses. Though Hale and Sabbagh (1991) and Hale (1991) have raised questions about their approach, Cantor and Land (hereafter C-L) (1991) have defended their work vigorously (Land *et al.*, 1995). Here I raise further questions about the C-L procedures. I then update their data set, add additional variables to it, and carry out further analyses of homicide and robbery rates in the United States during the years 1946–1997. Finally, I discuss the work of several other researchers who have used the C-L approach.

2. THE CANTOR–LAND APPROACH

C-L (1985) argue that earlier research dealing with the impact of unemployment on crime rates has led to weak and inconsistent findings because it has failed to take into account two possible ways unemployment might influence crime. Although the unemployed are expected to have greater motivation to violate the law, they might also spend more time at home, preventing burglaries and reducing their vulnerability to robbery, assault, and homicide[2] (an opportunity effect). C-L note that the two possibilities need not be mutually exclusive: unemployment could reduce the opportunities to violate the law while, at the same time, increasing the motivation to do so. If both effects are instantaneous, a coefficient representing the net effect of unemployment on crime might be small and insignificant even though both effects are substantial.

A linear relationship between the rate at which individual i commits crimes (C_i), and that individual's lawful opportunities and motivation at time t can be represented in the form of a regression equation with residual e_i:

$$C_{it} = a + b_1(\text{opportunity}) + b_2(\text{motivation}_{it}) + e_{it} \tag{1}$$

If opportunity at time t and motivation at time t are both proportional to unemployment at time t (U_t), a regression of C_t against U_t will yield an estimate of the sum $b_1 + b_2$. Without additional information, there is no way to estimate the individual coefficients b_1 and b_2.

C-L break the underdetermination by suggesting that opportunity effects should be instantaneous, while motivational effects are likely to be lagged. This is because most workers will have savings and welfare benefits to sustain them for a time after they lose a job. C-L represent the motivational factor with a term involving the difference in the unemployment rate, $\Delta U_t = U_t - U_{t-1}$, arguing that people will compare their current employment status with what it was in the past. Thus one can measure the motivational and opportunity effects of unemployment by using the expression $b_1 U_t + b_2 \Delta U_t$ to predict the crime rate at time t. The coefficient b_1 should be negative, while b_2 should be positive.

Analyzing nationally aggregated annual data for the years 1946–1982, C-L find evidence for trends in the crime rates, which they eliminate by taking first or second differences. The equations they consider thus take the form of

$$\Delta C_t = a + b_1 U_t + b_2 \Delta U_t + e_t \tag{2}$$

or

$$\Delta^2 C_t = a + b_1 U_t + b_2 \Delta U_t + e_t \tag{3}$$

C-L present results for both logged and unlogged crime rates. Values of adjusted R^2 for these models range from 0 (assault) to .1979 (larceny).

[2]A similar argument was presented by Cook and Harkin (1985).

Evidence of the predicted opportunity and motivational effects is found primarily for offenses involving illegal acquisition. In a subsequent analysis, Land *et al.* (1995) extend the time series to 1990, obtaining similar results. In Section 2, I point out several problems associated with the C-L procedures. Because there is something of a disconnect between the narrative in which C-L present their theoretical ideas and the equations they use to represent those ideas, I discuss both.

2.1. The Lag Structure of Unemployment

2.1.1. Distinguishing Between Opportunity and Motivation Effects

The validity of the C-L strategy for distinguishing motivational from opportunity effects rests on the accuracy of the proposition that most workers have savings and welfare benefits to sustain them for a time on losing a job. This may well be true of some workers, but it is surely not true of all. Evidence to this effect can be found in Conley's (1999) study of a cohort of subjects in the Panel Study of Income Dynamics. Among blacks with an income of \$15,000 or less in 1992, the median net worth of the family was zero (i.e., no assets). In the entire black subsample, the median assets excluding housing equity were \$2000. In 1998, the bottom 40% of households in the Federal Reserve Board's Survey of Consumer Finances had a mean net worth of \$1100 and a mean annual income of \$13,500. Among non-Hispanics, 14.8% of whites and 27.4% of African Americans had zero or negative net worth (Wolff, 2001). Clearly, many would face serious financial difficulties very quickly after losing a job.

In an unpublished study[3] using monthly crime and unemployment data, C-L (1987) found that changes in unemployment were positively related to changes in burglary and larceny just 1 month later. Longer-lagged effects were absent, apart from negative effects with a lag of 2 months. These results suggest that analyses of annual data may be insufficiently fine-grained to detect the motivational effects of unemployment and that lags as long as a year are too long to model them. If the various motivational effects of unemployment are felt very quickly, then it will be impossible to distinguish opportunity effects from motivational effects with annual data because they will both appear as contemporaneous effects.

If the motivational effect is indeed lagged, so that loss of a job in year $t-1$ increases the motivation to violate the law in year t, then one could represent the motivational effect with a term in U_{t-1}, and the underdetermination of coefficients would no longer be a problem. This is not the strategy C-L adopt, but it would appear to be a straightforward translation of

[3] I know its contents only through the summary by Land *et al.* (1991).

the ideas in their narrative into a statistical model. Because C-L found evidence that motivational effects have a time lag much shorter than a year, it is questionable whether they should be studied by introducing a term in unemployment lagged by as long as a year, though they could legitimately be modeled with much shorter lags (e.g., weekly or monthly). However, the procedure would still be substantively dubious.

To see this, consider three sets of individuals. Members of the first set lose their jobs at the end of year t and remain unemployed through the following year. Members of the second set are employed in year t but lose their jobs during year $t+1$. Members of the third set become unemployed at the start of year t but find jobs a year later and keep them. If the motivational effect of unemployment were to be expressed through an unemployment rate lagged by 1 year, members of all three groups would have low motivation to violate the law in year t because they would both be living on earnings until they lost their jobs (groups 1 and 2) or on savings and welfare (group 3). Groups 1 and 2 would have equally low motivation to violate the law in year $t+1$, even though members of the first group are unemployed for the entire year, while members of the second group are working part of the year. On the other hand, members of group 3 would have higher motivation to violate the law in year $t+1$, even though they are working throughout that year, because they were unemployed the previous year.

These implications seem implausible. A current job will provide income to meet the present needs, as well as a stream of income in the future that the job-holder may not want to jeopardize (however, see the discussion of low-wage jobs below). To be sure, someone who is currently unemployed and who was also unemployed in the previous year might have greater financial need than someone who had been employed for a long time prior to the current spell of unemployment. Such a person might be more likely to have debts or needs that cannot be met with current income. But that would also be true of some people in the year they become unemployed. Very likely a distributed lag dependence of motivation on unemployment is needed, or a nonlinear expression in which the coefficient expressing the effect of contemporaneous unemployment on motivation depends on earlier levels of unemployment.

Ignoring these complications, one would operationalize Eq. (1) by writing

$$C_t = a + b_1 U_t + b_2 U_{t-1} + e_t \tag{4}$$

Making use of the identity $\Delta U_t = U_t - U_{t-1}$, and grouping terms, we have

$$C_t = a + (b_1 + b_2)U_t - b_2 \Delta U_t + e \tag{5}$$

Examination of Eq. (5) shows that the coefficient of the contemporaneous unemployment term is the sum of the opportunity and motivation effects, while the coefficient of the differenced term enters with opposite sign from the coefficient of the lagged term in Eq. (4).

Because Eq. (5) follows logically from C-L's discussion of motivational effects, even if it is not their own mathematical formulation, the implications of this equation are worth considering. Ignore for a moment the fact that the left-hand member of Eq. (5) is a crime rate and not a difference in crime rate, and consider the Cochrane–Orcutt estimates that C-L (1991, p. 329) present for robbery and burglary in light of the present discussion. They estimate the contemporaneous coefficient for the effect of unemployment to be –8.3501 for robbery and –41.685 for burglary; the corresponding coefficients for the change in unemployment are 7.2727 and 36.613. They interpret the positive coefficients as consistent with motivational theory, but based on the reasoning just presented, both coefficients have the wrong sign. Moreover, the coefficients representing opportunity effects are not –8.3501 and –41.685 but $-8.3501 + 7.2727 = -1.0774$ and $-41.685 + 36.613 = -5.072$. Both coefficients are negative, consistent with opportunity theory, but they are much smaller in magnitude than the coefficients C-L identify with opportunity effects. Because I doubt that a lagged unemployment rate is the best way to capture the motivational effect of unemployment on crime rates, I do not want to stress this finding too much; I mention it to highlight a problem in the way C-L translate verbal expressions of their ideas into equations.

Now consider not the C-L narrative, but its mathematical representation. Instead of representing the motivational effect of unemployment by lagging unemployment, C-L represent it by a difference score, ΔU_t. Two points may be made about this procedure. The first is the implausibility of representing motivation with a difference score.[4] This procedure would imply that the motivation to commit crime is as strong among those who have been unemployed for a long time as among those who have been continuously employed for a long time. In each case, there is no change in unemployment status from 1 year to the next. C-L's suggestion that motivation arises through a comparison with one's previous employment status seems off the mark here. Whatever standard one uses for a mental comparison, unemployment leads to real needs among some people that may be expected to affect criminal motivation. Moreover, someone who is unemployed at time t but who finds a job the next year would, by virtue of the

[4]After completing my paper, I discovered that Pyle and Deadman (1994) have also expressed reservations about Cantor and Land's specification, commenting, "It is not apparent why motivation should be related to the change in unemployment rather than its level in a previous period" (p. 341).

improvement, be less motivated to commit a crime in year $t+1$ than someone who had always been employed. This implication, too, is implausible. It is also at variance with C-L's suggestion that unemployment is more criminogenic when it has lasted awhile than when it first occurs.

Next, suppose that the equation to be estimated is Eq. (2). If the motivational effects are represented by ΔU_t, then the equation represents change in unemployment as causing change in crime rates without a lag, contrary to the C-L narrative. A lagged model would use ΔU_{t-1} as a predictor, not ΔU_t. It follows that the mathematical representation of motivational effects is no more satisfactory than the narrative version.

To determine empirically whether the influence of change in unemployment might be lagged rather than contemporaneous, I updated C-L's data set and examined the cross-correlation function for ΔU_t and the differenced murder rate for the United States, for the years 1946–1996. There were suggestions that an increase in unemployment might reduce the murder rate with a lag of a year or 2, but none of the correlations was statistically significant at the .05 level, and in a regression of change in the murder rate on ΔU_{t-1} alone or in a model that also includes ΔU_{t-2}, the F statistic for the regression was not significant. Nor were any of the individual coefficients.

2.1.2. *Motivation and the Duration of Unemployment*

C-L were probably on the right track in suggesting that long-term unemployment may be a more powerful motivater of crime than short-term unemployment, as several studies have found that long-term unemployment increases involvement in crime, while short-term unemployment does not. To take account of this one needs a variable representing the duration of unemployment. Neither a difference score nor a lagged aggregate unemployment variable can substitute for such a measure. Conceptually they are quite distinct.

One can have a constant level of unemployment with no one's employment status changing between time 1 and time 2 or with such a high level of turnover in unemployment that no one is unemployed at both times. Where aggregate unemployment has increased between time 1 and time 2, the increase establishes a floor on the number of people who have been unemployed for just a short time, but the number could be substantially larger. If, for example, the unemployment rate in one year is 5% and that in the next year it is 6%, the number of people who lost jobs in the intervening year could be anywhere between 1 and 6%. For this reason, neither change in unemployment nor aggregate unemployment is a good proxy for

Table I. Cochrane–Orcutt Estimates of Coefficients and Summary Statistics for the Effects of Unemployment on Crime Rates, 1946–1996[a]

Dependent variable	Intercept	U_t	DUR_t	Adj. R^2	$\hat{\rho}$	DW
Dhomicide	1.325*	.049	−.120*	.310	.39	1.90
Drape	2.725*	−.022	−.151	.030	.41	1.88
Drobbery	41.988*	4.127	−5.009*	.439	.36	1.85
Dassault	24.029*	3.676*	−2.950*	.127	.32	2.02
Dburglary	221.788*	14.378	21.798*	.330	.40	1.69
Dauto	80.242*	−1.133	−4.989*	.300	.59	2.02

[a]All dependent variables are first-differenced crime rates, measured as numbers of crimes per 100,000 population. Intercepts and coefficients for U_t and DUR_t (duration of unemployment) are metric coefficients.
$*p < .10$.

duration of unemployment.[5] Were strength of motivation to be measured by the numbers of people who are unemployed, no matter for how long, this would not be an issue, but when long-term unemployment is assumed to increase motivation, then it is an issue.

Using the updated data set, I replicated C-L's regressions using the duration of unemployment, rather than change in unemployment, as a measure of motivation.[6] The results of such analyses for six index offenses (homicide, rape, robbery, assault, burglary, auto theft) are shown in Table I, which is constructed parallel to C-L's (1985) Table II.[7] None of the contemporaneous unemployment coefficients is both negative and statistically significant, as predicted by opportunity theory. In addition, all of the coefficients of DUR (duration of unemployment) are negative, five of them significantly. Motivation theory predicts that these coefficients should be positive. Thus, using these procedures there is no support for either motivational theory or opportunity theory. However, in the remaining part of this article I argue that the procedures themselves are flawed, so that the lack of support for either theory has little meaning.

[5]Empirically, the two variables are quite weakly related. Using data from the Executive Office of the President (1998) I computed the correlation between average number of weeks unemployed and the difference in levels of civilian unemployment using annual data for the United States for the period from 1950 to 1997. It was .17.

[6]Because the duration of unemployment does not provide information on how many people are experiencing unemployment of that duration, it is not an ideal measure of motivation. The product of the level of unemployment and the duration of unemployment would be a better measure. However, in our data set, the correlation between the product variable and the level of unemployment is .940; empirically it would be difficult to distinguish the two.

[7]As definitions of larceny–theft changed during the period of study, I elected to omit this offense from the analysis rather than adjust for the change, as C-L did.

Table II. Error Correction Model Estimates of Models for Homicide Rates, 1946–1997[a]

Independent variable	Model A	B	C	D	E	F	G
Constant	−.14	−.17	−.18	.68	.76	.41	.47
	(.39)	(.50)	(.54)	(1.97)	(1.82)	(.94)	(.92)
ΔDivorce	.29***	.34**	.32***	.28*	.29*	.29*	.29*
	(4.72)	(5.75)	(5.48)	(2.57)	(2.56)	(2.65)	(2.61)
Error	−.15	−.29**	−.26**	−.22*	−.22*	−.24*	−.25*
	(1.74)	(3.34)	(2.80)	(2.51)	(2.48)	(2.69)	(2.63)
PCTM1529	4.52*	5.16**	5.75**	1.90	1.39	3.38	3.00
	(2.45)	(2.94)	(3.22)	(1.28)	(.66)	(1.60)	(1.11)
U_t	−.16***	—	−.07	—	.02	—	.02
	(4.15)		(1.41)		(.36)		(.23)
U_{t-1}	—	−.18***	−.13*	—	—	−.07	−.07
		(4.92)	(2.67)			(.99)	(.94)
DUR	—	—	—	−.09**	−.09**	−.06	−.07
				(4.73)	(3.31)	(1.87)	(1.60)
R^2	.48	.53	.55	.56	.56	.57	.57
DW	1.65	1.70	1.65	1.51	1.49	1.52	1.52

[a]Coefficients are unstandardized regression coefficients; figures in parentheses are values of Student's *t*.

*$p < .05$.

**$p < .01$.

***$p < .001$.

2.2. The Treatment of Trends

During the years covered by the C-L and Land–Cantor–Russell studies, crime rates rose. Because trends in time series pose problems for statistical estimation, statisticians remove them before carrying out further analyses. C-L (1985) and Land *et al.* (1991) do this by taking first or second differences, a standard procedure. To show that this differencing poses a problem for the interpretation that Land and his collaborators give to their findings, assume for the sake of simplicity that the trend in crime rates is linear. If we add a term linear in t to Eq. (1), the terms involving opportunity and motivation represent the degree to which variation in these variables raises or lowers the crime rate above or below the trend line. Assuming that the opportunity effects are proportional to U_t and that the motivational effects are proportional to the duration of unemployment, estimation of this equation for the six offenses listed in Table I yields coefficients for the effect of unemployment that are consistently positive, and for the effect of duration of unemployment that are consistently negative, except for rape, where both estimates fail to achieve statistical significance. Because C-L (1985) found the best-fitting models for all six offenses we are considering to be ones in which the crime rates were differenced twice, I reestimated the equation after adding a quadratic term in year.[8] Except for burglary, none of the quadratic terms was statistically significant. All coefficients for the contemporaneous unemployment rate were positive and statistically significant at the .05 level; all those for the duration of unemployment were negative and statistically significant.[9]

These conclusions were reached by estimating regression equations containing deterministic linear or quadratic terms in time. Although this is a perfectly acceptable procedure, the trends can also be eliminated by taking first differences (or second differences if needed). If this is done, the intercept in the regression equation drops out, and the term in t becomes a constant. We are thus left with an equation in which a difference in the crime rates is predicted by a difference in the opportunity variable and a difference in the motivation variable. This is what is expected theoretically. Corresponding to a given level of opportunity and motivation there should be, in equilibrium, a corresponding level of illegality. A change in opportunity or in motivation should lead to a change in the volume of crime.

Contrast the procedure just outlined with the one that C-L adopt. They difference the crime rates in Eq. (1) once or twice to eliminate trends but carry out no differencing of the independent variables. This procedure is mathematically unacceptable. If one accepts Eq. (1) as a theoretical representation of the processes of interest, then operations that transform the left-hand member of Eq. (1) must also be performed on the right-hand member if the equality is to be preserved.

The equations on which Land and his collaborators base their conclusions lead to absurd implications because they difference only the crime rates, and not their predictors. Suppose that the trend being eliminated is linear, that it is Eq. (2) being estimated, and that there are no motivational effects. However, there are opportunity effects, so that b_1 is negative. Equation (2) says that a constant level of unemployment would lead to a steady drop in the crime rate. If the crime rates require second-differencing, Eq.

[8]To reduce multicollinearity between *year* and *year*^{2}, I subtracted 1972 from *year*, and used this centered variable and its square in the regression.

[9]For purposes of comparison with C-L (1985), I also estimated these models using U_t, ΔU_t, as well as the linear and quadratic terms in year as predictors. In this set of estimates, all the linear and quadratic terms in time were significant except for rape, where the quadratic term was not significant. Four of the six coefficients for U_t were negative, but only two of the six were statistically significant at the .10 level: the coefficient for rape was positive; the coefficient for auto theft was negative. Of the six coefficients for change in unemployment, only the coefficient for rape was negative (not significant); the remaining five were positive, with the coefficients for murder, robbery, and auto theft being statistically significant at the .10 level. Discrepancies from the results reported by C-L (1985) may be due to differences in the years covered.

(3) would be estimated. It would say, under the same conditions, that a constant rate of unemployment will lead to a deceleration in the increase of crime rates. In a world in which there are no opportunity effects, only motivational effects, Eqs. (2) and (3) also predict that a constant level of unemployment will lead to an increasing or decreasing crime rate [Eq. (2)] or an accelerating or decelerating crime rate [Eq. (3)], as long as the constant term in the regression, *a*, is different from zero. These predictions do not correspond to any reasonable notion of the way unemployment should affect crime rates.

In responding to criticism from Hale and Sabbagh, C-L (1991) offer a justification for differencing crime rates not given in their original paper: differencing could eliminate omitted variables responsible for the upward trend in crime rate, allowing them to concentrate on the effects of unemployment. Yet differencing undertaken for this reason must still be carried out for both left- and right-hand members of an equation if logical consistency is to be maintained and the equations are to retain their original meaning. In addition, Hale (1991) has pointed out that this procedure works only if the omitted variable has a constant trend but does not contribute at all to fluctuations around the trend line. Should an omitted variable have a random component as well as a deterministic trend, the differencing procedure will not eliminate it. Residuals for the differenced equation will have a negative first-order serial correlation, and estimates for the effects of unemployment will be biased if the random component is correlated with unemployment. Because virtually every imaginable social variable that might contribute to a trend in crime rates will have a random component, differencing cannot be considered a satisfactory way of eliminating omitted variables responsible for trends. One must, therefore, echo Hale's (1991) observation that "differencing is no substitute for modeling." If there are variables responsible for trends in crime, it is desirable that they be identified and introduced into one's model whenever possible.

2.3. Cointegration Issues

2.3.1. Nonstationarity and Unit Root Tests

When a time series is not stationary, classical statistical theory breaks down (Granger and Newbold, 1974; Phillips, 1986) and special procedures are needed. Consequently, one of the very first issues a researcher must confront when analyzing a time series is the question of whether it is stationary. "Unit root" tests allow one to determine whether a series is stationary, and if it is not, whether it is a random walk, a random walk with drift, or a random walk with drift and trend (Banerjee *et al.*, 1993; Holden and Perman, 1994; Harris, 1995, pp. 27–39; Charemza and Deadman, 1997, pp. 98–122; Greene, 1997, pp. 847–851; Johnston and DiNardo, 1997, pp. 223–228) . These tests consider whether the coefficient a in the equation $y_t = ay_{t-1} + \cdots + e_t$, $y_t = \mu + ay_{t-1} + \cdots + e_t$, or $y_t = \mu + ay_{t-1} + bt + \cdots + e_t$ is significantly different from 1. Equations in which the coefficient a is equal to 1 represent "unit root" processes.

When I carried out two such tests, the Augmented Dickey–Fuller test and the Phillips–Perron test, for the six crime rates (homicide, forcible rape, robbery, assault, burglary, auto theft) for the years 1946–1997, the tests failed to reject the null hypothesis of a unit root for each offense, consistent with each series being nonstationary.[10] When the tests were repeated on the differenced rates, the unit root hypothesis was rejected in each instance, suggesting that no further differencings were needed. The same tests for unemployment indicated that it was stationary, and required no differencing.

A question could be raised whether it is really possible for a crime rate to be a realization of a random walk process. The variance of a random walk time series increases without limit over time, and this seems implausible for crime. It is unrealistic to suppose, however, that the same generating process responsible for temporal changes in crime will continue unchanged forever. A random walk seems to fit these offenses over the half-century for which we have data. Changes in the causes of crime (including social control strategies) or in the strength of their effects could change the structure of the crime rate series in the future.

Before proceeding to discuss cointegration, it is worth reflecting on the theoretical importance of the finding that crime rates appear to be realizations of a unit root process. This means that there are no effective social processes tending to reduce crime rates if they grow too large or to increase them if they fall too low. Instead, they bounce about randomly, uninfluenced by the instantaneous level of crime, and without tending to return to an equilibrium level.

If a time series requires d differencings to achieve stationarity, it is said to be integrated of order d, denoted $I(d)$. Logical consistency requires that if crime rates are a realization of a unit root process, they must be explained by a unit root process. It is thus mathematically impossible for a crime rate that is $I(1)$ to be caused only by a function that is $I(0)$. If a crime rate is $I(1)$, at least one of the explanatory variables must also be $I(1)$, though additional predictor variables can be $I(0)$. This knowledge can help focus a search for explanatory variables.

If one estimates the effect of an $I(1)$ series X_t on an $I(1)$ series Y_t by regressing Y_t on X_t, one runs the risk of spurious regressions. Until recently,

[10] I treat a failure to reject the null hypothesis as equivalent to accepting the null hypothesis.

differencing both sides of the regression equation to eliminate the nonstationary, and then analyzing the stationary differences, was the recommended way to proceed. Yet this is not a satisfactory procedure because it removes all information about the long-run tendencies of the differenced variables. Often it is the long-run trends that are of much greater interest than short-time fluctuations; yet researchers following procedures needed to avoid spurious regressions focused all their attention on the short-run, ephemeral fluctuations, rather than the long-run tendencies. In criminology this has meant ignoring the causes of the large rise in crime rates between the early sixties and the early seventies, while focusing on year-to-year fluctuations in crime rates around the rise. Recent developments in statistical theory based on the concept of cointegration offer an appealing way to avoid this loss of information.

2.3.2. The Cointegration of Crime and Divorce

Cointegration theory is based on the insight that even if the series X_t and Y_t are individually nonstationary, a linear combination of the two series may be stationary. If there exists a constant β such that $Y_t - \beta X_t$ is $I(0)$, the two series are said to be cointegrated. Cointegrated series will tend to move together. If a disturbance leads to a short-run increase in the distance between them, an equilibrating force will tend to bring them back together again. The relationship between the two variables thus tends to maintain itself over the long term. Even though each variable drifts, they drift together and do not grow farther apart, as they would were they not cointegrated, and were random-walking independently of one another. Information about this long-term relationship is what is lost when the series are differenced (Banerjee *et al.*, 1993, pp. 136–140; Harris, 1995, pp. 52–75; Greene, 1997, pp. 851–859).

To consider cointegration for each of the six index offenses would extend the length of this paper unduly. Instead, I analyze just the homicide rate and the robbery rate in this light. Visual inspection of graphs for the homicide rate, the robbery rate, and the divorce rate strongly suggests that each crime rate is cointegrated with the divorce rate:[11] both crime rates move roughly in parallel with the divorce rate, although the parallel movement may have weakened some in recent years (see Figs. 1 and 2). Augmented Dickey–Fuller and Phillips–Perron tests confirm that the divorce rate is $I(1)$, and that when the homicide rate and the robbery rate are each

[11]I was encouraged to examine divorce by a graph showing the divorce rate and the robbery rate given by LaFree (1998, pp. 140–144). LaFree rests his argument on the relationship between various crime rates and other social indicators on the basis of general trends, without conducting any statistical analyses to test their relationships.

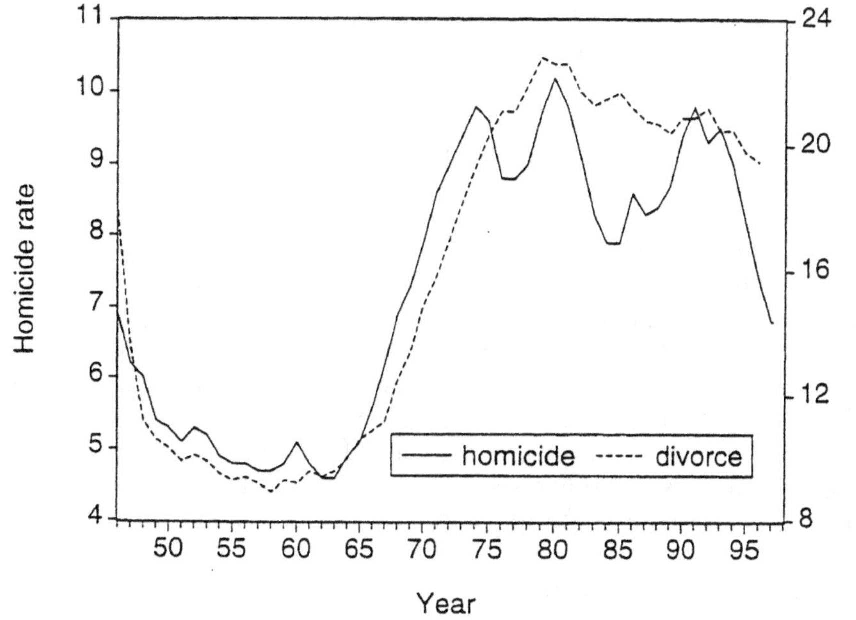

Fig. 1. Homicide rates and divorce rates.

Fig. 2. Robbery rates and divorce rates.

regressed on the divorce rate, the residuals are $I(0)$, i.e., stationary. If we denote the divorce rate by D_t, the cointegrating equation is

$$C_t = \alpha + \beta D_t + v_t \tag{6}$$

A Johanssen test for cointegration is consistent with each pair of series being cointegrated.

It does not seem likely that this relationship is a direct, causal one or that people who are divorcing have exceptionally high divorce rates. More likely, divorce is an indicator of a strain in a fundamental social institution—the nuclear family. It is this strain that leads some individuals to kill, whether or not they themselves divorce. The divorce rate in the United States rose dramatically between 1960 and 1980, a time when gender relations and ideologies were undergoing major transformations, putting great strain on many families and leading some of them to divorce. The upsurge in homcides and robberies in those years may have been responses to strains related to this shift experienced by people who did *not* divorce.[12]

2.3.3. Error Correction Models

Fluctuations around equilibrium can be assessed statistically through a transformation of a dynamical equation. For illustrative purposes, suppose that the crime rate C is influenced by the lagged and contemporaneous divorce rates, a contemporaneous term in unemployment, and a lagged crime rate. We thus write

$$C_t = \gamma_0 + \gamma_1 C_{t-1} + \gamma_2 D_t + \gamma_3 D_{t-1} + \gamma_3 U_t + e_t \tag{7}$$

Writing $C_t = C_{t-1} + \Delta C_t$ and grouping terms, we can express this equation as

$$\Delta C_t = \gamma_0 \gamma_2 \Delta D_t + (\gamma_1 - 1)\left[C_{t-1} - \left(\frac{\gamma_2 + \gamma_3}{1 - \gamma_1} \right) D_{t-1} \right] + \gamma_4 U_t + e_t \tag{8}$$

By evaluating Eq. (8) at its equilibrium ($C_t = C_{t-1}, D_t = D_{t-1}$) and comparing with Eq. (6), we see that the ratio $(\gamma_2 + \gamma_3)/(1 - \gamma_1)$ can be identified with the coefficient β, and that the expression in brackets is the deviation

[12]Because unmarried women are more likely than married women to hold jobs (Nakosteen and Zimmer, 1989), one might wonder whether some or all of the divorce effects are related to women's greater labor force participation, a possibility that is given particular relevance to the present analysis by research indicating that women's employment is positively related to crime in Australia (Kapuscinski *et al*., 1998). Although women's labor force participation and the divorce rate are positively correlated in the Unted States, they behave rather differently, and the women's labor force participation does not move together with the homicide rate or the robbery rate; the divorce rate does.

of the series from its equilibrium in the cointegration model. Equation (8) can thus be written more compactly as

$$\Delta C_t = \gamma_0 + \gamma_2 \Delta D_t + \varphi v_{t-1} + \gamma_4 U_t + e_t \tag{9}$$

where $\varphi = \gamma_1 - 1$ and v represents the quantity in brackets in Eq. (8). This "error correction" representation of Eq. (7) expresses short-run change in crime rates as an additive function of short-run change in the divorce rate, an error correction term that maintains the long-run tendencies of the model, and the exogenous variable U_t. Additional independent variables, such as a term in U_{t-1} or ΔU_t, can be added to the equation if that is appropriate, so long as they are $I(0)$.

Two points regarding Eq. (9) are noteworthy. First, if the coefficient φ is nonvanishing, the omission of the error correction term could lead to omitted variable bias. This term would be absent were one naively to write a simple regression equation in which a differenced divorce rate causes a differenced crime rate. Thus, differencing to deal with nonstationarity is not the recommended procedure when a pair of variables is cointegrated. Second, because all the variables in Eq. (9) are stationary, the equation can be estimated using OLS.

Equation (9) is the basis for the Engle–Granger two-step estimation procedure: one first estimates Eq. (6) to obtain the residuals, then uses them to estimate Eq. (9) (Engle and Granger, 1987). I carried out Engle–Granger estimations for various models involving, in addition to divorce, several stationary variables that might be expected to influence either criminal motivation or opportunity or both. For this purpose I chose the percentage of males between age 15 and age 29, the unemployment rate (various combinations of contemporaneous, lagged and differenced, but never all three at once, as only two of the three are linearly independent), and the duration of unemployment. This list of variables could, obviously, be extended, but with 51 observations, there are limits to what is practical. OLS estimates of these models are shown in Table II (homicide) and Table III (robbery).[13] F tests for those sets of models that are nested show that the most parsimonious and best-fitting models for both homicide and robbery are B (unemployment lagged by 1 year) and D (duration of unemployment). Adding additional measures of unemployment fails to yield a significant improvement in fit to these models.

The graphs in Figs. 3 and 4 show the actual changes in homicide rates and robbery rates alongside the rates predicted on the basis of model B.

[13]On the basis of LaFree's (1998, pp. 115–132) discussion of inflation, I also considered models in which percentage change in the consumer price index was used as a predictor, but it did not make a statistically significant contribution to the regressions. Estimates for these models are not listed in Tables II and III.

Table III. Error Correction Model Estimates of Models for Robbery Rates, 1946–1997[a]

Independent variable	Model A	B	C	D	E	F	G
Constant	−.72	−2.33	−1.71	22.15	31.65*	−1.24	5.38
	(.95)	(.24)	(.17)	(1.98)	(2.38)	(.10)	(.34)
ΔDivorce	7.69**	7.21**	7.42**	2.61	2.85	3.95	4.00
	(3.00)	(3.62)	(3.58)	(.76)	(.83)	(1.23)	(1.24)
Error	−.13	−.11	−.12	−.02	−.02	−.12	−.11
	(1.51)	(1.70)	(1.73)	(.22)	(.22)	(1.43)	(1.34)
PCTM1529	105.41	174.30**	164.86**	90.13	32.40	204.97**	166.38*
	(1.52)	(3.34)	(2.87)	(1.74)	(.48)	(3.31)	(2.05)
U_t	−3.71*	—	.60	—	2.63	—	1.44
	(2.59)		(.42)		(1.30)		(.74)
U_{t-1}	—	−6.27***	−6.60***	—	—	−6.69**	−6.28**
		(5.97)	(4.99)			(2.91)	(2.64)
DUR	—	—	—	−3.10***	−3.97***	−.36	−1.00
				(4.74)	(4.29)	(.32)	(.71)
R^2	.34	.58	.58	.53	.54	.61	.61
DW	1.43	1.35	1.36	1.12	1.39	1.32	1.31

[a]Coefficients are unstandardized regression coefficients; figures in parentheses are values of Student's *t*.
*$p < .05$
**$p < .01$
***$p < .001$

The models do a fairly good job at predicting changes in both rates, while failing to predict the sharp drop in the rates that occurred after 1993. Significantly, the increases of the 1960s are explained without any criminal justice system variables in the model. There is little here to suggest, for example, that Supreme Court decisions entitling indigent defendants to attorneys (*Gideon* v. *Wainwright*, 1963; *Escobedo* v. *Illinois*, 1964) and requiring the police to issue warnings to suspects (*Miranda* v. *Arizona*, 1966), had anything to do with those increases. Nor is there an unexplained increase in crime associated with the suspension of executions between 1967 and 1976 while the constitutionality of capital punishment was being challenged in the courts. I do not mean to imply that law enforcement variables had no effect on crime whatsoever, only that they do not seem to have been responsible for major shifts in levels of crime in these years.

The value in Tables II and III show that short-run increases in the divorce rate tend to produce short-run increases in both homicide and robbery (though in model D for robbery, the coefficient for divorce is not statistically significant). As expected, the error correction terms are negative in all the models, indicating that divorce and crime tend to move together—

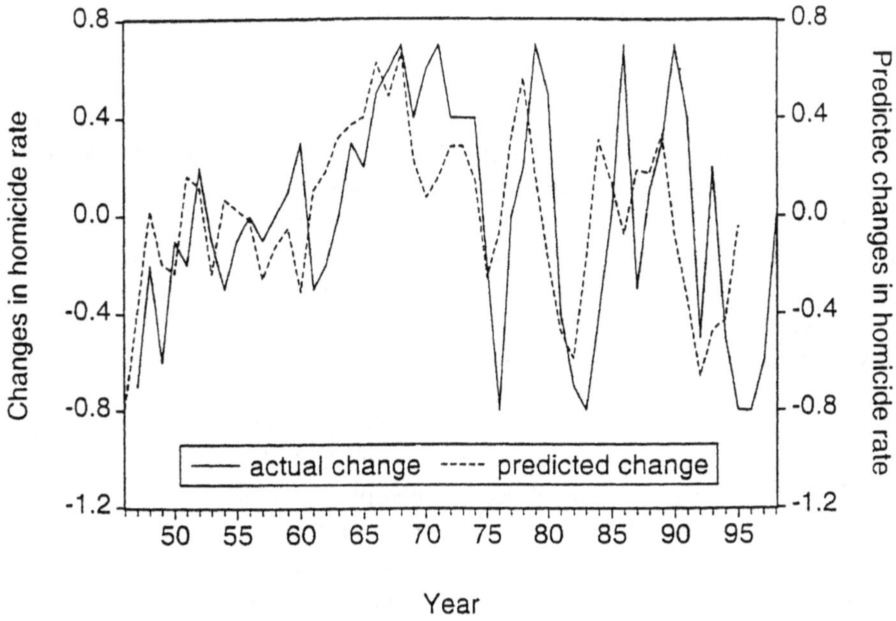

Fig. 3. Actual and predicted changes in homicide rates.

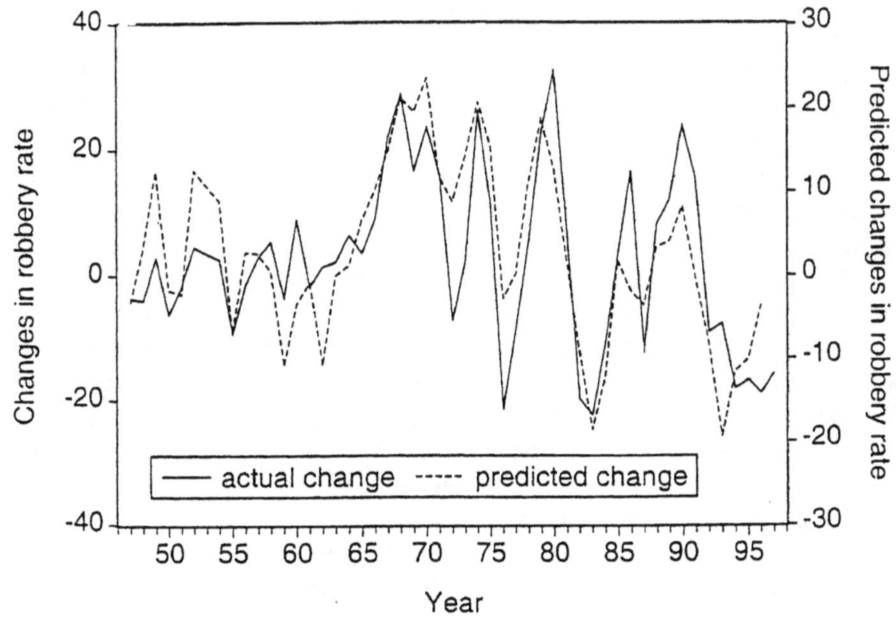

Fig. 4. Actual and predicted changes in robbery rates.

though in model D for robbery the coefficient is very small and not statistically significant.

The negative signs of the terms involving lagged unemployment and unemployment duration are opposite to what is expected of motivational effects, consistent with other studies (Ruhm, 1999; Raphael and Winter-Ebmer, 2001). Possibly the greater collective hardships of high or protracted unemployment strengthen social solidarity, reducing crime. Or it may be that unemployed people—especially those who have been unemployed for a long time—spend more of their time in public places, socializing in parks, and loitering and begging on the streets, discouraging crime by their presence. Consumption of alcohol rises in times of prosperity and drops when unemployment rises (Ruhm, 1995). Alcohol is a known disinhibitor and induces belligerence in some individuals. Unemployment might, then, curb violent crime by reducing the consumption of alcohol.

If the contemporaneous effect of unemployment measures the opportunity effect of unemployment, there is no unequivocal evidence for such an effect. Once the duration of unemployment or the lagged effect of unemployment is controlled, contemporaneous unemployment does not make a significant contribution.

How do these results compare with those of C-L (1985) and Land *et al.* (1995)? They found, in their first-differenced model incorporating both U_t and ΔU_t, that the instantaneous effect of unemployment was significantly negative, while the effect of change in unemployment was not. They also found a negative contemporaneous effect for robbery. If the Land *et al.* (1995) results are reparametrized in terms of U_t and U_{t-1} rather than U_t and ΔU_t to facilitate comparison of the estimates, their results are entirely consistent with mine: as discussed above, they find a contemporaneous effect that is positive, but very small and not statistically significant, and an appreciable negative effect of U_{t-1}.

For reasons that should be obvious from what has already been said, the results presented here are more credible and more informative than those presented by C-L (1985) and Land *et al.* (1995). The equation on which I base my analysis better represents a plausible theoretical model. The estimation procedure does not eliminate the drift in crime rates from the analysis but explains it. The resulting models reproduce the homicide and robbery rates reasonably well except that they do not predict the sharp drop in crime rates of the past few years.

That said, I do not want to exaggerate the strength of my findings. Because the correlations among unemployment, lagged unemployment, and duration of unemployment are high (between .75 and .80), it is difficult to assess their simultaneous effects with just 50 observations. The Durbin–

Watson statistics in Tables II and III lie in the "inconclusive" region, so the potential for omitted variable bia exists.[14]

3. USERS OF THE PARADIGM

The procedures developed by C-L for analyzing time series have been put to use by several researchers, notably Devine *et al.* (1988), Smith *et al.* (1992), and Britt (1994, 1997). Devine *et al.* use time series to study the impact of several variables on U.S. crime rates between 1948 and 1985. Following the standard recipe, Devine *et al.* difference the crime rates to eliminate what they consider trends. Probably the trends are actually manifestations of drift, but that is a distinction without a consequence here, as drift can be eliminated by differencing. In one set of models they introduce as independent variables change in the rate of male unemployment, the rate of inflation, the change in public relief, and the change in the imprisonment rate. Because all independent variables are measures of change, these models take the form of "change causes change" and do not raise problems of interpretation. In another set of models, Devine *et al.* add a static measure of opportunity and find that it makes a significant contribution to homicide, robbery, and some of the burglary models. However, as I have already argued, the use of a static measure of opportunity to explain change in the crime rate makes little sense.

Britt (1994) and Smith *et al.* (1992) apply the C-L paradigm to study the age-specific effects of unemployment on crime. This is a potentially valuable undertaking because recent crime rate changes have been highly age specific: increases in the murder rate in the years immediately after 1985 were restricted largely to people younger than age 25 (Blumstein and Rosenfeld, 1998), and recent decreases have been confined largely to the same age bracket (Butts, 2000). In these circumstances, an aggregate analysis that did not distinguish younger from older offenders could be quite misleading. Both studies take the number of arrests as a measure of the number of crimes committed, and regress it on the unemployment rate and the change in unemployment rate. Britt restricts his analysis to 16–19 year olds between 1958 and 1990 and considers all index crimes; Smith *et al.* consider four age categories—16–19, 20–24, 25–34, and 35–44—examining homicide, robbery and burglary. Each measures the crime rate by the arrest rate, and regresses it on the unemployment rate and the change in unemployment

[14]However, I did carry out Cochrane–Orcutt estimations of the error correction models that included first-order autocorrelations among the residuals, and the results were very similar to those presented in the text. Omitted variables often lead to serially correlated errors.

rate. Denoting arrests by A, and age and year by the subscripts i and t, this implies the estimation of an equation that takes the form

$$\Delta A_{it} = b_0 + b_1 U_{it} + b_2 \Delta U_{it} + e_{it} \tag{10}$$

Their findings are consistent: the contemporaneous effect of unemployment is negative, and the change effect positive, for all offenses. I comment on these studies below.

3.1. Britt's Analysis of the Age–Crime–Unemployment Relationship

In a further extension of this line of research, Britt (1997) analyzes age-specific U.S. arrest rates for the seven index offenses for the years 1958–1995 to test two propositions concerning the impact of unemployment on crime found in Greenberg's (1977, 1985) theoretical treatment of the age–crime relationship. Quoted verbatim from Britt's paper, the two propositions are as follows: (H1): "The unemployment–crime relationship will vary by age group, where youth and young adults are expected to show a greater motivational (positive) effect of unemployment on criminal behavior" and (H2) "The unemployment–crime relationship will vary over time, especially for youth and young adults, where the motivational (positive) effect of unemployment is expected to increase over time."

For several reasons, Britt's research does not provide a satisfactory test of Greenberg's ideas or these propositions. Here I summarize and then criticize Britt's research. My discussion deals with the following issues: (a) the extraction of propositions to be tested from Greenberg's narrative, (b) the translation of the discursive propositions into regression equations, (c) the operationalization of the variables in the regression equations, (d) the use of aggregate data to test propositions about individuals, and (e) the choice of a time frame for conducting the analysis.

3.1.1. The Extraction of Propositions from Greenberg's Narrative

Greenberg's (1977, 1985) model for the age dependency of crime draws on two major pillars of criminological theory to explain the age distribution of crime and the manner in which it has changed historically: strain theory and control theory. The model posits three types of institutional involvement or lack of involvement as sources of strain. It asserts that adolescent theft "occurs as a response to the disjunction between the desire to participate in social activities with peers and the absence of legitimate sources of funds needed to finance this participation" (p. 197). This is the first source of strain.[15] Greenberg argued that the intensity of this strain depends on age. Because adolescents lack the institutional affiliations that provide adults with alternative sources of self-esteem, participation in peer-focused social activities is expected to be more important to adolescents than to older adults.[16] The age stratification of American society has increased over time, so that this sort of strain should be greater now than in the past. These last two sentences form the basis of the two propositions Britt tests.

The model posits that a second source of strain—the denial of autonomy and the exposure to status degradation inflicted on students in school—is relevant primarily to the explanation of joy-riding, vandalism, acts of interpersonal violence, and seemingly irrational thefts in which the objects stolen are discarded or destroyed. Delinquency in response to this type of strain is also posited as contingent. It is primarily students who do not find compensating rewards and benefits from school (such as gratification from learning, extracurricular activities such as sports and clubs, socializing with peers, and future occupational rewards) who are expected to rebel against the restrictions and status degradations they encounter in school. Students who find school to be rewarding on balance, or who anticipate that it will enable them to achieve valued occupational goals, will tend to put up with its restrictions and status degradations. Any test of the theory must take these interaction effects into account. A third source of strain in the model is "masculine status anxiety," which intensifies at the end of the transition from adolescence to adulthood, when young males find that they cannot obtain jobs or discover that the jobs they can obtain pay badly and offer poor prospects for advancement. This source of strain is asserted to be relevant primarily to violent offenses. The control theory component of the argument focuses on the shift from juvenile court jurisdiction to the criminal court, which creates a substantially enhanced risk of serious punishment,

[15]Though not discussed by Greenberg (1977), the sale of illegal narcotics is another offense to which this reasoning might reasonably be expected to apply. Several studies have linked the sale of drugs by young people to their limited opportunities for earning income lawfully (Reuter *et al.*, 1990; Fagan, 1992; Myers, 1992; Hagedorn, 1994).

[16]This line of reasoning could be criticized on theoretical grounds for what it omits. Leisure-time social activities are usually considered discretionary. Someone—even a teenager—who cannot afford these activities might be unhappy but can survive: for most adolescents, paying for rent and food is not a serious problem, no matter what their employment status or personal finances may be, because someone else is paying for them. Homeless adolescents, who may have to steal to survive, would be exceptions (McCarthy and Hagan, 1992). In contrast, an adult who lacks financial resources may be unable to pay the rent or buy groceries. One might think that the strain induced by inability to pay for life necessities would be greater than the strain induced by inability to pay for leisure-time social activities. Greenberg's omission of this source of strain was intentional; a focus on life necessities would suggest that the peak age of involvement in theft should be in adulthood, not in adolescence, where it is in fact.

and on the informal sources of control associated with the institutions juveniles are able to establish or enter when they become adults: marriage and employment.

Several features of this argument are relevant to the present discussion. First, the relationship between strain arising from lack of income and employment is not simple, because employment is not the only source of legitimate income. Greenberg (1977, pp. 196, 198) remarks that as long as parents pay for their children's leisure-time social activities, children will not be strapped for cash even though they do not derive income from a job. It follows that if one wants to test Britt's propositions, one must assess variations in the extent to which parents subsidize their children. Parental ability and willingness to do this may well depend on their own employment circumstances.

When considering youths' aspirations toward conventional careers, the same problem arises. Fifteen-year-olds' aspirations may be influenced by the level of unemployment adults in their community experience, quite independently of their own employment statuses. If, for example, adolescents see that older adults in their communities are unable to find lawful jobs, they are likely to dismiss lawful employment as a possibility for themselves in the future. It follows that youthful involvement in crime may depend not only on their own employment, but on their parents' employment and income. Unfortunately, a model that incorporated the age-specific unemployment rates for both youths and individuals who belong to an older generation would be difficult to estimate with aggregate data because of severe multicollinearity: Britt notes that the correlation between the total annual unemployment rate and the unemployment rate for persons ages 16 to 19 between 1958 and 1990 is .98. This high correlation means that when Britt reports the effect of unemployment variables, we cannot be confident that the effects are those of the relevant age-specific unemployment rate, rather than those of the overall unemployment rate, or the unemployment rate for middle-aged workers who are parents of the 16- to 19-year-olds.

Second, the theory makes different predictions about the effects of unemployment for different kinds of crime. Unemployment is predicted to have the strongest effect on theft in adolescence but on interpersonal violence in young adulthood. For this reason, Britt's conclusion that the motivational effect of unemployment on homicide is greater at ages 18–24 (his Table III) than in earlier and later years is not at odds with Greenberg's theoretical model: quite the contrary (see further discussion below). Third, Greenberg's theory is explicitly multivariate. Estimating the effect of unemployment alone on illegality does not provide an appropriate test of a multivariate theory, unless the independent variables in the model are uncorrelated. The results reported in this paper suggest that the effect of unemployment on crime cannot be studied without taking into account the other factors that might influence crime rates.

In addition, a number of researchers have suggested that there is a relationship between adolescent employment and school experience. When high school students work long hours, their school performance may suffer, increasing their involvement in some kinds of illegal activities. Deficiencies in school performance may also lead some juveniles to take jobs. Because the Greenberg model posits irritating experiences in school to be criminogenic, these influences must be taken into account if the effect of unemployment is to be assessed. Regrettably, information about the relevant subjective variables is not to be found in nationally aggregated data sets. A better test of the model would use longitudinal data for individuals.

3.1.2. Formulating the Regression Equation

To test the two hypotheses reproduced above, Britt estimates equations in which differences in the age- and period-specific arrest rates are regressed on the age- and period-specific unemployment rates and on differences in these unemployment rates [see Eq. (10) above]. Each coefficient in the regression equation is expressed as the sum of a constant term and terms representing fixed effects for age and year. As written here, the subscripts for the regression coefficients arising from the fixed effects are omitted.

On carrying out the estimation, Britt finds no significant age dependence of the unemployment and differenced-unemployment coefficients for rape, larceny, and motor vehicle theft. For homicide and assault he finds the opportunity effect of unemployment, represented by b_1, to be negative for persons age 16 through 24 and positive for adults who are 25 or older. None of the motivational effects are significant for assault, but for homicide they are positive for ages 16–24, with the strongest effect at ages 18–19; at ages 25–34 they are negative but not significant.[17] Britt considers these homicide and assault findings to be "at odds with Greenberg's hypothesis that youth and young adults will have greater motivation to commit crimes in response to unemployment." Actually, Greenberg formulated no hypotheses about the age dependence of the opportunity effect; moreover, findings about the opportunity effect have no bearing whatsoever on the existence or nonexistence of a motivational effect, or about its strength.

[17]In fact, this is not exactly what Britt says about his findings. He says that the motivational effects for homicide have "a greater motivational effect on adults (25 years and older)." This statement is inconsistent with the figures in Britt's Table III. I strongly suspect that the reference to a motivational effect in this passage reflects an attention lapse while writing and base my remarks on the table, rather than the text.

Britt finds weak support for the motivational effect of unemployment on larceny being stronger for 16–17 year olds than for older people. The motivational effects of unemployment for rape, larceny, and motor vehicle theft did not vary significantly by age. For homicide, they were higher at ages 18–24 than at younger and older ages; for robbery and burglary they were higher at ages 20–24 than at earlier and older ages. Britt summarizes these findings by saying that they are generally consistent with the hypothesis that younger persons who are more likely to be excluded from the labor market will be more motivated to commit acts of theft. In contrast, the effect of unemployment on homicide and aggravated assault shows a greater motivational effect for older persons, suggestive of the possibility that adults may be faced with additional psychological pressures immediately upon being unemployed, which are not as pressing for younger individuals but lead to increased chances of homicide for adults. In fact, the homicide effects (strongest at ages 18–24) are exactly what Greenberg (1977) predicted as a consequence of masculine status anxiety.

Tests of the second hypothesis can be summarized more briefly: Britt finds no evidence that the impact of unemployment has been increasing over time. All these conclusions rest on the validity of Britt's translation of the discursive formulations of opportunity theory and motivational theory into the regression equation given in Eq. (10). In Section 2 I argue that this specification does not satisfactorily represent motivation theory; those arguments apply here as well. The equations that Britt and Smith *et al.* (1992) estimate, then, are not the equations that are appropriate for testing the theoretical ideas they wish to test. The coefficients they obtain are not measures of motivational effects or of opportunity effects.

This is not the only difficulty. It is implicit in Eq. (10) that opportunity effects are age specific. That is, the motivational contribution to the arrest rate in a given age bracket is assumed to be influenced only by unemployment levels of individuals in the same age bracket. This is as dubious theoretically as the notion that the motivational effects of unemployment are age specific (discussed earlier). Residences left unattended when a resident takes a job are easier to burglarize than residences where someone is cleaning and cooking during the day. People who are working at a job outside the home may have increased exposure to assault at the hands of strangers. These effects, however, are not expected to be age specific. Thus, if someone of a given age takes a job, leaving her apartment unattended while she is working, she is increasing her vulnerability to burglary and assault by perpetrators of all ages.

Of course, some opportunity effects of unemployment may be age specific. If teenagers are unemployed because they are attending school, they will be spending a sizable fraction of their waking hours in the company of others of roughly the same age, who are unemployed for the same reason. Their vulnerability to assault or theft at the hands of their peers may be influenced by the unemployment rate of their peers, but not so much by the unemployment rate of persons in other age brackets. Likewise, people who are working have opportunities to engage in employee theft that should be relatively uninfluenced by the unemployment rates of people in other age categories. But these possibilities do not refute my argument that for many kinds of crime, the unemployment rate in a given age bracket should affect opportunities of persons in all age brackets to commit crimes. These cross-age effects of unemployment must be taken into consideration in constructing a model. Failure to do so makes the interpretation of findings uncertain.

3.1.3. Operationalization of Variables

In testing a theory empirically, it is important that the variables be operationalized in such a way that they reasonably represent the variables in the theory. Serious discrepancies inevitably raise questions about the meaningfulness of the test. Britt justifies his use of arrests as a measure of crimes committed by citing studies that the age distribution of arrests is similar to the age distribution of offenses, However, the age categories used in some of these studies are crude (e.g., 21 and over), and so provide only a limited basis for assessing the accuracy with which the age distribution of arrests parallels that of offending behavior. In a study that Britt does not cite, Patterson and Arguer (1993) conclude on the basis of self-reports that the age distribution of arrests is not the same as the distribution of offenses.

The possibility that the probability of an arrest following the commission of a crime could be influenced by unemployment rates must also be taken seriously. Using data from the National Longitudinal Study of Youth, Glasser and Sarcerdote (1999) find that the effect of the local unemployment rate on whether the subject stole something worth less than $50, shoplifted in the last year, or had income from crime in the last year was negative but not statistically significant. The effect on whether the subject was charged with a crime or ever convicted (also negative), however, was highly significant. This result suggests the possibility that local enforcement practices are in some way influenced by the level of unemployment in a community. If this is so, a regression of arrest rates on unemployment might actually be measuring changes in enforcement practices, not changes in motivation or opportunities.

The operationalization of unemployment in all these studies is also problematic. Without discussion, Britt, like C-L and Devine *et al.*, simply takes unemployment rates produced by the U.S. Department of Labor's

Bureau of Labor Statistics as valid representations of unemployment as a theoretical variable. A closer examination of the way unemployment rates are defined demonstrates that this equivalence cannot be taken for granted.

As summarized above, in Greenberg's model, theft is a response to the strain associated with the exclusion of juveniles from the world of full-time adult work. When they get older, this strain diminishes for those young adults who are able to find full-time jobs. This claim cannot be tested adequately with unemployment rates produced by the Bureau of Labor Statistics. The Bureau of Labor Statistics derives unemployment rates from responses to the Current Population Survey of the civilian noninstitutional population that is 16 years of age or older. Respondents are counted as unemployed if they did not hold a job during a particular calendar week (Sunday through Saturday of the week that includes the 12th day of the month), "were available for work, except for temporary illness, and had made specific efforts, such as contacting employers, to find employment sometime during the 4-week period ending with the reference week," or "were waiting to be recalled to a job from which they had been laid off" even if they were not looking for a job (U.S. Department of Labor, 1997, p. 5). These criteria exclude from the ranks of the unemployed discouraged individuals who have given up looking for a job or who never sought one because they thought it unlikely that a search would be successful. Housewives and students who are not working or looking for a job because they are in school are not classified as unemployed. Part-time workers who are underemployed because they want a full-time job but cannot find one are not counted. Youths who are less than 16 years old are not counted because in most states they would be barred by law from most jobs (Nixon, 1968; U.S. Department of Labor, 1997). Individuals who are working for very low wages are also not counted. Moreover, some youth may be employed part-time at jobs that could hardly qualify as part of "the world of adult work" (e.g., babysitting, mowing lawns). From the point of view of testing the Greenberg model, many of these individuals should be counted as unemployed because they will not earn enough from their jobs to meet their subjectively defined target level of expenditures. But they are not counted by the Bureau of Labor Statistics criteria.

Many criminals hold such jobs. In the RAND study of persons arrested in Washington, DC, for selling drugs (the great majority of them being young black males), roughly two-thirds were employed at the time of their arrest, but at low-wage jobs in which the median pay was $800 a month. Narcotics trafficking supplemented this income (Reuter *et al.*, 1990). Other studies have reached similar conclusions (Greenberg, 2001). Crutchfield and Pitchford (1997) found that young adults employed in the secondary sector, where wages were low and employment irregular, had higher levels of criminal involvement than those employed in the primary sector. Workers who expected their employment to be of long duration were less likely to engage in crime. To complicate matters further, some of those counted as unemployed, along with many who are considered outside the labor market, may be working "off the books," in the so-called informal economy, or at illegal occupations, such as prostitution or drug selling (Sassen-Koob, 1989; Reuter *et al.*, 1990; Fagan, 1992, 1994, 1997; Edin and Lein, 1997, pp. 145–146, 172–178). The number of state and federal prisoners serving sentences for drug offenses—277,859 in 1997—most of them for selling (Mumola, 1999, p. 2), suggests that the number of individuals earning money illegally may be quite large.

The lack of correspondence between a theoretically relevant conception of unemployment and the definition employed by the Bureau of Labor Statistics becomes evident when one computes the correlation between the proportion of the total civilian population that is employed and the civilian unemployment rate. One might think, naively, that, by definition, the employment rate and the unemployment rate would be negatively correlated. If one drops, the other should rise correspondingly. Yet the correlation between these variables between 1950 and 1997 is a *positive* .513. This is possible because someone who is not working will not be counted as unemployed if not considered to be in the labor market. When large numbers of people are newly entering the labor market (as women have been doing in the past few decades), it is possible for the employment rate and the unemployment rate to rise simultaneously (Cook and Harkin, 1985).

Were the undercount to be uniform across age categories and years, it would make no difference that officially defined unemployment failed to coincide with exclusion from the world of full-time adult work: the two variables would be exactly proportional. However, there is no reason to think that this is so (Bowen and Finegan, 1965; Tella, 1965; Dernberg and Strand, 1966). The proportions of individuals who are defined as not in the labor force because they are in school, or keeping house, or retired surely vary by age. To use the official unemployment statistics is, therefore, to risk serious systematic bias in the analysis.

Realizing that the employment–unemployment contrast might be inadequate, Phillips *et al.* (1972) analyzed age-specific U.S. arrest rates for property offenses for the years 1952–1967 using this contrast and, also, using the contrast "in the labor force–not in the labor force." Models based on the latter contrast had quite a bit more explanatory power. Phillips *et al.* note that the labor force measure may be less transitory, as it is based on past as well as current work status. This measure merits further exploration.

3.1.4. The Level of Analysis

All the authors under discussion here use nationally aggregated data in their analyses. When one simply wants to determine whether changes in certain variables characteristic of a nation affect other variables characteristic of that nation, this procedure is unexceptional. It is more problematic, however, when adopted as a means of testing theories about individuals.[18] Criminal motivation theory is a theory about individuals, and opportunity theory, though it involves features of a community, rests on arguments about how those features affect the behavior of potential offenders, making it easier or more difficult for them to violate the law.

It has been understood for decades that relationships found in aggregated data may not hold for individuals (Robinson, 1950; Langbein and Lichtman, 1978). Evidence that arrest rates are high when unemployment is high, for example, need not imply that the unemployed have a higher rate of arrest than the employed. Conversely, a relationship found for individuals need not appear in aggregate data. Teenagers and young adults have a higher likelihood of committing homicide than those who are younger or older, yet national homicide rates for nations are not always elevated when the percentage of the population in these age brackets is high (Gartner, 1990; Gartner and Parker, 1990; Marvel and Moody, 1991; Pampel and Gartner, 1995). Males are more likely than females to commit crimes of violence, but in American cities, the sex ratio does not significantly influence the violent crime rate (Messner and Sampson, 1991). Some analyses of crime rates in SMSAs have found that the percentage of young males in the population either has a *negative* effect on crime (Crutchfield *et al.*, 1982; Messner and Blau, 1987) or fails to make a significant contribution (DeFronzo, 1983), contrary to what is found in studies of individuals. Someone who failed to find an aggregate relationship between the percentage of young people and the crime rate, and inferred that among individuals age was unrelated to crime, would reach a mistaken conclusion.

One can see why this might happen by considering the propensity to steal C_{ij} of individual i in community j as a function of his or her own wealth W_{ij} and the mean wealth of the community. We allow for the possibility that the effect of an individual's wealth might depend on the mean wealth of the jurisdiction in which he or she lives. Writing a regression equation for these

[18]In a private communication, Ken Land mentioned to me that his papers were not intended to test theories about individuals, only to examine the relationships among macro variables. The discussion of motivation in his papers involves reasoning about individuals. Motivation in the Cantor and Land papers is conceptualized as a characteristic of individuals. To the extent that his findings are interpreted as bearing on motivation to commit crime, they are tests of ideas about individuals.

effects, letting a bar over a variable represent its mean in jurisdiction j, and letting u represent the residual, we have

$$C_{ij} = a + b_1 W_{ij} + b_2 \bar{W}_j + b_3 W_{ij} \bar{W}_j + u_{ij} \tag{11}$$

Summing over individuals in each jurisdiction and dividing by the number of individuals in each jurisdiction gives us

$$\bar{C}_j = a + b_1 \bar{W}_j + b_2 \bar{W}_j + b_3 W_j^2 + \bar{u}_j = a + (b_1 + b_2)\bar{W}_j + b_3 W_j^2 + \bar{u}_j \tag{12}$$

With aggregate data alone, the individual coefficients b_1 and b_2 are not identified (only their sum is), and the interaction term in Eq. (11) cannot be distinguished from a quadratic contextual variable. As a result of these limitations, aggregate data alone cannot distinguish between the effect of an individual's unemployment on his or her own criminal behavior and that of the unemployment rate in the community. Moreover, nonlinear terms, product terms, and ratios do not aggregate in any simple way. That is, if an equation for individuals involves terms such as X_{ij}^2, $X_{ij} Y_{ij}$, and X_{ij}/Y_{ij}, aggregation to the level of the jurisdiction will not, in general, lead to an equation with corresponding terms involving the powers, products, or ratios of the averaged variables in each jurisdiction (Greenberg and Kessler, 1981). This has immediate implications for analyses of crime rates and unemployment rates, each of which is defined as a ratio.

It follows that when one wants to test a theory formulated for individuals, it is preferable to obtain data for individuals, not just data for aggregates. Social scientists have sometimes avoided doing so because it is difficult, but also because they have been misled by Durkheim's (1951) fallacious argument that a rate characteristic of a jurisdiction is a collective phenomenon that cannot be explained by the individual characteristics of the people living in that jurisdiction. A rate is computed by adding up the contributions of individuals. Those contributions may, of course, be affected by characteristics of the aggregate. It is possible to work with individual data and yet incorporate contextual effects into one's model, as is done in Eq. (11). Thus, methodological individualism need not imply a rejection of the sociological axiom that the collective properties of the groups in which people live are consequential.

When contextual effects are considered, it will often be the case that the relevant context is something smaller than the nation. In studying the opportunity effects of unemployment, for example, it is likely to be the local unemployment rate that is relevant; few prospective criminals will be enabled to commit crimes by opportunities arising from changes in unemployment in distant regions. Nor need the collection of individual data imply that individual behaviors are statistically independent of one another. With appropriate data, one could take into account the influence that respondents (e.g., best friends or fellow gang members) have on one another's activities.

Whether an individual-level model explains variation among aggregate units, such as SMSAs, states, or nations, is a question separate from the validity of the model. A theory about individuals might be correct in the sense that every assertion it makes about the effects of variables in the theory is valid, but it might be incomplete, failing to incorporate additional variables or effects that are also important. It might, for this reason, fail to explain aggregate-level variation fully. When one wants to see whether an individual-level equation accounts for aggregate differences, one must first estimate the individual-level equation, use it to generate predictions for the dependent variable that can be aggregated, and then compare the predictions for the aggregate with the reality. This is not the same as estimating a regression equation with the aggregated variables.

Another disadvantage to the use of aggregate data in criminological analyses concerns the distinction between rates of participation (whether someone violates the law) and frequency of violation on the part of the violators (Blumstein *et al.*, 1986, p. 55, 1988). The number of crimes committed is the product of the number of violators and the mean frequency at which they violate the law. The two can vary independently. When analyzing aggregate crime rates it is possible to study only the product. With individual data it is possible, at least in principle, to study both.

A second issue is not inherent in the use of aggregate data but is frequently characteristic of it: information about the mechanisms by which independent variables bring about their outcome is often lacking. C-L noted that they did not have direct information about criminal motivation and opportunities. Their analyses, like those by Devine *et al.* and Britt, make assumptions about the effects of unemployment on individual behavior yet cite no evidence to support these assumptions. Is it true that unemployment increases the time people spend at home? Studies of individuals have the potential for collecting this sort of information.

3.1.5. The Time Span of the Study

To determine whether there is a trend in the effect of unemployment on crime, as hypothesized in H2, it would be necessary to examine the relevant time period. Greenberg's discussion does not make the ahistorical claim that there is a general tendency for unemployment to influence crime more and more strongly as one decade follows another until the end of time. He claims that specific, historically located developments have had that effect. In arguing that the exclusion of juveniles from the world of adult work is of greater importance now than in the past, Greenberg called attention to the particular importance of child labor laws and mandatory school attendance legislation adopted during the first few decades of the twentieth century, as well as post-World War II affluence, with its culture of consumerism, and marketing targeted to adolescents (Greenberger and Steinberg, 1986). All these developments were in place by 1958, the first year in Britt's time series. Outside the South, for example, high school enrollment rates and graduation rates rose rapidly between 1910 and 1940, then leveled off (Goldin, 1998; Goldin and Katz, 1998). To study the effect of these developments it would be necessary to start the time series much earlier.

To be sure, college attendance rose substantially during the years of Britt's study, but one would not expect this trend to have the same consequences for the crime rate as the earlier increase in high school attendance, some of which was required by state law. Many college students work or are supported by parents, scholarships, and loans. Almost all are in college because of its immediate and long-term rewards. Historically, this has not been as true of high school attendance.

In explaining the historical trend toward a greater concentration of criminality in the youthful years, Greenberg notes that exclusion of juveniles from the world of adult work had been going on gradually for a long period of time—perhaps a century—and therefore might plausibly be explained not merely as the result of child labor and mandatory school attendance laws but, rather, as a consequence of a capitalist economy's failure to generate sufficient employment to put youth and adults to work. Recent research allows us to flesh out this sketchy explanation. Compulsory school attendance legislation, combined with child labor laws, did increase school attendance at the start of the twentieth century (Margo and Finegan, 1996). Child labor dropped very substantially over a period of several decades, starting around 1870 or 1880 (Carter and Sutch, 1996), though only in part because of legislation or a weakening demand for labor. Silberman (1965) charts the declining labor force participation of teenagers in the first half of this century, noting that by far the largest component of the drop occurred for farm workers. The decline of the family farm, accompanied by migration to the city, eliminated their jobs. In addition, as parents' incomes rose, they increased their investment in their children's future by educating them for longer periods, in the process, deferring their entrance into the labor market.

Though in recent decades the American economy has endured large numbers of plant closings and downsizings (Sordius *et al.*, 1981), resulting in the loss of millions of jobs, unemployment rates have not trended upward because an even larger number of new jobs has been created. Many of the new jobs, however, are in the service sector, teach few skills, pay badly, are repetitive and boring, carry few or no benefits or opportunities for advancement, and offer only irregular employment (Bluestone and Harrison, 1982;

Kasarda, 1988, 1989, 1990, 1992; Burtless, 1990; Reubens *et al.*, 1981; Taylor, 1997). The proportion of students working at such jobs has increased in recent decades: in the 1950s, about 5% of high school students worked after school; in the 1990s, this figure increased to about 25%. Possibly in response to the increased supply of teenage workers, teen wages have fallen relative to adult wages. There is also evidence that employers have substituted young workers for older ones in response to the wage differential (Kalachek, 1969; Hills and Reubens, 1983; Greenberger and Steinberg, 1986, pp. 65–68; Rothman, 1992). According to one observer, the youths taking these jobs are largely "media-savvy teenagers hungry for designer clothes and cellular phones, or saving for the rising costs of college" (Thomas, 1998).

Black males are the one exception to the upward trend in high school students holding part-time jobs; for them the trend has been downward. Greenberg noted that the trend in labor force participation had been different for black and white youths: black teenage labor market participation dropped dramatically between 1950 and 1973, while for white teenagers it remained stable. After noting this difference, Greenberg did not comment further on it. This article provides an occasion for doing so. For the years 1958–1995 (the time spanned by Britt's data), black male labor force participation rates continued to decline for 16–19 year olds, while for white males they *rose*. This racial difference in employment trends calls for an explanation (Adams and Mangum, 1978) that goes beyond Greenberg's off-hand reference to the "disaccumulationist" phase of the capitalist mode of production. Developments such as the loss of manufacturing jobs to low-wage foreign countries, cuts in public sector employment, increases in the minimum wage, skill deficits among youth educated in center-city public schools, spatial mismatch between jobs and potential workers, and the high incomes now available to youths selling illegal narcotics must figure in such an explanation (Goodman and Dolan, 1979, pp. 170–171; Wilson, 1987; Hagedorn, 1988; Hughes, 1989; Fagan, 1992, 1997; Fernandez, 1992; Kasarda, 1992; Peterson and Vroman, 1992; Hagan, 1997; Taylor, 1997).

With employment trends differing for black and whites youths, it is essential that a statistical analysis examine crime trends separately for blacks and whites, lest important effects be washed out in the mix. That the increases in homicide rates in the late eighties were larger for black males than for white males (Blumstein and Rosenfeld, 1998) may be related to the racial differences in employment trends. Presumably it is because of their more limited legitimate labor market prospects that black males were disproportionately drawn into street-level crack distribution, where unregulated competition has been accompanied by high levels of violent crime

(Fagan and Chin, 1990; Blumstein, 1995; Cook and Laub, 1998; Grogger and Willis, 1998).

4. CONCLUSION

I have identified numerous difficulties in the attempts to study the impact of unemployment on crime rates by analyzing nationally aggregated data. The regression equations in these efforts do not adequately represent the theoretical ideas they are designed to test, and the variables in the theory are not adequately represented by those available in official unemployment statistics. Nationally aggregated data are less than ideal when estimating relationships posited by theory to hold for individuals. For this reason, it is doubtful that much confidence can be placed in the conclusions reached in the studies discussed here.

The issues raised in this discussion transcend the handful of studies I reviewed. Recent advances in the econometric analysis of nonstationary time series suggest that many—perhaps most—sociological analyses of crime rate time series (and, very likely, other kinds of rates as well) suffer from serious methodological deficiencies. The methods they have used fail to reveal long-run tendencies or rely on misspecified models and improper estimation procedures. The cointegration revolution provides a solution to these difficulties. Researchers making use of this solution will still have to grapple with the other issues raised here, such as the operationalization of variables, the translation of ideas into mathematical representations, and the limitations of aggregate data for purposes of testing theories about individuals. Some of these difficulties may be harder to solve than the purely statistical problems posed by nonstationarity.

ACKNOWLEDGMENTS

I am grateful for Chris Hale and Robert Yaffee for helpful comments, to Thomas Marvell for furnishing data, to Nitsan Chorev for assistance in data collection, and to Susan Carlson for statistical advice.

REFERENCES

Adams, A. V., and Mangum, G. L. (1978). *The Lingering Crisis of Youth Unemployment*, W. E. Upjohn Institute for Employment Research, Kalamazoo, MI.

Banerjee, A., Dolado, J. J., Galbraith, J. W., and Hendry, D. F. (1993). *Co-Integration, Error Correction, and the Econometric Analysis of Non-Stationary Data*, Oxford University Press, New York.

Bluestone, B., and Harrison, B. (1982). *The Deindustrializing of America: Plant Closings, Community Abandonment, and the Dismantling of Basic Industry*, Basic, New York.

Blumstein, A. (1995). Youth violence, guns, and the illicit-drug industry. *J. Crim. Law Criminol.* 86: 10–36.

Blumstein, A., and Rosenfeld, R. (1998). Explaining recent trends in U.S. homicide rates. *J. Crim. Law Criminol.* 88: 1175–1216.

Blumstein, A., Cohen, J., Roth, J. A., and Visher, C. A. (eds.) (1986). *Criminal Careers and "Career Criminals,"* National Academy Press, Washington, DC.

Blumstein, A., Cohen, J., and Farrington, D. P. (1988). Criminal career research: Its value for criminology. *Criminology* 26: 1–35.

Bowen, W. G., and Finegan, T. A. (1965). Labor force participation and unemployment. In Ross, A. M. (ed.), *Employment Policy and the Labor Market*, University of California Press, Berkeley, pp. 115–161.

Britt, C. L. (1994). Crime and unemployment among youths in the United States, 1958–1990. *Am. J. Econ. Sociol.* 53: 99–109.

Britt, C. L. (1997). Reconsidering the unemployment and crime relationship: Variation by age group and historical period. *J. Quant. Criminol.* 13: 405–417.

Burtless, G. (ed.) (1990). *A Future of Lousy Jobs? The Changing Structure of U.S. Wages*, Brookings Institution, Washington, DC.

Butts, J. A. (2000). *Youth Crime Drop*, Urban Institute Justice Policy Center, Washington, DC.

Cantor, D., and Land, K. C. (1985). Unemployment and crime rates in the post-World War II United States: A theoretical and empirical analysis. *Am. Sociol. Rev.* 50: 317–332.

Cantor, D., and Land, K. C. (1987). Unemployment and crime rates: A bivariate seasonal ARIMA analysis of monthly data, 1969–1985. Unpublished paper.

Carter, S., and Sutch, R. (1996). Fixing the facts: Editing of the 1880 U.S. census of occupations with implications for long-term labor force trends and the sociology of official statistics. *Hist. Methods* 29: 5–24.

Charemza, W. W., and Deadman, D. F. (1997). *New Directions in Econometric Practice: General to Specific Modelling, Cointegration and Vector Autoregression*, Edward Elgar, Lyme, MA.

Conley, D. (1999). *Being Black: Living in the Red: Race, Wealth, and Social Policy in America*, University of California Press, Berkeley.

Cook, P. J., and Harkin, G. A. (1985). Crime and the business cycle. *J. Legal Stud.* 14: 115–28.

Cook, P. J., and Laub, J. H. (1998). The unprecedented epidemic in youth violence. In Tonry, M., and Moore, M. H. (eds.), *Youth Violence. Crime and Justice: A Review of Research, Vol. 15.* University of Chicago Press, Chicago, pp. 27–64.

Crutchfield, R. D., and Pitchford, S. R. (1997). Work and crime: The effects of labor stratification. *Social Forces* 76: 93–118.

Crutchfield, R. D., Geerken, M., and Gove, W. R. (1992). Crime rate and social integration: The impact of metropolitan mobility. *Criminology* 20: 467–478.

DeFronzo, J. (1983). Economic assistance to impoverished Americans: Relationship to incidence of crime. *Criminology* 21: 119–136.

Dernberg, T., and Strand, K. (1966). Hidden unemployment 1953–1962: A quantitative analysis by age and sex. *Am. Econ. Rev.* 55: 71–95.

Devine, J. A., Sheley, J. F., and Smith, M. D. (1988). Macroeconomic and social-control policy influences on crime rate changes, 1948–1985. *Am. Sociol. Rev.* 53: 407–420.

Durkheim, E. (1951). *Suicide* (G. Simpson, trans.), Free Press, New York.

Edin, K., and Lein, L. (1997). *Making Ends Meet: How Single Mothers Survive Welfare and Low-Wage Work.* Russell Sage Foundation, New York.

Engle, R. F., and Granger, C. W. J. (1987). Cointegration and error correction: Representation, estimation and testing. *Econometrica* 55: 251–276.

Executive Office of the President (1997). *Economic Report of the President*, US Government Printing Office, Washington, DC.

Fagan, J. (1992). Drug selling and licit income in distressed neighborhoods: The economic lives of street-level drug users and dealers. In Harrell, A. V., and Peterson, G. E. (eds.), *Drugs, Crime and Social Isolation*, Urban Institute Press, Washington, DC, pp. 99–146.

Fagan, J. (1994). Women and drugs revisited: Female participation in the cocaine economy. *J. Drug Issues* 24: 179–226.

Fagan, J. (1997). Legal and illegal work: Crime, work, and unemployment. In Weisbrod, B. A. and Worthy, J. C. (eds.), *The Urban Crisis: Linking Research to Action*. Northwestern University Press, Evanston, IL, pp. 33–80.

Fagan, J., and Chin, K. L. (1990). Violence as regulation and social control in the distribution of crack. In de la Rosa, M., Gropper, B., and Lambert, E. (eds.), *Drugs and Violence*, National Institute on Drug Abuse Research Monograph No. 103, U.S. Public Health Administration, Rockville, MD, pp. 8–39.

Fernandez, R. M. (1997). Spatial mismatch: Housing, transportation, and employment in regional perspective. In Weisbrod, B. A., and Worthy, J. C. (eds.), *The Urban Crisis: Linking Research to Action*. Northwestern University Press, Evanston, IL, pp. 81–99.

Gartner, R. (1990). The victims of homicide: A temporal and cross-national comparison. *Am. Sociol. Rev.* 55: 92–106.

Gartner, R., and Parker, R. N. (1990). Cross-national evidence on homicide and the age structure of the population. *Social Forces* 69: 351–371.

Glasser, E. L., and Sacerdote, B. (1996). Why is there more crime in cities? *J. Polit. Econ. Suppl. S* 107: S225–S258.

Goldin, C. (1998). America's graduation from high school: The evolution and spread of secondary schooling in the twentieth century. *J. Econ. Hist.* 58: 345–374.

Goldin, C., and Katz, L. (1998). Human capital and social capital: The rise of secondary schooling in America, 1910 to 1940. *J. Interdisc. Hist.* 29: 683–723.

Goodman, J. C., and Dolan, E. G. (1979). *Economics of Public Policy*, West, Minneapolis, MN.

Granger, M. C. W. J., and Newbold, P. (1974). Spurious regressions in econometrics. *J. Economet.* 2: 111–120.

Greenberg, D. F. (1977). Delinquency and the age structure of society. *Contemp. Crisis* 1: 189-223.

Greenberg, D. F. (1985). Age, crime, and social explanation. *Am. J. Sociol.* 91: 1–21.

Greenberg, D. F. (2001). Novus ordo saeclorum? *Punish. Soc.* 3: 81–93.

Greenberg, D. F., and Kessler, R. C. (1981). Aggregation bias in deterrence research: An empirical analysis. *J. Res. Crime Delinq.* 18: 128–137.

Greenberger, E., and Steinberg, L. D. (1986). *When Teenagers Work: The Psychological and Social Costs of Adolescent Employment*, Basic Books, New York.

Greene, W. H. (1997). *Econometric Analysis*, Prentice-Hall, Upper Saddle River, NJ.

Grogger, J., and Willis, M. (1998). The introduction of crack cocaine and the rise in urban crime rates. Working Paper 6353, National Bureau of Economic Research, Cambridge, MA.

Hagan, J. (1997). Crime and capitalization: Toward a developmental theory of street crime in America. In Weisbrod, B. A., and Worthy, J. C. (eds.), *The Urban Crisis: Linking Research to Action*, Northwestern University Press, Evanston, IL, pp. 287–308.

Hagedorn, J. M., with Macon, P. (1988). *People and Folks: Gangs, Crime, and the Underclass in a Rustbelt City*, Lake View, Chicago.

Hagedorn, J. M. (1994). Homeboys, dope fiends, legits, and new jacks. *Criminology* 32: 197–220.

Hale, C. (1991). Unemployment and crime: Differencing is no substitute for modeling. *J. Res. Crime Delinq.* 28: 426–429.

Hale, C., and Sabbagh, D. (1991). Testing the relationship between unemployment and crime: A methodological comment and empirical analysis using time series data from England and Wales. *J. Res. Crime Delinq.* 28: 400–417.

Harris, R. I. D. (1995). *Using Cointegration Analysis in Econometric Modeling*, Prentice–Hall, New York.

Hills, S. M., and Reubens, B. G. (1983). Youth employment in the United States. In Reubens, B. G. (ed.), *Youth at Work: An International Survey*, Roman and Allanheld, Totowa, NJ, pp. 269–318.

Holden, D., and Perman, R. (1994). "Unit roots and cointegration for the economist." In Rao, B. B. (ed.), *Cointegration for the Applied Economist*, St. Martin's, New York, pp. 47–112.

Hughes, M. A. (1989). Misspeaking truth to power: A geographical perspective on the "underclass" fallacy. *Econ. Geogr.* 65: 187–207.

Johnston, J., and DiNardo, J. (1997). *Econometric Methods*, 4th ed., McGraw-Hill, New York.

Kalachek, E. (1969). *The Youth Labor Market*, Policy Papers in Human Resources and Industrial Relations No. 12, Institute of Labor and Industrial Relations, University of Michigan–Wayne State University, Ann Arbor.

Kapuscinski, C. A., Braithwaite, J., and Chapman, B. (1998). Unemployment and crime: Toward resolving the paradox. *J. Quant. Criminol.* 14: 215–244.

Kasarda, J. D. (1988). Jobs, migration and emerging urban mismatches. In McGeary, M. G. H., and Lynn, L. E., Jr. (eds.), *Urban Change and Poverty*, National Academy Press, Washington, DC, pp. 148–198.

Kasarda, J. D. (1989). Urban industrial transition and the underclass. *Ann. Am. Acad. Polit.-Soc. Sci.* 501: 26–47.

Kasarda, J. D. (1990). Structural factors affecting the location and timing of urban underclass growth. *Urban Geogr.* 11: 234–264.

Kasarda, J. D. (1992). The severely distressed in economically transforming cities. In Harrell, A. V., and Peterson, G. E. (eds.), *Drugs, Crime, and Social Isolation: Barriers to Urban Opportunity*, Urban Institute Press, Washington, DC, pp. 45–97.

LaFree, G. (1998). *Losing Legitimacy: Street Crime and the Decline of Social Institutions in America*, Westview, Boulder, CO.

Land, K. C., Cantor, D., and Russell, S. T. (1995). Unemployment and crime rate fluctuations in the post-World War II United States: Statistical time series properties and alternative models. In Hagan, J., and Peterson, R. D. (eds.), *Crime and Inequality*, Stanford University Press, Stanford, CA, pp. 55–79.

Langbein, L. A., and Lichtman, A. J. (1978). *Ecological Inference*, Sage, Beverly Hills, CA.

Margo, R. A., and Finegan, T. A. (1996). Compulsory schooling legislation and school attendance in turn-of-the-century America: A "natural experiment" approach. *Econ. Lett.* 53: 103–110.

Marvell, T. B., and Moody, C. E., Jr. (1991). Age structure and crime rates: The conflicting evidence. *J. Quant. Criminol*, 7: 237–273.

McCarthy, B., and Hagan, J. (1992). Mean streets: The theoretical significance of situational delinquency among homeless youth. *Am. J. Sociol.* 98: 597–627.

Messner, S. F., and Blau, J. R. (1987). Routine leisure activities and rates of crime: A macro-level analysis. *Social Forces* 65: 1035–1052.

Messner, S. F., and Sampson, R. J. (1991). The sex ratio, family disruption, and rates of violent crime: The paradox of demographic structure. *Social Forces* 69: 693–713.

Mumola, C. (1999). *Substance Abuse and Treatment, State and Federal Prisoners, 1997*, Bureau of Justice Statistics, U.S. Department of Justice, Washington, DC.

Myers, S. L., Jr. (1992). Crime, entrepreneurship, and labor force withdrawal. *Contemp. Policy Issues* 10: 84–97.

Nakosteen, R. A., and Zimmer, M. A. (1989). Minimum wages and labor market prospects of women. *South. Econ. J.* 56: 302–314.

Nixon, R. A. (1968). An appreciative and critical look at official unemployment data. In Herman, M., Sadofsky, S., and Rosenberg, B. (eds.), *Work, Youth, and Unemployment*, Thomas Y. Crowell, New York, pp. 29–43.

Pampel, F. C., and Gartner, R. (1995). Age structure, socio-political institutions, and national homicide rates. *Eur. Soc. Rev.* 11: 243–260.

Peterson, G. E., and Vroman, W. (1992). *Urban Labor Markets and Labor Mobility*, Urban Institute, Washington, DC.

Phillips, L., Votey, H. L., and Maxwell, D. (1972). Crime, youth, and the labor market. *J. Pol. Econ.* 80: 491–504.

Phillips, P. C. B. (1986). Understanding spurious regressions in econometrics. *J. Econometr.* 33: 311–340.

Pyle, D. J., and Deadman, D. F. (1994). Crime and the business cycle in post-war Britain. *Br. J. Criminol.* 34: 339–357.s

Raphael, S., and Winter-Ebmer, R. (2001). Identifying the effect of unemployment on crime. *J. Law Econ.* (in press).

Reubens, B. G., Harrison, J. A. C., and Rupp, K. (1981). *The Youth Labor Force 1945–1995: A Cross-National Analysis*, Allenheld, Osmun, Totowa, NJ.

Reuter, P., MacCoun, R., and Murphy, P. (1990). Money from Crime: A Study of the Economics of Drug-Dealing in Washington, DC., Report R-3894, Rand, Santa Monica, CA.

Robinson, W. S. (1950). Ecological correlations and behavior of individuals. *Am. Sociol. Rev.* 15: 351–357.

Rothman, R. A. (1992). Working youths in the United States. In Warme, B. D., Lundy, K. L. P., and Lundy, L. A. (eds.), *Working Part-Time: Risks and Opportunities*, Praeger, New York, pp. 119–130.

Ruhm, C. J. (1995). Economic conditions and alcohol problems. *J. Health Econ.* 14: 583–603.

Ruhm, C. J. (1999). Are recessions good for your health? Unpublished paper.

Sassen-Koob, S. (1989). New York City's informal economy. In Portes, A., Castells, M., and Benton, L. A. (eds.), *The Informal Economy: Studies in Advanced and Less Developed Countries*, Johns Hopkins University Press, Baltimore, pp. 60–77.

Silberman, C. E. (1965). What hit the teenagers? *Fortune* April: 130–134, 228–230, 232, 234.

Smith, M. D., Devine, J. A., and Sheley, J. F. (1992). Crime and unemployment: Effects across age and race categories. *Sociol. Perspect.* 35: 551–572.

Sordius, J. P., Jarle, P., and Ferman, L. A. (1981). *Plant Closings and Economic Dislocation*, W. E. Upjohn Institute for Employment Research, Kalamazoo, MI.

Taylor, I. (1997). The political economy of crime. In Maguire, M., Morgan, R., and Reiner, R. (eds.). *The Oxford Handbook of Criminology*, Clarendon Press, Oxford, pp. 265–303.

Tella, A. (1965). The relation of labor force to employment. *Industr. Lab. Rel Rev.* April: 76.

Thomas, J. (1996). Experts take a 2d look at virtue of student jobs. *New York Times* May 13: A16.

U.S. Department of Labor (1997). *Bureau of Labor Statistics Handbook of Methods*, U.S. Government Printing Office, Washington, DC.

Wilson, W. J. (1987). *The Truly Disadvantaged*, University of Chicago Press, Chicago.

Wolff, E. N. (2001). Recent trends in wealth ownership, 1983–1998. In Shapiro, T. M., and Wolff, E. N. (eds.), *Assets and the Disadvantaged: The Benefits of Spreading Asset Ownership*, Russell Sage Foundation, New York (in press).

[4]
Long-Term Trends in Crimes of Violence

Empirical and theoretical issues posed by Mark Cooney's (2003) analysis of long-term trends in crimes of violence are discussed.

KEYWORDS: Violence, homicide, trends, individualization, informal social control

Listen to the yell of Leopold's ghost
Burning in hell for his hand-maimed host
Hear how the demons chuckle and yell
Cutting his hands off down in hell

—Vachel Lindsay, *The Congo*

Researchers analyzing long-term trends in crime rates comparatively are plagued by gaps in the archives, and imperfect recording of crimes (Cockburn, 1991; Sharpe, 1983, 1985). Population estimates for the centuries before there were censuses are at best rough. Quantitative data for the key explanatory variables are unavailable. The psychological capacity for self-control, which is central to Elias's ideas, and the strength of informal social control, which is important to Donald Black's, are not easily assessed from historical data. Historians do not agree on whether family solidarity in medieval England was strong or weak.

TRENDS IN VIOLENCE

Despite deficiencies in data, the long-term decline in homicide rates between thirteenth-century England (the earliest period for which they can be estimated) and present-day Western Europe and North America is so large and appears so consistently in various places that it cannot be dismissed as an artifact of inadequate records. If the earlier records are especially incomplete, the true drop would be even larger (Eisner, 2001, 2003). The possibility that later crime counts, deriving from urbanized societies where most people do not know one another, might be more inaccurate than those generated in small villages and rural regions, has not been considered, but it seems possible to me. Even so, the broad conclusion is clearly correct: If we ignore state-sponsored killings, there has been

I am grateful to Jo Dixon and Philippa Maddern for helpful assistance, to David Garland for comments on an earlier draft, and to Gary Jensen for making his homicide data set available.

far less lethal violence in modern Western Europe and North America than there was in the Middle Ages.

Official records fall short in not documenting crimes involving behaviors that, although technically illegal, were ignored by the courts. For example, large numbers of babies sent out to baby farms for wet-nursing in eighteenth- and nineteenth-century England, France, and Italy died from starvation (Behlmer, 1982; Scrimshaw, 1984), but their deaths rarely led to indictments. Trends in homicide rates might look different if they were to be included.

Finally, the downward trend has not occurred uniformly throughout time or space. An Augmented Dickey-Fuller Test for U.S. homicide rates for the years 1900–2000 shows them to be well described by a random walk with positive drift, i.e., short-term fluctuation with a stochastic tendency to increase. The homicide rate at the end of the century was five times higher than it was at the beginning. The current rate for New England is about four times higher than at the end of the seventeenth century (Roth, 2001). Homicide rates for individual American cities can be analyzed from various points in the nineteenth century to the present, and show no evidence of systemic downward trends. In 2001, they were twice as high as in New York City in 1820 and Philadelphia in 1839–1845 (Federal Bureau of Investigation, 2002; Lane, 1979:60; Monkkonen, 2001a). To speak of the recent drop in U.S. homicide rates as a resumption of an earlier downward trend mistakenly assumes that there has been such a trend. The short-term increases and decreases mentioned by Cooney (2003) are very likely due to the random walk, which for short stretches of time, can look like a trend. English homicide rates are now more than three times what they were in 1900 (Morris and Bloom-Cooper, 1967; Simmons, 2002). Some have suggested that the earlier downward trend in Europe has been replaced with an upward trend (Elias, 2000; Gurr et al., 1977), but neither Elias, nor Black, nor Cooney offers an explanation for it.

Trends in the percentages of homicides occurring within the family are less firmly established. For England, the percentages are 2% to 8% in the Middle Ages (Given, 1977; Hanawalt, 1979:159), 18% to 21% in early modern times (Cockburn, 1977; Sharpe, 1983), and 29.1% now (Home Office, 2000:81). Spierenburg (1994, 1996) also found a large increase in the percentage of intimate homicide victims in Amsterdam for the period 1651–1810. These figures are consistent with the upward trend claimed by Stone (1983) and Cooney (2003). However, the percentages are not reliable. Medieval and early modern English records generally do not identify step-relations, family relationships other than the closest, or master-servant and master-apprenticeship relationships (Cockburn, 1991; Hanawalt, 1979:159; Maddern, 2002; Sharpe, 1985). Descriptions of circumstances that might make it possible to identify a domestic relationship are sometimes missing. The Amsterdam percentages are based on trials, and the sample size is small: For the 1751–1810 period, there were just 34 cases. With a larger sample (500 trials), Castan (1971) found that 66% of homicides in early modern Toulouse were familial. An even higher percentage was found among the Bison-horn Maria, an aboriginal people of India (Elwin, 1966). In late medieval France, 12.5% of homicides were intrafamilial (Gauvard, 1991:618–619), a figure not much different from the 13.1% in the FBI's Supplemental Homicide Reports for 2001 or the 14.5% of homicides between spouses or romantic partners in New York 1800–1875 (Federal Bureau of Investigation, 2002; Monkkonen, 2001: 114-115).[1] In colonial America, 30 homicides were prosecuted before 1660. If infanticides are not counted, the proportion of intrafamilial homicides was low, even though the overall homicide rate was lower than in medieval Europe. Yet if domestic servants are considered part of the household (as they would have been at that time), then approximately half of all homicides were domestic (Chapin, 1983:111–114).[2] Nonlethal domestic violence, underreported now, was surely underreported even more in earlier times, when reasonable chastisement was lawful and, among men, normative (Hawkes, 2002; Maddern, 2002). That it is reported often in contemporary American survey research is weak evidence of an upward trend. The trend may well have been downward.

Although Cooney (2003) indicates that he wishes to exclude predatory violence from consideration, the evidence on which he rests his conclusions about the decline in the number of coparticipants in violent crime consists of tabulations that include such crimes. If, as some historians consider likely, most of the homicides in fourteenth-century England for which no perpetrator could be identified involved robbery or burglary, close to 30% of the homicides may have been theft-related. Robberies and burglaries were more likely than other crimes to be carried out by groups. Even so, most homicides involved one, two, or three perpetrators (Hanawalt, 1979:186–90).

I verified that this is true of the homicides recorded in the surviving coroner's rolls for various years in fourteenth-century London (Sharpe, 1913): 68.6% were committed by a lone killer, 14.4% had two suspects, and 9.2% had three. Just 7.8% were attributed to four or more people

1. The domestic homicide rate has fallen dramatically in recent years, possibly because it is now easier for women to leave abusive husbands (Dugan et al., 1999).

2. Cockburn (1991) notes that if one includes infants, servants, and apprentices as part of an extended family, no strong upward trend in the proportion of homicides occurring within the family is seen in Kent over the 400 years between the middle of the sixteenth century and the middle of the nineteenth.

acting in concert. Most of the homicides seem to have stemmed from arguments, not from the kind of disputes for which a court would be able to supply a remedy (e.g., property claims or injuries). The FBI's Supplemental Homicide Reports for 2001 show the comparable figures to be 85.5%, 8.4%, and 2.7%. Only 3.4% were attributed to larger groups. These figures evince a modest historic shift in the direction of individualization. Still, if the London figures are typical, few medieval urban homicides were perpetrated by gangs, mobs, clans, or political factions. Macfarlane (1979) has argued that medieval English society was substantially individualistic, much more so than Western Europe. That the differences are not larger may be a criminological reflection of that individualism.

A full study of trends in co-offending would have to attend to possible changes in practices of identifying parties present at the scene as co-offenders. Assuming for the sake of argument that the differences noted here are not due to differences in recording practices, it may be that where several co-offenders acted jointly in the Middle Ages, they did so because numbers conferred an advantage at a time when virtually all men carried swords or knives. Numbers probably became less important once thieves (or other assailants) could use guns to intimidate their victims.

THE ELIAS THESIS

Norbert Elias must be credited with having identified on the basis of qualitative materials a long-term reduction in violence that was later corroborated by quantitative research (Elias, 2000; Spierenburg, 2001). The reduction was contrary to the claims of modernization and social disorganization theory, and those flavors of Marxism that locate all social ills in capitalism. Elias also accurately noted that interpersonal violence declined in the aristocracy before it did among commoners. His thesis made sense of the squeamishness toward the public display of violence and the infliction of pain that gradually took hold in Western societies, leading to the end of public executions, and in many countries, to its abolition, as well as an end to corporal punishment (e.g., flogging), campaigns against cruelty to animals, and the rise of pacifism. Moreover, the theory's emphasis on self-control is consistent with a currently popular theory that attributes crime to impulsivity (Gottfredson and Hirschi, 1990). Notwithstanding the theory's difficulties (Geis, 2000; Greenberg et al., 2002), it enjoys a good deal of empirical support.

Yet a closer examination discloses difficulties with Elias's model. If the civilizing process started in the royal courts and spread to the aristocracy, why did homicide rates decline in colonial New England in the seventeenth century (Roth, 2001), where there were no courts or aristocracy? What are we to make of the barbarities committed against the indigenous peoples of Africa and the Americas in the early modern and modern eras? If the slave-traders and conquistadors are to be dismissed as relics of a medieval mentality, what about King Leopold II of Belgium, who, late in the nineteenth century, took possession of the Congo by having the hands or feet of hundreds of thousands cut off (Hochschild, 1998)? How do we account for the state-sponsored genocidal campaigns of twentieth-century Europe?

These examples point to a limitation of the studies that link violence with lack of self-control: They do not distinguish acting violently with inability to refrain from doing so. People can strike out because they literally cannot help themselves, or because they could abstain from violence but do not. Several studies of medieval interpersonal violence, which commonly originated in quarrels in such public places as taverns, conclude that it was often controlled and ritualized (Gauvard, 1991:705-752; Phythian-Adams, 1991), not uncontrolled. It may have been rational, although illegal. Violence can be effective in achieving a variety of goals, including discouraging others from attacking oneself, something not considered by Elias or Gottfredson and Hirschi. Culture can dictate its appropriateness as a response to challenges (Spierenburg, 1994, 2001).

WEAK STATES

The "culture of honor" that supports the use of violence flourishes when states are weak so that people must rely on their own resources to defend themselves, and social conditions create incentives for its use. This will be the case whether there is strong informal social control or not, and independently of the strength of partisanship. The homicide rates derived from the medieval European archives were not high because of partisanship and strong informal social control. Although feuding may have contributed to high levels of violence in some parts of medieval and Renaissance Europe (Stone, 1965), it did not figure importantly in the homicide records of medieval and early modern England. Homicides were processed by the courts, or occasionally through self-help, which sometimes included a family member or two, or an acquaintance or servant, but not by clan members or a political faction. The hue and cry was part of the formal law enforcement system. This system was weak for various reasons, including a very low rate of arrests and a high rate of acquittals. In the London coroner's rolls for the fourteenth century, the killers typically fled or took refuge in a church from which they later escaped. In the 153 homicide episodes I studied (a few of them involving more than one victim), only one death sentence was recorded. This weakness permitted high levels of homicide, in accord with classical deterrence theory.

Modern parallels can be found in the Mexican villages studied by Nash

(1967) and Schwartz (1972), where homicide levels were extremely high. These villages lacked strong informal social control, and homicides were individualized, not collective, even in the village that had partisan conflicts. Partisan conflicts were present in some towns of the American Old West, but even those that did not had very high rates of homicide. Many killings were themselves a form of informal control, but they were not usually a collective enterprise (McGrath, 1984)—for which reason I think they should not be called social control. Towns of the Old West had little of the informal social organization that could have prevented crime and very weak formal law enforcement. A weak state does not always imply the existence of strong informal control.

STATE CENTRALIZATION

The consolidation of power on the part of the European monarchs in the early modern period led to lower rates of personal violence through the introduction of more effective and efficient law enforcement, the curbing or disbanding of private armies, the military defeat of aristocratic challengers to royal authority, and efforts to discourage men from carrying weapons and fighting duels. In 1495, the *Reichstände* of the Holy Roman Empire proclaimed that all civil and criminal disputes had to be brought in court, not pursued privately (Selig, 1998). In the North countries, defendants lost the right of compurgation, self-defense, and of settling cases through private payments (Ylikangas, 2001). Elite-led religious repudiation of crimes of violence accompanying the Reformation and Counter-Reformation helped to erode the culture of honor further (Karonen, 2001; Muchembled, 1984, 1985). Firmer law enforcement helped to pacify the American West, as it did early modern Europe. The centralization of state power that increased the effectiveness of law enforcement also made possible the deaths of Elias's parents in the rationalized violence of Nazi concentration camps.

The relevance of the Black model to violence in inner-city minority neighborhoods is not so clear. These neighborhoods are not noted for strong informal social control. Neighborhoods that have it have less violence, not more (Sampson and Groves, 1989). High percentages of female-headed households do not suggest strong family solidarity. Apart from divisions between rival gangs, partisanship does not appear to be strong. Even the solidarity of the gang has been questioned (Yablonsky, 1959). It is middle-class people, not those with low incomes, who are reluctant to call the police (Baumgartner, 1988:42). African-American crime victims are no less likely than white victims to call the police (Avakame et al., 1999; Bachman and Coker, 1995; Baumer, 2002; Black, 1980; Felson et al.,

2002), and residents of the most socioeconomically disadvantaged neighborhoods are no less likely to do so than residents of the most advantaged neighborhoods (Baumer, 2002).

The very high rate of black imprisonment in the United States indicates that the state is far from absent or unavailable in minority neighborhoods, except perhaps for those who engage in illegal activity. Criminals' inability to request assistance with their disputes from the police is not distinct to minorities; it is also characteristic of mafia-type organized crime groups. High levels of homicide among low-income blacks are not primarily due to the absence of law enforcement, but to the same causes that lead to high levels of other crimes, such as robbery (see, for example, Sampson, 1987). Indeed the social conditions that predict high levels of homicide in census tracts also predict high levels of rape, robbery, assault, burglary, and motor vehicle theft (Miethe and Meier, 1994:103–107, 109–111). Law enforcement responds to these crimes, but its capacity to prevent them is limited.

RESEARCH AGENDA

To make further progress in our understanding of trends in violent crime, it will be important to specify the timing of changes in levels and patterns of crime, as Eisner (2001, 2003) does, and to relate these changes to indicators of explanatory variables. It should be able to explain, for example, why the percentage of homicides whose victims were adult family members began to rise in Kent a century later than the homicide rate started falling (Cockburn, 1991). Patterns that fail to fit a model should not be dismissed glibly[3]; they can provide important information regarding sources of variation.

It will be necessary to incorporate into the analysis factors not included in Cooney's discussion. One of these is demographic. If age-specific rates were anything like those of modern times,[4] this would boost early homicide rates because the life-span was shorter than it is now. Prior to the Black Death in 1349, the bulk of the English population was under age 35 (Hanawalt, 1979:127). A second is medical care. Improvements in the

3. I think Cooney does this in his remarks about intrafamilial homicide among the Buganda. It may be true that they had lived under English rule for a long time when Bohannan did his study. This was also true of the English in the thirteenth-fourteenth centuries. The critical question is how seriously this modified pre-conquest social patterns.

4. It is not clear that the age distribution of homicides in earlier times was similar to what it is now. In nineteenth-century Columbus, Ohio and New York City, it was radically different (Monkonnen, 1975, 2001b), but we do not know how typical these cities were, or what the distributions looked like in earlier centuries and in other countries.

treatment of trauma victims have increased the probability that someone injured in an assault will survive, reducing homicide rates (Cockburn, 1991; Harris et al., 2001; Spierenburg, 1996).

Lastly, gender must be incorporated into the analysis. The code of honor that called for a violent response to a challenge was a male code. Only infrequently did women commit homicide. This code has been invoked as a possible explanation of why men rarely killed their wives, but the explanation is uncertain. Law and culture permitted men the use of nonlethal physical violence to discipline their wives and children, and there appears to have been much of it. It may be that wives and children tried to avoid provoking their violent-prone husbands and fathers, and that the mutual functional dependence of spouses in a highly gendered division of labor inhibited lethal intra-familial violence.

REFERENCES

Avakame, Edem F., James F. Fyfe, and Candace McCoy
1999 Did you call the police? What did they do? An empirical assessment of Black's theory of mobilization of law. Justice Quarterly 16:765–792.

Bachman, Ronet and Ann Coker
1995 Police involvement in domestic violence: The interactive effects of victim injury, offender's history of violence, and race. Violence and Victims 10:91–106.

Baumer, Eric P.
2002 Neighborhood disadvantage and police notification by victims of violence. Criminology 40:579–616.

Baumgartner, M. P.
1988 The Moral Order of a Suburb. New York: Oxford University Press.

Behlmer, George K.
1982 Child Abuse and Moral Reform in England. Stanford, Calif.: Stanford University Press.

Black, Donald
1980 The Manners and Customs of the Police. New York: Academic Press.

Castan, Nicole
1971 La criminalité familiale dans le ressort du Parlement de Toulouse (1690-1730). In Crimes et criminalité en France sous l'Ancient Régime 17e-18e siècles. Paris: Librairie Armand Colin.

Chapin, Bradley
1983 Criminal Justice in Colonial America, 1606-1660. Athens: University of Georgia Press.

Cockburn, J. S.
1977 The nature and incidence of crime in England 1559-1625: A preliminary survey. In J.S. Cockburn (ed.), Crime in England 1550-1800. Princeton, N.J.: Princeton University Press.
1991 Patterns of violence in English society: Homicide in Kent, 1560-1985. Past and Present 130:70–106.

Cooney, Mark
2003 The privatization of violence. Criminology 41:1377–1406.

Dugan, Laura, Daniel Nagin, and Richard Rosenfeld
1999 Explaining the decline in intimate homicide. Homicide Studies 3:187–214.

Eisner, Manuel
2001 Modernization, self-control and lethal violence. British Journal of Criminology 41:618–638.
2003 Secular trends of violent crime: Evidence and theoretical interpretations. Crime and Justice: An Annual Review. In press.

Elias, Norbert
2000 The Civilizing Process: Sociogenetic and Psychogenetic Investigations. Cambridge, Mass.: Blackwell Publishers.

Elwin, Verrier
1966 Maria Murder and Suicide. Bombay: Oxford University Press.

Federal Bureau of Investigation
2002 Crime in the United States—2001. Washington, D.C.: U.S. Government Printing Office.

Felson, Richard B., Steven F. Messner, Anthony W. Hoskin, and Glenn Deane
2002 Reasons for reporting and not reporting domestic violence to the police. Criminology 40:617–647.

Gauvard, Claude
1991 'De grace especial': Crime, état et societé en France à la fin du Moyen Age. Paris: Sorbonne.

Geis, Gil
2000 On the absence of self-control as the basis for a general theory of crime: A critique. Theoretical Criminology 4:31–53.

Given, James Buchanan
1977 Society and Homicide in Thirteenth-Century England. Stanford, Calif.: Stanford University Press.

Gottfredson, Michael and Travis Hirschi
1990 A General Theory of Crime. Stanford, Calif.: Stanford University Press.

Greenberg, David F., Robin Tamarelli, and Margaret S. Kelley
2002 The generality of the self-control theory of crime. In Elin Waring and David Weisburd (eds.), Crime and Social Organization. Advances in Criminological Theory 10. New Bruswick, N.J.: Transaction.

Gurr, Ted Robert, Peter N. Grabosky, and Richard C. Hula
1977 The Politics of Crime and Conflict: A Comparative History of Four Cities. Beverly Hills, Calif.: Sage.

Hanawalt, Barbara
1979 Crime and Conflict in English Communities, 1400-1348. Cambridge, Mass.: Harvard University Press.

Harris, Anthony, Stephen H. Thomas, Gene A. Fisher, and David J. Hirsch
2001 Murder & medicine: The lethality of criminal assault 1960-1999. Homicide Studies 6:128–66.

Hawkes, Emma
2002 The "reasonable" laws of domestic violence in late medieval England. In Eve Salisbury, Georgiana Donavin, and Merral Llewelyn Price (eds.), Domestic Violence in Medieval Texts. Gainesville: University Press of Florida.

Hochschild, Adam
1998 King Leopold's Ghost: A Story of Greed, Terror, and Heroism in Colonial Africa. Boston, Mass.: Houghton Mifflin.

Home Office
2000 Criminal Statistics, England and Wales 1999. London: Her Majesty's Stationary Office.

Karonen, Petri
2001 A life for a life versus Christian reconciliation: Violence and the process of civilization in the kingdom of Sweden, 1540-1700. In Heikki Ylikangas, Petri Karonen, and Marti Lehti (eds.), Five Centuries of Violence in Finland and the Baltic Era. Columbus: Ohio State University Press.

Lane, Roger
1979 Violent Death in the City: Suicide, Accident, and Murder in Nineteenth-Century Philadelphia. Cambridge, Mass.: Harvard University Press.

Macfarlane, Alan
1979 The Origins of English Individualism: The Family, Property, and Social Transition. New York: Cambridge University Press.

Maddern, Philippa
2002 Interpreting silence: Domestic violence in the king's courts in East Anglia, 1422-1442. In Eve Salisbury, Georgiana Donavin, and Merral Llewelyn Price (eds.), Domestic Violence in Medieval Texts. Gainesville: University Press of Florida.

McGrath, Roger D.
1984 Gunfighters, Highwaymen and Vigilantes: Violence on the Frontier. Berkeley: University of California Press.

Miethe, Terence D. and Robert F. Meier
1994 Crime and Its Social Context: Toward an Integrated Theory of Offenders, Victims, and Situations. Albany: SUNY Press.

Monkkonen, Eric
1975 The Dangerous Class: Crime and Poverty in Columbus, Ohio, 1860-1885. Cambridge, Mass.: Harvard University Press.
2001a New standards for historical homicide research. Crime, Histoire & Sociétés - Crime, History & Society 5:5–26.
2001b Murder in New York City. Berkeley: University of California Press.

Morris, Terence and Louis Blom-Cooper
1967 Homicide in England. In Marvin Wolfgang (ed.), Studies in Homicide. New York: Harper and Row.

Muchembled, Robert
1984 Lay judges and the acculturation of the masses: France and the Southern Low Countries, Sixteenth to Eighteenth Centuries. In Kaspar von Greyerz (ed.), Religion and Society in Early Modern Europe, 1500-1800. Boston, Mass.: Allen and Unwin.

1985 Popular Culture and Elite Culture in France, 1450-1750. Tr. Lydia Cochrane. Baton Rouge: Louisiana State University Press.

Nash, June
1967 Death as a way of life: The increasing resort to homicide in a Mayan Indian community. American Anthropologist 69:455–470.

Phythian-Adams, Charles V.
1991 Rituals of personal confrontation in late-medieval England. Bulletin of the John Rylands Library 73:65–90.

Roth, Randolph
2001 Homicide in early modern England 1549-1800: The need for a quantitative synthesis. Crime, Histoire & Société - Crime, History & Society 5:33–57.

Sampson, Robert J.
1987 Urban black violence: The effect of male joblessness and family disruption. American Journal of Sociology 93:348–83.

Sampson, Robert J. and W. Byron Groves
1989 Community structure and crime: Testing social-disorganization theory. American Journal of Sociology 94:774–802.

Schwartz, Lola Romanucci
1972 Conflict without violence and violence without conflict in a Mexican mestizo village. In James F. Short, Jr. and Marvin E. Wolfgang (eds.), Collective Violence. Chicago, Ill.: Aldine Atherton.

Scrimshaw, Susan M.
1984 Infanticide in human populations: Societal and individual concerns. In Glenn Hausfater and Sarah Blaffer Hrdy (eds.), Infanticide: Comparative and Evolutionary Perspectiges. New York: Aldine.

Selig, Robert A.
1998 Eye for an eye? Crime and punishment in early modern Germany. German Life: Culture, History, Travel (Dec.):23–27.

Sharpe, J. A.
1983 Crime in Seventeenth-Century England: A Country Study. Cambridge, U.K.: Cambridge University Press.
1985 The history of violence in England: Some observations. Past and Present 108:206–215.

Sharpe, Reginald R.
1913 Calendar of Coroners Rolls of the City of London A.D. 1300-1378. London: Richard Clay.

Simmons, Jon (ed.)
2002 Crime in England and Wales 2001/02. London: Home Office.

Spierenburg, Pieter
1994 Faces of violence: Homicide and trends and cultural meanings: Amsterdam, 1531-1816. Journal of Social History 27:701–714.
1996 Long-term trends in homicide: Theoretical reflections and Dutch evidence, fifteenth to twentieth. In Eric A. Johnson and Erik H. Monkkonen (eds.), The Civilization of Crime: Violence in Town and Country Since the Middle Ages. Urbana: University of Illinois Press.
2001 Violence and the civilizing process: Does it work? Crime, Histoire & Société - Crime, History & Society 5:87–105.

Stone, Lawrence
1965 The Crisis of the Aristocracy, 1558-1631. Oxford: Clarendon Press.
1983 Interpersonal violence in English society 1300-1980. Past and Present 101:22–33.

Yablonsky, Lewis
1959 The delinquent gang as a near-group. Social Problems 7:108–117.

Ylikangas, Heikki
2001 What happened to violence? An analysis of the development of violence from medieval times to the early modern era based on Finnish source material. In Heikki Ylikangas, Petri Karonen, and Marti Lehti (eds.), Five Centuries of Violence in Finland and the Baltic Era. Columbus, Ohio: Ohio State University Press.

David Greenberg is Professor of Sociology at New York University. His current interests lie in the spatial and temporal dimensions of crime and punishment.

[5]
Modeling Criminal Careers

A stochastic model of criminal careers embodying the assumptions of Gottfredson and Hirschi (1986, 1988) is used as a tool to examine the arguments and claims that have been raised in the recent debate over the nature of criminal careers. The model is used to fit aggregate career data in different jurisdictions and to explain racial and sex patterns in recidivism data. Some of the arguments that have been deployed on both sides of this debate are shown to lack validity.

Nullius in verba.

—Motto of the Royal Society

THE CRIMINAL CAREERS CONTROVERSY

Criminal careers—the sequence of an individual's criminal violations over a period of time—have recently become the subject of active research (e.g., Blumstein et al., 1986). At the same time, the criminological significance of this research, and its implications for intervention policy, remains controversial.

Even the bare facts pertinent to the description of criminal careers have become the subject of dispute. Does it make sense to speak of careers starting, persisting, and ending? Do different factors explain entry into, and exit from, each of these career stages? Or does a common underlying attribute of criminality explain the temporal development of careers, as well as group and individual differences in levels of involvement in crime (Blumstein et al., 1988a, 1988b; Gottfredson and Hirschi, 1986, 1987, 1988)?

This paper will not address these questions directly. Rather, it will examine the evidence that the parties to this controversy have cited as supporting one or another position to the dispute. By developing a formal mathematical model for criminal careers, the paper shows that evidence that has been interpreted as favoring one side of the dispute is equally compatible with the position held by the other side. In other words, a good deal of the empirical evidence being cited in the dispute is entirely irrelevant to it. That this is

I am grateful to Douglas Smith for asking the question that led to this investigation; to Lyle Shannon for furnishing unpublished data; to Arnold Barnett, Chester Britt, Daniel Nagin, Marjorie Zatz, and two anonymous reviewers for comments on an earlier draft; and to David Rowe, D. Wayne Osgood, and Alan Nicewander for sharing their unpublished work along related lines.

so stems from the power of paradigmatic assumptions to shape the formulation of research questions and the interpretation of empirical evidence. Findings that seem to point to one conclusion can take on a different significance when viewed from a different perspective.

THE TWO POSITIONS

Two rival positions have dominated recent discussion of the temporal properties of criminality. One, associated with Alfred Blumstein and his collaborators, has been developed in the context of an ongoing program of longitudinal research on crime. This research has been motivated in part by the possibility that factors that influence early involvement in crime might become unimportant in later stages of a career. To take a hypothetical example, involuntary unemployment might impel someone to steal or sell illegal narcotics. Someone who found those illegal sources of income sufficiently lucrative might not abandon them should opportunities for lawful income later arise. Inability to earn income lawfully would then influence the onset of a criminal career, but be irrelevant to its persistence. Blumstein and his co-workers have argued that there actually are such factors.

In the early stages of their work, Blumstein and his co-workers modeled criminal careers by assuming that an individual can be characterized by his or her "criminal propensity," an attribute that influences an individual's level of involvement in crime. They also assumed that a population consists of several discrete groups with different sorts of criminal careers, their number to be established empirically. Blumstein and Moitra (1980) were able to fit recidivism data for a cohort of Philadelphia males by assuming that the population consisted of "innocents," who were never arrested, "desisters," who were arrested only once or twice, and "persisters," who were arrested three or more times. Similar models yielded good fits for recidivism data from London, Racine, Wisconsin, and Marion County, Oregon (Blumstein et al., 1985).

These models were essentially behaviorist in their approach to classification. Individuals were classified on the basis of whether they were arrested or convicted in a given span of time. Offenders who were not rearrested or reconvicted were categorized as desisting. This approach is problematic because of what statisticians call "right-hand censoring" of the data. In a finite time span, it is impossible to know that someone has permanently desisted from crime. Perhaps a seeming desister would commit a new crime if observed for a longer period of time (Zatz, 1982).[1] In more recent work, Blumstein and his co-workers overcome this difficulty by attributing to offenders a propensity to violate the law that is manifested behaviorally only stochastically, or probabilistically (Barnett et al., 1987, 1989). When that is

1. Rowe and Osgood (1990) also criticize this body of work on the same grounds.

done, the identification of an individual as a desister is always provisional, subject to correction with additional data.

This program of research has been challenged by Travis Hirschi and Michael Gottfredson as pointless and misleading. In their view, there is no need to classify offenders because the same theory of criminality—control theory—applies to all (Gottfredson and Hirschi, 1990). Nor do they see value in longitudinal research. This is so because they believe there already exists abundant evidence that "criminality"—the tendency to commit criminal acts—is highly stable, in the sense that criminal behavior at one time is strongly correlated with criminal behavior at later times.

Hirschi and Gottfredson also hold that criminality declines uniformly with time for all offenders, regardless of offense, region of the world, or historical epoch. For that reason, they argue, it is meaningless to speak of different stages in a criminal career, such as onset and desistance. As they see it, criminals don't desist; their propensity to commit crime simply diminishes continuously with time. Nor is there any reason to study the impact of such factors as unemployment on the development of careers; such impacts are nonexistent, or too weak to be of any substantial interest.

Blumstein and his collaborators find support for their approach in a number of pieces of empirical evidence. First, they find that simple stochastic models involving discrete classes of offenders with fixed probabilities of desisting or recidivating following an offense provide good fits to the distribution of offenses across offenders (Blumstein and Moitra, 1980; Blumstein et al., 1985). Second, they note that the correlation of such demographic characteristics as race, sex, and age with criminal participation (the proportion of a group that is criminally active in a given time period) is substantially higher than for the frequency of criminal violations *among participants*. Put differently, demographic variables have greater significance when explaining entry into a criminal career than when explaining persistence in crime (recidivism) for those who have already started (Blumstein et al., 1988b).

Third, they contend that the frequency of criminal offenses among active offenders does not decline with age. In their view, the declining aggregate involvement in crime with age does not reflect the uniform diminution of criminality that Hirschi and Gottfredson have proposed; rather it reflects the fact that some offenders abandon crime altogether, and those who continue to commit crimes at the same frequency as when they were younger. This observation suggests that research into social factors responsible for desistance might prove fruitful; for Hirschi and Gottfredson, it could not.

In responding to these claims, Gottfredson and Hirschi (1988) concede no ground. The correlations between various offender attributes and different indicators of criminal involvement are, they say, more or less the same for all the indicators. Moreover, they argue, Blumstein and Cohen's (1979) identification of a class of arrestees whose frequency of arrests did not decline as they got older was the product of bias in the selection of the sample. As for the first point, they ignore it. Although their table showing the distribution of offenses across offenders in the Richmond data displays the same features as the tables analyzed by Blumstein et al. (1985), they fail to comment on these features, leaving us uncertain as to whether their model can account for the observed patterns.

The issues raised in this debate are best addressed through the use of precisely formulated models whose predictions can be systematically assessed. To do this, I propose a simple stochastic model for criminal offenses that embodies the assumptions of Gottfredson and Hirschi's point of view. I derive its consequences and examine the adequacy of the model empirically. When this is done, it becomes apparent that this model is as good as that of Blumstein and colleagues in explaining much of the empirical evidence, and that all participants to the debate have misunderstood some of the implications of their ideas.

A COMPOUND POISSON MODEL OF CRIME

The model of offending proposed here entails three simple assumptions. First, individuals are characterized by a mean offending rate, lambda, that is constant over time.[2] This parameter can be identified with an individual's criminality or propensity to commit crime. This propensity is expected to depend on that individual's attributes, as well as characteristics of the social setting in which that individual lives. (These dependencies, which are the subject of standard etiological research on crime, are not explored here.) Second, criminal events occur independently and at random. In any given finite time span, an individual's offense rate may be higher or lower than lambda for reasons that lie outside the model (e.g., the existence of randomly occurring opportunities).

Together, these two assumptions imply that the probability of an individual characterized by lambda committing n offenses in time t is given by the Poisson distribution

$$p(n) = p_n = (\lambda t)^n \exp(-\lambda t)/n! \ . \tag{1}$$

The assumption that criminality is reflected in criminal behavior only randomly is not a particularly controversial one. It has been stressed by Hirschi and Gottfredson (1986). Though absent from the early work of Blumstein

2. In this paper, terms like "crime" and "offense" are used indiscriminately to refer to criminal violations, arrests, or convictions. The model is potentially applicable to all of these. The model can be extended to deal with more than one crime category, but that is not done here.

and his collaborators (Blumstein and Moitra, 1980; Blumstein et al., 1985), it has been adopted in their more recent work (Barnett et al., 1987, 1989).

For some purposes, the assumptions of the model are undoubtedly not strictly true. It is known, for example, that many crimes are committed by several offenders acting jointly (Reiss, 1986; Zimring, 1981). However, if it is understood that the equation applies to events, and that a crime committed by several individuals is to be counted as a single event, then no problem will arise. In practice, arrest and conviction data tend to count individual arrests or convictions as distinct, even if they arise from the same event, which creates a potential problem. Nevertheless, such distributions can be fit quite well on the assumption that a Poisson process is at work.

Temporal independence of crimes is also a dubious assumption. Sufficiently fine-grained analyses of criminal histories show that offenses often bunch together more closely than would be expected from a Poisson distribution, and that for some offense categories, a renewal process may make more sense than the Poisson (Lehoczky, 1986; Rolph and Chaiken, 1987:9–12). Yet, if data are aggregated over a period as long as a year, as is often done, this day-to-day or week-to-week bunching may be irrelevant.

The use of a continuous-time model for the temporal development of criminal careers is a departure from the approach taken by Blumstein and Moitra (1980), Blumstein et al. (1985), and Rowe et al. (1988).[3] They model recidivism as a geometric process. After committing an offense, an individual in offending group i is assumed, in their work, to have a recidivism probability p_i, with a corresponding desistance rate $1 - p_i$. Time does not appear explicitly. Consequently, groups are characterized by recidivism rates that do not take into account that some group members were in detention during part of the follow-up period and therefore unable to commit new offenses.[4]

Nor does the geometric model take into account the finite extent of the follow-up period during which recidivism can be observed. In a study that ends at age 18, as the Philadelphia cohort study did (see below), this period is shorter for a 17-year-old than for a 15-year-old. A juvenile who fails to

3. The revised, 1990 version of the Rowe et al. paper abandons the geometric model in favor of the Poisson process used here. The critique of the geometric model presented here was inspired in part by its use in the earlier version.

4. Some of the Philadelphia cohort were in detention during part of the period their arrests were being tracked (Barnett and Lofaso, 1985). Very likely this was true in other jurisdictions as well. The estimation procedure used here also neglects periods of detention, as well as times in which subjects were outside the jurisdiction. These sources of error are neglected because the relevant data are not available for some of the data sources analyzed here, and to facilitate comparison with the work of others who, in analyzing these data, also did not make these corrections. It is to be hoped that future work may be able to take "time out" into account. The most likely effect of doing so would be to introduce modest changes in the values of the parameter estimates. It is unlikely that any substantive conclusions would change.

recidivate during the short period before becoming an adult might well do so in later years (Barnett and Lofaso, 1985).[5]

The inadequacy of recidivism models that ignore time available to recidivate can be seen by means of a simple thought experiment. Consider a homogeneous group of individuals with a certain probability of recidivism. Imagine that some of this group are arrested early in a follow-up period. Others avoid arrest until one day before the follow-up period ends, when they are arrested and immediately released. It would be bizarre to suppose that each subgroup has the same likelihood of being rearrested in the time available for it to be rearrested. Nothing known about criminal behavior would support such a conclusion. Blumstein and his collaborators have abandoned the geometric model in their most recent work in favor of a Poisson process (Barnett et al., 1987, 1989), and so do I.

One noteworthy feature of the Poisson model is that there is no such thing as a true "innocent" or a true "desister." In time t, however, a proportion $p_o = \exp(-\lambda t)$ is expected to commit no offenses. As t increases, this proportion declines, so that individuals supposed to be "innocents" because they have had no arrests in a finite time span eventually "display their true colors" by recidivating.

The model does embody important features of the Gottfredson and Hirschi position. By taking lambda to be constant over time, the stability of criminality is guaranteed. To be sure, they maintain that lambda is not constant over time, but declines. I note, below, however, that many of the results obtained on the assumption of constancy are preserved when lambda is permitted to change uniformly for all individuals in the population. The assumption of constancy is made here for mathematical and expository simplicity.

As it happens, if all members of the relevant populations are assumed to have the same lambda, the Poisson distribution provides a poor fit to the distributions of arrests in the data sets that Blumstein et al. (1985), studied. Specifically, the Poisson formula predicts too many individuals to have a small number of arrests, and too few to have large numbers.

The third assumption of the model is intended to overcome this problem. The model assumes that the populations of interest are heterogeneous with respect to lambda. A number of different distributions for lambda have been studied in earlier research on criminality; one that has been widely used is the gamma function. It was first introduced by Greenwood and Yule (1920) in a study of accident proneness and later applied to criminological problems (Carr–Hill and Payne, 1971; Green and Martin, 1973; Greenberg,

5. There may be special offenses for which time might appropriately be treated as a discrete, rather than continuous, variable. Income tax fraud might be an example; most taxpayers can only do it once a year. Election fraud would be another logical candidate (Greenberg, 1979:259).

1979:259–287; Spilerman, 1970, 1971, 1972). Gamma is a two-parameter family of asymmetric, continuous curves defined by the properly normalized formula

$$p(\lambda) = \beta(\beta\lambda)^{\alpha-1}e^{-\beta\lambda}/\Gamma(\alpha), \qquad \lambda > 0. \qquad (2)$$
$$= 0 \qquad \lambda \leqslant 0.$$

Here, the parameters α and β are positive numbers. When α is an integer, $\Gamma(\alpha) = (\alpha - 1)!$ Otherwise, Γ interpolates between values of the factorial function. Depending on the values of the two parameters α and β, the curve either has a single maximum at some nonzero value of lambda, or it declines monotonically in the domain $\lambda > 0$. In either instance, the distribution has a right-hand tail even longer than that of Alice's mouse.[6] Graphs of the gamma distribution for typical values of α and β can be found in Derman et al. (1973:371–373) and Greenberg (1979:272).

The two parameters provide flexibility in fitting a range of empirical distributions. They are related to the moments of the gamma distribution by the following formulas:

$$\bar{\lambda} = \alpha/\beta \text{ and } \mathrm{var}(\lambda) = \alpha/\beta^2. \qquad (3)$$

Beta, therefore, is the ratio of the mean value of lambda in the distribution to its variance, and alpha is the ratio of the square of the mean value of lambda to the variance of lambda.

Mathematical tractability is another advantage of working with this particular distribution.[7] Thus, integration over lambda can be carried out analytically, leading to the Pareto, or negative binomial, distribution for the number of offenses:

$$p(n) = \int_0^\infty p(n|\lambda)p(\lambda)d\lambda = \frac{\Gamma(n+\alpha)\,(t/\beta)^n}{n!\,\Gamma(\alpha)\,(1+t/\beta)^{n+\alpha}}. \qquad (4)$$

As in the homogeneous Poisson distribution, some individuals with nonzero lambda will have no arrests. In time t, the proportion of such individuals is

$$1/(1 + t/\beta)^{\alpha},$$

which declines with increasing t.

Notwithstanding its venerable history, the assumption that lambda is a

6. " 'Mine is a long and a sad tale!' said the Mouse, turning to Alice, and sighing. 'It *is* a long tail, certainly!' said Alice, looking down in wonder at the Mouse's tail; 'but why do you call it sad?' "—Lewis Carroll, *Through the Looking Glass*.

7. Some of the attractive mathematical properties of this particular class of distributions are detailed in Holden (1983) and Lehoczky (1986).

continuous variable was, for reasons that are not altogether clear, dropped by Blumstein and his collaborators in favor of discrete distributions.[8] That there are distinct groups with sharply differentiated criminal propensities is, however, uncertain. Blumstein et al. (1985) interpret unexpected jumps or plateaus in the graph of recidivism rates $r(n)$ against offense number n as evidence for discontinuities in recidivism propensity that identify discrete groups. However, such humps and plateaus are by no means incompatible with a continuous distribution of lambda. In the model proposed here, in which lambda is continuous, $r(n) - r(n - 1)$ is appreciable when n is small, but small when n is large (see below).

Moreover, $r(n)$ is defined as the ratio of two proportions, the proportion of offenders having at least $n + 1$ offenses to the proportion having at least n. Should random fluctuations lead to a value of $r(n)$ that is slightly larger than expected on the basis of a cohort's criminal propensities because the numerator is, by chance, a bit high, then the denominator of $r(n + 1)$ will also be too high, tending to make $r(n + 1)$ smaller than expected. In the same way, a value of $r(n)$ that is, by chance, too low will tend to be followed by an $r(n + 1)$ that is too large. In this way, correlations between the components of these ratio variables can lead to spurious negative correlations among the ratios themselves, thereby leading to artifactual jumps and plateaus.

Though ethnographic studies of delinquency do suggest that many adolescents immerse themselves into distinct subcultures, each with its own social roles and characteristic modes of involvement in crime (Schwendinger and Schwendinger, 1985), it is also true that some of the predictors of delinquency are continuous, or have such fine gradations that they can be taken as continuous for all practical purposes. For example, low family income and low nonverbal IQ scores predict chronic delinquency in the London sample discussed below. But it is implausible that the effects of income and IQ are sharply discontinuous. Surely one pound sterling less in income, or a single IQ point less in intelligence, will not have a large impact on the probability that a child becomes delinquent. For this reason, it seems preferable to assume that the propensity to commit crimes varies continuously in most populations likely to be encountered.

Hirschi and Gottfredson have not commented on the specific mathematical form of the distribution of criminality across the population. The control theory they espouse (Gottfredson and Hirsch, 1990) suggests that the distribution of criminality should parallel the distribution of levels of control in the group of interest. They have not specified that distribution, but no problems are introduced by supposing that distribution to be continuous. The results

8. In a paper published after this study was completed, Blumstein and his collaborators abandon the assumption of discrete groups in favor of the gamma distribution for criminality (Ahn et al., 1990), though without offering a rationale.

to be derived here prove to be insensitive to this assumption; comparably good fits could be obtained by assuming a discrete distribution or a continuous distribution other than the gamma.[9] I make the assumption of a gamma distribution to establish continuity with earlier work and for mathematical convenience. Because control can vary from none at all to very high, an asymmetric, nonnegative distribution would seem to be quite appropriate.

FITTING THE DATA

In earlier research, the Pareto distribution has given good fits to the distribution of escapes from English training schools (Green and Martin, 1973) and racial disturbances in American cities (Spilerman, 1970, 1971, 1972). Does it also fit distributions of delinquent or criminal careers? The availability of several sets of published delinquency offense distributions makes it possible to address this question.

To do so, I first estimated the two parameters of the model separately for the distribution of delinquent offenses in Philadelphia, London, Richmond, California, and Racine, Wisconsin, using the procedures outlined in Appendix 1. I then computed a predicted offense distribution for each and compared it with the observed distribution by examining differences between the observed and predicted proportions for each number of arrests, as well as through a global chi-square test. Given the extremely large sample sizes in two of the three data sets, I did not use the chi-square statistic for purposes of rigorous significance testing with those models, but rather as an indication of relative goodness-of-fit for models having the same number of degrees of freedom.

The parameters of the model that best fit the Richmond, California, data had $\alpha = 0.316$. $\beta = 0.301$ (see Table 1). All proportions in the table were fit to better than .005, with a chi-square of 2.60. With 5 degrees of freedom, this is not statistically significant at the .05 level. When the sample size of 2,587 is taken into account, the fit is awesome.

Observed and predicted proportions of convictions for working-class London boys are shown in Table 2. The best fit here had $\alpha = 0.22$, $\beta = 0.19$, with a chi-square of 8.11. With 10 degrees of freedom, this is not statistically significant at the .05 level.

Table 2 also shows the fit for the Philadelphia cohort. Here, the best fit had parameters $\alpha = 0.280$, $\beta = 0.2745$. Although the chi-square of 68.69 for the model was highly significant at the .05 level, a value that large is not disturbing when account is taken of the sample size (just under 10,000).

9. Rowe et al. (1990) achieve equally good fits by assuming that the distribution of criminality follows a lognormal distribution.

Indeed, the ratio of chi-square to sample size—which measures the magnitude of discrepancies in the aggregate—is smaller for this sample than for the London sample.

Table 1. Offense Distribution in Richmond, California*

Number of Offenses	Observed Frequencies	Predicted Frequencies
0	.6300	.6298
1	.1531	.1529
2	.0816	.0773
3	.0429	.0459
4	.0255	.0291
5	.0189	.0193
6 or More	.0480	.0457

* N = 2,587, α = 0.316, β = 0.301, λ = 1.05, chi-square = 2.60.
SOURCE: Gottfredson and Hirschi (1988).

Substantively, the fit for this model is acceptable; only one difference between observed and predicted proportions was in excess of .01. Although the fit could be improved further by allowing for a slight departure from the gamma distribution, such a modification would probably be unique to the particular cohort at hand. For present purposes, there would be little point to such overfitting.[10]

10. One reason this is so is that tables are being modeled for rates of involvement that have been aggregated over offense categories. Suppose that participation in each kind of delinquency is governed by a Poisson process that operates independently of involvement in other kinds of delinquency and that the rate parameter for each process is gamma distributed with different parameters for each type of delinquency. The distribution for the aggregate rate will depart from a gamma distribution to the extent that the individual beta parameters are different from one another.

Table 2. Offense Distributions in London and Philadelphia

Number of Offenses	London[a] Observed	London[a] Predicted	Philadelphia[b] Observed	Philadelphia[b] Predicted
0	.6692	.6680	.6506	.6506
1	.1237	.1235	.1622	.1429
2	.0530	.0633	.0653	.0718
3	.0480	.0393	.0346	.0428
4	.0253	.0266	.0242	.0274
5	.0253	.0189	.0163	.0184
6	.0051	.0138	.0098	.0127
7	.0101	.0103	.0086	.0089
8	.0051	.0078	.0057	.0064
9	.0051	.0060	.0039	.0046
10	.0025	.0046	.0039	.0033
11 or More	.0276	.0179	.0148	.0102

[a] N = 396, $\alpha = 0.22$, $\beta = 0.19$, $\lambda = 1.16$, chi-square = 8.11.
[b] N = 9,945, $\alpha = 0.280$, $\beta = 0.2745$, $\lambda = 1.02$, chi-square = 68.69.
SOURCES: London cohort, from Blumstein et al. (1985). Philadelphia, from Wolfgang, et al. (1972:68, 162).

The Racine, Wisconsin, data set includes information on the criminal careers of girls as well as boys (Table 3). In the best-fitting model for nontraffic police contacts to age 30 in the 1942 female birth cohort, $\alpha = 0.20$, $\beta = 0.32976$, with a chi-square of 1.73. With 5 degrees of freedom, this is not statistically significant at the .05 level. The comparable best-fitting model for boys has $\alpha = 0.55$, $\beta = 0.14056$, with chi-square = 17.66. Although the fit is not as good as for girls, the differences between observed and predicted proportions are not statistically significant at the .05 level.[11]

11. Fits for total police contacts, including traffic offenses, were comparably good.

Table 3. Racine Offense Distributions, By Sex

	Females[a]		Males[b]	
Number of Offenses	Observed Proportions	Predicted Proportions	Observed Proportions	Predicted Proportions
0	.7653	.7566	.3006	.3162
1	.1264	.1138	.2135	.1525
2	.0397	.0513	.1096	.1036
3	.0217	.0283	.0815	.0772
4	.0181	.0170	.0506	.0601
5	.0289	.0330	.0225	.0479
6			.0309	.0389
7			.0225	.0319
8			.0140	.0264
9			.0281	.0220
10			.0169	.0184
11 or More			.1098	.1049

[a] $N = 277$, $\alpha = 0.20$, $\beta = 0.32976$, $\lambda = 0.61$, chi-square $= 1.73$.
[b] $N = 356$, $\alpha = 0.55$, $\beta = 0.14056$, $\lambda = 3.91$, chi-square $= 17.66$.
SOURCE: Shannon (1988:142).

DISCUSSION OF THE MODELS

The fits just obtained are perfectly adequate. Consequently, the good fits that Blumstein and Moitra (1980) and Blumstein et al. (1985) have obtained on the basis of different assumptions regarding criminal careers provide no clear support for the features of their model. In particular, the fits do not demonstrate that individuals involved in criminal activity either desist or continue committing crimes at approximately constant rates as they get older.

To examine the other issues at stake in the careers controversy, it is necessary to explore some of the implications of the compound Poisson model for recidivism. The discussion first considers the relationship between crime and demographic variables, then the nature of the age-crime relationship.

CRIME AND DEMOGRAPHIC VARIABLES

If the recidivism rate $r(n)$ is defined as the proportion of those who have committed n offenses who then go on to commit at least one additional offense in a given amount of time, it follows from the model that as n increases, $r(n)$ increases as well. This can be seen intuitively by noting that the offenders who commit n offenses can come from any part of the gamma distribution. Even an individual with a low lambda can, by chance, commit a large number of offenses in a short time. However, this is highly unlikely.

The higher the number of offenses, the higher the proportion of offenders that will have relatively high values of lambda. The proportion that will commit another offense in a given time span will consequently increase with n. This will happen even in the absence of reinforcement or "labeling" effects. It arises entirely from selection.

This intuitive reasoning can be made mathematically precise by invoking Bayes' Theorem, which relates the conditional probabilities $p(\lambda|n)$ and $p(n|\lambda)$ to the unconditional probabilities $p(\lambda)$ and $p(n)$:

$$p(\lambda|n) = p(n|\lambda)p(\lambda)/p(n). \tag{5}$$

Substituting from Equations (1), (2), and (4),

$$p(\lambda|n) = \frac{\beta(\beta\lambda)^{n+\alpha-1}(1 + t/\beta)^n e^{-(\beta+t)\lambda}}{\Gamma(n + \alpha)}. \tag{6}$$

For $n = 0$, this expression declines monotonically from $\lambda = 0$ to $\lambda = \infty$. For $n \geqslant 1$, the conditional probability density has a maximum determined by the condition $dp(\lambda|n)/d\lambda = 0$. Taking the derivative,

$$\lambda_{max} = (n + \alpha - 1)/(\beta + t). \tag{7}$$

An offender with n arrests is more likely to have a lambda that falls in an interval of given length that brackets *this* value of lambda than to have a lambda that falls in any other interval. If one had to guess an individual's lambda knowing only that he or she had experienced n arrests, this value of lambda would be the best guess.

The heterogeneous geometric distribution posited by Blumstein et al. (1985) also features recidivism that increases with offense number, but for a different reason. In their model, desisters drop out of the sample, leaving a population of relatively incorrigible persisters with high rates of recidivism. However, as seen earlier, one can reproduce recidivism rates that increase with offense number without assuming that there are any desisters. That the present model predicts recidivism rates that increase with n, but to a declining degree, can be seen in Figure 1, which shows the observed and predicted recidivism rates for the Philadelphia sample.[12]

It is noteworthy that λ_{max} increases linearly with n, approaching $n/(1 + \beta)$ asymptotically. The proportional change in λ_{max} for proportional change in α is $\alpha/(n + \alpha + 1)$. For even moderate n, λ_{max} is relatively insensitive to α. It

12. To avoid computing rates on the basis of very small cell frequencies, I have aggregated the rates for large n into the category $n = 5$ or more. The curves for London and Richmond are so similar that they cannot easily be shown on the same graph.

Figure 1. Observed and Predicted Recidivism Rates for the Philadelphia Cohort

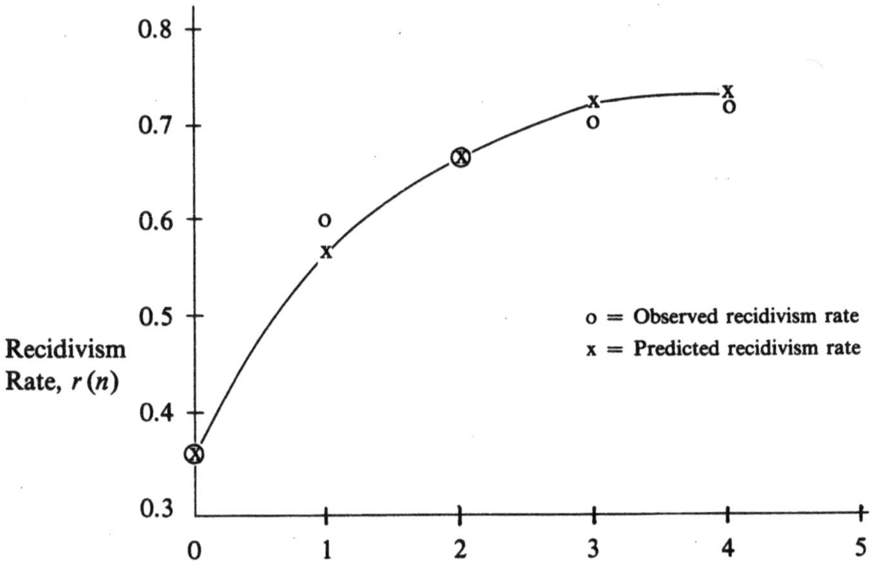

follows that when one has two populations that differ primarily in the parameter α, and one selects samples of these populations that have already committed some number of offenses, the two samples will have distributions of lambda that are more alike than the original distributions in the unselected populations. Consequently, the rates of recidivism in these samples will be closer to one another than in the unselected population.

This feature of the model provides a ready explanation of the finding that in multivariate analyses of parole performance, once other predictor variables are taken into account, the prisoner's race or ethnicity has little or no predictive value (Blumstein and Cohen, 1987; Blumstein and Graddy, 1982; Kassebaum et al., 1971:258, 270), even though blacks in the population have substantially higher rates of infraction for many types of offenses than do whites. Most inmates have committed quite a few offenses by the time they are imprisoned;[13] consequently, they will have been selected for prison in a manner that tends to filter out low-frequency offenders. This selection

13. For a substantial number of these offenses, they were not arrested; some arrests will have been dismissed or will have resulted in dispositions that did not involve imprisonment (acquittal, nonincarcerative sentences).

screens out more of the white population than the black, leaving white and black offenders who, for the most part, have high lambdas.

These principles can be seen at work by comparing the observed distribution of offenses for white and nonwhite youths in the Philadelphia cohort. The two empirical distributions are shown in Table 4, along with the predicted distributions obtained by fitting the observations to a negative binomial

Table 4. Philadelphia Offense Distributions by Race

	Blacks[a]		Whites[b]	
Number of Arrests	Observed Proportions	Predicted Proportions	Observed Proportions	Predicted Proportions
0	.4976	.4900	.7136	.7115
1	.1737	.1631	.1575	.1448
2	.0851	.0950	.0572	.0639
3	.0589	.0632	.0246	.0332
4	.0407	.0447	.0175	.0186
5	.0310	.0327	.0102	.0108
6 or More	.1130	.0327	.0195	.0172

[a] N = 2,902, $\alpha = 0.40$, $\beta = 0.202$, $\bar{\lambda} = 1.98$, chi-square = 7.66.
[b] N = 7,043, $\alpha = 0.30$, $\beta = 0.474$, $\bar{\lambda} = 0.63$, chi-square = 31.48.
SOURCE: Wolfgang et al. (1972:54).

separately for each group, using the procedure described in Appendix 1. The fit to the nonwhite sample is spectacular. The fit for the white youths is not as good, but considering the sample size, it is adequate.

Although the mean incidence of arrests (and hence the mean lambda) is about three times higher for nonwhites than for whites, the ratio of peak lambdas for nonwhites and whites who have committed one offense is just 1.55. For those who have committed five offenses, it is only 1.26.

Recidivism rates for nonwhites and whites also converge. The predicted recidivism rates of nonwhites and whites who have committed one offense are, respectively, 0.65 and 0.45; the rates for those who have committed five offenses are 0.78 and 0.66, a smaller difference. The observed rates match these predictions closely.

The same reasoning can be applied to sex differences. The mean number of arrests per person is 3.91 for the Racine males, 0.61 for the females, a ratio of 6.41. After one offense, there is still a substantial disparity between male and female recidivism rates: 0.69 compared with 0.46, but the ratio is much less than the ratio of arrest rates. After four offenses, the rates are 0.83 and 0.62. The convergence is slow because the difference in initial rates is so large, but as offense number increases, the rates come closer together.

Although the model predicts the convergence of recidivism rates of blacks and whites, and of males and females, as the number of prior offenses increases, for any finite number of prior offenses, there will be some disparity. The magnitude of this disparity can be assessed by supposing that individuals are observed for a period t_1, and then for a subsequent period t_2. It follows from the assumption of the model that offenses in the two time periods are independent. It can be shown (the derivation is in Appendix 2) that the probability that an individual who has committed n_1 offenses in the first time period will recidivate by committing one or more offenses in the second time period is

$$1 - \left(\frac{\beta + t_1}{\beta + t_1 + t_2} \right)^{n_1 + \alpha} .$$

By inserting the parameters for blacks and whites from the best-fitting models of Table 4, it is possible to compare the probability that blacks and whites who have committed any given number of offenses will recidivate in a follow-up period of given length. When this is done, one finds the probability of recidivism, given any specific number of previous offenses, to be higher for blacks in the Philadelphia study than for whites. This is exactly what was found (Wolfgang et al., 1972).[14]

It follows that a single conceptual framework is capable of accounting for pronounced racial differences in overall levels of participation in crime and for much more modest differences in recidivism.[15] Just as Hirschi and Gottfredson argue, there is no need to introduce separate explanations for different career stages. In light of their argument that longitudinal research is largely irrelevant for criminology (Hirschi and Gottfredson, 1983, 1986), it is ironic that this confirmation was obtained through the application of a temporal model for careers to longitudinal data for a cohort.

The above analysis makes clear that all parties to the careers debate have been mistaken about the implications of their assumptions for the correlation

14. Hirschi and Gottfredson (1985) have objected on political grounds to the statement that recidivism rates for blacks are higher than those for whites, but they have not offered reasons for thinking that the Philadelphia data are misleading on this point. The difference is predicted from a model that seems to embody the theoretical assumptions they themselves favor.

15. Rowe et al. (1990) have also noted that models of this general type can explain the racial patterns in recidivism observed in the Philadelphia cohort study. The observed relationship between socioeconomic status (SES) and criminality is not so readily accommodated within Gottfredson and Hirschi's unitary framework. A study of juvenile delinquency in a Sacramento birth cohort found that rates of involvement were slightly higher for low-SES youths than for others, but their rates of recidivism were lower (Wedge, 1981:31). This is evidence for the existence of social factors that impinge on career trajectories.

between demographic variables and different indicators of criminality. Blumstein et al. (1988a, 1988b) find support for their approach in the fact that correlations between criminality and such demographic variables as race and sex, change when criminality is measured by indicators that tap different dimensions of the career, for example, participation compared with the rate of involvement on the part of active criminals. Gottfredson and Hirschi (1988) accept this argument, but they deny that there are substantial differences in the correlations when different indicators of criminality are employed.

Both sides have accepted a premise that is mistaken. Because of the selection feature at work when recidivism is conditioned on number of previous offenses, recidivism rates are expected to show lower correlations with demographic variables than participation rates, even when a single, uniform process governs all phases of the career. If Gottfredson and Hirschi are correct, the correlations cannot be invariant across different indicators of a career. The evidence that there are some substantial differences in these correlations cannot be used to dismiss their approach.

THE AGE-CRIME RELATIONSHIP

As noted above, the nature of the age-crime relationship has been debated. In the aggregate, per capita arrest rates decline with age (Cline, 1980; Greenberg, 1977, Hirschi and Gottfredson, 1983). In the compound Poisson model analyzed here, there is no desistance from crime, and all lambdas remain constant with time. Under these circumstances the amount of crime committed by a set of offenders will not diminish with age, but will instead remain constant. This deficiency of the model can be remedied in several ways.[16] One is to let lambda depend explicitly on time. Copas and Tarling (1988) have proposed a convenient parameterization, in which $\lambda(t) = \lambda_{\infty}[1 + \sigma\exp(-\mu t)]$. Under this assumption, all offenders experience a uniform decline in criminality as they get older. This is exactly the pattern that Hirschi and Gottfredson (1983, 1985) hold to be the case empirically. One can preserve the distribution of cases across individuals by assuming that λ_{∞} is gamma distributed. Consequently, none of the results obtained thus far would be altered.

Before opting for this strategy, however, it should be noted that Hirschi and Gottfredson's conclusion that all offenders experience a uniform decline in offense rates over time has been vigorously disputed by Blumstein et al. (1988a, 1988b), who claim to have identified active offenders whose lambdas do not decline with time.[17]

16. A more complete discussion of some of these options, along with others, can be found in Holden (1983), Lehoczky (1986), and Copas and Tarling (1988).

17. Peterson and Braiker (1981) found that among prison inmates overall rates of offending declined with time, but offense-specific rates did not. Inmates tended to abandon

Although this disagreement cannot be fully resolved here, it is relevant that some of the evidence Blumstein and colleagues present can be given a very different interpretation. They compute the ratio of offenses per active offender and note that in the Philadelphia cohort, as well as in earlier research by Sheldon and Eleanor Glueck, the annualized lambda for active offenders computed on a year-by-year basis is roughly constant over time, even though the aggregate number of offenses committed by the entire cohort under consideration drops with time.[18] It appears, then, that among those actively violating the law, the rate of infractions does not decline with age. The aggregate decline is largely due to the desistance of some offenders.

From the point of view of the heterogeneous Poisson model, the distinction between an active and an inactive offender is dubious. Behaviorally speaking, one is only an offender while committing an offense. Defining as active offenders only those who have committed at least one offense in a given year seems arbitrary. Why a year? Are those who commit one offense every other year not offenders in alternate years? If the answer is no, why are those who commit an offense every other day considered offenders on their days off?

In the stochastic model developed here, the distinction between offenders and nonoffenders is meaningless. Everyone has a nonvanishing lambda, which may change over time, but by chance a fraction of the sample will fail to commit an offense in a given year. However, the model permits one to compute a crime rate per active offender using the Blumstein et al. definition.

For the entire population, the mean of a negative binomial distribution is given by $\bar{n} = \alpha/\beta$. This is the mean number of offenses per capita for the entire cohort. The mean number of offenses *per active offender* is computed by dividing this number by that proportion of the cohort that has at least one offense in the given year,[19] that is, $n^{\#} = \alpha/\beta(1 - p_0)$. From Equation (4), however, $p_0 = (1 + 1/\beta)^{-\alpha}$. Consequently,

$$n^{\#} = \alpha/\beta[1 - (1+1/\beta)^{-\alpha}]. \quad (8)$$

To see how $n^{\#}$ behaves when lambda changes with time, recall that the mean lambda in the gamma distribution is given by α/β. One can make this decline with time by letting this ratio decline. For illustrative purposes, suppose that in time period 1, $\alpha_1 = \beta_1 = 0.20$, figures comparable to those in the

some forms of crime, that is, to become more specialized with time. Greenberg (1985), Farrington (1986), and Steffensmeier et al. (1989) also present evidence that the rate of decline in criminal offense rates is not uniform for all offenders.

18. Gottfredson and Hirschi (1988) cite some of this evidence as well, evidently not realizing that it runs directly counter to their own claims about the age-crime relationship.

19. Blumstein et al. (1988b) attempted a similar procedure, computing $p_o = \exp(-\lambda t)$ from the Poisson distribution. Unfortunately, that procedure is inapplicable when the sample is heterogeneous with respect to lambda.

cohorts whose fits were presented here, and in the second time period, $\alpha_2 = 0.10$, $\beta_2 = 0.20$. In the first period, the mean lambda and mean offense rates will be one offense per year; half that in the second period. However, because the shape of the gamma distribution that represents the proportion of individuals with different propensities to commit crimes has shifted between times 1 and 2, more people in the second time period will abstain from committing an offense in that period.

Computing directly from Equation (8), $n_1^{\#} = (0.2)/(0.2)[1 - (6)^{-.2}] = 3.32$, and $n_2^{\#} = 0.1/(0.2)[1 - (4.33)^{-.1}] = 3.05$. Even though the offense rate has dropped by 50%, the effective lambda, or offense rate per active offender, has dropped by only 8%. It follows from l'Hospital's rule that in the limit where α approaches zero, $n^{\#} = 1/\beta[1n(1 + 1/\beta)]$. When $\beta = 0.2$, this is 2.79, or 84% of the value when $\alpha = 0.20$. It follows that an offense rate per active offender that remains relatively constant over time can be reconciled with a lambda that declines dramatically over time.

To say this is not to deny that some offenders may truly desist. Sudden conversions may be rare in the criminal world, but if Saul of Tarsus was capable of a radical conversion, so are run-of-the-mill criminals. Individuals who have abruptly abandoned a life of active crime are not altogether unknown to criminologists.[20] The pessimism that informs Hirschi and Gottfredson's position is not altogether unwarranted, but it is too extreme. Moreover, a modest decline in the predicted effective lambda is still a decline that cannot be reconciled with an observed constancy.

If this empirical constancy truly represents persistent violation of the law at constant frequency on the part of some subpopulation of offenders, and not behavior on the part of the police or courts, some other offenders must be desisting, or else lambda must be changing at rates that are not uniform across the offender population. It follows that there must be an element of truth to the Blumstein et al. position, even if there proves to be considerably less true desistance than they suggest.

Several possibilities for incorporating this desistance or change into the model can be suggested. One is to introduce positive reinforcement into the model. The Eggenberger–Polya model, in which $\lambda = (c + dn)/(1 + \sigma t)$, with c, d, and σ positive and n an integer, is particularly attractive for this purpose because it leads to a negative binomial distribution of cases across individuals, just as the stationary heterogeneous Poisson model does. In this

20. West (1978), for example, reports that half of the 40 high-rate juvenile thieves he studied had retired from criminality by age 20. As high-rate offenders, this would not be possible under the Hirschi and Gottfredson model. To all appearances, a couple of distinguished criminologists have also managed to desist from crime altogether, after intensive early involvement.

model, offenders' lambdas decline with time, but through positive reinforcement or labeling, they increase with offense number *n*. However, a linear dependence of lambda on *n* is implausible. More likely, there are saturation effects. Moreover, this model does not predict an aggregate decline in a cohort's offense rate with time. Consequently, a model that incorporates stronger time dependence is needed. The Copas–Tarling model may be better.

Another possibility is to let lambda depend explicitly on variables that are believed to influence levels of criminality and to use the gamma distribution (or some other family of curves) to model the residuals. These variables provide an avenue by which social influences on criminal careers can be introduced. Such variables will, in general, have a nontrivial time dependence that varies across individuals, and thus, they could cause lambda to decline for some individuals and not others. This approach would be one vehicle for introducing social influences into the model. However, given current uncertainties about the extent to which such variables can explain the age variation in criminal behavior (Hirschi and Gottfredson, 1983), it is possible that this approach could leave a substantial part of the variation, unexplained.

If one wishes to introduce true desistance, one might incorporate into the model a probability that an individual's lambda is instantaneously reduced to zero after a given offense or as a function of age (Barnett et al., 1987, 1989; Blumstein and Moitra, 1980; Blumstein et al., 1985). Perhaps some fraction of offenses will provide negative reinforcement (the attempted theft that yields no booty, the assault that ends with the assaulter being pummeled, the narrow escape from arrest or conviction, the criminal justice sanction that actually deters). Or, if total desistance is too strong an assumption, the switch might be to a low but nonvanishing lambda (Carr–Hill and Carr–Hill, 1972; Greenberg, 1978). These probabilities can be made conditional on other events happening, such as marriage, getting a job, joining the army, being sent to prison.[21]

The study of these models will require data for individuals, rather than the aggregates studied here, however.

FURTHER IMPLICATIONS

That the compound Poisson model can account for major features of recidivism data does not mean that it is correct. As shown, models based on different assumptions can also account for these features.[22] Nevertheless, the

21. Rand (1987) discusses the evidence that particular kinds of life events lead to desistance from crime. West (1978) found that desistance from high-intensity youthful theft in this sample was strongly associated with job and school status and entering into a "conventional relationship" with a woman.

22. Rowe et al. (1988), for example, were able to show that the convergence of white

success of the compound Poisson model so far suggests that it must be taken seriously as a model for the temporal evolution of criminal careers.

Assuming for the sake of discussion that the assumptions of the model are at least approximately valid, the reasons for this validity require explanation. The assumption that most requires such an exploration is obviously the gamma distribution for criminality. Statistical considerations readily explain its relevance to the lifetimes of complex machines (Parzen, 1962:132–34) and to certain problems in geology (Einstein, 1937). The reasons it works so well in modeling criminal careers in a number of geographically separated populations are less clear.

For the moment, then, the gamma distribution must be taken as an empirical generalization. Much like the inverse-square law of gravitational attraction, it helps to organize various pieces of information, and it allows one to make predictions. In the long run, it needs to be explained. The fact that the gamma distribution also provides a good fit to consumer purchases of nondurable goods (Ehrenberg, 1959), work-place accidents (Arbous and Kerrich, 1951; Greenwood, 1950; Newbold, 1927), scientific publications (Allison, 1980), episodes of psychiatric hospitalization for schizophrenia (Eaton, 1974; Eaton and Fortin, 1978), employee absenteeism (Arbous and Sichel, 1954), and criminal victimizations (Nelson, 1980) suggests that the explanation is not specifically criminological, but entails more general social processes.

As observed above, the gamma distribution's properties of being asymmetrical and nonnegative may be significant. Because so much of statistical theory has revolved around the normal distribution, analysts are accustomed to assuming that all variables of sociological interest should be distributed normally. Yet many are not. Arguably, many variables of sociological or criminological interest are nonnegative. Their distributions might well be approximated by the gamma.

The matter is made more complicated by the fact that other distributions of lambda provide comparably good fits to the aggregate recidivism data.[23] The flexibility provided by the existence of one or two free parameters is adequate to fit monotonically declining frequency distributions for many different families of functions. In principle, it would be desirable to distinguish among them; in practice, it is not easy to do. To see why, note that the number of

and nonwhite recidivism rates in the Philadelphia birth cohort could be explained by a model in which some proportion of offenders desist at random after each offense. This is essentially the assumption that Blumstein et al. (1985) made. In subsequent work, Rowe and his collaborators have abandoned this feature of their model.

23. See note 9 above.

offenses n that a given offender commits in time t can be considered a measurement of that offender's criminality. It is, however, an imperfect measurement. Consequently, one can write

$$n_t = \lambda + \epsilon_t. \tag{9}$$

The errors are random and independently distributed, with a variance that declines with time. To measure the distribution of lambda with precision requires measurements taken over a period of time. Although the precision of an estimate of *constant* lambda will improve with the duration of the collection period, so will the likelihood that lambda itself has changed during the collection period.

Further consequences of a measurement-error approach to the compound Poisson model are also noteworthy. The discrepancy between n_t and λ has implications for the prediction of criminal events (Lundberg, 1940; Newbold, 1927). Suppose Z is an exogenous individual attribute that gives rise to different levels of criminality in individuals. If criminality, or lambda, was measured with perfect accuracy, one could determine the usefulness of knowledge of Z in predicting lambda by examining the correlation between the two variables. However, when observations are made for a finite time span, one observes n, the number of offenses actually committed, rather than lambda.

If the correlation between Z and lambda is $r_{Z\lambda}$, the correlation between n and Z will be attenuated because of the measurement error. By direct computation of the correlation,

$$r_{nZ} = r_{\lambda Z}\sqrt{\text{var}(\lambda)/\text{var}(n)}.$$

When lambda is distributed as a gamma function, this can be shown to equal

$$r_{\lambda Z}\sqrt{t/(t + \beta)}.$$

In a multivariate problem, the standardized regression coefficients representing the effects of a vector of predictors $\{Z_k\}$ will also be attenuated. Because the partial regression coefficients depend nonlinearly on the zero-order correlations, this attenuation will not be uniform for all the regression coefficients; it will depend on the correlations among the predictors. Nonetheless, the attenuation will reduce the predictive power of the variables. In addition, this bias in the estimation of the regression coefficients will reduce the predictive accuracy of the estimated regression equation when applied to a later time period.

For much the same reason, even though an individual's criminality is assumed to be perfectly stable over time, the correlation between the criminal offenses individuals commit in time 1 and those they commit in time 2 will be (assuming the two periods are of equal duration), $\text{var}(\lambda)/\text{var}(n) = t/(t + \beta)$, which is less than 1. It follows that past criminal record is an imperfect predictor of future criminal record, even when individuals do not change at all over time. Some individuals who committed offenses in time 1 will not do so in time 2, and vice versa. Because the error variance declines with time, this loss of predictive accuracy will decline with the length of the follow-up. For follow-ups of given duration, the loss of predictive accuracy will be greatest for distributions in which beta is large, that is, in which the mean value of lambda is high relative to its variance.

POLICY CONSIDERATIONS

This analysis has addressed primarily scientific questions, not public policy. Yet, there may be policy implications that should not be altogether ignored. Although research on criminal careers can be undertaken for a variety of purposes, the work of Blumstein and his collaborators has had as one of its aims the exploration of a series of questions concerning a penal policy of selective incapacitation.

In themselves, neither the desistance model developed by Blumstein et al. nor the uniform decline model of Hirschi and Gottfredson requires that a policy of selective incapacitation be adopted, or even favors such a policy. To the degree that desistance occurs and is unpredictable, the model of Blumstein et al. would seem to weigh against such a policy, for if a crime career ends during the period of preventive confinement, the efficiency of incarceration in preventing crime will be reduced. If Hirschi and Gottfredson are correct in holding that criminality declines more or less uniformly with age, then many offenders will be "over the hill" by the time they are old enough to be plausible candidates for preventive incarceration.

Nevertheless, there is an aura surrounding the Blumstein model that in a certain sense does seem to favor selective incapacitation. This bias, which I believe is present regardless of whether Blumstein and his collaborators themselves actually favor selective incapacitation, arises from the assumption that offenders consist of discrete groups—innocents, desisters, and chronic or persistent offenders. Perhaps this is just a convenient analytical device—a mathematical assumption for building a model that fits some curves—as they themselves remark. Yet, it is only too easy to forget that these terms characterize a model and to assume that when Blumstein et al. (1985) are speaking of persistent, high-recidivism offenders, they are talking about a distinct species of offenders in the real world.

It is psychologically easier, I suggest, to overcome normative reservations about incarcerating on the basis of predicted future acts rather than past conduct, when one believes that those to be incarcerated are a different, criminal breed, not like the rest of us. If candidates for incarceration are members of a feared or despised minority group, as is often the case in American courts today, such beliefs are especially easy to accept.

Conversely, a model that views criminality as continuous imposes a higher psychological threshold to selective incapacitation. It does so because there is no "natural" and obvious cutting point to divide candidates for preventive detention from those to be released. Elegant, formal cost-benefit models can be worked out,[24] but given the practical difficulties of achieving precision in cost-benefit analyses of crime-control interventions,[25] any cutting point is bound to appear somewhat arbitrary and difficult to justify.[26]

This potential for bias becomes even stronger because of the tendency of naive laypersons to oversimplify, misunderstand, or lose sight of distinctions and qualifications that criminologists make about their work and consider important. This point was brought home recently when a scientist-colleague who is not a criminologist told me that he had heard Al Blumstein speak about criminal career research. He "learned" that we now have the capacity to identify "career criminals" with high precision while they are still very young, and he added that it was much to be regretted that public sentimentality about young children stood in the way of our solving the crime problem through very long periods of preventive imprisonment for such pre-career criminals.

Now, Blumstein and his co-workers have been extremely responsible in acknowledging the limits of prediction.[27] Their papers have never advocated a policy of this kind (see, e.g., Blumstein, 1983), and I do not believe that they have done so in oral presentations either.[28] But this may be the message that even highly educated noncriminologists carry away. Although criminologists cannot be blamed for laypersons' misunderstandings, those misunderstandings can themselves become a political reality that will have public consequences. Under these circumstances, it may be especially important that criminologists continue to explore a range of models for criminal careers.

24. For one example, see Blumstein et al. (1985).

25. See, for example, Greenberg (in press).

26. Whether this is good or bad will depend on how one assesses the desirability of such a policy.

27. Blumstein and Moitra (1980), for example, express skepticism about a selective incapacitation program on the basis of the difficulty they had in predicting who among the Philadelphia cohort subjects would be a "chronic offender."

28. Blumstein et al. (1985) note that it is inconceivable that juveniles would be subjected to imprisonment because they were having difficulty with school or came from families that had low incomes. Such predictors, they suggest, might more plausibly be made the basis for helpful, preventive measures.

REFERENCES

Ahn, Chul W., Alfred Blumstein, and Mark Scherbish
1990 Estimation of arrest careers using hierarchical stochastic models. Journal of Quantitative Criminology 6:131–152.

Allison, Paul David
1980 Processes of Stratification in Science. New York: Arno.

Arbous, A.G. and J.E. Kerrich
1951 Accident statistics and the concept of accident proneness. Biometrics 7:340–432.

Arbous, A.G. and H.S. Sichel
1954 New techniques for the analysis of absenteeism data. Biometrika 41:77–90.

Barnett, Arnold and Anthony J. Lofaso
1985 Selective incapacitation and the Philadelphia cohort data. Journal of Quantitative Criminology 1:3–36.

Barnett, Arnold, Alfred Blumstein, and David P. Farrington
1987 Probablistic models of youthful criminal careers. Criminology 25:83–108.
1989 A prospective test of a criminal career model. Criminology. 27:373–385.

Blumstein, Alfred
1983 Selective incapacitation as a means of crime control. American Behavioral Scientist 27:87–108.

Blumstein, Alfred and Jacqueline Cohen
1979 Estimation of individual crime rates from arrest records. Journal of Criminal Law and Criminology 70:561–585.
1987 Characterizing criminal careers. Science 237:985–991.

Blumstein, Alfred and Elizabeth Graddy
1982 Prevalence and recidivism in index arrests: A feedback model. Law and Society Review 16:265–290.

Blumstein, Alfred and Soumyo D. Moitra
1980 The identification of "career criminals" from "chronic offenders" in a cohort. Law and Policy Quarterly 2:321–334.

Blumstein, Alfred, David P. Farrington, and Soumyo D. Moitra
1985 Delinquency careers: Innocents, desisters, and persisters. In Michael Tonry and Norval Morris (eds.), Crime and Justice, An Annual Review of Research. Vol. 6.

Blumstein, Alfred, Jacqueline Cohen, Jeffrey A. Roth, and Christy A. Visher (eds.)
1986 Criminal Careers and "Career Criminals." 2 vols. Washington, D.C.: National Academy Press.

Blumstein, Alfred, Jacqueline Cohen, and David P. Farrington
1988a Criminal career research: Its value for criminology. Criminology 26:1–35.
1988b Longitudinal and criminal career research: Further clarifications. Criminology 26:57–74.

Carr–Hill, Roy A. and Clive D. Payne
1971 Crime: Accident or disease: An exploration using probability models for the generation of macro-criminological data. Journal of Research in Crime and Delinquency 8:133–155.

42 GREENBERG

Carr–Hill, G.A. and R.A. Carr–Hill
1972 Reconviction as a process. British Journal of Criminology 12:35–42.

Cline, Hugh
1980 Criminal behavior over the life span. In Orville Brim and J. Kagan (eds.), Constancy and Change in Development. Cambridge, Mass.: Harvard University Press.

Copas, John B. and Roger Tarling
1988 Stochastic models for analyzing criminal careers. Journal of Quantitative Criminology 4:173–186.

Derman, Cyrus, Leon J. Gleser, and Ingram Olkin
1973 A Guide to Probability Theory and Applications. New York: Holt, Rinehart & Winston.

Eaton, William W.
1974 Mental hospitalization as a reinforcement process. American Sociological Review 39:252–260.

Eaton, William W. and A. Fortin
1978 A third interpretation for the generating process of the negative binomial distribution. American Sociological Review 39:264–267.

Ehrenberg, A.S.C.
1959 The pattern of consumer purchases. Applied Statistics 8:26–41.

Einstein, Albert Jr.
1937 Der geschiebetrieb als Wahrscheinlichkeitsproblem. In Mitteilungen der Versuchanstalt für Wasserbau. Zürich: Eidgenössischen Technische Hochschule.

Farrington, David
1986 Age and crime. In Michael H. Tonry and Norval Morris (eds.), Crime and Justice: An Annual Review of Research. Vol. 7. Chicago: University of Chicago Press.

Gottfredson, Michael and Travis Hirschi
1986 The true value of lambda would appear to be zero: An essay on career criminals, criminal careers, selective incapacitation, cohort studies, and related topics. Criminology 24:213–234.
1987 The methodological adequacy of longitudinal research on crime. Criminology 25:581–614.
1988 Science, public policy, and the career paradigm. Criminology 26:37–56.
1990 A General Theory of Crime. Stanford: Stanford University Press.

Green, J.R. and D.N. Martin
1973 Absconding from approved schools as learned behavior: A statistical study. Journal of Research in Crime and Delinquency 10:73–86.

Greenberg, David F.
1977 Delinquency and the age structure of society. Contemporary Crises 1:189–224.
1978 Recidivism as radioactive decay. Journal of Research in Crime and Delinquency 15:124–125.
1979 Mathematical Criminology. New Brunswick: Rutgers University Press.
1983 Age and crime. In Sanford H. Kadish (ed.), Encyclopedia of Crime and Justice. New York: Macmillan.

1985 Age, crime, and social explanation. American Journal of Sociology 91:1–21.
In Press The cost-benefit analysis of imprisonment. Social Justice.

Greenwood, M.
1950 Accident proneness. Biometrika 37:24–29.

Greenwood, M. and G.U. Yule
1920 An inquiry into the nature of frequency distributions representative of multiple happenings with particular reference to the occurrence of multiple attacks of disease or of repeated accidents. Journal of the Royal Statistical Society 83:255.

Hirschi, Travis and Michael Gottfredson
1983 Age and the explanation of crime. American Journal of Sociology 89:552–584.
1985 Age and crime, logic and scholarship: Comment on Greenberg. American Journal of Sociology 9:22-27.
1986 The distinction between crime and criminality. In T. Hartnagel and R. Silverman (eds.), Critique and Explanation: Essays in Honor of Gwynne Nettler. New Brunswick, N.J.: Transaction Books.

Holden, T.R.
1983 Failure time models for criminal behavior. Unpublished paper, Sociology Department, Yale University, New Haven.

Kassebaum, Gene, David A. Ward, and Daniel M. Wilner
1971 Prison Treatment and Parole Survival: An Empirical Assessment. New York: John Wiley & Sons.

Lehoczky, John P.
1986 Random parameter stochastic process models of criminal careers. In Alfred Blumstein, Jacqueline Cohen, Jeffrey A. Roth, and Christy A. Visher (eds.), Criminal Careers and "Career Criminals." Vol. 2. Washington, D.C.: National Academy Press.

Lundberg, O.
1940 On Random Processes and Their Application to Sickness and Accident Statistics. Uppsala: Almquist and Wiksell.

Nelson, James F.
1980 Multiple victimization in American cities: A statistical analysis of rare events. American Journal of Sociology 85:870–891.

Newbold, Ethel M.
1927 Practical applications of the statistics of repeated events Particularly to industrial Accidents. Journal of the Royal Statistical Society 90:487–535.

Parzen, Emanuel
1962 Stochastic Processes. San Francisco: Holden–Day.

Peterson, Mark A. and Harriet B. Braiker, with Suzanne M. Polich
1981 Who Commits Crimes: A Survey of Prison Inmates. Cambridge, Mass.: Oelgeschlager, Gunn, and Hain.

Rand, Alice
1987 Transitional life events and desistance from delinquency and crime. In Marvin E. Wolfgang, Terence P. Thornberry, and Robert M. Figlio (eds.), from Boy to Man, from Delinquency to Crime. Chicago: University of Chicago Press.

Reiss, Albert J., Jr.
1986 Co-offender influences on criminal careers. In Alfred Blumstein, Jacqueline Cohen, Jeffrey A. Roth, and Christy A. Visher (eds.), Criminal Careers and "Career Criminals." Vol. 2. Washington, D.C.: National Academy Press.

Rolph, John E. and Jan M. Chaiken
1987 Identifying High-Rate Serious Criminals from Official Records. Santa Monica, Calif.: RAND.

Rowe, David C., D. Wayne Osgood, and Alan W. Nicewander
1988 A latent trait approach to unifying criminal careers. Paper presented to the American Society of Criminology. Chicago, Illinois.
1990 A latent trait approach to unifying criminal careers. Criminology 28:237–270.

Schwendinger, Herman and Julia Schwendinger
1985 Adolescent Subcultures and Delinquency. New York: Praeger.

Shannon, Lyle
1988 Criminal Career Continuity: Its Social Context. New York: Human Sciences Press.

Spilerman, Seymour
1970 The causes of racial disturbances: A comparison of alternative explanations. American Sociological Review 35:627–649.
1971 The causes of racial disturbances: Tests of an explanation. American Sociological Review 36:427–442.
1972 Strategic considerations in analyzing the distribution of racial disturbances. American Sociological Review 37:493–499.

Steffensmeier, Darrell J., Emilie Andersen Allan, Miles D. Harer, and Cathy Streifel
1989 Age and the distribution of crime: Variant or invariant? American Journal of Sociology 94:803–831.

Wedge, Robert F.
1981 Delinquency in a Sacramento Birth Cohort. Sacramento: California Youth Authority.

West, W. Gordon
1978 The short-term careers of serious thieves. Canadian Journal of Criminology 20:169–190.

Wolfgang, Marvin, Robert M. Figlio, and Thorsten Sellin
1972 Delinquency in a Birth Cohort. Chicago: University of Chicago Press.

Zatz, Marjorie S.
1982 Dynamic modeling of criminal processing histories. In John Hagan (ed.), Dynamic Modeling of Criminal Processing Histories: Innovations and Applications. Beverly Hills, Calif.: SAGE.

Zimring, Franklin
1981 Kids, groups and crime: Some implications of a well-known secret. Journal of Criminal Law and Criminology 72:867–885.

David F. Greenberg is Professor of Sociology at New York University. His most recent books include *The Construction of Homosexuality*, and *Linear Panel Analysis: Models of Quantitative Change* (with Ronald Kessler) and *Mathematical Criminology*. He is currently preparing a new edition of his *Crime and Capitalism*.

APPENDIX 1. PARAMETER ESTIMATION PROCEDURE

Standard textbooks on statistical distributions tell readers that the parameters α and β of a negative binomial distribution can be estimated from the mean and variance of the distribution of events by means of the formulas

$$\bar{n} = \alpha/\beta, \qquad \mathrm{var}(n) = (1 + t/\beta)\, \alpha t/\beta.$$

However, this procedure cannot be used when the observed distribution of events one wants to fit has been grouped. This is because the mean and variance of the distribution cannot be computed from these formulas when data have been grouped into open-ended categories like "6 or more arrests." The textbooks are silent about how to proceed under such commonly encountered circumstances. Consequently, it was necessary to improvise.

Setting $t = 1$ (the time scale is arbitrary and can be fixed for the convenience of the researcher), the predicted proportions for the negative binomial distribution for $n = 0$ and $n = 1$ are $p_0 = (1 + 1/\beta)^{-\alpha}$ and $p_1 = (\alpha/\beta)(1 + 1/\beta)^{-\alpha-1}$

The equation for p_0 can be solved for β, yielding the expression $(1 + \beta)^{-1} = 1 - p_0^{1/\alpha}$. In addition, $p_1/p_0 = \alpha/\beta(1 + 1/\beta) = \alpha/(\beta + 1)$. Eliminating the quantity $(1 + \beta)$ yields $(p_1/p_0) = \alpha(1 - p_0^{1/\alpha})$.

This equation cannot be solved analytically for α, but it can be solved numerically. Since the mean number of offenses per capita was given in the sources, once α was obtained numerically, β could be estimated from the equation $\beta = \alpha/\bar{n}$.

This procedure fits the observed proportions p_0 and p_1 exactly, but it does not necessarily provide an optimal fit to the entire distribution. From the point of view of minimizing chi-square, a difference of fixed magnitude between observed and predicted proportions is most damaging when it occurs for cells with small predicted frequencies. In this analysis, these are cells with large n. Consequently, α was varied systematically from the value obtained by this procedure, and that value was chosen that minimized chi-square for the distribution as a whole.

APPENDIX 2
RECIDIVISM PROBABILITIES

Under the assumption that offenses occurring in time periods t_1 and t_2 are statistically independent, the probability of an individual with criminality parameter lambda committing n_1 offenses in the first time period and n_2 in the second is

$$p(n_1,n_2|\lambda) = \frac{(\lambda t_1)^{n_1}}{n_1!}\frac{(\lambda t_2)^{n_2}}{n_2!}e^{-\lambda(t_1+t_2)}$$

To find the unconditional joint probability of committing n_1 offenses in the first time period and n_2 in the second, one must take the probability distribution of lambda into account:

$$p(n_1,n_2) = \int_0^\infty p(n_1,n_2|\lambda)\, p(\lambda)d\lambda$$

$$= \left(\frac{t_1}{\beta+t_1+t_2}\right)^{n_1}\left(\frac{t_2}{\beta+t_1+t_2}\right)^{n_2}\left(\frac{\beta}{\beta+t_1+t_2}\right)^{\alpha}\frac{\Gamma(n_1+n_2+\alpha)}{n_1!n_2!\Gamma(\alpha)}.$$

The conditional probability that someone who committed n_1 offenses in time t_1 will commit n_2 in time t_2 is then (Arbous and Sichel, 1954; Newbold, 1927):

$$\frac{p(n_1,n_2)}{p(n_1)} = \left(\frac{\beta+t_1}{\beta+t_1+t_2}\right)^{n_1\alpha}\left(\frac{t_2}{\beta+t_1+t_2}\right)^{n_2}\frac{\Gamma(n_1+n_2+\alpha)}{\Gamma(n_1+\alpha)n_2!}.$$

Now consider the special case of $n_2 = 0$. The conditional probability $p(0|n_1)$ represents the probability that someone who has committed n_1 offenses in the first time period commits none in the second period. Such a person has failed to recidivate during the follow-up period. The probability that such an individual does recidivate is the probability that he or she has committed one or more offenses in the follow-up period; it is simply 1 − (probability of not recidivating), or

$$1 - \left(\frac{\beta+t_1}{\beta+t_1+t_2}\right)^{n_1+\alpha}$$

Part II
The Effects of the Criminal Justice System

[6]
The Effect of Arrests on Crime: A Multivariate Panel Analysis

ABSTRACT

We estimate multiwave panel models for the effect of clearance rates and a vector of socioeconomic control variables on index crimes, using a sample of 98 U.S. cities for the years 1964–70. No consistent evidence of a substantial effect is found.

The effect of police practices on rates of law violation is a matter that has a practical bearing on crime prevention strategies. It can also enhance our understanding of the contributions made by formal methods of social control to conformity. Despite the importance of these concerns, surprisingly little is known about the effects of criminal justice institutions on crime rates. Indeed, only in recent years have researchers begun to study the degree to which crime can be reduced by marginal changes in police employment, expenditure, patrolling strategies, or efficiency in solving crimes.[1]

Statistical investigations of the relationship between aggregated rates of crimes known to the police and various indicators of police activity have employed various analytic strategies. Some researchers have analyzed cross-sectional data (Brown; Geerken and Gove; Sjoquist; Wilson and Boland, a, b); others have analyzed time series (Cloninger and Sartorius; Phillips and Votey) or panel data (Greenberg et al., a; Logan). The present analysis has been designed to meet methodological criticism of this body of research.

Critics of research dealing with the effect of law enforcement on crime rates have pointed to two important statistical sources of bias: speci-

We are grateful to Sheri L. Prupis and Barbara F. O'Meara for carrying out computer computations, and to Charles Logan for supplying data. Support for this research was received under Grants #79-NI-AX-0054 and #80-IJ-CX-0062 from the National Institute of Law Enforcement and Criminal Justice. Points of view are those of the authors and do not necessarily reflect the position of the U.S. Department of Justice. An earlier version of this paper was presented at the 1980 meeting of the American Society of Criminology.

fication bias arising from the omission of relevant variables, and simultaneous equation bias (Fisher and Nagin; Greenberg, a, c; Nagin).

Specification Bias
Since crime rates are expected to be influenced by social, economic, and demographic variables, the effect of sanction levels on crime rates can be assessed only if these other variables are taken into account. Some researchers have ignored this issue altogether, reporting analyses based only on the relationships between crime rates and sanction levels (e.g. Brown; Geerken and Gove; Greenberg et al., a, b). Other investigators have attempted to control for such effects by introducing in their equations a set of variables believed to influence crime rates. However, should variables that influence both the crime rate and the sanction level be omitted from the analysis, parameter estimates for the effect of sanctions on crime will be biased, perhaps badly.

Simultaneous Equation Bias
Ordinary least-squares (OLS) methods for estimating regression equations assume that independent variables are unaffected by the dependent variable. In the present context, this means assuming that the crime rate has no influence on the predictor variables included in a regression equation for the crime rate. There are reasons for thinking that at times this assumption may be false. It has been suggested, for example, that high levels of crime could strain the limited resources of law enforcement agencies, reducing effective sanction levels. It may also be the case that when crime rates rise, the criminal justice system responds with harsher or more certain punishment. If these, or other processes in which crime rates affect law enforcement exist, failure to take them into account could lead to seriously biased estimates for the effect of law enforcement on crime.

Simultaneous equation methods permit the effects of crime on sanctions and sanctions on crime to be determined even when feedback effects of this sort are present. However, these methods can be applied to cross-sectional or time series data only if stringent assumptions are made about the effects of exogenous variables on the jointly dependent endogenous variables. To estimate the effect of a criminal justice sanction on crime one must be able to specify a priori the precise effect that one or more exogenous variables has on crime. Since criminological theory typically does not make predictions about the magnitude of effects that are expected to be present, this is usually done by specifying that these exogenous variables have no effect at all on crime.

It is rare in criminological research that assumptions of this kind can be made with much confidence. Too little is known about the effects on crime of a good many variables for us to be able to assert with conviction that they do not influence the crime rate. Yet if the researcher makes an incorrect assumption about such effects, parameter estimates can be seriously biased. Statistical theory provides no method for discovering this bias from the parameter estimates themselves.

In their survey of the crime deterrence literature, Fisher and Nagin concluded that the assumptions made for the purposes of identifying simultaneous equation systems were often highly implausible on substantive grounds. Their conclusion that it will be difficult to arrive at an alternative set of more plausible assumptions underscores the desirability of using statistical techniques that do not entail such sharp limitations.

Researchers have begun to realize that panel data (collected for multiple units of analysis at a number of fixed times) can help to overcome the limitations of cross-sectional analyses. Thus Wilson and Boland (b) observe that information about changes in arrests and crime rates over a 5- or 10-year period would provide a surer basis for inferences about their reciprocal effects than the cross-sectional data they analyze; and Tittle, noting that the conclusions reached in his perceptual study of deviance deterrence are premised on assumptions about the causal order of variables that cannot be tested with his cross-sectional data, suggests that panel data would be helpful in this regard.

We have pointed out elsewhere (Greenberg and Kessler; Kessler and Greenberg) that panel data do not automatically resolve all questions of causal inference. One must still make some a priori statistical assumptions in order to estimate the effects of variables on one another. Under specific circumstances, though, multiwave panel data make it possible to identify simultaneous equation systems with weaker assumptions than those required when working with cross-sectional or time-series data. In addition, panel data permit partial tests of these assumptions, and allow information about the possible contribution of omitted exogenous variables to be extracted from the data.

These features make panel analysis a methodology of choice for studying the relationship between crime rates and sanctions. However, the panel analyses of crime rates published to date (Greenberg et al., a; Logan; Pontell) fail to control for the effect of exogenous variables on crime and sanctions. As we noted above, this failure can result in spurious correlations being treated as evidence of causal effects, and hence lead to biased estimates of the effect of arrests on crime. The present study deals with this possibility by extending an earlier panel analysis of crime rates and clearance rates (Greenberg et al., a) through the introduction of a set of socioeconomic control variables. The earlier study found no evidence that higher clearance rates led to lower crime rates. In the present study we are able to determine whether this conclusion holds up when appropriate control variables are taken into account.

Data and Procedures

DATA

Our analysis is based on information about crimes, clearances (crimes solved by the police, usually but not always through arrest), and a number of control variables, for a stratified random sample of 98 U.S. cities with populations of more than 25,000, for the years 1964 through 1970.[2] We explore the relationship between per capita rates for the seven index crimes and total index crimes (as measured by offenses recorded by the police), and the clearance rates for these offenses, defined as the ratio of offenses cleared to the number of offenses known to the police for that offense in that year.[3] Other influences on these variables are taken into account by introducing control variables believed on theoretical grounds to be relevant to crime causation and to police effectiveness in solving crimes.

The following variables are used in our analysis[4]:

1. *Population* (1967). A larger population implies a greater degree of anonymity, and hence weaker informal social controls. This in turn facilitates the emergence of a criminal subculture. In addition, police enforcement is less likely to be effective when victims do not know the identities of their victimizers.

2. *Population density* (1970). This variable is chosen for the same reason as *population*.

3. *Percent of the population below the age of 18* (1970). Arrest rates for teenagers are disproportionately high, probably because psychological and social stress associated with adolescence lead to higher rates of involvement in crime (Greenberg, b). Comparative lack of expertise in crime would be expected to increase the clearance rate of those in this age bracket.

4. *Percent of the labor force employed in manufacturing* (1970). We consider this variable to take account of the possible influence of labor force composition on crime. One might speculate that variability in the stress associated with different kinds of jobs is reflected in crime rates, and that blue collar parents socialize their children differently than white collar parents, in ways that have consequences for involvement in delinquency. In addition, Humphries and Wallace note that the ecological layout of manufacturing cities differs from that of cities with other kinds of economic activity in ways that can be expected to influence patterns of crime and law enforcement.

5. *Percent of the labor force that is unemployed* (1970). For offenses involving illegal acquisition, this variable measures one incentive to violate the law. Stress associated with unemployment may also be causally related to violent crimes. Individuals who are unemployed have, on the average, re-

duced prospects for future earnings, and thus risk less from an arrest than those who are presently employed. Reduced risk might be expected to result in higher crime rates.

6. *Median income* (1960). This is an index of potential victim stock for property crimes. To the extent that cultural evaluation of theft and violence are linked with socioeconomic status, median income will also control for cultural contributions to variation in crime rates. In addition, median income represents community resources available for law enforcement, and thus may indirectly influence the clearance rate.

7. *Percent of population with Spanish surnames* (1970). Minority group membership implies lower income and reduced prospects for future lawful achievement. Members of groups that have been victimized by discrimination are expected to accord less legitimacy to legal norms and law enforcement and, lacking internalized respect, less likely to conform to the law and its agents. In addition, the police may be less hesitant about arresting suspects who are members of minority groups.

8. *Percent of families headed by a female* (1970). Several delinquency theorists (Cohen; Miller) have argued that delinquency can originate in the reaction of adolescent males to a female-headed household. A household headed by a single parent may also possess fewer resources for supervising and controlling children.

9. *Skewness of income* (1970), as measured by the ratio of the standard deviation of income to median income.[5] Anomie theory (Merton) suggests that skewness of income holds out to those in low income brackets the possibility of receiving incomes that are higher than can be attained through legitimate means. This may lead to crime as an illegitimate means of achieving material goals in the absence of internalized inhibitions against stealing. Cloward and Ohlin contend that prospective thieves who fail at illegal enterprises involving theft or organized crime may turn to violence in frustration. This variable is thus potentially relevant to the genesis of violent crimes as well as theft. Inclusion of this variable is also dictated by conflict-theoretical arguments that wealthy elites strengthen police forces to cope with the threats to the social order created by economic inequality (Jacobs). The particular indicator of inequality we use has the desirable properties of being scale-free, and of being smaller for a given spread of income when overall incomes are higher.

10. *Percent of the population that is black* (1970). The rationale for the inclusion of this variable is the same as that for variable 7. We treat the two variables separately rather than lumping blacks and Hispanics into a single minority category because cultural differences and differences in family structure between the two groups may be relevant to crime causation.

11. *Regional dummy variable for northern cities.*[6] Region may be a proxy for cultural differences relevant to crime causation (e.g., subculture of violence) and law enforcement effectiveness, as well as for aspects of social structure that distinguish different regions of the U.S., but that are not fully taken into account by the other variables.

12. *Regional dummy variable for southern cities.*[7] This variable is included for the same reason as variable 11. Cities not classified as either northern or southern are western.

Comparison with the control variables employed in studies conducted by economists shows that our list taps dimensions of social life that they have not included.[8]

PROCEDURES

Because there is reason to think that the lagged and instantaneous effect of crime on clearances might be of opposite sign, we estimated models that included both lagged and instantaneous effects.[9] As theory does not tell us precisely what time-lag to expect, we estimated models with lags of one, two, and three years. We found that the autocorrelations among crime rates a year apart were extremely high—so high, in fact, that the correlation matrix could not be inverted. This means that the effect of other variables on these rates is too low over the space of a year for this effect to be distinguished statistically, given our sample size. For this reason, we examined models involving lags of two and three years.

All the models considered were variations on the model shown in Figure 1, a three-wave model involving per capita crime rates (C), clearance rates (A), and a set of exogenous control variables (Z) assumed to influence C and A. To avoid complicating the figure, the exogenous variables are omitted, and correlations among errors are not shown; however, the models estimated did take into consideration the possible existence of cross-sectional and serial correlations among error terms and higher-order autoregressive terms (e.g., the effect of A_1 on A_3, where the subscripts label the waves of observation). Models with two-year lags were estimated with data for the years 1964, 1966, 1968 and 1970; models with three-year lags, with data for 1964, 1967 and 1970.

The computer program LISREL IV (Jöreskog and Sörbom) was used to estimate all the models discussed below. We began our analysis by estimating four-wave models with a two-year time span between each wave, for each index offense separately, and for total index offenses. In these models we assumed that high-order autoregressive terms were absent, and that all correlations among errors were zero. When correlations among variables were too high to permit inversion of the correlation matrix, we considered three-wave, three-year lag models instead.

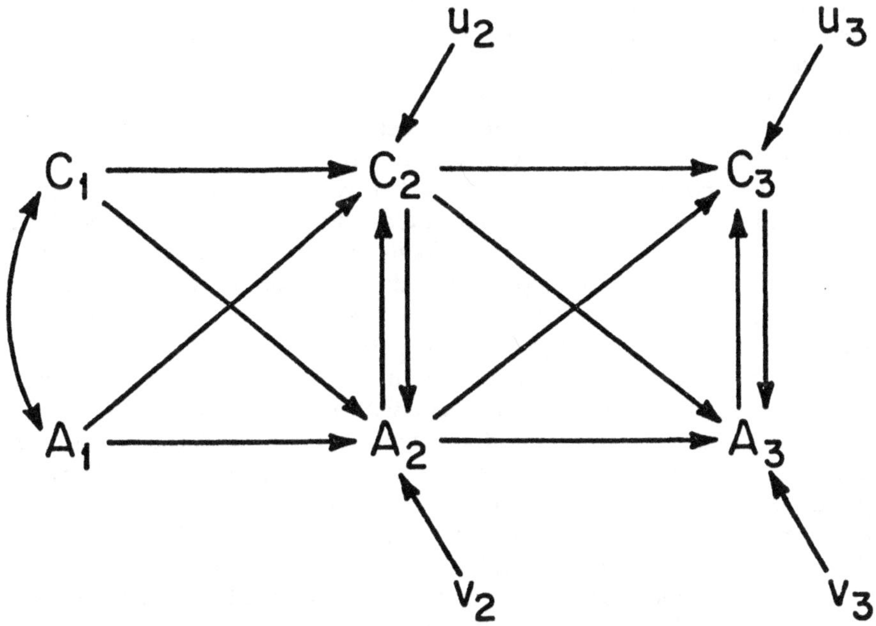

Figure 1. THREE-WAVE PANEL MODEL FOR CRIME RATES, ARREST RATES, AND EXOGENOUS CONTROL VARIABLES

In estimating the four-wave models we assumed that instantaneous standardized regression coefficients (e.g., for the influence of A_t on C_t) remain constant over time. Cross-lagged effects linking time 1 with time 2 were unconstrained, but those linking time 2 with time 3 were assumed to equal those linking time 3 with time 4. A comparison of the estimates linking times 1 and 2 with those linking 2 and 3 (or 3 and 4) then permits a partial test of the constancy assumption. No constraints were imposed on the first-order autoregressive terms, but cross-lagged effects lagged by two or more waves were assumed to be absent.

Equilibrium Conditions

Provided the crime rates–clearance rates system is not in equilibrium, these models are overidentified, with every parameter either just-identified or overidentified, even though no assumptions have been made about the magnitude of the effect of any exogenous variable on crime or on clearances. In equilibrium, on the other hand, the normal equations used to estimate model parameters are redundant, so that insufficient information is available to identify the model. Intuitively, this happens because in equilibrium multiple waves of data do not provide the additional information

778 / Social Forces Volume 60:3, March 1982

needed to identify equations; in a sense, one is seeing the same thing in each wave, so that the over-time information of panel data does not add to the information contained cross-sectionally.[10]

The assumption that the relationship between crime rates and clearance rates was not in equilibrium between 1964 and 1970 is reasonable on substantive grounds. Crime patterns began to change markedly in the early sixties. For instance, homicide rates, which had been declining for three decades, began to rise in 1963, and continued to increase through the early seventies. Victims were more likely than before to be unknown to perpetrators, slain in connection with street robberies; and were proportionally less often than before spouses or friends of the perpetrator. Clearance rates began to decline in the same period.

Some commentators have attributed changes in crime patterns in the early sixties to the disillusionment with the failure of the civil rights movement to achieve more rapid gains in the status of blacks, and declining clearance rates to restrictions imposed on the police by the U.S. Supreme Court in these years. For purposes of the present analysis, it is immaterial what the reasons were for these changes. What is important is that an external shock or constraint of some sort generated disequilibrium among our variables, at least for a time. Internal evidence from our estimates suggests that the assumption of disequilibrium is not unreasonable.

Model Revision

The models on the basis of which we draw our inferences were arrived at through a series of analyses. We first estimated the initial model described above for each offense. Where the initial model fit the data poorly, the model was revised by adding serial correlation of errors, higher-order autoregressive effects, or causal effects linking crime rates and clearance rates separated by more than one wave. The technical output provided by the LISREL program provided guidance as to which additional effects would prove helpful in improving the fit. Once an acceptable fit was obtained, effects that were small and consistent with zero at the *0.05* significance level were fixed at zero. These revised models were then reestimated. This process was repeated until a good fit was achieved *parsimoniously*. Comparison of the chi-square statistics for good-fitting models in which the effect of clearances on crime were estimated, with identical models in which these effects were fixed at zero, enabled us to determine whether a significant crime-prevention effect was present.

There is a danger that in fitting and trimming a model in this way, one will overfit the data. To protect against fitting what are essentially sampling fluctuations, a useful rule-of-thumb is to incorporate only effects that are fairly consistent over time. Some of the models arrived at by our procedure violate this principle. In some of the models, for example, we found that an effect linking time 1 and time 2 variables proved to be significant, while the corresponding effects linking time 2 with time 3 and time 3 with time 4 were small and insignificant. We decided to consider such models despite the danger of over-fitting, since the alternative was to accept models that fit the data poorly. In that case, interpretation of parameter estimates would be uncertain, and we would be faced with substantial ambiguity in model specification as well. It remains true, though, that where a given effect is found for one pair of waves but not for other pairs in the panel, our confidence that it represents a genuine effect is greatly reduced.

Findings

The best-fitting models for each offense are summarized in Table 1, which contains parameter estimates for the models with 2-year lags, and Table 2, which contains parameter estimates for the models with 3-year lags.[11]. Where more than one model provided an acceptable fit, all are shown in the table. We discuss for each offense the effect of arrests on crime, the effect of crime on arrests, and the effect of exogenous control variables on arrests and crime. Stability coefficients are given in a table in the appendix, as they are of less interest.

THE EFFECT OF ARRESTS ON CRIME

If arrests at time t reduce crime rates at time t' (where t' may or may not be the same as t), the estimated standardized coefficient $A_tC_{t'}$ should be negative and statistically significant. This proves to be true in only one of the two models that provide an acceptable fit to the murder data (Table 1). In model (a), one lagged effect is negative and statistically significant ($A_1C_2 = -.356$), but the other lagged effects (for A_2C_3 and A_3C_4) and the instantaneous effects are all consistent with zero. In model (b), all parameters for the effect of clearances on crime are fixed at zero. Model (a) fits the data significantly better than (b), but both models provide quite good fits. Evidence for a possible crime-prevention effect here is clearly very limited. The lack of consistency in the estimates for model (a), and the good fit obtained for the null model (b) lead us to conclude that we have no persuasive evidence in our data for the existence of a crime-prevention effect for murder.

For burglary, we find good fits with two different models. In model (a), the lagged effect A_1C_2 is estimated while all other lagged effects are fixed at zero; and the instantaneous effects A_tC_t are constrained to be equal. The lagged effect is extremely small, providing a check on the assumption that the parameters A_2C_3 and A_3C_4 are zero. The instantaneous effect is negative and statistically significant, but quite small in magnitude.

780 / Social Forces Volume 60:3, March 1982

Table 1. ACCEPTABLE MODELS FOR CRIME RATES (C) AND CLEARANCE RATES (A) WITH TWO-YEAR LAGS[a]

Parameter	Offense: Murder (Model I)	Murder (Model II)	Rape	Burglary (Model I)	Burglary (Model II)	Grand Larceny
A → C						
A_1C_2	-.356*			.017		
A_2C_3						
A_3C_4						
A_2C_2				-.085*		
A_3C_3				-.085*		
A_4C_4				-.085*		
C → A						
C_1A_2	-.365*			-.096		
C_2A_3						
C_3A_4						
C_1A_4	-.081					
C_2A_4			-.329*			
C_2A_2			-.291*	-.034		
C_3A_3				-.034		
C_4A_4				-.034		
C ↔ A						
C_1A_1	-.173	-.173	-.105	-.255*	-.255*	-.451*
C_2A_2	.065	.074			-.074*	
C_3A_3	-.193*	-.193*			-.052*	
C_4A_4	-.019	-.023			-.038	
Fit Statistics						
χ^2	12.47	23.14	17.46	29.06	28.13	21.81
d.f.	14	17	16	16	17	17
probability level	.50	.10	.30	.02	.02	.10
largest $S-\Sigma^b$				.068	.091	

[a] X_iY_j represents the standardized regression coefficient for the effect of X_i on Y_j.

[b] $S-\Sigma$ is the difference between the observed and predicted covariance matrix. Cell entry is the largest element in the difference matrix. Entries are given only for models in which the probability level is greater than 0.05.

*Statistically significant at the 0.05 level.

Table 2. ACCEPTABLE MODELS FOR CRIME RATES (C) AND CLEARANCE RATES (A) WITH THREE-YEAR LAGS[a]

Parameter	Offense Aggravated Assault	Robbery	Auto Theft	Total Index
A → C				
A_1C_2	.077			
A_2C_3	-.143*			
C → A				
C_1A_3			.239*	
C ↔ A				
C_1A_1	-.177*	-.215*	.456*	-.346*
C_2A_2	.053			-.012
C_3A_3	.055			-.100*
Fit Statistics				
X^2	11.09	13.82	39.61	7.37
d.f.	5	9		8
probability level	.02	.30	<.001	.30
largest $S-\Sigma^b$	.127		.070	

[a]X_iY_j represents the standardized regression coefficient for the effect of X_i on Y_j.

[b]$S-\Sigma$ is the difference between observed and predicted covariance matrix. Cell entry is the largest element in the difference matrix. Entries are given only for models in which the probability level is greater than 0.05.

*Statistically significant at the 0.05 level.

In model (b), all effects in which *A* influences *C* are fixed at zero, but cross-sectional correlations among errors are estimated (in model (a) they were fixed at zero). The fit here is also good, but not significantly better than in model (a). Thus the evidence for a crime prevention effect here is ambiguous, and the effect is small in any event.

For aggravated assault (Table 2), our best-fitting model differs significantly from the observed correlation matrix; but since the fit is substantively quite good, we proceed to interpret parameter estimates. We find a statistically significant estimate $A_2C_3 = -.143$, consistent with a crime-prevention effect. However, the estimate for A_1C_2 is smaller, positive and not statistically significant (*.077*). The lack of consistency here makes us re-

782 / Social Forces Volume 60:3, March 1982

luctant to interpret the estimate for A_2C_3 as evidence for a crime-prevention effect.

In all other offense categories, good fits to the data were obtained for models in which crime prevention effects were small and not statistically significant. When these effects were then fixed at zero and the models reestimated, good fits were still obtained; subtraction of the chi-square statistics for the two models showed the crime prevention effects to be statistically insignificant.

THE EFFECT OF CRIME ON CLEARANCE RATES

Estimates of the parameter C_tA_t, provide evidence regarding the effect of crime rates on clearance rates. For several of the models in Tables 1 and 2, we find isolated estimates for C_tA_t, parameters that are negative and statistically significant; for example, in model (a) for murder (Table 1), the parameter C_1A_2 is $-.365$, statistically significant. But the other seven parameters are either not significant ($C_1A_4 = -.081$) or consistent with zero. Thus there is no consistent evidence for a saturation effect, or for a process in which rising crime rates enhance the efficiency of law enforcement efforts. In other models such as murder (b), burglary (b), and grand larceny (Table 1), and aggravated assault, robbery, and total index offenses (Table 2), all parameters are consistent with zero.

THE EFFECT OF EXOGENOUS VARIABLES

The effect of exogenous variables can be studied in our models in two ways: through parameter estimates for the influence of control variables on our endogenous variables, and through the correlations of errors in models where these were estimated. Since the focus of this paper is on the impact of law enforcement on crime, we report our findings for the effect of the control variables on crime rates and clearance rates somewhat cursorily.[12]

With only a few exceptions, the effects of the control variables on crime rates and clearance rates were neither large nor consistent from one year to the next. A few of the variables did show consistent effects that were more than miniscule in magnitude (statistically significant at the *0.05* level or having an absolute value of at least *.10*); we confine our discussion to these contributions.

The effect of city population on murder, rape, and robbery was positive, but no such effect was found for the other offenses. The effect of population density on robbery was also positive, while its effect on clearances for murder, assault, robbery, larceny, and total index offenses was negative. Contrary to expectation, the proportion of the population below the age of 18 had no effect on crime rates. It tended to reduce the clearance rate for assault, but to increase it for auto theft.

Proportion of the labor force employed in manufacturing was found to have no consistent, substantial effect on crime rates. It did increase the clearance rate for assaults, but reduced it for auto thefts. Percent of the labor force that is unemployed had a positive effect on murder, but not on any of the other offense rates. Median income had a negative effect on rape, a positive effect on burglary, but no consistent effect on the other crime rates. The effect of this variable on clearances for rape and auto theft was negative.

Percent of the population with Spanish surnames was positively related to rape and assault; it tended to reduce clearance rates for rape, but to increase them for assaults. Percent of the population that is black was positively associated with murder, assault, robbery and auto theft, as well as with clearances for assault and robbery.

Percent of families headed by a female had no consistent effects on crime rates, but had a positive effect on clearances for robbery and larceny. Skewness of income had a negative effect on rape and no consistent effect on other crime rates. It did tend to reduce clearances for larceny and auto theft. Cities in the North had higher robbery rates and clearance rates for robbery, but lower clearances for auto theft; cities in the South had lower rates of rape and clearances for rape.

Given that the correlations of control variables with crime rates and clearances are neither negligible nor inconsistent, this failure to find stronger and more consistent effects may seem surprising. The reason for this finding, however, can readily be seen by considering the unstandardized structural equation for the crime rate:

$$C_t = a + b_1C_{t-1} + b_2A_t + b_3A_{t-1} + b_4Z_t + u_t. \tag{1}$$

For simplicity, the equation includes only a single control variable Z, but the argument will not be affected if additional control variables are present. If we subtract the quantity C_{t-1} from left-hand and right-hand members of the equation, we have

$$\Delta C_t = C_t - C_{t-1} = a + (b_1 - 1)C_{t-1} + b_2A_t + b_3A_{t-1} + b_4Z_t + u_t. \tag{2}$$

We see that the coefficient $(b - 1)$ measures the effect of the level of C on change in C, while the remaining coefficients are direct measures of the effect of A_t, A_{t-1} and Z_t on change in C. When we estimate equation (1), then, we are not estimating the effect of Z on C, but the effect of Z on *change* in C. Once this is understood, the paucity of statistically significant coefficients for the effect of our control variables on crime rates is less mysterious. We might expect, for example, that a certain level of unemployment would generate a corresponding level of crime in a city. But we would not expect a fixed level of unemployment to lead to steadily *increasing* levels of crime. The same is true for our other control variables.

Even where the control variables did contribute significantly to the regressions, their contributions were almost always quite modest. Hardly any of the standardized effects were as large as *.30* in magnitude. Comparing regressions with all control variables deleted from the regressions (reported in Greenberg et al., a) with those reported here, we find increments in the variance explained of roughly 5 percent, not a large amount. Moreover, our conclusions about the effect of arrests on crime are not substantially changed by the inclusion of these variables. In the earlier study, good fits were obtained for all offenses with models in which the effect of clearances on crime rates was fixed at zero. Here, such effects are either consistent with zero or quite small in magnitude.

The insensitivity of these conclusions to the inclusion or exclusion of the twelve control variables used here gives us confidence that our findings are unlikely to be badly biased by the omission of additional causes of crime.[13] Our confidence that this is so is strengthened by our estimates of the correlations among contemporaneous eror terms of crime rates and clearance rates. Good fits for rape, burglary (a), grand larceny, robbery, and auto theft were obtained for models in which these correlations of errors were fixed at zero; in models for murder (a), murder (b), burglary (b), aggravated assault and total index offenses these correlations were estimated; but as seen from the entries in Tables 1 and 2, the estimates proved to be invariably small. In no case did they exceed *.20* in magnitude, and in most instances they were considerably smaller. The amount of bias in estimates for the parameters A_tC_t, that could be present as a result of the omission of variables responsible for these correlations of errors could not be large.

Discussion

Our analysis finds no consistent evidence for the proposition that higher arrest clearance rates result in substantially lower index crime rates. Where parameter estimates for the effect of arrests on crime are consistent (as in the model for aggravated assault), they are quite small. When effects are larger in magnitude (as in one of the two models for murder), they are not consistent over time. For most of our models we did not even find inconsistent evidence for a crime-prevention effect of arrests.[14]

Our failure to find evidence for a crime-prevention effect contrasts with the econometric studies based on cross-sectional or time-series data, which have found evidence consistent with a crime-prevention effect. We attribute these discrepant findings to the dubious assumptions made in the econometric analyses. Cloninger and Sartorius assume that crime rates are entirely uninfluenced by socio-economic variables, and thus that law enforcement variables *alone* influence crime rates. As noted earlier, Phillips and Votey control for labor force participation alone, neglecting all other social influences on crime. Sjoquist considers a wider range of control variables, but neglects the possible reciprocal effect of crime on arrests.

In the most careful cross-sectional analysis to date, one which finds that arrests reduce crime for robbery but not for burglary, and only inconsistently for auto theft, Wilson and Boland (b) assume that police patrol strategy is affected by a city's political climate but not by its crime rate; and that patrol strategy affects the crime rate only by changing the probability of an arrest, not directly. They frankly concede that their analysis depends on the validity of these assumptions, and while they find them plausible, they cannot demonstrate that they are true. We think Wilson and Boland's assumptions are at least debatable. Crime has become a hot political issue over the last fifteen years. In this atmosphere, a city's political climate and police patrol strategies may well have been influenced by its crime pattern. Police can deter crime by appearing on the street, even if they make no arrests; indeed, it is a common experience that highway drivers will slow down when they see a squad car, even if they do not see any cars being ticketed.

Our approach, based on panel data, has obviated the need for assumptions as stringent as those made in earlier work, solely for reasons of statistical convenience. This is not to say that the present approach is entirely free from assumptions. The method we outline here assumes that parameters are stationary, and our parameter estimates are not entirely consistent with it. Fortunately, this assumption is not needed in the null models. We have assumed also that lagged effects are felt within the space of a few years; were the correct time-lag closer to a century, we would be unlikely to see any signs of a causal effect. Here our everyday knowledge about the duration of social processes comes to our aid to exclude such possibilities.

Since the assumptions we make are less stringent and more plausible than those made in earlier studies, we are inclined to attribute the discrepant findings to model misspecification in the earlier work. We were able to verify in our own data that an inappropriate cross-sectional analysis could lead to biased parameter estimates consistent with a crime-prevention effect. We did this by estimating multiple regression equations for the crime rates in 1970 using 1970 clearance rates and the 12 control variables as predictors. Here lagged endogenous variables are not included among the predictors, and no attempt is made to model the short-run effect of crime on clearances.[15] In these models, the estimated standardized regression coefficients for the effect of clearances on crime rates were: murder, −*.004*; rape, −*.128*; assault, −*.177**; robbery, −*.232**; burglary, −*.213**; auto, −*.142*; grand larceny, −*.319**; and total index offenses, −*.232** (starred parameters are significant at the *0.05* level). All eight estimates are negative, and five of them are statistically significant. This contrasts with our failure to find consistent negative estimates for these parameters in the panel analysis.

Although we find no evidence that marginal changes in clearance rates have an appreciable impact on crime rates, we are far from claiming that police practices have no effect on crime. Part of the appeal of the deterrence doctrine in its current revival at the hands of economists is that we all know from introspection and from everyday observation, that people can be made to conform by threatening them with undesirable consequences. It may be that we fail to see evidence of this in the present data because the clearance rate is too poor an indicator of the probability of an arrest for us to detect a prevention effect. Another possibility is that marginal changes in risk are not communicated very well to prospective offenders. Since systematic information about risks is not at all easy for prospective offenders to obtain, this may well be the case. Where information about changes in penalties is not communicated, we can hardly expect those changes to result in changed deterrence.

Once we acknowledge that information about penalties and how they change can be highly inaccurate, our failure to find substantial and consistent evidence that clearances reduce crime becomes understandable. It can still be the case, however, that crime is deterred by mistaken beliefs about penalties. There is an old joke about the small hamlet that purchased a sign reading "Radar used to apprehend speeders"—but couldn't afford the radar equipment. Our findings cannot say whether that investment was a sound one. A sign in a store warning that "shoplifters will be prosecuted" may reduce theft even if the store owner never apprehends or prosecutes shoplifters.

What we can say is that given the sort of publicity about law enforcement practices that now prevails, marginal increases in clearance rates—those that are on the order of the differences observed among the clearance rates of the cities in this sample—are unlikely to lead to measurable reduction in index crimes. More substantial changes in clearance rates, or in the sanctions imposed at later stages of the criminal justice system (or propaganda campaigns about the risk of crime, whether empirically founded or not) might well have a greater effect.

Notes

1. Research dealing with the effect of law enforcement on crime rates is often advertised as "deterrence research." In fact, most of this work does not study the deterrent effect of sanctions alone, but the net effect of law enforcement on crime, regardless of the process by which enforcement creates this effect. The possible contributions of rehabilitation and incapacitation (restraint), reinforcement of the collective conscience, and so forth, are not eliminated in analyses of the aggregate relationships between crime rates and sanction levels.
2. For details of the sampling procedure, see Greenberg et al. (a). On the basis of a separate analysis of data for all 50 states as well as the data for the sample of cities analyzed here, we

argue elsewhere (Greenberg et al., b) that data for cities are less likely to be subject to aggregation bias.

3. Roland Chilton has recently argued that ambiguities in the definition of a clearance make it less satisfactory than the ratio of arrests to crimes (although an arrest is the most common way the police clear a crime, there are other ways as well). However, the latter ratio is not entirely satisfactory either. Since a single crime can be cleared by the arrest of more than one individual, the ratio of arrests to crimes is not identical to the theoretically relevant probability that a crime will be followed by an arrest. We consider it an open question at this time which indicator is the most appropriate in studying the impact of arrests on crime.

4. Although we had initially planned to include indices for poverty and for high income, these variables proved to be highly correlated with our other control variables and were consequently excluded from the analysis. Data for some of the control variables included were available for both 1960 and 1970. However, correlations among observations at the two times proved to be quite high (ranging from *0.70* to over *0.90*). To avoid problems of multicollinearity, data for only one of the two time points were used. We employed 1970 data for all variables except median income; 1960 values were used for this variable because they were not as highly correlated as the 1970 values with other variables. Data for all the control variables were drawn from the Bureau of the Census.

5. These quantities are computed on the basis of the proportions of families earning less than \$3,000, between \$3,000 and \$4,999, between \$5,000 and \$6,999, between \$7,000 and \$9,999, between \$10,000 and \$14,999, between \$15,000 and \$24,999, and over \$25,000. For computing purposes, the upper limit of the highest-income category was taken to be \$35.000.

6. Cities located in the following states were classified as northern: Connecticut, Illinois, Indiana, Iowa, Massachusetts, Michigan, Minnesota, Missouri, New Hampshire, New Jersey, New York, Ohio, Pennsylvania, Vermont and Wisconsin.

7. Cities were classified as southern if located in Alabama, Arkansas, Florida, Georgia, Kentucky, Louisiana, Mississippi, North Carolina, South Carolina, Texas, Virginia. Cities were classified as western (neither northern nor southern) if located in California, Nebraska, Nevada, New Mexico, North Dakota, Oklahoma, Utah and Washington.

8. For example, Phillips and Votey introduce only a single control variable, an indicator of labor force participation; Sjoquist fails to include indicators of such theoretically relevant variables as age distribution of the population, the degree of affluence in a community, inequality of income, occupational distribution, broken homes, and region of the United States.

9. We have shown elsewhere (Greenberg and Kessler) that parameter estimates may have the wrong sign in models that have incorrectly specified lags. In the present context, there is reason for thinking that lagged and instantaneous effects of crime on sanctions may be of opposite sign, since saturation effects, if they exist, should be short-run (instantaneous), while pressure to increase the efficiency of policing in response to rising crime rates is expected to be effective only gradually, over a period of time. If these two opposite-sign effects are lumped together in a model that included only an instantaneous effect or only a lagged effect, the two processes would tend to cancel one another.

10. As the system of equations approaches equilibrium, the standard errors of parameter estimates increase rapidly, so that even moderately large parameters fail to achieve statistical significance in large samples. We did not encounter this in our estimates. At the point where equilibrium is reached, our models become underidentified. Intuitively, this happens because in equilibrium, multiple waves of data do not provide the additional information needed to identify equations. For a more mathematical treatment of approach to equilibrium in multi-wave panel models, see Kessler and Greenberg.

11. Models involving lags of three years were estimated only when the correlation matrix with variables lagged at two-year intervals could not be inverted.

12. We do not provide estimates for the effects of control variables on crime rates or clearance rates here (there are several dozen such estimates for each offense), but restrict our discussion to the most noteworthy features of the estimates. The first-named author will provide tables of these estimates upon request.

13. Given this argument one may wonder whether our use of panel models renders our analysis equally insensitive to the effect of *arrests* on crime. The answer is no. If the true structural equation governing crime rates is $C_t = a + b_1A_t + b_2Z_t + e_t$, where e is an error term, and

one subtracts from this the same equation lagged by one time unit and rearranges terms, one obtains the equation

$$C_t = C_{t-1} + b_1(A_t - A_{t-1}) + b_2(Z_t - Z_{t-1}) + (e_t - e_{t-1}).$$

This equation tells us that the coefficients of A_t and Z_t represent the respective effects of change in A and Z on change in C. If Z_t and Z_{t-1} are correlated and only Z_t is included in the analysis, its contribution will be suppressed by the factor

$$(l - r_{Z_t Z_{t-1}}).$$

Where the correlation between Z_t and Z_{t-1} is high, as it is in our data, this suppression is high. Since A_t and A_{t-1} were not highly correlated in our data, both were included in our initial models, and one or the other deleted only when its contribution was negligible. Here the low correlation between lagged and instantaneous values reduces the suppression effect.

14. We also examined models involving offense rates for individual offenses and arrest clearance rates for total offenses. The rationale for considering these models was the possibility that an arrest for one offense might deter someone contemplating the commission of another offense. Moreover, if criminals switch crime categories (and there is reason to believe that some do), the arrest and incarceration of someone charged with a given offense may eliminate offenses in other crime categories through the restraining (incapacitative) function of imprisonment. None of these models yielded evidence suggesting the existence of a crime-prevention effect for arrests.

15. Our panel analyses suggest that no serious error is likely to result from the neglect of reciprocal causation. Any discrepancy between the cross-sectional analysis and the panel analysis, therefore, must arise from the inclusion of the lagged endogenous variable in the latter analysis.

To see the circumstances under which the two approaches will yield the same conclusions about the effect of predictor variables on the criterion, consider the panel equation $y_2 - y_1 = a_1y_1 + a_2x + a_3z$. If the variables have reached equilibrium, so that $y_1 = y_2$, we can set the left hand member equal to zero, and solve the resulting equation for y_1, obtaining $y_1 = -(a_2/a_1)x - (a_3/a_1)z$. The coefficients for x and z are in the correct proportion, although their magnitudes will in general be biased. Thus it is only in equilibrium that the static and dynamic approaches yield comparable results.

References

Brown, D. W. 1978. "Arrest Rates and Crime Rates: When Does a Tipping Effect Occur?" *Social Forces* 57(December):671–82.

Bureau of the Census. 1972. *County-City Data Book*. Washington: GPO.

Chilton, R. 1980. "The Limitations of Arrests per Offense Ratios in the Analysis of Urban Crime Data." Unpublished paper presented to the American Society of Criminology.

Cloninger, D., and L. C. Sartorius. 1979. "Crime Rates, Clearance Rates and Enforcement Effort." *American Journal of Economics and Sociology* 38(October):389–402.

Cloward, R. A., and L. E. Ohlin. 1960. *Delinquency and Opportunity: A Theory of Delinquent Gangs*. New York: Free Press.

Cohen, Albert K. 1955. *Delinquent Boys: The Culture of the Gang*. New York: Free Press.

Fisher, F., and D. Nagin. 1978. "On the Feasibility of Identifying the Crime Function in a Simultaneous Model of Crime Rates and Sanction Levels." In Alfred Blumstein, Jacqueline Cohen, and Daniel Nagin (eds.), *Deterrence and Incapacitation: Estimating the Effects of Criminal Sanctions on Crime Rates*. Washington: National Academy of Sciences.

Geerken, M., and W. R. Gove. 1977. "Deterrence, Overload, and Incapacitation: An Empirical Evaluation." *Social Forces* 56(December):424–47.

Greenberg, David F. a:1977. "Deterrence Research and Social Policy." In Stuart Nagel (ed.), *Modeling the Criminal Justice System*. Beverly Hills: Sage.

———. b:1977. "Delinquency and the Age Structure of Society." *Contemporary Crises: Crime, Law and Social Policy* 2(April):189–223.

———. c:1979. *Mathematical Criminology*. New Brunswick: Rutgers University Press.

Greenberg, D. F., and R. C. Kessler. 1981. "Panel Models in Criminology." In James A. Fox (ed.), *Methods in Quantitative Criminology*. New York: Academic Press.

Greenberg, D. F., R. C. Kessler, and C. H. Logan. a:1979. "A Panel Model of Crime Rates and Arrest Rates." *American Sociological Review* 44(October):843–50.

———. b:1981. "Aggregation Bias in Deterrence Research: An Empirical Analysis." *Journal of Research in Crime and Delinquency* 18(January):128–37.

Humphries. D., and D. Wallace. 1980. "Capitalist Accumulation and Urban Crime, 1950–1971." *Social Problems* 28(December):179–93.

Jacobs, D. 1979. "Inequality and Police Strength." *American Sociological Review* 44(December):913–24.

Jöreskog, K. G., and D. Sörbom. 1979. *LISREL IV: Analysis of Linear Structural Relationships by the Method of Maximum Likelihood*. Sweden: University of Uppsala Department of Statistics.

Kessler, Ronald C., and David F. Greenberg. 1981. *Linear Panel Analysis: Models of Quantitative Change*. New York: Academic Press.

Logan, C. H. 1975. "Arrest rates and Deterrence." *Social Science Quarterly* 56(December):376–89.

Merton, R. K. 1938. "Social Structure and Anomie." *American Sociological Review* 3(October):672–82.

Miller, W. B. 1958. "Lower Class Culture as a Generating Milieu of Gang Delinquency." *Journal of Social Issues* 14(November):5–19.

Nagin, D. 1978. "General Deterrence: A Review of the Empirical Evidence." In Alfred Blumstein, Jacqueline Cohen, and Daniel Nagin (eds.), *Deterrence and Incapacitation: Estimating the Effects of Criminal Sanctions on Crime Rates*. Washington: National Academy of Sciences.

Phillips. L., and H. L. Votey, Jr. 1972. "An Economic Analysis of the Deterrent Effect of Law Enforcement on Criminal Activity." *Journal of Criminal Law, Criminology, and Police Science* 63(September):330–42.

Pontell, H. N. 1978. "Deterrence: Theory versus Practice." *Criminology* 16(May):3–22.

Sjoquist, D. L. 1973. "Property Crime and Economic Behavior: Some Empirical Results." *American Economic Review* 63(June):439–46.

Tittle, Charles R. 1980. *Sanctions and Social Deviance: The Question of Deterrence*. New York: Praeger.

Wilson, James Q., and Barbara Boland. a:1978. "The Effect of the Police on Crime." *Law and Society Review* 12(Spring):367–90.

———. b:1979. *The Effect of the Police on Crime*. Washington: GPO.

Appendix

The stability coefficients for the two-year lag models summarized in Table 1 are given in Table A.1; those for the three-year lag models summarized in Table 2, in Table A.2.

790 / Social Forces Volume 60:3, March 1982

Table A.1. STABILITY COEFFICIENTS FOR TWO-YEAR LAG MODELS FOR CRIME RATES (C) AND CLEARANCE RATES (A)[a]

	Offense					
Parameter	Murder (Model I)	Murder (Model II)	Rape	Burglary (Model I)	Burglary (Model II)	Grand Larceny
C_1C_2	.334	.382	.267	.840	.856	.927
C_2C_3	.368	.368	.213	.854	.893	.796
C_3C_4	.273	.274	.621	.621	.650	.904
C_1C_3			.236			
A_1A_2	.356	-.288	.173	.568	.606	.568
A_2A_3	.237	.237	.069	.594	.608	.334
A_3A_4	.183	.189	.218	.670	.673	.687
A_1A_3		.427		.301	.303	.386
A_1A_4			-.206			
A_2A_4			.166			

[a] X_iY_j represents the standardized regression coefficient for the effect of X_i on Y_j.

Table A.2. STABILITY COEFFICIENTS FOR THREE-YEAR LAG MODELS FOR CRIME RATES (C) AND CLEARANCE RATES (A)[a]

	Offense			
Parameter	Aggravated Assault	Robbery	Auto Theft	Total Index
C_1C_2	.760	.771	.912	.847
C_2C_3	.660	.689	.986	.825
A_1A_2	.467	.256	.638	.606
A_2A_3	.557	.196	.713	.513
A_1A_3	.269	.140	1.015	

[a] X_iY_j represents the standardized regression coefficient for the effect of X_i on Y_j.

[7]
The Incapacitative Effect of Imprisonment: Some Estimates

I. INTRODUCTION

Recent research on the functions of imprisonment has begun to provide quantitative, empirical knowledge of its rehabilitative and deterrent effects.[1] Much less is known, however, about the incapacitative effect of imprisonment. While it has long been understood that the physical segregation of prison inmates prevents them from engaging in some criminal activity (as well as much non-criminal activity) during the period of their confinement, quantitative estimates of the size of this effect have been lacking.[2] Leaving aside all deterrent or rehabilitative and counter-rehabilitative effects, it is of some interest to know whether the incapacitative function of imprisonment is large or small.

Here we present some quantitative estimates of the incapacitative effect of imprisonment on the rate at which the seven F.B.I. index offenses are committed. These estimates may be of

An earlier version of this paper, "Parole Recidivism and the Incapacitative Effects of Imprisonment," was presented at the 1974 meeting of the Society for the Study of Social Problems. I am grateful to Dorothy R. Jaman for information on homicide rates in the California prison system, to Stevens H. Clarke and Robert Martinson for comments on the earlier version of the paper, and to James O. Robison for encouragement and general assistance. Part of this research was funded by grants from the Field Foundation and New World Foundation.

1. For several recent surveys of this research, see Robert Martinson (1974a), Douglas Lipton *et al.* (1975), Morris Silver (1974), Gordon Tullock (1974), David F. Greenberg (1974a) and David F. Greenberg (1975).
2. Following the completion of this research, I discovered Isaac Ehrlich's attempt to identify an incapacitative effect of imprisonment (1973). Ehrlich regressed reported index crime rates for states against a number of social, economic and punishment variables, finding evidence that punishment reduced crime rates. Within the framework of a particular model, he found that the incapacitative effect accounted for less than 10% of the coefficients expressing the crime reduction effect of imprisonment, thus establishing an independent deterrent effect. His findings would appear to be consistent with mine.

   In addition, Stevens H. Clarke (1974) has drawn on unpublished data for the Philadelphia male birth cohort studied by Wolfgang, Figlio and Sellin (1972) to estimate the incapacitative effect of juvenile incarceration. He finds the effect to be small, not surprising in view of the low rate at which juveniles are incarcerated. The present study is confined to adult offenders.

some interest in connection with current proposals for substantial reductions in the size of the prison population, although they will not ultimately settle the question of whether such decarceration is advisable. In the process of developing our estimates, we will have occasion to provide a new interpretation of parole recidivism data. This interpretation will indicate the salience of the labeling perspective in deviance theory for the study of recidivism.

It is helpful, in discussing incapacitation, to distinguish what may be called "selective" incapacitation from "collective" incapacitation. By selective incapacitation, we mean the prevention of crime through physical restraint of persons selected for confinement on the basis of a prediction that they, and not others, will engage in forbidden behavior in the absence of confinement. By contrast, collective incapacitation refers to crime reduction accomplished through physical restraint no matter what the goal of confinement happens to be (deterrent, rehabilitative, incapacitative, etc.), and where decisions about who is to be imprisoned need not necessarily entail predictions as to future conduct.

II. SELECTIVE INCAPACITATION

The concept of selective incapacitation is at the center of many recent proposals for criminal justice reform. Several prison administrators, claiming that at most 10 to 15 percent of inmates now in prison present a threat of personal injury to the public at large, have suggested that the remainder could be released to the community (Goldfarb and Singer, 1973: 179-180; Mitford, 1973: 286). In essence, this is a recommendation for the selective incapacitation of the 10 to 15 percent of the current prison population who would not be released to the community because of the injury they would do were they not incarcerated.

The National Council on Crime and Delinquency has made a similar recommendation. In a policy statement issued by the Board of Directors in October, 1973, the Council took the position that:

> Confinement is necessary only for offenders who, if not confined, would be a serious danger to the public. For all others, who are not dangerous and who constitute the great majority of offenders, the sentence of choice should be one or another of a wide variety of non-institutional dispositions (1973: 449).

Whether non-institutional dispositions are indeed appropriate for all but those offenders who pose a threat of serious danger to the public (presumably this means violence, the statement doesn't say) presumably turns on issues beyond the scope of this paper (such as the importance attached to other aims of sentencing). However, *the recommendation for deciding who is to be incarcerated on the basis of the threat such individuals would represent if released could be implemented only if it were possible to predict how a given prisoner would behave if released.* A number of recent studies of the recidivism of released prisoners allow us to examine the present state of the art of prediction.

We begin by examining returns to prison for a national sample of parolees. Information about the fate of 25,602 male parolees released in 1970 is now available (National Probation and Parole Institutes, 1972). After a year at large, 40 of the 25,602 male parolees released in 1970 had been returned to prison on a new homicide or negligent manslaughter conviction or allegation. Only 3 of those 40, or 7.5% of the total, had an initial homicide or negligent manslaughter commitment. Since those with a homicide or negligent manslaughter commitment comprise 7.4% of the parolees released, it appears that the prior conviction for homicide or manslaughter bears little or no relation to the subsequent commitment for an offense of this kind. Only 6 of the homicides and manslaughters were committed by someone whose initial offense involved violence of any kind. Thus, continued imprisonment of only the violent offenders would have prevented a very limited amount of homicide, at the cost of imprisoning several thousand offenders whose initial offense involved violence, but who did not, to the best of our knowledge, become involved in a new homicide or manslaughter after release.

Returns with new rape or aggravated assault convictions are somewhat more highly correlated with original convictions for those offenses than is the case with homicide, but for those too, preventive confinement of those who committed the initial offense would have eliminated only a small fraction of the subsequent offenses, at the cost of imprisoning many who did not, so far as we know, commit another offense of that kind.[3]

Prior commitment offense, of course, is only one source of predictive information that might be used in making a decision

3. Of the population, 3519 had a commitment offense involving violence (willful homicide, negligent manslaughter, aggravated assault and forcible rape) and another 2937 an offense involving potential violence (armed and unarmed robbery). The parolees in this study were released from prison in all but two of the fifty states, and Puerto Rico. The two missing states were Alaska and Connecticut; states that submitted only partial information were Alabama, California, Indiana, Maryland, Michigan, New York, Ohio, Pennsylvania, Wisconsin, Arkansas, Delaware, New Jersey, North Carolina, Puerto Rico, Rhode Island, and Tennessee.

whether to incarcerate in order to prevent future violent offenses, or indeed, offenses of any kind. Much of the recent research in the prediction of criminal behavior has been conducted under the auspices of the Research Division of the California Department of Corrections. As described in one of the publications of the Research Division (1971a):

> In 1958, initially under the guidance of Leslie Wilkins from England, the Research Division of the California Department of Corrections entered the field of parole outcome prediction from base expectancies. The base expectancy scale assigns a score to each inmate according to possession or absence of certain historical characteristics. It predicts from past observation the percentage of inmates for each particular BE score who will have favorable outcomes; the higher the score, the greater the possibility of favorable parole outcome . . . . BE61A was created to predict favorable parole outcome within two years after release. In general, favorable outcome was defined as no return to any prison from parole, no jail sentence of 90 or more days, or not PAL (parolee-at-large) over six months. The scale scores range from 0 - 76, with the specified points accumulated for whichever of the following characteristics are applicable:
>
> 12 arrest-free period of five or more consecutive years
> 9 no history of any opiate use
> 8 not more than two jail commitments
> 7 not committed for burglary, forgery or checks
> 6 no family criminal record
> 6 no alcohol involvement
> 5 not first arrested for auto theft
> 5 six or more consecutive months for one employer
> 5 no aliases
> 5 first imprisonment under this serial number
> 4 favorable living arrangement
> 4 not more than two prior arrests
>
> . . . BE61A continues to be a valid measurement and predictive device for male felon parolees . . . the percent favorable outcome for each year's releases is higher at any level than the percent observed for the same year's lower levels. Although the BE was created to predict favorable outcome within two years, it has some validity for predicting returns to prison, in that the percent of returns generally increases as the BE score level decreases.
>
> Even though the BE61A scale accounts for less than 20% of the variation in parole outcomes, its predictions for favorable outcome are better than chance. Therefore, it can be helpful to administrators and in program evaluations.

An evaluation of the usefulness of the base expectancy score for choosing which prisoners to confine in order to prevent them from engaging in violent behavior upon release must take into account the fact that a predictive device of this kind can make two kinds of errors. It can release individuals predicted not to recidivate but who in fact do so (false negatives); also, it can fail to release individuals predicted to recidivate, but who would not recidivate if released (false positives).

For some purposes, the question of false positives can be safely ignored. When millions of children are innoculated with polio vaccine to protect them from contracting infantile paralysis, there need be little concern that few of those children would become polio victims if not vaccinated. Since the injection is inexpensive, harmless, and only slightly and briefly painful, it is clearly better to be safe than sorry. In utilizing predictions of criminal conduct to decide who is to be imprisoned, the consequences of ignoring the false positives are clearly much more serious—possible long-term erroneous confinement and stigmatization. Under this circumstance, one cannot neglect consideration of the false positives generated by a prediction method without implicitly assuming that the suffering of the persons mistakenly confined need not be taken into account. As Caleb Foote (1970: 52-53) observed:

> It is a prerequisite for any system of preventive detention that you assume that those detained are going to be second-class citizens. The false positives are viewed as more expendable in the debates on preventive detention. Judges and psychiatrists who support preventive detention assume that a mistaken identification of one actually safe person who is predicted to be dangerous is much less serious than the release of one actually dangerous person. The operating rationale, therefore, is much like that of a search-and-destroy mission. Some dangerous Viet Cong may be eliminated, and the civilians and children are expendable.

This observation would appear to be no less appropriate at the post-conviction stage, when a disposition is being selected by the judge, or in decisions involving the continuation of confinement on grounds of predicted behavior for someone already in custody, than at the pretrial stage, where preventive confinement proposals have been debated. This should be kept in mind when we consider the implications of using the California base expectancy score as a predictive device to aid decision-making about selective incapacitation. Information is available on the parole success of the 5910 men released to parole from California prisons in 1967 (Research Division, 1971b). Using return to prison with a new felony commitment within two years after release as the outcome to be prevented by refusing to release inmates predicted to recidivate, Table 1 shows the consequences of not releasing different groups of inmates.

TABLE 1

Hold BE Level	Number of Inmates Held	% of Recidivists Held	% of Non-Recidivists Held	% of Non-Recidivists Among Those Held	% of Total Decisions in Error
F	179	3.3%	3.0%	87%	14%
EF	1065	19.7%	17.8%	87%	25%
DEF	2012	37.2%	33.6%	87%	37%
XDEF	4313	79.8%	72.1%	87%	66%

Source: Derived from *Research Division 1971b.*

Since the predictive device is fallible, the only way the parole board could retain *all* recidivists in prison would be to release no one. As this might be impractical (it is necessary to release prisoners to make room for new commitments), the parole board would have to release at least some prisoners.[4] With base expectancy score as the criterion governing release, the table indicates what the consequences would be of choosing different base expectancy scores as cutting lines to decide on questions of release. For example, if only base expectancy levels E and F were detained, just under 20% of the recidivists would be kept in prison, as would a slightly smaller proportion of the non-recidivists. As the number of persons detained declines, the number of non-recidivists confined declines as well (a presumably desirable result), but so does the percentage of recidivists, no matter where the line is drawn, a majority of those detained will be non-recidivists.[5] Fortuitously, for this population, 87% of those held will be non-recidivists at each level of confinement. This implies a ratio of false positives to true positives of 6.7 to 1.

Since 12% of the 5910 men were returned to prison with a new felony commitment within two years, if the parole board were to make the decision concerning detention by random selection from the prisoner population, 88% of those detained could be expected to be non-recidivists. Thus when the base expectancy score is used as a device for deciding who should be released from prison, the percentage of non-recidivists confined drops from the 88% obtained through a random selection to 87%, an improvement of just one percent. It would be an understatement to point out that this is hardly impressive.

Since the ratio of false to true positives (and therefore the cost-effectiveness of preventive confinement) does not change with the risk levels retained in this particular instance (assuming for the sake of simplicity that there are neither economies nor diseconomies of scale), the board might consider choosing a cut-

4. In practice, it is likely that release rates would be strongly influenced by commitment rates, for if the former substantially exceeded the latter over a period of time the prison population would be seriously depleted, while if the latter persistently exceeded the former, an intolerable increase in population density would result.

5. In light of this finding, it should be pointed out that in a civil commitment hearing held to deprive someone of liberty on grounds of mental illness and dangerousness to others, the government must establish dangerousness with a degree of certainty traditionally given by the "preponderance of evidence" test, which would require decisions to be more often right than wrong if made on the basis of the evidence introduced. Some courts have begun to require the more stringent "reasonable doubt" standard in civil commitment cases. Greenberg (1974c: 265, note 129.) The accuracy of the base expectancy score is so poor that it would not meet even the lesser of these standards.

ting line so as to minimize the number of erroneous decisions. It would appear from the table that this could be done by retaining only the worst risk level, since then only 14% of all decisions would be in error, even though preventive confinement that detained only 3% of the recidivists might seem not worth the trouble. However, if the aim were simply to minimize error, the board could do better by releasing *all* the inmates, since it would then be wrong only 12% of the time.[6]

In the analysis just described, the criterion of parole failure was simply return to prison with a new commitment. The advocates of selective incapacitation do not have in mind imprisoning *all* those who are at present returned to prison with a new commitment of *any* kind—only those whose new commitments are for violence offenses. How accurately can these be predicted?

The most elaborate attempt to develop methods for predicting violent recidivism was that of Wenk and Robison, who studied the violent recidivist offenses of California Youth Authority wards (Wenk and Robison, 1971; Wenk *et al.*, 1972). These youths have a higher rate of over-all recidivism (at the end of fifteen months 38.9% were parole violators) and a higher rate of return to violence than adult parolees, making them a logical target for a policy of selective incapacitation.

Wenk and Robison had access to unusually complete biographical data for more than 4,000 wards—an advantage, since the accuracy of predictions might be expected to increase with the number of individuals and the amount of information about them fed into the construction of prediction equations. Six sizable subgroups with particularly high rates of violent recidivism were identified: those who had a psychiatric referral for evaluation of violence potential, a history of actual violence, those with four or more admissions to the Youth Authority, a violent admission offense, Mexican-Americans, and those with a severe alcohol problem. The category "history of actual violence" is particularly noteworthy Comprising a fifth of the entire population, it includes half the subjects who became violent, with a violent recidivism rate three times as high as the rest of the wards. Yet, confining this group would have entailed confining 19 apparently non-violent youths for every youth who recidivated violently (a much higher rate of false positives than when returns to prison with a new commitment were being considered), and would have resulted in the release of half of those who became violent.

6. I have been drawing on James O. Robison's unpublished analysis of parole decision-making and outcomes.

By confining only the subgroup with the highest rate of violent recidivism, those committed on the basis of a psychiatric referral, the false positive ratio could be reduced slightly to 15 to 1, but this would drastically reduce the effectiveness of the confinement since then only 16 of the 104 violent recidivists in the population would be confined, and three times as many erroneous decisions would be made than would occur were everyone to be released.

As a multivariate analysis could be expected to improve the quality of the predictions, a statistician and a psychologist were each asked to develop predictions using multivariate techniques, with half the sample used to validate the prediction formula developed from the first half of the sample. The statistician's best predictions identified 7.7% of the violent recidivists, with a false positive ratio of 12 to 1. He concluded pessimistically:

> Considering the rarity of the phenomenon (only one in forty exhibits subsequent violence), it is difficult to imagine that, even with the most refined techniques, one could do much better than, say, to double the best rates obtained here. This lack of precision of our selection process seems inherent in the limitations of the quantifiable variables we have in this study (Wenk and Emrich, 1972: 192).

Using a different approach, the psychologist developed a multiple regression prediction using 18 variables, in which the ratio of true positives to false positives did not exceed 0.06, no better than in the simple analysis taking one variable at a time. Nevertheless, the psychologist concluded:

> It is apparent that this set of data offers numerous encouraging leads on the constitution and possible identification of potentially violent parolees. These results strongly suggest that a useful violence index could be constructed although a great deal more research is obviously necessary . . . In sum, it appears to be feasible to develop, in this sample, at least, an index of violence prone-ness that would correctly identify over 50 percent of those individuals violating parole by violent offenses at the cost of mis-classifying no more than 10 percent of those not returned for violent offenses (Wenk and Robison: 1971:47).

Wenk and Robison point out, however, that the high proportion of nonviolent offenders in the group implies that even should this accuracy eventually be attained, the ratio of false to true positives would still be 8 to 1, which is very high.

The state of prediction is evidently rather poor. Implementation of a policy of selective confinement based on predictions of dangerousness would clearly founder on the gross inaccuracies of prediction.[7] While it is certainly possible that with additional

7. It is beyond the scope of this article to discuss precisely what degree of predictive accuracy would be required before it would be acceptable to use predictive methods in making decisions about selective

information about offenders, and more sophisticated, possibly nonlinear, statistical techniques, predictive accuracy could be improved, there are some fundamental limitations to the degree to which improvement is likely to be possible. These limitations include (a) the extreme practical difficulties and high cost of improving the accuracy of data to be used in predictions, and (b) the interactional nature of much recidivist crime, and in particular, of violent crime. If a particular individual's recidivism depends not only on his or her own personal traits, but also on largely unforseeable contingencies such as how others (spouses, prospective employers, etc.) behave toward that individual, the information that would be essential for an accurate prediction would be omitted from the actuarial analysis that forms the basis for a prediction. The meagre results obtained after fifty years of research in the prediction of parole behavior from the characteristics of individual parolees strongly suggest that these contingencies may be at least as important as biographical data in determining parole success of failure.

III. COLLECTIVE INCAPACITATION— THE VISIBLE TIP OF THE ICEBERG

Although the analysis of the preceding section suggests the unfeasibility of a policy of *selective* incapacitation, it leaves open the possibility that there may still be a sizable collective incapacitation effect from imprisonment. If, for example, a high proportion of criminals were confined, rates of crime repetition were high, and a great deal of switching from one form of crime to another took place, predictions of a particular variety of recidi-

incapacitation. For a provocative discussion of this question see Andrew von Hirsch (1972); a parallel discussion of the use of predictions in civil commitments appears in Greenberg (1974b). The following argument, however, should suffice to indicate that the issue is not necessarily qualitatively different at the post-conviction level than it is at the pre-conviction level. Consider a man released from prison who is now accused of another crime. No one would question that when he is tried for this new offense, the appropriate standard in reaching a verdict should be the reasonable doubt test, just as in the first trial. Suppose, however, that instead of having been accused of committing a crime that has already taken place, the man had been predicted to engage in some crime at a later date. Here we not only do not know whether this man will commit the crime, we do not even know for certain that it will take place. Why would we tolerate a lesser degree of certainty with regard to the incarceration of someone predicted to engage in a crime that may not take place at all, than we would when someone is accused of a crime that we know has taken place? If this reasoning is persuasive, the reasonable doubt criterion would have to be used for decisions involving selective incapacitation. Since this criterion could virtually never be met for predictions of the future, preventive commitments would have to be eschewed. I am indebted to Andrew Von Hirsch for this argument.

vism (say violent recidivism) might be poor, but the collective incapacitation effect of imprisoning offenders without regard to the likelihood of repetition could still be substantial. In estimating how substantial, we will use parole recidivism statistics extensively (National Probation and Parole Institutes, 1972). Since women comprise only 6.3% of the parolee sample under study, the bulk of the analysis will be devoted to male parolees; however, differences in the nature of male and female recidivism will be pointed out.

Published parole success rates are not available for the individual reporting agencies, so that state by state comparisons are not possible. However, such comparisons would be uninformative in the absence of information about the composition of the respective prison populations. For example, one state might have a higher recidivism rate than another not because its prisons were more criminogenic than another, but because of differences in the criminal populations of two states, unemployment levels, efficiency of police departments, or criteria used in selection for probation. Instead of success rates for the individual agencies, we have them for the national sample as a whole. The rates, then, represent a national average of successes and failures from states with possibly different prison populations, and release and revocation policies. Four our purposes, this is not entirely disadvantageous: the lumped data are less likely to reflect the idiosyncratic policies or unusual crime picture of any particular state. On the other hand, the conclusions drawn may not be equally valid for all states.

Table 2 reports the fate one year after release of the male parolees released in 1970 for whom agencies made information available to the compilers of *Uniform Parole Reports.* Inspection of the table indicates that at the end of one year, 18.9% of the parolees had been returned to prison, either as technical violators, or with a new major conviction. This represents a slight decline from the 1969 male parolee one year return rate—19.6% (National Probation and Parole Institutes, n.d.). An additional 0.6% of the 1970 parolees were continued on parole after conviction for a new major offense. By conventional definitions, the recidivism rate for the first year after release would be close to 20%.

Two years after release, 27% of the 1969 male parolees had been returned to prison, indicating that in the second year after release, even when depletion of the sample due to the return to prison of almost 20% of the parolees during the first year is taken into account, the recidivism rate declines substantially from its value during the first year[8] (National Probation and Parole Institutes, 1973). These figures suggest, though they do not rigorously prove, that at the point of release from prison, many prisoners do not become intensely involved in crime.

Since the magnitude of the numbers just cited for parolee recidivism are substantially smaller than those often cited, it must be emphasized that a recidivism *rate* is not be confused with the percentage of parolees who are *eventually* reconvicted or returned to prison. The rate involves not only the number of violators or violations, but the period of time over which the violations occur as well. Thus, the finding that the recidivism rate was no more than 20% in the first year and less thereafter would not contradict a statement that more than half of all parolees are *eventually* returned to prison.

TABLE 2

1970 MALE PAROLEES, FATE AFTER ONE YEAR

FATE	NUMBER	PERCENT
CONTINUED ON PAROLE		
no difficulty or sentence less than 60 days	18,789	73.4%
with new minor conviction(s)	290	1.1%
with new major conviction(s)	156	0.6%
ABSCONDER	1,517	5.9%
RETURN TO PRISON AS A TECHNICAL VIOLATOR		
no new conviction(s) and not in lieu of prosecution	2,400	9.4%
new minor or lesser conviction(s) or in lieu of prosecution	592	2.3%
in lieu of prosecution of new major offense(s)	645	2.5%
RETURN TO PRISON, NO VIOLATION	12	0.1%
RECOMMITTED TO PRISON WITH NEW MAJOR CONVICTION(S)	1,201	4.7%
TOTAL	25,602	100.0%

Further inspection of the table is instructive. We learn that of those returned to prison, only 25% were returned with a new

8. If incidents taking place during the first year, but which do not lead to deprivation of liberty until the second year were taken into account, this number might be somewhat larger. The numerical importance of these "pending" cases would be large only so long as the analysis is confined to short follow-up periods. I have no nationwide data on "pending" cases, but can illustrate the point with California data on 1966 parolees. At six months, 8.9% had been returned to prison, and 5.1% had cases pending; at one year, 21.0% had been returned to prison, and 3.3% had cases pending. At two years, the respective figures were 36.0% and 1.1% (Research Division, 1971b: 8, 15, 19).

major conviction; all others were returned as technical violators (a technical violator is one who breaks a regulation to which parole agencies require parolees to conform; these violations are not criminal offenses).[9] As parole agencies sometimes return someone to prison as a technical violator even when a new crime has been committed, so as to avoid the expense and trouble of a new trial, some of these technical violators might well have been convicted of a new crime had a trial been held. Yet, even if it is assumed that *all* those returned in lieu of prosecution for a new major offense would have been proved guilty in court had the agency not revoked parole on grounds of a technical violation, we would still have a minority (38%) of the parole revocations triggered by reason of involvement in a new major offense.

Actually, a study of parole revocation decisions suggests that in at least some instances, parole may be revoked on grounds of suspicion even when reason exists to believe that the parolee had *not* been involved in criminal activity.[10] Other revocations —roughly an eighth of the total—occur in response to suspicion of involvement in, or conviction for a minor crime, one that would not involve imprisonment had the violator not been on

9. State correctional systems differ greatly in parole revocation practices. For some states, the proportion of returns to prison attributable to technical violations would be much smaller than for the United States as a whole. Thus, in Wisconsin, about ¼ of all persons returned to prison have new commitments, the remainder being technical violators (Division of Corrections, 1971) and in Michigan, only 30.2% of parole violators returned had new sentences (Department of Corrections, 1970), while in New York about 60% of persons returned to prison were arrested for some new crime (Clark and Rudenstine, 1975: 160), and in the federal system, 74.3% of parole violator warrants were for violations of laws (Federal Bureau of Prisons, 1974).

10. The following case summary illustrates such a revocation: S. was convicted for second-degree burglary and served two years . . . After completing eighteen months on parole he was arrested two blocks from his home at 11:00 P.M. He was on his way home from a nearby bar where he had just spent two or three hours. The police were looking for someone who had committed a burglary several blocks away about an hour earlier. When they discovered that S. had a record for burglary he was taken to jail and charged with this crime. When his alibi was established and there was no evidence to connect him with the crime except for his being in the neighborhood, the judge dismissed the charge and admonished the arresting officers.

    S.'s parole was cancelled, however, and he was returned to prison. When he appeared before the A.A. [Adult Authority, i.e. the parole board] for a parole-violation hearing he was asked if he knew why he had been returned. He replied that he did not. The A.A. member became irritated with him and told him that just because he "beat the charge" in court did not mean that he was not guilty, and that the best thing he could do was to admit that he was guilty. He refused to do this and tried to explain to the member that the judge clearly believed him to be innocent and that he could prove this from the transcript of the preliminary hearing.

    S. was denied parole consideration and postponed for another year . . . (Irwin, 1970:56-57).

parole. For example, one of the men killed during the Attica rebellion was a check forger whose parole had been revoked for driving without a license. Men are not customarily sent to Attica for driving without a license. (Personal communication to the author from Andrew Von Hirsch, on file with the author.)

Most striking, the table indicates that fully half the parolees returned to prison were not even suspected, much less found guilty, of involvement in a new offense, minor or serious. Instead, they were returned to prison for violating a parole regulation. Some examples will illustrate the circumstances that can result in revocation. A common parole regulation forbids "association with individuals of bad repute."[11] Another parole regulation, imposed on some, but not all California parolees, forbids the use of alcoholic beverages.[12]

From the recidivism data and available case studies, we learn that if recidivism is defined as new known involvement in serious

---

11. Consider the following excerpt from a parole agent's recommendation to the California Adult Authority that a parolee be returned to prison for violating this rule:

> Subject is running around with Indian girls again and is getting himself very dirty. He has a very low regard for himself and cannot feel comfortable in the company of anyone but Indians. . . . His dissolute action continued unabated with the keeping of late and unusual association with drunk Indians, promiscuous sex activities with Indian girls. . . . He does not take advantage of or avail himself of the many fine opportunities for wholesome recreation in this area, nor of the religious or socially uplifting events. . . . His habits have become less acceptable socially. . . . He seldom bathes and has sex with girls of low status. . . . (Kassebaum, *et al.*, 1971: 189).

Eliot Studt (1973: 159-60) describes the revocation of a 17-year old black youth who violated this rule:

12. This parolee had been released from prison approximately three months earlier; the agent discovered during the first interview that the man had injured his back so seriously that he was in extreme pain. Welfare aid was obtained, and the parolee was housed in a run-down ghetto hotel full of winos, the only housing resource in that area for single, unemployed men. Medical appointments were made but, before the parolee could get to a doctor, he was arrested for being drunk on the sidewalk and taken to jail. When the police discovered the physical state of the parolee, and learned that the drinking had occurred, at least in part, to dull the pain pending the receipt of medication, they recommended to the judge that the charges be dismissed. The judge dismissed the case, recommending that no further action be taken against the parolee. After this event, the agent made arrangements for the transfer of the parolee to the care of the Veteran's Administration as soon as the admitting examinations, scheduled for six weeks ahead, were completed. Because the parolee had violated his 5b condition, the agent also wrote a report to the Board, outlining the circumstances and the plans for medical care, and recommending continuance on parole. To the agent's dismay the Adult Authority revoked the parole.

Studt (1973:21) describes the youth, "in severe pain . . . standing in handcuffs with tears running down his cheeks" after having been told that he was being returned to prison.

criminal activity, rather than as a return to prison (the administrative action), the recidivism rate is rather low—somewhere between 5 and 8% in the first year after release (neglecting cases pending at the end of the year), less in subsequent years. For women parolees released in 1970, the rates are even lower. At the end of one year, 13.9% had been returned to prison (a lower rate than for male parolees), and another 0.23% were continued on parole after a new major conviction. Yet, of those returned to prison, only 16.4% were returned with a new major conviction, 8.9% in lieu of prosecution for a new major offense, 12.7% with a new minor conviction or in lieu of prosecution for a new minor offense, and an astonishing 60% as technical violators with no new convictions and not in lieu of prosecution (National Probation and Parole Institutes, 1972).

It appears that for male parolees, and even more so for the female parolees, the proverbially high rate of recidivism (as defined by returns to prison, the usual measure) is in large part an artifact created by the parole system itself, since many of the returnees were sent back to prison for behavior that is not forbidden to the general public, for suspicion of an offense where guilt was not proved in court, and at least sometimes when the parolee had already been tried and acquitted, or when the offense was minor and would not have resulted in imprisonment had the offender not been on parole. (See table 1).

These results suggest that parole recidivism is best understood within the framework of the labeling approach to the study of deviance, with its emphasis on the study of organizational processes and their effects on outcomes (Schur, 1971: 82-99). They clearly demonstrate that parolees are not usually returned to prison as the result of a reactive response by law enforcement agencies to the commission of new felonies. Persons returned to prison are in a legal sense far from homogeneous. Some have been found to have committed felonies, others misdemeanors, and the majority have not been found to have violated the law at all. Some have been returned to prison through judicial, and others through administrative procedures. Without an examination of the procedures by which parolees, parole agents, and parole board members interact to produce official recidivism statistics, and absent an investigation of the standards these decision-makers actually employ, a very misleading picture of parolee behavior would be obtained.

It is of some interest to note the rationale for having a parole system that permits parolees to be returned to prison in the absence of proof of any criminal violation. Parole was instituted in the decades following 1870, and reflects views of crime causation held in the late nineteenth and early twentieth centuries. Criminologists and reformers of that period compared crime to a disease, and penal administrators to physicians who could cure criminals of the personal pathology that led to their initial involvement with crime. Since a successful cure would benefit the criminal as well as the public, due process protections associated with the criminal trial and limitations on the severity of punishment derived from retributive and deterrent philosophies of punishment could safely be ignored.

The parole system was seen as an administrative device that would simpultaneously permit the retention in prison of those whose disease had not been cured and the speedy return to prison of those who were beginning to relapse. No sense in waiting until a new crime had actually been committed; act at once, as soon as pathological behavior begins to manifest itself. The class biases of penal administrators led them to label as symptoms of impending criminality such routine features of lower class existence as occupational and residential mobility, sexual experience outside marriage, and association with "disreputable" people. These assumptions were not verified before the system was implemented, and have long been abandoned by most criminologists.[13] Nevertheless, thousands of released prisoners continue to be returned to custody for violating rules never enacted by a legislature, and to which a considerable portion of the population no longer subscribes.

The labeling perspective in deviance theory is often linked with symbolic interactionist social psychology. It is argued that the denunciations and degradation ceremonies accompanying the official labeling of someone as deviant affect the self-concept in such a way as to increase the likelihood of future deviance. In the case of the parole system two other mechanisms seem to be at work. One involves the transformed *social* identity of the incarcerated. Regardless of the consequences of imprisonment for self-concept or behavior patterns, imprisonment and subsequent release on parole subject the individual to a far more stringent set of rules (with much weaker due process safeguards) than those imposed on the general public. Behavior that would not result in imprisonment for the average citizen results in long-

13. Norman Holt (1974) has recently pointed out that technical violators not returned to prison but kept on parole were no more likely to be rearrested than parolees freshly released from prison; the technical violation, therefore, had no predictive value.

term imprisonment for the ex-felon. In other words, the parole agency organizes social responses to parolee behavior so that the behavior is not interpreted according to the conventional rules operative for most citizens, but according to a different set of rules applicable because of the parolee's behavior at some time in the past, perhaps years earlier. Regardless of the attitudes of particular individuals, the normal operation of the agency turns the parolee status into a master identity, which over-rides other considerations and places the parolee in jeopardy of imprisonment without crime.

The second mechanism, the existence of which is more difficult to demonstrate empirically, involves the effect of the high recidivism rates generated by the parole system in reinforcing public stereotypes of released prisoners as especially dangerous. This image contributes to the difficulties faced by released prisoners in such areas as employment and social life. It is quite possible that the new crime rate of parolees would be lower in the absence of a parole system continuously generating high recidivism rates. To the hard-liner, high recidivism is a demonstration of the need for longer sentences to protect the public; to the reformer, they show the need for increased appropriations to fund new rehabilitation programs. Thus, the same data serve as resources for parties at both ends of the policy spectrum. Neither realizes that in constantly calling to the attention of the public numbers that are to a great extent artifacts of administrative action, public prejudice against ex-convicts may be intensified.

Since parole agents possess considerable discretion in responding to technical violations (as well as in the interpretation of such vaguely worded expressions as "individuals with bad reputation") revocation rates can be manipulated to achieve organizational objectives. One such instance of manipulation has been documented by Paul Takagi (1967: 158-161). California had been experimenting with small parole caseloads in the hope that these would reduce recidivism. When investigation disclosed that recidivism was not lower despite the small caseloads:

> The chief of the agency stated that henceworth the units in the agency will compete against one another to see who can produce the lowest technical violation rate. In order to reduce the technical violation rates among the small case-load agents, the supervisors will be required to hold a detailed case conference with the agent recommending a technical violation and explore what alternatives are available in the community so a parolee need not be returned to prison. If the supervisor agrees with the agent's recommendations to return the client to prison, then the supervisor must state in writing a justification for the recommendation. Such a case, however, will then be reviewed by the

> regional administrator with the view toward disagreeing with the field recommendations. If the regional administrator should agree with the return recommendations, then he, too, must state why he agrees.
>
> The further requirement was made that copies of such reports will be forwarded to headquarters for review and training purposes and that the material will be utilized to evaluate the performances in the field. The chief of the agency added one final note. All future promotions will be considered in terms of how well the district supervisors and the regional administrators have provided leadership in reducing the technical violation rates. At this juncture in the meeting, my informant indicated one of the participants at the meeting responded to these unwritten policy requirements with an exclamatory "Bullshit!" The chief of the agency turned to the man and said: "Mr. C———, you hold a responsible position in this organization; and if that is the way you feel, perhaps you should not be in that position."
>
> Headquarters' pressures upon the regional administrators and the small-caseload supervisors served effectively to reduce the technical violation rates in the subsequent months.

Although a recidivism rate of 5 to 8% a year (as defined by return to prison because of a new major conviction or allegation of a new major crime) does not seem especially high, it may be worthwhile to examine the offenses for which recidivists are returned to prison, for if these offenses were especially serious, even a recidivism rate of this magnitude might be considered alarming. As the previously cited national sample of parolees records the new commitment offense or allegation (in the case of a technical return in lieu of prosecution) for the 1970 male parolees returned to prison, we can examine this question. Of the 25,602 men in the sample, only 0.73% were returned for conviction or suspicion of a violent offense (homicide, manslaughter, forcible rape, aggravated assault); another 1.1% were returned for potentially violent offenses (armed or unarmed robbery). The bulk of the returns were for property crimes not involving confrontation with a person, or violations of the drug laws (National Probation and Parole Institutes, 1972).

More than one interpretation of these figures is possible. It might be argued that recidivism is low because the parole system is highly effective in preventing released prisoners from returning to crime—whether through its helping or surveillance function is immaterial. This explanation, along with another—that only the best risks are released on parole—can be excluded by research indicating that prisoners released mandatorily after parol denial recidivate at roughly the same frequency as prisoners released on parole (Carney, 1967; Mueller, 1965; Clark and Rudenstine, 1975: 1962:3; Research Division, 1968), and that intensity of parole supervision does not seem to influence the rate of return to crime (Greenberg, 1974a).

Another possibility is that the prison system, rather than being a school for crime, is quite successful in rehabilitating prisoners or in deterring them from further criminal activity. Our knowledge of such effects is still far from complete. However, most rehabilitation programs have shown no measurable effect on recidivism, and in the few cases where a measurable effect has been shown, the effect was not large (Greenberg, 1974a). In addition, recidivism rates of released prisoners are about the same as those of matched probationers (Wilkins, 1958; Hammond, 1958; Babst and Mannering, 1965; Shoham, 1966: 193; Lamb and Goertzel, 1974), and one recent study (Berecochea, *et al.*, 1973) found that length of time served in prison had no effect on recidivism[14] Prisons may be terribly unpleasant, psychologically destructive, and at times dangerous to life and limb, but there is no compelling evidence that imprisonment substantially increases (or decreases) the likelihood of subsequent criminal involvement.

If taken at face value, then, official statistics on parole recidivism suggest that the collective incapacitative effects of punishment on crime rates are truly infinitesimal. On the assumption that all prisoners would recidivate at the same rate as the roughly 25,000 parolees in the sample under study, we can calculate that if all the approximately 200,000 prisoners in the United States were released, at the end of a year only about 1,460 would have been returned for conviction or suspicion of a violent offense. In 1970, 384,701 such offenses were reported to police (Federal Bureau of Investigation, 1972: 62-53). One major flaw in this line of reasoning is that offenses leading to imprisonment are only the tiny, most visible tip of a very large iceberg of offenses that do not lead to a police report, arrest, conviction, or imprisonment. In 1970, for example, there were 1,551,300 arrests for index crimes in the United States (Federal Bureau of Investigation, 1971: 119), but only about 77,000 persons were sentenced to prison in that year, and not all of them for index offenses (Federal Bureau of Prisons, n.d.). The clearance rate for index offenses was only 20% in 1970 (Federal Bureau of Investigation, 1971: 115), and this figure would be even smaller were crimes not reported to police included in the measure of likelihood that

14. Since this study involved only a six month reduction in sentences averaging several years, it cannot indicate what the effect of a larger variation in sentence length might be. In addition, it is possible here, as with many rehabilitation studies, that different members of the prison population were differently affected by the treatment, so that a positive effect for some was cancelled out by a negative effect for others. Berecochea *et al.* (1973) were not able to identify any such groups but that does not mean they did not exist.

an offense will result in an arrest. Official parole statistics indicating only rates of return to prison understate the amount of recidivist crime committed by parolees. Insofar as an estimate of the absolute amount of crime prevented through incapacitation of prisoners is concerned, an inclusion of these hidden offenses could only increase the estimate.

If one is concerned not with the absolute amount of parolee crime, but rather with the fraction of crimes for which parolees are responsible, it is less clear what the effect of including undetected offenses will be. For if parolees are frequently not apprehended for their crimes, non-parolees also escape apprehension. It could be argued that those who violate the law more frequently will be more likely to be caught and imprisoned. If this is so, the fact that many crimes are undetected would not necessarily lead to a small incapacitative effect, for the most active criminals would be those taken out of circulation. On the other hand, imprisonment may depend as much on lack of aptitude or skill as on frequency of violating the law. If this is so, the incapacitative effect of imprisonment would not tend to be very large. To settle the issue, a more quantitative approach is required.

IV. ESTIMATION OF UNDETECTED RECIDIVIST OFFENSES—MODEL 1

In this section, we present the first of two independent estimates of the volume of undetected recidivist crime parolees commit. Because data are most complete for index crimes (non-negligent homicide, forcible rape, aggravated assault, robbery, burglary, auto theft, and larceny over $50), we will attempt to estimate the rate at which released prisoners commit index crimes, and the corresponding magnitude of the incapacitative effect of imprisonment, assuming that the recidivist crimes would not be committed were the parolees not released. It must be admitted that the use of index crimes is not entirely satisfactory. On the one hand, some serious offenses (e.g. kidnapping) are not included; in addition, a high volume of less serious offenses may not be entirely inconsequential, and these too are excluded from the crime index. On the other hand, the index itself weights equally crimes of very different gravity; the social consequences of an act of grand larceny or auto theft are quite different from the consequences of such assaultive crimes as homicide and rape. Since most of the current interest in incapacitation concerns offenses against the person, it must be pointed out that most of the index offenses are offenses involving theft where no confrontation with a victim occurs. Even with these limitations, an estimate may be of some interest, and will provide a consistency check on the second model we will present, which yields separate estimates for each of the index crimes.

As numerical values for some of the variables required by the model are unavailable, simplifying assumptions will be needed. While the assumptions appear reasonable, the reader should keep in mind that new empirical research could require the modification of some of the assumptions and a refinement or correction of the conclusions reached here. To assist the reader in keeping track of the notation, definitions of the symbols defined in the text are collected in Table 3.

We begin by defining a minor offense. A minor offense is an offense (such as drunkenness or disorderly conduct) that rarely if ever results in a prison sentence, and for which the chances of the subsequent offense being an index offense are particularly small. As crime-switching matrices adequate for our purposes are not available, we shall have to rely on common-sense knowledge about crime patterns to distinguish minor from non-minor offenses.[15] Let A be the number of persons arrested annually for a non-minor offense. We assume that released prisoners commit index crimes at the same rate as all persons arrested for non-minor offenses, whatever the disposition of their cases; call this rate r.[16]

15. We classify homicide, rape, robbery, aggravated assault, burglary, larceny, auto theft, other assaults, arson, forgery and counterfeiting, fraud, embezzlement, possession of stolen property, weapons, narcotics, and gambling as non-minor offenses. Minor offenses include vandalism, prostitution, sex offenses (except rape and prostitution), offenses against the family and children, driving under the influence, liquor laws, drunk, disorderly, vagrancy, suspicion, curfew and loitering, runaways, and all others except traffic.

16. The approximate validity of this assumption is suggested by F.B.I. data on crime careers (Federal Bureau of Investigation, 1971: 36-38) and the general lack of effect of disposition on outcome (Greenberg, 1974a). Nevertheless, the available data are sufficiently poor to leave one with the feeling that this assumption is somewhat treacherous. On the one hand, defendants are more likely to be imprisoned if their offense is an especially serious one, and the rate of recidivism is lower for the more serious crimes: it has long been known, for example, that persons convicted of homicide have an especially low rate of return to crime. In addition, recidivism is highest among youthful offenders, who are less likely than adults to be incarcerated. On the other hand, recidivism also increases with prior record, and persons with longer records are more likely to be incarcerated. Probationers do seem to return to crime less often than ex-prisoners; on the other hand, an F.B.I. six year follow-up on persons brought into, and released from the federal criminal justice system in 1963 indicated that persons who were acquitted or dismissed had a higher re-arrest rate than parolees, and the re-arrest rate for the sample as a whole was a few percentage points higher than for the parolees. No information about possible differences in

Let V be the annual number of virginal arrests for a non-minor crime. A virginal arrest is an arrest of someone who has never before been arrested on a non-minor charge (the individual may, however, have been arrested previously for a minor charge). We assume for the sake of simplicity that persons arrested on non-minor charges all commit index crimes at a uniform rate for T years and then stop. This assumption is somewhat crude, since criminal activity need not be of uniform intensity or character throughout the crime career. Indeed, we have already noted that official parole recidivism data suggest that recidivism rates decline with time, and it has long been known that involvement in criminal behavior declines with age. It is reasonable that in many instances, cessation of involvement in crime would be gradual, not abrupt. Nevertheless, the crudeness of the data make the assumption of uniformity as reasonable as any other.

We also assume that the chances of apprehension remain constant throughout the crime career. A more realistic model would allow this number to vary as the character of crimes committed changed, and as the criminal became both more skilled and better known to law enforcement agencies. We shall denote by p the probability that a non-virgin (someone who has been arrested previously for a non-minor offense) who commits an index offense will be arrested for it. In addition, we shall need to assume that all the quantities of the theory change slowly over a period of time T (the length of the crime career). The plausibility of the assumption will depend somewhat on the magnitude of T.

Since rp represents the annual rate at which non-virgins are arrested on index charges, the reciprocal of this quantity represents the average time interval between arrests. Also, rpT represents the number of additional lifetime index arrests a person arrested for the first time on a non-minor charge will undergo. Blumstein and Larsen (1969) have estimated the number of subsequent index offenses arrests that 20-year-old virgins arrested on index charges will experience, utilizing earlier studies of the recidivism of federal prisoners, and Minnesota state prisoners. The number of subsequent index arrests depends somewhat on the initial offense, rapists and robbers being the least likely to be arrested again (2.2 subsequent index arrests) and auto thieves the most likely (2.8 or 2.9 subsequent index arrests). For our

the rearrest offenses is provided. (Federal Bureau of Investigation, 1970: 38). With better information on the recidivism patterns of different dispositions, our assumption could easily be modified, if necessary.

purposes the difference between these numbers isn't very important. We will take rpT = 2.5 for all non-minor virgin arrests.[17]

An empirical value of rp for juvenile males is obtained from the recently published cohort study of roughly 10,000 Philadelphia boys whose delinquent careers were followed to age 18. Among those arrested for an index offense at least twice, the average time lapse between index arrests was 14.5 months (Wolfgang *et al.*, 1972: 232-233). Comparable information for adults can be obtained from F.B.I. Crime Career data. For the F.B.I.'s sample of nearly a quarter of a million persons arrested on federal or state charges in the period 1970-1972 there had been on the average four arrests up to and including the present arrest, over a period of five years, for an average time lapse between arrests of 1.67 years (Federal Bureau of Investigation, 1973: 38). As not all these arrests would have been for index offenses, for this sample rp would have had some value less than 1/1.67 = 0.6. Indeed, in a five year follow up of offenders released from the federal criminal justice system in 1963, it was found that of those who were arrested (63% of the total), only 43% were arrested for violent crimes (11%) or property crimes (32%). (Federal Bureau of Investigation, 1969: 39).

Unlike subsequent editions, the 1965 edition of *Uniform Crime Reports* distinguishes index from non-index arrests in summarizing information about crime careers. For this year, rp took on a value close to 0.5. It is this value that will be adopted here, rather than the larger value (12/14.5 = 0.86) obtained from the study of Philadelphia juvenile arrests. Even though the Crime Career arrests are not necessarily representative of all adult arrests it seems likely that they would be more representative of non-minor adult arrests than the sample of Philadelphia juveniles. The smaller value of rp for adults is consistent with the tendency of arrest rates to decline with increasing age. Using rp = 0.5, we obtain T = 5 years.[18]

17. This number may be compared with the crime career data provided by the F.B.I. for "known repeaters" arrested in 1966-67, on charges of murder, felonious assault, robbery, burglary, auto theft, and rape. These had an average number of crime index offenses ranging from 3 (auto theft) to 5 (burglary), with the remainder having 4 index arrests, over crime careers ranging between 7 and 11 years. As not all individuals can be assumed to have reached the termination of their crime careers, the ultimate number of average index arrests would presumably be larger. However, the sample is defined as consisting of "known repeaters" (not further defined), and thus is presumably biased toward persons with longer crime careers (Federal Bureau of Investigation, 1968: 35).

18. It should be noted that the crime career as defined here is conceptually not the same as the length of the crime career used in F.B.I.

Next we want to estimate the value of r. From the value for rp just obtained we infer that r cannot be smaller than ½ index offense per year (since p cannot exceed 1). This gives us a lower limit on the amount of recidivist crime: there cannot be less than half an index crime per year for every person released from prison.[19] Since p can be quite a bit less than 1, this lower limit does not exclude the possibility that there are substantially more index crimes per year per ex-prisoner.

We next obtain an upper limit for r. We can do this by noting that an index crime can be committed by persons in any of the following categories: (a) those who have already acquired an arrest record on a non-minor charge, i.e. non-virgins, (b) virgins who are committing an index offense for the first time and who are arrested for it, (c) virgins who are not arrested for the index crime they commit. This group may include professionals who are never arrested, or "amateurs" who commit one or two crimes and then desist without ever experiencing arrest (self-reporting studies of teen-agers suggest that a substantial fraction fall within this category), and some of the persons who have acquired arrest records for minor offenses. If we assume that *all* index crimes are committed by persons in categories (a) and (b), we can obtain an upper limit to the rate at which the non-virgins commit index crimes.

To proceed, we note that the number of persons with non-minor arrest records and whose crime careers have not ended is VT, while the number of crimes each commits is r, each year. Denoting by V the annual number of virginal arrests for an index crime, we have the following inequality:

$$C > V_I + rVT$$

where C represents the annual number of index crimes committed in the United States. Combining this with our previous result for rpT, we obtain

$$p > \frac{2.5V}{C - V} = \frac{2.5V/A}{\frac{C}{A} - \frac{V_I}{A}}$$

publications. For us, crime career measures the time between a first non-minor arrest and the end of a criminal career. The F.B.I., on the other hand, looks at the length of past arrest records of all those arrested in a single year. In general, these need not coincide because not all those represented in the F.B.I. sample will have completed their careers, and because those with very short crime careers will be under-represented in a retrospective calculation, since they tend to drop out of the sample. Numerical examples are given in Blumstein and Larson (1972). The length of the F.B.I.-defined crime career has been falling rapidly in recent years.

19. This result does not imply that every parolee commits at least half an index crime in the year after release. Some will commit none, others one or more. The lower limit says nothing about the proportion of parolees who become involved in new criminal activity.

If we can estimate the value of the ratios in the right-hand member we can compute a lower limit for p and then obtain an upper limit for r.

TABLE 3

NOTATION FOR MODEL 1

A	=	number of persons arrested annually for a non-minor offense
V	=	annual number of virginal arrests for a non-minor crime
V_I	=	annual number of virginal arrests for an index crime
C	=	number of index crimes committed annually
r	=	rate at which persons arrested for non-minor offenses commit crimes
p	=	the probability that a non-virgin who commits an index offense will be arrested for it
T	=	the average length of a crime career from first to last non-minor arrest

There is no published information indicating what percentage of all arrests in a given year are virginal. Of the 1965 arrests represented in the Crime Career file, about 25% were virginal (Federal Bureau of Investigation, 1966: 28); the corresponding figure in 1972 was about 35% (Federal Bureau of Investigation, 1973:38). However, not all the prior arrests were necessarily non-minor, reporting on the part of police agencies is not always perfect, and extrapolation to a national population would be uncertain. Nevertheless, the 1965 value of V/A should indicate the general magnitude of V/A to be expected, though the 1972 value is suggestive of changes in the crime picture.

Actually, consistency compels us to set V/A somewhere in this vicinity. To see this, note that the reciprocal of V/A represents the total number of non-minor career arrests a person arrested for the first time on a non-minor charge will experience. Since not all non-minor arrests are for index offenses, this quantity will be somewhat larger than the number of index arrests a person arrested for a virgin non-minor offense will experience in a career. Consequently we have the inequality $A/V > rpT + 1 = 3.5$, or $V/A < 1/3.5$. Since the majority of non-minor arrests are for index offenses, we can set $V/A = 1/4$, consistent with the 1965 federal data. V_I/A must be smaller than this. We set V_I/A somewhat arbitrarily at $1/5$, noting that p is insensitive to the precise value of this quantity, since the denominator will be dominated by C/A.

C, it will be recalled, was defined as the number of index crimes taking place annually. It is well known that not all crimes are reported to the police. A victimization study conducted in 1965 by the National Opinion Research Center concluded that slightly fewer than half of all index crimes were reported to the police. Other studies of victimization, conducted in Washingon D.C., Chicago, and Boston, found varying degrees of unreporting: in some areas there were 1.5 times as many crimes reported by victims as were reported to the police, while in other areas the rate of non-reporting was 3 or more (President's Commission, 1967: 20-22). The National Crime Panel Surveys conducted by the Census Bureau for the Law Enforcement Assistance Adminstration have begun to provide more recent information on rates of victimization in large cities. With some variation in rates of non-reporting from one city to another, it was found that for 1972, roughly half of crimes of violence and burglary of households were reported to the police, 75-80% of commercial thefts were reported, and about a quarter to a third of personal larcenies (Law Enforcement Assistance Administration, 1974a; 1974b).

Current rates of non-reporting for reporting areas outside the largest cities have not yet been published. In analyzing 1965 data, we will take the ratio of index crimes committed to those reported to be 3; for 1972, we will allow the ratio to vary between 2 and 3. In 1965, 2.78 million index crimes were reported to the police; we assume this corresponds to 8.34 million index offenses committed (Federal Bureau of Investigation, 1966: 3). By 1972, the number of index crimes reported had risen to 5.9 million, which we assume corresponds to somewhere between 11.8 and 17.7 million index offenses.

In 1965, 5.03 million arrests were reported by agencies for jurisdictions encompassing a total population of 135 million. By our criteria, 27% of these arrests were non-minor (Federal Bureau of Investigation, 1966: 112). Extrapolating to the entire U.S. population of 194 million, we find 1.94 million non-minor arrests in 1965. For 1972, the extrapolation is already performed by the F.B.I., and indicates 3.15 million non-minor arrests (Federal Bureau of Investigation, 1973: 119).

From these numbers we obtain $p > 0.15$ and $r < 3.33$ index offenses per year for 1965. For 1972, we find $p > 0.116$ with half of all index crimes assumed non-reported, and $p > 0.176$ if a third of all index crimes are reported. The respective upper limits for r are 4.3 and 2.84. Should the appropriate value for V/A for 1972 turn out to be ⅓ instead of ¼, the lower limits for p would be increased by a factor 1.33, and the upper limits for r would be decreased by the same factor. For definiteness in discussion, we will use the 1965 upper limit in subsequent discussion.

Taking together the lower limit for r established earlier, and the upper limit just established, we have succeeded in bracketing the "true" recidivism rate between 0.5 and 3.33 index offenses per year. If the assumption is correct that released prisoners commit index offenses at the same rate as all non-virgins, the release of N prisoners will result in the commission of somewhere between 0.5N and 3.33N index offenses per year.

It is of some interest to see whether a person previously arrested on a non-minor charge is more or less likely than someone who has not been so arrested to escape apprehension following the commission of an index crime. The chances of apprehension for a person who has such a prior record have just been determined to be larger than 15%. Again assuming that in 1965 the ratio of unreported to reported index crimes was two to one, we find the chances of someone (with or without a prior non-minor arrest) being arrested after committing an index crime to be 6.7% (based on a clearance rate of about 20%). This number, of course, represents an average for all index offenses, and would be much higher for some index offenses than for others. We conclude, then, that a parolee who commits an index crime is more than twice as likely to be arrested for it as someone not on parole.

It may therefore be inferred that if criminal techniques are learned in prison, they do not suffice to overcome ineptitude or the increased jeopardy an official record bestows. Those with serious police records are more likely to be suspected when a crime is reported. As their photographs will be on file in police headquarters, their likelihood of being identified (or mis-identified) by a victim increases. Parolees are subject to unusually intensive surveillance. Their homes and persons can be searched without a warrant. In addition, criminal skills can grow rusty when not practiced during a period of imprisonment. Although communication of criminal skills can and does take place in prison, losers are not necessarily the best teachers.

What can be concluded from these findings about the incapacitative effects of imprisonment? Assume the number of men confined in prison today to be 200,000. Suppose this number were to be cut in half by halving the average sentence length, which is now about two years. Neglecting general deterrence effects, how much extra crime could be anticipated? From the 100,000 men released we could expect somewhere between 50,000 and 333,000 index crimes. Were all prisoners to be freed, and deterrence effects neglected, the crime increment would be double this. Were additional women to be released, their contribution would be smaller, as suggested by the parole recidivism data cited earlier. Since our assumptions about the magnitude of under-reporting implied that in 1965 there were about 8.34 million index crimes, this would represent a total incapacitative effect of imprisonment of between 1.2 and 8%. Were jails and juvenile institutions included, the number would be slightly larger. The same numbers can be used to indicate the decline in crime rates that could be anticipated were prison populations increased by raising sentences.[20]

From the model parameters obtained through our analysis, something can be said about the number of criminals active at any point in time. The number so obtained will help us in deciding where in the range between 0.5 and 3.33 the most likely value of r lies. If the number of index crimes committed in 1965 was 8.34 million, the number of persons committing them was 8.34 million divided by r. The lower limit for r corresponds to 16.68 million criminals; the upper limit, to about 2.5 million; the magnitude of the total incapacitative effect of imprisonment is then equal to the fraction of this population that is imprisoned—8% in the case of the upper limit for r. Now with a crime career of 5 years, in a steady-state model, ⅕ of this population of criminas abandons crime every year, and is replaced by novices just entering criminal careers. Thus, the number of persons entering criminal careers would vary between 3.3 million and 0.5 million depending on the value for r chosen. The larger of these numbers is clearly impossible: not enough males (who, if arrest records are believed, commit most of the index offenses) are born every year. The smaller of the numbers does not seem particu-

20. In making this assertion, we are making some technical assumptions that may not be entirely valid. One is that the duration of imprisonment has no effect on the length of a crime career. Another involves the demand for criminal activities. When criminals are taken out of circulation in substantial numbers through imprisonment, market forces may attract non-criminals into criminal activity. To the extent that this happens, imprisonment will not reduce crime through incapacitation; it will simply create a turn-over in the composition of the criminal labor force. For homicide and other crimes of violence not incidental to the commission of a theft, this effect is probably non-existent. However, for thieves who, through fences, supply a market, and for suppliers of illegal goods and services, this effect may well be important. Thus, according to Lt. Samuel Carter, head of the gambling squad of the Washington D.C. police force, police activity had little impact on the level of gambling activity in that city: "Nothing we've been able to do so far has made much difference. We closed more than 2,000 gambling cases last year, some of big operators. We might be able to tighten things up for a few days or weeks, but there's always somebody else to take their place. It's a never-ending process." (The Washington Post, November 15, 1972). Robert Martinson (1974b) has also discussed this phenomenon in general terms.

larly unreasonable, and appears generally consistent with Christenson's estimates of the distribution of arrests and conviction in the general population (1967: 216). Of course, if a substantial fraction of index crimes are committed by persons who never acquire a non-minor arrest—and for the property offenses this is not an outlandish proposition—the number 0.5 million just obtained would decrease, as would the most plausible value for r.

V. ESTIMATION OF UNDETECTED RECIDIVIST OFFENSES—MODEL 2

An independent, though somewhat crude estimation of the amount of recidivist crime can be obtained using parole recidivism data. In this model we attempt to determine from information about returns to prison with new commitments or allegations something about the magnitude of involvement in new crimes, whether or not detected, for each of the seven index offenses individually. We assume that a parolee's chances of being arrested after committing an index crime will be the same as those of someone in the general population. As our previous discussion indicates, this is a generous assumption, since the evidence suggested that a parolee was more apt than a member of the general public to be arrested after committing an index crime. However, we want to avoid using the lower limit on likelihood of arrest for an index crime previously obtained so as to have an entirely independent calculation. If the other assumptions of this model are valid, the probable consequence of this procedure will be to over-estimate the amount of parolee crime by at least 100%. By making this assumption, however, we can utilize national clearance rates for index offenses.

The official clearance rate allows us to link the number of reported crimes with the number of arrests. However, the clearance rate cannot be simply identified with the fraction of crimes resulting in an arrest, since some crimes are cleared when no arrest takes place, and since a single crime may be cleared by the arrest of more than one person. The correction factor for the nation as a whole can be obtained by comparing index crimes cleared with the number of arrests for index offenses; the ratio of these two quantities is about 0.7. However, when a crime involving a parolee is solved by the arrest of more than one person, there is no reason to assume that all those arrested will be parolees. Consequently it seems preferable to neglect this correction factor, lest one over-correct.

Parole recidivism data tell us the number of returns to prison for index offenses. Tom complete the inferential chain, we need to know the likelihood that a parolee arrested for an index crime will be returned to prison with a new index commitment or allegation. Since parolees are treated quite differently from members of the general public when arrested for a crime, we cannot use the ratio of imprisonments to arrests for the country as a whole.

Some information, though not quite in the form we require, is provided by a study of the California parole system. This study attempted to answer the following question: if a parolee whose original commitment was for crime X is arrested while on parole, how likely is it that the arrest will result in a return to prison (whether the return is technical or with a new commitment). The answer was found to depend somewhat on the nature of X, the original commitment offense. For non-rape sex it was 37.4%, for homicide, 61.6%, and most of the figures for other offenses fell in the range 40 to 50% (Kolodney *et al.*, 1970).

We, however, are interested in the return rate as it depends on the *new* charge, not the old one. It seems reasonable to suppose that at least some of the variation in return rates reflects the nature of the new charge; the variation in return rates with the original charge would then be at least in part a consequence of a (somewhat weak) correlation between the rate of return and the original charge; presumably the more serious the original charge, the more scope it would allow under indeterminate sentencing for giving the parolee extra time without the complications of a trial. In any event, since the variation with original charge is not too drastic, we cannot go too far astray. For definiteness, we assume that 60% of the new homicide charges and 45% of the other index arrests result in a return to prison.[21]

On the basis of these assumptions, we are in a position to construct Table 4. Totalling the number of crimes committed, we find 32,698 index crimes committed by the 25,602 parolees, or 1.28 index offenses per person per year. To achieve comparability with the estimates made earlier, we multiply this figure by 1.5. The reason for this is that Table 3 utilizes the NORC

21. These figures are drawn from California, 1964. Unpublished data made available to me by John Berecochea for California parole revocation actions in 1971-72 show very little change in these numbers. It is anybody's guess whether they are valid for other states. Parole agencies simply do not publish information on the rate at which their parolees are arrested on specific charges. By extrapolating from one state to the nation as a whole, I am clearly skating on thin ice. At present there is no alternative. Should other states be found to imprison a smaller percentage of their arrested parolees, the estimate of crimes prevented by imprisonment obtained using this model would have to be revised upward.

data on nonreporting, which indicates a somewhat smaller degree of nonreporting than the surveys utilized in preparing the other estimates. When this adjustment is made, we find approximately 2 index offenses per year per person. We note that this number would have had to be increased somewhat had the roughly 20% of the parolee sample returned to custody during the first year after release remained at large, since some of those returned would undoubtedly have committed additional offenses had they not been returned to prison. Since it is reasonable to assume that those apprehended and returned to prison would have committed more crimes on the average than those who remained at large, the correction might be larger than the allowance for the 20% sample depletion alone would suggest.

Despite the uncertainty surrounding various aspects of this model calculation, it is noteworthy that the figure obtained falls within the lower and upper limits established by the previous

TABLE 4

1970 MALE PAROLE RECIDIVISM, ONE YEAR, UNDETECTED CRIME ESTIMATE (25,602 parolees)

Offense	Return to Prison New Commitment (s) or Allegations	Number of Arrests*	Crimes Reported to Police**	Crimes Committed***	Percent Crime Increase if 100,000 Men are Released
non-negligent homicide	36	58	67	67	1.65%
forcible rape	28	62	112	448	1.16%
robbery	277	617	2160	3240	2.42%
burglary	594	1320	7000	21000	1.26%
aggravated assault	120	266	399	798	0.47%
grand larceny	255	566	3110	4665	0.69%
auto theft	189	420	2480	2480	1.05%

*The manner in which the number of arrests is obtained from the number of commitments is described in the text.

**Clearance rates as reported in *Uniform Crime Reports* vary only slightly from one year to the next. We have used the following values: homicide 86%, rape 55.4%, robbery 28.5%, assault 66.7%, burglary 18.9%, larceny 18.2%, auto theft, 17%.

***Here we approximate NORC victimization data to determine rates of non-reporting. Specifically, we assume all homicides are reported, 25% of all rapes, 67% of all robberies, 50% of all aggravated assaults, 1/3 of all burglaries, 2/3 of all larcenies, and all auto thefts. It should be noted that the entries in the final column do not depend on these numbers.

calculation, performed with an entirely different set of assumptions. One would be inclined to place greater confidence in it, were it not so heavily dependent on numbers derived from a single state.

In the final colum of Table 4, we indicate the percentage increase in each of the index offenses that might be anticipated on the basis of this calculation were 100,000 men to be released from prison. The increase ranges from a fraction of a percent for aggravated assault and larceny to as much as 2.42% for robbery. Were the size of the prison population to be increased by increasing sentence lengths, the same table would indicate the corresponding reduction in crime that might be expected, again ignoring all deterrence effects and possible effects of imprisonment on the length of crime careers (about which nothing is known).

The magnitude of the crime prevented through incapacitation must be reduced by the amount of crime committed as a result of imprisonment, by inmates against other inmates and guards, and by guards against inmates. There are no statistics available concerning such crime rates for the nation as a whole, but an idea of their magnitude can be obtained from statistics concerning homicides committed by California prisoners in 1971 against guards and other prisoners. During that year, 17 inmates and 7 guards were killed (Research Division, 1973). On June 30, 1971, the institutional population of California prisons was 21,789. Taking this to be the average population of the California prison system for that year, we find the incapacitative effect of prison on homicide reduced by 42%. Were information on homicides committed by guards against prisoners available, the reduction might be even larger. Of course there was more violence in 1971 in California prisons than there had been in earlier years, and it is possible that other states have lower rates of violence. Nevertheless, it is clear that when one resorts to imprisonment to solve the crime problem, the crime problem reappears within the prison. If crimes against prisoners are no less worth preventing than crimes against non-prisoners, this phenomenon cannot be neglected in a consideration of the incapacitative effects of imprisonment.

VI. DISCUSSION

Subject to the uncertainties of the data base and the limitations of the assumptions employed, the two model calculations presented here provide order-of-magnitude estimates of the collective incapacitative effect of imprisonment, quite apart from any deterrent effect. It was concluded that the amount of index crime prevented by the physical restraint of the present population of prisoners amounted to no more than 8% of the total. An increase of a year in the present average sentence length of 2 years could be expected to increase this figure by about 4%; a corresponding decrease in sentence lengths would reduce it by the same amount. Our analysis of the inaccuracies of crime prediction suggests that selective confinement on a predictive basis is not a promising direction for improving the incapacitative effectiveness of penal incarceration.

Whether variations in crime rates of this magnitude are substantively important is a matter of judgment. From one perspective, they are equivalent to setting the calendar a year or so ahead or back, since reported crime rates regularly increase by this much from one year to the next. From another perspective, the absence of firm evidence of a deterrent effect leaves open the possibility that the incapacitative effect is a major component of the reduction in crime rates attributable to law enforcement activity.

Two factors limit the size of the incapacitative function of imprisonment. One is the low rate of return to serious crime among parolees. This low rate has been disguised by rates of return to prison for technical violations of parole regulations. This rate may indicate that many inmates are nearing the end of their crime careers by the time they are sent to prison.

The other factor is the low rate of imprisonment for index crimes. In part this reflects low clearance rates; in part, it reflects prosecutorial discretion to drop charges or reduce them to misdemeanors, and judicial reluctance to impose prison sentences. This reluctance is especially high in the case of juvenile defendants, who comprise a large and increasing part of our serious crime picture. Were all adults and juveniles found to have committed index crimes deprived of liberty for a period as long on the average as the sentences served by those now imprisoned (or even somewhat shorter), the incapacitative effect of imprisonment would surely increase by a substantial amount.

Another conceivable route to increasing the incapacitative function of imprisonment would be a "throw away the key" policy. Were all persons now imprisoned held for life, the incapacitative function of imprisonment would again be larger. To determine just how large, we would have to know the percentage of persons involved in serious crime who have been in prison. Strictly speaking, little is known about the characteristics of individuals who commit serious crimes, but subject to dangers arising from possible biases in the sampling, we can say something about those who become involved in the criminal justice system. The percentage of such persons who have previously been in prison is just the percentage by which crime would be reduced were a "throw away the key" policy to be put into effect, leaving aside deterrent and labor market considerations.

Of the national sample of male parolees released in 1970, 67% had no prior prison experience, though only 27% had no prior non-prison sentences (National Probation and Parole Institutes, 1972). This figure varies from one state to another. In California, 74.3% of the male prisoners newly received from the courts had no prior prison commitment (Research Division, n.d.); in Wisconsin, 69.9% of sentenced offenders admitted to adult correctional institutions in 1970 had no previous experience in a penal institution (Division of Corrections, 1971). For Michigan commitments in 1969, the corresponding figure was 62% (Department of Corrections, 1970), and in New York in 1964, it was 53.6% (Commission of Corrections, 1965). Were the prison population a representative sample of the criminal population, one would be able to say that on a nationwide basis, perpetual confinement of all felons would eliminate about a third of all felonies; and in states like New York, where an unusually high percentage of prison inmates have been in prison before (this is probably a consequence of greater willingness to grant probation), the percentage might approach half.

There are two reasons, however, why this reasoning is incorrect. Since the decision to impose a prison sentence may itself be influenced by the defendant's prior record, it is instructive to look at the characteristics of defendants at an earlier stage in processing.[22] Here data are more scarce, but one finds, for

22. Indeed, this suggests an alternative approach to the incapacitation problem. With a representative sample of arrests for index crimes, one could determine the fraction of such crimes that would have been prevented had the prison population been expanded by extending all sentences for one year by noting what percentage of arrestees had been released from prison within the preceding year, and the consequences of indefinite confinement from the percentage of arrestees who had ever been in prison. Only California provides information of this sort. For 1971, 5.5% of all persons arrested for homicide were on parole and 17.4% had been in prison; comparable figures for rape were 5.4% and 16.9%; for robbery 7.3% and 21.0%; for aggravated assault 2.6% and 12.3%; for burglary, 7.2% and 22.0%; for grand larceny 6.0% and 19.3%; for auto theft 5.1% and 18.4% and for drug offenses 2.6% and 9.6%. (Governor's Select Committee, 1973: 99-130). Since roughly 95% of felons released from prison in California are released on parole, and since most parolees do two years or more on parole (unless returned to prison earlier), one would infer an incapacitative effect of one additional year in prison to be 3-4%, consistent with the figures obtained in

example, that in 1969, only 23.6% of all defendants convicted in federal district courts had a prior prison record (Administrative Office, 1971). In California in 1970, only 22.6% of Superior Court defendants had no prior criminal record of any sort, but only 14.% had a prior prison record. This represents a decrease from 1966, when 19.6% of California Superior Court defendants had a prior prison record (Bureau of Criminal Statistics, n.d.: 45).

These records are not fully trustworthy because of possible incomplete recording. Were juvenile incarcerations included, the percentage with prior institutional experience would be somewhat larger. Nevertheless, if one is concerned with the incapacitative effect of indefinitely extending *adult* sentences—and we have been concerned throughout only with the incapacitative effect of adult prisons—it is appropriate to exclude juvenile commitments. Since a certain amount of selection takes place before one becomes a defendant, and since prior prison record may be a selection criterion at these earlier stages as well, even the above figures, which suggest a crime reduction effect of 15-25% for perpetual confinement, may be an overestimate.

All of the above figures are drawn from those agencies in the criminal justice system that process adults. A major fraction of index crimes—indeed, a majority of crimes involving theft without violence—involve juveniles. Since juveniles have had less time to accumulate a record, it comes as no surprise that they are less likely than adults to have a commitment record. Comparing the prior commitment records of juveniles committed to the California Youth Authority in 1964 with the records of adults committed the previous year to the Department of Corrections, we find 78% of the juveniles committed for homicide had no prior record of any kind, as compared with 34% for the adults; for robbery, the respective figures were 63% versus 17%; for assault, 59% versus 17%, for burglary, 54% as compared with 6%, and for auto theft, 47% versus 1%. (Space—General Corpotion, 1965: 213-214). This greatly reduces the degree to which crimes can be reduced by extending the period of confinement for adults—or for juveniles (since a smaller percentage of juveniles have entered the institution in the first place). Moreover, one sees that it is for the more serious offenses that the percentage of inmates with prior prison experience is lowest. Thus extended confinement—or an equivalent policy (execution,

our first model; and a crime reduction of about 20% for a "throw away the key" policy of lifetime imprisonment for all those now sent to prison. If parolees are caught more often than other felons, the result would be correspondingly smaller.

exile, perfect rehabilitation) that permanently removed individuals from the population of active criminals—would be least effective for the crimes one presumably cared most about reducing.

Our estimates here are much lower than those implicit in claims about the criminal justice system previously published by former U.S. Attorney General Ramsey Clark. According to Clark:

> Much of our crime is caused by the inhumanity of our prisons and by our failure to rehabilitate those we send to them . . . . The most important statistic on crime is the one which tells us that 80 per cent of all felonies are committed by repeaters. Four-fifths of our major crimes are committed by people already known to the criminal justice system . . . If only one-half of the repeated crime we now suffer could be eliminated, society would be free of 40 per cent of all serious crime (Clark, 1970: 215).

Clark goes on to state (1970: 229) that "better than one-half of all the people who leave prisons return convicted of a subsequent crime . . . ."

This is an extremely misleading depiction of our crime problem. More than half of those who leave a prison do not return with a new criminal conviction. The rate of return to prison is indeed high, but most returns are not the result of new convictions. Moreover, no method is presently known to reduce repeated crime by half through rehabilitation. The statement that prisoners should be successfully rehabilitated has about the same status as the statement that terminal cancer patients should be cured: the wish does not provide the means for accomplishing it.

Clark's assertion that 80 percent of all felonies are committed by repeaters does not imply that such a high proportion of offenders have been in prison. Of those arrested for serious crimes, the majority have been arrested previously, but these arrests need not have been for a serious offense, and could have taken place long before the felony arrest. The number of persons arrested each year on *some* charge is extremely large. In 1972, an estimated 8.7 million non-traffic arrests were made (Federal Bureau of Investigation, 1973: 115). It was estimated that 47% of the male population would be arrested sometime during a lifetime, and that this figure, estimated almost ten years, ago, was rising (Christenson, 1967: 216). That a high proportion of persons arrested on felony charges have at some time in the past been arrested for something is consequently not very informative. Since many of those persons had charges against them dismissed, or were acquitted, or were convicted of a crime insufficiently serious to lead to long-term involvement with the penal system, it seems somewhat unfair to attribute their subsequent involvement in a felony to the prison. There are certainly no grounds for blaming the inhumanity of the prison and its failure to rehabilitate for much of our crime. And the reduction in crime rates by a factor of 5 that Clark implicitly anticipates from a perfect rehabilitation system for prisoners is clearly a gross exaggeration. Ten to fifteen percent perhaps, but hardly more—unless the system were applied to all arrested and convicted persons, including probationers, persons fined, and those sent to jail, or otherwise sentenced to a disposition not involving imprisonment.

The implications of our estimates for public policy are not entirely clear. The proponent of incapacitation might use them to argue for a substantial increase in the size of the prison population. Someone else might argue that the prison population could safely be reduced, since crime would increase by only a small amount. Since the benefits of imprisonment (reduced crime) and its costs (taxpayer costs and costs to those confined) are distributed to different populations, it would be difficult to use standard cost-effectiveness techniques to decide on appropriate trade-offs between costs and benefits. How much suffering through imprisonment can be legitimately imposed on offenders to reduce rates of victimization by some amount is a judgment not easily made.

In the author's view, questions about the severity of punishment are best governed by the gravity of the offense. Unlike street lighting, which may also reduce crime, imprisonment imposes very heavy costs on a limited number of individuals; for this reason it cannot be treated as a simple problem in social engineering. Even in Biblical times, it was recognized that it would be immoral to punish offenders with a severity in excess of the harm that they had themselves inflicted. The concept that the interests of offenders cannot be sacrificed to an unlimited degree even if to do so is socially advantageous would seem to be as essential a protection against the Leviathan now as when the authors of the Declaration of Independence insisted that some rights were inalienable. In the extreme, few would dissent from this proposition: even if it were known that life imprisonment effectively discouraged parking offenses or shoplifting, it would stil be rejected as an unjust punishment because of its disproportionality to the seriousness of the offense. If these essentially retributive notions of punishment retain their importance, as I believe they do, empirical knowledge of the effects of punishment on crime rates would be of subsidiary importance, perhaps of relevance in deciding between alternate punishments of roughly equal severity, but otherwise beside the point. For the more utilitarian-minded, the estimates presented here may have greater bearing on questions of policy.

Our findings do have considerable bearing, however, on the parole system. Parole seems incapable of performing either of the two functions for which it was initially intended. It is incapable of making accurate predictions about behavior after release, and consequently is unable to make rational decisions of the kind required by a system of selective incapacitation. This inability presently results in the wrongful continued imprisonment of many inmates. In addition, parole supervision seems incapable of preventing released prisoners from returning to crime. Instead it functions as an obstacle, preventing those who have once been given a deviant social identity from returning to a normal existence. The revolving door from which released inmates find it so difficult to escape is in significant measure a product of parole. It would be a step forward for inmates were parole abolished, along with any attempt to utilize predictive methods in the determination of sentences. Following release, ex-prisoners would then be subjected to the same laws and surveillance as other citizens, with the parole agency functioning as a strictly voluntary helping organization to assist released inmates (when asked) with reentry problems—finding a job, locating a residence, coping with bureaucratic hassles, making friends, and the like.

REFERENCES

BABST, D.V., and J.W. MANNERING (1965) "Probation versus Imprisonment for Similar Types of Offenders—a Comparison by Subsequent Violations," 2 *Journal of Research in Crime and Delinquency* 60.

BERECOCHEA, John E., Dorothy R. JAMAN, and Welton A. JONES (1973) *Time Served in Prison and Parole Outcome: An Experimental Study*. Sacramento: California Department of Corrections Research Division.

BLUMSTEIN, Alfred and Richard LARSON (1969) "Models of a Total Criminal Justice System," 17 *Operations Research* 199.

——— (1972) "Problems in Modeling and Measuring Recidivism," 8 *Journal of Research in Crime and Delinquency* 124.

BOARD OF DIRECTORS, NATIONAL COUNCIL ON CRIME AND DELINQUENCY (1973) "The Nondangerous Offender Should Not be Imprisoned," 19 *Crime and Delinquency* 449.

BUREAU OF CRIMINAL STATISTICS, *Crime and Delinquency in California, 1970*. Sacramento: California Department of Justice.

CARNEY, Francis J. (1967) "Predicting Recidivism in a Medium Security Correctional Institution," 58 *Journal of Criminal Law, Criminology and Police Science* 338.

CHRISTENSON, Ronald (1967) "Projected Percentage of U.S. Population with Criminal Arrest and Conviction Records," in President's Commission on Law Enforcement and the Administration of Justice, *Task Force Report: Science and Technology.* Washington D.C.: Government Printing Office.

CLARK, Ramsey (1970) *Crime in America.* New York: Simon and Schuster.

———— and David RUDENSTINE (1975) *Prison Without Walls: Report on New York Parole.* New York: Praeger.

CLARKE, Stevens H. (1974) "Getting 'Em Out of Circulation: Does Incarceration of Juvenile Offenders Reduce Crime?" 65 *Journal of Criminal Law and Criminology* 528.

COMMISSION OF CORRECTIONS (1965) *Thirty-Eighth Annual Report for the Year 1964.* Ossining: State of New York.

DEPARTMENT OF CORRECTIONS (1970) *1969 Criminal Statistics.* State of Michigan.

DIVISION OF CORRECTIONS (1971) *Offenders Admitted to Adult Correctional Institutions Calendar 1970.* Madison: Wisconsin Bureau of Planning, Development and Research.

EHRLICH, Isaac (1973) "Participation in Illegitimate Activities: A Theoretical and Empirical Investigation," 81 *Journal of Political Economy* 521.

FEDERAL BUREAU OF INVESTIGATION (1966) *Uniform Crime Reports-1965.* Washington D.C.: Government Printing Office.

———— (1968) *Uniform Crime Reports-1967.* Washington D.C.: Government Printing Office.

———— (1969) *Uniform Crime Reports-1968.* Washington D.C.: Government Printing Office.

———— (1971) *Uniform Crime Reports-1970.* Washington D.C.: Government Printing Office.

———— (1972) *Uniform Crime Reports-1971.* Washington D.C.: Government Printing Office.

———— (1973) *Uniform Crime Reports-1972.* Washington D.C.: Government Printing Office.

FEDERAL BUREAU OF PRISONS (n.d.) *State Prisoners: Admissions and Releases,* 1970. Washington D.C.: U.S. Department of Justice.

———— (1974) *Statistical Reports Fiscal Year 1973.* Washington D.C.: U.S. Department of Justice.

FOOTE, Caleb (1970) "Comments on Preventive Detention," 23 *Journal of Legal Studies* 48.

GOLDFARB, Ronald and Linda SINGER (1973) *After Conviction.* New York: Simon and Schuster.

GOVERNOR'S SELECT COMMITTEE ON LAW ENFORCEMENT PROBLEMS (1973) *Controlling Crime in California.* Sacramento, California.

GREENBERG, David F. (1974a) "Much Ado About Little: The Correctional Effects of Corrections," Unpublished paper prepared for the Committee for the Study of Incarceration.

———— (1974b) "Involuntary Psychiatric Commitments to Prevent Suicide," 49 *N.Y.U. Law Review* 227.

———— (1975) "Theft, Rationality, and the Methodology of Deterrence Research," to be presented at the Annual Meeting of the American Sociological Association.

HAMMOND, W.H. (1969) *The Sentence of the Court.* London: Her Majesty's Stationery Office.

HOLT, Norman (1974) "Rational Risk-Taking: Some Alternatives to Traditional Correctional Programs," Paper presented to the American Correctional Association Conference on Parole-Corrections Project, San Antonio, Texas.

IRWIN, John (1970) *The Felon.* Englewood Cliffs: Prentice-Hall, Inc.

KASSEBAUM, Gene, David A. WARD, and Daniel M. WILNER (1971) *Prison Treatment and Parole Survival.* New York: John Wiley and Sons.

KOLODNEY, Steve E., Paul L. PATTERSON, Douglas DAETZ, and Robert L. MARX (1970) "A Study of the Characteristics and Recidivism Experience of California Prisoners," in *Parole Board Reform in California*, Report of the Select Committee on the Administration of Justice. Sacramento: Assembly of the State of California.

LAMB, H.R. and V. GOERTZEL (1974) "Ellsworth House: A Community Alternative," 131 *American Journal of Psychiatry* 64.

LAW ENFORCEMENT ASSISTANCE ADMINISTRATION (1974a) *Crime in the Nation's Five Largest Cities.* National Crime Panel Surveys of Chicago, Detroit, Los Angeles, New York, and Philadelphia. Advance Report. Washington, D.C.: U.S. Department of Justice.

——— (1974b) *Crime in Eight American Cities.* National Crime Panel Surveys of Atlanta, Baltimore, Cleveland, Dallas, Denver, Newark, Portland, and St. Louis. Advance Report. Washington D.C.: U.S. Department of Justice.

LIPTON, Douglas, Robert MARTINSON, and Judith WILKS (1975) *The Effectiveness of Correctional Treatments.* New York: Praeger Publishers.

MARTINSON, Robert (1974a) "What Works?—Questions and Answers about Prison Reform," 35 *The Public Interest* 22.

——— (1974b) "On Incapacitation—Physical Restraint in Crime Control," Unpublished paper.

MITFORD, Jessica (1973) *Kind and Usual Punishment.* New York: Alfred A. Knopf.

NATIONAL PROBATION AND PAROLE INSTITUTES (1972) *Uniform Parole Reports Newsletter.* Davis: National Council on Crime and Delinquency (November).

——— (1973) *Uniform Parole Reports Newsletter.* Davis: National Council on Crime and Delinquency (February).

PRESIDENT'S COMMISSION ON LAW ENFORCEMENT AND THE ADMINISTRATION OF JUSTICE (1967) *The Challenge of Crime in a Free Society.* Washington D.C.: Government Printing Office.

RESEARCH DIVISION (1968) *California Prisoners 1964-6.* Sacramento: California Department of Corrections.

——— (1971a) "Parole Outcome of Felon Releases to California Parole in 1968-1970." Unpublished document of the California Department of Corrections.

——— (1971b) "Parole Outcome of Felon Releases to California Parole 1962-1969 by Parole Office of Release," Unpublished document of the California Department of Corrections.

——— (1973) "Number of Persons Fatally Injured Due to Assaultive Incidents," Unpublished document of the California Department of Corrections (March 21).

SCHUR, Edwin M. (1971) *Labeling Deviant Behavior.* New York: Harper and Row.

SHOHAM, Shlomo (1966) *Crime and Social Deviance.* Chicago: Henry Regnery.

SILVER, Morris (1974) "Punishment, Deterrence and Police Effectiveness: A Survey and Critical Interpretation of the Recent Econometric Literature," unpublished paper.

SPACE-GENERAL CORPORATION (1965) *Prevention and Control of Crime and Delinquency, Final Report.* El Monte, California: Space-General Corporation.

STUDT, Eliot (1973) *Surveillance and Service in Parole.* Washington D.C.: Law Enforcement Assistance Administration.

TAKAGI, Paul (1967) *Evaluation Systems and Adaptations in a Formal Organization.* Ph.D. Dissertation, Department of Sociology, Stanford University.

TULLOCK, Gordon (1974) "Does Punishment Deter Crime?" 36 *The Public Interest.*

VON HIRSCH, Andrew (1972) "Prediction of Criminal Conduct and Preventive Confinement of Convicted Persons," 21 *Buffalo Law Review* 717.

WENK, Ernst A. and Robert L. EMRICH (1972) "Assaultive Youth: An Exploratory Study of the Assaultive Experience and Assaultive Potential of California Youth Authority Wards," 9 *Journal of Research in Crime and Delinquency* 171.

WENK, Ernst A., and James O. ROBISON (1971) "Assaultive Experience and Assaultive Potential: An Exploratory Study," Unpublished paper prepared for the National Council on Crime and Delinquency.

WENK, Ernst A., James O. ROBISON, and Gerald W. SMITH (1972) "Can Violence Be Predicted?" 18 *Crime and Delinquency* 393.

WILKINS, Leslie T. (1958) "A Small Comparative Study of the Results of Probation," 8 *British Journal of Delinquency* 201.

WOLFGANG, Marvin, Robert M. FIGLIO, and Thorsten SELLIN (1972) *Delinquency in a Birth Cohort.* Chicago: University of Chicago Press.

Part III
Understanding the Criminal Law and Criminal Justice System

[8]
The Dialectics of Crime Control

THEORETICAL PERSPECTIVES ON CRIME CONTROL

Although criminologists have generally agreed that the explanation of crime control is one of the central tasks of criminology, our understanding of why changes in criminal law and its enforcement take place remains theoretically primitive. Historians have carried out many case studies of such changes, but often they have abstained from explaining the events they describe. Sociologists, on the other hand, commonly devise explanations for a particular change of interest without considering how widely the explanations can be generalized. Textbook treatments typically survey these explanations but without reconciling or synthesizing discrepancies of perspective.

Until these matters are clarified, the continued multiplication of case studies will make only a limited contribution to our understanding of crime control. It is in the hope of contributing to this clarification that we point to deficiencies in the explanations currently in vogue, and show how Marxian theory can contribute to an understanding of historical changes in the scope, methods, and legitimating ideologies of crime control. The framework we develop will be used to discuss changes in crime control in England and the United States from the industrial revolution to the present.[1] Because of space limitations, our treatment will necessarily be somewhat schematic; we focus on those features of selected developments that are of analytical significance.

We begin by examining the logic of explanations for changes in crime control that appear often in the literature. Broadly speaking, these explanations fall into two types: systems theories and theories concerned with agency. We consider each in turn.

Systems theories

Systems theories explain the features of a social system in terms of the functional needs of the system—the needs that must be met if the system is to continue functioning as a system. For example, laws prohibiting murder have been explained by the assertion that in the absence of such laws people would kill one another off to the extent that society itself would disappear.

Systems theorists typically assume that crime control mechanisms prevent or contain disruptive or disequilibrating tendencies that arise from within the social system or from outside it. Criminal justice is thus a self-correcting or restorative mechanism (Parsons, 1951; Parsons and Gerstein, 1977). Functionalist sociologists who have interpreted repressive punishment in terms of its presumed effects of reinforcing normative consensus and restoring social solidarity in the face of deviance use this reasoning (Durkheim, 1893:67–72, and 1895:70–110; Erikson, 1966; Inverarity, 1976). Although Marxists have criticized the functionalist characterization of society as consensual, and have argued against the proposition that a mode of production based on exploitation can be stabilized in the long run, some Marxian theorists have discussed crime control in similar terms. Thus Poulantzas, following Althusser, discusses the "state apparatuses" (which include the police, the courts, the prison system, and the army) in terms of their "principal role," which is "to maintain the unity and cohesion of a social formation by concentrating and sanctioning class domination, and in this way reproducing social relations, i.e. class relations" (Poulantzas, 1974: 25). Whereas earlier Marxist writings tended to argue that this was true because state officeholders were themselves capitalists or were directly subservient to them, the more recent structuralist Marxist literature holds that the constraints on state policy are so large that this will be true no matter what the social backgrounds of officeholders.

It is the essence of a systems theory that the explanation of a social phenomenon does not refer to the meanings or goals of the members of the society.[2] It does not see change as a consequence of the purposeful activity of identifiable social actors, but as a spontaneous and unwitting convulsion of the entire social system. Nor does it explain how or why anyone realizes what a system or a mode of production needs and insures that these needs are met. Thus the system or mode of production must itself be endowed with omniscience and omnipotence. (In this sense, systems theories reify social relations. Moreover, in supposing that a mode of production is always capable of securing its own reproduction, systems theories leave inexplicable the replacement of one mode of production by another. The Marxian notion of contradiction makes explicit the possibility that a mode of production will not be able to reproduce itself (Hirst and Hindess, 1975).)

Since systems theories also fail to specify how the outcome (crime control) is connected to the cause (functional need of the system), they are at best incomplete. The implied assumption that there is always no more than one way to fulfill a given need remains to be demonstrated. One must also question whether an observed criminal prohibition is in fact always vital to the survival of the society. Is it plausible, for example, that in the absence of repressive legislation, homosexuality in late-nineteenth-century England

and the United States would have increased to the point where it threatened population growth or destroyed the nuclear family? Nothing of the sort happened in France, where the Napoleonic Code abolished all legal prohibitions against homosexual activity among consenting adults. Can it be argued persuasively that the prohibition of alcohol was necessary for the survival of American capitalism in 1920, but not necessary a little more than a decade later when the Eighteenth Amendment was repealed? Claims such as these would not be credible. To understand this legislative history we must look beyond the "needs" of the social system, though without abandoning the obviously valuable insight that a society's social control machinery is in some way related to the character of the society in question.

Theories of agency

Theories of agency derive from Becker's (1966) observation that legal rules prohibiting specified conduct do not create themselves, but are instead the product of "entrepreneurs" who crusade for the adoption of the rules they wish to see enacted, perhaps at the expense of others. In the words of one non-Marxian conflict theorist:

> If there were no groups trying to control the activities of other groups and trying to enforce their wills upon those other groups through the legislative processes, there would be no laws making some activities "crimes" and there could, consequently, be no "criminals." ... the criminal laws are specifically enacted by the middle and upper classes to place the poorer classes under the more direct control of the police. (Douglas, 1971:xvii)

Theories of agency identify the social agents responsible for changes in criminalization and specify why they seek change. In this respect, they supply what is missing in systems theories.

Becker's suggestion has been extended to include group or collective entrepreneurs as well as individuals, and case studies have implicated a number of different groups who have at one time or another widened or narrowed the scope of crime control, including government bureaucracies (Dickson, 1968; Belknap, 1977; Embree, 1977), professional interest groups (Humphries, 1977) and status groups (Gusfield, 1963; Zurcher and Kirkpatrick, 1976).

The Marxian literature, on the other hand, has paid more attention to class as the most salient category. Thus Quinney (1977:45) holds that "law ... is an instrument of the state that serves the interest of the developing capitalist ruling class.... Law and legal repression are, and continue to serve as the means of enforcing the interests of the dominant class in the capitalist state." Many instances where the historical evidence suggests that law did indeed serve dominant class interests have been located; for the best single summary of this literature, see Chambliss (1974).

Many of the non-Marxian analyses of agency are vulnerable to criticism on grounds of voluntarism. Becker (1963), for example, never indicates why a particular entrepreneur chooses a particular category of behavior as the target of a campaign. The choice appears completely arbitrary and unrelated to any objective social conditions.[3] There is no conception of social structure other than a kaleidoscope of groups defined by all kinds of criteria (age, race, sex, wealth, religion, etc.). Why groups form on the basis of any particular criterion, and why one group succeeds in its entrepreneurial efforts while another group fails is not addressed. The assertion that rules are made by "the powerful" (found in much of the labeling theory literature) doesn't take us very far in the absence of a theory of the sources of power (Liazos, 1972; Thio, 1973).

Marxists conceptualize social structure more clearly, but their works frequently pose serious problems. As we noted earlier, many of the empirical studies carried out by non-Marxists show us groups defined along lines other than class. Marxists have largely neglected the implications that the existence of such groups have for a theory in which the only social differentiation recognized is that of class.

Another set of problems revolves around the assumption made by some Marxist writers (e.g., Hepburn, 1977; Quinney, 1977; and with some minor reservations, Michalowski and Bolander, 1976) that the capitalist class is unified, all-powerful, and invariably capable of ensuring that legislation reflects its interests alone.[4] Since at times capitalists are visibly divided, and since some legislation has been adopted despite capitalist opposition (much labor legislation, some consumer legislation, and recent environmental protection measures), this view can be sustained only if one is willing to suppose that the ruling class pretends to be divided and shrewdly decides to let other classes win a few legislative battles in order to deceive them into thinking that they really do have a chance to influence legislative outcomes. Surely this is preposterous.

As Spitzer (1980) and Fine (1979) have noted, even when a crime control measure does embody the interests of a class, the form that the measure takes can rarely be explained in terms of the interest alone. In pursuing its interest, a class is checked by many constraints (e.g., the costs of implementation and the resources available for meeting them, the level and forms of class struggle, the character of the state, the need to legitimate its actions to other classes.)

Insufficient attention has been given in this literature to the gradual and largely nonconflictual processes through which the appropriate targets and methods of crime control are redefined in response to changed social circumstances. If systems theorists err by neglecting consciousness entirely, theorists of agency err by neglecting the processes through which consciousness forms and actors acquire subjective interests. Seeing entrepreneurs, theorists attribute changes in public perception of social conditions to the entrepreneurs, without considering that the perceptions of the entrepreneurs themselves must be explained. In short, a theory of interests, and indeed, of consciousness generally, is missing from much of this work.

What is needed in a theory of historical change in crime control is implicit in the criticisms we have raised of earlier work. A theory must locate agents of change structurally, specify how they come to regard a particular form of change as desirable, and show why they are able or unable to achieve what they seek. Marxism can aid in the task of developing such a theory.

A Marxian framework

CLASS AND CONTROL Marxist theory begins with the social relations of production. When direct producers are separated from the means of production, and distribution is not collective, society is divided into classes. The class that does not produce, but expropriates the surplus produced by others, is characterized as an exploiting class; while the producers, deprived of the use of their full product, are regarded as an exploited class. As several modes of production (e.g., capitalist, feudal, slave, and petty commodity production) may coexist in a single social formation (Marx, 1858:106–7), there is typically a multiplicity of classes.

Since classes are postulated to have opposing interests with regard to the use of the means of production and the distribution of the product, a source of instability is present in all class societies. It follows that exploitative modes of production do not reproduce themselves through economic means alone. An exploited class will seek to reduce or eliminate its exploitation. On the other hand, an exploiting class will attempt to preserve exploitative class relations.

Criminalization is one tactic among many that an exploiting class will attempt to use in doing this. Exploiting classes will thus define as illegal, and try to punish, actions that threaten its interests. For example, it may seek to eliminate forms of appropriation of wealth that are inconsistent with the mode of production in question by defining them as theft and attaching penal sanctions to those who "steal." This strategy, of course, requires that the state define as criminal those actions that run counter to the interests of the exploiting class. Marxists have generally held that the state will do just that.

An exploited class need not necessarily accept the views of the exploiting class as to what actions should be criminalized. The exploited may oppose the views of the exploiters and attempt to gain acceptance for views that embody their own class interests. Lacking the financial and political resources of the exploiting class, however, they are likely to be relatively less successful. They thus may be compelled to rely on extra-legal or illegal methods of control, such as strikes and industrial sabotage. The exploiting class will in turn attempt to frustrate these attempts through its own control measures, ranging from firings to injunctions and criminal prohibitions.

We thus have a dynamic picture of crime control as both the subject of class conflict and the instrument of class control. As class conflict evolves, so will the scope and forms of control employed by both exploiting and exploited classes.[5]

Marxist theory does not exclude the possibility that the factual premises from which a class defines its interests and formulates control strategies may be wrong. Marx's comment to the reader of *Capital* is worth recalling here:

> If, as the reader will have realized to his great dismay, the analysis of the actual intrinsic relations of the capitalist process of production is a very complicated matter and very extensive; if it is a work of science to resolve the visible, merely external movement into the true intrinsic movement, it is self-evident that conceptions which arise about the laws of production in the minds of agents of capitalist production and circulation will diverge drastically from these real laws and will merely be the conscious expression of the visible movements. The conceptions of the merchant, stockbroker, and banker, are necessarily quite distorted. Those of the manufacturers are vitiated by the acts of circulation to which their capital is subject, and by the levelling of the general rate of profit. Competition likewise assumes a completely distorted role in their minds. (Marx, 1894:312—13)

The same may of course be true of other classes as well. As a consequence, crime control strategies cannot be a simple reflection of the "objective" needs of a class. One must at times examine the ways in which the relations of production give rise to misconceptions that shape crime control.

We must also note that the reproduction of class relations may require that a dominant class criminalize the actions of *its own members*. For example, the survival of individual capitalists would be jeopardized if a single capitalist were to gain control over an entire sector of the economy and use this control to raise prices to other capitalist purchasers or to undersell competitors. To prevent this, capitalists may support anti-monopoly legislation. It is likewise important to individual capitalists that no single capitalist gain control of the state and use this control to the detriment of all the others. Capitalists may thus support political arrangements that restrain the state, such as checks and balances between branches of government, and popular elections.

The same is true of the working class. Its members have a common interest in discouraging workers who may be tempted to sacrifice the interests of their class for personal advantage, and thus may support criminal penalties for thieves and narcotics merchants who prey on members of their community.

It need not be the case that classes will disagree about every aspect of crime control. After noting the existence of three classes in nineteenth-century Europe—the feudal aristocracy, the bourgeoisie, and the proletariat—each with its distinctive morality, Engels notes (in a passage that should lay to rest the notion that Marxism can be refuted by evidence that classes agree about the wrongfulness of certain crimes) that the classes' moral theories have much in common:

> These moral theories represent three different stages of the same historical development, and have therefore a common historical background, and for

> that reason alone they necessarily have much in common. Even more. In similar or approximately similar stages of economic development moral theories must of necessity be more or less in agreement. From the moment when private property in movable objects developed, in all societies in which this private property existed there must be this moral law in common: Thou shalt not steal. (Engels, 1878:271)

This is so because workers no less than capitalists have an interest in holding on to their belongings. It is only where class interests diverge that we should expect class differences in attitudes toward crime control.

In pursuing one interest, a class must not jeopardize more important interests. Thus slaveowners cannot use imprisonment to punish their slaves, because to do so would deprive them of the use of their investments. Consequently, slaves in the American South were disciplined primarily with summary corporal punishment, not with imprisonment (Sellin, 1976; see also the reading by Shelden in this volume). Likewise, to consistently use brutal punishments might provoke slaves to revolt. Consequently, Southern legislatures passed laws protecting slaves from their masters in limited ways.[6]

To win broad support, a rising class must appeal to interests wider than its own. Thus Marx notes that no class can achieve the status of a ruling class

> unless it can arouse, in itself and in the masses, a moment of enthusiasm in which it associates and mingles with society at large, identifies with it, and is felt and recognized as the *general representative* of this society. Its aims and interests must genuinely be the aims and interests of society itself, of which it becomes in reality the social head and heart. It is only in the name of the general interest that a particular class can claim general supremacy. (Marx, 1844a:55—56; emphasis in original.)

Note that it cannot merely *pretend* to serve general interests or assert that it does so. The aims and interests of the dominant class must "genuinely" be those of society. The dominant class must become "the social head and heart" "in reality."

No doubt this passage is overstated and one-sided. A class need not gain universal enthusiasm to rule. But if it is to retain the support of its allies in a "historical bloc" of classes (to use the language of Gramsci, 1971), it must accommodate the interests of other classes. Thus it cannot establish forms of control that will evoke strong opposition from allied subordinate classes. As the example of the slave South illustrates, there are limits to the forms of control that can be imposed on exploited classes if class rule itself is not to be jeopardized. Engels (1890:404) noted the relevance of this consideration for the form that legal control takes: "A modern state law must not only correspond to the general economic condition and be its expression, but also be an *internally coherent* expression which does not, owing to inner contradictions, reduce itself to nought" (emphasis in original). He goes on to say that in order to achieve this the faithful reflection of economic conditions suffers increasingly. All the more so the more rarely it happens that a code of law is the blunt, unmitigated, unadulterated expression of the domination of a class—this in itself would offend the "conception of right." Even in the Code Napoleon the pure, consistent conception of right held by the revolutionary bourgeoisie of 1792–96 is already adulterated in many ways and insofar as it is embodied there, daily has to undergo all sorts of attenuation, owing to the rising power of the proletariat.

THE IDEOLOGY OF CONTROL Although our discussion has been couched in terms of interest, much of the advocacy of change in social control is posed in other terms. Indeed, the phenomenon of the reformer who purports to be disinterested or altruistic has often been noted in studies of historical change in social control. It has, however, become fashionable to regard claims to disinterestedness as cynical cover-ups for the pursuit of self-interest. In many instances, this cynicism may be warranted. After all, an appeal to humanitarianism could be a strategy to gain support for a policy favored on other grounds. Yet there is a problem of evidence. Where no documentation of hidden motivation can be found, the motivation has generally been inferred from the sometimes repressive consequences of the reform. But if consequences cannot always be anticipated because the relevant actors have a limited and perhaps mistaken understanding of social process, such inferences may be wrong.

Marx's own writings do not require us to assume that all action springs from economic interest. When Marx proposes that "Life is not determined by consciousness, but consciousness by life" (Marx and Engels, 1846:247) and that consciousness arises on the foundations of a society's economic structure (Marx, 1859), he is not reducing consciousness to interest, nor life to economics. His conception of human nature certainly allows for sentiments of solidarity, but it views these sentiments and the forms in which they are expressed as being socially conditioned.

Even when ideas do advance the interests of a class, their proponents are not necessarily aware that they do so. Thus Engels comments in letters responding to inquiries about Marxist theory:

> The reflection of economic relations as legal principles is necessarily also a topsy-turvy one: it goes on without the person who is acting being conscious of it; the jurist imagines he is operating with a priori propositions, whereas they are really only economic reflexes, so everything is upside down.... It seems to me obvious that this inversion, which so long as it remains unrecognized, forms what we call *ideological outlook*.... (1890:404; emphasis in original.)
>
> Ideology is a process accomplished by the so-called thinker consciously, it is true, but with a false consciousness. The real motive forces impelling him remain unknown to him; otherwise it simply would not be an ideological process. Hence he imagines false or seeming motive forces. (1893:408)

In these terms, many ideas about crime and its control have been ideological. This is not to say that they are mistaken, or that they have been disseminated for the purpose of deceiving anyone. Ideology is not necessarily propaganda. Rather, ideology consists of ideas that originate in social experience—particularly the experience of class relations—without the originator of the ideas being aware of it.[7] In short, it is not bourgeois interests but bourgeois society that is the source of bourgeois ideas. These ideas may contain or express class interest, but cannot be reduced to class interest.

NON-CLASS ACTORS Thus far we have assumed that historical change is always brought about by *classes*. Insofar as crime control is concerned, this is not always the case. As we noted earlier, collective actors that are *not* classes have frequently been important. However, Marxist theory views class consciousness as variable. Subjective classes—those whose members are aware of common class interests and share common political goals—form over time through struggle. The obstacles to the formation of class consciousness are many (and in some of Marx's writings were seriously underestimated).

When class consciousness is weak, we can expect to see other entities, such as class fractions, or groups that cut across class lines, seeking change in crime control.[8] Occupational groups are especially likely to be important, because communication on the job, as well as through conventions and trade journals, strengthens identification with the occupation and facilitates the dissemination of conceptions of occupational interest. Professionals' high incomes provide them with greater financial resources in seeking or obstructing change than people in other occupations have, while the long period of professional training strengthens their identification with the profession. Furthermore, the mystique associated with the greater conceptual elaboration of occupational knowledge and the "service ethic" of the professionals provide advantages to the professions over other occupations in seeking support for social change. At various times physicians, psychiatrists, lawyers, and social workers have mobilized to gain acceptance for their own occupationally-derived conception of how society should respond to crime.

Marxian theory suggests that the state would also be a relevant actor in promoting change. Although at times Marx and Engels wrote as if the state could be viewed as a simple tool of a single class, and therefore not an independent actor in its own right, on other occasions they recognized that this view was too simple. Thus, according to Engels:

> Society gives rise to certain common functions which it cannot dispense with. The persons appointed for this purpose form a new branch of the division of labor *within society*. This gives them particular interests, distinct, too, from the interests of those who empowered them; they make themselves independent of the latter and—the state is in being. . . . The new independent power,

> while having, in the main, to follow the movement of production, reacts in its turn, by virtue of its inherent relative independence—that is, the relative independence once transferred to it and gradually further developed—upon the conditions and course of production.... The new political power ... strives for as much independence as possible. (Engels, 1890:402–3)

State officeholders may use this "partial autonomy" to advance their own immediate interests or to gain political support by advancing the interests of other social groups, such as classes. The enormous financial resources of the state, its ability to gain exposure for its views in the mass media, and its near monopoly on the means of violence give it an enormous importance in influencing the scope and forms of crime control.[9]

The mobilization of both class and non-class actors has often been the work of individuals or small groups who construct theories of crime causation, devise strategies of control and decontrol, and organize support for these strategies. Because this ideological and political work is ordinarily too time-consuming to be undertaken by those directly involved in material production, it is often carried out by others[10]—hence the prominence in nineteenth-century American and British reform movements of clergy, members of the landed gentry, and the wives and daughters of wealthy men. In the twentieth century, the financial support given to these functions by private philanthropic foundations and the federal government permits intelligentsia drawn from wider social backgrounds to undertake these tasks so long as their proposals pose no direct threat to dominant class interests.[11]

As Embree (1977) notes, however, the mere existence of "entrepreneurs," moral or otherwise, is not sufficient to guarantee their success. Groups seeking to change the scope and methods of crime control constantly appear, but not all of them achieve their goals. The success of such entrepreneurial efforts hinges on the ability of the entrepreneur to frame conceptions of deviance and devise strategies of control that mesh with the subjective interests and world view of those with sufficient resources to carry through an initiative and overcome possible opposition.

These considerations derived from the writings of Marx and Engels provide a vocabulary and insights that can be useful in understanding historical change in the scope, ideology, and forms of crime control. To illustrate their usefulness, we show how they can be applied to selected changes in these aspects of crime control over roughly the last two hundred years in England and the United States.

COMPETITIVE INDUSTRIAL CAPITALISM

The industrial revolution transformed the forces and relations of production in the late eighteenth and nineteenth centuries, first in England and then in Europe and the United States. Technical innovations led to a more complex division of labor and increased labor productivity; factory production replaced domestic industry; wage labor largely supplanted remuneration in kind; and the capitalist mode of production became dominant. Petty commodity production persisted as a subordinate mode of production, along with slavery in the U.S. South, until 1865.

In the course of the industrial revolution major changes in the scope, ideology, and methods of social control occurred. These changes originated in the contradictions of mercantile capitalism; they contributed to and were transformed by the process of industrialization.

The scope of control

REDUCTION OF CONTROL OVER THE ECONOMY The mercantile economy was subject to far-reaching state control. Wages and prices were regulated, imports and exports were controlled, and labor mobility was discouraged. Criminal penalties, at times severe, were imposed for violations. However, the growth and commercialization of the economy created a mass of small manufacturers and merchants who began to campaign against the legally enforceable monopolies, patents, and licenses that had been granted to large merchants by the cash-starved Stuarts in the early seventeenth century. Some mercantilists supported these efforts on the grounds that monopolies raised prices and restricted output, thereby reducing exports.

Parliament responded to these pressures by abolishing industrial monopolies, but owing to pressure from the great merchant capitalists who lent money to Parliament, nothing was done to "liberate" commerce. After the 1660s, the restrictive regulations concerning guilds and apprenticeships were no longer enforced, except in agriculture—another concession to the growing power of the smaller manufacturers. In 1688 the old commercial monopolies were finally abolished in response to industrialists' complaints that monopolies choked the expansion of industry (Hill, 1961:154,204,262). Other mercantile restrictions, such as wage controls and regulations concerning the quality of goods, remained in effect. But by the middle of the eighteenth century, the fixing of wages by the state had become exceptional in London, primarily because the economy had expanded to the point where regulation had become unworkable (Heckscher, 1931:311).

Yet only with the political victory of the middle class in 1832 was anything resembling a true laissez-faire policy adopted. The Corn Laws were repealed, tariffs were reduced, land became a commodity, slavery was abolished throughout the empire, legislation prohibiting the emigration of workers and the export of machinery was repealed, and the welfare payments that interfered with the free play of labor market forces ended. The flow of factors of production was now to be governed not by punitive legislation, but by the impersonal regulation of supply and demand.

This flowering of economic freedom was predicated on the success of state intervention in the economy in preceding centuries. Ever since the mid-fourteenth century, the supply of labor had been secured through criminal legislation. So long as it was possible to survive by begging, gambling, or peddling, by cultivating wasteland, or by using the commons, forests, ponds, and game preserves to gain a livelihood, it was possible to avoid becoming a wage laborer (Thompson, 1975:240–41). To close off these possibilities, Parliament had enacted severe penalties for vagrancy in the sixteenth century (Marx, 1867:734–40) and for poaching, stealing fruit from trees, taking fish from ponds, and gathering wood from forests in the eighteenth century (Thompson, 1975: Ignatieff, 1978:26–27). The criminal law thus became a means for separating potential laborers from the means of production, leaving them no other possible source of income than a wage. Once this task had been fully accomplished, the wage agreement no longer had to be subject to the direct regulation of the state:

> Direct force, outside of economic conditions, is of course still used, but only exceptionally. In the ordinary run of things, the labourer can be left to the "natural laws of production," i.e. to his dependence on capital, a dependence springing from, and guaranteed in perpetuity by, the conditions of capitalism themselves. (Marx, 1867:271)

At least in theory, the role of the state with regard to the economy was to be restricted to enforcing voluntary contractual agreements and maintaining the currency.

The bourgeoisie favored this restriction on the role of the state because it prevented the state from giving any individual capitalist a competitive advantage over the others, and because the supply of labor was now sufficient to keep wages down; but laissez-faire policy had wider backing. Working-class support for the repeal of the Corn Laws was won by the promise of cheaper bread, while the middle class supported repeal in the hope that wages could be reduced if the cost of workers' subsistence were to decline.

In practice, the state was never as limited in its control functions as laissez-faire theory required. Thus in England, child labor was restricted by the Factory Act of 1819 and by subsequent legislation; factory inspection was begun in 1833; and hours legislation was passed in 1844. These protective measures were achieved, despite the opposition of most manufacturers,[12] by an alliance of workers, artisans hostile to the factory, paternalistic Tory gentry resentful of the industrialists' victory in 1832, physicians and public health professionals, Anglican clergy concerned with retaining the loyalty of working-class worshippers, and even a handful of industrialists who were afraid that the working class would fail to reproduce itself unless working conditions were improved (Marx, 1867:270, Perkin, 1969:363, 401; Ward, 1970). The abundant supply of labor from the countryside, however, made the latter consideration irrelevant to most industrialists.

The economies of the American colonies were, on paper, highly regulated as well, but not always effectively. The scarcity of labor, for example, turned wage regulation codes into a dead letter, since employers were willing to pay higher wages to attract workers. Later, during the Jacksonian period, laissez-faire doctrines spread, but even then they did not go so far as to exclude an active role for the state in subsidizing private entrepreneurial efforts that promised public benefit. Doctrines critical of governmental control over the economy had their greatest legal impact outside the criminal law (e.g., in contract law).

ALCOHOL AND SELF-CONTROL In limiting state interference with the economy, the petty bourgeoisie secured one of the structural conditions it needed for its survival as a class. But individual entrepreneurs needed something more. In an individualistic, competitive economy, success required the possession of appropriate character traits. Entrepreneurs had to be self-motivated to take advantage of market opportunities. It was crucial for entrepreneurs who operated their businesses on thin margins to work hard for long hours and to eliminate the distractions and costs associated with unnecessary personal consumption (Howe, 1976). With labor costs comprising a large fraction of the cost of doing business, it was equally important for employers to minimize the wages paid to employees. Thus the emphasis placed on cultivating self-mastery, assertiveness, industriousness, thrift, frugality, and abstemiousness, and the stress on avoiding laziness and ostentatious consumption in literature written for middle-class male audiences in the early nineteenth century reflected the needs of the individual entrepreneur quite accurately.[13]

As the weakening of community and extended kinship ties had reduced the effectiveness of external sources of control, and the increased industrial production of low-cost goods multiplied temptations to spend one's earnings, powerful *internal* sources of control were required. A sense of duty had to supply what neither formal nor informal external sources of control could continue to provide.

This development can be seen in nineteenth-century British and American thought concerning drunkenness. Levine (1978) has noted that American attitudes toward the consumption of alcohol shifted drastically at the end of the eighteenth century and in the early part of the nineteenth. The American colonists, including the Puritans, had valued alcohol for the contributions it made to health and conviviality. It was widely consumed by all social classes. Work discipline for artisans and craftsmen in the petty commodity mode of production was not rigorous, and it included drinking rituals as part of a noncompetitive work culture. As the capitalist mode of production became dominant, these rituals disappeared among the middle class, and work discipline was tightened—though drinking remained an important element of male working-class culture. Fear that drunkenness would lead to the loss of self-control led to a rejection of alcoholic consumption by the middle class.[14] Temperance societies were formed in both England and the United States to encourage moderation in drinking, and later, abstinence; and heavy chronic drinking came to be explained as the consequence of a pathology entailing the loss of self-control. The hysterical tone of much prohibition literature reflected the precariousness of middle-class status and the danger to that status that uncontrolled drinking posed.[15]

Following the American Civil War, industrialization shifted the emphasis of the petty bourgeois temperance movement away from an exclusive preoccupation with self-control. The expansion of capitalism gave the large corporation an increasingly prominent role in the economy; and the industrial proletariat grew rapidly, swelled by culturally alien immigrants attracted by high wages. Upwardly mobile fractions of the working class adopted the abstinence patterns of the middle class they aspired to join, and in some cases they became active prohibitionists, though most of them did not.[16]

Middle-class women, now fully excluded from the public economy (as they had not been at the time of independence), gave Prohibition strong support. Given women's financial dependence on men, wives' class positions were jeopardized by male drinking to the same extent as their husbands'. Furthermore, the association between the saloon and prostitution posed a potential threat of venereal disease. And, as an exclusively male preserve, the saloon symbolized male prerogative and privilege (Levine, 1979). Much of the leadership of the post—Civil War temperance movement came from women, as well as from evangelical clergy who were able to draw on the organizational resources of their churches to mobilize lower-middle-class support for the cause, and whose involvement may have been provoked by their own declining occupational status (Hofstadter, 1956: 150—53).

With the backbone of the movement remaining a middle class that was being squeezed economically and politically between labor and capital, antiliquor agitation began to embody middle-class fears of the working class.[17] The liquor trust, denounced for profiting by promoting human misery, became a symbol of capitalist greed (Isaac, 1965:123; Blocker, 1976). Middle-class Prohibitionists also linked alcohol with working-class crime, labor militancy,[18] industrial efficiency and accidents, the level of wages (it was hoped that if workers stopped drinking, wages could be lowered and class conflict reduced), and political corruption (the saloon played a major role in the urban ethnic political machines). Thus alcohol control became joined with class control (Ostrander, 1957; Gusfield, 1963; Timberlake, 1963). Many states adopted prohibition legislation, and ultimately Prohibition was established nationally. This last development will be discussed below, when we take up crime control in the early stages of monopoly capitalism.

NARCOTICS LEGISLATION The earliest legislation against smoking opium also grew out of the social conflicts engendered by competitive industrial capitalism, but through a different process. During the nineteenth century tens of thousands of Chinese immigrants had come to California to work in railroad construction, mining, and agriculture. So long as the economy remained prosperous, opium-smoking Chinese laborers attracted little attention. Then, as the labor market contracted during the depression of the 1870s, white workers organized to exclude new Chinese immigrants, whom they believed were taking away their jobs. These white workers gained support from the white petty bourgeoisie, who also suffered from competition when unemployed Chinese workers opened small retail businesses. (They simultaneously suffered from the completion of the transcontinental railroad, which opened the California market to factory-produced goods made in the East). A considerable body of anti-Chinese legislation was passed at local, state, and federal levels in response to this sentiment. It was in this atmosphere that local and state legislation against the smoking of opium was adopted—in San Francisco, in 1875; in Virginia City, Nevada, in 1876; and in California, in 1881. Ingestion of opium and its derivatives by other means than smoking remained lawful; only the usage associated with the Chinese was banned. Until early in the twentieth century, the only federal restrictions on opium consisted of tariffs on its importation (Helmer, 1975; Morgan, 1976; Embree, 1977).

We see here a process in which an economic crisis occurs at a time of weak class consciousness, engendering conflict within the working class along lines of race, national origin, language, and class experience before immigration. Cultural practices of groups regarded as different but not deviant before the crisis become more salient in the face of economic competition, and by association with the competitor fraction of the class, come to be viewed as reprehensible in themselves. It is this ideological process that leads to the criminal prohibition of cultural traits associated with the politically weaker fractions of the class.[19]

The ideology of control

FORMAL LEGAL EQUALITY The campaign to reduce state control of the economy in late-eighteenth and early-nineteenth-century Britain was waged in the name of a theory that claimed general social benefits for laissez faire. According to the theory, as individuals pursued private gain, an "invisible hand" would maximize social well-being—provided that all exchanges were consensual. External interference with the terms of these mutually agreeable exchanges could only be detrimental. In a *formal* sense, this ideology is radically democratic, for it grants equal legitimacy to every individual's preferences for goods and services and is grounded in the realities of the marketplace, where what counts is cash, not the personal attributes of its possessor.[20] The individualism of this philosophy had its origins in the progressive penetration of commodity exchange relations into communities where collectivist values had earlier prevailed.

Laissez-faire philosophy provided a new rationale for the existence of the state and its control apparatus. Since the rational pursuit of gain would lead individuals to acquire wealth through nonconsensual taking, the state was needed to prohibit and penalize unwilling private exchanges. Thus the calculated balancing of potential costs and gains provided the theoretical explanation for the existence of crime and the justification for its repression. As individuals enter the theory only abstractly (through having the abstract faculty of rationality) and therefore equally, the sanctions for such exchanges were to be formally equal as well. To avoid unnecessary costs in repressing crime, penalties were to be limited to what was necessary to outweigh the potential gain from the offense.

These ideas were first developed by some of the leading figures of the French Enlightenment—Montesquieu, Voltaire, Helvetius, Diderot, d'Alembert—whose thinking had been influenced by the growth of commerce and industry. Generally loyal to the aristocracy or monarchy, they wanted to rationalize and depersonalize the state administration. Beccaria (1764) gave this "classical school of criminology" its most coherent and influential formulation.

Scion of an old noble family, Beccaria expressed the ideology of that fraction of the aristocracy that had begun to engage in capitalist agriculture. These aristocrats were thus allied with the "new bourgeoisie," which consisted of small commercial and industrial capitalists (mainly textile manufacturers) producing outside the guilds, and with the modernizing administration of the Austrian Hapsburgs, who wanted to revive the economy of Lombardy so that taxation could pay for the costs of administering the territory (Candeloro, 1956). Theirs was an ideology that simultaneously affirmed de facto privilege in the form of property ownership while denying de jure privilege in the form of legally recognized rank. It was a utopian response to a feudal order that was disintegrating politically and economically.

Later, the doctrine of formal legal equality would be embraced by middle-class English reformers to legitimate the control apparatus against working-class criticism (see below). But it is doubtful that this was a major consideration for Beccaria, since the lower classes posed no threat in northern Italy when he was writing. The tenets of classical criminology seem to be less a defense of class interests than a reflection of the penetration of bourgeois ideology into the consciousness of the aristocracy.

SCIENTISM The writings of the classical criminologists enjoyed great popularity in the U.S. around the time of the War of Independence. Then, as capitalism became the dominant mode of production, explanations of crime began to shift away from abstract rational calculation toward attempts to differentiate criminals from noncriminals on the basis of personal traits. For many writers, criminals were incapable of restraining themselves when faced with temptation (Boostrum, 1974; Currie, n.d.). Some attributed this inability to parental overindulgence and the subsequent failure to develop self-control. Thus the upbringing of a man released from a New York prison in 1831 after serving a sentence for attempted rape is characterized as follows: "Lived with his parents who indulged him too much for his good; was a very wild unsteady boy; fond of company and amusements; when he could not get his parents' consent, would go without it" (quoted in Rothman, 1971:70).

Other writers paid more attention to other causes of weak self-control, ranging from inherited deficits to pathological social environments. These writings tell us little about crime, but say much about bourgeois preoccupation with such matters as raising children, resisting impulses in the face of temptation, and working-class movements for higher wages.

Eclectic and empirically unsupported though these explanations tended to be, they mark the beginnings of an attempt to account for crime in scientific terms. The striking advances in technology made possible by discoveries in the physical sciences gave impetus to those who sought comparable understanding and control of socially troublesome populations.

The individualism of nineteenth-century explanations of crime may have reflected the atomism of the physical sciences, but it is perhaps more plausible that both reflect the social importance of the petty bourgeoisie and the individualizing tendencies of competitive capitalism. The greatest conceptual borrowings, though, came from biology. Lamarckian doctrine (the hereditary transmission of acquired characteristics), hereditary degeneracy, and Darwinian biology shaped explanations of crime in the nineteenth century. As immigration and the sharpening of class conflict in late-nineteenth-century America increased the social distance between working-class criminals and middle-class citizens, explanations of crime gave greater prominence to the role of biological defects, but without slighting environmental factors.

Although it was increasingly cast in scientific *form*, it must be kept in mind that little of the nineteenth-century literature on crime met what would today be considered minimal scientific standards of methodological adequacy. For the most part, prescientific concepts of causality and elements of lay morality were simply cloaked in scientific trappings until well into the twentieth century.

The methods of control

THE POLICE Throughout the eighteenth century, poor harvests, the abolition of usufruct rights to land, forests, and streams, the discharge of soldiers at the end of wars, the export of wheat during times of shortage, the forestalling and engrossing by landowners and merchants, fluctuations in the supply and demand for manufactured goods, and the introduction of labor-saving machinery, all led to periods of rising food prices, unemployment, and social dislocation for the laboring poor. The weakening of paternalistic regulation of the economy exacerbated these problems (Rose, 1961; Thompson, 1963; Shelton, 1973).

Excluded by property qualifications from voting or holding office, and therefore from using lawful political methods to deal with these developments, agricultural and industrial laborers rioted to enforce the "just price" of the vanishing "moral economy" (Thompson, 1971; Stevenson, 1975). And in the latter part of the eighteenth century, as capitalist social relations became more firmly established, they rioted for higher wages (Shelton, 1973:8). So long as their aims remained limited, however, riots were not treated as major threats; indeed, members of the upper classes even encouraged, manipulated, and at times led them (Thompson, 1963:74; Silver, 1967; Shelton, 1973).[21]

When riots got out of hand and threatened landed estates or houses of industry, magistrates called out associations of gentry with their servants (in essence, another mob) to put them down—a form of control based on personal authority. At times the militia and army were also used; but magistrates mistrusted the loyalty of the militia, since its members' social backgrounds were similar to those of the mob, and the large landowners feared that a standing army or bureaucratic police force would strengthen the centralized state, weakening their own political power (Silver, 1967; Shelton, 1973).

When it was first proposed in the late eighteenth century, a permanent, salaried civilian police force was unacceptable to the gentry because it would have tended to undermine their personal authority. Already weakened by the effects of the commercialization of rural society, their patrimonial authority was sustained by personal domination of law enforcement: by pardoning criminals and declining prosecution, the gentry could win popular gratitude (Hay, 1975).

However, personal forms of enforcement had drawbacks as well as advantages. The hostilities generated in putting down riots continued to divide communities afterward, since the parties to the conflict all resided in the community. Calling out the army was too much an all-or-nothing affair; it risked exacerbating the conflict and escalating events unnecessarily. As the expanded reproduction of capitalism drew more and more of the population into capitalist social relations and exposed increasing numbers of the lower classes to the vicissitudes of the marketplace, labor militancy and radicalism grew. Conspiracies sprang up. Fear of a revolution, intensified by the French example, ultimately led the landowners to accept the creation of a regular police force, since the army would have been incapable of coping with a domestic uprising if it had had French support (Shelton, 1973; Stevenson, 1977).

Merchants and industrialists concerned about riot and theft also supported the establishment of a police force. As Spitzer and Scull (1977a) note, riot was extremely disruptive to the marketplace. Farmers and middlemen traders would tend to avoid rural markets that had been threatened by mob action. In addition, owners of factories threatened with destruction by displaced craftsmen wanted protection (Shelton, 1973).

Beyond the threat of riot, however, merchants wanted to reduce the costs of theft. Colquhoun (1795, 1800), the leading turn-of-the-century police reformer, bemoaned the enormous losses merchants suffered in the rapidly growing commercial centers. As the geographical extent of trade grew, private protection on an individual basis became less feasible. Yet, as Spitzer and Scull (1977a) point out, the "free rider" problem made collective private arrangements unfeasible.[22] The existing system of enforcement, which relied heavily on rewards to informers, recovery of stolen goods for a fee paid by the victim, and private prosecution, had sprung up unplanned as the commercial revolution eroded the traditional enforcement arrangements based on communal solidarity. But it was ineffective, and may even have encouraged crime. A tax-supported, salaried police patrol was thus adopted as the only feasible solution to the problem of riot and theft in rural market and industrial towns and in commercial cities in the final stages of the transition from a mercantile to a competitive capitalist economy.

Despite the clear and widely discussed advantages that a public police had for capitalist interests, for several decades only minimal steps to strengthen the existing system of enforcement were taken (Donajgrodzki, 1977); for instance, not until 1829 was the Metropolitan Police Force finally established in London.[23] Opposition to strengthening the police came not only from those who feared the restoration of absolutism, but also from elements of the nascent working class, and from London officials who resisted the loss of patronage jobs that abolishing the watch and ward system would entail (Manning, 1977). Sir Robert Peel, a Tory politician and landowner, *and* son of a large textile manufacturer, was perfectly positioned to weld the alliance of landowners, manufacturers, and fractions of the petty bourgeoisie that finally succeeded in establishing a bureaucratic police force in England.

The establishment of a salaried, preventive patrol was significant not merely as a more *efficient* way of carrying out social control. Policing represented two qualitatively new developments: rule through impersonal, bureaucratically administered general law; and a deeper, more finely tuned penetration of formal control into everyday social life (Spitzer, 1979).

A bureaucratic mode of enforcement had become possible in a politically decentralized society because economic change had weakened patrimonial sources of authority in the countryside while exacerbating class conflict to the point where the propertied classes realized that they needed a new form of control—particularly one that was depersonalized. The landowner who, as magistrate, dispersed the mob was too readily identified with the interests he defended.[24] A salaried police force, these classes felt, could more effectively claim to represent a law that embodied general interests rather than those of a particular class, since it would not be a direct party to the disputes that erupted into riots. The creation of the new police thus had an important ideological dimension having to do with the legitimation of control. Reformers argued that those who were punished would acknowledge the fairness of their punishment and feel guilty only if it were evident that the law was enforced impartially (Ignatieff, 1978:70–75). By remunerating the police with wage payments, bureaucratization also enhanced the legitimacy of enforcement, (as well as its efficiency). Abandoning the "service for fee" system made it possible for the laboring classes to file complaints—an opportunity they used to a substantial degree (Philips, 1977:125–28).

The creation of a police force also permitted the state to adjust its response to the magnitude of a perceived threat with greater precision. Thus the establishment of the police represented an attempt to bring the social control machinery itself under greater control. Furthermore, as a proactive force, the police were to *prevent* crime rather than merely respond to it after it had occurred. This was to be done by bringing a visible personification of the law into working-class communities *on a regular basis.*[25] Traditional popular working-class culture, a source of resistance to the discipline of the factory, was reinterpreted as a generating milieu of crime, and the police were called upon to eliminate it.[26] The bureaucratization of enforcement made this possible, for the police could arrest and prosecute without regard to the wishes of complainants. Outside the context of bureaucratized enforcement this assault on working-class culture would have been unthinkable.

The circumstances surrounding the establishment of police departments along the Eastern seaboard in the United States before the Civil War were quite similar to those in England. Riots were a frequent occurrence in preindustrial Boston, New York, Philadelphia, Baltimore, St. Louis, and Cincinnati (Lane, 1967; Richardson, 1970; Walker, 1977). As riots in these cities took on social and political overtones in the decades preceding the Civil War, proposals for establishing a police system something like that of London were adopted. Again it took some years before reformers could overcome fears that the police would be used to establish a tyranny and the reluctance of local political leaders to lose patronage jobs.

As Harring notes (chapter 4 in part 3) the mere establishment of police forces in preindustrial American cities did not necessarily have much practical consequence, since often little more was involved than a formal reorganization of existing watch systems under a single agency, with little administrative change. Before the invention of the telegraph and the telephone, administrative decentralization was a technological necessity. Moreover, budgetary constraints limited the growth of police departments.

It was the post–Civil War strife that overcame capitalist reluctance to pay for increased protection with higher taxes. Together with petty bourgeois shopkeepers and professionals, American industrial capitalists lobbied successfully for appropriations to increase the size of urban police forces and helped to develop new strategies of deployment in response to strife involving factory workers and their employers.[27] In times of crisis, the police could now be called on to intervene on behalf of owners.

The extent to which a police force actually carries out class control functions is always limited by organizational and political factors. In nineteenth-century American cities, bribes paid by saloon keepers, who were important figures in urban politics, substantially nullified the enforcement of laws against saloons and vice, though not necessarily against drunkenness.[28] One might expect that the widening of suffrage would have limited the use of the police against the working class. On occasion (e.g., in Boss Tweed's New York), big city mayors did refuse to use the police to break strikes. The loyalty of the police, who were themselves drawn from working-class backgrounds, could not always be guaranteed in actions against strikers; but in large cities, the conservatism of the larger middle class, and the inability of unnaturalized immigrants to vote, limited the ability of the working class to influence policing policy. The national divisions that separated the police from the policed, along with a variety of organizational strategies designed to preserve the loyalty of the force, generally sufficed to ward off large-scale political defection. In smaller industrial towns, on the other hand, the working class was proportionately larger and often had middle-class support during strikes. Under those circumstances, the small local police forces could not be used to repress strikers, and capitalists consequently relied more heavily on private forces (Gutman, 1963; Spitzer and Scull, 1977b).

PROPORTIONALITY IN PUNISHMENT Proposals to abolish the death penalty in England for most offenses and to establish a rough proportionality between the gravity of the offense and the severity of the penalty reflected concerns for both the legitimacy and the effectiveness of the law. The carnival-like atmosphere at executions, as well as occasional riots and defiance on the part of the condemned, seemed to erode respect for the majesty of the law (Cooper, 1974; Linebaugh, 1975; Ignatieff, 1978). In addition, eighteenth-century juries apparently refused to convict petty thieves to avoid sending them to the gallows. Frequent pardons further reduced the certainty of punishment.

Insisting that these conditions jeopardized property by undermining the deterrent effect of the law,[29] the petty bourgeoisie and capitalists from all over England flooded Parliament with petitions urging a reform of sentencing in the second decade of the nineteenth century (Rustigan, article 8 in this volume). In alliance with reforming Tory landlords, who were equally concerned with the legitimacy of the law, this middle class successfully pressured Parliament into eliminating the death penalty for most offenses. By the time Parliamentary reform gave the middle class formal political representation in 1832, much of this reform had already been carried out, though business interests continued to press for further reductions in capital punishment in succeeding decades (Cooper, 1974:41).

The early-nineteenth-century argument for reducing the use of the death penalty was also posed on humanitarian grounds. Rusche and Kirchheimer (1939) attribute this humanitarianism to the industrial revolution, which increased the demand for labor and thus raised the social value of a human life. There is probably some truth to this explanation. The death penalty had been much less used in the American colonies than in England in the eighteenth century, possibly reflecting the comparative scarcity of labor in the colonies, though perhaps more plausibly reflecting the absence of a panicky landed gentry.

But this is to take too narrow a view of the matter. The humanitarianism of the reformers was part of a shift in religious ideology associated with their upward mobility. The break from the Calvinist doctrine of predestination in favor of the belief that anyone could be saved came as the petty bourgeois dissenters prospered and became well-to-do capitalists. Their humanitarianism was a response to the contradiction between their former ascetic, self-denying orientation to the world, adopted by a lower middle class and sustained by religious doctrine, and the economic success that adhering to this doctrine facilitated. So instead of using wealth for personal enjoyment, they used it for public service. Humanitarian reform was a way of expressing a common humanity with the poor and outcast. At the same time, the new class position of the reformers gave a strong social control component to their paternalistic humanitarianism (Ignatieff, 1978:58).[30]

Pashukanis (1929:180–81) has argued that there is a deep structural connection between the principle of proportionality in punishment advocated by eighteenth and early-nineteenth-century criminal law reformers, and the development of industrial capitalism:

> Deprivation of freedom, for a period stipulated in the court sentence, is the specific form in which modern, that is to say bourgeois capitalist, criminal law embodies the principle of equivalent recompense. This form is unconsciously yet deeply linked with the conception of man in the abstract, and abstract human labour measurable in time. Industrial capitalism, the declaration of human rights, the political economy of Ricardo, and the system of imprisonment for a stipulated term are phenomena peculiar to one and the same historical epoch.

Here Pashukanis does not assert that imprisonment for fixed periods was in the interest of capitalists, but rather that the reduction of human labor to abstract, interchangeable "labor time" in the industrial phase of capitalism in general lead members of a capitalist society toward specific notions of appropriate sanctions based on the metaphor of commodity exchange. Thus it was in the period when the capitalist mode of production became fully established that imprisonment for fixed periods of time proportional to the injury caused by the crime became a major form of criminal punishment.

Since the doctrine of proportionality gained as wide an acceptance in Catholic parts of Europe as in Protestant regions, Pashukanis's attribution of the doctrine to the ideological effects of capitalism is by no means implausible. Yet it is important not to forget that public sentiment regarding punishment was translated into new penal practices only insofar as that sentiment was manifested politically. In England, this took the form of acquittals of defendants (made possible by the jury system, a precapitalist survival), petitions to Parliament, and representation in Parliament, after 1832. The gentry, who enacted the Bloody Code in the eighteenth century and whose political authority was reinforced by gaining pardons for clients, had to be defeated politically before the new system could be established.

THE PENITENTIARY The prison system devised by these English reformers reflected the same concerns that informed their campaign against the death penalty. To legitimate punishment, all prisoners had to be treated equally, regardless of social rank. Equal treatment meant eliminating prisons operated privately under contract from the state, for in these, a prisoner's standard of living was governed by the payments the prisoner made to the jailkeeper (Sheehan, 1977). The prison, like the police, was now to be impartially administered through a system of formal rules established by a bureaucratic government agency. Abuses of authority were to be prevented by opening the prison to public inspection (Ignatieff, 1978:77–78).

Based on a vision of reconciliation between classes that economic and social change had driven apart, the prison was to reform miscreants, not demolish them (Ignatieff, 1978:210). Since crime was attributed to indolence, avarice, the decline of authority, and irreligiosity—that is, to the vices of the laboring classes—the new prison discipline was to consist of a regimented daily routine, hard labor, an abstemious alcohol-free diet, submission to authority, and religious exhortation. Since popular working-class culture was believed to sustain crime, prisoners were to be cut off from the outside world and from one another: visitors and correspondence were restricted, and the cell system and rule of silence were imposed to prevent even the slightest communication among inmates.[31]

The Federalist merchants (Quakers and other Protestants) who created the American penitentiary were motivated by somewhat similar concerns. To restore the social order that the conflicts of the Jacksonian era seemed to be destroying, they built prisons and other confining institutions, and organized systems of discipline (known as the Philadelphia and Auburn systems) that British and European administrators were to copy (Lewis, 1970; Rothman, 1971).

Both the English and the American prisons were established as a response to a crisis in preindustrial capitalism.[32] The architectural form that the prison took and the disciplinary methods it adopted, however, were not entirely determined by that crisis. They were also governed by the theories of crime causation then prevalent, and by the organizational innovations being introduced in connection with the industrial revolution. The failure of the houses of correction to turn a profit for the outwork masters who were given contracts for the use of inmate labor, had, along with the continuing difficulty of supervising cottage industry, stimulated the introduction of the factory. Many of the new disciplinary techniques the English reformers introduced into the penitentiary had first been introduced as solutions to administrative problems in "free" production,[33] as well as in the schools, hospitals, and other institutions that the same group of reformers managed for the poor (Hartwell, 1971:77; Ignatieff, 1978:32,62).[34]

As in the case of the police, the prison evolved in a direction that diverged greatly from the plans laid by the founders because of economic and political developments connected with the evolution of capitalism—developments which the founders were neither able to anticipate nor to control (see the selection by Petchesky in this volume).

THE TRANSITION TO MONOPOLY CAPITALISM

At the end of the nineteenth century, the American economy underwent a transition to what has conventionally been called monopoly capitalism.[35] The size of business enterprises grew, and many sectors of the economy came to be dominated by a handful of giant corporations. With the domestic market for commodities saturated, farmers and industrialists began to seek markets abroad. The labor movement, recovering from its defeat in the late 1880s, was becoming increasingly large, organized, militant, and political. Employees working for capitalists constituted an increasing proportion of the labor force. The substantial middle-class stratum of self-employed businessmen and professionals that remained was under growing pressure from both labor and big business.

The scope of control

REGULATION OF THE ECONOMY The movement toward deregulating the economy that characterized the competitive phase of industrial capitalism was substantially reversed in the transition to monopoly capitalism. The state began to play a larger role in determining the price and quality of goods and the terms of the labor contract.

Different classes and class fractions sought regulation on behalf of diverse goals. Labor had begun to seek economic gains through legislation to improve wages, hours, and working conditions in the post–Civil War decades, hoping that its political strength (votes) could be used to overcome its economic weakness. Labor support for state protection persisted in the Progressive Era (Ratner, 1981), but was by no means unanimous: many union leaders feared that state regulation would be detrimental to unionism and might limit the gains that the organized working class could win on its own (Weinstein, 1968:43–44; Domhoff, 1970:177–78). Some corporate leaders, academics, and clergy supported labor legislation in this period, even though it penalized employers for engaging in prohibited practices, since they hoped that modest improvement in the income and working conditions of workers would stem labor militancy. The major opposition came from small manufacturers, who could less easily bear higher labor costs. Although much protective legislation was struck down by the U.S. Supreme Court on the grounds that it violated the contractual freedom of workers, ultimately legislation protecting wages, hours, and working conditions was put into effect.

Having failed to eliminate competition through cartels and mergers, large corporations lobbied for regulation of business to stabilize the economy, with the support of middle-class consumers who had been alarmed by scandals of the sort revealed in Upton Sinclair's *The Jungle*. Farmers and small businessmen also sought regulation in the hope of offsetting the economic power of the railroads and other large corporations. In essence they wanted regulation to restore the competition that the growing power of the large corporations had destroyed. A host of state and federal regulations was adopted in the late nineteenth and early twentieth centuries in response to pressure from these constituencies (Kolko, 1963; Tipple, 1963; Weinstein, 1968).[36]

REGULATION OF ALCOHOL, PROSTITUTION, AND NARCOTICS The Prohibition movement, having abandoned its anticorporate rhetoric (i.e., having abandoned the attempt to build an alliance with labor), revived in the years 1907–1919 after a period of dormancy. It gained broad support from a middle class whose anxieties over immigration and class conflict grew as industrial violence intensified (Blocker, 1976). Some historians have maintained that business funding of the movement at this stage was critical to its success:

> Around 1908, just as the Anti-Saloon League was preparing for a broad, state-by-state drive toward national prohibition, a number of businessmen had contributed the funds essential for an effective campaign. The series of quick successes that followed coincided with an equally impressive number of wealthy converts, so that as the movement entered its final stage after 1913, it enjoyed not only ample financing but a sudden urban respectability as well. Substantial citizens now spoke about a new discipline with the disappearance of the saloon and the rampaging drunk. Significantly, prominent Southerners with one eye to the Negro and another to the poorer whites were using exactly the same arguments. (Wiebe, 1967:290–91)

In this interpretation, the Eighteenth Amendment, establishing Prohibition on a national scale, was the work of the Progressive coalition of businessmen and middle classes.[37] According to Pivar (1973), the crackdown on red light districts in cities throughout the country in the early twentieth century had similar sponsorship. The business and middle classes wanted to end the political corruption that surrounded vice and alcohol and that was bankrupting city treasuries (as well as forcing businesses to pay bribes to politicians) and to encourage a more virtuous, hygienic urban environment.

Other criminal legislation arose from America's growing involvement in foreign affairs. Although physicians and pharmacists had taken some steps to regulate the consumption of narcotics for reasons having much to do with advancing their occupational interests (Embree, 1973; Musto, 1973:13–23), it appears that the 1914 Harrison Act criminalizing the possession and non-medical dissemination of opiates was adopted primarily in connection with American commerce in the Far East (Embree, 1973, 1977; Musto, 1973:24–68). The U.S. State Department sought a treaty prohibiting international traffic in opium because it wished to deprive England of the revenue it earned by importing opium into China. Since China had little interest in buying British manufactured goods, England depended on the opium trade to finance its foreign trade deficit with China. The State Department also hoped to advance the Open Door policy (opening Chinese doors to American products) by supporting the Chinese government's attempt to protect its own population from opium. The Harrison Act was adopted in fulfillment of America's treaty obligations under the International Opium Convention. The prohibition of domestic narcotics use was an outcome of the legislation, but not the main reason for its adoption.

The greater industrial productivity achieved through the technical and organizational innovations of the Progressive Era (e.g., the assembly line), together with rising wages and a shift in the composition of the labor force toward managerial and clerical positions, began to undermine the social basis for the asceticism of the self-denying middle class. Business advertising encouraged hedonistic consumerism, not abstention. At the same time, political repression and curtailment of immigration after the First World War relieved middle- and upper-class anxieties over class conflict. These developments, together with the discovery that Prohibition had worsened rather than eliminated problems of corruption and crime, undermined support for Prohibition, leading to its repeal in 1933 (Blocker, 1976:13).

Similar forces have undermined other legal restrictions. The recent trend toward repeal of laws forbidding marijuana, contraception, abortion, and homosexuality has at its origin a cultural shift from abstinence to consumption associated with the transition from competitive to monopoly capitalism (Reed, 1978:61–62). It is a trend, however, that is resisted by the middle-class and working-class aristocracies, whose economic position continues to rest in part on the inculcation of the traditional middle-class virtues.

The ideology of control

Two competing political philosophies coexisted in the nineteenth-century America. The first, that of classical liberalism or laissez faire, has already been described. Based on the formal equality of all adult citizens, it prescribed a minimal role for the state with respect to the economy. The second was derived from medieval Christian notions of moral stewardship. In Puritan doctrine, the elect were to govern the community for its own good, using compulsion when necessary to prevent sin. Although the secularization of society weakened this doctrine in the nineteenth century, it never entirely died out. Thus, even though laissez-faire doctrine continued to be voiced during the Progressive Era, clergy and intellectuals began to reassert a vision of the state as an institutional expression of the general will, a super-parent who would guide the nation toward perfection (Hopkins, 1940; Levine, 1971). The doctrines of individualism and Social Darwinism were thus to be abandoned in favor of a Reform Darwinism in which social evolution was to be planned. The state was to stand above and reconcile conflicting parties, and to lead society toward social harmony. The anarchy of unregulated big business was thus to be rejected, along with the anarchy of the working class, in favor of state regulation (Fine, 1956). Such notions had in fact been expressed earlier (Lester Ward, one of the founding fathers of American sociology, had begun to articulate this position as early as

1869); but this projected expansion of state function only gained wider acceptance when the growth of giant corporations undermined the institutional basis for individualism, and the fear arose that capitalism would be destroyed if class conflict were to go unchecked (Schwendinger and Schwendinger, 1974).

Another major ideological development concerned the explanation of crime. As we noted above, nineteenth-century explanations of crime increasingly centered on biological defects. This doctrine gave scientific legitimacy to methods of controlling deviants that in their combination of coercion and ostensibly benevolent paternalism could not have been legitimated by philosophical individualism, though little along these lines was done until the early twentieth century (see below).

It is likely that the appeal of hereditary degeneracy and evolutionary atavism as explanations for crime and other social problems in the late nineteenth century had much to do with the legitimacy these notions gave to the political and economic supremacy of the Anglo-Saxon American upper and middle classes (and at the end of the century, to imperial expansion). As the economy was transformed during the course of the nineteenth century, ideological explanations of crime were revised to correspond with the changing legitimation requirements of these classes. So long as much of the economy consisted of small enterprises whose capital was derived from family savings, success could plausibly be linked with will power and self-control, and crime with the absence of weakness of these faculties. But as the capital requirements of business grew and occupational success increasingly involved promotion as an employee in a bureaucratic hierarchy, success could no longer be attributed to such voluntaristic qualities alone. Thus degeneracy and atavism came to be regarded as relevant to criminality because of their implications for *intellectual* power, rather than for will power. The attention given to low intelligence as a cause of crime in the early twentieth century, particularly after the introduction of IQ testing, reflected these developments (Gonzalez, 1977; Hahn, 1978).

Since symbolic and material rewards accrued to occupations that were able to gain jurisdiction over the control of deviance, old and new occupations—law, medicine, psychology, and social work—jockeyed for position by asserting the relevance of their specialized knowledge to the problem of coping with crime. Ideologies explaining deviance and justifying strategies for its control or decontrol thus came to be linked with occupational interests. State and private agencies charged with controlling deviance likewise developed conceptual systems in order to gain or maintain support for their organizational mandate, and to legitimate or defend strategies for managing their subject populations. Thus:

> New categories and sub-categories of deviance and control are being created. . . . All these agencies—legal and quasi-legal, administrative and professional—are marking out their own territories of jurisdiction, competence and referral. Each set of experts produces its own "scientific" knowledge: screening devices, diagnostic tests, treatment modalities, evaluation scales. And

> all this creates new categories and the typifications which fill them.... These creatures are then fleshed out—in papers, research proposals, official reports—with sub-systems of knowledge and new vocabularies.... (Cohen, 1979:358)

This process began with the need to manage the diverse categories of "idlers" locked up during the Great Confinement in the mercantile era (Foucault, 1965; Scull, 1977). It continued during the age of competitive capitalism and increased as the scope of control widened in the monopoly stage of capitalism. As the targets of control have widened, and the agencies of control have multiplied, so has the terminology of control.

The methods of control

The transition to monopoly capitalism brought several new developments having to do with the methods of social control. Our discussion will take note of three: the establishment of state regulatory agencies, the indeterminate sentence, and the juvenile court.

REGULATORY AGENCIES Regulatory agencies were the Progressive Era's solution to the problem of controlling business in a manner that did not delegitimize capitalism by tarnishing capitalists with the stigma of criminality. The first such agency, the Inter-State Commerce Commission, was established in 1887 in response to pressure from farmers, businessmen, and labor leaders whose interests were all injured by the economic power of the railroads (Wiebe, 1967:53). The Federal Trade Commission followed in 1914, again in response to business pressure (Kolko, 1963); now there are more than fifty federal regulatory agencies.

The agencies' use of civil rather than criminal procedures, and the combination of legislative, executive, and judicial functions in a single agency permitted the achievement of greater substantive (technical) rationality in control than the formally rational procedures developed in the competitive stage of capitalism allowed. At a point when corporate capital was sufficiently powerful that it no longer needed procedural due process to protect itself from the state, it was willing to do without some of the protections that the bourgeoisie had demanded in earlier periods. Legitimation for this development came not from the formal equality of individuals, as in the competitive stage of capitalism, but from the ideological conception of the state as a neutral harmonizer of conflicting and not necessarily equal interests.

INDETERMINATE SENTENCING The movement to revise criminal sentencing began in England in the 1840s and 1850s, and spread to the United States in the decades following the Civil War.[38] Consistent with their belief that crime was due to weak impulse control, reformers criticized the Philadelphia and Auburn systems of prison discipline as too mechanical to reform criminals.

By releasing prisoners at the expiration of a judicially fixed term, these systems gave prisoners no incentive to reform. Though infractions of institutional regulations were punished (quite harshly at Auburn), only outward, behavioral compliance was gained, not an inner conversion.

As an alternative, reformers proposed that release from custody should occur in stages, with the duration of the sentence to depend on the comportment of the prisoner (Hill, 1857; Carpenter, 1864; Eriksson, 1976:81–97). Reducing custody in stages would permit prisoners to develop the power of self-control under supervision, while the rewards of greater liberty and early release would reinforce good behavior.

The value of such an arrangement for controlling inmates at a time when corporal punishment of prisoners was drawing criticism was readily appreciated by penal administrators. Yet its deeper significance lay in its relationship to the creation of an appropriately motivated labor force (Currie, n.d.). The classical social contract theorists had supposed that all members of the society innately possessed the personal qualities required by capitalist social relations (notably rationality). As industrialization began and encountered resistance from workers unaccustomed to the discipline of the factory, however, it became clear that the production of appropriately motivated workers had to be secured through institutions not directly involved in the production process, namely the family, the school, and the church. When these institutions failed, as nineteenth-century crime and pauperism showed they sometimes did, the prison had to step in. Architecture alone could not do the trick, as the Jacksonians had believed. A system of discipline was needed that would more closely resemble the capitalist economy outside the prison. Rewards for performance in prison fulfilled this need. This phase of reform, then, reflected the contradiction between the capitalist-derived notion of punishment as exchange for past injury (equal punishment for equal offenses), and the individualization required by the social control function the prison was to serve in a capitalist society.

The adoption of "time off for good behavior" systems adopted in many states in mid-nineteenth century may have been due to these considerations, but they did not go far enough to suit post–Civil War reformers. Comparing crime to a disease, these reformers wanted sentences that were open-ended, regardless of offense.[39] "As it is clearly impossible to predict the date of a sick man's restoration to bodily health," they argued, "so it is no less impossible to foretell the day when a moral patient will be restored to moral soundness" (Wines, 1880:620). Prisoners were to be held until reformed and supervised after release so that they could be reincarcerated at the first sign of relapse, without the necessity of waiting for a new crime to be committed. With the increased emphasis on hereditary degeneracy or atavism as a major cause of crime in the late nineteenth century, the indeterminate sentence would also allow the permanent incarceration of the incurable "born criminals."

As criminals were deemed to lack responsibility, the concepts of blame, retribution, and even deterrence were considered to be irrelevant to the social control response. Indeed, imprisonment was no longer to be considered a punishment at all, but a treatment bestowed on the prisoner by a benevolent state. The adversarial relationship between the criminal and the state that formed the basis for criminal procedure in the competitive stage of capitalism was now to be dissolved by the interest both were presumed to hold in the criminal's being cured. Consequently, limits on the state's power to coerce were no longer to be needed (Brockway, 1912:375–76; AFSC Working Party, 1971).

Penologists campaigned vigorously for sentencing reform along these lines in the late nineteenth century, and won wide support from middle-class and capitalist constituencies who were attracted by the possibility of dealing more effectively with crime, insanity, pauperism, and labor and political unrest. But indeterminate sentencing was also favored by Populists (John Altgeld) and anarchists (Emma Goldman), who were presumably persuaded by the paternalistic dimension of the proposals (Currie, n.d.).

Despite this impressive support, implementation remained extremely limited for several decades. Indeterminate sentencing bills fared badly in the legislatures and the courts. Not until the first two decades of the twentieth century were indeterminate sentencing and parole supervision widely adopted. Funding for research and publicity provided by leading capitalist families may have helped to gain wider acceptance for these reforms,[40] though the broader middle-class Progressive acceptance of social engineering on the part of the positive state at the turn of the century is likely to have been at least as important.

A possible explanation for the persistence of punishment based on the retributive equivalence of crime and punishment is suggested by Pashukanis. If popular retributive thought, including the principle of proportionality, is rooted in the exchange relations of an economy based on commodity production, then resistance to the full medicalizing of crime will persist as long as the social relations of commodity exchange persist (Pashukanis, 1978: 181–82). Monopoly pricing power and state regulation of the capitalist economy may lead to departures from the exchange of equal values, but only to a limited degree. If this reasoning is correct, the implementation of true indeterminate sentencing would necessarily remain limited, so long as sentencing systems are responsive to public opinion.

THE JUVENILE COURT Chicago's juvenile court, the first in the nation, was established in 1899; twenty years later similar courts had been established in almost every state (Caldwell, 1961). According to the leading sociological treatment of this development (Platt, 1969, 1974), the juvenile court was established by upper- and middle-class reformers as part of a wider effort to stabilize corporate capitalism. This innovation is supposed to have worked to the detriment of the children it ostensibly aimed to help by depriving them of criminal due process, and subjecting them to punishment for noncriminal status offenses.

Subsequent research on the Chicago court (Fox, 1970; Parker, 1976), as well as on the juvenile courts of Milwaukee (Schlossman, 1977), Oklahoma (Bryant, 1968), Memphis (Shelden, n.d.), Toronto (Hagan and Leon, 1977), and Norway (Dahl, 1974), requires some revision of this formulation. Although members of the upper class were involved in the court movement in Chicago, Milwaukee, Memphis, and Norway, they were not involved in Denver, Oklahoma, or Toronto. The Chicago court's procedural informality was not an innovation,[41] and the establishment of juvenile courts elsewhere did not necessarily increase the number of reformatory commitments; in Buffalo (Almy, 1902) and Toronto (Hagan and Leon, 1977) it did not do so.

The establishment of the American juvenile court reflected several distinct, though related developments. Organized labor and businesses that did not employ children secured the passage of laws forbidding child labor—in the former case to reduce competition for jobs; in the latter case, to raise the labor costs of competitors. This effort drew wider support from reformers and the public, who feared that child employment would increase adult unemployment and would weaken the race at a time when expansion abroad placed a premium on physical strength and vigor. These efforts and others on behalf of juveniles led contemporaries to call the reformers "child-savers," a label they accepted for themselves. To insure that children would receive the education demanded by a technologically advancing economy, and to aid the cultural and political assimilation of immigrants, these same forces joined to lobby successfully for mandatory school attendance laws toward the end of the nineteenth century (Felt, 1965; Levine and Levine, 1970). Given that parents would not necessarily be willing or able to force their children to go to school, enforcement had to be placed in the hands of the state.[42]

During the nineteenth century, children and adolescents were increasingly coming to be seen both as innocent and as subject to greater social influence than adults, a tendency no doubt related to the prolonged education that middle-class children began to receive. Special courts and specialized reformatories for juveniles were logical consequences of this view of children, as was the age-of-consent legislation of the turn of the century (Hamoway, n.d.).

Though not entirely new, the procedural informality of the juvenile court and its orientation to the individual treatment needs of the child were in keeping with the tendency toward individualized, technical rationality in adult sentencing. This trend could be carried farther for juveniles than for adults because of the popular conception of children as not responsible for their actions. This conception grew in the nineteenth century as more and more children lost their social responsibilities as a result of child labor laws (Greenberg, 1977).

Regarding the reformatory as a failure, the Progressive Era child-savers who campaigned for the creation of juvenile courts did not want to place more children in it, but to keep them out if at all possible.[43] For this reason (and presumably to obtain salaried jobs for themselves), reformers made state funding for paid probation officers one of their major goals. The probation officers were to supervise children in their own communities, and through the children, were to cultivate American manners in their parents. Only where the family had disintegrated or could not be reformed did the child-savers want to remove the child from its family and place it in a family-like institution. The court was thus to be an agent of assimilation and uplift—an extension of benevolent, though coercive control into the community.

In this respect, the juvenile court shared with campaigns against saloons, prostitution, and corruption in municipal government the goal of eradicating unsavory features of immigrant, working-class existence, and transforming public life along middle-class lines. Many of the same reformers were active in all of these causes (Odegaard, 1966:85). Amelioration of class conflict was one aspect of this transformation, but not the only one. Like the settlement house, the playground, the extension of public education to the masses, and probation for adults—all begun or adopted by the Progressives—the juvenile court involved the recognition that positive social engineering could not be achieved through a purely repressive institution like the police (see the reading by Stark in this volume).[44]

DISCUSSION

We have not aimed to present a *history* of how crime control changed as mercantile capitalism was transformed into competitive and then monopoly capitalism; as such, our work would be entirely inadequate. Instead, we have presented an *interpretation* of selected changes in the scope, ideology, and forms of control in Marxian terms. It is the logic used in explaining the events, not the events themselves, that is our main focus here.

Contrary to popular misconception, Marxian theory asserts neither that the ruling class manipulates the criminalizing process at will on behalf of its interests, nor that the economy wholly determines a society's crime control arrangements. It must be recalled that in the passage where Marx introduces the famous "base-superstructure" metaphor (1859:20–21), he asserts only that "The mode of production in material life determines the *general character* of the social, political and spiritual processes of life" (emphasis added), not necessarily their every detail.

The historical record seems to confirm this. Broad trends in crime control correspond to successive stages in the development of capitalism. State control of the economy expands in the mercantile stage, contracts in the competitive stage, and expands again with monopoly capitalism. New forms of crime control, such as the police and the prison, are associated with the transition from one stage to another. Explanations of crime causation become scientific rather than religious under the impact of capitalist industrialization, and the formal qualities of sanctions (e.g., formally or substantively rational) are transformed too.

But many developments are not uniquely tied to a single stage. The police and the prison are present in both competitive and monopoly stages of capitalism, though their character is somewhat different in the two stages. The Volstead Act prohibiting alcohol and its repeal both occurred in the monopoly phase of capitalism. Temperance movements appeared in many countries in connection with competitive industrial capitalism, but very few adopted total prohibition. It follows that the explanation of such changes cannot be restricted to the analysis of the economy narrowly defined, but must also take into account such considerations as the character of the state, the content and degree of adherence to popular ideologies, the level of class consciousness, and the degree and forms of class mobilization of *all* classes (not just the ruling class), as well as divisions and alliances among classes and class fractions. This does not mean that political and social "factors" that are unrelated to purely economic "factors" should be "added in." On the contrary, they are all influenced by the forces and relations of direct material production, but are not totally determined by them.

Taken by itself, a mode of production is too limited a concept to tell us much about crime control (Greenberg, 1975). Suppose, for example, one wanted to explain the legislation prohibiting opium derivatives in the U.S. in the early twentieth century. There is nothing about the concept of the capitalist mode of production that tells us that opium exists, that many Chinese smoked it in the nineteenth century, that Chinese laborers immigrated to the United States, or that these immigrants and other Americans used opium. Given all this information, one can still not deduce the passage of a law against opium on the basis of the implications of opium use for capitalist production and distribution. Many of the problems associated with heroin use today appear to be a consequence of the prohibition itself, and thus cannot have been a cause of it. Even if one were to concede that opium use had some negative consequences for capitalism (e.g., by reducing workers' efficiency or undermining their health), we would have to recall that opium was widely used as an all-purpose nostrum in the late nineteenth century without noticeably interfering with the rapid expansion of industrialization. Drug use remains widespread today despite the prohibition. Tobacco and alcohol are believed to be injurious to the user's health, and the costs to business and to the general public of excessive consumption of alcohol have been given wide publicity. Yet neither tobacco nor alcohol is prohibited.

Nevertheless, one cannot understand how the Chinese came to smoke opium without understanding the role that the opium trade played in British economic imperialism. The Chinese immigration to America cannot be understood except in terms of the demand for labor created by the expansion of industrial capitalism in the United States. And, as Embree (1977) has argued, the prohibition of opium derivates under the Harrison Act is only comprehensible in terms of America's imperial expansion into the Pacific, a response undertaken by the state in response to tendencies toward stagnation in the American economy (Oglesby and Schaull, 1967).

Capitalism provides the class experience from which ideologies of control are developed; thus the classical principles of formal equality and proportionality, and the "treatment model" which denies these principles, are both related to stages in capitalist development, though it is questionable whether either could be rigorously deduced from the concept of capitalism. The same is true of such social control methods as the police, the prison, the juvenile court, and the regulatory agency.

If one were to borrow the language of variable analysis, these observations imply that a general Marxian theory of historical change in crime control cannot be framed in such a way that mode of production is treated as the independent variable. Social control must be understood in terms of social formations (containing an articulated set of modes, along with the political and ideological "levels"). Yet here too, the distinction between dependent and independent variables is somewhat misleading, for crime control is itself a part of a social formation, and thus the social formation cannot be considered as entirely prior to it, either logically or empirically. Indeed, the *mode of production* is not entirely distinct from social control conceptually, for crime control can be (though is not always) part of the forces and relations of production (consider penal slavery, prison labor, factory discipline). We are thus faced with a complex problem involving joint or reciprocal determination, rather than unidirectional causality.

Notes

1 Social control in the mercantile era is treated from the same viewpoint in Humphries and Greenberg (1980).

2 Thus according to Poulantzas (1973:77), "political class struggle has nothing to do with a ... process ... 'acted' by ... the class subject."

3 For example, Dickson (1968) never explains why the Federal Bureau of Narcotics chose to expand its bureaucratic empire by seeking to prohibit marijuana instead of aspirin. See Galliher and Walker (1977) for a reinterpretation of Dickson's data.

4 Chambliss (1969:10) is one of the few Marxist criminologists to criticize this position explicitly: "it would be a mistake to [assume] that all laws represent the interests of persons in power at the expense of persons less influential ... laws are passed which reflect the interests of the general population and which are antithetical to the interest of those in power."

5 For example, vagrancy law was created in fourteenth-century England as a form of wage control in the interests of feudal landlords (Foote, 1956; Chambliss, 1964), presumably because earlier forms of control, such as the manorial courts, had been weakened by the growth of cities to which serfs could escape. The efforts of a propertied class to frustrate a control strategy adopted by the working class can be seen in the legislative history of the Texas Minimum Wage Law, which for the first time subjected the wage contract in Texas to governmental control: "In 1915 two minimum wage bills were introduced in the legislature. Employers' opposition became aroused and no vote was taken. In 1917 a bill was again introduced and the retail merchants prevented its coming to a vote. In 1918 the state Federa-

tion of Labor demanded of all candidates for the legislature a pledge to vote for a minimum wage law, and the Democratic Party in the state included it in its platform. In the following year a law was passed.... The employers, however, continued their opposition to the law... [and] asked for delay in putting the rates into effect.... The legislature in 1921 asked the Commission to delay actions.... The Texas law came to an end before any rates were actually put into effect" (Brandeis, 1935:517–18, quoted in Ratner, 1981).

6 However, to avoid undermining the authority of the owners, slave testimony was not admissible as evidence in court, a restriction that partly undermined the value of the protective legislation and damaged other interests of slaveowners (Genovese, 1974:40).

7 Sumner's (1979) treatment of ideology is consistent with our position. We note that experience itself involves interpretation, and thus makes use of concepts and ideas previously acquired. Consequently, ideas do not generally mirror social relations as they exist at any moment. Residues or traces of earlier forms of social relations can survive in consciousness long after the relations themselves have become extinct.

8 Cutler et al. (1977:232) note that leading Marxist theorists, including Marx and Lenin, recognized that the contending parties in political conflict were not always classes, but did not deal adequately with this fact in their more general theoretical statements about classes and politics.

9 In earlier historical periods the state did not enjoy all of these resources, at least not to the degree that it does today. For a discussion of how the weakness of the English state in the mercantile era limited its ability to implement its policies, see Humphries and Greenberg: (1980). The degree to which the state has been autonomous from dominant class control is, of course, historically variable (Weisser, 1979).

10 In *The German Ideology* Marx and Engels assert that one part of the ruling class "appears as the thinkers of the class (its active, conceptive ideologists) who make the perfecting of the illusions of the class about itself their chief sources of livelihood, while the others' attitude to these ideas and illusions is more passive and receptive, because they are in reality the active members of this class and have less time to make up illusions and ideas about themselves" (quoted in Miliband, 1977:58). Although this oversimplifies the functions of intellectuals, it does suggest, consistent with our view, that classes must legitimate their domination to themselves as well as to subordinate classes.

11 For example, the Rockefeller Foundation played a major role in drawing up legislative proposals for ending Prohibition (private communication from Harry G. Levine) and for decriminalizing abortion and contraception (Humphries, 1977). It also helped to fund the development of methadone as a strategy for controlling heroin addiction (Klein, 1976). Criminal sentencing reform proposals have grown out of policy analyses financed by both private foundations and the federal Law Enforcement Assistance Administration. While these proposals need not *represent* dominant class interests, they cannot directly challenge them. Control over the distribution of financial resources thus implies a substantial measure of control over ideological resources and helps to shape the definitions of deviance and proposals for social control that enter into public discussion and receive political consideration.

12 By 1861, many of the manufacturers who had opposed factory legislation a few decades earlier admitted that it had not had the pernicious consequences they had anticipated, and they were now happy to have it (Ward, 1970).

13 As Marx put it, "The science of a marvelous industry is at the same time the science of *asceticism*" (1844b:171; emphasis in original).

14 Boyer (1978) argues that fear of downward mobility in the middle class was responsible for other sorts of efforts aimed to bolster self-control in the Jacksonian era as well.

15 Gusfield (1963:36–44) points out that in the first two decades of the nineteenth century, temperance was promoted by Calvinist ministers and Federalist lay leaders concerned with

the cultural dimensions of their own displacement by the new middle classes. They, however, had been unable to gain wide popular support for temperance.

16 For documentation of working-class involvement in the American temperance movement see Isaac (1965:55) and Timberlake (1963:80–91); for the British temperance movement, see Harrison (1971). Isaac (1965:36) also notes the support of black leaders, such as Frederick Douglass, for Prohibition. Working-class and black leaders shared the belief that drinking interfered with the struggle for group advancement.

17 Several historians have shown that Gusfield's (1963) claim that the temperance movement was primarily based in the rural middle-class is wrong. The relationship between urbanism and Prohibition sentiment was weak; the important variables were class and ethnicity.

18 Within months of the great Chicago riot of 1877, the middle classes had inititiated "a broad movement of reform, directed toward temperance legislation and Christian missions and charity societies and the public school system, all oriented toward converting workingpeople to middle class notions of work and thrift, sobriety and respectability" (Kann, n.d.). In addition, they strengthened the police force and state militia.

19 Economic competition between Mexican and Anglo laborers in the American Southwest in the 1930s gave rise to marijuana legislation through a similar process (Helmer, 1975).

20 In a substantive sense, this is not necessarily true: formal equality does not take real social differences into account, and may lead to very unequal consequences for different parties to an agreement. In *Capital,* Marx claimed to show that the wage contract, though formally equal, nevertheless had as its consequence the capitalist exploitation of workers.

21 According to Shelton (1973), landowners and industrialists channeled popular discontent toward middlemen, who were made scapegoats for economic hardship. As long as riots were directed against middlemen, the holders of major wealth were not threatened.

22 Attempts along these lines were made. Thus, manufacturers in eighteenth-century industrial towns formed associations to finance the prosecution of laborers accused of offenses connected with the "putting out" system, such as embezzlement of raw materials (Shelton, 1973:71).

23 The first police force for the entire city of Paris was established in the same year (Weisser, 1979:161).

24 The lower gentry who as parish judges sympathized with the rioters and did little to suppress them*failed* to serve the interests of property (Shelton, 1973:95). The local militia posed much the same problem. When called upon to put down rioters who were their own family and neighbors, their loyalty could not be trusted. The reformers who urged the creation of a police force hoped that full-time employees salaried by the state would be more loyal than a militia of community residents who were not paid by the state.

25 The fathers of the English police saw the force not merely as a deterrent to crime. The police were also to engage in moral exhortation, and lead the poor to adopt middle-class morals and living habits (Donajgrodzki, 1977).

26 Thus Philips (1977:84–87) notes: "Studies of the introduction of new police forces into communities suggest that one immediate effect which they produce is a marked increase in prosecutions for minor public order offences—brawls, drunkenness, disorderly conduct in public, etc." In the industrial Black Country of northern England the establishment of a "new" police force led to "a general campaign against drunkenness, disorderly behavior and fighting in the streets, and against the hitherto tolerated blood sports [bullbaiting, prizefighting, cockfighting and dogfighting]. Middle class opinion had moved decisively against such "barbarous" sports.... The new police played an important role in stamping out these sports ... the police sought them out, broke them up, arrested and prosecuted the participants" (Philips, 1977:86). The police carried out similar campaigns against working-class culture in Boston (Lane, 1975), Salem (Ferdinand, 1972), and other Northeastern industrial cities of the United States (Harring, article 10 in this volume).

27 Policing in the Black Country was reorganized in the nineteenth century in much the same way (Philips, 1977:57–60).

28 The necessarily decentralized character of police patrol always reduces the organization's ability to gain officers' compliance with organizational policy. In this period, however, police corruption seems to have been less a case of individual police refusing to enforce the law in return for payoffs, than an organizational policy of nonenforcement in return for bribes at the highest levels of the administrative hierarchy.

29 The merchants who petitioned Parliament blamed the upswing in crime after 1815 on the weakness of law enforcement, but with little basis. The increase is now generally attributed to the difficulty that soldiers discharged at the end of the Napoleonic War had in finding employment.

30 A similar combination of pragmatic and humanitarian concerns seems to have been responsible for the campaign against the death penalty in the United States just after the War of Independence. In New York, for example, the campaign of businessmen was led by Thomas Eddy, a prosperous Quaker merchant (Lewis, 1965:4). For evidence concerning a similar shift in religious doctrine in the United States and a discussion of the effect of this shift on the way crime and punishment were viewed, see Davis (1957) and Griffin (1960).

31 To achieve this strict control, imprisonment for debt had to be abolished. Since debtors had not been convicted of a crime, they could not be subjected to the rigorous discipline of the penitentiary (Ignatieff, 1978:31). As business indebtedness and bankruptcy were becoming a more normal feature of the capitalist economy, imprisonment for debt also came under increasing criticism from business classes.

32 Most of the committals to the Gloucester penitentiary between 1792 and 1809, for example, involved breaches of labor discipline on the part of agricultural workers and workers in the "putting out" system (Ignatieff, 1978:108–9, 179–83).

33 Geis (1972) notes that Jeremy Bentham's Panoptican design for penitentiaries and workhouses was adapted from a plan his brother Samuel had devised to stop carpenters employed in a shipyard from pilfering materials.

34 For similar diffusion of control strategies in the French prisons see Foucault (1975).

35 We follow the conventional usage in characterizing the economy during this period as "monopoly capitalism," even though the concentration of capital in most sectors of the economy never reached the point of complete monopolization.

36 Chambliss (1976) has noted that support for federal regulation of the meat-packing industry came from the industry itself. The larger meat packers hoped that inspection would increase their sales by reassuring foreign customers that American meat was safe. Since smaller meat packers could not afford the methods required by the new regulations, federal regulation gave the larger meat-packers a competitive advantage. According to Wiebe (1962:212), "at least one segment of the business community supported each major program for federal control" of the economy.

37 On the other hand, Boyer (1978:214, 348–49) argues that active business support for Prohibition was exceptional, and cites evidence that in some localities the business community strongly opposed Prohibition, since it threatened investments in tourism, real estate, hotels and restaurants, and the liquor industry. Divisions on this issue within the capitalist class may have given the middle classes greater political strength than would otherwise have been the case. An additional factor in the success of the Prohibition movement was clearly the liquor industry's failure to put together a unified opposition. The wine, beer, and liquor sectors of the industry could not agree on a common strategy; indeed, the liquor industry was the one major sector of manufacturing that had not developed a national trade association.

38 A few reformers, such as Samuel Gridley Howe, had already publicized the British experiments before the Civil War, but not until after the war were they given much attention.

39 They really meant this. Macdonald (1893:32), a leading figure in this movement, noted that sentences totally indefinite in length would permit someone convicted of drunkenness to be imprisoned for life should that prove desirable.

40 Major contributors included such names as Adler, Astor, Carnegie, Dodge, Guggenheim, Harriman, Letchworth, Lowell, Morgan, Rockefeller, Schiff, and Vanderbilt, along with foundations established by these and other leading capitalist families (Hahn, 1978).

41 Juveniles were being committed to asylums in the absence of a criminal conviction even in the Jacksonian era. The Pennsylvania Supreme Court upheld the practice in *Ex parte Crouse* (1838). In Chicago this was the practice from 1855 to 1870, when a court decision based on laissez-faire doctrine severely curtailed the state's powers to incarcerate juveniles not convicted of a crime. Proceedings involving juveniles after this date still appear to have been procedurally informal (Fox, 1970).

42 Working-class salaries in this period did not rise very much with age. Consequently, parents often depended on their children's income (private communication from Steven Dubnoff) and would have been reluctant to send their children to school. Even when willing, they might not have been able to control their children. Lacking substantial capital, working-class parents were able to do relatively little to secure their children's future, and thus were much less able to control them than were peasant parents in Europe, who could bequeath land to their children. It is noteworthy that in the early years of the juvenile court, many parents filed complaints against their adolescent children, alleging refusal to work or to turn over their earnings (Schultz, 1973; Schlossman, 1977). Thus parents responded to the weakening of their traditional sources of authority over children by turning to the new institutional source of control for assistance.

43 Platt (1969) appears to have erred on this point because of his tendency to overlook changes in the child-saving movement between the Jacksonian and Progressive eras. In this classical study of the origins of the juvenile court, Platt maintains that its originators wanted to send more youths to reformatories. This was true of pre–Civil War reformers, but was no longer true at the end of the nineteenth century.

44 Recent discussions of the child-saving movement have given too much attention to the class backgrounds of the movement's leaders and participants (Platt, 1969, 1974; Hagan and Leon, 1977). The native middle and upper classes shared a common perspective on most aspects of the Progressive program, including this one. Ben Lindsey, for example, the founder of the Denver juvenile court, came from a poor family background and entered the middle class by becoming a lawyer. A leading figure in the Progressive movement, he campaigned nationally for the juvenile court, and hobnobbed with corporate executives and national political figures such as Theodore Roosevelt. Heavy upper-class involvement did not preclude significant political defeats for the movement, as in Illinois (Fox, 1970). While capitalist support for the movement may have been helpful, it was not essential, as the examples of Denver, Toronto, and Oklahoma illustrate. We know of no theoretical reason to think it should have been. The middle class is quite capable of acting politically on its own, without upper-class leadership.

References

AFSC Working Party
1971 *Struggle for Justice*. New York: Hill and Wang.

Almy, Frederick
1902 "Juvenile Courts in Buffalo." *Annals of the American Academy of Political Science* 20:279–85.

Beccaria, Cesare
1764 *Of Crimes and Punishments*. Indianapolis: Bobbs-Merrill, 1963.

Becker, Howard S.
1963 *Outsiders: Studies in the Sociology of Deviance.* New York: Free Press.

Belknap, Michael R.
1977 "The Mechanics of Repression: J. Edgar Hoover, the Bureau of Investigation and the Radicals, 1917–1925." *Crime and Social Justice* 7:49–58.

Blocker, Jr., Jack S.
1976 *Retreat from Reform: The Prohibition Movement in the United States,* 1890–1913. Westport, Conn.: Greenwood Press.

Boostrum, Ronald
1974 "The Personalization of Evil: The Emergence of American Criminology, 1865–1910." Ph.D. dissertation, University of California, Berkeley.

Brandeis, Elizabeth
1935 "Labor legislation." In John R. Commons (ed.), *History of Labor in the United States, 1896–1932*, vol. 3. New York: Macmillan.

Brockway, Zebulon Reed
1912 *Fifty Years of Prison Service: An Autobiography.* Montclair, N.J.: Patterson Smith, 1969.

Bryant, Jr., Keith L.
1968 "The Juvenile Court Movement: Oklahoma as a Case Study." *Social Science Quarterly* 49:368–76.

Caldwell, Robert G.
1961 "The Juvenile Court: Its Development and Some Major Problems." *Journal of Criminal Law, Criminology and Police Science* 51:493–511.

Candeloro, Giorgio
1956 *Storia dell' Italia Moderne*. vol. 1, *Le Origini del Risorgimento*. Milano: Feltrinelli.

Carpenter, Mary
1864 *Our Convicts*. Montclair, N.J.: Patterson Smith, 1969.

Chambliss, William J.
1964 "A Sociological Analysis of the Law of Vagrancy." *Social Problems* 11:67–77.
1969 *Crime and the Legal Process*. New York: McGraw-Hill.
1974 "The State, the Law, and the Definition of Behavior as Criminal or Delinquent." In Daniel Glaser (ed.), *Handbook of Criminology*. Chicago: Rand McNally, pp. 3–44.

Cohen, Stanley
1979 "The Punitive City: Notes on the Dispersal of Social Control." *Contemporary Crises* 3: 339–63.

Colquhoun, Patrick
1795 *A Treatise on the Police of the Metropolis.* Montclair, N. J.: Patterson Smith, 1969.
1800 *A Treatise on the Commerce and Police of the River Thames*. Montclair, N.J.: Patterson Smith, 1969.

Conrad, Peter, and Joseph W. Schneider
From Badness to Sickness: Deviance in American Society. St. Louis: C. V. Mosby, 1980.

Cooper, David D.
1974 *The Lesson of the Scaffold: The Public Execution Controversy in Victorian England.* Athens: Ohio University Press.

Currie, Elliot Park
n.d. "Managing the Minds of Men: The Reformatory Movement, 1865–1920." Ph.D. dissertation, University of California, Berkeley.

Cutler, Antony, Barry Hindess, Paul Hirst, and Athar Hussain
1977 *Marx's "Capital" and Capitalism Today*, vol. 1. London: Routledge and Kegan Paul.

Dahl, Tove Stang
1974 "The Emergence of the Norwegian Child Welfare Law." *Scandinavian Studies in Criminology* 5:83–98.

Davis, David Brion
1957 *Homicide in American Fiction, 1798–1860: A Study in Social Values*. Ithaca: Cornell University Press.

Dickson, Donald T.
1968 "Bureaucracy and Morality: An Organizational Perspective on a Moral Crusade." *Social Problems* 16:143–56.

Domhoff, G. William
1970 *The Higher Circles: The Governing Class in America*. New York: Random House.

Donajgrodzki, A. P.
1977 "'Social Police' and the Bureaucratic Elite: A Vision of Order in the Age of Reform." In A. P. Donajgrodzki (ed.), *Social Control in Nineteenth Century Britain*. Totawa: Rowman and Littlefield, pp. 51–76.

Douglas, Jack
1971 *Crime and Justice in American Society*. Indianapolis: Bobbs-Merrill.

Durkheim, Emile
1893 *The Division of Labor in Society*. New York: Free Press, 1964.
1895 *The Rules of Sociological Method*. New York: Free Press, 1964.

Embree, Scotty
1973 "The Politics of Expertise: A Profession and Jurisdiction." Ph.D. dissertation, New York University.
1977 "The State Department as Moral Entrepreneur: Racism and Imperialism as Factors in the Passage of the Harrison Narcotics Act." In David F. Greenberg (ed.), *Corrections and Punishment*. Beverly Hills: Sage, pp. 193–204.

Engels, Friedrich
1878 "Herr Eugen Dühring's Revolution in Science," Ch. 9. In Lewis S. Feuer (ed.), *Karl Marx and Friedrich Engels' Basic Writings on Politics and Philosophy*. Garden City: Anchor, 1959, pp. 270–79.
1890 "Letter to Conrad Schmidt." In Lewis S. Feuer (ed.), *Karl Marx and Friedrich Engels' Basic Writings on Politics and Philosophy*. Garden City: Anchor, 1959, pp. 403–7.
1893 "Letter to Franz Mehring." In Lewis S. Feuer (ed.), *Karl Marx and Friedrich Engels' Basic Writings on Politics and Philosophy*. Garden City: Anchor, 1959, pp. 407–9.

Erikson, Kai T.
1966 *Wayward Puritans: A Study in the Sociology of Deviance*. New York: Wiley.

Eriksson, Torsten
1976 *The Reformers: An Historical Survey of Pioneer Experiments in the Treatment of Criminals*. New York: Elsevier.

Felt, Jeremy P.
1965 *Hostages of Fortune: Child Labor Reform in New York State*. Syracuse: Syracuse University Press.

Ferdinand, Theodore N.
1972 "Politics, the Police, and Arresting Policies in Salem, Massachusetts since the Civil War." *Social Problems* 19:572–88.

Fernbach, David
1973 "Toward a Marxist Theory of Gay Liberation." *Socialist Revolution* 28: 29–41.

Fine, Bob

1979 "State and Punishment: A Marxist Critique of Economism." In Bob Fine et al. (eds.), *Capitalism and the Rule of Law: From Deviancy Theory to Marxism*. London: Hutchison, pp. 29–45.

Fine, Sidney

1956 *Laissez Faire and the General Welfare State*. Ann Arbor: University of Michigan Press.

Foote, Caleb

1956 "Vagrancy-type Law and Its Administration." *University of Pennsylvania Law Review* 104:603–50.

Foucault, Michel

1965 *Madness and Civilization: A History of Insanity in the Age of Reason*. Tr. Richard Howard. New York: Pantheon.

1975 *Discipline and Punish: The Birth of the Prison*. Trans. Alan Sheridan. New York: Pantheon, 1977.

Fox, Sanford J.

1970 "Juvenile Justice Reform: An Historical Perspective." *Stanford Law Review* 22:1187–1239.

Galliher, John F., and Allyn Walker

1977 "The Puzzle of the Social Origins of the Marihuana Tax Act of 1937." *Social Problems* 24:367–76.

Geis, Gilbert

1972 "Jeremy Bentham." In Hermann Mannheim (ed.), *Pioneers in Criminology*, 2d ed. Montclair, N.J.: Patterson Smith, pp. 51–68.

Genovese, Eugene D.

1974 *Roll, Jordan, Roll: The World the Slaves Made*. New York: Pantheon.

Gonzalez, Gilbert G.

1977 "The Relationship between Monopoly Capitalism and Progressive Education." *The Insurgent Sociologist* 7:25–41.

Greenberg, David F.

1975 "On One-dimensional Marxist Criminology." *Theory and Society* 3:610–21.

1977 "Delinquency and the Age Structure of Society." *Contemporary Crises* 2:189–223.

Griffin, Clifford S.

1960 *Their Brothers' Keepers: Moral Stewardship in the United States, 1800–1865*. New Brunswick: Rutgers University Press.

Gusfield, Joseph R.

1963 *Symbolic Crusade: Status Politics and the American Temperance Movement*. Urbana: University of Illinois Press.

Gutman, Herbert G.

1963 "The Worker's Search for Power: Labor in the Gilded Age." In H. Wayne Morgan (ed.), *The Gilded Age: A Reappraisal*. Syracuse: Syracuse University Press, pp. 38–68.

Hagan, John, and Jeffrey Leon

1977 "Rediscovering Delinquency: Social History, Political Ideology and the Sociology of Law." *American Sociological Review* 42:587–98.

Hahn, Nicolas Fischer

1978 "The Defective Delinquent Movement: A History of the Born Criminal in New York State, 1850–1966." Ph.D. dissertation, State University of New York at Albany.

Hamowy, Ronald

n.d. "Medicine and the Criminalization of Sin: 'Self-abuse' in Nineteenth Century America." Unpublished paper.

Harrison, Brian

1971 *Drink and the Victorians: The Temperance Question in England, 1815–1872*. Pittsburgh: University of Pittsburgh Press.

Hartwell, R. M.

1971 *The Industrial Revolution and Economic Growth*. London: Methuen.

Hay, Douglas

1975 "Property, Authority and the Criminal Law." In Douglas Hay et al. (eds.) *Albion's Fatal Tree: Crime and Society in Eighteenth Century England*. New York: Pantheon, pp. 17–63.

Heckscher, Eli F.

1931 *Mercantilism*, vol. 1. New York: Macmillan, 1955.

1935 *Mercantilism*, vol. 2. New York: Macmillan, 1955.

Helmer, John

1975 *Drugs and Minority Oppression*. New York: Seabury Press.

Hepburn, John R.

1977 "Social Control and the Legal Order: Legitimate Repression in a Capitalist State." *Contemporary Crises* 1:77–90.

Hill, Christopher

1961 *The Century of Revolution, 1603–1714*. Edinburgh: Thomas Nelson and Sons.

Hill, Matthew Davenport

1857 *Suggestions for the Repression of Crime*. Montclair, N.J.. Patterson Smith, 1975.

Hirst, Paul, and Barry Hindess

1975 *Precapitalist Modes of Production*. Boston: Routledge and Kegan Paul.

Hofstadter, Richard

1956 *The Age of Reform: From Bryan to F.D.R.,* New York: Random House.

Hopkins, Charles Howard

1940 *The Rise of the Social Gospel in American Protestantism, 1865–1915*. New Haven: Yale University Press.

Howe, Daniel Walker

1976 "Victorian Culture in America." In Daniel W. Howe (ed.), *Victorian America*. Philadelphia: University of Pennsylvania Press, pp. 3–28.

Humphries, Drew

1977 "The Movement to Legalize Abortion: An Historical Account." In David F. Greenberg (ed.), *Corrections and Punishment*. Beverly Hills: Sage, pp. 205–24.

Humphries, Drew and David F. Greenberg

1980 "Social Control and Social Formations: A Marxian Analysis." In Donald Black (ed.), *Toward a General Theory of Social Control*. New York: Academic Press.

Ignatieff, Michael

1978 *A Just Measure of Pain: The Penitentiary in the Industrial Revolution, 1750–1850*. New York: Pantheon.

Inverarity, James

1976 "Populism and Lynching in Louisiana, 1889–1896: A Test of Erikson's Theory of the Relationship between Boundary Crises and Repressive Justice." *American Sociological Review* 41:262–80.

Isaac, Paul E.

1965 *Prohibition and Politics: Turbulent Decades in Tennessee, 1885–1920*. Knoxville: University of Tennessee Press.

Kann, Kenneth

1877 "The Big City Riot in 1877: Chicago." Unpublished paper.

Klein, Dorie

1976 "The Rise of Methadone: The Medical Model and Crime Control." Unpublished paper presented to the American Society of Criminology.

Kolko, Gabriel

1963 *The Triumph of Conservatism: A Reinterpretation of American History, 1900–1916.* New York: Free Press.

Lane, Roger

1975 *Policing the City: Boston, 1822–1885.* New York: Atheneum.

Levine, David

1971 *Jane Addams and the Liberal Tradition*, Madison: State Historical Society of Wisconsin.

Levine, Harry Gene

1978 "The Discovery of Addiction: Changing Conceptions of Habitual Drunkenness in America." *Journal of Studies on Alcohol* 39:143–74.

1979 "Temperance and Women in 19th Century United States." In *Research Advances in Alcohol and Drug Problems*, vol. 5. New York: Plenum.

Levine, Murray, and Adeline Levine

1970 *A Social History of Helping Services*. New York: Appleton-Century-Crofts.

Lewis, W. David

1965 *From Newgate to Dannemora: The Rise of the Penitentiary in New York, 1796–1848.* Ithaca: Cornell University Press.

1970 "The Reformer as Conservative: Protestant Counter-subversion in the Early Republic." In Stanley Cohen and Lorman Ratner (eds.), *The Development of an American Culture.* Englewood Cliffs, N.J.: Prentice-Hall.

Liazos, Alexander

1972 "The Poverty of the Sociology of Deviance: Nuts, Sluts and Preverts." *Social Problems* 20:103–20.

Linebaugh, Peter

1975 "The Tyburn Riots against the Surgeons." In Douglas Hay et al. (eds.), *Albion's Fatal Tree*. New York: Pantheon, pp. 65–118.

Macdonald, Arthur

1892 *Abnormal Man*. Washington, D.C.: Government Printing Office.

Manning, Peter

1977 *Police Work: The Social Organization of Policing*. Cambridge: M.I.T. Press.

Marx, Karl

1844a *Contribution to the Critique of Hegel's Philosophy of Right*. "Introduction." In T. B. Bottomore (ed.), *Karl Marx, Early Writings*. New York: McGraw-Hill, 1964, pp. 55–56.

1844b Economic and Philosophical Manuscripts. In T. B. Bottomore (ed.), *Karl Marx, Early Writings*. New York: McGraw-Hill, 1964, pp. 61–219.

1858 *Grundrisse: Introduction to the Critique of Political Economy*. Tr. Martin Nicolaus. New York: Vintage, 1973.

1859 A Contribution to the Critique of Political Economy. In Lewis S. Feuer (ed.), *Marx and Engels' Basic Writings on Politics and Philosophy*. Garden City: Anchor, 1959, pp. 42–46.

1867 *Capital: A Critique of Political Economy*, vol. 1. Trans. Samuel Moore and Edward Aveling. New York: International Publishers, 1967.

1894 *Capital: A Critique of Political Economy*, vol. 3. New York: International Publishers, 1967.

Marx, Karl, and Friedrich Engels

1846 "The German Ideology." In Lewis S. Feuer (ed.), *Marx and Engels' Basic Writings on Politics and Philosophy.* Garden City: Anchor, 1959, pp. 246–61.

Michalowski, Raymond J., and Edward J. Bohlander

1976 "Repression and Criminal Justice in Capitalist America." *Sociological Inquiry* 46: 95–106.

Miliband, Ralph

1977 *Marxism and Politics*. Oxford: Oxford University Press.

Morgan, Patricia A.

1976 "The Legislation of Drug Law: Economic Crisis and Social Control." Unpublished paper presented to the Society for the Study of Social Problems.

Musto, David F.

1973 *The American Disease*. New Haven: Yale University Press.

Oglesby, Carl, and Richard Schaull

1967 *Containment and Change*. New York: Macmillan.

Ostrander, Gilman M.

1957 *The Prohibition Movement in California, 1848–1933*. Berkeley: University of California Press.

Parker, Graham

1976 "The Juvenile Court Movement: The Illinois Experience." *University of Toronto Law Journal* 26:253–306.

Parsons, Talcott

1951 *The Social System*. New York: Free Press.

Parsons, Talcott, and Dean R. Gerstein

1977 "Two Cases of Social Deviance: Addiction to Heroin, Addiction to Power." In Edward Sagarin (ed.), *Deviance and Social Change*. Beverly Hills: Sage, pp. 19–57.

Pashukanis, Evgeny B.

1929 *Law and Marxism: A General Theory*. Tr. Barbara Einhorn. London: Ink Links, 1978.

Perkin, Harold

1969 *The Origins of Modern English Society, 1780–1880*. London: Routledge and Kegan Paul.

Philips, David

1977 *Crime and Authority in Victorian England: The Black Country 1835–1860*. Totowa, N.J.: Rowman and Littlefield.

Pivar, David J.

1973 *Purity Crusade: Sexual Morality and Social Control, 1868–1900*. Westport, Conn.: Greenwood.

Platt, Anthony M.

1969 *The Child Savers: The Invention of Delinquency*. Chicago: University of Chicago Press.

1974 "The Triumph of Benevolence: The Origins of the Juvenile Justice System in the United States." In Richard Quinney (ed.), *Criminal Justice in America: A Critical Understanding*. Boston: Little, Brown, pp. 356–89.

Poulantzas, Nicos

1973 *Political Power and Social Classes*. London: Sheed and Ward.

1974 *Classes in Contemporary Capitalism*. Tr. David Fernbach. London: Verso.

Quinney, Richard

1977 *Class, State and Crime: On the Theory and Practice of Criminal Justice*. New York: McKay.

Ratner, Ronnie S.

1981 *The Rise and Growth of Wage and Hours Standards Laws in the U.S., 1900–1973*. New Brunswick: Rutgers University Press.

Richardson, James F.

1970 *The New York Police, Colonial Times to 1901*. New York: Oxford University Press.

Rose, R. B.

1961 "Eighteenth Century Price Riots and Public Policy in England." *International Review of Social History* 6:277–82.

Rothman, David J.

1971 *Discovery of the Asylum: Social Order and Disorder in the New World*. Boston: Little, Brown.

Rusche, Georg, and Otto Kirchheimer

1939 *Punishment and Social Structure*. New York: Russell and Russell, 1969.

Schlossman, Steven L.

1977 *Law and the American Delinquent: The Theory and Practice of "Progressive" Juvenile Justice, 1825–1920*. Chicago: University of Chicago Press.

Schultz, J. Lawrence

1973 "The Cycle of Juvenile Court History." *Crime and Delinquency* 19:457–77.

Schwendinger, Herman, and Julia Schwendinger

1974 *The Sociologists of the Chair: A Radical Analysis of the Formative Years of American Sociology, 1883–1922.* New York: Basic Books.

Scull, Andrew

1977 "Madness and Segregative Control: The Rise of the Insane Asylum." *Social Problems* 24:337–51.

Sellin, Thorsten

1976 *Slavery and the Penal System*. New York: Elsevier.

Sheehan, W. J.

1977 "Finding Solace in Eighteenth-Century Newgate." In J. S. Cockburn (ed.), *Crime in England, 1550–1800.* Princeton: Princeton University Press, pp. 229–45.

Shelton, Walter J.

1973 *English Hunger and Industrial Disorders*. Toronto: University of Toronto Press.

Silver, Allan

1967 "The Demand for Order in Civil Society: A Review of Some Themes in the History of Urban Crime, Police and Riot." In D. J. Bordua (ed.), *The Police: Six Sociological Essays*. New York: John Wiley and Sons, pp. 1–24.

Spitzer, Steven

1979 "The Rationalization of Crime Control in Capitalist Society." *Contemporary Crises* 3:187–206.

1980 "'Left-wing' Criminology—An Infantile Disorder?" In James A. Inciardi (ed.), *Radical Criminology: The Coming Crises.* Beverly Hills: Sage.

Spitzer, Steven, and Andrew Scull

1977a "Social Control in Historical Perspective: From Private to Public Responses to Crime." In David F. Greenberg (ed.), *Corrections and Punishment*. Beverly Hills: Sage, pp. 265–86.

1977b "Privatization and Capitalist Development: The Case of the Private Police." *Social Problems* 25:18–29.

Stevenson, John

1975 "Food Riots in England, 1792–1818." In R. Quinault and J. Stevenson (eds.), *Popular Protest and Public Order: Six Studies in British History, 1790–1920*. New York: St. Martin's Press, pp. 33–74.

1977 "Social Control and the Prevention of Riots in England, 1789–1829." In A. P. Donajgrodzki (ed.), *Social Control in Nineteenth Century Britain.* London: Croom Helm, pp. 27–50.

Sumner, Colin

1979 *Reading Ideologies: An Investigation into the Marxist Theory of Ideology and Law*. New York: Academic Press.

Thio, Alex

1973 "Class Bias in the Sociology of Deviance." *The American Sociologist* 8:1–12.

Thompson, E. P.

1963 *The Making of the English Working Class*. New York: Vintage Books.

1971 "The Moral Economy of the English Crowd in the Eighteenth Century." *Past and Present* 50:76–136.

1975 *Whigs and Hunters: Origins of the Black Act*. New York: Random House.

Timberlake, James H.

1963 *Prohibition and the Progressive Movement, 1900–1920*. Cambridge: Harvard University Press.

Tipple, John

1963 *The Gilded Age: A Reappraisal*. Syracuse: Syracuse University Press.

Walker, Samuel

1977 *A Critical History of Police Reform*. Lexington, Mass.: Lexington.

Ward, J. T.

1970 "The Factory Movement." In J. T. Ward (ed.), *Popular Movements c. 1830–1850*. London: Macmillan, pp. 54–77.

Weinstein, James

1968 *The Corporate Ideal in the Liberal State, 1900–1918*. Boston: Beacon.

Weisser, Michael R.

1979 *Crime and Punishment in Early Modern Europe*. Atlantic Highfields, N.J.: Humanities Press.

Wiebe, Robert H.

1962 *Businessmen and Reform: A Study of the Progressive Movement*. Cambridge: Harvard University Press.

1967 *The Search for Order, 1877–1920*. New York: Hill and Wang.

Wines, Enoch C.

1880 *The State of Prisons and of Child-Saving Institutions in the Civilized World.* Montclair, N.J.: Patterson Smith, 1968.

Zurcher, Jr., Louis A., and R. George Kirkpatrick

1976 *Citizens for Decency: Antipornography Crusades as Status Defense*. Austin: University of Texas Press.

[9]
The Dynamics of Oscillatory Punishment Processes

In a recent paper, Blumstein, Cohen and Nagin present two homeostatic models of the imprisonment process inspired by Durkheim's conception of society as a normatively integrated self-regulating mechanism.[1] Comparing the imprisonment rates predicted by their models with Canadian data for the period 1925–1960, the researchers found a good agreement for one of their models. It is the purpose of this paper to propose an alternative explanation of the observed imprisonment rates.

In both the models discussed by Blumstein *et al.*, the number of criminals at large in society is regulated by the imprisonment of criminal law violators. When the number of violators in prison declines, the number at large increases. Society then responds to this increase with more incarcerations, thereby reducing the number of criminals (and presumably the amount of crime) present outside the prison system. However, the two models differ in the detailed assumptions made about the imprisonment process.

Both models generate second order autoregressive equations[2] for the per capita imprisonment r_t. These equations have the general form

$$r_t = \phi_1 r_{t-1} + \phi_2 r_{t-2} + \delta' + \epsilon_t, \qquad (1)$$

where ϕ_1, ϕ_2 and δ' are constant coefficients, t is the time, and the disturbance terms ϵ_t are assumed to be independently distributed. When empirical values or plausible estimates of the parameters of the two models are inserted into the expressions derived theoretically for the coefficients, numerical predictions for their values are obtained.

Blumstein, Cohen and Nagin find that the model most consistent with the Canadian data (their model II) yields the coefficients

$$\phi_1 = 1.31, \qquad \phi_2 = -0.43, \qquad \delta' = 5.0 \times 10^{-5},$$

in rather good agreement with the values

$$\hat{\phi}_1 = 1.23, \qquad \hat{\phi}_2 = -0.43, \qquad \hat{\delta}' = 9.17 \times 10^{-5}$$

they obtain from a least squares fit to the observed imprisonment rates.

Blumstein, Cohen and Nagin's work has major theoretical and practical implications. First, Durkheim's belief that punitive justice strengthens social cohesion by reinforcing the collective conscience, although influential, has rarely been empirically tested. Durkheim himself argued that it is primarily in societies characterized by mechanical solidarity that punishment serves this function;[3] since he believed that society was evolving toward a division of labor based on organic solidarity, it is unclear that he would expect punishment to play a major role in strengthening norms and preventing crime in the modern world. To be sure, the model proposed by Blumstein *et al.* does not depend entirely on the proposition that collective acts of repression strengthen norms; they allow for the possibility that legal norms themselves may change. Nevertheless, in finding support for the existence of a self-regulating mechanism, they do provide at least partial confirmation of some of Durkheim's ideas and more generally for a functionalist theoretical orientation.

Second, Durkheim's writings on crime are commonly taken as representing a "consensus

* Research for this paper was conducted under a grant from the Russell Sage Foundation. I am grateful to Daniel Nagin for a helpful conversation, and to Jacquelyn Cohen for pointing out several errors in an earlier version.

** Assistant Professor, Sociology Department, New York University.

[1] Blumstein, Cohen & Nagin, *The Dynamics of a Homeostatic Punishment Process*, 68 J. CRIM. L. & C. 317 (1976).

[2] An autoregressive equation is one in which the dependent variable is regressed on its own earlier variables.

[3] E. DURKHEIM, THE DIVISION OF LABOR IN SOCIETY (G. Simpson trans. 1933).

theory" approach to crime and law enforcement. It is norms that are widely shared by the community that repression strengthens. Decades ago, George Herbert Mead pointed out[4] that in a pluralistic society characterized by normative dissensus, the enforcement of controversial rules might not have this effect at all. By punishing actions thought by some significant group not to be wrong, the state would tend to evoke resentment and hostility, weakening identification with the collectivity. To the extent that inhibition against crime depends on a sense of identification with rule-makers and with potential victims, the enforcement of some norms might increase rather than decrease the level of violations.

The Blumstein, Cohen and Nagin findings suggest that the "Meadian conflict model" did not operate in Canada during the years of study and thus might be taken as confirming the validity of a consensus perspective; however, the Blumstein, Cohen and Nagin model [hereinafter cited as the BCN model] is capable of accommodating some conflicting elements. Blumstein *et al.* argue that when too large a proportion of the population is imprisoned, norms may change in such a way as to shift the boundary between criminal and non-criminal activities, with lesser offenses being decriminalized. This would reduce the number of criminals through a process of redefinition, rather than repression. Class or interest group conflict could play a role in the social process of redefinition. Blumstein *et al.* also argue that when too few individuals are punished, "the basic identifying values of the society will not be adequately articulated and reinforced, again leading to social instability" creating "pressures for stricter law enforcement and perhaps more severe punishments."[5] This pressure could as easily come from particular groups in the society as from the society as a whole.

Implicit in the above quotation is the view that the punishment of crime is a vital necessity for society; if the number of individuals singled out for punishment falls below some level, "social instability" will result. The BCN model thus seems to legitimate state punishment practices. It does, however, call into question some widely held ideas about the effectiveness of particular punishment practices. In the most successful model, the size of the mean criminal population is extraordinarily insensitive to the recidivism rate, indicating that neither the rehabilitation nor the special deterrence of a prison population roughly as large as is found in Canada would have a substantial impact on the crime rate. The size of the mean criminal population also proves to be insensitive to wide variation in the rate of admissions to and releases from prison, though the prison population is extremely sensitive to variations in these parameters. The model is, however, consistent with the possibility that enforcement makes a contribution to conformity through its general deterrent effect, though it does not provide any information concerning the magnitude of this contribution, if it exists.

Although the BCN model suggests that the mean size of the criminal population is not very responsive to short-run changes in policy concerning prison admissions and releases, it does attribute changes in the size of the criminal population at large to variation in the size of the prison population. In this sense, the model projects an air of complacency. On the one hand, we do not need to be excessively alarmed by increases in crime, because the normal workings of popular pressure will bring about corrective measures just as in the past; extraordinary steps going beyond what has been done in the past are not needed. On the other hand, in the short-run it is primarily through the state's *punishment* policies that the number of criminals in society is regulated. While it is consistent with the BCN model to undertake other programs that might increase the population's motivation to conform, that is probably a long-term proposition, with little immediate impact on either crime rates or punishment levels.

Despite the elegance of the models that Blumstein *et al.* present and the impressive agreement between prediction and observation that they find, final judgment as to the adequacy of their model must be reserved until alternative models of the processes that generate imprisonment rates are examined. Such an examination of one set of alternative models will suggest the need to revise at least some features of the BCN model.

Taken together, a set of assumptions about releases and admissions comprise a model for

[4] Mead, *The Psychology of Punitive Justice*, 23 AM. J. SOC. 577 (1918).

[5] Blumstein, Cohen & Nagin, *supra* note 1, at 320.

changes in the size of the prison population. In examining alternative models, releases from prison will first be considered, and then admissions will be considered.

Releases from Prison

P_t, A_t and R_t represent, respectively, the prison population, the number of admissions to prison and the number of releases from prison at time t. Neglecting the small number of inmate deaths, the change in prison population at time t equals the admissions at time t less the releases at time t. Although time is a continuous variable, data concerning prison admissions and releases are available only in aggregated form, as annual rates. This requires that we make use of the discrete-time approximation

$$P_t - P_{t-1} = A_t - R_t, \tag{2}$$

where we have implicitly assumed that time is measured in years.

The first assumption about releases we consider is that the number of prisoners released is proportional to the prison population in any given year. Thus, when the prison population is high, the number of prisoners released will be correspondingly high as well. This assumption can be expressed through the equation:

$$P_t - P_{t-1} = A_t - bP_t.$$

Lagging the time by one year and taking the difference between the above equation and the lagged equation, we obtain the second order difference equation:

$$P_t - 2P_{t-1} + P_{t-2} = A_t - A_{t-1} - b(P_t - P_{t-1}),$$

or

$$P_t - \frac{(2+b)}{(1+b)}P_{t-1} + \frac{1}{(1+b)}P_{t-2} = \frac{A_t - A_{t-1}}{1+b}. \tag{3}$$

During the period under study, the mean sentence length was about two years which corresponds to the value $b = {}^1/_2$.

Next we transform equation (3), which relates prison populations and prison admissions, to an equation for the per capita prison population r_t and the per capita prison admission rate a_t. Assuming with Blumstein, Cohen and Nagin that the population T_t grows exponentially at rate g, the transformation can be accomplished using the rules:

$$\begin{aligned} P_t &= r_tT_t \\ P_{t-1} &= (r_{t-1} - gr_t)T_t \\ P_{t-2} &= (r_{t-2} - 2gr_{t-1} + g^2r_t)T_t \\ A_t &= a_tT_t \\ A_{t-1} &= (a_{t-1} - ga_t)T_t. \end{aligned}$$

These rules are valid to order g. As g for Canada is approximately 0.02, terms of order g^2 can be omitted as negligible. We then find:

$$r_t = \frac{(2+b+2g)}{\{1+b+g(2+b)\}}r_{t-1} - \frac{1}{\{1+b+g(2+b)\}}r_{t-2} + \frac{a_t(1+g) - a_{t-1}}{\{1+b-g(2+b)\}}.$$

Inserting observed values of b and g, we find:

$$\phi_1 = 1.64, \qquad \phi_2 = -0.65.$$

Since the predicted value of ϕ_1 lies outside the ninety-nine percent confidence limits of its observed value, the model is clearly untenable.

As this model has not led to good predictions, the assumption made about releases must be modified. Instead of assuming that the number of releases is proportional to the number of prisoners, we assume that the lengths of the sentences served in prison are geometrically distributed. This means that of a cohort of prisoners admitted at the same time, a fraction α will be released after one year, a fraction α^2 after two years, and a fraction α^n after n years.[6] This approximates the observed distribution of sentences, which is highly skewed. Many prisoners have sentences which are comparatively short, with a small minority serving sentences that are much longer.

With this assumption, equation (2) becomes:

$$P_t - P_{t-1} = A_t - \alpha A_{t-1} - \alpha^2 A_{t-2} \cdots - \alpha^n A_{t-n} \cdots \tag{3}$$

Because the infinite series in the right hand member is awkward to handle, it is best to

[6] In a continuous time model, the equivalent assumption would be that sentences are exponentially distributed. *See, e.g.*, Shinnar & Shinnar, *The Effects of the Criminal Justice System on the Control of Crime: A Quantitative Approach*, 9 L. & SOC'Y REV. 581 (1975). In a study of prison sentences, a geometric distribution assumption may actually be better than an exponential distribution assumption because prison sentences are usually a year or more in length (in the United States at least) and tend to cluster at the integers (two years, three years etc.).

eliminate it using a trick based on the Koyck transformation for handling problems involving distributed lags in econometrics. The trick consists of rewriting equation (3) with t replaced by t − 1, and multiplying the result by the quantity α. This gives us:

$$\alpha(P_{t-1} - P_{t-2}) = \alpha A_{t-1} - \alpha^2 A_{t-2} \cdots - \alpha^n A_{t-n} \cdots \quad (4)$$

Subtracting equation (4) from equation (3), we find:

$$P_t - (1 + \alpha)P_{t-1} + \alpha P_{t-2} = A_t - 2\alpha A_{t-1}. \quad (5)$$

When written in terms of the per capita prison population, this becomes

$$r_t - \frac{(1 + \alpha + 2\alpha g)}{1 + (1 + \alpha)g} r_{t-1} + \frac{\bar{\alpha}}{1 + (1 + \alpha)g} r_{r-2} = \frac{a_t(1 + 2\alpha g) - 2\alpha a_{t-1}}{1 + (1 + \alpha)g}. \quad (6)$$

The quantity α can be estimated from the mean sentence length S through the equation

$$S = \alpha/(1 - \alpha)^2.$$

During the period under study, the mean sentence length was approximately two years, corresponding to $\alpha = 1/2$. Inserting this value and the empirical value of g in equation (6), we find:

$$\phi_1 = 1.48, \qquad \phi_2 = -0.48.$$

Although the value of ϕ_1 just obtained is about twenty percent higher than the observed value, it does fall within the ninety percent confidence limits for $\hat{\phi}_1$.

It must be emphasized that these predictions for ϕ_1 and ϕ_2 do not depend in any way on assumptions concerning crime rates, recidivism rates, or the rates at which individuals in the population at large initiate or abandon criminal activity. It has simply been assumed that sentence lengths decline geometrically, and that the population grows slowly at an approximately constant rate.

As the Canadian population growth was indeed slow, and as the coefficients are insensitive to the details of the growth pattern, a comparison of the model predictions with observation is primarily a test of the assumption that sentence lengths decline geometrically. A discrepancy between observed and predicted values of ϕ_1 and ϕ_2 might, therefore, indicate little more than a pattern of sentencing that deviates from the pure geometric distribution assumed in the model.[7] In any event, the reasonably good agreement found in this model for the two coefficients ϕ_1 and ϕ_2 demonstrates that the good agreement Blumstein *et al.* find in their model for the same coefficients is not strong evidence in favor of their model.

Any additional dynamic assumptions to be incorporated in our model must take the form of assumptions about the behavior of a_t, the per capita rate of prison admissions. It is to this topic that we turn next.

Commitments to Prison

Perhaps the simplest assumption that might be made about commitments to prison is that the per capita commitment rate fluctuates randomly about a constant level. With this assumption, we can write

$$a_t = a + \nu_t, \quad (7)$$

where the ν_t are independently and identically distributed with zero mean and constant variance, and a is a constant.

With this assumption, the right hand member of equation (6) becomes

$$\frac{a(1 + 2\alpha g - 2\alpha)}{1 + (1 + \alpha)g} + \frac{(1 + 2\alpha g)\nu_t - 2\alpha\nu_{t-1}}{1 + (1 + \alpha)g}.$$

Substituting $\alpha = 1/2$ and $g = 0.02$, we find $\delta' = 0.02a$. The average per capita rate of admissions to prison was approximately twenty per 100,000 per year; consequently the model predicts $\delta' = 0.4 \times 10^{-5}$. This is too small by a factor of more than twenty.

This large discrepancy between predicted

[7] It follows that a better fit for the coefficients ϕ_1 and ϕ_2 can be obtained by slightly modifying the assumptions made about sentences. For example, in making the assumption that sentences are geometrically distributed, it is implicitly assumed that no account is taken of the number of people in prison when decisions are made about release. By assuming that the release rate is increased when the prison population is high, one additional parameter is added to the model, and the fit for both coefficients is improved. Some evidence for a departure from a pure geometric distribution of sentences has been found for a sample of prisoners drawn from five California prisons. *See* J. Chaiken, Distribution of Time Spent in Prison (1977) (unpublished Rand Working Paper).

and observed value of δ' is not as alarming as it appears. The prediction for δ' is quite sensitive to the value of α. For example, if $\alpha = 0.45$ instead of 0.50, we would predict $\delta' = 2.3 \times 10^{-5}$, which, though still too small, lies within the ninety-five percent confidence limit for the observed value. Secondly, the predicted value for δ' depends strongly on the predicted values for ϕ_1 and ϕ_2. Because the values we obtained for these two parameters were slightly too large in magnitude, we expect to find a value for δ' that is somewhat too small.

To see this, we note that the solution to the equation

$$r_t = \phi_1 r_{t-1} + \phi_2 r_{t-2} + \delta'$$

can be written as the sum of any particular solution to this equation, plus the general solution to the reduced equation obtained by setting $\delta' = 0$. We can find a particular solution to the above equation by letting $r_t = C$, a constant. We then find

$$\delta' = C(1 - \phi_1 - \phi_2).$$

C can be found by noting that when the general solution to the reduced equation is oscillatory, as it is in the BCN model II, the mean of the general solution will be zero. Consequently, we must have $C = \bar{r}$, the mean value of the r_t. The prison population is thus predicted to oscillate around a constant value.

Using the values of $\hat{\phi}_1$ and $\hat{\phi}_2$ that Blumstein *et al.* obtained from their least squares analysis, and noting that the mean incarceration rate was roughly forty-six prisoners per 100,000 population, we find $\delta' \approx 9.2 \times 10^{-5}$. In our "geometric sentences" model, the coefficient $1 - \phi_1 - \phi_2$ vanishes (to within rounding error). Consequently, the least squares value of δ' computed under the constraint that the model's predictions for ϕ_1 and ϕ_2 are correct would lead to the value $\delta' = 0$, which is much closer to the model's prediction for the coefficient.

The assumption that the error terms in equation (7) are statistically independent leads to the prediction that there is first order serial correlation among the error terms ϵ_t in equation (1), with

$$r_{\epsilon_t,\epsilon_{t-1}} = -{}^1/_2,$$

and vanishing serial correlations of higher order. This would appear to be a bad prediction, as Blumstein *et al.* report finding no serial correlation among the error terms from their least squares fit.[8]

A consistent treatment of errors in the BCN model, however, also leads to the conclusion that the error terms should be negatively correlated, with a magnitude that depends on the relative accuracy with which the model predicts crime rates and imprisonment rates. As it is not known how accurately their model predicts crime rates, no precise prediction for the magnitude of autocorrelation in the error terms can be made for their model. However, it is possible to establish the limits

$$-6/13 < r_{\epsilon_t, \epsilon_{t-1}} < 0$$

for their model.

A more serious difficulty with the assumption that admissions fluctuate randomly about a constant level is that with coefficients ϕ_1 and ϕ_2 of the magnitude predicted by the "geometric sentence" model, the solution will not be oscillatory. Yet a visual inspection of the annual per capita prison populations suggests random fluctuation about a sinusoidal oscillation. There are two ways such oscillatory behavior can be produced. One is through a self-regulating process of the sort hypothesized by Blumstein, Cohen and Nagin. Another way is for prison admissions to be driven by a variable that is exogenous to the crime-punishment system, and which oscillates sinusoidally.

The distinction between these two possibilities can be clarified through the use of a physical analogy. Suppose I suspend a weight from a spring in the presence of the earth's gravitational field, and let the weight and spring come to equilibrium. If I then displace the weight, stretching or compressing the spring, and release it, the weight will bob up and down without any further intervention on my part. In the absence of friction, the weight will oscillate with a fixed amplitude and fixed frequency indefinitely. Another way I can get the weight to move in an oscillatory manner is by holding it with my hand and moving my hand up and down.

The BCN model is somewhat analogous to the first possibility, though the analogy is im-

[8] It is possible that the stepwise estimation procedure adopted by Blumstein, Cohen and Nagin, in which the autoregressive coefficients of the model were estimated first and the error terms then examined for autocorrelation, led to an underestimation of serial correlation among the error terms.

perfect. Since changes in the criminal population at large are influenced by changes in the prison population, and vice versa, the system actually behaves like two coupled springs. However, the oscillatory movement of each variable in the crime-punishment system arises from the internal dynamics of the self-regulation. The second possibility would constitute a mechanical analogue to the prison population if there is some variable that causes prison admissions to oscillate in the same way that my hand causes the weight to oscillate. To consider this possibility we must see whether there are any variables that might influence prison admissions and which also oscillate with an appropriate frequency.

There are many variables that might be expected to influence the rate of prison admissions, such as a community's demographic composition, the amount of resources it can expend on punishment, the prevailing political sentiment, the crime rate and so on. Most such variables change slowly and not necessarily in a sinusoidal fashion. Whatever contribution they might make to an explanation of the mean level of a community's incarceration rate, they would not cause that rate to oscillate. On the other hand, *those variables that characterize the state of the business cycle do show the required behavior,* because periods of economic expansion alternate with periods of contraction in capitalist economic systems.

Moreover, there are reasons to expect prison admissions to depend strongly on the phase of the business cycle. One reason is suggested by microeconomic theory. When the economy is in a period of contraction, unemployment rises. Persons who are unemployed can be assumed to have a greater incentive to steal than those who are not. In addition, they may risk less when they engage in crime, for they cannot lose their jobs if they are caught.[9] If this reasoning is correct, crime rates will increase during periods of unemployment. Assuming that the probability of arrest, conviction and imprisonment following an offense remain unchanged, more violators will be sentenced to prison during periods of high unemployment. It is also possible that when the crime rate increases, judges will respond to this increase by imposing prison sentences more frequently, in the hope that this will help to reduce the crime rate.

Another reason prison admissions might be expected to vary with the business cycle is suggested by Rusche and Kirchheimer,[10] whose historical survey of punishment practices suggest that long-term changes in the form and intensity of state-imposed punishment reflect the supply and demand of labor. When the supply of labor is high relative to demand, this perspective would suggest that the rate of imprisonment would be increased, with the goal of taking excess labor off the market.

These arguments suggest that of the many indices that might be used to measure the phase of the business cycle, unemployment is likely to be superior to others (*e.g.*, the gross national product or aggregate investment). We therefore take the unemployment rate as an indicator of the state of the economy. For the period 1945–1959, we find that the correlation between per capita admissions to prison and the proportion of the labor force seeking employment is $r = 0.92$; this strongly confirms the hypothesis.[11] When the period is extended back to 1938, the earliest year for which the relevant data are available, the correlation is still positive but not as strong; apparently the relationship is distorted by the Depression and War years.

As can be seen from inspection of Figure 1, which shows both prison admission rates and unemployment rates for the years 1945–1959, the high correlation between unemployment and commitments to prison is not a trend effect, created by causally unrelated monotonic increases or decreases in both variables. Both rates move up and down, prison commitments following changes in unemployment quite closely, with some evidence of prison admissions lagging a bit behind unemployment. This may be a consequence of court delay.

A similar relationship has been shown to hold for prison admissions in the United States; for the period 1960–1972, the correlation between the unemployment rate and the rate of first admissions to federal prison was 0.91, and for first admissions to state prison, 0.86.[12]

[9] *See* Ehrlich, *Participation in Illegitimate Activities: A Theoretical and Empirical Investigation,* 81 J. POL. ECON. 521 (1973).

[10] G. RUSCHE & O. KIRCHHEIMER, PUNISHMENT AND SOCIAL STRUCTURE (1939).

[11] Unemployment rates and prison admission rates per population, for ages 16 and over, are taken from M. URQUHART & K. BUCKLEY, HISTORICAL STATISTICS OF CANADA 61, 644, 656 (1965). Data for more recent years are not available.

[12] *See* W. H. ROBINSON, P. SMITH & J. WOLF,

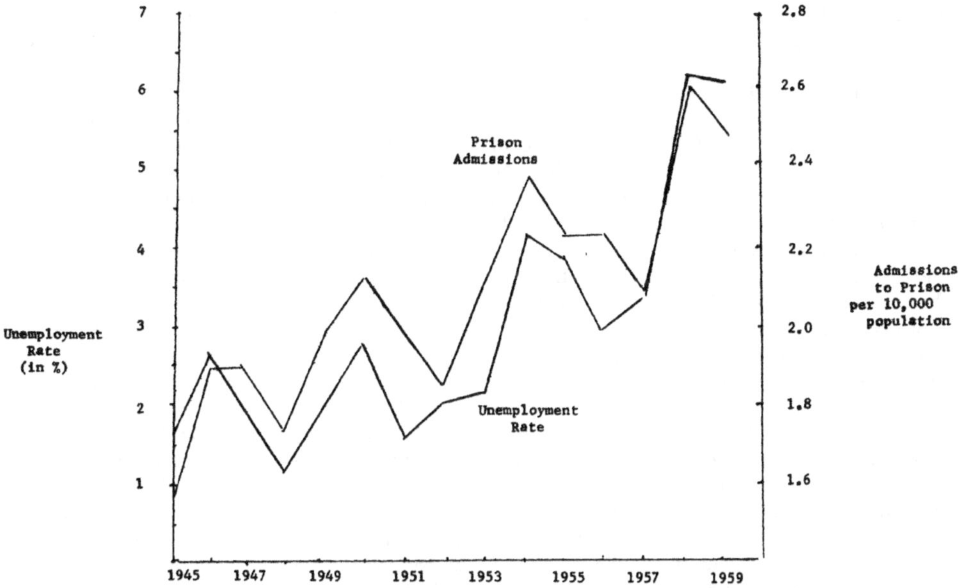

FIGURE 1. Prison Admissions and Unemployment Rate in Canada, 1945–1959.

Again, this was not a trend effect; prison admissions rose and fell with the unemployment rate.

For the Canadian data, the correlation between per capita prison *population* and the unemployment rate is also positive but considerably weaker than for per capita prison admissions ($r = 0.28$; when unemployment is lagged by one year, $r = 0.36$). This is hardly surprising. When the mean sentence length is not short as compared to the period of business cycle, the prison population at a given time will contain cohorts admitted at different stages of the cycle. Also, each cohort will contain prisoners with sentences of different lengths. Both effects will tend to wipe out the population, partially obliterating the effect of unemployment.

Because of the moderately strong positive first order autocorrelation among unemployment rates ($r_{u_t, u_{t-1}} = 0.654$), the serial correlation among the error terms of equation (1) will be much smaller in this model than in the random admissions model.

Having verified the existence of a strong relationship between prison admissions and unemployment, one may ask how this relationship can be explained. In arguing that the prison admission rate and the unemployment rate might be related, we suggested several possible causal processes that might lead to such a relationship. One possibility involved a relationship between the crime rate and the unemployment rate. This model suggests that the crime rate increases with the unemployment rate. With constant conditional probabilities of arrest and conviction, more offenders will be brought into court and sentenced when unemployment is high, increasing the number of admissions to prison. For more than a hundred years, writers who analyzed the relationship between crime and unemployment using data on officially labeled offenders, have assumed that this is the model they were testing.

If this "workload" model is correct, we should find a high correlation between the unemployment rate and the crime rate, a high correlation between the crime rate and the conviction rate, and a high correlation between the conviction rate and the imprisonment rate. The data necessary to test all these predictions are not available. However, partial tests can be carried out. Empirically, the correlation between the per capita rate of admissions to prison and the per capita rate of convictions is

PRISON POPULATIONS AND COSTS—ILLUSTRATIVE PROJECTIONS TO 1980 (1974).

approximately 0.01, in total disagreement with the final prediction.[13] High rates of commitment to prison during periods of unemployment thus cannot be explained as a passive judicial response to a larger caseload.

Reported crime rates for the full range of offenses are not available for Canada, but the *U.N. Demographic Yearbook* does report annual homicide rates for Canada. For the years 1953–1970, the correlation between the homicide rate and the unemployment rate is 0.22. This is in the predicted direction but not strong enough to support the "workload" model.

We cannot fully test the hypothesis that judges respond to perceptions of a higher crime rate with increased sentences, but this explanation is consistent with the observed correlations only if perceptions of the crime rate are far more strongly related to the unemployment rate than to the reported crime rate, at least to the extent that the homicide rate is an index of the overall crime rate. We know too little about perceptions of crime to fully assess this possibility, but on the surface it appears somewhat implausible.

Of course it may be that the homicide rate is not a good index of the overall crime rate. Homicide occurs infrequently by comparison with theft offenses, and may be more weakly related to unemployment than the latter. If so, the overall crime rate, for which we have no data, may be more strongly related to unemployment than the homicide rate, for which the correlation is small.

The American data, however, suggest that prison sentences may not be closely related to perceived crime rates. During the mid to late 1960's, a period of economic expansion, crime rates and arrest rates rose. Since increased crime rates were the subject of extensive public discussion and figured in national political campaigns, it is likely that judges were aware of this increase. Yet admissions to prison declined during this period. With the recession of the early 1970's, crime rates continued to rise, but no more rapidly than before, and prison commitments increased dramatically.

It thus appears that in both Canada and the United States, changes in commitments to prison can be explained almost entirely by changes in the unemployment rate. Changes in the number of cases entering the criminal justice system and potentially available for imprisonment seem to be unimportant, as does the crime rate, at least as far as we can measure it.

Rusche and Kirchheimer's proposal that penal policies are governed by labor market considerations irrespective of the problems crime poses for society is not contradicted by the data, but nevertheless seems implausible for the period under consideration, for it requires that we assume that Canadian and American judges, almost without exception, orient their sentencing policies to the requirements of the labor market and that they agree on how this can best be done. For the present period, this assumption is farfetched. Perhaps the absolute monarchs of seventeenth century Europe could instruct judges to commute sentences in order to obtain galley slaves,[14] but neither the prime minister of Canada nor the president of the United States exercises comparable authority over sentencing.

For the present era, it is more plausible to assume that judges are less willing to grant probation to offenders when they are unemployed, or that unemployment affects levels of community tolerance toward offenders, to which judges respond in sentencing. The data needed to determine whether this speculation has merit are unfortunately not at hand.

Discussion

We have shown that a model in which prison sentences are geometrically distributed, and in which admissions to prison are governed by the unemployment rate, fares reasonably well when compared with a least squares fit to a second order autoregressive equation for the per capita imprisonment rates. As the difference equation predicted by the model is not of precisely the same form as the one for which the least squares fit was obtained (because the model involves a time-dependent driving term), the comparison must be taken as merely suggestive.[15]

It follows from the analysis presented here that the testing of a model that contains assumptions about admissions and releases from prison must be undertaken with caution. In

[13] Annual conviction rates are reported in M. Urquhart & K. Buckley, *supra* note 11, at 643.

[14] *See* G. Rusche & O. Kirchheimer, *supra* note 10, at 53–71.

[15] This reservation does not apply to our findings concerning the relationship between unemployment and prison admissions.

the models presented here, separate tests of the assumptions made about releases and admissions were possible. However, the test of the assumptions made about releases was not as strong as it would have been possible had detailed information about the distribution of sentence lengths been available.

In the BCN models, separate tests of the various model assumptions are less easily performed. Blumstein, Cohen and Nagin's best model does lead to good predictions for the coefficients of equation (1), but as we have seen, this may be true of alternative models as well. A stronger test would involve a comparison of crime rates and imprisonments with those predicted by the model.

Unfortunately, annual crime rates do not appear to be available for Canada for the years in question. However, the analysis of prison admissions presented here does cast doubt on the validity of the assumptions made in the BCN model about the admissions process. We find that whatever effect punishment may have on crime, oscillations in the rate of admissions to prison in Canada in recent years have been governed almost entirely by changes in the unemployment rate. The same relationship appears to hold in the United States as well. In light of this cross-national similarity, further investigation to determine whether the same pattern is found in other nations appears warranted.

The relationship between unemployment and admissions to prison discovered here is of particular interest in connection with the labeling perspective in deviance theory, which has, among other things, directed attention to the role of extra-legal contingencies in criminal justice dispositions. For the most part, attention has focused on the effect of *individual* offenders' extra-legal attributes on the dispositions they receive. However, extra-legal considerations may also influence the dispositions received by offenders *collectively*. In the short run, it appears that economic considerations have an important bearing on the likelihood that someone who has been convicted will be sentenced to prison or will receive a non-prison disposition.

Our findings have implications for reformers who seek to reduce prison populations. In recent years, reformers have sought to "divert" offenders from prison by creating "alternative" dispositions, not involving incarceration. Yet in recent years, prison populations have risen to historically unprecedented levels. Moreover, accumulating evidence suggests that many of those sentenced to diversion programs would not have been sentenced to prison in the absence of diversion programs. Instead, their cases would have been dismissed, or they would have been granted probation. It thus appears that the development of diversion programs may be an ineffective way of changing the size of the prison population. Although we are not accustomed to thinking about the manipulation of the state's fiscal and monetary policies as a way of influencing judicial sentencing patterns, such an approach might prove more effective than strategies now being employed, if it could be implemented.

The major difficulty here will be the obvious fact that levels of employment are governed by other considerations besides penal policy. Corporations make investment decisions on the basis of profit considerations, and federal policies that impact on unemployment take into account the needs of continued capital accumulation, the balance-of-payments problem, the exigencies of election year politics and so on. These are problems that surely carry much greater weight with policy-makers than considerations of penal policy.

The counterposing of "conflict theory" and "consensus theory" approaches to criminology has often been framed as if the crucial question at issue was whether the population was united or divided on such matters as the substantive content of the criminal law and the appropriate methods of enforcement. Notwithstanding such issues, the analysis presented here shows that conflict theory may be relevant to an understanding of the criminal justice system in another way. High levels of employment function to reduce income to the working class and prevent rising wages because of eroding business profits,[16] and the business cycle which plays such a large role in determining the rate of admissions to prison is a feature of capitalist economic systems, that is, of a particular kind of class system. Moreover, the bulk of the prison population is drawn from the working class. Thus, the notions of class and class conflict are directly relevant to an understanding of the functioning of the prison system.

[16] Boddy & Crotty, *Class Conflict and Macro-Policy: The Political Business Cycle*, 7 REV. RADICAL POL. ECON. 1 (1975).

[10]
The Prison as a Lawless Agency

In a remarkably prophetic passage, W. E. B. DuBois described, more than half a century ago, the desperate plight of black people trying to free themselves from the suffocating confinement of social imprisonment:

> It is difficult to let others see the full psychological meaning of caste segregation. It is as though one, looking out from a dark cave in a side of an impending mountain, sees the world passing and speaks to it; speaks courteously and persuasively, showing them how these entombed souls are hindered in their natural movement, expression, and development; and how their loosening from prison would be a matter not simply of courtesy, sympathy, and help to them, but aid to all the world. One talks on evenly and logically in this way, but notices that the passing throng does not even turn its head, or if it does, glances curiously and walks on. It gradually penetrates the minds of the prisoners that the people passing do not hear; that some thick sheet of invisible but horribly tangible plate glass is between them and the world. They get excited; they talk louder; they gesticulate. Some of the passing world stops in curiosity; these gesticulations seem so pointless; they laugh and pass on. They still either do not hear at all, or hear but dimly, and even what they hear they do not understand. Then the people within may become hysterical. They may scream and hurl themselves against the barriers, hardly realizing in their bewilderment that they are screaming in a vacuum unheard and that their antics may actually seem funny to those outside looking in. They may even, here and there, break through in blood and disfigurement, and find themselves faced by a horrified, implacable, and quite overwhelming mob of people frightened for their own very existence.[1]

DuBois could as easily have been describing the almost insurmountable difficulties today's actual, not metaphorical, prisoners face in communicating the nightmares of their lives to those outside the walls, and the violent repression of even their slightest efforts to obtain some breathing space for themselves. The simi-

---

The views expressed herein are those of the authors and do not necessarily reflect the position of the Committee for the Study of Incarceration.

1. W. DuBois, Dusk of Dawn 130-31 (1968).

larity in the situation of prison inmates and that of black people in the larger society is too striking to be written off as merely metaphorical. Convicted criminals were the one category to which the thirteenth amendment's prohibition of involuntary servitude explicitly did not apply. Exploitation of prisoners' slave labor in the form of chain gangs and the convict lease system continued after chattel slavery had been ended, and survives today in the form of lucrative "Prison Industries," which return substantial profits to state and federal treasuries because of their exemption from minimum wage laws. The parallel reaches much farther, extending even to the reactions of those in power when the oppressed reach for emancipation. In each case those with unanswered and longstanding grievances began to take matters into their own hands, acting in response to a "long train of abuses and usurpations"; in each case the official response has been "shoot first and ask questions later." Whether initiated by those in prison or those outside, attempts to achieve social change were met with arrests, beatings, killings, with newspaper editorials deploring "excesses" and admonishing restraint and patience, with official investigating committees representing anyone but those who suffer, and with a flurry of public concern polarized between those advocating even harsher repression and those wishing to save the system with a few inconsequential reforms—but which in any event dissipates in days or weeks leaving nothing changed. The parallel is doubly striking in that, likely as not, the prisoner is black or brown.

The significance of these parallels, as well as their implication for an understanding of American society, deserves exploration. The significance of racial discrimination in the South was vigorously debated in the early days of the civil rights movement. Was Mississippi an "aberration" of the American system? So contended the liberals. Was it simply America writ large? So contended the radicals. The same question can be asked of the prison system. Are the horror stories acted out in so many prisons mere "exceptions" to a usually benign "correctional" system, or do they on the contrary reflect something essential to the entire prison system, if not to American society as a whole? Is Attica an anomaly, or is it the crux of the entire system, reaching out to those on parole, and beyond them to the man or woman in the ghetto or barrio or slum or political movement, whose physical location is far from the penitentiary?

PRISON AS LAWLESS AGENCY

A. *Leviathan and the Rule of Law*

We can answer this question only by examining the prison system in its relation to society. The text which perhaps poses this problem best for us was written more than three hundred years ago by Thomas Hobbes, who asserted that unless human greed and aggression were curbed by fear of punishment, civilization itself would disintegrate:

> [D]uring the time men live without a common Power to keep them all in awe, they are in that condition which is called Warre; and such a warre, as is of every man, against every man. . . .
>
> . . . In such condition, there is no place for Industry; . . . no Arts; no Letters; no Society and which is worst of all, continuall feare, and danger of violent death; And the life of man, solitary, poore, nasty, brutish, and short.[2]

Hobbes argued that social cohesion could be created and maintained through intimidation, to be accomplished by an immensely powerful unitary state apparatus, the Leviathan.

Contemporary Americans are in an excellent position to assess Hobbes' contention. We are all aware of the extent to which the fear of state-imposed punishment constrains our action and leads us to toe the line; in this respect Hobbes' faith in the Leviathan was not unjustified. At the same time, fear of punishment has never succeeded in eliminating domestic violence or theft. Furthermore, the last four decades have seen a steady growth in the strength of the executive branch of government. Hundreds of thousands of Asians have died under its bombs and bullets in a war that has raged unabated for a decade, despite its overwhelming unpopularity in recent years. Traditional vehicles of protest and opposition politics have had little if any impact on its continuation. Nor have they had substantially greater impact on domestic problems of poverty or racism. The system's inflexibility in the face of efforts to bring about changes by "working within the system" has led to pervasive feelings, shared by black, brown, white, young, intellectual, and many others, that the executive is unrestrainable, unlimitable, unstoppable. New techniques of protest and expression of dissent and opposition flow from a deep and empirically well-founded belief that the old ones have had very limited utility.

2. T. Hobbes, Leviathan ch. 13, at 62 (1651).

Living in the belly of the Leviathan, American prisoners have reason to be more acutely aware than perhaps anyone else of what Hobbes' philosophy has meant. Is it not those who are most firmly in the grip of Leviathan who live in "continuall feare, and danger of violent death"; those most rigidly controlled by the State whose lives are "solitary, poore, nasty, brutish and short"? The facts speak for themselves.

A recent federal court decision in the Eastern District of Virginia documented many instances of abuse suffered by prisoners in that state; we quote only one:

> The Court finds that in late August of 1970, Lassiter was placed in a meditation cell by reason of the fact that he was mentally disturbed and his behavior was sometimes uncontrollable. . . . Breeden, through an inmate named Marsh Whitney, secured copies of records of Lassiter's psychiatric care over the three prior years.
>
> Between August 25th and Lassiter's death, while Lassiter was confined to a meditation cell, he screamed day and night apparently seeking help. . . .
>
> Efforts were made by Breeden to bring to the attention of the prison nurse the records he had secured from inmate Whitney. On August 27th Breeden spoke to a lieutenant and subsequently gave him a copy of what purported to be a doctor's letter diagnosing Lassiter's condition as chronic schizophrenia. On August 29th Breeden wrote to Superintendent R.M. Oliver about the case.
>
> Lassiter continued to scream for help until he died on August 31st.[3]

Similar circumstances and events have been reported elsewhere.[4] In San Quentin George Jackson and two other prisoners

3. Landman v. Royster, 333 F.Supp. 621, 638 (E.D. Va. 1971).

4. According to a San Quentin inmate:

> For years San Quentin has been a chamber of horrors to convicted felons hapless enough to be placed here. The nightmares that take place have never been related except in whispers late at night among the cons themselves; in whispers because to discuss these atrocities openly might cost one more than he can afford. His life. Those who become aware the quickest are the ones who don't readily adjust to harsh treatment and eventually wind up in one punishment center or another. This is where education about life in San Quentin begins. You never forget the screams late in the night, the bloody pulp that was once a man hurried out on a stretcher before daybreak, the report of accident or suicide in the newspaper a few days later, the smirking nightshift guard standing on the tier giving a blow-by-blow description to his dayshift buddy. Once you hear how a certain guard paid a convict a few cartons of cigarettes to kill another, your education is complete. From then on, when an officer grabs a convict and pushes him around, you don't wonder why so few fight back.

G. Saladin in R. Minton, Inside: Prison American Style 97-98 (1971).

were slain last August. Two days after their deaths, the following affidavit was released by all 26 inmates who were in the Adjustment Center where the three slain men were incarcerated.

> We, the undersigned, each being held incommunicado because of suffering from both wounds and internal injuries inflicted on our persons by known and unknown agents of Warden Louis S. Nelson.
>
> That Warden Louis S. Nelson and Associate Warden James W. L. Park, through their agents did, on August 21, 1971, kill one George Jackson, and conspired to murder the undersigned who refused to join in the state official's conspiracy.
>
> That Officers Doe 1, Doe 2 and Doe 3 did open the cell gates and order the undersigned to come from their cells, thereafter gunshots or what appeared to be gunshots went off and all went into the cells in the back of the same building to avoid being shot. Thereafter the prison guards, armed with guns, entered the cell block and ordered the undersigned to come out or be killed. The undersigned was ordered by the officers to take off all their clothes and walk from the cell one at a time. Each of the undersigned received vicious physical beatings by prison guards with blackjacks, clubs and guns. Each of the undersigned was handcuffed and made to lay on the ground naked from approximately 4 o'clock P.M. to 10 o'clock P.M., at which time, one inmate, Allen Mancino, who was hand- and leg-chained on the ground was begging the guards to loosen the handcuffs cutting him, and was told to keep his mouth shut by the officer guard who shot part of his leg off with a rifle. There, Mancino was made to lay, begging for a doctor for approximately an hour before the guard would allow him moved. Thereafter, the undersigned was made to lay on the grounds while prison guards threatened to kill them and shot all around the undersigned; beating the undersigned in such a way wounds and injuries still show on them, their bodies, and they still suffer from aforesaid beatings, and are being held incommunicado by Warden Louis Nelson. While being held incommunicado, the undersigned are being constantly threatened by prison guards.
>
> That the undersigned are suffering from the wounds, injuries and living in an atmosphere of fear by reasons that have been heretofore stated.
>
> That the undersigned are denied the right to have legal papers, and seek permission from this court to further offer affidavits in testimony upon hearing, if heard by this court.
>
> That defendant Nelson will continue his beastly acts while the court grant the relief sought. I declare under penalty of perjury the foregoing is true and correct.[5]

5. The affidavits are in E. MANN, WHY IS GEORGE JACKSON DEAD? 14 (1971).

Nor is San Quentin unique in the California prison system. The following statements were written by prisoners in the Correctional Training Facility at Soledad:

> O Wing. Where guards beat on guys for almost nothing, where one Doctor hack took convicts by force out of their cells and gave them shock treatments strapped on a common barber shop chair. Where convicts were thrown gas bombs in their cells after being beaten to subdue them they called it. Where guards opened convict cell doors on purpose with others they knew would fight, or stab, or kill each other . . . .
>
> . . . .
>
> A black inmate by the name of P. refused to come out of his cell and was repeatedly tear-gassed until he passed out. He was then taken to the officers' area and when he regained consciousness a struggle insued and inmate P. was wantonly beaten and was called "nigger" repeatedly. He was then taken to the hospital; he died the same day. His death was passed off as heart failure.
>
> After the murder of P. by prison officials there were never more than six Blacks allowed on Max Row which houses 24 inmates thus the remaining 18 cells were occupied by Anti-Black Caucasian and Mexican inmates who race-talk us in shifts so that its done 24 hours a day. On their exercise periods they spit, throw urine, and feces in our cells while the officials stand by in indifference and approval. They, the officials, call us HAMMERS and NIGGERS (both mean the same thing).
>
> The prison officials here stopped serving the meals and they immediately proceeded to poison our meals by filling food to be issued to us with cleanser powder, crushed glass, spit, urine and feces while the officials stood by and laughed.
>
> . . . .
>
> On the 28th of December a list was passed out announcing the opening of the Max Row exercise yard on the 29th. It didn't open because there was still some work yet to be done. But I did notice that white inmates and officials were awfully cheerful for some reason or another and they continuously didn't forget to remind us of the yard opening soon.
>
> On January 13, 1970, seven Blacks and eight Caucasians were released to O Wing yard for exercise. There was no gang fight as was reported to the news media; only seven inmates actually engaged in physical combat to the best of my knowledge. The first shot killed N. who was only a few feet from me and as I turned to go to him and see how bad he was hurt E. and M. were only a short distance from me and yelled to me to watch out and I turned

> to face the attack directed at me by two Caucasians who were running towards me. E. started for N. to presumably see how badly he was hurt and to protect him from being attacked while he was down. But he was shot dead a few feet from N., before he reached him and M. was shot dead trying to come to my assistance. There were NO warnings of any kind given before the shooting, there was NO ganging up on any inmate by Blacks. The guard in the tower leaned out of the window with his gun from the time the first Black inmate arrived on the yard.
>
> I looked at the tower guard and he was aiming the gun toward me and I thought then that he meant to kill me too, so I moved from the wall as he fired and went over to stand over inmate M., all the time looking the guard in the gun tower in the face. He aimed the gun at me again and I just froze and waited for him to fire, but he held his fire. After I saw he was not going to fire, I pointed to where inmate M. lay, with two other Black inmates bending over him, and started to walk toward the door through which we had entered the yard, and the tower guard pointed the gun at me and shook his head. I stopped and begged him for approximately ten minutes to let me take M. to the hospital but all he did was shake his head. Then I started forward with tears in my eyes, expecting to be shot down every second. The tower guard told me, "That's far enough." Then another guard gave me permission to bring M. off the yard and I was ordered to lay him on the floor in the officer's area and go to my cell, which I refused to do until M. was taken to the hospital.[6]

These reports are only a tiny fraction of those arriving in a steady stream at the law offices of attorneys engaged in prison litigation.[7] We wish they were exceptional; unfortunately they are not. What has been reported here could be documented in most prison systems throughout the country. Any effort to make sense of these stories, whose unreality and unbelievability is matched only by the similar incredible and paralyzing surrealism of reports from Nazi concentration camps,[8] must begin with an analysis of Leviathan's failure to secure human freedom, dignity, or even physical survival for prison inmates.

One might begin such an analysis with Montesquieu's discovery that both freedom and security could be enhanced and multiplied by the multiplication and dispersion of power:

6. The documents quoted are available from the Prison Law Project, 5406 Claremont Ave., Oakland, Cal. 94618.

7. *See, e.g.,* MAXIMUM SECURITY: LETTERS FROM PRISON (E. Pell ed. 1972), *noted in* 21 BUFFALO L. REV. 1007 (1972).

8. H. ARENDT, THE ORIGINS OF TOTALITARIANISM 437-59 (1958).

> To prevent this abuse [of power], it is necessary from the very nature of things that power should be a check to power.[9]

Etched deeply into the minds of the Founding Fathers of the United States, this insight resulted in a system of checks and balances being built into the government they designed. Aware that power undivided, unopposed, unchecked could only lead to tyrany, they wrote safeguards into the Constitution.

B. *Lawlessness Within the Prison*

In recent decades those safeguards have proved utterly incapable of controlling the growing power of the executive. Neither Congress nor the judiciary has been able or willing to check a war conducted without a shred of legality. In the prison system, the absence of checks or balances is nothing new. Legislatures have never had an abiding interest in the subject. The courts have traditionally refused to intervene in what they have found convenient to consider the prerogative of the executive. This attitude is only beginning to change.

Screened from public visibility and immune from effective accountability to other branches of the government, the predictable abuses took place and continue to occur. There is almost nothing the prison cannot do, and does not do to inmates, including keeping them beyond the expiration dates of their sentences (via procedures declaring them dangerous or mentally ill). It can and does transfer them far from their families; limit and restrict their visitors; censor what they read, what they may write; decide whom they may associate with inside, what medicine or other medical care they will or will not receive, what education they may or may not have, whether they will be totally locked up, for weeks, months, occasionally even years, or enjoy limited physical freedom. Inmates' personal property may be misplaced and destroyed, incoming and outgoing letters sometimes not delivered, and, in the extreme, prisoners may be starved, brutalized and killed.

Administrative decisions within the prison including punitive measures such as transfer and solitary confinement are not subject to due process procedures and are ordinarily immune from judi-

9. C. DE MONTESQUIEU, THE SPIRIT OF LAWS bk. XI, pt. 4 (T. Nugent transl. 1949). *See also* the discussion in H. ARENDT, ON REVOLUTION ch. 4 (1963).

cial review. In most jurisdictions judges have wide latitude in fixing the length of sentence (except in California where the Adult Authority sets the sentence), and parole boards have similar latitude in determining how much of the sentence will be served in prison. Parole boards may deny or grant parole on the basis of information unavailable to prisoners or their attorneys, on the basis of criteria which, if they exist at all, are secret. On the grounds that parole is a privilege, not a right, these decisions are ordinarily not reviewable by the courts. In short, prisoners are at the mercy of the prison system. The monolithic Leviathan has brought in its wake all the abuses Hobbes intended it to remedy.

Does this mean that every administrator is malevolent or every guard brutal? That every prisoner is denied medical care, or every prisoner sent to the hole is falsely accused? That every prison is a Soledad or San Quentin? Certainly not. There are a few "good men" in corrections and some sensitive guards, though the constraints of their occupations seriously limit the impact of their sensitivity or "goodness." There are also prisoners who abuse other prisoners. For that matter, there were inmates of Nazi concentration camps who exploited other inmates, and there were Nazis who refused to kill. There was even a showcase concentration camp which the Red Cross was allowed to inspect.[10] This hardly mitigated the atrocities. Free from any other constraints, the humanitarian sentiments of some prison employees have simply not acted as effective restraints against abuses.

According to Philip Selznick,

> The essential element in the rule of law is the restraint of official power by rational principles of civic order. . . . Legality imposes an environment of constraint, of tests to be met, standards to be observed, ideals to be fulfilled.[11]

By this definition, whatever the statutes may say, whatever reformers have hoped, prisons have been and are *lawless agencies.* This has been the characterization of almost all observers not directly connected with prison administration, and indeed from some correctional personnel as well. In his recent law review article, William B. Turner, Assistant Counsel of the NAACP Legal and Educational Fund, Inc. (San Francisco) opens with Simon Sobel-

10. H. Arendt, Eichmann in Jerusalem 82 (1963).
11. P. Selznick, Law, Society, and Industrial Justice 11 (1969).

off's statement that Acton's classic proverb about the corrupting influence of absolute power is true of prison guards, and closes by referring to the "lawless sphere of our system of criminal justice." [12]

Most agencies of government, no matter how abusive, how oppressive, are ultimately accountable, reviewable, finally responsive in some definable way, to the processes of "law"—that is, some body of limiting rules, regulations, restraint—whether flowing from the Constitution, public opinion as expressed through representatives, court decision, or through other processes which are understood and enforceable, at least to some extent, by those whom the agency affects. The prison system is almost totally non-responsive to "due process of law" or "law" itself.

Prison administrators understand the vulnerability and powerlessness of inmates, parolees, and their families. Indeed, reprisals can be so severe against prisoners who attempt to obtain redress in any way but the most supplicant manner that many used to prefer (and some still do) to suffer in silence, rather than risk years in solitary or a denial of parole. Administrators act with total, arbitrary authority to avoid any action—whether legislative or judicial, or from the community or from attorneys—which asserts an inmate's rights or desires as against the desires of the prison system. The taxpayer's money is spent to pay the Attorney General to oppose any attempts in court to change these conditions, whether it be to get access to prisoners' files, or have inmates represented at the parole hearing, or to permit the public to see the strip cells or hear the prisoners testify in open court as to these conditions.

Access to the prisons is denied to almost all, and the few taken on tours are presented carefully constructed tableaux. The prison has two distinct faces: one for the public, which it presents through skilled public relations personnel and a budget provided by taxpayers for that purpose alone; the other, to prisoners. In the wake of lies about the way hostages at Attica died and a host of contradictions in official stories about the death of George Jackson, one can only ask whether *anything* prison officials say is believable.

In the late sixties the federal courts began, very slowly, and

12. Turner, *Establishing the Rule of Law in Prisons: A Manual for Prisoners' Rights Litigation,* 23 STAN. L. REV. 473, 518 (1971). *See also* Hirschkop & Millemann, *The Unconstitutionality of Prison Life,* 55 VA. L. REV. 795 (1969).

under tremendous pressures from prison rebellions with their attendant publicity and public interest, from numerous pro se petitions by prisoners, and from extremely carefully designed lawsuits brought by attorneys working with the National Lawyers Guild, American Civil Liberties Union, NAACP Legal Defense and Educational Fund, and private attorneys for such prisoners as Martin Sostre, George Jackson and John Clutchette, to abandon the unqualified "hands-off" doctrine which had previously characterized their approach to all prison problems.

The sweeping decision of United States District Judge Motley, in *Sostre v. Rockefeller,*[13] although seriously cut back by the Second Circuit, heralded some change in judicial attitudes toward the seething mass of discontent and the continual allegations of brutality and administrative abuse in the prisons. Despite some favorable decisions [14] upholding prisoners' first amendment rights and indicating an intent to put some limits on the conditions prevailing in solitary confinement and the length of time prisoners could be kept there, the actual situation in most prisons did not change much.

Thus, several years ago, a Soledad inmate sued Superintendant Cletus Fitzharris for inflicting cruel and unusual punishment upon him by keeping him in a tiny strip cell without light, ventilation, clothes or body covering, where he was forced to sleep naked on a cold concrete floor, deprived of any way to clean himself, and forced to eat in the stench and filth caused by his own vomit and body wastes. In finding Fitzharris guilty, the court said:

> [W]hen, as it appears in the case at bar, the responsible prison authorities in the use of the strip cells have abandoned elemental concepts of decency by permitting conditions to prevail of a shocking and debased nature, then the court must intervene . . . to restore the primal rules of a civilized community in accord with the mandate of the Constitution of the United States.[15]

Today one is told that there are no more strip cells at Soledad, but the letters already quoted from inmates describe condi-

13. 312 F. Supp. 863 (S.D.N.Y. 1970), *rev'd in part sub nom.,* Sostre v. McGinnis, 442 F.2d 178 (2d Cir.) (en banc), *cert denied,* 92 S. Ct. 719 (1971).

14. Palmigiano v. Travisono, 317 F. Supp. 776 (D.R.I. 1970); Clutchette v. Procunier, 328 F. Supp. 767 (N.D. Cal. 1971), *appeal docketed,* No. 71-2357 (9th Cir., Aug. 30, 1971); Landman v. Royster, 333 F. Supp. 621 (E.D. Va. 1971).

15. Jordan v. Fitzharris, 257 F. Supp. 674, 680 (N.D. Cal. 1966).

tions the same or worse; worsened by repeated tear-gassings of the entire tier of O Wing, sometimes directly into the faces of the prisoners. Today inmates have toothbrushes, but sometimes the guards come into their cells while the inmates are at court or visiting relatives, and mix their tooth powder with cleanser. Mr. Fitzharris, so sharply censured by the court, has recently been promoted to the position of Deputy Director of the Department of Corrections of the State of California.

The lack of substantive change was due to many factors, most of them interrelated, including the ability of prison administrators to engage, at public expense, in dilatory appeals to avoid instituting court-ordered reforms; the reluctance of the court to enforce detailed orders or to look into the same practice under a different label, for example, punitive or disciplinary segregation now called "administrative segregation"; and the massive ability of administrators to circumvent court-imposed limitations by such methods as the mooting of a case which looked as though it might set a precedent limiting the authorities' powers, and simply ignoring court orders. Most prisoners are indigent, and the few attorneys working in the field cannot file an order to show cause every time there is a violation of a court order.

As with the judicial victory in *Jordan v. Fitzharris,*[16] the authorities in California found a way around the ruling of the district court in *Grady v. Procunier,*[17] enjoining the Soledad administrators from interfering with confidential communications with attorneys. The background of the *Grady* case is instructive as to the pressures which result in some judicial intervention. Shortly after the killing of three black inmates in Soledad's O Wing exercise yard on January 13, 1970, various inmates, including survivors of the incident itself, began trying to write to attorneys and relatives concerning the incident. The prison authorities held up much of this mail altogether. An injunction was secured on behalf of the named plaintiff and the other inmates, and for almost a year much of Soledad's inmate mail to attorneys did leave the prison sealed. Some—there is no telling how much—did not. When the Department of Corrections first implemented the rule state-wide, and permitted sealed letters to attorneys from all prisons in California,

16. *Id.*
17. No. C-70-298 ACW (N.D. Cal., Mar. 20, 1971).

then revoked the rule in April of 1971, Robert Charles Jordan, Jr. (the same Jordan who brought the 1966 case) instituted suit which is presently pending in the California Supreme Court. In the Attorney General's return in that matter, the state filed exhibits purporting to show the dangers to security of inmate-attorney confidential correspondence. The state attached xeroxed copies of letters which had purportedly gone out sealed from inmates during the period when the sealed letter rule was in effect.

The treatment of Black Muslims is another example of prison intransigence in the face of court orders. Although the religious rights of Black Muslims were upheld in several decisions, pork continued to be served frequently in the prisons. Many Muslims were put in segregation or denied parole in reprisal for their religious affiliation and activities, although the paperwork in their files may have carefully avoided mention of this, and would typically include a range of accusations, including conspiracy to agitate or overthrow the prison administration.

During the negotiations over the inmate discipline plan ordered by Judge Zirpoli (the Ninth Circuit twice refused to stay implementation of this plan, which was required to implement the rudimentary attributes of due process in the San Quentin disciplinary proceedings), and in discussions between Department of Corrections personnel and legislators concerning the Adjustment Center Bill,[18] prison authorities and the Director of Corrections were frank to say that they would simply put men into solitary confinement by the administrative segregation route if too many limits were placed on the use of solitary confinement as punitive discipline.

They have done so. Many inmates, most of them black, but including brown and white, were put into indefinite segregation, immediately after the death of George Jackson on August 21, 1971, and remain in solitary confinement at this writing (January, 1972).

18. The Adjustment Center Bill, AB 2904, SB 1610, introduced by Assemblyman John Dunlap (D. Vallejo) and Senator Mervyn Dymally (D. Los Angeles) in the 1971 California legislative session, incorporated some of the features of Judge Zirpoli's decision in *Clutchette,* and added restrictions on the use of solitary confinement. Its most novel feature required the prison authorities to show cause, in superior court, with the right to counsel and cross-examination, etc., that the inmate was a danger to himself or others, if the authorities wished to keep him in solitary confinement more than 30 days in any 6 month period. The bill passed the Assembly, 42-32, picking up a good deal of Republican as well as Democratic support, passed the Senate Judiciary Committee, 7-5, and died in the Senate Finance Committee.

The Department acknowledges that most of them committed no in-prison offense of any kind, but asserts the right of prison administrators to lock-up anyone—indefinitely—whom they "feel" is dangerous, or whom any custodial personnel "feel" "might" contribute to tension in the prison. Lawsuits challenging this widespread practice at three different prisons are at present pending in the state and federal courts in California: *Bly v. Procunier* (San Quentin),[19] *In re Henderson* (Folsom),[20] and *In re Hutchinson and Irvin* (Deuel Vocational Institution (DVI)).[21]

Circumvention or outright violation of court orders is by no means unique to California. Following the massacre at Attica in September, 1971, a federal district court judge in Buffalo ordered Attica authorities to admit a group of lawyers and physicians seeking to provide counsel to inmates who might be interviewed by state police investigators. They were not admitted, and the order was later vacated.[22] At a Conference on Prisoners' Rights held in November, 1971 under the sponsorship of the American Civil Liberties Union, attorneys engaged in prisoners' rights litigation frequently asked "How does one get a court decision implemented?" It had been their experience that refusal on the part of prison administrators to implement court-ordered reforms was pervasive.

In addition to its frank communication that it would by-pass the Adjustment Center bill and other prison reform bills if passed, the California Department of Corrections vigorously lobbied—at public expense—in opposition *to every single one of 175* prison bills introduced into the 1971 session of the California State Legislature. It is certain that some would have passed without this extremely well-planned and coordinated opposition. The very fact of a Corrections Department lobbying against prison reform bills in the legislature (and by-passing the intent of them if they are passed) presents serious problems in the light of a concept of

19. No. C-71-2019 (N.D. Cal., filed Oct. 21, 1971) (submitted and now pending before Judge Zirpoli).

20. Petition dismissed by Superior Court, Sacramento County, order to show cause pending in Court of Appeals, Third Appellate District, therein numbered 3 Crim. 6461.

21. Complaint not acted upon by Superior Court, San Joaquin County, order to show cause pending in Court of Appeals, Third Appellate District, therein numbered 3 Crim. 6427, 6428; petition for writ of mandamus to compel disclosure to petitioners' counsel of the central files relied upon by prison authorities to continue indefinite lock-up, *denied* by California Supreme Court January 14, 1972.

22. N.Y. Times, Sept. 15, 1971, at 33, col. 2.

an even-handed legal process. What is the rationale for a Department of Corrections to lobby in the legislature? When the courts announce that a particular prison problem may be one for the legislature, it is probable that they do not consider the fact that the administrators have a sophisticated and vigilant lobby in that legislature.

Since the administrators can, and do, perform favors and give special dispensations to various of each legislator's constituents upon the legislator's request (made possible by the discretionary system of justice we criticize later), many of the legislators fear to attack the Department or press strongly against the Department's wishes. The recent spectacle of a liberal California legislator praising the Director of Corrections publicly—privately admitting that the situation is deplorable—would appear to manifest another indication of lawlessness, signalling the closing off of yet another channel of possible redress for prisoners, that of reform through the legislature.

C. *Lawlessness and the Minority Experience*

There is, no doubt, a certain paradoxical quality to the suggestion that a law enforcement agency should itself be lawless, operating in total disregard for and in frequent violation of the law. This seeming paradox will not, however, be unfamiliar to blacks and other minorities who have been well educated, as victims, in the abuses of the law, evasions of the law, and violations of the law on the part of law enforcement agencies.

Victimization of black people at the hands of law enforcement is nothing new in the United States. As slaves, they had the legal status of cattle or real estate and were totally unprotected by the criminal law, though masters' property rights in their chattel were fully protected. Freed Negroes hardly fared much better. They were tried in separate courts, and could be enslaved as punishment for criminal offenses, as well as for nonpayment of fines or taxes. Slave patrols were empowered to punish freed Negroes without trial. After the Civil War, emancipated slaves were doubly victimized by a repressive and discriminatory system of law enforcement, and by the widespread extra-judicial use of Lynch's Law.

In many instances, summary justice was imposed with the encouragement if not the participation of law enforcement officials, and not merely in the South. To quote only two examples, a Congressional Committee investigating the pogrom which broke out in East St. Louis in 1917 reported that:

> [S]o great was the indifference of the few policemen who remained on duty that the conclusion is inevitable that they shared the lust of mob for negro blood, and encouraged the rioters by their conduct . . . .[23]

After citing a number of incidents where police beat and shot Negroes without cause, the report concludes:

> Many other cases of police complicity in the riots could be cited. Instead of being guardians of peace they became a part of the mob by countenancing the assaulting and shooting down of defenseless negroes and adding to the terrifying scenes of rapine and slaughter.[24]

Following a riot in Harlem in the spring of 1935, the Mayor's Commission on Conditions in Harlem commented on police relations with the community they were charged with protecting:

> While one would not expect the policemen in Harlem to show any appreciation or understanding of the sociological factors responsible for crime in the community, the discipline of the Police Department should see to it that they do not become the persecutors and oppressors of the citizens of the community. Nevertheless, it is true that police practice aggressions and brutalities upon the Harlem citizens not only because they are Negroes but because they are poor and therefore defenseless.[25]

The reports of the National Advisory Commission on Civil Disorders or newspaper accounts of pre-dawn raids on Black Panther Party headquarters and apartments in various cities make clear to the doubting that police lawlessness has by no means disappeared. The badge provides immunity from prosecution or conviction: police homicide is almost by definition "justified."

Nor is lawlessness within the criminal justice system confined

23. B. Johnson, J. Raker, M. Foster & H. Cooper, Report on the Special Committee Authorized by Congress to Investigate the East St. Louis Riots, H.R. Doc. No. 1231, 35th Cong., 2d Sess. 8 (1918), *quoted in* The Politics of Riot Commissions 1917-1970, at 69 (A. Platt ed. 1971).

24. *Id.* at 70.

25. The Mayor's Commission on Conditions in Harlem, The Negro in Harlem: A Report on Social and Economic Conditions Responsible for the Outbreak of March 19, 1935 ch. IX (New York Municipal Archives, unpublished), in The Politics of Riot Commissions 1917-1970, at 178 (A. Platt ed. 1971).

to the police department. There is discrimination in the setting of bail, exclusion of minority groups from jury panels, and blatant prejudice and outright illegality on the part of the minor judiciary in courts throughout the land. While the legal profession has been energetic in proposing ways to control obstreperous defendants, the far more widespread and serious problem of controlling judges has not even been addressed.[26]

Disraeli's phrase, "The Two Nations" seems entirely appropriate when speaking of American criminal justice. In the sensitive and profoundly juridical and political introduction to the volume *Life at the Bottom,* Gregory Armstrong points out that the poor and the ostracized minorities have been taught to accept the *justice* of their debased condition, a condition in which:

> Black skin, brown skin, powerless, poor housing, cheap clothes, bad teeth, chronic debilitating illness, all the other stigmata of poverty, in terms of the actual functioning morality of the American culture . . . are the equivalent of criminal acts. . . . There are two Americas, one governed by law, conferring certain basic human right on its citizens; the other without law or justice, its citizens completely deprived of even the most rudimentary human rights. . . . In the reality of American daily life they are just as totally excluded from all the rituals and functions that confer the rights and privileges of humanity.[27]

For the last three hundred years, law and lawlessness have gone hand in hand in contributing to the oppression of persons of color. The law itself has often been openly discriminatory and repressive, but repression has never been confined to the law. While many of the *legal* disabilities created by *openly* discriminatory legislation have been repealed or struck down by the courts, illegal acts of repression and discrimination as well as legal but covert forms of these activities continue unabated. As an example of the latter we refer to the public defender system created when the Supreme Court ruled that indigent defendants must be provided legal counsel. The ruling has been satisfied formally, but defendants are still denied adequate, effective legal representation. Only the appearance has changed. Veiled from public consciousness by secrecy and insulated from other pressures, the prisons have not even had to change the appearances.

26. Schwartz, *Judges as Tyrants,* 7 CRIM. L. BULL. 129 (March 1971).
27. G. ARMSTRONG, LIFE AT THE BOTTOM XII-XIII (1971).

D. *The Social and Political Context of Lawlessness*

Of all major contemporary political ideologies, only fascism elevated official lawlessness to a basic principle of political ideology and practice.[28] The State itself was subordinated to the Party, and the Party to the Führer or Party Leader, whose commands overruled and superseded law. German law and the Weimar Constitution were by no means repealed when the Nazis came to power,[29] though this could easily have been done. To have operated according to law, even Nazi law, would have been too limiting, too constraining. It was more convenient not to have any, so the laws were simply ignored. The resulting elimination of all fixed rules and regulations with their accompanying predictability had enormous advantages in implementing a reign of terror. This terror was not unleashed purely out of sadism or nihilism, though both elements were certainly present, but on behalf of an ideology of racism, which achieved its fullest realization in the extermination camps, motivated by the necessity of atomizing a population so as to neutralize and eliminate possible sources of countervailing power, with the ultimate aim of overcoming class conflict—without, however, abolishing classes.[30]

Both in Italy and in Germany, fascism in power served the needs and interests of the monopoly capitalists.[31] In the name of the *Volk,* conflicting classes and interests were to be united harmoniously by a social organization which incorporated them and which excluded and even exterminated those who for biological or political reasons could not be incorporated in the consensus, for example, Jews, gypsies, Communists. In practice, it would have been impossible to serve incompatible interests at the same time, and fascism did not even bother to try. The victory of fascism in Germany and Italy may be traced to the collapse of socialist and communist movements in the face of the cultural crisis of modernization, the political crises associated with the end of the First World

28. Lawlessness was also pervasive in Stalinist Russia, but was never elevated to a basic principle of political conduct.

29. H. ARENDT, THE ORIGINS OF TOTALITARIANISM 394 (1958).

30. H. MARCUSE. *The Struggle Against Liberalism in the Totalitarian View of the State,* in NEGATION 3 (J. Shapiro transl. 1968), *originally published* ZEITSCHRIFT FUR SOZIALFORSCHUNG, vol. III (1934).

31. H. MARCUSE, REASON AND REVOLUTION 410 (1941); F. NEUMANN, BEHEMOTH: THE STRUCTURE AND PRACTICE OF NATIONAL SOCIALISM (1942).

War, and the economic crises of post-war Europe.[32] Traditional liberal ideology was not capable of coping with these crises either. Its sustaining tenets of laissez-faire economics had little relevance to the economic collapse and its ideology was no longer capable of holding things together.[33] Faced with this situation, some liberals held firmly to their principles no matter what, unable to accept an ideology which proclaimed:

> The individual, so we teach today, has as such neither the right nor the duty to exist, since all rights and all duties derive only from the community.[34]

Others abandoned the ideology which was no longer able to provide protection for their property rights as it had in the past. Thus Giovanni Gentile, the liberal educator and philosopher, addressing a letter to Mussolini at the time the former joined the Fascist Party, writes:

> As a liberal by deepest conviction, I could not help being convinced, in the months in which I had the honor to collaborate in the work of your government and to observe at close quarters the development of the principles that determine your policies, that liberalism as I understand it, the liberalism of freedom through law and therefore through a strong state, through the state as ethical reality, is represented in Italy today not by the liberals, who are more or less openly your opponents, but to the contrary by you yourself. Hence I have satisfied myself that in the choice between the liberalism of today and the Fascists, who understand the faith of your Fascism, a genuine liberal, who despises equivocation and wants to stand to his post, must enroll in the legions of your followers.[35]

Fascist ideology, then was one solution to a crisis to which traditional liberal thought had become irrelevant. Liberalism had admirably represented the interests of competitive entrepreneurial capitalism; fascism was better suited to the highly centralized monopoly capitalism which had come to dominate the economic life of all industrialized western nations in the early decades of this century.

32. I. Silone, Postwar Socialism in Neither Liberty nor Bread: The Meaning and Tragedy of Fascism 10-11 (F. Keene ed. 1940).

33. K. Polanyi, The Great Transformation (1957).

34. H. Marcuse, *supra* note 31, at 413, *quoting* O. Dietrich in Volkesche Beobachter, Dec. 11, 1937.

35. H. Marcuse, *supra* note 30, at 11, *quoting* 4 Aufbau 233 (F. Karsen ed. 1931).

The United States economy is likewise highly centralized; its manufacturing and financial sectors are dominated by oligopolies, mostly operating on a multi-national scale. Through a small interlocking elite, these enterprises are well-integrated with the government, which defends their interests.[36] In this respect the United States resembles fascism. There are of course differences, but similarities as well. Like the fascist states, the United States is openly imperialist. While racism in the United States has a different character than it did in Germany (since blacks are not regarded as enemies of society to be exterminated, but rather are hated, feared, and yet have been too valuable as sources of cheap labor to be annihilated), the connection between lawlessness, racism, and imperial expansion is characteristic of both societies. American prisons are not, of course, extermination camps, but the differences between the O Wing of Soledad and the concentration camps should not be exaggerated either.

Unlike Germany or Italy under fascism, the United States is at least formally a parliamentary democracy, though many of the most significant public issues are decided outside the formal framework of government, with the corporate elite often playing a decisive role at the highest levels.[37] Opposition politics and freedom of the press, of speech, etc., have not been eliminated, as in the totalitarian states, so much as they have been bypassed. The elite's command of vast wealth and its control of major universities and news media, as well as its access to almost unlimited resources of government and its legacy of legitimacy, enable its ideas and programs to dominate the public forum almost free from challenge.

Though there are doubtless many reasons for the comparatively conservative temper of American working people, surely part of the explanation resides in the extraordinary heterogeneity of the working population. Although the elite is rather homogeneous and is predominantly white, Anglo-Saxon and Protestant, workers by contrast have been differentiated along racial, religious, ethnic, and cultural lines. These divisions have helped to inhibit the development of a *class* consciousness, as distinguished from a racial, national or religious identity. Historically, these divisions

36. G. William Domhoff, Who Rules America (1967) and The Higher Circles: The Governing Class in America (1970); J. Weinstein, The Corporate Ideal in the Liberal State: 1900-1918 (1968).

37. *Id.*

were exploited by the business elite and encouraged by it, since it was advantageous to keep workers divided. Only in the last decade, in response to growing black militancy, radicalization and resort to extra-legal tactics, has part of the ruling elite changed its valuation of racial separation and has instead begun to foster racial integration.

Because of its heterogeneity, different segments of the working population experience quite different aspects of American social reality, and develop correspondingly different conceptions of that reality.[38] Thus George Jackson could in all honesty sign his letters [39] from Soledad, "From Dachau with love," while middle class readers could in equal honesty react with bewilderment because they were not able to discern any signs of fascism in their suburb.[40] Indeed, many were led to believe that George Jackson and others like him, rather than the dominant elite, were the primary threat and cause for concern. This misperception has led many individuals to support the political and economical system although they could benefit by changing it.

Only when repression becomes so visible that all the nation sees it—as it did during the Democratic Party Convention in Chicago in August, 1968, at Kent State and Jackson State in May, 1970, or at Attica in September, 1971—does much of the population receive even an inkling of what prisoners, or radicals or black people and other minorities face every day. This was, of course, the reason why the slogan, "The whole world is watching" had such significance to demonstrators in Chicago. It wasn't so unusual for demonstrators to be clubbed or arrested by police; what was novel was the knowledge that television screens across the country would show what was happening. This is infrequent, however, and what seems to be the isolated character of these events then gives them the appearance of inexplicable aberrations from what is assumed to be usually fair and impartial law enforcement practices. Cognitive dissonance contributes to the readiness with which such events are dismissed as atypical; if taken as symptomatic, many cherished and time-honored beliefs about American society would have to be abandoned. Furthermore, the world-view which a more accurate

38. Marx & Engels, *The German Ideology* in K. MARX & F. ENGELS, BASIC WRITINGS ON POLITICS AND PHILOSOPHY 246 (L. Feuer ed. 1959).

39. SOLEDAD BROTHER: THE PRISON LETTERS OF GEORGE JACKSON (1970).

40. This specific formulation is due to Eric Mann, (private communication).

perception of reality might suggest would very likely make personal demands which many individuals might not wish to face. These phenomena contribute to what Marxists have called "false consciousness."

The genius of the American criminal justice system has been the extent to which it has accommodated itself to the heterogeneity of the American population. It might be very difficult to sustain lawlessness in prisons or in court if all of us were exposed to it. But this never happens. Most Americans are never processed by the police, courts and prisons. With few exceptions, this unenviable experience is reserved for those with dark skin, little money, for cultural deviants, and those with threatening ideas. Indeed, more than one-third of all prisoners are black,[41] though blacks constitute only about 12% of the population; other minority groups are similarly over-represented. The reason is not that these groups are the most criminal in our society; the explanation lies in the systemic biases and discriminatory institutional practices which characterize the enforcement of the law as well as its legislation.[42]

In the context of existing law enforcement practices, the prison system helps to sustain the myth that certain groups of people (for example, blacks, the Spanish-speaking, Indians, poor whites) are inferior, defective, dangerous, not to be trusted: it discourages challenges to the existing political and economic order by reminding members of those groups that the violence of the state can and will be unleashed against them if they get out of line. Through the systematic non-enforcement of laws against business and governmental crime it not only helps to sustain the existing political and economic order but allows that order to clothe itself with a false mystique of lawfulness. The sophistication of the legal system enables it to accomplish many of these goals without violating the law, but when these methods are inconvenient or unavailable, illegal methods can be used.

On the whole the system has worked remarkably well; the government and the economy have been more stable than in many countries. In recent years this system has come under attack—pri-

41. Federal Bureau of Prisons, National Prisoner Statistics, Characteristics of State Prisoners 1964.

42. Struggle for Justice: A Report on Crime and Punishment in America 107-12 (prepared for the American Friends Service Committee 1971).

marily from racial and ethnic minorities and students, but from others as well. This has been true within the prison. Strikes, protests, revolts, have taken place in numerous prisons throughout the country. Many aspects of the prison system have been challenged by those outside as well. Much of the lawlessness in prison has been directed at those who are suspected of involvement in such efforts, or who could be tempted to such involvement in the future and need to be discouraged in advance.

Thus, in California, where a variety of political groups ranging from the Black Panther Party to the United Prisoners Union have engaged in organizing inside the prison system, the reaction of officials after George Jackson's killing has been severe. The underground press has been banned, book censorship tightened, lawyers' visits sharply restricted, and new restrictions on correspondence imposed. At most prisons, black and Chicano groups previously authorized have been disbanded and leaders subjected to "bus therapy"—transfer to other institutions. To prevent new collectives from replacing those disrupted by transfers, many prisoners suspected of political activity are transferred not just once, but repeatedly. Hundreds of others suspected of agitation and organizing have been locked up and subjected to extreme conditions, as indicated in the following affidavit:

> Until October 8, 1971 I was a prisoner on the mainline of California Men's Colony-East CMC, a medium security prison in San Luis Obispo, where I had been for about 2½ years with a clean disciplinary record. . . . October 8 I was awakened at 1:00 A.M. by about 8 to 10 guards . . . shackled and without a coat taken to a bus. I was one of the first to arrive at the bus and I watched thirty other Black men arriving two at a time from the four different quads at CMC; many were under escort of 15 guards . . . . All thirty-one of this group at CMC had been active members of the Afro Unity Association (AUA), which had been a recognized Black ethnic organization, which had authorization from the prison to exist. I have learned that after we were transferred that organization was totally disbanded by the prison officials at CMC . . . . Early that same morning we arrived at Soledad Prison and were taken to O Wing, the Soledad Adjustment Center . . . . I was put in a cell which had water on the floor upon my arrival. The toilet was cracked with sharp edges protruding upward, and filth from human waste was . . . on the floor.
>
> On that same day that we arrived in Soledad we appeared before the "Rover Board," composed of officials from the Depart-

ment of Corrections in Sacramento. They said that we were all under suspicion for disrupting the activities of CMC and considered a threat by the administration. They gave no greater detail to support their claim, and concluded by saying that we would be sent to different prisons throughout the state; . . . after remaining in O Wing for almost one week, I was transferred to San Quentin with nine other men. Some of this group was taken directly to B Section segregation unit and the Adjustment Center . . . . The next day . . . four other men . . . and I were taken . . . to B Section segregation unit (the hole), with no reason given for this move. I was put in a cell on the fourth tier. I had no sheets or pillow . . . . I had no eating implements, *i.e.,* plastic spoon or drinking cup. I had to eat and drink out of my hands and I was denied soap to wash my hands with. These conditions remained the same throughout my stay in B Section.

On October 20, 1971 I went before a committee in B Section. I was told of a plot to kill members of the administration at CMC in which I was alledgedly [sic] involved. No details were given and no evidence was put forward to support these serious accusations. The committee members merely repeated that my involvement in the alleged plot was documented and refused to specify what form the "documentation" took. They further accused me of making "threats of death" on other prisoners, similarly without any specifics . . . none of these accusations ever resulted in my being given a disciplinary write up. . . .

On October 21, 1971 I was moved to A Section and put under close custody. I was put into a cell which has water leaking from the face bowl. I have asked to have the damage repaired and to be moved to another cell many times. I have newspapers on the floor an inch thick and they are soaked with water, and the smell is overpowering. Because of the dampness and cold from many broken windows and inadequate heating, I stay under the bed covers most of the day. Roaches have taken up residence because of the filth. Nothing can be put on the floor and walking to the toilet, a distance of only two feet, is miserable. I have been electrically shocked by the loose hanging wire from the light fixtures over a half dozen times when passing it. Prison officials have made no effort to fix this either.[43]

In New York, an ultra-security "maxi-maxi" is under serious consideration for prisoners suspected of radicalism, and in California there is a move afoot to transfer all Adjustment Center inmates to the California Medical Facility at Vacaville, where a facade of psychiatry and treatment may be used to prevent access to this

43. Reported in THE STAFF 16 (P.O. Box 46090, Los Angeles, Cal. 90046, Dec. 10, 1971).

facility and its maximum security sections. In Illinois the old Joliet Branch of the Illinois State Penitentiary has already been converted into such an institution, and three guards were fired for informing the press that prisoners were being starved, beaten and tortured. The secrecy and tight security planned for all these institutions will make it easier for authorities to perpetrate lawless violence against prisoners.

On the outside, whether and to what extent a framework of legality is retained is likely to depend on the extent and seriousness of the challenge the dominant elite must face. At present the challenge is not yet serious and is moreover confined to limited strata of the population. Thus it seems unlikely that the government will resort to the kind of total lawlessness experienced under Nazism; it is more likely to use the law as an instrument of repression increasingly—as it is already doing—and merely supplement this repression with illicit means when there are particularly strong reasons for doing so. To the extent that legitimated authority breaks down, however—and this has certainly been the trend of the last decade—violence may be the only alternative open to the government if it wishes to avoid collapse. In any event, lawlessness in American prisons—and outside them—is anything but an anomaly; like lawlessness in Nazi Germany or Fascist Italy, it serves very real functions in the defense of an imperialist, oligopoly capitalism based on racism and exploitation.

What often seems like an "over-reaction" to challenge may seem less functional, and may spring from irrational elements in human motivation as well as from systematic elements in decision-making. Racial prejudice may have been promoted for the most crass economic motives, but it can hardly be denied that many believed in the tenets of racism. Bernard Diamond has described from a psychoanalytic viewpoint, how attitudes toward the moneyless and helpless may be characterized on the one hand by guilt-induced love and a desire to help, and on the other hand, by hatred, which in turn leads to fear:

> The concurrent hatred implies fear—deep, primitive, unconscious fear—that the very existence of the poor and weak in society threatens the existence of that society. Punitive sanctions must then be applied to control those whom one fears, to make certain that they do not grow and prosper and gain the strength to fulfill their threat of usurpation of power. As the individual most fears death

> and annihilation, so society most fears anarchy and revolution. The poor and dependant, as a class, become endowed with magical, destructive powers totally out of proportion to reality. They become sacrificial recipients of scapegoated sins, but at the same time they are tabooed objects who cannot be destroyed without dire consequences.[44]

This hypothesis may help to explain the similarity in the response of early nineteenth century American communities to the indigent, to orphans, the aged, the insane, and criminals, all of whom were for the first time, subjected to incarceration.[45] On the other hand, while the "magical, destructive powers" of criminals imputed to be dangerous have often been exaggerated (in the case of blacks possibly by a fear that they would treat whites as they had themselves been treated), the loving component of this dialectic has often been missing. Criminals, it seems plausible, were preserved in institutions beginning in the early nineteenth century not because they were "tabooed objects who cannot be destroyed without dire consequences" but rather because the prison, asylum, reformatory seemed like admirable places to assimilate immigrant cultures to an older, native American culture, and in particular to discipline potential workers for the farms and industries of a labor-short economy.

It is equally plausible that what seems like "over-reaction" can be interpreted as a perception on the part of authorities that their exploitative practices and mystifying ideology are extremely vulnerable to coherent organized opposition, which must therefore be suppressed at all costs. Opposition must therefore be coopted and absorbed, or else crushed. Its survival would be too threatening.

E. *The Failure of Liberal Ideology*

The inability of whites and other middle class individuals to understand the experiences of minority groups has its roots not only *directly* in the very different experiences of these groups, but also indirectly, in the failure of the political thought to which the population is exposed during its education, to assess accurately

44. Diamond, *The Children of the Leviathan: Psychoanalytic Speculations Concerning Welfare Law and Punitive Sanctions,* 54 CALIF. L. REV. 357, 362 (1966).

45. D. ROTHMAN, DISCOVERY OF THE ASYLUM: SOCIAL ORDER AND DISORDER IN THE NEW REPUBLIC (1971).

the significance of certain developments which have taken place in modern political institutions. The system of checks and balances devised by the framers of the Constitution was devised before the profusive growth of administrative agencies within the executive branch of government. These agencies have not been brought under effective control by that system, nor have new effective controls been instituted.

Although the American bourgeoisie, in contrast to its European counterpart, never had to wage a revolutionary struggle against an incumbent, economically anachronistic feudal aristocracy or monarchy, it was deeply influenced at the time of its War of Independence by the ideas formed in Europe in the course of the struggle there—particularly by such ideas as the rule of law, due process, and equality before the law. These ideas were intended to limit the state as to occasions on which it could interfere with individuals and also in the manner of that intervention. They were also intended to eliminate the elite privileges which the feudal aristocracy and clergy had enjoyed. These concepts were at the core of eighteenth century penal theory [46] and were embodied in the French Penal Code of 1791 as well as in the American Constitution.

The extent to which the attempt to implement some of these principles in the European judicial system was linked with class struggle is indicated by the manner in which the drive against informality and judicial discretion lost its momentum and fizzled out as the bourgeoisie who had mounted it consolidated their political power:

> Both the principle of proportion and the refined methods of criminal procedure were products of the bourgeois revolutions. Formalization of criminal justice offered many advantages in the central European countries where feudal-absolutist forces still retained much of their strength, as well as in the western countries where political power was long an object of struggle between different groups. The independence of the judiciary and the rationalization of criminal law were excellent weapons in the struggle against the remnants of feudalism and absolutist bureaucracy. . . . The refinement of procedural methods was one of the most effective ways of protecting the acquisition and extension of economic power by means which were sometimes questionable even from

46. J. Heath, Eighteenth Century Penal Theory ch. 1 (1963)

> the standpoint of the ruling classes. In the struggle against the lower classes, on the other hand, the independence of the judiciary, drawn solely from the upper classes, revealed itself to be not too great an obstacle in spite of formalism of method. In countries like England, informal patriarchal procedures were retained for petty offenders, that is to say, for lower-class crimes. . . .
>
> The end of the nineteenth century marks the close of the period of antagonism between the last remnants of feudalism and the administrative bureaucracy on the one hand and the middle class on the other. As the latter strengthened their hold over the machinery of government and administration, it became less and less necessary to continue the process of formalizing criminal law as a guarantee of their social and economic position. . . . It was no longer necessary to protect the bourgeoisie against the arbitrariness of the administration, now that the two were largely identical.[47]

In the United States, where the highest echelons of the capitalist class felt confident of controlling the administrative apparatus of the state they were content to leave its operation unfettered by formal rules and legal restrictions; thus the business regulatory agencies were accorded wide discretion because the business community felt assured that the agencies would operate in the interests of the industries they were intended to regulate.[48] Where the wealthy felt less confident of their control, they insisted on the most meticulous and thorough development of rules and their uniform application, as in tax law.

As described in *Struggle for Justice*,[49] a recent report on crime and punishment prepared for the American Friends Service Committee, from which we draw extensively in this section, the interests of the dominant class in the area of criminal law administration, were best served by providing judges, prosecutors and parole boards with vast unreviewed and unchecked discretionary powers, ostensibly justified as meeting the needs of the individual defendant—treating the criminal, not the crime. Since members of this class knew that lawyers, prosecutors and judges tended to be drawn from their own ranks or else were totally subservient to them, there was little doubt in their minds that this slogan would

47. G. Rusche & O. Kirchheimer, Punishment and Social Structure 142-44 (2d ed. 1968).

48. *See* G. William Domhoff, The Higher Circles: The Governing Class in America chs. 5 & 6 (1970).

49. For a description of these discretionary powers, see Struggle for Justice, *supra* note 42, at 124-44.

provide a respectable cover for ignoring or wrist-slapping the upper and middle class criminal who posed no political threat to the established order, while allowing the full weight of law enforcement to be brought to bear against those without money or power to fight back, that is, against the group the elite was especially concerned to deter—not so much because they were worried about petty violations of the law but rather because they saw in this class the potential seedbeds for revolution. Under the discretionary system of justice they devised, individuals in low income brackets who committed minor crimes were often punished with a severity far exceeding that meted out to those who committed far more serious offenses, for example, waging illegal war, price-fixing on a massive scale, pollution of the environment, placing unsafe cars on the road, maintaining dangerous working conditions, leasing slum apartments, practicing racial discrimination, etc.

In his extensive writings studying the relationship of legal institutions to their social and economic context, Max Weber viewed the question of discretion somewhat differently. Although recognizing that:

> 'Equality before the law' and the demand for legal guarantees against arbitrariness demand a formal and rational 'objectivity' of administration, as opposed to the personally free discretion flowing from the 'grace' of the old patrimonial domination . . .[,] [50]

he nevertheless asserts that

> [t]he propertyless masses especially are not served by a formal 'equality before the law' and a 'calculable' adjudication and administration, as demanded by 'bourgeois' interests. Naturally, in their eyes justice and administration should serve to compensate for their economic and social life-opportunities in the face of the propertied classes. Justice and administration can fulfill this function only if they assume an informal character to a far-reaching extent.[51]

While Weber was correct in seeing a connection between the rise of rationalized law and the commercial interests of the bourgeoisie, which demanded predictability, the middle class is certainly not the only group in society to benefit from certainty, due

50. M. WEBER: ESSAYS IN SOCIOLOGY 220 (H. Gerth & C. Wright Mills eds. 1946).
51. *Id.* at 221.

process or equality under law. The "propertyless masses," to the extent that they are aware of the problem, understand that their social disadvantages are at present held *against* them by criminal justice functionaries, and that a non-discretionary system would be to their advantage because they would then gain the benefits now enjoyed by the well-to-do. Thus, a reduction in the discretionary powers of prison officials and parole boards was demanded by Attica prison inmates, and constitutes an important part of the demands raised by other groups, such as the United Prisoners Union, and the women who went on strike at the Federal Reformatory for Women in Alderson, West Virginia.

The upper classes were not alone in wanting a system of discretionary justice; the concept had very wide support. To punitively-oriented police officials and prosecutors it meant the ability to hold criminals they regarded as especially dangerous for periods of time far longer than rule of law would make possible or retributive principles of sentencing legitimate. It provided prison administrators with a perfect control apparatus. Where variation in the length of sentence and inequality of treatment have been legitimated on the basis of supposed treatment needs, they can be, and are manipulated to secure good behavior. It is ordinarily not necessary to beat prisoners to make them behave; it is only necessary to threaten parole denial.

Liberal penologists and reformers liked the discretionary system because it meshed so perfectly with their goal of rehabilitating prisoners during their incarceration. This aim had roots in religious and humanitarian sentiment in the early part of the nineteenth century, and indirectly in English utilitarian philosophy. It received enormous impetus from the positivistic school of criminology, with its deterministic models of human behavior and its tendency to view crime as analogous to disease, and the criminal as a patient, to be cured. Adherents of this school implicitly assume that empirically identifiable factors distinguish criminals from non-criminals, and can be used to classify the former for treatment strategies. It is assumed that these exist or can be devised, and that one can tell when the treatment has succeeded. Although these premises may have seemed plausible fifty or a hundred years ago when sociologists were deeply impressed by the determinism of the physical sciences, none of them has been confirmed and the prospects for their confirmation in the foreseeable future are not bright.[52]

Although the policy of confining prisoners in order to treat them has yet to prove itself in the form of an effective treatment program, it has nevertheless retained an extraordinary hold on correctional thinking despite this practical failure. This may be attributed to the covert functions the ideology serves. It helps liberals relieve their guilt feelings over having to punish people, it allows prison employees to feel they are doing something useful by "helping" their charges, and as already mentioned it provides an admirable control device. In addition it serves to discredit prisoners by convincing both them and the public at large that prisoners are incarcerated because of some personal rather than a social defect. Finally, it provides prison administrators with a language of euphemisms with which to disguise practices which the public might find unpalatable if labeled honestly. (Instead of the hole, we have the "meditation room" or the "Adjustment Center.")

The link between the treatment philosophy and positivist criminology was a consequence of the recognition that not all criminals are alike. It was then argued that judges ought to have substantial discretionary powers to devise a sentence based on the individual treatment needs of the criminal being sentenced. Later it was argued that experts should make such decisions, and so the parole board was given the power to determine how long a prisoner actually served. This system reached its pinnacle in California where the Adult Authority fixes the sentence within a very wide range specified by the legislature (for example, one to life, ten to life, one to fifteen), grants and revokes parole, and can refix the original sentence.

The resulting unequal treatment of prisoners in a curious way ended up mirroring inequalities outside the prison. Prisoners who conform to all expectations, who come from white, middle class backgrounds (there aren't that many of them but there are some) are given favorable consideration for placement in halfway houses, minimum security institutions and early release on parole. Those who get into trouble or are black or hold the wrong political views are placed in high security institutions and are de-

52. For a critique of the individualized treatment philosophy, see STRUGGLE FOR JUSTICE, *supra* note 42, at ch. 6.

nied release. The resulting differentiation of prisoners along lines of class, race and privilege helps to keep them divided just as the identical divisions among those on the outside help to keep workers divided. Guards are well aware of this and have often encouraged racial hostility between prisoners on the basis of a "divide and conquer" philosophy.[53] The official fostering of racial hostility is only part of a broader policy of keeping inmates divided. In the words of a noted penologist, it is the aim of prison administrators

> to keep inmate society as unorganized as possible, to prevent individuals from joining forces. To this end, psychological solitary confinement is substituted, to the fullest extent possible, for physical isolation. This permits inmates to work and to participate in prescribed activities, but it minimizes the danger of violence, revolt or riot. To facilitate the state of unorganization or anomie, administrators always admonish inmates to "do your own time," and consistently, officially distribute rewards such as parole and good-time allowances to inmates who remain isolated from other prisoners.[54]

This atomization helps to keep prisoners powerless, as in any other totalitarian society.[55] In fact, "classification," a standard item in the rehabilitationist repertoire, is actually a sophisticated control device. In a prison system composed of a number of different prisons, the difference between a Soledad or San Quentin and a minimum security farm helps to insulate different classes of prisoners from one another, and contributes to conformity by creating the threat of transfers for misbehavior.

With support from diverse elements—from criminologists, liberals, reformers, police officials, prosecutors, judges, prison administrators—a web of discretionary power was created that in effect largely placed prisoners outside the protection of the law and increased their powerlessness. Equality under law, due process, predictability have all disappeared.

Accustomed by the discretionary system to making decisions free from any accountability, prison officials were placed in an environment conducive to lawlessness—not just the lawlessness of

53. *See, e.g.*, Minton & Rice, *Race War at San Quentin*, RAMPARTS, Jan. 1970 at 18; Wessner, *Racism in Federal Prison*, THE PEACEMAKER, May 2, 1970.

54. Donald R. Cressey, in the foreward to the reissued text of the classic work by D. CLEMMER, THE PRISON COMMUNITY 59 (1958).

55. H. ARENDT, *supra* note 9, at 59.

parole boards, transfers or disciplinary proceedings, but also the lawlessness of physical violence. There is no little irony in this outcome. A discretionary treatment system was promoted by liberals on the grounds that it would help prisoners and at the same time let them out earlier—as soon as they were cured. Many reformers managed to convince themselves that by converting the punitively oriented prison functioning in the framework of a rigid, non-discretionary system to a rehabilitative or treatment-oriented discretionary system, they could somehow humanize the prison experience.

These reformers overlooked the obvious: treatment is not the opposite of punishment; reward is the opposite of punishment, and no one has seriously proposed rewarding prisoners. The view that imprisonment for punishment should be regarded as a barbaric anachronism while imprisonment for treatment is benign and progressive can be sustained only by denying the experience of the prisoner, who is subjected to the same indignities, deprivations and humiliations under either system. Indeed, the therapeutic regime brings with it new hardships and humiliations. The uncertainty over the length of confinement significantly adds to the psychological hardship of incarceration, while the view of the criminal as sick, not in control of his or her own actions, is demeaning and insulting to human dignity. Furthermore, since treatment is defined as help, and help cannot be punitive, those who are incarcerated in order to be treated are stripped of legal protections which as criminals they would enjoy.[56] This process is carried to its ultimate in so-called civil commitments which because they are supposedly motivated by benevolence, are not considered punitive, even when imposed coercively and involve physical environments indistinguishable from prisons.

By ignoring the reality of treatment as experienced by its recipients and by distinguishing "good" from "bad" prisons by the motives of society's judges and jailers, the ultimate dehumanization of prisoners has been achieved: they are literally not there. Historical evidence suggests that powerlessness actually bestows a kind of invisibility; those without power disappear from view as if they wore a magical cloak. At a time when slavery flourished, one

56. N. Kittrie, The Right to be Different: Deviance and Enforced Therapy (1971); T. Szasz, Law, Liberty and Psychiatry (1963).

English traveler could write about his trip through America with the words:

> In a course of 1200 miles I did not see a single object that solicited charity.[57]

Only by rebelling, by stepping out of their place of powerlessness and acting together, generating the power of collective action, do those who "dwell in darkness" (Brecht) step into the spotlight of history and in so doing shed their cloak of invisibility. Rebelling prisoners have been doing just that.

In essence, the reformers who supported this system of vast, unchecked discretion placed their faith in some assumed inevitable benevolence of those in power, naively overlooking the more realistic conclusion that unchecked power is susceptible of abuse no matter what its motives, and that when the motives seem most benevolent, the abuses may be all the more dangerous because they are unchecked by any humanitarian constraints. (Why should I be limited in what I do to you when it's for your own good?) Criminal justice functionaries were of course well aware of these considerations of power; it was precisely because the reforms in question strengthened them at the expense of convicts that they supported the reforms. Prisoners are becoming increasingly aware of the pitfalls of a discretionary system, and the connections between their own powerlessness and their victimization on the part of the lawless prison system it created. It is this realization which accounts for the shift in demands from those which have traditionally been raised by prisoners in the past and which can be satisfied without upsetting the power relations of the prison (for example, better food) to those which seek to limit the discretionary power of authorities and shift the balance toward the prisoners.

The foregoing analysis leads to several conclusions. First, the prison system is indeed no aberration, but a rather central element to American society. It has been shaped, and in turn reinforces

57. H. Arendt, *supra* note 9, at 63-64, which also quotes John Adams:

> The Poor man's conscience is clear; yet he is ashamed. . . . He feels himself out of the sight of others, groping in the dark. Mankind takes no notice of him. He rambles and wanders unheeded. In the midst of a crowd, at church, in the market . . . he is in as much obscurity as he would be in a garret or a cellar. He is not disapproved, censured, or reproached; *he is only not seen* . . . .

See also R. Ellison, Invisible Man (1952) (a contemporary fictional representation of the same phenomenon).

and supports the perpetuation of a status quo characterized by racism, inequity and exploitation. The lawlessness of that system was not an accidental by-product or an oversight, but actually crucial to the social functions the prison has performed. It is clear that a return to rule by law, rather than rule by men, or lawlessness, would represent a significant victory for those who are now most seriously victimized. It would seriously handicap those now in control of the prisons by limiting their ability to take reprisals against those engaged in political activity within the prisons, and in so doing it would create space for those activities.

This is, of course, a transitional, not a final, goal. Due process and uniform application of unambiguous rules are by themselves incapable of eliminating the disadvantages moneyless individuals or members of feared or hated minorities will experience in court as a result of their status. A law against armed robbery means one thing to an unemployed black male living in an impoverished ghetto and quite another thing to someone with a secure job and steady income. This is not, as Weber believed, an argument in favor of discretion, since under the present socio-economic system such discretion will inevitably turn such social disadvantages into liabilities in the courtroom. It does, however, point to the limitations of formal equality under conditions of social inequality. This limitation is one that jurists have been reluctant to realize.

Although implicit in many legal treatises, this limitation is glaringly visible in C. K. Allen's introduction to the Oxford University World Classic Edition of Henry Sumner Maine's *Ancient Law*,[58] the first modern comparative study of early legal institutions, written, interestingly enough, by a British colonial administrator. Allen reflects a prevalent agreement that "it is not too much to say that with the appearance of this book modern historical jurisprudence was born." [59] Prior to Maine's study, first published in 1861, England had produced a theory of law which by "its exclusion of historical considerations from the province of jurisprudence led it into the radical fallacy of regarding all systems of law as being typified by Western European monarchical states." This work deeply influenced the development of British anthropology: Maine's skepticism concerning "any attempt to establish

58. H. MAINE, ANCIENT LAW (introduction by C. Allen 1931).
59. *Id.* at IX.

a single, invariable scheme of development for the human race in all its branches" [60] and his attempts to relate legal to other social institutions were congenial to the structuralist viewpoint.[61]

Although Maine had attempted to place all legal systems on an equal footing, the development of English jurisprudence as well as American Constitutional theory grew out of the study of white institutions and historical development, and came to define systems in which a white minority exercised power over whites and blacks, with the latter having little or no participation in the formulation of ideas, ideals, ideology, law, or power relations except as recipients, defendants, prisoners, victims.

Maine himself was by no means immune from culture-laden value judgments. His conclusion (later elaborated by such scholars as Weber [62] and Durkheim [63]) that "[t]he movement of the progressive societies has hitherto been a movement from Status to Contract" [64] exhibited a certain ethnocentricity. (In fact, its self-congratulatory Hegelianism was welcome to Western legal theorists and historians.) Professor Allen's introductory text comments:

> [Maine's] aphorism sufficiently expresses a principle with which no historical jurist nowadays has any quarrel—namely the emergence of the self-determining, separate individual from the network of family and group ties; or, in the briefest terms, the movement from group to individual . . . . It is to be observed that Maine guardedly said that this movement had *hitherto* been characteristic of the progressive societies. Many are now asking, with complacency, whether the contrary movement, from contract to status is not setting in. It is quite certain that the absolute self-determination of the individual, which nineteenth century *laissez-faire* enshrined in the hallowed phrase 'freedom of contract' has become much modified in our own day; and the place of the individual in society is governed far more extensively by the particular grouping, in which, not always by his own free choice, he finds himself, than it was when *Ancient Law* was written. It may be that when the part which was once played by the family nidus will be played in the future by the syndical nidus; it may be that Maine's famous principle will some day be regarded simply as a parenthesis in social history. Whether this, if it should happen, will be the

60. *Id.* at XXI.
61. Goddard, *Limits of British Anthropology,* 58 NEW LEFT REV. 79 (Nov.-Dec. 1969).
62. M. WEBER, ON LAW IN ECONOMY AND SOCIETY (M. Rheinstein ed. 1967).
63. E. DURKHEIM, THE DIVISION OF LABOR IN SOCIETY (G. Simpson transl. 1964).
64. H. MAINE, *supra* note 58, at ch. XXVI.

> mark of progressive or of retrogressive societies is a controversial question very fitting for every thinking man's contemplation. . . .[65]

These remarks fail to distinguish between limiting and emancipating group ties, and overestimate the historical impact of "freedom of contract." Even at its zenith, this freedom was in reality quite limited; it certainly never applied to slaves, for example. Like the laissez-faire liberal theories of classical economics, we have here a philosophy which enshrines the idea of free individuals entering into contracts under conditions of *formal* equality, but which overlooks the actuality of unequal social status (for example, black, brown, poor) to which a system of laws is then in theory uniformly applied. The resulting economic inequalities and differential distribution of political power are inexplicable and unresolvable within the framework of liberal theory. When faced with the kind of a crisis which developed in post-World War I Europe, the theory collapses, giving way to new ideologies such as fascism. The resolution of this difficulty requires a transformation of society, though not the transformation fascism sought. Only when wealth, income and power are distributed with at least approximate uniformity can freedom of contract be something other than a mystified, fetishized version of inequality.

The significance of these comments is amplified when we consider the relevance of Maine's description of the role which the study of law plays in the history of nations and in the development of the intellectual faculties, to the prison setting. Maine writes:

> there are two subjects of thought—the only two perhaps with the exception of physical science—which are able to give employment to all the powers and capacities the mind possesses. One of them is metaphysical inquiry, which knows no limits so long as the mind is satisfied to work on itself, the other is Law, which is as extensive as the concerns of mankind. It happens that, during the very period indicated, the Greek-speaking provinces were devoted to one, the Latin-speaking provinces to the other, of these studies. I say nothing of the fruits of speculation in Alexandria and the East, but I confidently affirm that Rome and the West had an occupation in hand fully capable of compensating them for the absence of every other mental exercise . . . . We should reflect that the

65. *Id.* at XXVI-XXVII.

> earliest intellectual exercise to which a young nation devotes itself is the study of its laws.[66]

This was certainly the case in colonial America.

There is some irony in the fact that one of the major preoccupations of the convicted class is increasingly the study of laws. This interest is hardly surprising: convicts are condemned through the processes of law and criminal justice administration; by mastering these tools they hope to understand how they are victimized, the better to combat that victimization. Because of the basic lawlessness of the court, prison and parole system, the possible uses of law are very limited at present, though they represent the only alternative to the risks of direct action. More striking, this increased sophistication in the law is advancing in precisely the same proportion as the convicted class becomes aware of itself as a status, as a "nation." The concept of a "Bill of Rights" for prisoners, extending constitutional protections and legal guarantees to members of the convicted class, has been central to the work of Prisoners Unions, for example. And the developing black organization, consciousness, power, entity—nation if you will—also increasingly devotes itself not only to self-expression, economic advancement and the pursuit of political power, but to the study of laws. *But to whose laws?* So long as the distribution of power and wealth is unchanged, resort to an exclusively legalistic approach to change is likely to be at best an ineffectual, defensive strategy. On the other hand, as part of a strategy aimed at the acquisition of power on the part of a self-conscious class—blacks or prisoners—resort to legal tactics may be far more effective. In the civil rights movement, for example, attacks on racial discrimination in the courts were complemented by picketing, boycotts, marches and demonstrations and other forms of pressure from an aroused community.

F. *Prison Issues and Social Change*

In the context of the prison this suggests several things. First, attempts to alleviate oppressive prison conditions cannot avoid dealing with questions of power. A mere improvement in the physical conditions of confinement will do little to alleviate the lawlessness which the lack of power invites. The relevant concept here is

66. *Id.* at 299-300.

"prisoners' rights"—*rights,* not privileges which can be manipulated or withdrawn as a control device and which tend to set against one another those who need to act in unison.

Second, the struggle around prison-related issues cannot be separated from struggles around other social issues. The society in which prisoners are brutalized and killed at Soledad and San Quentin and Attica and Tucker Farm in Arkansas is the same society which slaughtered Indians and then Vietnamese, in which Panther leaders are shot to death while they sleep, in which voter registration workers are killed in Mississippi. It is a society in which both unemployment and corporate profits are high and the possibility of satisfying work is denied to the many while urgent social needs go unmet. More than a century ago Marx described the industrial proletariat as:

> a class with *radical chains,* a class of civil society which is not a class of civil society, . . . a sphere which has a universal character by its universal suffering and claims no *particular right* because no *particular wrong* but *wrong generally* is perpetrated against it; which can invoke no *historical* but only its *human* title, . . . a sphere, finally, which cannot emancipate itself without emancipating itself from all other spheres of society, and thereby emancipating all other spheres of society, which, in a word, is the *complete loss* of man, and hence can win itself only through the *complete re-winning of man.*[67]

This is true today of prisoners. While smaller victories can and must be pursued, the Soledads and Atticas can be relegated to the dustbins of history only as part of a far-reaching transformation of the entire society.

An important part of any effort to build a liaison between the prisoner movement and those working for social change outside the prison must be an attempt to open the prison to the outside. The community, through its leaders, representatives and ordinary members, must have access to prisoners, and have free and private communication, in person and by letters, with inmates. Prisoners must be allowed visitors of their choice—at convenient times of course, but under conditions of privacy allowing for uninhibited communication. If medical treatment is at issue, private physicians must be allowed access to inmates. Competent legal represen-

67. Marx, *Toward the Critique of Hegel's Philosophy of Right,* in K. MARX & F. ENGEL, *supra* note 27, at 264-65.

tation must be allowed and provided in all matters of privilege denial or other disciplinary and punitive treatment. By stripping away the cover of secrecy from the prison, these steps would contribute significantly to curbing the present lawlessness of the prison, and would increase society's awareness of what is now done in its name.

At the corner stone of a dialectical understanding of historical process is the concept that the existing society already contains within it and even produces those elements which will contribute to social change. Imperial domination leads to national liberation movements, domestic racism to a new sense of identity and self-assertion on the part of minority groups. America is producing people who cannot live satisfying lives unless the character of the nation is altered; consequently they attempt to effect those alterations. The prison itself has produced the prisoner movement. This movement is still in its infancy; prisoners are only just now coming to an informed sense of identity and a consciousness of the possibilities of collective action. Prisoners unions, strikes, revolts —these are the first visible signs of these stirrings. It is from the prisoner movement, the ex-convict movement, that leadership will come in struggles relating to the prison—and no doubt in other struggles as well. But support from all of us is needed, and must be forthcoming, not only for prisoners' sakes, but for our own. For the prison indeed oppresses not just those who are locked behind its bars. It reaches out to every one of us.

[11]
Punishment, Division of Labor, and Social Solidarity

Introduction

A long-standing sociological tradition considers the type of social control measures utilized in a society to be determined by its more fundamental features. For Durkheim (1933, 1992), it is the division of labor in a society and the degree of absolutism of its government that determine collective responses to violations of social rules. To social scientists inspired by Marx, the mode of production in a society, the demand for exploitable labor, and the kinds and intensity of class conflict are fundamental determinants (Rusche and Kirchheimer 1939; Fine 1980; Melossi and Pavarini 1980; Miller 1980; Williams 1980; Adamson 1984). In recent years Donald Black (1976) and his followers (Horwitz 1990) have been extending this research program by positing the influence of a number of social characteristics on levels and styles of social control.

At best, the insights furnished by this approach have been partial. One need not reject those insights to recognize that some recent developments in crime control policy cannot be fully understood in these reductionist terms. Without abandoning it altogether, I want to explore a different way of thinking about criminal sanctions by suggesting that some features of punishment policy and practices can be understood as components of political strategies for *changing* a society. It is an intended *future* social structure and culture, not its current condition, that shapes the strategies. These strategies are not directed to crime alone, but also to an array of other social issues, such as welfare, education, and immigration. They rely on assumptions about the way society functions, or could function. Their ability to attract wide support rests in part on their congruence with popular conceptions of justice, and beliefs about the way society operates.

Tough Punishment

Until the early 1970s, American prison populations rose and fell over the decades, yet remained within bounds, without any long-run trend (Blumstein and Cohen 1973; Blumstein, Cohen and Nagin 1976). After declining appreciably for much of the 1960s, incarceration rates began to rise, and have been outpacing population growth steadily ever since. At the end of 1996, more than 1.6 million people were in prison or jail, and another 3.5 million were on probation or on parole. This is the population of a large city. Not content with this expansion, some politicians and policy analysts call for further expansion (e.g., DiIulio 1995).

A clearer picture of carceral growth can be had by examining trends in rates. In 1972, there were 93 sentenced prisoners per 100,000 residents in state and federal institutions (Maguire and Pastore 1996:556); at the end of 1995, there were 409 (Gilliard and Beck 1996:3). This is the highest incarceration rate in the industrialized world. Many of those committed to prison have been convicted of relatively minor offenses[1] (Austin and Irwin 1991).

This enormous increase is all the more remarkable in that it has come at a time when governments have been facing strong pressures to cut budgets.[2] The punishment system appears to have spun out of control. Predictions made a decade ago that the growth in prison populations "will taper off before long" for demographic reasons have failed the test of time (Blumstein 1987). Whatever the factors were that kept prison populations within limits in previous generations, they are no longer operating (Blumstein 1988). Prisons are being built and filled for political reasons, not because of demographic considerations.

Prison expansion is only one of many ways punishment policy has been toughening. Increasingly, states are adopting legislation allowing juveniles to be tried as adults, and are removing the confidentiality of juvenile court records (Butterfield 1996a). A number of states have started to hold parents responsible for offenses committed by their children (Kotlowitz 1994; Applebome 1996; Torbet et al. 1996). Educational programs for prison inmates are being eliminated in budget cuts (Kunen 1995). Federal legislation has excluded some addicts from Social Security benefits and from welfare payments. "Three strikes" legislation adopted by some states provides life sentences without parole for felons with two prior felony convictions, no matter how long ago, and sometimes without regard to the seriousness of the earlier offenses[3] (Shichor and Sechrest 1996). In 1995, Alabama restored the chain gang (Bragg 1995), a form of penal servitude long regarded as an instrument of racial oppression. After a moratorium on executions between 1967 and 1977 while the U.S. Supreme Court was considering the constitutionality of the death penalty, executions have resumed; the number of prisoners currently awaiting execution now exceeds 3000. In another decision, the Supreme Court ruled that judges can legitimately extend someone's sentence on the basis of charges of which the defendant has been acquitted.

In addition, public funding to finance appeals of death sentences brought by indigent defendants has been eliminated. The U.S. Senate has approved legislation limiting the rights of state prisoners to argue in the federal courts that they were unconstitutionally convicted or sentenced. This restriction on the right of *habeus corpus* would prevent a federal judge from stopping the execution of a state prisoner sentenced to death, even if new evidence is uncovered indicating that the prisoner is probably not guilty, or if the conviction was obtained through an incorrect ruling in the state trial court (Lewis 1995). Another bill limits the power of judges to turn the supervision of prison conditions over to a court-appointed special master.

Explaining Toughening

How to explain these developments? Homicide rates, considered the most accurate of all reported crime statistics, have changed little since 1980. Reported rates for other offenses did rise, but since victimization surveys show no parallel increase during the 1970s and 1980s, the increase in reported rates may reflect nothing more than an increased willingness of victims to notify the police (Orcutt and Faison 1981; O'Brien 1996).

That increases in reported crime rates do not necessarily lead to higher incarceration rates is demonstrated by the drop in prison populations during the late 1960s while reported crime rates were rising (at least partly for demographic reasons); and they are rising now, even though reported crime rates have been falling for five years in a row.[4]

The inability of crime rates to account fully for trends in prison populations is equally evident when considering trends comparatively. Since

1950, rates of reported serious crime have risen virtually in parallel in the Netherlands and in England/Wales; yet trends in prison populations have been quite different. The Dutch prison population was about the same in 1990 as in 1950, while in England and Wales it doubled (Downes 1988: 7, 34).

A court can sentence to prison only those offenders who are actually brought into the criminal justice system. Could it be that more people are being imprisoned because the police are arresting more criminals? In 1972, the arrest rate for index offenses per 100,000 population was 883.4; in 1995 it was 1132.7[5] (FBI 1973:126, 1996:209). This increase of 28 percent can hardly explain a more than four-fold increase in the incarceration rate.

A very large increase in arrests on narcotics charges has certainly contributed.[6] But imprisonment rates have increased for other offenses as well. Many states have adopted legislation mandating longer sentences for convicted criminals, and restricting or eliminating parole. Judges have been ladling out prison sentences more generously, and parole authorities have been revoking parole more readily (Shane-Dubow, Brown and Olsen 1985; Tonry 1988; Pillsbury 1989; Langen 1991; Wicharaya 1995; Marvell and Moody 1996). As a result, prison populations have grown at an historically unprecedented rate (Blumstein 1988; Langan 1991; Zimring and Hawkins 1995).

This trend is clearly inexplicable within the framework of Durkheim's (1933) model of legal evolution. That model sees the basis for social solidarity gradually shifting from "mechanical" to "organic" solidarity. In societies with mechanical solidarity, similarity in occupations and life circumstances is supposed to lead social members to identify strongly with one another, and to punish any infraction of social norms passionately, vigorously, and harshly. Societies with organic solidarity are supposed to be based on complementarity of function in a complex division of labor. Here demand for punishment is supposed to be milder, ameliorated by humanitarian sentiments; and social control places increased emphasis on restitution, less on retribution. Order is secured primarily through market exchanges rather than forcibly secured similarity, although punishment does not disappear.

It has long been known that long-term trends do not fit this model (Barnes 1965; Sheleff 1975; Spitzer 1975), and it clearly furnishes no insights that would help us to understand increased punitiveness now. Though the division of labor in contemporary United States is complex, the demand for severe punishment is high. Between 1972 and 1978, the percentage of respondents in a national survey saying that the courts were not harsh enough toward criminals rose from 66 percent to 85 percent (Hindelang, Gottfredson, and Flanagan 1980:196–7) and then leveled off. Support for the death penalty has risen over the past generation[7] for reasons that are not related to changes in the division of labor, at least not in the way Durkheim envisioned. It is not because American society is becoming less differentiated that it is becoming more punitive.

Increased punitiveness might, however, be explained by increasing inequality. Generalizing from diverse literatures, Donald Black (1976), has proposed that punishment will be more intense the higher the degree of economic inequality in a society, and that it will be harsher the lower the financial status of the person being punished.

A crossnational study of prison populations based on a global sample has found them to be larger where economic inequality is higher[8] (Killias 1986), consistent with this proposition.[9] Because political conditions in the less-developed countries are often quite different from those in the developed world, a crossnational study based on a globally representative sample of nations runs the risk of mixing apples and oranges, possibly obscuring patterns that may be distinct to the developed nations. Yet it is patterns for the developed world that might help us to understand recent American developments.

To determine whether the results Killias found hold for the developed world, I collected data for the nations[10] defined by the World Bank as having "high income," and computed the correlation between the imprisonment rate and economic inequality.[11] It is evident from figure 13.1 that there is a moderately strong positive relationship between imprisonment rates and economic inequality; the correlation between these two variables is 0.47. When the United States, which is clearly an outlier, is deleted from the sample, the correlation rises to 0.69. The correlations are quite similar if one measures punitiveness by the ratio of the imprisonment rate to the crime rate rather than by the imprisonment rate.

This correlation is not due to countries with high inequality having high crime rates and hence more people in prison: with the United States deleted from the sample, the correlations between inequality and the homicide and burglary rates are small and statistically insignificant. Only the auto theft rate[12] has a non-trivial correlation with inequality (0.28). Moreover, the crime rates are virtually unrelated to the level of imprisonment. Although a number of crossnational studies of crime rates have found higher rates to be associated with economic inequal-

FIGURE 13.1
Imprisonment Rates by Inequality

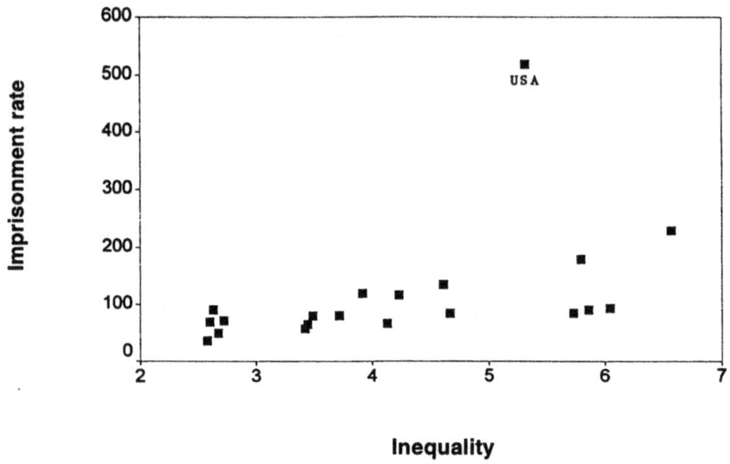

ity, this relationship is not found among the "high income" nations[13] (see figures 13.2, 13.3, and 13.4). Though the United States is among the more stratified nations in this sample, its overall crime rate is not unusually high.[14]

Nor does the relationship between punishment and inequality arise because highly unequal societies are also unusually wealthy, and therefore better able to afford the cost of building and maintaining prisons. Statistical controlling for gross national product (GNP) per capita hardly changes the correlation between inequality and the imprisonment rate.[15] Nor does it appear that the international differences can be wholly explained by differences in the kinds of crime the countries face. For specific kinds of crime, such as robbery, some countries imprison much more readily than others and for longer periods (Downes 1988:36–40; Downes 1990; J. Lynch 1988; Muncie and Sparks 1991).

Economic trends in the United States are consistent with a positive relationship between income inequality and prison population. Over the past two decades, as the prison population has risen, the distributions of income and wealth have become appreciably more skewed[16] (Winnick 1989; Burtless 1990; Phillips 1990:3–31; Karoly 1992, 1993; Krugman 1992, 1994; Danziger and Gottschalk 1993; Bradsher 1995; Westergaard 1995; Wolff 1995a, 1995b; Head 1996).

FIGURE 13.2
Homocide Rates by Inequality

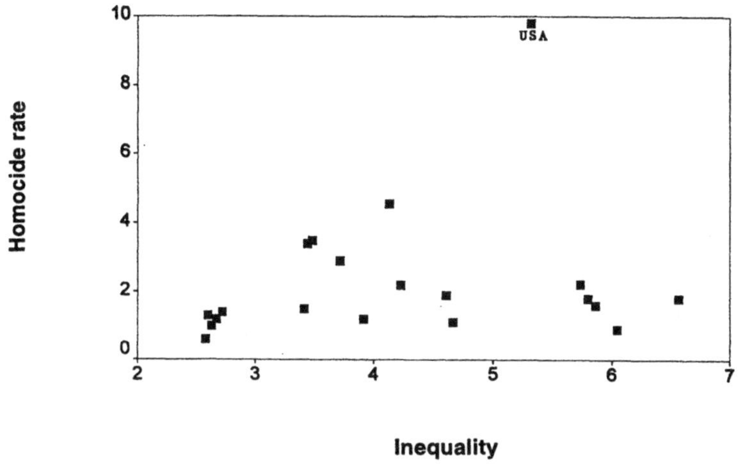

This skewing reflects two simultaneous trends: the rich have grown a good deal richer, while the poor have become somewhat poorer. The trends are the same when income is measured by earnings alone and by incomes from all sources. Between 1977 and 1988, incomes of the upper 1 percent of the population grew by 49.8 percent in constant dollars, while incomes of the bottom 80 percent fell, with the highest drop—14.8 percent—sustained by the bottom tenth (Phillips 1990:17). Between 1973 and 1995, average weekly earnings of "production and nonsupervisory workers," adjusted for inflation, fell by 18 percent, while "the real annual pay of corporate chief executives increased by 19 percent, and by 66 percent after taxes" (Head 1996). Between 1977 and 1989, average family income for the bottom quintile dropped by 9 percent; for those in the top 5 percent, it rose by 24 percent, and for those in the top 1 percent, it rose by 103 percent (Krugman 1992).

Children have been especially hard hit by this drop (Lichter and Eggebeen 1993): according to a report issued recently by Columbia University's National Center for Children in Poverty (1997), the number of children under age six living in poverty grew from 3.5 million to 6.1 million between 1979 and 1994. One in four children in that age bracket now live in poverty, a higher percentage than in other Western democracies.

FIGURE 13.3
Burglary Rates by Inequality

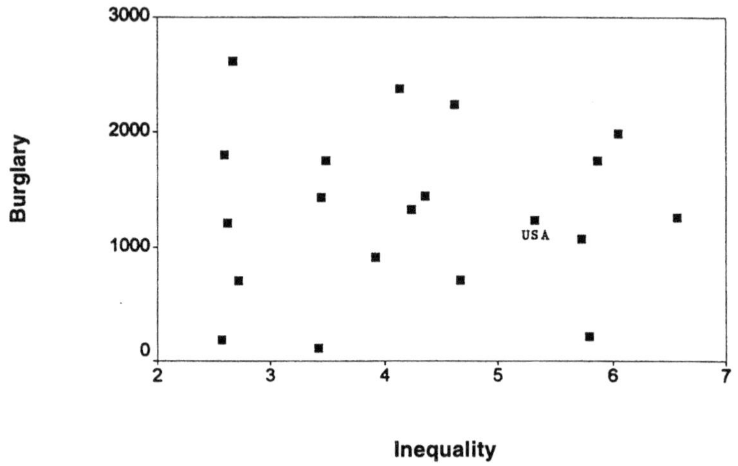

Trends for punishment and inequality are thus consistent with a cross-sectional relationship between inequality and punishment levels among the nations. Yet it is equally apparent from figure 13.1 that the relatively high level of economic inequality alone cannot explain why the United States dishes out punishment so generously. Its prison population is far larger than can be explained by economic inequality alone.

Moreover, sentencing research does not entirely support the expectation that low-income defendants are punished more harshly. Though British judges are more likely to incarcerate defendants convicted of minor crimes when they are unemployed (Crow et al. 1989); in the United States, employment status appears to have little effect on this decision (Klein et al. 1990).

It is possible, of course, that punishment will be harsher where inequality is greater even if low-income defendants are not punished more severely than defendants with higher incomes. It could be that in less egalitarian societies, everyone is punished more severely, though it is unclear from Black's writings just why this should occur. He himself does not offer any explanation as to why this relationship should be found.[17]

Others have offered explanations, but they can hardly be called satisfactory. Instrumental Marxists have argued that the ruling class in

FIGURE 13.4
Auto Theft Rates by Inequality

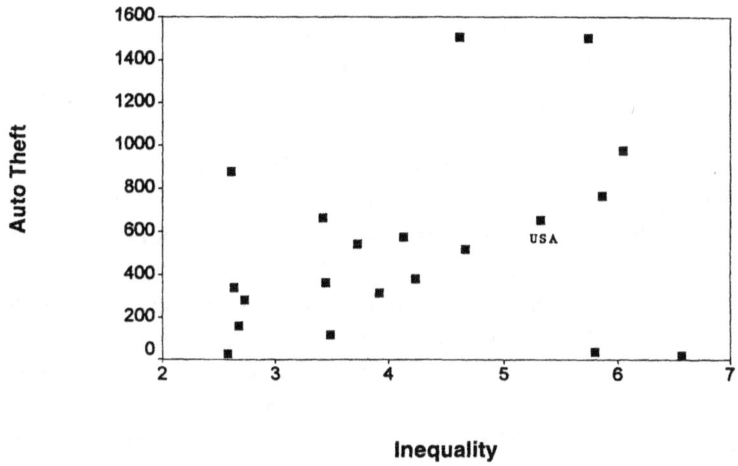

highly stratified societies must punish criminals harshly to prevent exploited and impoverished workers from rebelling against poverty and exploitation (Chambliss and Seidman 1980; Quinney 1977:131–34). The positive correlation found in time series and panel analyses between unemployment and the size of prison populations[18] in a number of market economies[19] (Greenberg 1977a; 1989; Jankovic 1977; Box and Hale 1982, 1985, 1986; Hale 1989; Inverarity and Tedrow 1987; Laffargue and Godefroy 1989; Sabol 1989; Yeager 1979; Wallace 1981; Cappell and Sykes 1991) is consistent with this explanation. Yet the instrumental Marxist answer does not strike one as adequate in nations where the courts operate with a good deal of institutional independence from capitalist control, in which judges are not necessarily drawn from the capitalist class themselves, and in which the poor are not rebelling.

Moreover, the Marxist model, which attributes an expansive penal policy to a small ruling class, fails to account for the widespread belief among the American public that judges and parole boards are too lenient (Warr 1995). In the 1991 General Social Survey[20] (a nationally representative survey covering many issues), only 3.2 percent of 1326 respondents disagreed with the statement that lawbreakers should get stiffer sentences. 83.9 percent thought that the courts are too lenient, only 2.8 percent that they are too harsh. In a recent survey of Texas residents, 76.9

percent favored building more prisons; 93.2 percent disagreed with sentences being made shorter; 87.3 percent disagreed with the greater use of probation; 88.0 percent favored death for murder; and 50 percent favored death for rape (Farnworth, Bennett, and West 1996).

The extent of this support for severe punishments, however, does little to explain variability in the level of punishment across space and time. Why does the United States imprison so much more readily than other nations? Why so much more now than a quarter-century ago?

At first glance, it might seem that another of Black's generalizations could conceivably be relevant: it is that punishment will be greater when there are large differences in status and culture between those who punish and those who are punishing. One would expect the dominant groups in society—those who make and enforce the laws—to punish those they regard as unlike them more harshly. Where groups are ranked hierarchically in prestige or moral repute, those in lower ranked groups should be more vulnerable to imprisonment.

In many countries, minority populations are disproportionately represented in arrest, conviction, and prison statistics (Home Office 1990; Carr-Hill 1987; Biles 1986; Albrecht 1987; Junger 1988; Hudson 1993; Tonry 1993, 1997; Chiricos and Crawford 1995; Jackson 1995). Those who make and enforce American laws are white and have relatively high incomes; those who are punished are disproportionately nonwhite[21] and have low incomes. Well-off white citizens can endorse tough law enforcement measures, confident that they will not be subjected to police abuse, unfair and discriminatory prosecutorial and judicial procedures, long sentences, and harsh prison conditions. Perhaps the United States has so much larger a prison population than the other high-income nations because the others do not have comparable racial-ethnic or class divisions.

Studies of sentencing in the criminal courts might be construed as failing to give consistent support to this idea. A number of statistical studies of criminal sentences have found that on average, the race of the defendant has little or no impact on the outcome (Hagan 1974; Kleck 1981; Blumstein, Cohen, Martin, and Tonry 1983; Wilbanks 1987). On the other hand, other research has found evidence for invidious racial discrimination at various stages of criminal justice processing, unmitigated by the introduction of sentencing guidelines intended to eliminate prejudice (Chiricos and Crawford 1995; Jerome Miller 1996:78). With prosecution and sentencing decisions decentralized, practices are likely to vary with jurisdiction. Generalization on the basis of data from a single jurisdiction should probably be avoided.

The existence of discrimination in the criminal justice system, however, is not central to Black's proposition. In a hypothetical world in which no discrimination whatsoever takes place, knowledge that the recipients of harsh punishment are unlikely to be people like oneself could still lead to support for harsher punishment. This may be as much so in a world where disproportionate minority presence in the ranks of the punishment is due to their high levels of involvement in crime rather than to discrimination within the criminal justice system. Less-punitive nations like Denmark, Sweden, the Netherlands, and Japan are ethnically more homogeneous than the United States.[22]

Research showing that racial prejudice is associated with support for the death penalty (Vidmar and Ellsworth 1974, R. Young 1991; Barkan and Cohn 1994) suggests that greater prejudice may explain America's unusual punitiveness. However, this punitiveness is not required by difference alone. The significance attached to ethnic, racial, and cultural differences is culturally variable. Racial, ethnic, and cultural differences need not preclude solidarity or empathetic identification.

American punitiveness need not be related to cultural difference. Cultural differences between whites and blacks—as measured by educational attainment, for example—have diminished with time. They are surely less now than they were in 1970, making it doubtful that the repression of cultural difference could, by itself, explain why American penal policy has become tougher since then.

Leslie Wilkins (1984:72–73) has proposed a cultural explanation of the relationship between penal practices and income differentials based on the observation that the dispersion of incomes in a society establishes a scale for rewarding valued behavior. In societies where valued performances are rewarded with relatively high salaries, the scale for translating value into monetary awards is more extended than in societies where remuneration is more equal. This same scale should apply when behavior that is disvalued and condemned is punished. Where income inequality is especially high, one should also find draconian penaltes for disvalued behavior. Wilkins thus predicts a positive association between the severity of penal sanctions and income inequality. Insofar as longer sentences tend to produce higher prison populations, one would also expect a positive correlation between the size of prison populations and income inequality. This is just what we found.

Some caution is in order with regard to Wilkins' implicit assumption that in each society there exists a broad consensus about rewards and punishments, or that public opinion determines the distributions of incomes and punishments.[23] One cannot conclude from the mere existence of a high degree of inequality in income that the population as a whole accepts this inequality as just. Growing economic inequality in the United States has been deplored by some commentators[24] (Phillips 1990; Wolff 1995b; DeParle 1996a; David Gordon 1996). Moreover, it is unclear from Wilkins's analysis why the scale for rewarding American performances (positively and negatively) has changed so dramatically in the space of a single generation.

If inequality is to be understood as a direct cause of the imprisonment rate, then it is immaterial why some nations are more unequal than others. Whatever the factors responsible for high inequality, it leads to more punishment. However, the relationship can be understood as something other than simply and directly causal. To consider this alternative possibility it becomes relevant to ask why inequality has grown in the United States. In considering this question, it is relevant to note that inequality has not grown in some of the other "high income" industrial nations such as England and France (Wolff 1994:21–26). It is not an intrinsic feature of a technologically advanced economy.

Various factors have been invoked to explain the growth of inequality in the United States after some decades in which it declined or remained stable: increased returns to education and to nonsalary sources of income such as stocks, bonds, and real estate investments; the loss of blue-collar jobs as corporations have shifted investment abroad; increased competition among blue-collars workers resulting from immigration; a decline in union membership; reductions in welfare benefits; a decline in the real minimum wage; and higher rates of divorce—which can leave mothers and small children in poverty. Researchers are still assessing the precise contributions of these and other factors (Wilson 1987; Moffitt 1990; Levy and Murnane 1992; Danziger and Gottschalk 1993, 1995; Juhn, Murphy and Pierce 1993; Borjas 1994; Freeman 1993; Krugman 1994; Bluestone 1995; Card and Krueger 1995: ch. 9; Borjas, Freeman and Katz 1996; DiNardo, Fortin and Lemieux 1996; David Gordon 1996; Mishel and Schmitt 1996; Tilly 1996; Nielson and Alderson 1997; McCrate 1997); they need not concern us here.

What is critical is that disposable incomes depend not just on extragovernmental social and economic factors, but also on the distribution of the tax burden and of governmental subsidies, including direct transfer payments and tax benefits. Constant exposure to condemnations of welfare for the poor makes it easy to forget that there are large (and largely unpublicized) subsidies to middle- and upper-income groups. Income tax deductions for interest paid on home mortgages are as much a subsidy as the provision of public housing. The federal government currently spends $66 billion a year on tax deductions for property taxes and interest paid on mortgages, quadruple the amount spent on low-income housing. According to DeParle (1996a), "more than two-thirds of it goes to families with incomes above $75,000." Bailouts for failing businesses are as much subsidies as unemployment compensation (Glasberg and Skidmore 1997). Federally guaranteed student loans, and payments to farmers for not planting their fields, are as much subsidies as unemployment compensation and AFDC (aid to families with dependent children) payments. Subsidies to business add up to $85 billion a year (Fischer et al. 1996:145). In addition to direct subsidies, such state interventions as minimum wage laws, tariffs, import quotas, and immigration policies affect economic outcomes indirectly through their effects on supply and demand for labor and commodities.

According to one estimate, in 1991, American households with incomes under $10,000 received a total of $5,690 in tax benefits and direct transfer payments, while households with incomes over $100,000 received $9,280—almost twice as much. Were indirect subsidies and the provision of public goods and services that largely benefit middle- and upper-income households to be taken into account, the figures would change but the disparity would almost surely be even larger (Beeghley and Dwyer 1989).

This disproportionality has increased over time. Between 1980 and 1991 federal outlays to households with incomes under $10,000 dropped by 7 percent in constant dollars, while those to households with incomes over $200,000 doubled (Howe and Longman 1992). If incomes are becoming more unequal, we may infer not only that some forms of income-producing activity have become more lucrative than others, but also that the government has not intervened effectively to compensate for this trend. In many ways, the government exacerbates it. No political movement has mobilized effective opposition to this exacerbation.

Income distributions, then, are as much an outcome of "politics" as of "economics." The direction and extent of state intervention to increase or reduce economic inequality may be taken as a measure of the degree to which a concern for the well-being of low-income strata has been made a goal of public policy. These policies thus indicate the extent to which a state is a class state. Formally, that is, in law, the United States does not have a class state. Eligibility to vote and to hold public office are not restricted by class, and at least in principle, citizens of all classes are protected equally by law. Still, the benefits of citizenship are very unequally distributed.

Some economists have argued otherwise. In the long run, they contend, redistributive welfare policies do a disservice to the poor. By reducing the incentive to invest in physical or human capital, and by reducing the supply of potentially productive labor, high minimum wage laws and generous welfare policies supposedly slow economic growth (Gilder 1981; Alesina and Rodrik 1994; Henderson 1997). In the long run, they prevent the pie that feeds all classes from expanding.

Unlike the subsidies to the rich, those that benefit the poor are denounced as being especially pernicious. According to anthropologist Marvin Harris (1981:131), in providing aid to families of dependent children, "the federal government places its stamp of approval on both the fatherless inner-city family and the pursuit of crime as the solution to black men's unemployment problems."

Consistent with this anti-welfare position, the more egalitarian European countries have higher levels of unemployment and lower levels of new job creation than the less egalitarian United States. In our sample, the correlation between inequality and GNP per capita is 0.31. Yet, a more systematic analysis of the evidence does not seem to support the antiredistribution argument. One reason the European countries have higher unemployment rates than the United States is that the United States more readily imprisons its unemployed, and prisoners are not counted in unemployment statistics (Western and Beckett 1997). Higher levels of inequality reduce nations' economic growth for reasons unrelated to redistribution (such as making education unaffordable to those in low-income brackets). In some circumstances, redistributive policies can enhance economic growth, or at least have no detrimental impact (Blank 1994; Chang 1994; Persson and Tabellini 1994; Fischer et al. 1997; Bénabou, forthcoming).

Just as a society's concern for those with little money is manifested in its welfare policy, its willingness to execute and to imprison readily and for long periods indicates the extent to which the well-being of criminal offenders figures into governmental response to violations of the law. Many of those punished for law violation are drawn from low-income brackets, and so concern for the well-being of one group is not unrelated to concern for the other.

One may thus see the comparative leniency of the Dutch and Scandinavian criminal justice systems and their low degree of economic inequality (which is substantially a product of their generously funded welfare systems[25]) as manifestations of a high degree of empathic identification and concern for the well-being of others. Where this identification and concern are high, citizens will tend to support social-democratic measures that partly detach economic well-being from fate in the marketplace. They will think that a member of the polity is entitled to an adequate standard of living simply by virtue of being a member of society, independently of any individually earned or inherited merit. Market outcomes themselves will be seen as the product of multiple contingencies, such as fluctuations in labor market conditions, that lie outside an individual's control and that should not play too large a role in determining someone's life chances. Principles of redistributive justice moderate commodification of labor in a market economy.

Citizens in the more collectively oriented societies will also tend to identify with criminals, not just with their victims. They will tend to see criminal conduct as stemming in part from social, economic, and familial conditions over which law violators exercise little control. Operating on the principle, "there but for the grace of God go I," citizens will be less prone to insist on harsh punishment for those who break the law. In arguing that identification with victims in homogeneous societies will lead to harsh punishment, Durkheim neglected to consider that identification with perpetrators who are members of the same society would tend to mute punitiveness.

Recent trends in American penal practices reflect changes in the level of this identification. In the mid-1960s, civil rights legislation gained the support of a substantial fraction of the white population, and the president launched a war on poverty. Both developments signal increased empathetic identification with minority and low-income populations. In the same years, prison populations dropped appreciably and support for the death penalty fell, even as reported crime rates and arrest rates were rising.

The significance of both trends may be highlighted by recalling one of the critical insights of Durkheim's discussion of organic solidarity. Market exchanges, Durkheim observed, are not self-enforcing. Where they occur as part of an ongoing relationship, fairness may need no external guarantees because each partner will find it advantageous to retain the good will of the other. But in a complex market economy, many business dealings do not occur in the context of an ongoing relationship. And the informal pressures and constraints that might operate in a small-scale band or tribal society, or in a small town in a capitalist society into which the impersonality of the market has not fully penetrated, cannot be counted on to uphold transactions or ensure fairness. Thus parties may succumb to the temptation to back out of an earlier agreement, or to exploit or cheat others when it is advantageous. Hence the state may be needed to enforce contracts, and to ensure that contracts meet standards of fairness. This insight can be generalized more broadly. In the complex conditions of modern society, distributional fairness is not something that market institutions can be counted on to supply. It requires the intervention of the state. However, as we have seen, state intervention does not necessarily bring about distributional equality or fairness. On the contrary, it can itself give rise to, or exacerbate, inequality and unfairness.

In Durkheim's model of social evolution, a complex division of labor is not created by the state; it occurs when unsuccessful competitors in existing occupations devise new occupations. However, the origins of modern market economies cannot be understood through this model of social evolution. An alternative model can be constructed by drawing on Durkheim's discussion of what he calls "abnormal forms" of the division of labor.

Abnormal Forms of the Division of Labor

Writing broadly of France at the end of the nineteenth century, Durkheim (1933:354–88) maintained that the division of labor brought about by the industrial revolution was neither mechanical nor organic. Instead, it was "abnormal." The growth of industry had been so rapid that new norms to govern industry had not had time to evolve; hence the division of labor was "anomic"—unregulated. In the absence of economic planning, investment decisions were vulnerable to miscalculation, triggering economic crises. The scale of business enterprises had grown to the point where communication between workers and employers had broken down. Instead of cooperation, the classes fought.

In traditional society, people were, according to Durkheim, satisfied with the station in life into which they were born. Now no longer willing to stay in their customary place, they were nevertheless excluded from many career lines. Where there were no formal barriers, obstacles such as lack of educational qualifications and financial assets could still prevent them from taking up certain occupations: "Even today among the most cultivated peoples, there are careers which are either totally closed or very difficult to be entered into by those who are bereft of fortune" (Durkheim 1933: 378).

When individuals cannot choose their occupations on the basis of their interests and talents, roles are allocated inefficiently, and the division of labor is "forced." Inequalities of wealth also open the door to exploitation. Rewards are incommensurate with efforts. If one social class is obliged, in order to live, to offer its services at any price, while the other can do without them, thanks to the resources at its disposal, which are not however necessarily due to any social superiority, the second unjustly dominates the first. In other words, there cannot be rich and poor at birth without there being unjust contracts (Durkheim 1933:384).With an abnormal division of labor, "only an imperfect and troubled solidarity is possible."

Although several sociologists have stressed the theoretical importance of Durkheim's discussion of the abnormal forms of the division of labor (Taylor, Walton, and Young 1973; Pearce 1989), Durkheim's failure to incorporate the abnormal forms into his model of legal evolution has allowed sociologists to ignore them when explicating Durkheim's analysis of law.[26]

Though deeply indebted to Marxian critiques of capitalism, Durkheim's decision to refer to the division of labor characteristic of his own day as "abnormal" suggested—contrary to Marxian analyses—that irrationality and exploitation were transient and ephemeral features of industrial capitalism, rather than essential to it (Schwendinger and Schwendinger 1974). They were, in other words, the result of an adaptive lag. Industrialization had taken place so rapidly that society had not had time to develop the institutions and norms needed to cope with the unprecedented problems it created. Hoping that the state would take up the challenge of these new problems, Durkheim did not need to incorporate them into his model charting long-term trends in legal evolution. It is, however, not difficult to do so.

As Durkheim argued, early human societies had a relatively low division of labor, but that does not mean cooperation and mutual dependence was absent. Because every member of a small-scale society is important to the survival of the collective, and because members are linked to one another in long-lasting multiplex relationships that extend cooperation and dependence across different social functions (work, ritual, reproduction, socialization), dispute resolution tends to emphasize conciliation and restitution. Harsh punishment is rare because it would rupture these relationships and alienate those punished from the group, along with their families, friends and allies. Solidarity in such societies is based in part on interdependence (organic solidarity), but affiliation to kinship groups within a tribe (lineage or clan, for example) is also an important source of identity and loyalty, and strongly influences responses to norm violations. Culturally mandated redistributive processes may prevent stratification from destroying this solidarity. Such societies combine some of the features Durkheim links with organic solidarity with some of those he associates with mechanical solidarity.

As human societies become more productive, and as the size of the group increases, the division of labor becomes more complex. Inequalities of stratification and power appear, and with them the state forms as a specialized social agency[27] (Engels 1942). States try, and often succeed, to establish their own authority and gain new sources of revenue by replacing retaliatory and conciliatory dispute-processing procedures with compulsory, punitive procedures under their own control.[28] They may give formal recognition to such social cleavages as castes and estates, and limit mobility between them through legal proscriptions. Class divisions based on the forcible extraction of surplus from slaves or serfs define the division of labor as forced and exploitative.

In societies where a forced division of labor is formally recognized in law, punishment will typically be harsher than in the more egalitarian small-scale primitive societies. The enlarged scale of the group means that individual norm violators may be considered expendable. The death penalty may be applied far more generously than in a band or tribal society. Punishment may also entail assignment to a degraded social status and to forced labor, e.g., penal slavery (Sellin 1976; French 1997).

In the usual case, offenses committed by individual members of the lower orders against their social superiors will be treated more harshly than vice versa, but this is not always the case. Elites may be expected to adhere to higher standards of conduct, and may be punished more heavily when they violate them. In the ancient Hindu Laws of Manu, for example, Brahmins are punished more harshly for certain infractions than members of other castes.

Where the state is not too powerful, many rule violations may be punished privately rather than publicly. A citizen head of household, for example, may hold the authority to punish members of his household, including slaves as well as wives and children. Even where the household head has the authority to kill his dependents—as the Roman *pater familias* did in certain cases—his interest in not losing an heir, or the services of a wife or slave, or the political support of his wife's family, might induce him to overlook an offense or to chastise the offender mildly. In the antebellum South, for example, slave-holders disciplined their slaves by whipping them, but had an incentive not to kill or incapacitate them. After the slaves were emancipated, their former masters, now their employers and landlords, had no such incentive. According to William E. Strong, Inspector General of the Freedmen's Bureau:

> The freedmen are in a worse position than they ever were as slaves. When they were held in bondage they were, as a rule, treated well; cases of extreme cruelty were very rare.... Now it is quite different, they have no interest in them, and seem to take every opportunity to vent their rage and hatred upon the blacks. They are frequently beaten unmercifully, and shot down like wild beasts, without any provocation.... (O. Howard 1866, quoted in Simon, 1991)

In many societies characterized by politically formalized abnormal divisions of labor, social movements developed to eliminate the formal distinctions between classes or estates. On the whole they have enjoyed striking success. Throughout most of the world feudalism and slavery have been abolished. In many countries, labor movements and socialist movements mobilized to reduce or abolish the exploitative class relationships implicated in the forced division of labor, with varying degrees of success.

Law has played a critical role in the transition toward a society in which occupational choice is unrestricted, and in which the conditions of work are not exploitative. It was through legal enactments that feudalism and slavery were abolished, and legal impediments to the employment of certain categories of people (such as women or members of religious and racial minorities) ended. Through legislation prohibiting discrimination in employment on the basis of race, sex, religion, and national origin, the state acted to remove long-standing public and private barriers to participation in the market economy.

In the United States, further legal steps were taken to remove the most glaring obstacles to full participation in social and political life.[29] Voting rights were extended to blacks and women, and equality of citizens before the law was established as a constitutional principle. The Supreme Court struck down state legislation prohibiting racial intermarriage. The segregation of schools, public transportation, public facilities, and housing was ended. Public higher education expanded to give opportunities to classes of students who did not have them previously.

Minimum wage laws were adopted to prevent exploitation at the workplace. Numerous legal measures, including hours restrictions, child labor laws, and occupational safety and health regulation, were adopted to protect the physical and mental well-being of workers. Unemployment compensation, compensation for on-the-job injuries, and grants to parents of dependent children were instituted to give workers and their families a source of financial support independent of employment. Regulations were put in place to protect consumers against fraud, unsafe products, and oligopolistic or monopolistic pricing practices. When first proposed, many of these steps were resisted, sometimes violently. Some of them were sought because they offered advantages to capitalists rather than workers or consumers. Nevertheless, the long-run trend has been one of eliminating particularistic barriers to full social participation, and of providing limited shelter from the vicissitudes of the capitalist market economy.

All these steps can be seen as elements of a broad trend to move society from one with an abnormal, forced division of labor to one more closely approximating Durkheim's description of organic solidarity. In recent years this trend continued with the establishment of affirmative action programs in employment and education, and minority set-asides for government contracts, justified by the belief that in a society with a centuries-long history of legally enforced white supremacy, mere formal legal equality would not suffice to bring about equal outcomes or genuine organic solidarity in any reasonable time period.

Though these efforts have not brought about full parity of the races or sexes, though they have not removed all obstacles to freedom of occupational choice or advancement, or fully protected workers, they have had partial success. Welfare programs, denounced by conservatives for fostering dependency and sanctioning immorality, have made major inroads on poverty. Crossnational research shows that the higher the welfare benefits in a nation, the greater the ability of recipients to escape poverty (Duncan et al. 1993). A recent evaluation of such American welfare programs as food stamps, housing assistance, school lunch programs, the earned-income tax credit, Social Security, and Aid to Families with Dependent Children, based on Census Bureau data, concluded that: "federal and state antipoverty programs have lifted millions of children out of poverty. Many of those who remained poor were significantly less poor than they would have been without government assistance" (Primus et al. 1996:1; also see Ozawa 1995). Open admissions to the City University of New York, begun in 1970, enabled thousands of students who would otherwise have been excluded from higher education, to obtain bachelors' degrees and better jobs (Arenson 1996a).

Between 1971 and 1985, the black-white gap in high school completion narrowed dramatically—from 23 to 6 percentage points (with a slight widening—to 7 points—after that) (National Center for Education Statistics 1995:72–73). The black middle class is now substantially larger than it was a generation ago (Landry 1987) and larger than it would have been in the absence of such programs as subsidized loans for higher education, affirmative action, and federal civil rights legislation (Lavin and Hyllegard 1996; "A Small Ripple" 1996). The number of marriages between blacks and whites, though low, has risen appreciably, pointing to increased social interaction, and growing acceptance of intermarriage (Kalmijn 1993; Holmes 1996a). Black representation in Congress, and in state and local government, has grown. Even though black arrest rates are substantially higher than white rates, over time the gap has narrowed.[30]

Equally dramatic gains have been made in relation to gender equality. All the Western democracies have extended the right to vote to women. Though the Equal Rights Amendment to the U.S. Constitution, intended to give authoritative backing to the equality of the sexes, was defeated, women have entered the labor force in large numbers, and many are pursuing careers in the professions, government, and the business world. The gap in wages between women and men has gradually narrowed (Kemp 1994:175). According to government figures, the number of women and racial minorities in corporate management has tripled over the last thirty years (Myerson 1997).

Durkheim argued that as the division of labor became more complex, the collective conscience would weaken, ameliorating punitive impulses. Humanitarian movements would seek to reclaim the criminals who were being destroyed in public exhibitions of power. Arguably, these movements developed only at the point where the expansion of the market economy made it appear practical to deal with large numbers of offenders without killing them or sending them into exile (Rusche and Kirchheimer 1939). Moreover, penal reformers' motivations were not exclusively benevolent and altruistic. The reformers who campaigned to replace executions, penal slavery and transportation to overseas penal colonies with prison sentences, half-way houses, and job-training programs were often alarmed by lower-class criminality, and threatened by the prospect of lower-class radicalism. However, their agenda of instituting more effective control over criminals, workers, and immigrants (Platt 1969; Foucault 1977; Ignatieff 1978: 58; Humphries and Greenberg 1981; Garland 1985; Polsky 1991; Simon

1993) does not necessarily mean that "humanitarian" concerns were altogether absent. Regardless of the complex factors that made it possible, the transformation of sentiment occurred.

Consider John Howard, the Bedfordshire sheriff who documented the filth and squalor of eighteenth-century English and continental jails. At a time when degrading jail conditions were widely known but considered inevitable—and perhaps desirable as a deterrent—Howard (1780) argued that the indiscriminate mixing of inmates exposed the innocent and the novice to the influence of hardened criminals, thereby promoting crime. Clean, orderly, disciplined jails, he contended, could reform criminals. This was a pragmatic argument, not an appeal to humanitarian sentiment. Yet, following a religious conversion, Howard also felt acutely that he was as much a sinner as were the prisoners, and shared with them a common humanity. Writing in an unpublished manuscript, he thanked God for making "such a worm" as himself "the Instrument of alleviating the miseries of my fellow creatures and to connect more strongly the social bond by mutual exertions for mutual relief" (quoted in Ignatieff 1978:56). There is little reason to think Howard was being hypocritical when writing this private document. In the previous generation, the Anglican priest John Wesley also felt a common sense of humanity with prisoners, but confined his efforts on their behalf to preaching sermons for them at the gallows (Ignatieff 1978:55). Whereas Wesley sought to save lost souls for the world to come, Howard wanted to lead them to a more virtuous life in this world, through better jail conditions (and stricter discipline within them).

In the following century, when novelist Charles Dickens sent letters to the *Daily News* arguing for the abolition of capital punishment, he insisted that abolition was "for the advantage of society, for the prevention of crime, and without the least reference to, or tenderness for any individual malefactor whatever." Yet in one of those letters he also wrote that after he and his friends had witnessed the hanging of a murderer, one whose treachery they detested:

> if any one among us could have saved the man (we said so, afterwards, with one accord) he would have done it. It was so loathsome, pitiful, and vile a sight, that the law appeared to be as bad as he, or worse; being very much the stronger, and shedding around it a far more dismal contagion. (quoted in Collins 1968:226)

Dickens' public disavowal of sentimentality probably reflected his defensiveness in the face of Thackeray's attacks on death penalty abolitionists for being effeminate.

Similar themes appear in the writings of American penal reformers. The Constitution of the Philadelphia Society for Alleviating the Miseries of Public Prisons (1787) announced that the obligations of benevolence, "founded on the precepts and example of the author of Christianity, are not canceled by the follies or crimes of our fellow-creatures" and called for the extension of compassion to suffering prisoners (Pillsbury 1989). They and like-minded reformers had an assimilationist agenda; they sought to incorporate wrong-doers into the social body rather than to expel them. It is true that the incorporation did not usually challenge class inequality in any fundamental way. Thus Elizabeth Fry, the Quaker who brought solace to women prisoners in early nineteenth-century England, and lobbied for prison reform, wrote about her servants that "We are not their familiars or equals in the things of life, for we have reason to believe that difference in our status is ordered by a wiser [one] than ourselves" (Simeral 1916:154). Reformed punishment could, indeed, be considered a more sophisticated and effective instrument of class rule than the cruder methods relied upon previously.

It is also true that the incorporation was to be on the reformers' terms, that it required assimilation to their culture, and that it was to be implemented coercively. Their moralism and their concentration on helping individuals while failing to change social-structural sources of marginalization doomed many of their efforts to uplift the poor and steer criminals to the straight-and-narrow. All this has had major implications for the character of the programs reformers proposed and implemented. Nonetheless, their agenda was premised on a humanity that controllers and controlled shared.

Though some penologists and criminologists of the late nineteenth and twentieth centuries openly embraced doctrines of racial inferiority (Lombroso 1871, 1876) this was never a prominent element in the reformist agenda. In the last half-century reformers have generally endorsed the goal of full citizenship and participation of those being reformed. This democratic goal is radically different from those sought by state punishment systems and their defenders in early modern Europe (Foucault 1977; Langbein 1977; Spierenberg 1984, 1991).

As with measures to benefit workers and consumers, the reformers' agendas were rarely implemented in full, but over the past two centuries much was accomplished. Fines, imprisonment, probation, and parole became the primary state sanctions, largely replacing execution, exile, and corporal punishment. Rehabilitative programs were introduced into the prison, albeit on a very modest scale. Juvenile courts and reformatories were established, and juvenile arrest records were sealed to protect juveniles from the stigma of a conviction.

To protect the innocent and to ensure fairness, the Supreme Court extended due process protections to suspects and defendants in criminal cases. To prevent punishment from disrupting ties to family and community, and to facilitate offender "re-integration," reformers argued for the creation of "alternatives to incarceration" located in the community (Alper 1974; Perlstein and Phelps 1995). Concerned that prosecutors and judges were discriminating invidiously against blacks and other minorities, reformers proposed restrictions on the exercise of judicial discretion in sentencing (American Friends Service Committee Working Party 1971).

The toughening of criminal justice policy reverses a number of these trends, just as reversals of incorporative trends are taking place on policies not directly related to crime, where the state has been promoting a transition from a forced division of labor toward organic solidarity. Consider regulation, which, ever since the Progressive Era, has been a major instrument for the protection of workers and consumers. President Ronald Reagan established a Task Force on Economic Competitiveness charged with the elimination of regulatory measures that imposed excessive costs on business. Under President George Bush, its successor, the Council on Competitiveness, made numerous changes in regulations drafted by the Environmental Protection Agency, many of them taken directly from documents prepared by the companies being regulated. The Council eliminated a proposed ban on incinerating lead batteries, and recycling provisions for new incinerators. It speeded up the Food and Drug Administration's approval procedure for new medical drugs, blocked attempts to regulate genetically engineered microbes, drugs and foods, and sponsored a bill to end all laws regulating the environment as infringing on property rights protected by the constitution (Tokar 1992).

Limits on welfare benefits for the poor and for immigrants have been enacted into law, with support from both major political parties. The federal income tax schedule has been made more regressive. Democratic and Republican politicians call for further tax cuts for the middle and upper classes, while ignoring the greater need of low-income citizens. Federal legislation has barred lawyers in federally financed Legal Services offices from handling class action suits on behalf of the poor (Greenhouse 1996). City governments have repressed begging in public places, and used zoning regulations to stop religious institutions from operating soup-kitchens to feed the homeless (Kress 1994).

Legislatively imposed budget cuts have forced retrenchment in public higher education. At a time when the stock of low-income rental housing has shrunk, federal funding for subsidized housing has been cut back sharply (O'Flaherty 1996; DeParle 1996b). In response to court decisions curbing preference programs, minority set-aside programs intended to help minority contractors obtain government contracts have been dismantled, resulting in the closing of large numbers of minority-owned businesses (Pear 1990; Hinds 1991; Holmes 1996b).

In California, a referendum calling for an end to affirmative action programs in state institutions passed in a popular vote, and has now gone into effect after surviving a court challenge. Though legal protection against discrimination in employment remains in effect, staff cuts at the Equal Employment Opportunity Commission ostensibly made for budgetary reasons have led to a large and growing backlog of unresolved cases[31] (Kilborn 1994). In much the same way, lack of enforcement of sanitation rules for farm workers—including requirements that employers provide toilet facilities and fresh drinking water—have effectively nullified the protections nominally provided by the Occupational Safety and Health Act (Noble 1988).

Collectively, these measures represent a withdrawal from public commitment to transform society from an abnormal division of labor to one based on organic solidarity. Where regulatory enforcement is weakened, businesses operate anomically; the interests of consumers in purchasing safe and reliable products, of employees in working in a safe work environment, and of all residents in an environment that is not dangerously polluted, are sacrificed to profit maximization.

In principle, injured parties can still seek remedies through private law suits, but long backlogs in the courts and the high cost of litigation make this remedy impractical, if not unattainable, for many potential plaintiffs.[32] To avoid the costs of litigation and the risk of losing law suits, many businesses are requiring as a condition of employment that employees sign away their rights to bring court cases alleging discrimination (Myerson 1997).

The fall in real wages that many workers have experienced over the last two decades, paralleled by rising productivity and growth in profits, and increases in wealth and income for the rich, indicates that capitalist firms are becoming more exploitative. Ostensibly, some of the new measures—such as the lifetime limit on welfare imposed by federal legislation in 1996—are intended to encourage those who now lie outside the division of labor to enter it by removing disincentives to job-seeking. There is, however, little reason to think that millions of new jobs for new workers with limited skills and work experience will be created quickly. The gap between needs and the welfare support to be withdrawn is far in excess of what private charities can conceivably supply. In New York City alone, almost 470,000 adults were on welfare in August, 1996. Under the new federal law just signed, at least 80 percent of these will lose welfare benefits within five years. Labor market specialists assert that the paid labor market is capable of absorbing only a small fraction of this number when their eligibility for welfare ends[33] (Finder 1996).

To the extent that welfare recipients do seek employment, they will exert downward pressure on wages, increasing the number of working poor with incomes below the poverty line, and intensifying exploitation. The denial of further benefits to welfare mothers who bear additional children, which some states have adopted, may or may not reduce out-of-wedlock births, but will surely leave families into which such children are born even more impoverished. The exclusion of children of illegal immigrants from public schools—a proposal not yet enacted into law—is more likely to create a new generation of illiterates and innumerates than it is to curtail illegal immigration. Work requirements for welfare, supposedly intended to prepare recipients for jobs, are interfering with recipients' efforts to earn the college degrees that will help them achieve upward mobility (Arenson 1996b).

For many of those who do not inherit substantial wealth, education is crucial to upward mobility. Rapid rises in college tuition at a time when federal loans for college are being cut are making it more difficult for prospective students to attend college, and force them to choose colleges on the basis of financial considerations, rather than for educational reasons (Geraghty 1997). Escape from the lower class through education is becoming more difficult.

On average, poor children do not perform as well in school, and independently of their performance and talents, are less likely to attend college (Sewell and Shah 1967; Persell 1977; Hill and Sandford 1995; Alexander and Entwisle 1996). In the absence of outside intervention, the children of the lower classes will largely remain in their class of origin. With reduced intergenerational mobility, the United States will more closely approximate a caste system, one sustained not by formal barriers between castes, but by *de facto* barriers arising from differences in the advantages that accrue to current class positions.[34]

The developments in criminal justice and those concerning welfare and inequality feed on one another. Prisons are expensive to build and to operate. The billions spent on police and prisons have created a "prison-industrial complex" that lobbies for further spending increases (Christie 1993; Lilly and Knepper 1993; Donziger 1996:85–96). At a time when politicians are loath to raise taxes or to increase deficit spending, a vast expansion in prison costs implies a corresponding contraction in the availability of funds for welfare or education.[35] Funds spent building new prisons are unavailable for opening new colleges that might admit students who believe they are being deprived of a college education by affirmative action programs.

The ban on the use of Pell grants to enable prison inmates, many of whom have serious educational deficits, to take college courses, which was put in place by the 104th Congress, will make it harder for ex-convicts to repair these deficits while in prison. A criminal record can further damage prospects for future employment and lawful earnings.[36] Trying juvenile offenders in criminal courts and imprisoning those convicted will enlarge the pool of people who have limited prospects of improving their returns in lawful labor markets. Given current arrest and imprisonment patterns, this labor market damage will impinge very disproportionately on black and Latino males.

Where prospects for lawful remunerative stable employment and upward mobility are restricted, the incentive to acquire income illegally through theft, prostitution, and the sale of narcotics is enhanced;[37] and—leaving aside the effect of "repeat offenders" legislation—those with a criminal record have less to lose from a subsequent arrest or conviction.

High crime rates in a neighborhood discourage business investment, and provide incentives for current residents and businesses who can afford to relocate to do so, increasing the spatial segregation that high economic inequality tends to promote. Because jobs are often found through contacts with those who already have them, these developments further reduce economic opportunities for local residents who cannot move (Bénabou 1993).

Individually and in the aggregate, levels of violence rise with poverty (e.g., Eberts and Schwirian 1968; Loftin and Hill 1974; Braithwaite 1979; Braithwaite and Braithwaite 1986; Messner 1980, 1982; Kick and LaFree 1985; Blau and Blau 1982; Bailey 1984; Simpson 1985;

Avison and Loring 1986; Krahn, Hartnagel and Gartrell 1986; Rosenfeld 1986; Peterson and Bailey 1988b; Maume 1989; Unnithan and Whitt 1992; Reiss and Roth 1993:130–31), and are reduced by government support for the poor (DeFronzo 1983; Rosenfeld 1986). Poverty increases the incidence of child abuse and domestic violence (Elmer 1967; Gil 1970; Gelles 1974; Maden and Wrench 1977; Straus and Gelles 1990; Straus, Gelles, and Steinmetz 1980). Thus, a decline in the economic well-being of the lower classes can be expected to increase levels of violence.[38] To the extent that the prevention of victimization is a reason or a pretext for more punishment, the new anti-welfare policies will help to keep violence and victimization at appropriately high levels.

It could be objected that the deteriorating economic circumstances of the lower classes did not lead to large increases in theft and violence in the recent past. Apart from a modest increase in violence in the late 1980s, almost certainly related to the crack trade, homicide rates were quite stable between 1970 and 1990. The illegal drug market undoubtedly made it possible for many nominally unemployed individuals to avoid stealing, and the expansion of the prison system took many criminals out of circulation. Just how much prison expansion contributed to keeping crime rates from getting out of hand is not entirely clear, but it may have done a good deal through deterrence and incapacitation of prospective law violators (Marvell and Moody 1994; Spelman 1994; Wicharaya 1995; Levitt 1996). The argument often made by opponents of further prison construction—that the stability of crime rates in the face of an enormous expansion in the prison population proves the ineffectiveness of imprisonment at stopping crime—neglects the possibility that crime rates might have grown a great deal for reasons having to do with the state of the economy, had the prison populations not risen.[39]

Why the Backlash?

Social trends do not halt or reverse automatically. It is often easier to continue or expand an effort than to turn it around. Yet government crime policy did reverse course. While punishment was a major component of crime policy during the 1960s, it was not the only component of the crime-fighting strategy that Presidents Kennedy and Johnson were devising. Even while fashioning new law-enforcement initiatives, they also proposed an anti-poverty program as another important element of their strategy. In the interests of fairness, they proposed to give defendants more rights in court. As U.S. Attorney General, Robert F.

Kennedy proposed that the federal government should make it possible for indigent defendants to be represented by attorneys in court (Calder 1982; Steel and Steger 1988). The Kerner Report, issued in the aftermath of large-scale rioting, proposed new initiatives to improve black employment prospects, education, housing and welfare, and to prevent abusive behavior on the part of the police (National Advisory Commission, 1968). Yet, once Richard Nixon took office in 1968, strategies for reducing crime that tried to alter its "root causes" no longer had presidential backing, and criminal justice proposals originating in the White House entailed strengthening, not weakening, enforcement capabilities. This reversal, alongside a reversal of welfare policy, calls for explanation.

Ask someone who supports the abandonment of egalitarian social policies and favors more punitive penal strategies why ameliorative policies lost favor, and you will be told that the old policies were obviously failing. Billions of dollars had been spent in the War on Poverty, yet welfare rolls rose,[40] and so did crime. Instead of helping recipients to become self-supporting, welfare undermined the work ethic. Instead of bringing about integration, mandatory school bussing hastened "white flight," leaving schools segregated and cities deprived of tax revenues (Coleman, Kelly, and Moore 1975; Henig 1994:102). Liberal elitist judges were flouting the will of the people on such issues as school prayer, school desegregation, and abortion rights. Minimum wage laws and pollution control cost jobs. The breakdown of traditional morality, and Supreme Court decisions favoring criminals, were leading to promiscuity, illegitimacy, drug use and violence. Programs to rehabilitate criminals did not work. The public became aware of these difficulties, and demanded that politicians reverse course (Gilder 1981; Murray 1984; Van den Haag 1975; Wilson 1975; Mead 1992).

Many of these claims do not withstand close scrutiny. Efforts to reduce poverty and eliminate discrimination accomplished much, and would have accomplished more had more resources been devoted to implementation and enforcement. There is little evidence that overly generous welfare provisions increased welfare rolls, discouraged recipients from seeking jobs, or increased teenage pregnancies (Wilson 1987; Moffitt 1990; Hacker 1992; Jencks 1992; Tonry 1995:12–17; Luker 1996). Some research suggests that the minimum wage law, criticized by economists for increasing youth unemployment, does not in fact do so (Card and Krueger 1995; Blinder 1996). The bussing of school children probably had little impact on white flight (Rosell 1975–1976;

Pettigrew and Green 1976). Many government initiatives and regulatory interventions have demonstrably improved public health and safety, and have benefitted the public in other ways (Kuttner 1996).

Although conservative critics denounced the Supreme Court for handcuffing police by requiring that defendants be informed of their rights, that indigent defendants be given attorneys, and that illegally obtained evidence could not be introduced in trial, these decisions did little to hinder law enforcement (Fyfe 1983; van Duizend, Sutton, and Carter 1984:91; Gordon 1990:34–36). The attacks on the Supreme Court were made without any basis in research whatsoever.

Changes in incarceration policy were not required by clear research results, and some of them were made notwithstanding experts' serious reservations about their consequences (Pillsbury 1995). The flat assertion that "rehabilitation doesn't work" (Robison and Smith 1971; Martinson 1974) was quickly seen to be an overstatement. Some treatment evaluations did show signs of effectiveness, though many did not (Ross and Gendreau 1980; Jenkins and Brown 1988; Cullen and Gendreau 1989; Whitehead and Lab 1989, 1990; Andrews et al. 1990a, 1990b). A research report claiming that the death penalty was a powerful deterrent of homicide (Ehrlich 1975) was promptly shown to rely on questionable statistical procedures (Passell and Taylor 1975; Bowers and Pierce 1975; Klein, Forst and Filatov 1978; Bowers 1988).

Studies showed that city crime rates were unresponsive to increases in the size of the police force (Greenberg, Kessler, and Logan 1979, Greenberg and Kessler 1982; Rich, Lineberry, and Jacob 1982), making the hiring of more police a dubious way to reduce crime. Cost-effectiveness assessments asserting that imprisonment was a good investment because it prevented losses greatly in excess of its costs (Zedlewski 1985, 1987) were shown to rest on equally dubious assumptions (Zimring and Hawkins 1988; Greenberg 1990). It appears that early intervention programs such as training parents of children at risk for delinquency, and providing incentives to discourage early school-leaving, would be far more cost-effective than mandatory prison sentences for repeat offenders (Greenwood 1996).

Of course, just because doubts have been raised about conservative, hard-line claims does not mean that they are entirely lacking in substance. One need not be a conservative to recognize that some regulatory agencies were captured by the industries they were supposedly regulating, or that they failed to protect the public (Fellmuth 1970; McAvoy 1976; Wilson 1981). Introspection will convince most people that the threat of punishment has some deterrent value, and common sense indicates that when active law-breakers are confined behind bars, some crime is prevented by virtue of their incarceration. Surely some people who could work exploit the welfare system. Yet, even if all the liberal efforts had been failures, failure need not require the abandonment of an enterprise. If an intervention is considered worthwhile, failure can be met with further experimentation. In some circumstances it may indicate the need for more far-reaching intervention.

It is an oversimplification to assert, as James Q. Wilson (1975) has, that politicians were forced to take tough stands because leniency was failing, and that the public was frightened by rising crime. Some hard-line proposals—notably narcotics control measures—retain their popularity with politicians and public despite failures that have been noted by critics over and over again. Popular support for gun control has not swayed politicians who fear retribution from the National Rifle Association. Moreover, public opinion, though increasingly punitive in recent years, has not been univocal. When the newly elected President Reagan announced in 1980 that "the public wants criminals clobbered, and that is what we are going to do" (quoted in Steel and Steger 1988), he was distorting what opinion polls showed the public to want. Alongside support for the death penalty and less leniency, substantial support for preventive and rehabilitative programs remained (Duffee and Ritti 1977; Riley and Rose 1980; Warr and Stafford 1984; Cullen, Clark and Wozniak 1985; Gottfredson and Taylor 1987; Cullen, Cullen, and Wozniak 1988; Skovron, Scott, and Cullen 1988; Cullen, Skovron, Scott, and Burton 1990; McCorkle 1993).

Still, this does not mean that popular feelings about an issue have been irrelevant. Politicians may exaggerate the punitiveness of their constituents, perhaps because constituents who are most fearful or most sanguinary are the most likely to communicate their convictions to their government representatives. However, in one of the studies demonstrating politicians' exaggeration of public punitiveness (Gottfredson and Taylor 1987), only a third of the respondents opposed new prison construction. There is no substantial constituency in favor of less punishment, whose existence is unknown to the politicians.[41]

Critics of the argument that politicians had to respond to public concern note that when conservative politicians began to call for expanded law enforcement capabilities and the nullification of Supreme Court decisions on defendants' rights, few citizens identified crime as the nation's most important problem when surveyed (Chambliss 1994,

1995). In fact, the percentage identifying crimes or drugs as the most serious problem is quite volatile; it rises sharply when news media highlight instances of horrendous violence, and when politicians harp on the perils of rising crime rates in their speeches, quite independently of any changes in levels of reported crime[42] (Alderman 1994; Beckett 1994; Chambliss 1994, 1995; Flanagan 1996).

Yet this measure is an imperfect indicator of public concern about crime,[43] and does not demonstrate the absence of spontaneous concern based on personal experience and the experience of one's associates. Nor does it prove that demands for punishment are irrational. Between 1960 and 1970, the numbers of each of the seven index offenses rose by factors of two to three. Ordinary citizens are not criminologists, and do not necessarily pay close attention to each and every fluctuation in crime rates. But when theft and violence increase regularly year after year for more than a decade, chances of victimization climb, and awareness of the increases diffuses through the population.

Increases of this magnitude and regularity could hardly have failed to make an impact on levels of fear, and on assessments of the seriousness of crime as a social problem. In the same years that index crime rates climbed, American cities were wracked by riots,[44] and major public figures, including a president, were assassinated. These events are often overlooked by scholars who try to refute the existence of any "objective" basis for fear of crime by examining crime rates for the years after the early 1970s, when the crime rates had leveled off.

More critical than the existence of concern are the implications that follow from that concern. One response to the riots following the assassination of Rev. Martin Luther King, Jr. was to prevent crime by "getting at its cause; slums, unemployment, run-down schools and houses" (Hubert Humphrey, quoted in Chambliss 1995). Another was that of the conservative senators and congressmen who sponsored the Omnibus Crime Control and Safe Streets Act allowing wiretapping without a court order, and exempting law enforcement agencies from the Civil Rights Act of 1964 (Chambliss 1995). These were measures, it might be noted, that had no conceivable relevance to the prevention of riots or more common kinds of crime. To the extent that the wiretapping provision had a policy goal, its goal was to strengthen federal capacity to deal with organized political opposition, of which there was then a great deal.

What is true for politicians is equally true for the public at large. It does not follow from the mistaken public view that crime has been increasing steadily that support for rehabilitation should have declined, while support for more punishment rose (Gerber and Engelhardt-Greer 1996).

That the brief and modest trend toward leniency in criminal justice policy and toward incorporation and reduced social inequality should have evoked some opposition is hardly surprising. When social change injures the interests of a sector of the population, or they believe that it does; and when it challenges the principles on which the old order is based, countermovements opposed to the change emerge calling for a return to "the good old days," or if that appears impractical, for an attainable alternative. The precise nature of the backlash, and the interests that are at stake, are of some interest.

To understand the increased punitiveness of the last twenty-five years we must consider both the politicians who call for punitive measures and the responsiveness of the public to these calls. Before doing so, though, we must note that for some backers of a hard-line approach this was nothing new. When civil rights measures were adopted in the 1960s, a substantial fraction of the country strongly opposed them. Many congressmen, including George Bush, voted against the 1964 Civil Rights Act. Their later opposition to affirmative action is easily understood as a continuation of their earlier opposition to formal racial equality. When a politician who opposed the legal equality of the races in 1964 now condemns affirmative action as "reverse discrimination," a violation of the principle that governments should treat all citizens equally, one must suspect that the condemnation really stems from long-standing opposition to government measures that will help blacks, not from commitment to formal legal equality. Public opinion has simply changed to the point where the earlier racist sentiment cannot be voiced in public. Having lost the battle to maintain white supremacy openly, they seek to preserve it covertly, in the name of the formal equality that they had long opposed. Likewise, a significant fraction of the population approved highly punitive penal methods all along, and opposed restrictions on law enforcement. As early as 1966, New York City voters defeated an all-civilian police board by a large margin in a referendum in which the Patrolmen's Benevolent Association led the opposition (Viteritti 1973); and a proposal for community control of the police lost even in Berkeley, one of the most liberal of all American towns.

One must also keep in mind that many people have not abandoned "liberal" positions. Ameliorative and redistributive programs still enjoy support in some quarters. College administrators still tend to favor affirmative action in admissions (Lederman 1996a, 1996b), and many public figures have condemned the new welfare provisions as ill-advised. Surveys show majorities in favor of affirmative action by spreads of 10 to 15 percentage points[45] (Harris 1995). In a referendum held in Houston in the fall of 1997, voters approved affirmative action programs by a majority of 54 to 46 percent. The city's business leaders and politicians had all supported the programs[46] (Verhovek 1997a). When asked whether the government needs to make a greater effort to try to rehabilitate criminals who commit violent crimes, or to punish them and put them away, 32 percent say "rehabilitate" and another 8 percent say "both equally" (compared to 49 percent who say "punish").[47]

Initially, it was conservative Republican and Southern Democratic politicians who campaigned for tougher law enforcement measures. They attacked the Supreme Court for favoring criminals by upholding or extending defendants' rights, possibly to discredit the Court for its invalidation of legislation upholding segregation. The conservatives called for preventive detention, longer sentences for narcotics offenses and for the use of a weapon in a crime, for limiting bail and the insanity defense, and for permitting wire-taps.

By contrast, in 1968, Democratic Presidential candidate Hubert Humphrey called for redistributive programs and equal rights for all citizens as a way to deal with crime. In 1972, the Democrats opposed the death penalty, and called for prison reform and a ban on hand-guns. Candidates like Hubert Humphrey, George McGovern, and George Dukakis, who held the more "liberal" positions, all lost. Although their defeats were surely not due to their stands on crime issues alone, it is quite understandable in light of this history that in his first term, President Bill Clinton protected his reelection bid by introducing a crime control act providing funds for 100,000 more police. A more principled liberal opposition to hard-line proposals might have left their proponents vulnerable to accusations of lacking empathy for crime victims.

In advancing the conservative agenda at a time when the public appears not to have been overly concerned about routine crime, politicians sought votes by linking conventional illegality with cultural and political developments that worried many voters. Republican Barry Goldwater's 1964 presidential campaign ran television ads conflating civil rights demonstrations with street crime and riots. In 1967, Vice President Spiro Agnew (1969:40) returned to this theme by lambasting "muggers and criminals in the streets, assassins of political leaders, draft evaders and flag burners, campus militants, hecklers and demonstrators against candidates for public office and looters and burners of cities." By rhetorically associating political opposition to American participation in the War in Vietnam with conventional crime, Nixon and Agnew were able to discredit the opposition and make the threat of crime appear larger and more worrisome. This threat was then used as the basis for arguing that the repressive capacities for the state had to be strengthened.

Similar campaigns have been conducted on economic issues. Proponents of free markets have long argued against state interference with market transactions, contending that government can best promote economic efficiency and growth by not interfering with private choices. Taxes and subsidies, the free-marketers contend, should not be used to alter distributions of income produced in competitive marketplaces; doing so merely introduces inefficiencies by discouraging productive activity. Government bureaucracies, they say, impose burdensome costs on businesses, making it difficult for them to compete in a global economy; and often fail to protect the public. Opponents of affirmative action programs charge them with failing to reward merit, heightening group consciousness, damaging the self-esteem and career prospects of those they try to help, and illegally discriminating on the basis of race and sex (Sowell 1975; Capaldi 1985; Eastland 1990; F. Lynch 1989; Steele 1990; Carter 1991; Yates 1994). Under the Reagan and Bush presidencies, the critics of liberal policies became more vocal and gained broader influence on public policy.

Representations—or misrepresentations—of crime in the mass media helped to make the public more receptive to the claims of politicians that crime rates were soaring (Antunes and Hurley 1977; Fishman 1978, 1981; Ericson, Baraneku, and Chan 1991; Surette 1992; Beckett 1994; Chambliss 1994, 1995; Schlesinger 1994; Chernak 1995; Murphy and DeStefano 1996). Television and film dramas—both in fiction and in news reporting—exaggerate the extent to which crimes involve violence, and through their "realism," leave viewers feeling threatened and insecure. Television and film depict due process constraints on law enforcement only as obstacles in apprehending and punishing criminals, not as protections for "honest" citizens (Crew 1990). One reason that many Americans have believed that crime rates have been growing rapidly is that television networks have devoted more time to crime news (Donziger 1996:69). Active criminals and ex-convicts are poorly positioned to oppose these representational distortions.

We need not assume that politicians who rail against "welfare queens," who wax with indignation at the supposed unfairness of affirmative action, and who ask a rival candidate for public office how he would feel were his wife to be raped, actually believe the myths they circulate, feel the emotions they display before audiences, or expect much from the programs they advocate; some of them may have adopted conservative positions opportunistically. Without believing what they say about welfare, race or crime, the hard-liners know that they can use these issues to further their prospects in the next election. If voters can be made to fear violence and resent immigrants and welfare recipients, they will vote for politicians who support longer sentences, and restrictions on immigrants and welfare.

Politicians' proposals for dealing with crime, however, suggest that more may be at stake than career promotion. Jacksonian-era figures who sponsored the building of penitentiaries and asylums saw them as small-scale models of the ideal society—hierarchical, authoritarian, disciplined. They hoped that once the success of the prison, mental asylum, and poor house had been demonstrated, the model would be adopted by other institutions in "free" society, such as the family and the school (Rothman 1971). The same may be true today. Conservative politicians' agenda is to shore up threats to authority and inequality. The criminal law appeals to them as a way of gaining consent. It entails one class of people—those who hold government office—telling other people what to do, threatening disobedience, and punishing those who fail to conform. The criminal justice system is designed to gain compliance through coercion from those who will not conform on the basis of the law's legitimacy, or on the basis of positive incentives. When a policy analyst proposes to increase the number of police in the United States from half a million to five million (Walinsky 1995), one may suspect that the proposal does not reflect a rational strategy for protecting lives, but a fascination with the idea of government by armed men wearing uniforms.

Through its punishment rituals, criminal law validates the moral superiority of those who make and administer the rules. Due process constraints on law enforcement are a symbolic challenge to this superiority. In allocating rights to suspects, they undercut this moral hierarchy. Similarly, state-mandated welfare implies—as private charity does not—that recipients have a right to a certain standard of living independently of their submission to the authority of an employer. The conservatives hope to create a world in which rights play a less important role in society, and coercion and legitimate authority play a larger role.

The conservatives have been able to gain exposure to their views on issues like taxes, welfare, and regulation because business corporations provide massive funding to conservative foundations and think-tanks, which in turn promote books and newspaper articles that advance the conservative agenda (Blumenthal 1986; Miller 1996). Possibly because left-wing critics of welfare and treatment programs had advertised their control functions so persistently (Piven and Cloward 1971; Platt 1969; American Friends Service Committee Working Party 1971), liberals did not take the strong stands against the backlash they might otherwise have made. The rich have been less active in promoting repressive criminal justice policies than in lobbying for the deregulation of business, probably because policing and prisons have less relevance to their class interests than taxation and regulation.

Some of the support these measures receive from the public can be attributed to simple self-interest. It is quite rational for people who feel threatened by violence to suppose that they will be safer with more people in prison. If tax-payers are being squeezed by declining real incomes, cuts in welfare programs and taxes might sensibly be seen as offering relief. Part of the white opposition to affirmative action programs stems from the belief that they or their children are being denied access to good jobs and elite schools (Bobo and Kluegel 1993). It is advantageous to this constituency to argue that affirmative action programs discriminate against whites, and that college admissions and financial aid decisions should be made on the basis of "merit," not on the basis of allegedly irrelevant criteria such as race and ethnicity.

In the last two decades, middle-income voters have faced job insecurity and a gradual decline in real wages. As corporate "down-sizing" jeopardized white middle-class jobs (Newman 1988), whites became increasingly concerned with preserving their own class position, and less concerned with helping others. Thinking only of themselves and of the immediate short-run implications of admissions and hiring practices while forgetting the long-run social consequences, they have been less willing than before to foster upward mobility for the poor, and more vigorous in seeking tax cuts. Given this stance on social issues, it would be quite rational to want to put more criminals in prison. If redistributive and preventive measures are to be excluded, what else can one do?[48]

This reasoning, however, overlooks the high costs of the hard-line approach. Once these are figured in, it is not likely that the tough approach is rational when viewed in a purely material light. While self-interest may explain some opposition to welfare payments and affirmative action, it fails to account for the low-income citizens who oppose welfare, and those blacks who oppose affirmative action. Nor does it explain why some middle- and upper-class people have supported welfare, civil rights, and affirmative action. In the absence of support that extended beyond the beneficiaries, these measures would never have been adopted.

The rational actor model overlooks the emotional loadings that accompany positions on all these issues. For many people, crime policy, welfare policy, race relations policy, all touch on fundamental beliefs and values, and are heavily weighted with emotion. Attempts to understand public responses to these issues that neglect their emotional and often irrational dimensions may be doomed to fail.

Chancer and Donovan (1996) have recently attempted to explain the moral outrage over crime and the demand for stringent punishment by arguing that "the general insecurities" of a middle-class anxious "about its own economic precariousness, status, and general life situation" are critical in gaining mass support for retributive policies. The aggression provoked by these insecurities is channeled toward criminals, whose open hostility toward authority make them unconscious objects of fascination and admiration.

This analysis focuses too narrowly on the lower middle-class, which is no more punitive than other classes. In two studies, support for retributivism was not significantly related to socioeconomic status (Warr and Stafford 1984; Grasmick et al. 1992). In the 1991 General Social Survey, however, respondents whose total family income is high have significantly higher support for stiffer sentences, though the effect is small. Those whose financial circumstances had recently improved were more likely to think the courts were not harsh enough, and that criminals deserve stiff punishment, but these differences were also small.

Chancer and Donovan's focus on economic anxiety may be misplaced. Neither anxiety over one's status, nor economic difficulty, nor punitiveness, is a monopoly of the middle class. Rossi, Simpson and Miller (1985) found punitivism to be little affected by respondents' race, sex, income, and household income. Those who had experienced a negative life event such as unemployment, serious illness, or a death in the family were significantly more likely to be punitive, suggesting that anxiety or frustration from multiple sources might lead to punitive feelings. However, it is unclear how much this anxiety is due to economic restructuring under conditions of uncertainty.

If economic declines produce punitive feelings, one would have an explanation for the relationship between the business cycle and rates of admission to prison found in several capitalist countries, as well as the emotional appeal of punishments. The low sentences found in Scandinavia, the Netherlands, and Japan may reflect a lower popular demand for punishment in societies whose economic systems do not engender high levels of insecurity. In Scandinavia or the Netherlands the welfare system is relatively generous (de Haan 1990; Downes 1992), and in Japan unemployment is very low and jobs are often assured for life.

A direct test of this reasoning would require comparable data about levels of economic insecurity in different societies, and such data are not currently available. However, to focus too exclusively on fears about one's job or income may be to slight the process through which fears and anxieties are directed toward particular issues by politicians and the mass media. The emphasis they have given to crime, welfare, and affirmative action has focused anxiety on those issues, rather than—for example—on the military budget, or defects in the economic system.

In trying to explain why American prison populations soared, while those in West Germany declined modestly over the same years. Joachim Savelsberg (1994) has argued that politicians and the mass media play an important role in structuring popular beliefs about crime and crime control. Savelsberg notes that countries vary in the extent to which politicians and newspapers highlight crime as a social problem and call for harsher measures to deal with it. In the more corporatist societies, different political factions or bodies are formally recognized and represented politically. Attempts are made to accommodate their interests through explicit bargaining and concessions.

Politicians in such societies should be less likely to try to win support through inflammatory campaign rhetoric that exaggerates the magnitude of social problems. Because all the major parties share in the responsibility for dealing with these problems, they will not have strong incentives to misrepresent them. For the same reasons, they will refrain from attacking the existing policies as being outrageously misguided. Publics in these societies are not as fearful of crime, and are less likely to make demands on the state for more stringent penalties.[49]

Differences in political arrangements make sense not only of the contrast between West Germany and the United States, but also of the low levels of incarceration in the Netherlands during the decades in which its "pillarized" political system was in place. In that system, major political decisions were made through behind-the-scenes agreements between the major political parties (Downes 1988; de Haan 1990). As this system has weakened in recent years, Dutch prison populations have risen, though not to the extent that they have in the United States.

A test of the importance of corporatism in structuring social responses to crime can be conducted using our sample of data for the affluent nations. When the per capita prison population is regressed on inequality, GNP, the crime rate, and a measure of corporatism measuring the extent to which different sectors of society engage in explicit bargaining and compromise agreements, (Pampel, Wiliamson, and Stryker 1990), corporatism is found to reduce the prison population significantly, while inequality no longer has a significant influence (see table 13.1). The more corporatist societies are less punitive. The United States is the second least corporatist society in the entire sample, and the most punitive.[50] Were the Democrats and Republicans to work out the main outlines of punishment policy behind closed doors, it is unlikely that Presidential candidate George Bush would have run television advertisements taxing his opponent George Dukakis for the crime Willie Horton committed on prison furlough (Anderson 1995).

Of course, the United States would also have ranked low on cor-

TABLE 13.1
Multiple Regression of Incarceration Rates*

Variable	**Standardized Regression**	***Coefficient*****
Corporatism	–.80	–.78
	(2.15)	(2.20)
GNP	.63	.58
	(2.08)	(1.99)
Inequality	.00	.05
	(.00)	(.14)
Homicide Rate	–.08	
	(1.03)	
Total Crime Rate	–.193	
	(1.06)	
R^2	.65	.68
adjusted R^2	.52	.56

*Pairwise deletion, United States deleted from sample

**Figures in parentheses underneath regression coefficients are Student's *t* statistics.

poratism three decades ago, when the incarceration rate was far lower than it is now, and declining. In itself, a culture of individualism and a more competitive political system need not lead to panics about crime, or to punitive policies. Crime became a public issue because racial conflict, radical political challenges, cultural changes including wider use of recreational drugs, the rise of feminism, and the weakening of sexual restrictions were occurring at the same time reported crime rates were rising rapidly.

Social changes of this magnitude would surely have elicited concern and opposition from substantial sections of the population even in the absence of political exploitation. They posed a challenge to the values, moral and political beliefs and familiar ways of life of many. The fear and anger aroused by cultural change and political opposition became joined to the fear aroused by crime and riots through framings posed by conservative politicians and amplified by misrepresentations on the part of those same politicians, and by depictions in the mass media.

Other countries encountered many of the same problems. In May 1968, the French New Left came close to toppling the government. The New Left in Germany and Italy was much more violent than in the United States. But politicians in those countries did not turn these threats into a general war against crime. Where repression took place, it was more narrowly focused on the political threat.

The more corporatist societies are not only less punitive; they are also more egalitarian and have more far-reaching redistributive policies. In our sample, the correlation between the corporatism score and inequality is –.66.[51] Welfare policies in the corporatist societies enjoy stronger public support. When asked whether the government should provide everyone with a "guaranteed basic income," support was far higher in Britain (59 percent), the Federal Republic of Germany (51 percent), and the Netherlands (48 percent) than in the United States (20 percent) (Smith 1990).

Obviously, these correlations pose a chicken-and-eggs problem. Corporatist political arrangements are not distributed among the nations at random, and they cannot necessarily be treated as exogenous to economic equality. It is in societies where it is considered important to accommodate diverse interests, including those of workers and people who cannot support themselves, that corporatist political arrangements tend to be found. The culture that gives rise to corporatism, and in turn to greater tolerance of deviance, shows a good deal of stability over time. The Netherlands had a lower rate of execution than England in the eighteenth through nineteenth centuries, and abolished capital punishment much earlier (Downes 1988: 69). English society has been exceptionally individualist for hundreds of years (Macfarlane 1979); France has been known for its identification of the people and the centralized state. Possibly there is something about the cultures of some countries that make them more amenable to corporatism and to egalitarian economic policies.

However they come about, once corporatist political arrangements are in place, they tend to perpetuate themselves. Just as politicians will tend to refrain from demonizing criminals, they will tend to avoid attacks on welfare recipients, and citizens will recognize that, despite its costs, it benefits them. In Norway, where welfare benefits are extravagant by American standards, and taxes to pay for them are equally high, businesses support the welfare state because they value the social peace it has brought them[52] (Ibrahim 1996). Making sure that a minimum standard of living is maintained, if necessary through the welfare system, becomes part of the national identity, valued for its own sake, just as "individualism" comes to be valued as an element of Americans' political identity.

On the other hand, sometimes political culture changes. For the first half of this century, the Netherlands had a higher incarceration rate than England and Wales, even though it had less crime (Downes 1988). Between 1968 and 1971, the value placed on social equality rose in national surveys of the American people; then in the 1970s it fell relative to such personal values as having a comfortable life, a sense of accomplishment, and excitement, possibly because awareness grew that equality came at a price. When real incomes began to fall, those costs came to be seen as unacceptable by a substantial fraction of the white population (Rokeach and Ball-Rokeach 1989).

Punitive Attitudes, Models of Society, and Principles of Justice

Because penalties for crime are imposed very disproportionately on members of minority groups, some observers have argued that the war on crime is really a war on blacks and Latinos (Miller 1996). It is, however, difficult to reconcile this argument with surveys showing that support for integration and equal treatment of the races has been growing gradually over the decades (Schuman et al. 1985; Firebaugh and Davis 1986; DiMaggio, Evans, and Bryson 1996; Quillian 1996).

Only limited support for the "war on blacks" thesis can be found in survey research. In the 1991 General Social Survey, respondents who supported residential racial segregation and who said that they would not vote for a qualified black presidential candidate nominated by their party were more likely to believe that the courts are not harsh enough, but the differences were tiny: for segregation, 81.8 percent versus 80.9 percent; for the presidential vote, 87.5 percent versus 84.1 percent. Whites were more likely than blacks to think the courts not harsh enough, but here too the differences were small (84.7 percent versus 79.8 percent).

Support for the death penalty was more strongly influenced by racial attitudes: 91.6 percent of strong supporters of racial segregation supported the death penalty for murderers, compared to 68.6 percent of strong opponents. 83.7 percent of those who would not vote for a black candidate favored capital punishment compared to 74.5 percent of those who would. The differences among the races were also stronger: 58.9 percent of black respondents supported the death penalty compared to 77.5 percent of whites.

These results suggest that one source of support for harsh punishment may be racist feelings, but it is clearly not the only one. A majority of blacks favor it. A large majority of blacks support stiffer punishment for criminals, as do a large majority of racists and nonracists. The percentage of the population endorsing strongly racist views is relatively small. Few Americans now advocate legal segregation of neighborhoods and public schools. Even were racists' views on punishment to be more distinctive than they are, those who endorse explicitly racist views would contribute relatively little to overall sentiment regarding punishment. Even in their absence, public sentiment for tough punishment would be strong—strong among blacks, and strong among those who reject racism. If it is not credible to suppose that blacks are supporting a war on blacks, perhaps another view of white support for the war on crime is called for.

Because a disproportionate percentage of blacks—approximately 28 percent—receive means-tested welfare support—it might be suspected that opposition to welfare could be motivated by antipathy to blacks. However, the race of the welfare mother has been found unrelated to views of welfare spending (Gilens 1996). A substantial majority of whites (69 percent) thinks that most welfare recipients are not truly needy, but are taking advantage of the system; so do a majority of blacks (62 percent). More whites than blacks think welfare for low-income families should be kept, but the difference is not large (55 percent versus 46 percent) (Gallup 1995:38).

The emphasis on explaining differences in the standard social-science statistical procedures provides limited insights when it is a pattern of similarity one seeks to explain. In attitudes toward punishment and welfare, the most striking feature is not that there are some modest differences between the races, or between those holding different views of race relations, but the similarities. There is strong support for stiff punishment and cuts in welfare budgets among all groups. Some insights into the sources of this support can be gleaned from the rhetoric that is deployed on behalf of penal policy positions.

Many factors surely contribute to the attitudes people hold about crime, punishment, and welfare. Yet the texts in which policy stances on these issues are defended reveal the common themes, suggesting that greater punitiveness may be one component of a larger policy shift toward an anomic and forced division of labor. It would be too much to say that individual views on crime, welfare, affirmative action, and other social policies always appear in tandem. The positions people hold on social policy issues are not always logically coherent and consistent. Sometimes they are idiosyncratic. Policy stands are correlated in predictable ways, but imperfectly. It is the common themes on which I focus here.

The notion that the courts are justified in punishing convicted criminals proportionately to the wrongfulness of their crimes has won a wide following among penological theorists in recent decades. Wrongdoers, they argue, should be punished because they deserve to be punished on the basis of what they have done. In so arguing, "just deserts" theorists do not contend that these principles are optimal for preventing crime, but rather that justice requires them. It is the wrongfulness of criminal acts, not social utility, that should govern the severity of punishment (Frankel 1972; Fogel 1975; Twentieth Century Fund 1976; von Hirsch 1976, 1985; Gross 1979).

Ordinary citizens rarely elaborate the subtle distinctions to be found in the essays of the just deserts theorists, but they too draw on conceptions of justice. Consider the recent letter to the editor of the *New York Times* that complained of "convicts wearing prison-supplied Nikes while watching cable television and exercising in gyms that surpass many high school facilities," indulgences that lead the author to wonder "if there is a punitive element in America's penal system" (Brennan 1997). Brennan's grievance is not that it is wrong to watch cable television or that public safety will be jeopardized by turning prisoners into couch potatoes. He fumes because he thinks that prisoners do not deserve to live so comfortably.

The same concern with justice figures prominently in reasons that supporters of the death penalty give to explain their support. "Murderers deserve punishment," they say; "an eye for eye; a life for a life" (Lotz and Regoli 1980; Finckenauer 1988; Steel and Steger 1988). Many of those who say they favor capital punishment to protect the public also say that they would not withdraw their support were evidence that it failed to deter homicide to emerge (Vidmar and Ellsworth 1974; Ellsworth and Ross 1983; Longmire 1996). Their belief that capital punishment deters may be a consequence of their belief that murderers deserve to die rather than a cause of their belief.[53]

Debates over affirmative action are also phrased in the vocabulary of deserts. Opponents argue that students with high grades and test scores deserve to be admitted to the best colleges. Admitting students with lower grades and test scores over those who are better qualified because they are classified as minority group members unjustly confers a benefit on the basis of what ought to be irrelevant. As Michael Levin (1989) put it, "it is *unfair* to bypass white males...who are not themselves responsible for the plight of blacks and women" (emphasis added). The laws should not set out to disadvantage anyone on account of their race. The current cohort of students did not create the historic pattern of segregation whose consequences affirmative action seeks to overcome; they should not be punished by the adoption of remedial measures that impair their life chances.

Though opponents of affirmative action point to what they contend will be long-term pernicious consequences of affirmative action (racial polarization, stigmatizing of minority students and job-holders, inefficiency in the use of educational resources), they also argue that college admission should be a reward for individual achievement or ability, not an instrument for improving society.

Overlaps between populations thought unworthy result in stereotypes through which a deficiency in relation to one activity sphere discredits those in other activity spheres. The belief that poor people are lazy discredits the claim that they turn to crime from necessity, not maliciousness; and reduces white support for welfare spending (Gilens 1996), presumably because of the belief that a large proportion of welfare recipients are black,[54] perhaps criminal. Conscious and unconscious prejudice against blacks can stigmatize all criminals, and all welfare recipients through a contamination of categories with overlapping membership.

All of these stands—those on punishment, those on welfare, those on affirmative action—rest on assumptions about questions of fact that do not withstand close scrutiny, and on the applicability of particular normative framings. A desert-based punishment scheme based on criminal behavior alone assumes that it is equally easy for everyone to comply with the law.[55] To the extent that this assumption is rendered false by the existence of discrimination and structured inequality not chosen by a defendant, equal proportional punishments no longer correspond to equal desert.[56] Just deserts theorists have long been aware of this difficulty (von Hirsch 1976:143–51), but have found no way to resolve it. Sentencing reform was potentially attainable through advocacy and lobbying; economic redistribution was not. Better to lobby for what is attainable even if the result falls short of standards that supposedly justify the scheme.[57]

Opponents of affirmative action in college admissions assume that grades and test scores adequately measure aptitude, and that restitution for past discrimination, compensation for inferior education and cultural devaluation or familial disadvantage should not be taken into account. Presumably better study habits could have raised grades and test scores, independently of a child's life circumstances. Or if one rejects this farfetched notion, one might simply accept continued racial stratification as a consequence of the formal equality. By that logic, universities and governments should not take accidents of birth into account, even though the continuing consequences of slavery, racial discrimination and economic disadvantage will ensure that individuals' life chances are greatly influenced by historical events over which they have no control.

Views of welfare also rest on assumptions about the recipients. Those who think welfare mothers are lazy, and believe that most people are poor because "they don't try hard enough to get ahead" are less sympathetic to welfare spending than those who think that people are poor "because they don't get the training and education they need"[58] (Gilens 1996).

Contrary to claims made by critics of welfare policy and affirmative action, class origin has a large influence on tests that supposedly measure intellectual ability (Fischer et al. 1995:79–88), and expensive coaching can improve test scores substantially. Class and race have large influences on someone's chances of being arrested, prosecuted, and convicted of crime. The suggestion that a better substitute for affirmative action in college admissions and in employment would be an upgrading of the public schools and the reconstitution of the black family (Sullivan 1995) is made without any realistic plan for accomplishing these goals.

The assumption in many discussions of affirmative action that in the absence of special programs a "level playing field" exists runs counter to evidence about discrimination in hiring and promotion (Kilborn 1995). The important role of friends and relatives in obtaining jobs is overlooked. A suggestion made by Shelby Steele (1990) that stepped-up prosecutions against discriminators could make affirmative action in hiring unnecessary ignores the higher standards of proof required in a criminal trial and the small likelihood that significant prosecutorial resources will be devoted to the prosecution of discriminating employers.

The critics of these programs hold a utopian view of American society. In the absence of state intervention, conscientious parents will raise children who will buckle down, overcome any and all obstacles, and triumph over adversity. Employers will always want the best-qualified employees, and therefore will avoid prejudicial discrimination. Those who do not will be driven out of business by their competitors. No shortage of adequately remunerative jobs stands in their way; or if there is a shortage, it is a product of minimum wage laws that make it too expensive for employers to hire marginally productive job applicants.

This is a world of wishful thinking. Would that all these interventions were unnecessary! Much money and much effort could be saved. Violation of appealing abstract principles of formal equality could be avoided. If the substantial efforts already undertaken have not yet brought a fair world into being, how much easier to persuade oneself that it has already done so. To acknowledge that it does not exist might impose burdensome moral obligations that many might prefer not to have to shoulder.

This fantastic utopianism lends a peculiar quality to the move toward a more "abnormal" division of labor. In earlier historical eras, people's placement in the stratification system was attributed to divine will. The secularization of culture made it impossible to sustain gross inequalities of wealth and power on this basis. Explanations of stratification as resting on innate differences in virtue and talent offered an alternative legitimation, one which held a good deal of appeal in the age of imperialism. The power of this explanation to legitimate hierarchy was almost completely nullified in the course of the twentieth century by its association with colonial rule and genocide (Arendt 1951). Though attempts have been made to revive it (Michael Young 1958; Herrnstein and Murray 1994), the strength of democratic egalitarian ideology has limited the influence of these attempts. The sway of doctrines of racial inferiority in the United States is now largely limited to politically impotent, marginal white militias.

In contemporary discussions of crime policies and allocation controversies one rarely encounters genetically-based arguments.[59] In contrast to early twentieth-century criminological writings, almost all contemporary criminologists agree that inherited traits at best play a minor role in explaining differences among individuals in illegal behavior (Katz and Chambliss 1991), and do not explain differences in racial and ethnic involvement. Differences between the races in unemployment and poverty are widely understood to reflect social and cultural factors, not racial differences in aptitude. Debates on immigration policy revolve around issues of language, the labor market and tax burdens, not on the issues of racial or national inferiority. When claims of intrinsic racial difference have been introduced into analyses of crime and economic inequality (Herrnstein and Murray 1994; Wilson and Herrnstein 1985; Rushton 1990, 1995a, 1995b), they have been very widely, even vitriolicly, attacked (Fraser 1995; Jacoby and Glauberman 1995).

We have then, not a push toward the reestablishment of a society based formally on racial or class distinctions. The opponents of affirmative action do not propose a return to Jim Crow law; whether honestly or hypocritically, they endorse legal equality, while opposing those measures that could make this equality more than formal. They see no inconsistency in this advocacy because they believe that remedial measures are no longer necessary.[60]

If, as all indicators suggest, this view is mistaken, the result will be to leave in place a division of labor that is *de facto* forced, costumed as an organic division of labor based on complementarity. One of the very few tools left in such a society for managing the strains of actual inequality is punishment. Other options would require an acknowledgment that the Eden of equal possibility has not yet arrived, potentially undermining the legitimacy of many social arrangements.

With this conjunction of a culture of formal legal equality and social structure of high and stable inequality, the proportion of the population processed by the state punishment system expands, and the intensity of punishment increases. Inequality of social outcomes persists or increases, secured through legislation that appears to apply equally to all, but impacts differentially on different social strata; and through the discriminatory exercise of police, prosecutorial and judicial discretion. Packaged and promoted as a "war on crime," escalation in punishment of the magnitude the United States has seen in the past quarter-century is the mark of a society at war with itself.

Particular conceptions of justice make such a war widely acceptable. There is nothing in any given policy domain to determine the framing that makes a particular justice scheme applicable. In the communes of medieval Italy, crimes involving interpersonal violence were routinely managed through compensatory and conciliatory cash payments to injured parties or their families, not through state-imposed retribution. Poverty was the basis for a reduction in the compensation paid[61] (Blanshei 1981, 1982). Today everyone takes for granted that the state should punish violent offenders.

A hundred years ago, positivist criminologists urged the abandonment of Enlightenment-era formal equality in punishment based on the seriousness of the offense on the grounds that it represented an anachronistic survival of metaphysical thinking. Scientific advances, they contended, undercut the epistemological basis for attributing responsibility to offenders, and thus made considerations of justice irrelevant to the disposition of criminal cases (Ferri 1900:87–8; Parmalee 1908:190; Lombroso 1911:361–3, 379–84). The interests of crime prevention, they thought, could be served best by ignoring questions of justice, and focusing instead on utilitarian concerns, which could be advanced through incapacitation and rehabilitation of offenders. In recent years dissatisfaction with some of the consequences of this utilitarian framework (American Friends Service Committee Working Party 1971) have motivated a return to older "metaphysical" principles of retributive justice.

A hundred years ago the courts handled civil suits involving on-the-job injuries within a legal system that required the establishment of blame for the accident. The unpredictability of jury awards stimulated the replacement of intent-based procedures and standards with a no-fault system (Friedman and Ladinsky 1967), that in recent years has been extended to automobile insurance.

Supporters of affirmative action have likewise argued for the irrelevance of merit. "Admission to graduate school is not a reward for the meritorious. It is—or ought to be—a method of selecting students who will do the most good for the population at large" (Henkin 1989). The purpose of affirmative action is not to affirm an abstract principle of formal equality, but to remedy an intolerable situation in which distinct sectors of the population are seriously underrepresented in the more prestigious and lucrative occupations because of a long history of discrimination. Perhaps prizes in piano competitions and golf contests should go to the competitors who play best, but for the supporters of affirmative action it isn't obvious that this principle should determine who goes to college. A consistent moral justification for programs to widen college attendance should not be attempted, because none can be given (Fish 1996).

Whatever one thinks of Fish's argument, his hope that beliefs about justice and fairness can be dropped from a debate at will is probably as vain as was the hope of the Italian positivists that they could be abandoned in the criminal sphere. For policies to be based on a judgment as to what distributional outcomes are socially useful rather than on earned "desert," whether positive or negative, would require the acceptance of a logic that is at odds with the justifications given for disparate outcomes in a market economy. If it is not worrisome that competition of differently equipped and differently motivated individuals in a formally equal labor market gives some people higher incomes than others, then why should it be a cause for concern if the number of minority students attending the better universities and professional schools drops dramatically,[62] so long as the drop results from a race-blind policy?

To a limited extent it has been possible to depart from principles of universalism. No one has ever mounted a media campaign denouncing the violations of universalism that occur when owners of businesses preferentially hire and promote members of their own family, or colleges give preference to applicants who are children of alumni ("legacies"). In these cases, the violations benefit groups who are not tainted by the stigma of laziness, dependence, and criminality; and they tend to reproduce, rather than challenge, the existing stratification order.

Some departures from market principles and from retributive punishment have also been introduced even when the beneficiaries are stigmatized in this way, for example, when welfare payments are made on the basis of need, and when juvenile delinquents are sentenced on the basis of supposed treatment considerations. However, these departures are insecurely grounded and are proving vulnerable to attack. This vulnerability has increased as the proportion of blacks among the recipients of welfare and the children brought into juvenile court has increased. It is the familiarity and acceptability of allocating goods on the basis of needs and social utility in the Dutch and Scandinavian welfare systems that enables those nations to distribute "bads" in a manner that relies less on a retributive logic. It is not merely that the scale for rewarding and punishment behavior is compressed in these countries, as Wilkins has suggested, but that less weight can be given to the logic of rewards and punishment.

The belief that harsh penalties will effectively deter—held by many proponents of tough punishment—is also the logic of the market. Employers attract employees by outbidding other employers. Entrepreneurs induce investors to invest capital by promising profits on their investment. The greater the inducement, the stronger its motivating force. This is the flip side of the logic of crime deterrence. The appeal of harsh punishment, notwithstanding its high cost and its inefficiency, is its consistency with the logic that works every day in the business world.

Change or Stability

Will current trends continue? The political strength of those sectors of the population most damaged by highly punitive crime policies is weakened by the disenfranchisement of convicted felons and by poor voting turn-outs in low-income neighborhoods.[63] As both major political parties increasingly frame their policies to appeal to wealthy campaign contributors, low-income voters, who are also the least punitive, are less and less likely to think that their vote will make a difference.

A culture that attributes success to individual virtues builds in psychological satisfactions for better-off sectors of the population, to supplement the material benefits they receive. Those who are doing well receive cultural confirmation that their success is due to their own virtues. Those who do not can preserve their egos by attributing their failures to affirmative action programs, however modest and limited their impact.

Empirically, affluence is positively associated with the belief that society is fair (Jackman and Jackman 1983; Jackman 1994), and white Americans are more likely to think society fair than black Americans (Schuman, Steeh, and Bobo 1985; Kluegel and Smith 1986; Sigelman and Welch 1991). Such beliefs are psychologically satisfying because they imply that those who have done well have done so by their own merits. By implication, those who have not done as well are less meritorious. Ward Connerly, a black businessman and regent of the University of California, justified his opposition to affirmative action in higher education by claiming, "Nobody ever gave me any race or sex preferences when I came into the cold world fifty-six years ago, and I made it anyway—high school, college, my own big business, important friends. If I could make it, anybody can...." (Ayres 1996). Since "anybody" isn't making it, his own accomplishment is magnified. Connerly's assumption that if one person can do something, there are no structural obstacles to everyone doing so, is of course a fallacy. Likewise those whose good luck or good behavior enable them to avoid being arrested can have their virtue confirmed through the moral downgrading of those who are punished. The wretched living conditions of those eking out a subsistence on welfare, or who will be deprived of welfare support altogether, only confirm the virtues of all the Connerlys, indeed, of all those who are not at the very bottom. When changes in the economy make it more difficult for many people to feel that they are being validated by their occupational successes, validation by degrading others may offer compensatory satisfactions.

Could moral outrage stir those who gain materially and psychologically from current trends? In principle this is possible. However, some of the most forceful expressions of outrage in recent years have been provoked only by the victimization of someone in the same subgroup. It was blacks and Latinos who rioted after the acquittal of white Los Angeles police officers accused of beating black motorist Rodney King. The beating was widely perceived to be a manifestation of pervasive police mistreatment of black civilians.[64] The acquittal of the officers charged with the beating, following a trial in which a videotape of the beating was introduced as evidence, was understood as a refusal to convict officers responsible for brutality toward blacks, no matter what the evidence. The rioting was fueled by anger toward long-standing abusive police practices toward which the Los Angeles police department had proved indifferent, and against which the courts had provided no protection—not just by the verdict in a particular case (Koon 1992; Gooding-Williams 1993; Ogletree et al. 1995).[65] It was not the population at large, but gays, who rioted in San Francisco after Dan White was convicted on a lesser charge for killing Mayor George Moscone and Supervisor Harvey Milk, who was one of the gay community's most visible, popular, and powerful political leaders (Shilts 1982; Koon 1992; Gooding-Williams 1993).

The belief that these episodes did indeed exemplify systemic injustice rather than individual aberrancy was not universal. Whites, for example, were more likely than blacks to think that the beating of Rodney King was justified, and to believe O.J. Simpson guilty of murder. Whites and blacks differ in attitudes toward capital punishment and toward police use of deadly force (Gallup 1994:213–16, 241–42, 1995:113–16; Cullen et al. 1996).[66] These differences are rooted in the differing histories and experiences of blacks and whites with the police and courts that shape not just abstract principles of justice, but their application to events of the day[67] (Skolnick 1995).

These limited responses are what is expected when the division of labor is forced. Outrage based on similarity—the response Durkheim suggested associated with a low division of labor—continues to occur when the division of labor is complex. But when that complexity embodies systematic disadvantage, exploitation, discrimination, and exclusion, empathetic identification is substantially restricted to members of the group with whom one identifies. That identification may be on the basis of any sort of group membership, not necessarily occupational similarity. Victimization of an out-group member will elicit no reaction, or a much weaker reaction.

The attenuation of outrage when out-group members are victimized is, of course, not total. Many whites were distressed by the Rodney King beating, but they did not respond with the same emotional intensity; their identification with King was reduced. Their outrage does not appear to have been as widely shared or as intense as when black civil rights demonstrators in the South were beaten, shocked with electric cattle prods, set upon by police dogs, and killed in the early 1960s. A generation of anger at crime, welfare recipients, and supposed beneficiaries of preferential hiring, and their ideational linkage with blacks, weakened the sympathy white liberals had for civil rights demonstrators in the 1960s.

Perceptions of the social exclusion and cultural disparagement that accompany forced divisions of labor generate defensive counter-ideologies deprecating dominant groups and affirming the worth, sometimes even the superiority, of the excluded groups. Within these groups, as among dominant groups, solidarity is felt largely with other group members, not with outsiders, who may be viewed with hostility and rejected as allies. In the mid-1960s the appeal of separatism and the growth of anti-white and anti-Jewish sentiment among blacks, followed by similar responses in other groups (e.g., lesbian separatists) created additional barriers to the building of a coalition that might reverse current trends (Gitlin 1995).

Eventually, of course, the cost of new prison construction will prove unsustainable. The vast sums allocated to the military budget during the cold war, however, show that a great deal of room remains for further expansion as long as the population believes it is in danger. With levels of violence and theft falling dramatically, fear may moderate, and enthusiasm for expansion may slacken. However, it is not clear that this will happen as long as politicians and the mass media shape perceptions of crime. In the absence of major changes in American political life, it is difficult to envision a change in the role they play.

Appendix A
Data Sources for the High-Income Nations Sample

Homicide rates are for 1989–92, and are taken from United Nations (1995:484–503) except for Israel, Denmark and Switzerland, whose homicide rates are taken from Interpol (1992). Burglary and auto theft rates are taken from Interpol (1992). I have used 1990 rates except where unavailable. The Australian auto theft rate is from Clarke and Harris (1992). The Australian auto theft rate is for 1987/8; the burglary rate for New Zealand is for 1984, and for Belgium is for 1983. Income data represent income after taxes and transfer parents, and are from World Bank (1994:221). GNP per capita is for 1990, and taken from World Bank (1995). Imprisonment rates are taken from Mauer (1995b) except for Norway, whose rate is taken from Young and Brown (1993). The Israel prison population includes approximately a thousand Israeli "security prisoners," but excludes more than 3000 from the occupied territories.

Notes

Parts of this paper were presented to the 1996 meeting of the Eastern Sociological Society. I am grateful to Lynn Chancer, Robert Stanley, Valerie West and Leslie T. Wilkins for comments on that paper, and to Slawomir Redo for assistance in finding data.

1. Just under half of state prisoners in 1993 were committed for an offense involving interpersonal violence of any sort (Snell 1995:11), while only 28.5 percent of new court commitments were for violent offenses (Gilliard and Beck 1994:10). As the number of drug offenders sent to prison has risen the percentage of violent offenders has fallen dramatically; in 1980, it was 48.2 percent.
2. In 1992, state governments spent $18.75 billion on corrections, up from $4.26 billion in 1980 (Maguire and Pastore 1995:13). Notwithstanding this large increase, the percentage of the population that thinks more should be spent has risen slightly (Maguire and Pastore 1995:161). Scull (1977) argued that the fiscal crisis of the state was leading to decarceration for criminals and psychiatric patients. However, the large-scale deinstitutionalization of psychiatric patients that may have been motivated by cost considerations has not been paralleled by comparable deinstitutionalization for prisoners.
3. In Great Britain the Tories have introduced similar legislation calling for a mandatory life sentence on a second conviction for an offense involving sex or violence.
4. Between 1961 and 1968, U.S. prison populations fell from 220,149 to 182,102 (Maguire and Pastore 1995:540). Index crimes known to the police increased over that period from 2,087,500 to 4,477,200 (Federal Bureau of Investigation 1972:61). Diana Gordon (1990) also notes the inability of crime rates to explain trends in prison populations. In the Netherlands, Australia, England and West

Germany there were also periods when prison populations dropped while crime rates rose (Downes 1988; Savelsberg 1994).

5. To preserve compatibility between the 1972 and 1995 figures, I have deleted arrests for arson from the 1995 rates. With arson included, the 1995 rate is 1140.3 per 100,000.
6. Arrest rates for drug violations rose from 9.5 per 100,000 in 1965 to 317.3 in 1974, falling after that to 147.3 in 1992 (Maguire and Pastore 1995:413). Between 1980 and 1993, the number of inmates in state prisons for drug offenses rose from 19,000 to 186,000—almost a tenfold increase (Snell 1995:11).
7. Support for the death penalty has increased from its lowest point—less than 45 percent—in 1966, to about 79 percent in 1987, its highest in this century (Bohm 1991; Warr 1995; Longmire 1996).
8. Prison populations are not an ideal measure of punitiveness (J. Lynch 1988). They depend on both the number of people sentenced and the length of time they are imprisoned; and are not normed for the number of offenders eligible for imprisonment. Our analysis is limited by the information available about prison populations in different countries.
9. Similar findings are also reported by Wilkins and Pease (1987) and Gottfredson and Clarke (1990:119–25).
10. The nations are New Zealand, Israel, Spain, Hong Kong, Singapore, Australia, United Kingdom, Italy, the Netherlands, Canada, Belgium, Finland, France, Germany, United States, Norway, Denmark, Sweden, Japan, Switzerland. United Arab Emirates was deleted from the sample because it does not publish statistics for crime rates or the distribution of income.
11. Inequality is here measured by the ratio of the disposable income received by the upper 10% to that received by the bottom 20 percent. Sources for the data used in the analyses based on this sample are listed in Appendix A.
12. One might be concerned that rates of auto theft should not be computed on the basis of a country's population, but on the number of automobiles. However, this may not make much difference. Clarke and Harris (1992) give auto theft rates for 19 high-income nations in 1987/8 per 1000 people, and per 1000 cars. I computed the correlation between these two rates; it was 0.905. Earlier studies that found a relationship between inequality and homicide rates computed inequality on the basis of income before taxes and transfer payments, while it is income after taxes and transfer payments that would appear to have the greater theoretical relevance. We have used the latter.
13. These results are based on reported crime rates, and must therefore be considered uncertain. There is no good reason for supposing rates of reporting and recording crimes to be similar in different countries. A number of the countries with rates of reported crime that are higher than those in the United States have rates of reported victimization that are lower than those in the United States, suggesting that reporting and recording rates may vary crossnationally (Van Dijk, Mayhew and Killias 1991).
14. The "crime rate" is defined as the sum of the homicide rate, the burglary rate and the auto theft rate. It is dominated by the two property offense rates, which are not exceptionally high in the United States. Rates of violence, however, are unusually high in the United States. Michalowski and Pearson (1990) and Ouimet and Tremblay (1996) have found homicide rates to be good predictors of imprisonment rates of the U.S. states in cross-sectional analyses. Changes in U.S. homicide rates, however, are essentially unrelated to changes in imprisonment rates.
15. Van Dijk and Mayhew (1992), Young and Brown (1993) and Mauer (1995a, 1995b) reach a similar conclusion.

16. According to the annual report on the state of the economy of the President's Council of Economic Advisors, this trend halted and slightly reversed in the years 1993–1995, as the lowest-income wage-earners gained disproportionately to others. The report attributes this gain to rising employment, the earned-income tax credit, and legislation specifying a higher minimum wage. However, reports issued in 1996 by the University of Michigan and by the Census Bureau show the gap between rich and poor to be widening (Hershey 1997). Data collected by the Federal Reserve Board suggest that income growth between 1992 and 1995 occurred disproportionately in middle-income brackets (Wessel 1997). In the face of these discrepant findings, it is not clear what the most recent trends are.
17. It is the absence of any specification of mechanisms or processes linking one variable to another in Black's writings that leads critics to contend that his ideas, whatever their validity, do not constitute a theory (Greenberg 1983; Hunt 1983). *Felix qui potuit rerum causas cognoscere*!
18. This relationship has become controversial. Galster and Scaturo (1985) and Parker and Horwitz (1986) find no evidence for the existence of a relationship between unemployment and prison admissions among the American states, in panel analyses for short time spans (1974–1979 for Parker and Horwitz), once common trends are removed from the data. However, six years is a short time-span over which to assess the existence of such a relationship. More damaging, Jacobs and Helms (1996) find no support for a relationship between unemployment or inequality and prison admissions between 1950 and 1990, contrary to Black's (1976) proposition. Chiricos and Delone (1992) survey a number of studies, finding the evidence to be mixed. For several reasons, unemployment statistics are less than ideal as indicators of a threatening population. They fail to count many who are not working, e.g., those who have given up on finding work, and they may count some who are working "off the books." Many of those who are unemployed are not a threat, e.g. middle- and upper-class workers who have savings, a network of family and friends who can help out, and options for other sources of employment. If prison admissions respond to a perceived threat, overall unemployment figures may be a poor measure of it.
19. This correlation is not found in non-market economies, such as Poland in the decades after the Second World War (Greenberg 1980), or in the Netherlands, where a generous welfare system has been in place (de Haan 1990).
20. All analyses of the 1991 General Social Survey reported here have been carried out by me.
21. In 1992, 54.3 percent of the new court commitments to prison in thirty-eight states in 1992 were black (Maguire and Pastore 1995:553). Nationally, approximately almost 7 percent of black men are in prison on any given day, (New York Times 1995) and 25 percent of black American men between the ages of twenty and twenty-nine are under correctional supervision (Mauer 1990). In some states and age-brackets the percentages are much higher: in California, almost 40 percent of black men in their twenties are in prison, on probation or parole (Butterfield 1996b). In addition, between 1977 and 1993, 121 white prisoners and 87 black prisoners were executed (Stephan 1994:11).
22. Insofar as ethnic homogeneity is a source of identification and solidarity based on similarity, one might expect greater punitiveness in such societies on the basis of Durkheim's analysis of mechanical solidarity. The observed pattern is just the opposite.
23. In a private communication, Wilkins assures me that his current thinking on this issue does not assume the existence of societal consensus on rewards and punishments.

24. Aggregating data from 1985, 1990 and 1993 from the General Social Survey I find that 45 percent of the respondents who expressed an opinion thought that the government should *not* redistribute income, while 31.8 percent that the government should. These were the only three years in which the question was asked. No trend is evident in the responses.
25. Higher rates of child poverty in the United States compared to other industrialized nations reflect differences in transfer payments and wage structures (Rainwater 1995).
26. They are not mentioned, for example, by Inverarity, Lauderdale and Feld (1982:148), who say, "Durkheim distinguished between two forms of social solidarity, which he called mechanical and organic," or by Treviño (1996).
27. Much effort has been invested in developing alternative models of state formation (Carneiro 1970; Service 1975). Whatever the details, the relationship between stratification and state formation is empirically sound.
28. In the early stages of this transition, the logic of compensation may be preserved. Payment is made to the state (as well as to a private injured party) to make amends for "the breach of the king's peace" (Goebel 1976; Knepper 1991).
29. A parallel account, differing only in detail, could be provided for European countries.
30. The ratio of black to white arrests declined from 3.13 in 1965 to 2.34 in 1992 (Maguire and Pastore 1995:378).
31. In the year ending 30 September 1996, the Equal Employment Opportunity Commission handled 160 bias cases, compared to 643 in 1990 (Myerson 1997).
32. Supreme Court decisions of the 1980s increased the difficulty of proving discrimination and of bringing a class action suit. However, the Civil Rights Act of 1991 made it easier to prove discrimination, and increased the size of a potential award. In response, the number of class action suits alleging discrimination has risen. Nevertheless, discrimination is often difficult to prove, and in many cases it remains difficult to find an attorney willing to bring a complaint (Myerson 1997).
33. A further problem is that many welfare recipients already do work. In one study, 43 percent of a nationally representative sample of AFDC recipients earned income by working an average of thirty-four hours a week. They worked in spurts because continuous employment was not continuously available, or was impractical because of life circumstances such as illness and family responsibilities. Had the recipients worked full-time, their wages would not have been high enough to raise a family of three over the poverty line (Spalter-Roth 1994; Edin 1991).
34. It is very likely the higher degree of economic inequality found in the United States that accounts for its exceptionally low mobility between generations. In a study of intergenerational mobility in Britain, Canada, Finland, Germany, Malaysia, Sweden, and the United States, Björklund and Jäntti (1997) found that the United States and Britain had the lowest rates.
35. A Rand Corporation study of the likely impact of California's new "Three Strikes" legislation projected that it would add between $4.5 billion and $6 billion to the state budget. With new taxes politically impossible, the study noted that the funds would most likely come from higher education, parks, environmental preservation, and other regulatory agencies (Pillsbury 1995).
36. It might be argued that because many of those who acquire criminal arrest, conviction, and imprisonment histories have limited job prospects for reasons unrelated to their criminal records (educational deficits, shortage of jobs), a criminal record cannot have much impact. However, the criminal justice system casts its net widely, especially in minority communities. One study found that two-thirds of nonwhite adult males in California had been arrested before reaching the age

of thirty (Tillman 1987). There is evidence that a criminal record reduces labor market prospects for some individuals (Lott 1990, 1992; Waldfogel 1994a, 1994b; Grogger 1992, 1995), and increases rates of recidivism in the current and subsequent generation (Hagan and Palloni 1990; Laub and Sampson 1993).

37. An econometric analysis based on data from the National Longitudinal Survey of Youth concludes that the level of lawful income available to a youth strongly influences a youth's decision to desist from crime (Pezzin 1995; see also Votey 1991).
38. Research findings regarding the effects of unemployment on crime are less consistent. For time series research using aggregate data, see Cantor and Land (1985), Chiricos (1987), Hale (1991), Hale and Sabbagh (1991) and Land, Cantor and Russell (1995). A panel study by Parker and Horowitz (1986), using aggregate data, also failed to find evidence for an effect of unemployment on criminality. However, unemployment data are notoriously poor. Moreover, many of those who are unemployed are not in serious economic difficulty. They have left one job to seek another; they have savings and financial support from family. Moreover, these studies focus on the instantaneous effects of marginal changes in the unemployment rate. The effects of long-term unemployment and destitution are quite another. Studies of individuals have yielded mixed results. Gottfredson (1985) concluded that juvenile employment had little or no effect on involvement in crime. On the other hand, several other studies found that employment did reduce adult involvement in crime (Rossi, Berk, and Lenihan 1980; Berk, Lenihan, and Rossi 1981; Jurik 1983; Thornberry and Christenson 1984; Votey 1991).
39. Prisons are, of course, not the only element of law enforcement that can potentially contribute to crime prevention. Police officials have maintained that the drop in crime rates of the past five years is due to newly aggressive policing. It may have contributed, though crime rates have also dropped in cities like Los Angeles, where aggressive policing is nothing new (Karmen 1996; Barrett 1997). The possible contribution of employment gains in an economy that has been expanding since 1991, when homicide rates began to drop, has received little attention in this discussion, but may also have played a role.
40. Between 1965 and 1975, AFDC monthly caseloads went from 1 million to 3.5 million, and the number of food stamp recipients from 0.4 million to 17.1 million (Moffitt 1990).
41. In a national survey conducted in 1972, only 10 percent of the respondents said that they would be less likely to vote for a candidate who advocated tougher sentences for lawbreakers, compared to 79 percent who said that they would be more likely. In a Harris poll conducted in 1970, 64 percent thought the courts dealt too leniently with criminals, compared to 3 percent who thought them too severe (Hindelang et al. 1975:206–297). Convicted felons, who might tend to favor lenient policies, are disenfranchised; politicians can safely ignore their policy preferences. Low-income and minority groups, who are somewhat less punitive, are also less likely to vote.
42. The percentages indicating that crime and violence were the most important problem facing the country in the Gallup poll rose from 2 percent in March of 1991 to 5 percent in March of 1992, to 9 percent in January of 1993, to 37 percent in January of 1994, to 52 percent in August of 1994, and then fell to 27 percent in January of 1995. The number of index crimes reported to the police fell steadily over these years. Similarly, the percentages indicating that drugs and drug abuse were the most important problem facing the country rose from 2 percent in January of 1985 to 38 percent in November of 1989, and then fell to 6 percent in January of 1993 (Maguire and Pastore 1995:140).

43. The proportion of respondents identifying crime as the most important problem can change even when public concern about crime is highly stable, because concern about other issues, such as war and unemployment, have declined.
44. By one count, 673 riots occurred in American cities between 1961 and 1968, with 141 taking place in 1968 alone (Spilerman 1971).
45. When the policy implications of the text of the California Civil Rights Initiative, which passed in November, 1996, were explained to survey subjects a year before the vote, many withdrew their support for the measure (L. Harris 1995).
46. A week later, a similar program maintained by the county in which Houston is located, was declared unconstitutional by a Federal judge (Verhovek 1997b).
47. There is more support for attempting to lower the crime rate by spending money on social and economic problems (52 percent) than for spending money on police, prisons, and judges (39 percent) (Maguire and Pastore 1995:171).
48. This question has occurred even to hard-liners. John Dilulio (1996) has recently argued that with welfare being cut back, even the prisons will not be able to stop black crime. The solution, he thought, must come from the black churches. This is surely an instance of a drowning man grasping at straws.
49. In special circumstances, crime may remain off-limits for ideological reasons even when the political system is not corporatist. Ajzenstadt (1996) notes that in the hotly contested national elections just held in Israel, crime was not made an issue by any of the political parties because both embrace a Zionist ideology of inclusiveness. This ideology provides the basis for social work and assimilative efforts directed toward delinquency, which is believed to occur disproportionately among immigrant youth.
50. Even when its low level of corporatism is taken into account, the United States remains an outlier in this regression so long as the analysis is restricted to linear terms in the independent variables.
51. The correlation between corporatism and rankings for redistributiveness, based on data for income taxes, indirect taxes, social service expenditures and redistributive effects taken from Hewitt (1977), is 0.74.
52. High revenues from oil exports have enabled Norway to pay for its welfare state without putting too large a crimp in middle- and upper-class lifestyles. Global competition has placed pressure on other nations to cut back on welfare benefits.
53. This would explain why people resist new knowledge that challenges their attitudes toward capital punishment. It is their attitudes toward the death sentence that is fundamental, not their belief about its effectiveness (Lord, Ross and Lepper 1979).
54. In a national survey, the median guess for the percentage of poor people who are black was 50 percent; the correct figure is 28 percent (Gilens 1996).
55. The impact of these beliefs on popular views of punishment can be seen in the 1991 General Social Survey 9.4 percent of those who believed that people cannot change the course of their lives agreed that the courts are too harsh, compared to 2.8 percent of those who strongly disagreed. The figures for strongly agreeing that law-breakers deserve stiff punishment were 41.5 percent and 48.3 percent.
56. There is a strong relationship between social class and involvement in crime (Braithwaite 1981), suggesting that the assumption of equal ease of compliance is far from valid.
57. Von Hirsch argued that deserts-based sentencing, even if not fully just, would be better for blacks than highly discretionary sentencing systems. In the intervening years, the proportion of prisoners who are black has risen. This may

reflect the structure of the penalties built into the new sentencing schemes. Federal sentencing guidelines, for example, penalize the sale of crack cocaine much more heavily than the sale of the powder form, even though the U.S. Sentencing Commission recommended an equalization. In 1994, just 3.5 percent of federal crack defendants were white, compared to 29.7 percent of the defendants charged with selling powdered cocaine (Jones 1995).

58. In the 1991 General Social Survey, 23.8 percent of those who strongly agree that people can't change the course of their lives strongly support government action to help the poor, compared to 15.One percent of those who strongly disagree.
59. Nelkin and Lindee (1995) point to passages in popular and academic discourse that explain crime genetically, but do not show that they are common or increasing. Perhaps policymakers and analysts give limited attention to research in this area because it offers so little in prevention or control strategies that could be implemented now or in the near future.
60. In a 1995 national survey, 62 percent of whites said that affirmative action programs are no longer needed to overcome discrimination, compared to 11 percent of blacks. Whites were more likely than blacks to think that black children have as good a chance as white children to obtain a good education (85 percent versus 64 percent) and to find a job for which they are qualified (75 percent versus 52 percent) (Gallup 1996:44).
61. When it came to power in thirteenth-century Bologna, the *popolo*, or popular party, was able to introduce state-administered punishment, probably in order to reduce political violence instigated by the feudal magnates, but the new legislation was weakly enforced and eventually abandoned.
62. Linda Wightman has estimated that if law school admissions were to be made only on the basis of grades and test scores (the main criteria for white applicants), the percent of admissions who are black would fall from 26 to 3. Asian-American admissions would fall from 26 to 15 percent, Mexican-American admissions from 32 to 9 percent, and Puerto Rican admissions from 24 to 6 (Strosnider 1997). Restrictions on the use of affirmative-action criteria in admissions decisions at the University of California system imposed in the aftermath of the passage of Proposition 209 in November of 1996, and at the University of Texas Law School following a federal court decision in the Hopwood case have already led to dramatic reductions in the number of black and Hispanic students admitted to law school at UCLA, the University of California at Berkeley, and the University of Texas (Higginbotham 1988; Rosen 1998).
63. According to one recent study, 14 percent of black men cannot vote because they are in prison or have a felony conviction (Butterfield 1997).
64. The belief is empirically well justified (Skolnick and Fyfe 1993; Ogletree et al. 1994).
65. Residents of South Central Los Angeles, where the riot occurred in 1992, were not as moved in 1997 when O.J. Simpson was convicted in a civil trial of causing wrongful death. The large differences in wealth and lifestyle between Simpson and the great majority of black Angelenos reduced their identification with him and muted their response (Goldberg 1997).
66. The racial differences in beliefs about the Rodney King case were smaller than in the O.J. Simpson case, no doubt because the videotape evidence left less room for interpretive maneuver.
67. These differences in experience are also manifesting themselves on juries in criminal trials. There are persistent reports of black jurors who are skeptical of testimony by police officers, and will not vote to convict black defendants even when the evidence is persuasive (Butler 1995; Rosen 1977).

References

Adamson, Christopher. 1984. "Toward a Marxian Penology: Captive Criminal Population or Economic Threats and Resources." *Social Problems* 31:435–58.

Agnew, Spiro T. 1969. *The Wisdom of Spiro T. Agnew*, New York: Ballantine.

American Friends Service Committee Working Party. 1971. *Struggle for Justice: A Report on Crime and Punishment in America*. New York: Hill and Wang.

Ajzenstadt, Mimi. 1996. "Social Control and the Welfare State: Discipline and Regulations in Israel, 1930–1970." Paper presented to the International Conference on Law and Society, Glasgow, Scotland.

Albrecht, Hans-Jorg. 1987. "Foreign Minorities in the Criminal Justice System in the Federal Republic of Germany." *Howard Journal* 26:272–86.

Alderman, J. 1994. "Leading the Public: The Media's Focus on Crime Shaped Sentiment." *The Public Perspective* 5:26–28.

Alesina, A. and D. Rodrik. 1994. "Distributive Policies and Economic Growth." *Quarterly Journal of Economics* 109:465–90.

Alexander, Karl L. and Doris R. Entwisle. 1996. "Early Schooling and Educational Inequality: Socioeconomic Disparities in Children's Learning," pp. 63–79 in J. Clark (ed.) *James S. Coleman*. London: Falmer Press.

Alper, Benedict S., ed. 1974. *Prisons Inside-Out: Alternatives in Correctional Reform*. Cambridge, MA: Ballinger.

Anderson, David C. 1995. *Crime and the Politics of Hysteria: How the Willie Horton Story Changed American Justice*. New York: Times Books.

Andrews, D. A., Ivan Zinger, Robert D. Hoge, James Bonta, Paul Gendreau and Francis T. Cullen. 1990a. "Does Correctional Treatment Work? A Clinically Relevant and Psychologically Informed Meta-Analysis"? *Criminology* 28:369–404.

———. 1990b. "A Human Sciences Approach or More Punishment and Pessimism: A Rejoinder to Lab and Whitehead." *Criminology* 28:419–29.

Antunes, George and P. Hurley. 1977. "The Representation of Criminal Events in Houston's Two Daily Newspapers." *Journalism Quarterly* 54:756–60.

Applebome, Peter. 1996. "Parents Face Consequences As Children's Misdeeds Rise." *New York Times* (April 10):A1, B8.

Arendt, Hannah. 1951. *The Origins of Totalitarianism*. London: Thames and Hudson.

Arenson, Karen W. 1996a. "Study Details CUNY Successes from Open-Admissions Policy." *New York Times* (May 7):A1, B4.

———. 1996b. "Workfare Rules Cause Enrollment to Fall, CUNY Says." *New York Times* (June 1):A1, A25.

Austin, James and John Irwin. 1991. *Who Goes to Prison?*. San Francisco: National Council on Crime and Delinquency.

Avison, William R. and Pamela L. Loring. 1986. "Population Diversity and Cross-National Homicide: The Effects of Inequality and Heterogeneity." *Criminology* 24:733–49.

Ayres, B. Drummond, Jr. 1996. "Fighting Affirmative Action, He Finds His Race an Issue." *New York Times* (April 18):A1, A19.

Barkan, Steven E. and Steven F. Cohn. 1994. "Racial Prejudice and Support for the Death Penalty by Whites." *Journal of Research in Crime and Delinquency* 31:202–9.

Barnes, J. A. 1965. "Durkheim's Division of Labour in Society." *Man* N.S. 1:158–75.

Barrett, Wayne 1997. "Not So Magic Stats: Did Rudy Cut the Murder Rate Himself?" *Village Voice* (January 14):15.

Beckett, Katherine. 1994. "Setting the Public Agenda: 'Street Crime' and Drug Use in American Politics." *Social Problems* 41:425–47.

Beeghley, Leonard and Jeffrey W. Dwyer. 1989. "Income Transfers and Income Inequality." *Population Research and Policy Review* 8:119–42.

Bénabou, Roland. 1993. "Workings of a City: Location, Education, and Production." *Quarterly Journal of Economics* 108:619–51.

———. forthcoming. "Inequality and Growth." *NBER Macro Annual.*

Berk, Richard A., Kenneth J. Lenihan and Peter H. Rossi. 1980. "Crime and Poverty: Some Experimental Evidence from Ex-Offenders." *American Sociological Review* 45:766–86.

Black, Donald. 1976. *The Behavior of Law*. New York: Academic Press.

Blau, Judith R. and Peter M. Blau. 1982. "The Cost of Inequality: Metropolitan Structure and Violent Crime." *American Sociological Review* 47:114–29.

Bailey, William C. 1984. "Poverty, Inequality and City Homicide Rates." *Criminology* 22:531–50.

Biles, David. 1986. "Prisons and Their Problems." In D. Chappell and P. Wilson (eds.) *The Australian Criminal Justice System, the mid-1980s*. Sydney: Butterworths.

Björklund, Anders and Markus Jäntti. 1997. "Intergenerational Mobility of Economic Status: Is the United States Different?" Paper presented to the American Social Sciences Association.

Blank, Rebecca. 1994. "Does a Larger Social Safety Net Mean Less Economic Flexibility?" pp. 157–87 in R. Freeman (ed.) *Working under Different Rules*. New York: Russell Sage Foundation.

Blanshei, Sarah Rubin. 1981. "Criminal Law and Politics in Medieval Bologna." *Criminal Justice History: An International Review* 2:1–30.

———. "Crime and Law Enforcement in Medieval Bologna." *Journal of Social History* 16:121–38.

Blinder, Alan S. 1996. "The $5.15 Question." *New York Times* (May 23): A27.

Bluestone, Barry. 1995. "The Inequality Express." *The American Prospect* 20 (Winter):81–93.

Blumenthal, Sidney. 1986. *The Rise of the Counter-Establishment: From Conservative Ideology to Political Power*. New York: Basic Books.

Blumstein, Alfred. 1987. "Sentencing and the Prison Crowding Problem," pp. 161–78 in S.D. Gottfredson and S. McConville (eds.) *America's Correctional Crisis*. New York: Greenwood Press.

———. 1988. "Prison Populations: A System Out of Control?" pp. 231–66 in M. Tonry and N. Morris (eds.) *Crime and Justice: A Review of Research*, vol. 10. Chicago: University of Chicago Press.

Blumstein, Alfred and Jacqueline Cohen. 1973. "A Theory of the Stability of Punishment." *Journal of Criminal Law and Criminology* 64:198–207.

Blumstein, Alfred, Jacqueline Cohen, Susan E. Martin, and Michael Tonry, eds.1983. *Research on Sentencing: The Search for Reform*, vol. 1. Washington, DC: National Academy Press.

Blumstein, Alfred, Jacqueline Cohen, and Daniel Nagin. 1976. "The Dynamics of a Homeostatic Punishment Process." *Journal of Criminal Law and Criminology* 68:317–34.

Bobo, Lawrence and James R. Kluegel. 1993. "Opposition to Race-Targeting: Self-Interest, Stratification Ideology, or Racial Attitudes." *American Sociological Review* 58:443–64.

Bohm, Robert M. 1990. "American Death Penalty Opinion, 1936–1986: A Critical Examination of the Gallup Polls," pp. 113–45 in R.M. Bohm in *The Death Penalty in America: Current Research*. Cincinnati: Anderson.

Borjas, George B. 1994. "The Economics of Inequality." *Journal of Economic Literature* 32:1667–1717.

Borjas, George B., Richard B. Freeman, and Lawrence F. Katz. 1996. "Searching for the Effect of Immigration on Labor Markets," *American Economic Review* 86:246–51.

Bowers, William G. 1988. "The Effect of Executions is Brutalization, Not Deterrence," 49–89 in K.C. Haas and J.A. Inciardi (eds.) *Challenging Capital Punishment: Legal and Social Science Approaches*. Newbury Park, CA: Sage.

Bowers, William G. and Glenn L. Pierce. 1975. "The Illusion of Deterrence in Isaac Ehrlich's Research on Capital Punishment." *Yale Law Journal* 85:187–208.

Box, Stephen and Chris Hale. 1982. "Economic Crisis and the Rising Prison Population." *Crime and Social Justice* 18:20–35.

———. 1985. "Unemployment, Imprisonment, and Prison Overcrowding." *Contemporary Crises* 9:209–228.

———. 1986. "Unemployment, Crime and Imprisonment, and the Enduring Problem of Prison Overcrowding," pp. 72–96 in R. Matthews and J. Young (eds.) *Confronting Crime*. London: Sage.

Bradsher, Keith. 1995. "Widest Gap in Incomes? Research Points to U.S." *New York Times* (Oct. 27): D2.

Bragg, Rick. 1995. "Chain Gangs to Return to Roads of Alabama." *New York Times* (Mar. 26):I.16.

Braithwaite, John. 1979. *Inequality, Crime, and Public Policy*. Boston: Routledge and Kegan Paul.

———. 1981. "The Myth of Social Class and Criminality Reconsidered." *American Sociological Review* 46:36–57.

Braithwaite, John and Valerie Braithwaite. 1986. "The Effect of Income Inequality and Social Democracy on Homicide." *British Journal of Criminology* 20:45–53.

Brennan, Mark G. 1997. "Lax Punishments." *New York Times* (Jan. 9): A20.

Burtless, Gary. 1990. "Earnings Inequality over the Business and Demographic Cycles," pp. 77–122 in G. Burtless (ed.) *A Future of Lousy Jobs?*. Washington, DC: Brookings Institution.

Butler, Paul. 1995. "Racially Based Jury Nullification: Black Power in the Criminal Justice System." *Yale Law Journal* 105:677–725.

Butterfield, Fox. 1996a. "States Revamping Laws on Juveniles as Felonies Soar." *New York Times*, Section 1 (May 12):1, 24.

———. 1996b. "Study Examines Race and Justice in California." *New York Times* (Feb. 14): A12.

———. 1997. "Many Black Men Barred From Voting." *New York Times* (Jan. 30): A12.

Calder, James B. 1982. "Presidents and Crime Control: Kennedy, Johnson and Nixon and the Influences of Ideology." *Presidential Studies Quarterly* 12:574–89.

Cantor, David and Kenneth C. Land. 1985. "Unemployment and Crime Rates in the Post-World War II United States: A Theoretical and Empirical Analysis." *American Sociological Review* 50:317–23.

———. 1991. "Exploring Possible Temporal Relationships of Unemployment and Crime: Comment on Hale and Sabbagh," *Journal of Research in Crime and Delinquency* 28:418–25.

Capaldi, Nicholas. 1985. *Out of Order: Affirmative Action and the Crisis of Doctrinaire Liberalism*. Buffalo, NY: Prometheus.

Cappell, Charles L. and Gresham Sykes. 1991. "Prison Commitments, Crime, and Unemployment: A Theoretical and Empirical Specification for the United States, 1933–1985." *Journal of Quantitative Criminology* 7:155–99.

Card, David and Alan B. Krueger. 1995. *Myth and Measurement: The New Economics of the Minimum Wage*. Princeton, NJ: Princeton University Press.

Carneiro, Robert. 1970. "A Theory of the Origin of the State." *Science* 169:733–38.

Carter, Steven L. 1991. *Reflections of an Affirmative Action Baby*. New York: Basic Books.

Chambliss, William J. 1994. "Policing the Ghetto Underclass: The Politics of Law and Law Enforcement." *Social Problems* 41:177–94.

———. 1995. "Crime Control and Ethnic Minorities: Legitimizing Racial Oppression by Creating Moral Panics" pp. 235–58 in D.F. Hawkins (ed.) *Ethnicity, Race, and Crime: Perspectives across Time and Place*. Albany: State University of New York Press.

Chambliss, William J. and Robert Seidman. 1990. *Law, Order, and Power*, 2d ed. Reading, MA: Addison-Wesley.

Chancer, Lynn and Pamela Donovan. 1996. "A Mass Psychology of Punishment: Crime and the Futility of Rationally Based Approaches." *Social Justice* 21:50–71.

Chang, Roberto. 1994. "Income Inequality and Economic Growth: Evidence and Recent Theories." *Economic Review* (Federal Reserve Bank of Atlanta) 79:1–10.

Chernak, Steven. 1995. *Victims in the News: Crime and the American News Media*. Boulder, CO: Westview Press.

Chiricos, Theodore G. 1987. "Rates of Crime and Unemployment: An Analysis of Aggregate Research Evidence." *Social Problems* 34:187–212.

Chiricos, Theodore G. and Charles Crawford. 1995. "Race and Imprisonment: A Contextual Assessment of the Evidence," pp. 281–309 in D.F. Hawkins *Ethnicity, Race, and Crime: Perspectives Across Time and Place*. Albany: State University of New York Press.

——— and Miriam Delone. 1994. "Labor Surplus and Punishment: A Review and Assessment of Theory and Evidence." *Social Problems* 39:421–46.

Christie, Nils 1993. *Crime Control as Industry*. London: Routledge.

Clarke, George R. G. 1995. "More Evidence on Income Distribution and Growth." *Journal of Development Economics* 47:403–27.

Clarke, Ronald V. and Patricia M. Harris. 1992. "Auto Theft and Its Prevention," pp. 1–54in M. Tonry (ed.) *Crime and Justice: A Review of Research*, vol. 16. Chicago: University of Chicago Press.

Coleman, James S., S. Kelly, and J. Moore. 1975. *Trends in School Segregation, 1968–1973*. Washington, DC: The Urban Institute.

Collins, Philip. 1968. *Dickens and Crime*. Bloomington: Indiana University Press.

Crew, B. Keith. 1990. "Acting Like Cops: The Social Reality of Crime and Law on TV Police Dramas," pp. 131–42 in C.R. Sanders (ed.) *Marginal Conventions: Popular Culture, Mass Media and Social Deviance*. Bowling Green, OH: Bowling State University Press.

Crow, I., P. Richardson, C. Riddington and F. Simon. 1989. *Unemployment, Crime, and Offenders*. New York: Routledge.

Cullen, Francis T., Liqun Cao, James Frank, Robert H. Langworthy, Sandra Lee Browning, Renée Kopache, and Thomas J. Stevenson. 1996. "'Stop Or I'll Shoot': Racial Differences in Support of Police Use of Deadly Force." *American Behavioral Scientist* 39:449–60.

Cullen, F. T., G. A. Clark, and J. F. Wozniak. 1985. "Explaining the Get Tough Movement: Can the Public Be Blamed?" *Federal Probation* 49:16–24.

Cullen, F. T., J. B. Cullen and J. F. Wozniak. 1988. "Is Rehabilitation Dead? The Myth of the Punitive Public." *Journal of Criminal Justice* 16:303–17.

Cullen, Francis T. and Paul Gendreau. 1989. "The Effectiveness of Correctional Rehabilitation." In L. Goodstein and D. L. MacKenzie (eds.) *The American Prison: Issues in Research Policy.* New York: Plenum.

Cullen, F. T., S. E. Skovron, J. E. Scott, and V. S. Burton, Jr. 1990. "Public Support for Correctional Treatment: The Tenacity of the Rehabilitative Ideology." *Criminal Justice and Behavior* 17:6–18.

Danziger, Sheldon and Peter Gottschalk, eds. 1993. *Uneven Tides: Rising Inequality in America.* New York: Russell Sage Foundation.

DeFronzo, James. 1983. "Economic Assistance to Impoverished Americans: Relationship to Incidence of Crime." *Criminology* 21:119–36.

DeParle, Jason. 1996a. "Class Is No Longer a Four-Letter Word." *New York Times Magazine* (March 17):40–43.

———. 1996b. "Slamming the Door." *New York Times Magazine* (Oct. 16):52–57, 68, 94, 105.

DiMaggio, Paul, John Evans and Bethany Bryson. 1996. "Have Americans' Social Attitudes Become More Polarized?" *American Journal of Sociology* 102:690–755.

Dilulio, John J., Jr.. 1994. "The Question of Black Crime." *The Public Interest* 117:3–32.

———. 1995. "White Lies about Black Crime." *The Public Interest* 118:30–44.

———. 1996 "Black Youth Crime: Churches Are the Answer." New York University. Fortunoff Colloquium.

DiNardo, John, Nicole M. Fortin and Thomas Lemieux, "Labor Market Institutions and the Distribution of Wages, 1973–1990: A Non-Parametric Approach," *Econometrica* 64:1001–1044.

Donziger, Steven R. 1996. *The Real War on Crime: The Report of the National Criminal Justice Commission.* New York: HarperPerrenial.

Downes, David. 1988. *Contrasts in Tolerance: Post-War Penal Policy in the Netherlands and England and Wales* Oxford: Clarendon Press.

———. 1990. "The Case for Going Dutch: The Lessons of the Post-War Penal Policy." *Political Quarterly* 63:12–24.

Duffee, David and R. Richard Ritti. 1979. "Correctional Policy and Public Values." *Criminology* 14:449–60.

Duncan, Greg J., B. Gustaffson, R. Hauser, G. Schmauss, M. Messenger, R. Muffels, B. Nolan and J. C. Ray. 1993. "Poverty Dynamics in Eight Countries," *Journal of Population Economics* 6:215–34.

Durkheim, Émile. 1933. *The Division of Labor in Society.* Trans. George Simpson. New York: Macmillan.

———. 1992. "Two Laws of Penal Evolution." Tr. T. Anthony Jones and Andrew T. Scull. Pp. 21–49 in M. Gane (ed.) *The Radical Sociology of Durkheim and Mauss.* New York: Routledge.

Eastland, Terry. 1990. *Ending Affirmative Action: The Case for Colorblind Justice.* New York: Basic Books.

Eberts, Paul and Kent P. Schwirian. 1968. "Metropolitan Crime Rates and Relative Deprivation." *Criminologica* 5:43–52.

Edin, Kathryn. 1991. "Surviving the Welfare System: How AFDC Recipients Make Ends Meet in Chicago." *Social Problems* 38:462–74.

Ehrlich, Isaac. 1975. "The Deterrent Effect of Capital Punishment: A Question of Life and Death." *American Economic Review* 65: 397–417.

Ellsworth, Phoebe and Lee Ross. 1983. "Public Opinion and Capital Punishment: A Close Examination of the Views of Abolitionists and Retentionists." *Crime and Delinquency* 29:116–69.

Elmer, E. 1967. *Children in Jeopardy: A Study of Abused Minors and their Families.* Pittsburgh: University of Pittsburgh Press.

Engels, Frederick. 1942. *The Origins of the Family, Private Property and the State.* New York: International Publishers.

Ericson, Richard Victor, Patricia M. Baranek, and Janet B. L. Chan. 1991. *Representing Order: Crime, Law, and Justice in the News Media.* Toronto: University of Toronto Press.

Farnworth, Margaret, Katherine Bennett, and Vincent M. West. 1996. "Mail vs. Telephone Surveys of Criminal Justice Attitudes: A Comparative Analysis." *Journal of Quantitative Criminology* 12:113–33.

Federal Bureau of Investigation. 1996. *Crime in the United States—1995.* Uniform Crime Reports, Department of Justice. Washington, DC: USGPO.

———. 1973. *Crime in the United States—1972.* Uniform Crime Reports, Department of Justice. Washington, DC: USGPO.

Fellmuth, Robert C. 1970. "The Regulatory-Industrial Complex." In B. Wasserstein (ed.) *With Justice for Some.* Boston: Beacon.

Ferri, Enrico. 1905. *Socialism and Positive Science (Darwin, Spencer,Marx).* Edith C. Harvey, trans. London: The Socialist Library.

Finckenauer, James O. 1988. "Public Support for the Death Penalty: Retribution as Just Deserts or Retribution as Revenge?" *Justice Quarterly* (March):81–100.

Finder, Alan. 1996. "Welfare Clients Outnumber Jobs They Might Fill," *New York Times* (Aug. 25):1, 46.

Fine, Bob. 1980. "The Birth of Bourgeois Punishment," *Crime and Social Justice* 13 (Summer):19–26.

Firebaugh, Glenn and Kenneth E. Davis. 1988. "Trends in Anti-black Prejudice, 1972–1984: Region and Cohort Effects." *American Journal of Sociology* 94:251–72.

Fischer, Claude S., Michael Hout, Martín Sánchez Jankowski, Samuel R. Lucas, Ann Swidler and Kim Voss. 1996. *Inequality by Design: Cracking the Bell Curve Myth.* Princeton, NJ: Princeton University Press.

Fish, Stanley. 1996. "When Principles Get in the Way." *New York Times* (Dec. 26):A17.

Fishman, Mark. 1978. "Crime Waves as Ideology." *Social Problems* 25:531–43.

———. 1981. "Police News: Constructing an Image of Crime." *Urban Life* 9:371–94.

Flanagan, Timothy J. 1996. "Public Opinion and Public Policy in Criminal Justice," pp. 151–158 in T.J. Flanagan and D. R. Longmire (eds.) *Americans View Crime and Justice: A National Opinion Survey.*Thousand Oaks, CA: Sage.

Fogel, David. 1975. *"...We Are the Living Proof...": The Justice Model for Corrections.* Cincinnati: W. H. Anderson.

Foucault, Michel. 1977. *Discipline and Punish: The Birthday of the Prison.* Trans. Alan Sheridan. New York: Pantheon.

Frankel, Marvin E. 1972. *Criminal Sentencing: Law Without Order.* New York: Hill and Wang.

Fraser, Steven, ed. 1995. *The Bell Curve Wars: Race, Intelligence, and the Future of America.* New York: Basic Books.

Freeman, Richard. 1993. "How Much Has Deunionization Contributed to the Rise in Male Earnings Inequality?" pp. 100–21 in S. Danziger and P. Gottschalk (eds.) *Uneven Tides: Rising Inequality in America.* New York: Russell Sage Foundation.

French, Howard W. 1997. "The Ritual Slaves of Ghana: Young and Female." *New York Times* (Jan. 20):A1, A5.

Friedman, Lawrence M. and Jack Ladinsky. 1967. "Social Change and the Law of Industrial Accidents." *Columbia University Law Review* 7:50–82.

Fyfe, James J. 1983. "The NIJ Study of the Exclusionary Rule." *Criminal Law Bulletin* 19:253–60.

Gallup, George, Jr. 1994. *The Gallup Poll: Public Opinion 1993*. Wilmington, DE: Scholarly Resources.

———. 1995. *The Gallup Poll: Public Opinion 1994*. Wilmington, DE: Scholarly Resources.

———. 1996. *The Gallup Poll: Public Opinion 1995*. Wilmington, DE.: Scholarly Resources.

Galster, G. A. and L. A. Scaturo. 1995. "The U.S. Criminal Justice System: Unemployment and the Severity of Punishment." *Journal of Research in Crime and Delinquency* 22:163–89.

Garland, David. 1985. *Punishment and Welfare*. Aldershot: Gower.

Gelles, Richard J. 1974. *The Violent Home*. Beverly Hills, CA: Sage.

Geraghty, Mary. 1997. "Finances Are Becoming More Crucial in Students' College Choice, Survey Finds." *Chronicle of Higher Education* (Jan. 17): A41.

Gerber, Jurg and Simone Engelhardt-Greer. 1996. "Just and Painful: Attitudes toward Sentencing Criminals." *Americans View Crime and Justice: A National Public Opinion Survey*. Thousand Oaks, CA: Sage.

Gil, David. 1970. *Violence against Children: Physical Child Abuse in the United States*. Cambridge, MA: Harvard University Press.

Gilder, George F. 1981. *Wealth and Poverty*. New York: Basic Books.

Giles, Martin. 1996. "'Race Coding' and White Opposition to Welfare." *American Political Science Review* 90:593–604.

Gilliard, Darrel K. and Allen J. Beck. 1994. *Prisoners in 1993*. Bureau of Justice Statistics Bulletin. U.S. Department of Justice. Office of Justice Programs.

———. 1996. *Prison and Jail Inmates, 1995*. Washington, DC: U.S. Department of Justice, Office of Justice Programs.

Gitlin, Todd. 1995. *The Twilight of Common Dreams*. New York: Henry Holt.

Glasberg, Davita Silfen and Dan Skidmore. 1997. *Corporate Welfare Policy and the Welfare State: Bank Regulation and the Savings and Loan Bailout*. Hawthorne, NY: Aldine de Gruyter.

Goebel, Julius, Jr. 1976. *Felony and Misdemeanor: A Study in the History of Criminal Law*. Philadelphia: University of Pennsylvania Press.

Goldberg, Carey. 1997. "Geography and Class in Two Simpson Verdicts." *New York Times* (Feb. 7): A20.

Gooding-Williams, Robert, ed. 1993. *Reading Rodney King, Reading Urban Uprising*. New York: Routledge.

Gordon, Diana R. 1990. *The Justice Juggernaut: Fighting Street Crime, Controlling Citizens*. New Brunswick, NJ: Rutgers University Press.

Gordon, David M. 1996. *Fat and Mean: The Corporate Squeeze of Working Americans and the Myth of Managerial "Downsizing"*. New York: The Free Press.

Gottfredson, Denise C. 1985. "Youth Employment, Crime, and Schooling: A Longitudinal Study of a National Sample." *Developmental Psychology* 21:419–32.

Gottfredson, Don M. and Ronald V. Clarke. 1990. *Policy and Theory in Criminal Justice*. Brookfield, VT: Gower.

———. 1989. "Imprisonment and Unemployment: A Comment." *Journal of Quantitative Criminology* 5:187–92.

Gottfredson, Stephen D. and Ralph B. Taylor. 1987. "Attitudes of Correctional Policymakers and the Public," pp. 57–75 in S.D. Gottfredson and S. McConville (eds.) *America's Correctional Crisis: Prison Populations and Public Policy*. New York: Greenwood Press.

Grasmick, Harold G., Elizabeth Davenport, Mitchell B. Chamlin and Robert J. Bursik, Jr. 1992. "Protestant Fundamentalism and the Retributive Doctrine of Punishment." *Criminology* 30:21–46.

Greenberg, David F. 1977a. "The Dynamics of Oscillatory Punishment Processes." *Journal of Criminal Law and Criminology* 68:643–55.

———. 1977b. "The Correctional Effects of Corrections: A Survey of Evaluation Studies," pp. 11–48 in D.F. Greenberg (ed.) *Corrections and Punishment.* Beverly Hills: Sage.

———. 1980. "Penal Sanctions in Poland: A Test of Alternative Models." *Social Problems* 28:194–204.

———. 1983. "Donald Black's Sociology of Law: A Critique." *Law and Society Review*: 17:337–68.

———. 1989. "Unemployment and Imprisonment: A Comment." *Journal of Quantitative Criminology* 5:187–91.

———. 1990. "The Cost-Benefit Analysis of Imprisonment." *Social Justice* 17:49–75.

Greenberg, David F. and Ronald C. Kessler. 1982. "The Effect of Arrests on Crime: A Multivariate Panel Analysis." *Social Forces* 60:771–90.

Greenberg, David F., Ronald C. Kessler and Charles H. Logan. 1979. "A Panel Analysis of Crime Rates and Arrest Rates." *American Sociological Review* 44:843–50.

Greenhouse, Linda. 1996. "How Congress Curtailed the Courts' Jurisdiction." *New York Times* (Oct. 27): E5.

Greenwood, Peter. 1996. *Diverting Children from a Life of Crime: Measuring Costs and Benefits*. Santa Monica, CA: Rand.

Grogger, Jeffrey. 1992. "Arrests, Persistent Youth Joblessness, and Black/White Employment Differences," *Review of Economics and Statistics* 74:100–106.

——— 1995. "The Effect of Arrests on the Employment and Earnings of Young Men." *Quarterly Journal of Economics* 110:51–71.

Gross, Hyman. 1979. *A Theory of Criminal Justice.* New York: Oxford University Press.

de Haan, Willem. 1990. *The Politics of Redress: Crime, Punishment and Penal Abolition.* Boston: Unwin Hyman.

Hacker, Andrew. 1992. *Two Nations: Black and White, Separate, Hostile, Unequal.* New York: Scribner.

Hagan, John and Alberto Palloni. 1990. "The Social Reproduction of a Criminal Class in Working-Class London circa 1950–1980." *American Journal of Sociology* 96:265–99.

Hale, Chris. 1989. "Unemployment, Imprisonment, and the Stability of Punishment Hypotheses: Some Results Using Cointegration and Error Correction Models." *Journal of Quantitative Criminology* 5:169–86.

———. 1991. "Unemployment and Crime: Differencing Is No Substitute for Modeling." *Journal of Research in Crime and Delinquency* 28:426–29.

Hale, Chris and Dima Sabbagh. 1991. "Testing the Relationship between Unemployment and Crime: A Methodological Comment and Empirical Analysis Using Time Series Data from England and Wales." *Journal of Research in Crime and Delinquency* 28:400–17.

Harris, Louis. 1995. "Affirmative Action and the Voter." *New York Times* (July 31): A13.

Harris, Marvin. 1981. *America Now: The Anthropology of a Changing Culture.* New York: Simon and Schuster.

Head, Simon. 1996. "The New, Ruthless Economy." *The New York Review of Books* (Feb. 26):47–52.

Henderson, David R. 1997. "Canada's High Unemployment Rate Is No Mystery." *Wall Street Journal* (Feb. 7): A19.

Henig, Jeffrey R. 1994. *Rethinking School Choice.* Princeton, NJ: Princeton University Press.

Henkin, Josh. 1989. "The Meretricious Origins of Merit: Or, Why Jewish Males Oughtn't Be So Smug." *Tikkun* 4.1:53–7.

Herrnstein, Richard J. and Charles Murray. 1994. *The Bell Curve: Intelligence and Class Structure in American Life*. New York: The Free Press.

Hershey, Robert D., Jr. 1997. "Clinton Aides Say That Income Gap Narrows." *New York Times* (Feb. 11): D3.

Hewitt, Christopher. 1977. "The Effect of Political Democracy and Social Democracy on Equality in Industrial Societies: A Cross-National Comparison." *American Sociological Review* 42:450–64.

Higginbotham, A. Leon, Jr. 1998. "Breaking Thurgood Marshall's Promise." *New York Times Magazine* (Jan. 18):28–9.

Hindelang, Michael J., Christopher S. Dunn, Alison L. Aumick, and L. Paul Sutton, eds. 1975. *Sourcebook of Criminal Justice Statistics—1974*. U.S. Law Enforcement Assistance Administration, National Criminal Justice Information and Statistics Service. Washington, DC: Government Printing Office.

Hindelang, Michael J., Michael R. Gottfredson, and Timothy J. Flanagan, eds. 1981. *Sourcebook of Criminal Justice Statistics—1980*. U.S. Department of Justice, Bureau of Justice Statistics. Washington, DC: U.S. Government Printing Office.

Hinds, Michael deCourcy. 1991. "Minority Business Set back Sharply by Courts' Rulings." *New York Times* (Dec. 23): A1, A15.

Holmes, Steven A. 1996a. "Study Finds Rising Number of Black-White Marriages." *New York Times* July 4): A16.

———. 1996b. "In New Guide, U.S. Retreats on Contracts for Minorities." *New York Times* (May 23):A26.

Home Office. 1990. *Prison Statistics: England and Wales, 1989*. London: HMSO.

Horwitz, Allan V. 1990. *The Logic of Social Control*. New York: Plenum.

Howard, John A. 1780. *The State of the Prisons in England and Wales*. Warrington: W. Eyres.

Howard, O. O. 1866. *Report of the Assistant Commissioners of the Freedmen's Bureau*. Senate Executive doc. no. 27, 39th congress, 1st sess. (Senate Executive Documents, vol. 2, Serial 1238).

Hudson, Barbara A. 1993. *Penal Policy and Social Justice*. Toronto: University of Toronto Press.

Humphries, Drew and David F. Greenberg. 1981. "The Dialectics of Crime Control." In D.F. Greenberg (ed.) *Crime and Capitalism: Readings in Marxist Criminology*. Palo Alto: Mayfield.

Hunt, Alan. 1983. "Behavioural Sociology of Law: A Critique of Donald Black." *Journal of Law and Society* 10:19–33.

Ibrahim, Youssef M. 1996. "Welfare's Cozy Coat Eases Norwegian Cold." *New York Times* (Dec. 13): A1, A12.

Ignatieff, Michael. 1978. *A Just Measure of Pain: The Penitentiary in the Industrial Revolution, 1750–1850*. New York: Pantheon.

Interpol. 1992. *International Crime Statistics, 1989–1990*. Saint Cloud, France: Interpol.

Inverarity, James, Pat Lauderdale, and Barry C. Feld. 1983. *Law and Society: Sociological Perspectives on Criminal Law*. Boston: Little Brown.

Inverarity, James and L. M. Tedrow. 1987. "Unemployment, Crime and Imprisonment: A Pooled Cross Section and Time Series Analysis." Paper presented to the Society for the Study of Social Problems.

Jackman, Mary R. 1994. *The Velvet Glove: Paternalism and Conflict in Gender, Class and Race Relations*. Berkeley and Los Angeles: University of California Press.

Jackman, Mary R. and Robert W. Jackman. 1983. *Class Awareness in the United States*. Berkeley and Los Angeles: University of California Press.

Jackson, Pamela Irving. 1995. "Minority Group Threat, Crime, and the Mobilization of Law in France," pp. 341–59 in D.F. Hawkins (ed.) *Ethnicity, Race, and*

Crime: Perspectives across Time and Place. Albany: State University of New York.

Jacobs, David and Ronald E. Helms. 1996. "Toward a Political Model of Incarceration: A Time-Series Examination of Multiple Explanations for Prison Admission Rates." *American Journal of Sociology* 102:323–57.

Jacoby, Russell and Naomi Glauberman, eds.1995. *The Bell Curve Debate: History, Documents, Opinions*. New York: Times Books.

Jankovic, Ivan. 1977. "Labor Market and Imprisonment." *Crime and Social Justice* 8:17–31.

Jenkins, Richard L. and Waln K. Brown. 1988. *The Abandonment of Delinquent Behavior*. Westport, CT: Greenwood Press.

Jencks, Christopher. 1992. *Race, Poverty and the Underclass*. Cambridge, MA: Harvard University Press.

Junger, Marianne. 1988. "Racial Discrimination in the Netherlands." *Sociology and Social Research* 72:211–16.

Jones, Charisse. 1995. "Crack and Punishment: Is Race the Issue?". *New York Times* (Oct. 28): 1,10.

Juhn, Chinhu, Kevin M. Murphy, and Brooks Pierce. 1993. "Wage Inequality and the Rise in Returns to Skill," *Journal of Political Economy* 101:410–42.

Jurik, Nancy C. 1983. "The Economics of Female Recidivism: A Study of TARP Female Offenders." *Criminology* 21:603–22.

Kalmijn, Matthijs. 1993. "Trends in Black/White Intermarriage." *Social Forces* 72: 22–41.

Karmen, Andrew. 1996. "What's Driving New York's Crime Rates Down?" *Law Enforcement News* (Nov. 30):8–10.

Karoly, Lynn A. 1992. "Changes in the Distribution of Individual Earnings in the United States, 1967–1986." *Review of Economics and Statistics* 74:107–15.

———. 1993. "The Trend in Inequality among Families, Individuals, and Workers in the United States: A Twenty-five Year Perspective" pp. 1–97 in S. Danziger and P. Gottschalk (eds.) *Uneven Tides: Rising Inequality in America*. New York: Russell Sage Foundation.

Katz, Janet and William J. Chambliss. 1991. "Biology and Crime," pp. 245–71 in J.F. Sheley (ed.) *Criminology: A Contemporary Handbook*. Belmont, CA: Wadsworth.

Kemp, Alice Abel. 1994. *Women's Work: Degraded and Devalued*. Englewood Cliffs, NJ: Prentice-Hall.

Kick, Edward L. and Gary D. LaFree. 1985. "Development and the Social Context of Murder and Theft." *Comparative Social Research* 8:37–58.

Kilborn, Peter T. 1994. "Backlog of Cases Is Overwhelming Jobs-Bias Agency." *New York Times* (Nov. 25): A1.

———. 1995. "White Males and Management: Report Finds Prejudices Block Women and Minorities." *New York Times* (Mar. 17): A14.

Killias, Martin. 1986. "Power Concentration, Legitimation Crisis, and Penal Severity," pp. 95–117 in W.B. Groves and G. Newman (eds.) *Punishment and Privilege*. New York: Harrow and Heston.

Kleck, Gary. 1981. "Racial Discrimination in Criminal Sentencing: A Critical Evaluation of the Evidence on the Death Penalty." *American Sociological Review* 46:783–805.

Klein, Lawrence R., Brian Forst, and Victor Filatov. 1978. "The Deterrent Effect of Capital Punishment: An Assessment of Estimates," pp. 336–60 in A. Blumstein, J. Cohen, and D. Nagin (eds.) *Deterrence and Incapacitation: Estimating the Effects of Criminal Sanctions on Crime Rates*. Washington, DC: National Academy of Sciences.

Klein, S., J. Petersilia, and S. Turner. 1990. "Race and Imprisonment Decisions in California," *Science* 247:812–16.

Kluegel, James R. and Eliot R. Smith. 1986. *Beliefs about Inequality: Americans' Beliefs about What Is and What Ought to Be*. New York: Aldine de Gruyter.

Knepper, Paul. 1991. "A Brief History of Profiting from the Punishment of Crime." Paper presented to the American Society of Criminology.

Koon, Stacey, with Robert Deitz. 1992. *Presumed Guilty: The Tragedy of the Rodney King Affair*. Washington, DC: Regnery Gateway.

Kotlowitz, Alex. 1994. "Their Crimes Don't Make Them Adults." *New York Times* (Feb. 13):VI:40–41.

Krahn, Harvey, Timothy J. Hartnagel and John W. Gartrell. 1986. "Income Inequality and Homicide Rates: Cross-National Data and Criminological Theories." *Criminology* 24:269–95.

Kress, June B. 1994. "Homeless Fatigue Syndrome: The Backlash against the Crime of Homelessness in the 1990s." *Social Justice* 21:85–108.

Krugman, Paul R. 1992. "The Rich, the Right, and the Facts," *The American Prospect* 11 (Fall):19–31.

———. 1994. *The Age of Diminished Expectations*. Cambridge, MA: MIT Press.

Kunen, James S. 1995. "Teaching Prisoners a Lesson." *The New Yorker* (July 10):34–39.

Kuttner, Robert. 1996. *Everything for Sale: The Virtues and Limits of Markets*. New York: Alfred A. Knopf.

Lab, S. P. and J. T. Whitehead. 1990. "From 'Nothing Works' to 'The Appropriate Works': The Latest Stop on the Search for the Secular Grail." *Criminology* 28:405–17.

Laffargue, B. and T. Godefroy. 1989. "Economic Cycles and Punishment: Unemployment and Imprisonment." *Contemporary Crises* 13:371–404.

Landry, Bart. 1987. *The New Black Middle Class*. Berkeley and Los Angeles: University of California Press.

Langan, Patrick A. 1991. "America's Soaring Prison Population." *Science* 251:1568–73.

Langbein, John H. 1977. *Torture and the Law of Proof: Europe and England in the Ancien Regime*. Chicago: University of Chicago Press.

Laub, John H. and Robert J. Sampson. 1993. "The Long Term Effect of Punishment." Unpublished paper.

Lavin, David E. and David Hyllegard. 1996. *Changing the Odds: Open Admissions and the Life Chances of the Disadvantaged*. New Haven, CT: Yale University Press.

Lederman, Douglas. 1996a. "Split on Racial Preferences: Federal Courts Are Rejecting Affirmative Action, But Colleges Vow to Defend It," *Chronicle of Higher Education* (April 5):A25, A29.

———. 1996b. "College Leaders Plan Strategy to Defend Affirmative Action." *Chronicle of Higher Education* (May 31): A24.

Levin, Michael. 1989. "Affirmative Action vs. Jewish Men." *Tikkun* 4.1:50–3.

Levitt, Steven D. 1996. "The Effect of Prison Population Size on Crime Rates: Evidence from Prison Overcrowding Litigation." *Quarterly Journal of Economics* 111:319–51.

Levy, Frank and Richard J. Murnane. 1992. "U.S. Earnings Levels and Earnings Inequality: A Review of Recent Trends and Proposed Explanations." *Journal of Economic Literature* 30:1333–81.

Lewis, Anthony. 1995. "Is It a Zeal to Kill?" *New York Times* (Dec. 8): A31.

Lichter, Daniel T. and David J. Eggebeen. 1993. "Rich Kids, Poor Kids: Changing Income Inequality among American Children." *Social Forces* 71:761–80.

Lilly, J. Robert and Paul Knepper. 1993. "The Corrections-Commercial Complex." *Crime and Delinquency* 39:150–66.

Lipton, Douglas, Robert Martinson and Judith Wilks. 1975. *The Effectiveness of Correctional Treatment: A Survey of Treatment Evaluation Studies*. New York: Praeger.

Loftin, Colin and Robert H. Hill. 1974. "Regional Subculture and Homicide: An Examination of the Gastil-Hackney Thesis." *American Sociological Review* 39:714–24.

Lombroso, Cesare. 1871. *L'uomo bianco e l'uomo di colore: letture sull' origine e le varietà delle razze umane*. Padua: F.Sacceto.

———. 1876. *L'uomo delinquente*. Milan: Hoepli.

———. 1911. *Crime: Its Causes and Its Remedies*. Trans. Henry P. Horton. Boston: Little Brown.

Longmire, Dennis R. 1996. "America's Attitudes about the Ultimate Weapon," pp. 93–108 in T.J. Flanagan and D.R. Longmire (eds.) *Americans View Crime and Justice: A National Public Opinion Survey*. Thousand Oaks, CA: Sage.

Lord, C., L. Ross, and M. Lepper. 1979. "Biased Assimilation and Attitude Polarization: The Effects of Prior Theories on Subsequently Considered Evidence," *Journal of Personality and Social Psychology* 37:2098.

Lott, John R., Jr. 1990. "The Effect of Conviction on the Legitimate Income of Criminals." *Economic Letters* 34:381–5.

———. 1992. "An Attempt at Measuring the Total Monetary Penalty from Drug Convictions: The Importance of an Individual's Reputation." *Journal of Legal Studies* 21:159–87.

Lotz, R. and Robert M. Regoli. 1980. "Public Support for the Death Penalty." *Criminal Justice Review* 5:55–65.

Luker, Kristin. 1996. *Dubious Conceptions: The Politics of Teenage Pregnancy*. Berkeley and Los Angeles: University of California Press.

Lynch, Frederick R. 1989. *Invisible Victims: White Males and the Crisis of Affirmative Action*. New York: Greenwood Press.

Lynch, James P. 1988. "A Comparison of Prison Use in England, Canada, West Germany and the United States: A Limited Test of the Punitive Hypothesis." *Journal of Criminal Law and Criminology* 79:180–219.

Macfarlane, Alan. 1979. *The Origins of English Individualism: The Family, Property, and Social Transition*. New York: Cambridge University Press.

Maden, M. F. and D. F. Wrench. 1977. "Significant Findings in Child Abuse Research." *Victimology* 2:196–224.

Maguire, Kathleen and Ann L. Pastore, eds. 1996. *Sourcebook of Criminal Justice Statistics 1995*. U.S. Dept. of Justice, Bureau of Justice Statistics. Washington, DC: USGPO.

Martinson, Robert. 1974. "What Works? Questions and Answers about Prison Reform," *Public Interest* 10:22–54.

Marvell, Thomas B. and Carlisle E. Moody, Jr. 1994. "Prison Population Growth and Crime Reduction." *Journal of Quantitative Criminology* 10:109–40.

———. 1996. "Determinate Sentencing and Abolishing Parole: The Long-term Impacts on Prisons and Crime." *Criminology* 34:107–28.

Mauer, Marc. 1990. *Young Black Men and the Criminal Justice System: A Growing National Problem*. Washington, DC: The Sentencing Project.

———. 1995a. "The International Use of Incarceration." *Prison Journal* 75:113–23.

———. 1995b. *Americans Behind Bars: The International Use of Incarceration, 1992–1993*. Washington, DC: Sentencing Project.

Maume, David J., Jr. 1989. "Inequality and Metropolitan Rape Rates: A Routine Activity Approach." *Justice Quarterly* 6:513–27.

McAvoy, Paul W. 1976. *The Crisis of the Regulatory Commission*. New York: Norton.

McCorkle, R. C. 1993. "Research Note: Punish and Rehabilitate? Public Attitudes toward Six Common Crimes." *Crime and Delinquency* 39:240–52.

McCrate, Elaine. 1997. "Welfare and Women's Earnings." *Politics and Society* 25:417–42.

Mead, Lawrence A. 1992. *The New Politics of Poverty: The Nonworking Poor in America*. New York: Basic Books.

Melossi, Dario and Massimo Pavarini. 1980. *The Prison and the Factory*. London: Macmillan.

Messner, Steve F. 1980. "Income Inequality and Murder Rates: Some Cross-National Findings." *Comparative Social Research* 3:185–98.

———. 1982. "Societal Development, Social Equality and Homicide." *Social Forces* 61:225–240.

Michalowski, Raymond J. and Michael A. Pearson. 1990. "Punishment and Social Structure at the State Level: A Cross-Sectional Comparison of 1970 and 1980." *Journal of Research in Crime and Delinquency* 20:73–85.

Miller, Jerome. 1996. *Search and Destroy: African-American Males in the Criminal Justice System*. New York: Cambridge University Press.

Miller, Martin B. 1980. "Sinking Gradually into the Proletariat: The Emergence of the Penitentiary in the United States." *Crime and Social Justice* 14 (Winter):37–43.

Mishel, Robert and John Schmitt. 1996. "Cutting Wages by Cutting Welfare: The Impact of Reform on the Low-Wage Labor Market." Briefing Paper, Economic Policy Institute, Washington, DC.

Moffitt, Robert A. 1990. "The Distribution of Earnings and the Welfare State," pp. 201–30 in G. Burtless (ed.) *A Future of Lousy Jobs?* Washington, DC: Brookings Institution.

Muncie, John and Richard Sparks. 1991. "Expansion and Contraction in European Penal Systems." In J. Muncie and R. Sparks (eds.) *Imprisonment: European Perspectives*. New York: St. Martin's Press.

Murphy, William and Anthony M. DeStefano. 1996. "It's 'Open Season' to Snipe at Judges." *Newsday* (Feb. 27): A6.

Murray, Charles. 1984. *Losing Ground: American Social Policy, 1950–1980*. New York: Basic Books.

Myerson, Allen R. 1997. "As Federal Bias Cases Drop, Workers Take Up the Fight." *New York Times* (Jan. 12): A1, A14.

National Center for Children in Poverty. 1997. *One in Four: America's Youngest Poor*. New York: Columbia University School of Public Health.

National Center for Education Statistics. 1995. *The Condition of Education, 1995*. Washington, DC: U.S. Department of Education.

Nelkin, Dorothy and M. Susan Lindee. 1995. *The DNA Mystique: The Gene as a Cultural Icon*. New York: W. H. Freeman.

Nielson, Francois and Arthur S. Alderson. 1997. "The Kuznets Curve and the Great U-Turn: Income Inequality in U.S. Counties, 1970 to 1990." *American Sociological Review* 62:12–33.

Newman, Katherine. 1988. *Falling from Grace: The Experience of Downward Mobility in the American Middle Class*. New York: The Free Press.

New York Times. 1995. "Nearly 7% of Adult Black Men Were Inmates in '94, Study Says," (Dec. 4): A15.

Noble, Kenneth B. 1988. "Farm Workers Fault Lack of Enforcement of Sanitation Rules" (Oct. 4): A1, A18.

O'Brien, Robert M. 1996. "Police Productivity and Crime Rates: 1973–1992." *Criminology* 34:183–208.

O'Flaherty, Brendan. 1996. *Making Room: The Politics of Homelessness*. Cambridge, MA: Harvard University Press.

Ogletree, Charles J., Jr., Mary Prosser, Abbe Smith, William J. Talley, Jr. 1995. *Beyond the Rodney King Story: An Investigation of Police Misconduct in Minority Communities*. Boston: Northeastern University Press.

Orcutt, James D. and Rebecca Faison. 1981. "Sex-Role Attitude Change and Reporting of Rape Victimization, 1973–1985." *Sociological Quarterly* 29:589–604.

Ouimet, Marc and Pierre Tremblay. 1996. "A Normative Theory of the Relationship between Crime Rates and Imprisonment Rates: An Analysis of the Penal Behavior of U.S. States from 1972 to 1992." *Journal of Research in Crime and Delinquency* 33:109–25.

Ozawa, Martha N. 1995. "Antipoverty Effects of Public Income Transfers on Children." *Children and Youth Services Review* 17:43–59.

Pampel, Fred C., John B. Williamson and Robin Stryker. 1990. "Class Context and Pension Response to Demographic Structure in Advanced Industrial Democracies." *Social Problems* 37:535–47.

Parker, Robert Nash and Allan V. Horwitz. 1986. "Unemployment, Crime, and Imprisonment: A Panel Approach." *Criminology* 24:751–73.

Parmalee, Maurice. 1908. *The Principles of Anthropology and Sociology in their Relations to Primitive Procedure*. New York: Macmillan.

Passell, Peter. 1975. "The Deterrent Effect of the Death Penalty: A Statistical Test." *Stanford Law Review* 28:61–80.

Pear, Robert. 1990. "Courts are Undoing Efforts to Aid Minority Contractors." *New York Times* (July 16): A1.

Pearce, Frank. 1989. *The Radical Durkheim*. London: Unwin Hyman.

Perlstein, Gary R. and Thomas R. Phelps, eds. 1975. *Alternatives to Prison: Community-Based Corrections*. Pacific Palisades, CA: Goodyear.

Persell, Caroline Hodges. 1977. *Education and Inequality: A Theoretical and Empirical Synthesis*. New York: The Free Press.

Persson, Torsen and Guido Tabellini. 1994. "Is Inequality Harmful for Growth? Theory and Evidence." *American Economic Review* 48:600–21.

Peterson, Ruth D. and William C. Bailey. 1988b. "Forcible Rape, Poverty, and Economic Inequality in U.S. Metropolitan Communities." *Journal of Quantitative Criminology* 4:99–119.

Pettigrew, Thomas F. and Robert C. Green. 1976. "School Desegregation in Large Cities: A Critique of the 'White Flight' Thesis." *Harvard Education Review* 46:1–53.

Pezzin, Liliana E. 1995. "Earnings Prospects, Matching Effects, and the Decision to Terminate a Criminal Career." *Criminology* 11:29–50.

Phillips, Kevin. 1990. *The Politics of Rich and Poor: Wealth and the American Electorate in the Reagan Aftermath*. New York: Harper Perennial.

Pillsbury, Samuel H. 1989. "Understanding Penal Reform: The Dynamic of Change." *Journal of Criminal Law and Criminology* 80:726–80.

———. 1995. "Why Are We Ignored? The Peculiar Place of Experts in the Current Debate about Crime and Justice." *Criminal Law Bulletin* 31: 305–36.

Piven, Frances Fox and Richard A. Cloward. 1971. *Regulating the Poor: The Functions of Public Welfare*. New York: Pantheon Books.

Platt, Anthony M. 1969. *The Child Savers: The Invention of Delinquency*. Chicago: University of Chicago Press.

Polsky, Andrew J. 1991. *The Rise of the Therapeutic State*. Princeton, NJ: Princeton University Press.

Primus, Wendell, Kathryn Porter, Margery Ditto and Mitchell Kent. 1996. *The Safety Net Delivers*. Washington, DC: Center on Budget and Policy Priorities.

Quillian, Lincoln. 1996. "Group Threat and Regional Change in Attitudes toward African-Americans," *American Journal of Sociology* 102:816–60.

Quinney, Richard. 1977. *Class, State and Crime: On the Theory and Practice of Criminal Justice*. New York: David McKay.

Rainwater, Lee. 1995. "Poverty and the Income Package of Working Parents: The United States in Comparative Perspective." *Children and Youth Services Review* 17:11–41.

Reiss, Albert J., Jr. and Jeffrey A. Roth. 1993. *Understanding and Preventing Violence*. Washington, DC: National Academy Press.

Rich, Michael J., Robert L. Lineberry, and Herbert Jacob. 1982. "Police Policies and Urban Crime." In H. Jacob and R. L. Lineberry (eds.) *Crime and Governmental Responses in American Cities*, Washington, DC: National Institute of Justice.

Riley, P. J. and V. M. Rose. 1980. "Public vs. Elite Opinion on Correctional Reform: Implications for Social Policy." *Journal of Criminal Justice* 8:345–56.

Robison, James O. and George Smith. 1971. "The Effectiveness of Correctional Programs." *Journal of Research in Crime and Delinquency* 17:67–80.

Rokeach, Milton and Sandra J. Ball-Rokeach. 1989. "Stability and Change in American Value Priorities, 1968–81." *American Psychologist* 44:775–84.

Rosell, Christine. 1975–6. "School Desegregation and White Flight." *Political Science Quarterly* 90:675–95.

Rosen, Jeffrey. 1997. "One Angry Woman." *New Yorker* (24 Feb. and 3 Mar.3):54–64.

———. 1998. "Damage Control." *New Yorker* (23 Feb. and 2 Mar.):58–68.

Rosenfeld, Richard. 1986. "Urban Crime Rates: Effects of Inequality, Welfare Dependency, Region, and Race," pp. 116–30 in J.M. Byrne and R.J. Sampson (eds.) *The Social Ecology of Crime*. New York: Springer-Verlag.

Ross, Robert and Paul Gendreau. 1980. *Effective Correctional Treatment: A Survey of Treatment Evaluation Studies*. New York: Praeger.

Rossi, Peter H., Richard A. Berk, and Kenneth J. Lenihan. 1980. *Money, Work and Crime: Experimental Evidence*. New York: Academic Press.

Rossi, Peter H., Jon A. Simpson, and JoAnn L. Miller. 1985. "Beyond Crime Seriousness: Fitting the Punishment to the Crime." *Journal of Quantitative Criminology* 1:59–90.

Rothman, David J. 1971. *Discovery of the Asylum*. Boston: Little, Brown.

Rusche, Georg and Otto Kirchheimer. 1939. *Punishment and Social Structure*. New York: Columbia University Press.

Rushton, J. Philippe. 1990. "Race and Crime." *Canadian Journal of Criminology* 32:315–34.

———. 1995a. "Race and Crime: An International Dilemma." *Society* 32:37–41.

———. 1995b. *Race, Evolution and Behavior: A Life History Perspective*. New Brunswick, NJ: Transaction Publishers.

Sabol, William J. 1989. "The Dynamics of Unemployment and Imprisonment in England and Wales, 1946–1985." *Journal of Quantitative Criminology* 5:147–68.

Savelsberg, Joachim. 1994. "Knowledge, Domination, and Criminal Punishment." *American Journal of Sociology* 99:911–43.

Schlesinger, Philip. 1994. *Reporting Crime: The Media Politics of Criminal Justice*. New York: Oxford University Press.

Schuman, Howard, Charles Steeh, and Lawrence Bobo. 1985. *Racial Attitudes in America*. Cambridge, MA: Harvard University Press.

Scull, Andrew T. 1977. *Decarceration: Community Treatment and the Deviant—A Radical View*. Englewood Cliffs, NJ: Prentice-Hall.

Schwendinger, Herman and Julia Schwendinger. 1974. *Sociologists of the Chair: A Radical Analysis of the Formative Years of North American Sociology (1883–1922)*. New York: Basic Books.

Sellin, J. Thorsten. 1976. *Slavery and the Penal System.* New York: Elsevier.
Service, Elmer R. 1975. *Origins of the State and Civilization: The Process of Cultural Evolution.* New York: W. W. Norton.
Sewell, William H. and Vimal P. Shah. 1967. "Socioeconomic Status, Intelligence, and the Attainment of Higher Education." *Sociology of Education* 40:1–23.
Shane-Dubow, Sandra, Alice P. Brown, and Erik Olsen. 1985. Sentencing Reform in the United States: History, Context, and Effect. Washington, DC: Government Printing Office.
Sheleff, Leon. 1975. "From Restitutive to Repressive Law." *Archive Européenes de Sociology* 16:6–45.
Shichor, David and Dale K. Sechrest, eds. 1996. *Three Strikes and You're Out: Vengeance as Public Policy.* Thousand Oaks, CA: Sage.
Shilts, Randy. 1982. *The Mayor of Castro Street.* New York: St. Martin's Press.
Sigelman, Lee and Susan Welch. 1991. *Black American's Views of Racial Inequality.* New York: Cambridge University Press.
Simeral, Isabel. 1916. *Reform Movements in Behalf of Children in England of the Early Nineteenth Century, and the Agents of Those Reforms.* New York: Columbia University Ph.D. diss.
Simon, Jonathan. "DON'T SHOOT ME, PLEASE, MR. STAGOLEE!: Violence, Discipline, and the Bodies of Young Black Men." Paper presented to New York University Law and Society Colloquium.
———. 1993. *Poor Discipline: Parole and the Social Control of the Underclass, 1890–1990.* Chicago: University of Chicago Press.
Simpson, Myles E. 1985. "Violent Crime, Income Inequality, and Regional Culture: Another Look." *Sociological Focus* 18:199–208.
Skolnick, Jerome. 1995. "A Durkheimian Moment: O.J. Simpson and the Collective Conscience." Paper presented to the American Society of Criminology.
Skolnick, Jerome and James J. Fyfe. 1993. *Above the Law: Police and the Excessive Use of Force.* New York: The Free Press.
Skovron, S. E., J. E. Scott, and F. T. Cullen. 1988. "Prison Crowding: Public Attitudes toward Strategies of Population Control." *Journal of Research in Crime and Delinquency* 25:150–69.
"A Small Ripple or a Large Wave? The Effect of Law on the Economic Progress of Minorities." 1996. *Researching Law: An ABF Update* 72:1,6.
Smith, T. W. 1990. "Social Inequality in Cross-National Perspective," pp.21–31 in J. W. Becker, J. A. Dais, P. Estes, and P. P. Mohler (eds.) *Attitudes to Inequality and the Role of Government.* Rijswijk, the Netherlands: Social en Cultural Planbureau.
Snell, Tracy L. 1995. *Correctional Populations in the United States, 1993.* NCJ-156241. Washington, DC: Bureau of Justice Statistics.
Sowell, Thomas. 1975. *Affirmative Action Reconsidered: Was It Necessary in Academia?.* Washington, DC: American Enterprise Institute for Public Policy Research.
Spalter-Roth, Roberta. 1994. "The Real Employment Opportunities of Women Participating in AFDC: What the Market Can Provide." *Social Justice* 21:60–70.
Spelman, William. 1994. *Criminal Incapacitation.* New York: Plenum.
Spierenberg, Petris Cornelis. 1984. *The Spectacle of Suffering, Executions, and the Evolution of Repression: From a Preindustrial Metropolis to the European Experience* New York: Cambridge University Press.
———. 1991. *The Prison Experience: Disciplinary Institutions and their Inmates in Early Modern Europe.* New Brunswick, NJ: Rutgers University Press.
Spilerman, Seymour. 1971. "The Causes of Racial Disturbances: Tests of an Explanation." *American Sociological Review* 36:427–42.

Spitzer, Steven. 1975. "Punishment and Social Organization: A Study of Durkheim's Theory of Penal Evolution." *Law and Society Review* 9:613–35.

Steel, Brent S. and Mary Ann E. Steger. 1988. "Crime: Due Process Liberalism Versus Law-and-Order Conservatism," pp. 74–110 in R. Tatalovich and B.W. Daynes (eds.) *Social Regulatory Policy: Moral Controversies in American Politics*. Boulder, CO: Westview Press.

Steele, Shelby. 1990. "A Negative Vote on Affirmative Action." *New York Times Magazine* (May 13):46–9, 73–9.

Stephan, James. 1994. *Capital Punishment 1993*. Washington, DC: Bureau of Justice Statistics.

Straus, Murray A. and Richard J. Gelles. 1990. *Physical Violence in American Families: Risk Factors and Adaptations to Violence in 8,145 Families*. New Brunswick, NJ: Transaction Publishers.

Straus, Murray A., Richard J. Gelles, and Susan Steinmetz. 1980. *Behind Closed Doors: Violence in the American Family*. New York: Anchor.

Strosnider, Kim. 1997. "Minority Law-School Enrollment Would Drop without Affirmative Action, Study Finds." *Chronicle of Higher Education* (Jan. 31): A28.

Sullivan, Andrew. 1995. "Let Affirmative Action Die." *New York Times* (July 23):A15.

Surette, Ray. 1992. *Media, Crime, and Criminal Justice: Images and Realities*. Pacific Grove, CA: Brooks/Cole.

Taylor, Ian, Paul Walton, and Jock Young. 1973. *The New Criminology: For a Social Theory of Deviance*. New York: Harper and Row.

Thornberry, Terence P. and R.L. Christenson. 1984. "Unemployment and Criminal Involvement: An Investigation of Reciprocal Causal Structures." *American Sociological Review* 49:398–411.

Tillman, Robert. 1987. "The Size of the 'Criminal Population': The Prevalence and Incidence of Adult Arrests," *Criminology* 25:561–80.

Tilly, Chris. 1996. "Workfare's Impact on the New York City Labor Foundation." Working Paper no. 92. Russell Sage Foundation, March 1996.

Tokar, Brian. 1992. "Regulatory Sabotage." *Z Magazine* (April):20–5.

Tonry, Michael. 1988. "Structured Sentencing," pp. 267–337 in M. Tonry and N. Morris (eds.)*Crime and Justice: A Review of Research*, vol. 10. Chicago: University of Chicago Press.

———. 1993. "Racial Disproportion in U.S. Prisons." *British Journal of Criminology*:

———. 1995. *Malign Neglect—Race, Crime, and Punishment in America*. New York: Oxford University Press.

———. 1997. "Ethnicity, Crime, and Immigration," pp. 231–59 in M. Tonry (ed.) *Ethnicity, Crime, and Immigration: Comparative and Cross-National Perspectives*. Chicago: University of Chicago Press.

Torbet, Patricia, Richard Gable, Hunter Hurst IV, Imogene Montgomery, Linda Szymanowski and Douglas Thome. 1996. *State Responses to Serious and Violent Juvenile Crime*. Washington, DC: Office of Juvenile Justice and Delinquency Prevention.

Treviño, A. Javier. 1996. *The Sociology of Law: Classical and Contemporary Perspectives*. New York: St. Martin's Press.

Twentieth Century Fund Task Force on Criminal Sentencing. 1976. *Fair and Certain Punishment*. New York: McGraw-Hill.

United Nations. 1995. *1993 Demographic Yearbook*. New York: Nations.

Unnithan, N. Prabha and Hugh P. Whitt. 1992. "Inequality, Economic Development and Lethal Violence: A Cross-Sectional Analysis of Suicide and Homicide." *International Journal of Comparative Sociology* 33:182–96.

Van den Haag, Ernest. 1975. *Punishing Criminals*. New York: Basic Books.

van Dijk, Jan J. M. and Pat Mayhew. 1992. *Criminal Victimization in the Industrialized World: Key Findings of the 1989 and 1992 International Crime Surveys.* The Netherlands: Ministry of Justice.

van Dijk, Jan J.M., Pat Mayhew, and Martin Killias. 1991. *Experiences of Crime across the World.* Boston: Kluwer.

van Duizend, Richard, L. Paul Sutton, and Charlotte A. Carter. 1984. *The Search Warrant Process: Preconceptions, Perceptions, Practices.* Williamsburg, VA: National Center for State Courts.

Verhovek, Sam Howe. 1997a. "Referendum in Houston Shows Complexity of Preferences Issues." *New York Times* (Nov. 6): A1, A26.

———. 1997b. "Judge Kills Texas Affirmative Action Plan." *New York Times* (Nov. 14): A33.

Vidmar, Neil and Phoebe Ellsworth. 1974. "Public Opinion and the Death Penalty." *Stanford Law Review* 26:1245–70.

Viteritti, Joseph P. 1973. *Police, Politics, and Pluralism in New York City: A Comparative Case Study.* Beverly Hills, CA: Sage.

von Hirsch, Andrew. 1976. *Doing Justice: The Choice of Punishments* New York: Hill and Wang.

———. 1985. *Past or Future Crimes: Deservedness and Dangerousness in the Sentencing of Criminals.* New Brunswick, NJ: Rutgers University Press.

Votey, Harold, Jr. 1991. "Employment, Age, Race, and Crime: A Labor-Theoretic Investigation." *Journal of Quantitative Criminology* 7:123–53.

Waldfogel, Joel. 1994a. "The Effect of Criminal Conviction on Income and the Trust 'Reposed in the Workmen.'" *Journal of Human Resources* 29:62–81.

———. 1994b. "Does Conviction Have a Persistent Effect on Income and Employment?" *International Review of Law and Economics* 14:103–9.

Walinsky, Adam. 1995. "The Crisis of Public Order." *The Atlantic Monthly* (July):39–44.

Wallace, Don. 1981. "The Political Economy of Incarceration Trends in Late U.S. Capitalism: 1971–1977." *Insurgent Sociologist* 10:59–66.

Warr, Mark. 1995. "The Polls—Poll Trends: Public Opinion on Crime and Punishment." *Public Opinion Quarterly* 59:296–310.

Warr, Mark and Mark Stafford. 1983."Public Goals of Punishment, and Publicly Preferred Penalties for Crimes." *Sociological Quarterly* 24:75–91.

Westergaard, John. 1995. *Who Gets What? The Hardening of Class Inequality in the Late Twentieth Century.* Cambridge, MA: Polity.

Wessel, David. 1997. "America's Wealth Is Being Distributed a Bit More Evenly, Fed survey Shows." *Wall Street Journal* (Jan. 24): A2.

Western, Bruce and Katherine Beckett. 1997. "How Unregulated Is the U.S. Labor Market? The Dynamics of Jobs and Jails, 1980–1995." Unpublished paper.

Whitehead, J. T. and S. P. Lab. 1989. "A Meta-Analysis of Juvenile Correctional Treatment." *Journal of Research in Crime and Delinquency* 26: 276–95.

Wilbanks, William. 1987. *The Myth of a Racist Criminal Justice System.* Monterey, CA: Brooks/Cole.

Wilkins, Leslie T. 1984. *Consumerist Criminology.* Totawa, NJ: Barnes and Noble.

Wilkins, Leslie T. and Ken Pease. 1987. "Public Demand for Punishment." *International Journal of Sociology and Social Policy* 7:16–29.

Williams, David. 1980. "The Role of Prisons in Tanzania: An Historical Perspective." *Crime and Social Justice* 13 (Summer):27–38.

Wicharraya, Tamasak. 1995. *Simple Theory, Hard Reality: The Impact of Sentencing Reforms on Courts, Prisons, and Crime.* Albany, NY: State University of New York Press.

Wilson, James Q. 1975. *Thinking about Crime*. New York: Basic Books.

———. 1981. "The Dead Hand of Regulation." *The Public Interest* 25:39–58.

Wilson, William Julius. 1987. *The Truly Disadvantaged: The Inner City, the Underclass, and Public Policy*. Chicago: University of Chicago Press.

Winnick, Andrew J. 1989. *Toward Two Societies: The Changing Distributions of Income and Wealth in the United States since 1960*. New York: Praeger.

Wolff, Edward N. 1995a. "How the Pie Is Sliced: America's Growing Concentration of Wealth." *The American Prospect* 22 (Summer):58–64.

———. 1995b. *Top Heavy: A Study of the Increasing Inequality of Wealth in America*. New York: The Twentieth Century Fund.

World Bank. 1994. *World Development Report 1994: Infrastructure for Development*. New York: Oxford University Press.

——— .1995. *World Tables, 1995*. Baltimore, MD: Johns Hopkins University.

Yates, Steven. 1994. *Civil Wrongs: What Went Wrong with Affirmative Action*. San Francisco: Institute for Contemporary Studies.

Yeager, Matthew G. 1979. "Unemployment and Imprisonment." *Journal of Criminology and Criminal Law* 70:586–88.

Young, Michael Dunlop. 1958. *The Rise of the Meritocracy, 1870–2033*. London: Thames and Young.

Young, Robert L. 1991. "Race, Conceptions of Crime and Justice, and Support for the Death Penalty." *Social Psychology Quarterly* 54:67–75.

Young, Warren and Mark Brown. 1993. "Cross-National Comparisons of Imprisonment," pp. 1–49 in M. Tonry (ed.) *Crime and Justice: A Review of Research*, vol. 17. Chicago: University of Chicago Press.

Zedlewski, Edwin W. 1985. "When Have We Punished Enough?" *Public Administration Review* 45:771–9.

———. 1987. *Making Confinement Decisions*. Washington, DC: U.S. Department of Justice, National Institute of Justice.

Zimring, Franklin E. and Gordon Hawkins. 1988. "The New Mathematics of Imprisonment." *Crime and Delinquency* 34:425–36.

——— 1995. *Incapacitation: Penal Confinement and the Restraint of Crime*. New York: Oxford University Press.

[12]
State Prison Populations and their Growth, 1971–1991

We extend earlier analyses of the factors that explain differences among the U.S. states in imprisonment rates by demonstrating the importance of state culture and political arrangements to the explanation of imprisonment rates, and growth in those rates, for the years 1971–1991.

The explanation of spatial and temporal variation in society's punishment practices has been a long standing challenge to social theorists. We take up this challenge by studying variation in punishment intensity among the 50 American states between 1971 and 1991. For this purpose, we focus on states' generosity in the use of imprisonment, for almost all offenses, the most serious penalty prescribed by criminal law. Although this generosity could be measured in various ways (sentence length, admission rates), we focus on the imprisonment rate—a measure of the stock of people incarcerated at any one time. The larger this stock relative to the state's population, the more punitive the state.

There is plenty of variation in imprisonment rates to explain. In recent decades, the ratio of the largest state imprisonment rate to the smallest in any given year has hovered around 7.0.[1] There has also been much temporal variation. Between 1970 and midyear 2000, the federal and state imprisonment rate increased by a factor of almost five, from 98 per 100,000 to 476 per 100,000 (Beck and Karberg, 2001:2; Cahalan and Parsons, 1986:29). These national figures disguise much variation among states in the rates of growth. In Oklahoma, for example, the imprisonment rate in 1981 was just 17% higher than it had been ten years earlier, whereas in Montana, it was 196% higher. Over the next decade, state prison populations continued to grow, but at remarkably disparate rates.

We are grateful to Bennie F. Brewer and JoAnn Van Atta of the Federal Bureau of Investigation, and Kirby G. Posey of the U.S. Bureau of the Census for providing us with unpublished data, to Mary Bernstein for data on religious affiliations, and to Katharine Beckett, Charles Cappell, Susan Carlson, Lynn Chancer, Ted Chiricos, Jo Dixon, David Garland, Karen Gelb, Michael Jacobson, Valerie Jenness, Richard Lempert, Thomas Marvell, Bruce Western, and the anonymous reviewers for helpful comments.

1. North Dakota had the lowest rate in 1971, 1981, and 1991. North Carolina had the highest rate in 1971; it was displaced by South Carolina in 1981 and 1991.

In 1991, the imprisonment rate in West Virginia was only 4% higher than it had been in 1981; in New Jersey, it was 127% higher. Although several researchers (e.g., Jacobs and Helms, 1996) have analyzed factors affecting national growth rates, differences among the states have largely been ignored.

Previous research on state differences in imprisonment rates (summarized more fully below) has focused on a small number of explanatory variables—state crime rates, racial composition, and economic conditions (unemployment or labor force participation, income level). Although these studies have identified some of the state characteristics associated with variation in imprisonment, they have tended to conceive this relationship mechanically, as if state conditions automatically produced a given type and level of penal response. In so doing, this work slights the policy choices that structure a state's response to its circumstances. Our work extends the theoretical scope of this body of research by building on the work of political scientists who have studied state policymaking. Their work has demonstrated the importance of a state's culture and political arrangements to policy outcomes in a number of different domains, such as welfare. Our work examines the relevance of a state's religious composition, the political beliefs of its residents, and its poverty policy to the explanation of its imprisonment practices.

PREVIOUS RESEARCH ON IMPRISONMENT

The antecedents of imprisonment have been much studied. We restrict our review to research on state differences in imprisonment rates, ignoring studies of admissions to prison, and time series analyses of national U.S. imprisonment rates.

The cross-sectional studies find imprisonment rates to be positively related to violent crime rates (Arvanites and Asher, 1998; Beckett and Western, 2001; Biles, 1979; Michalowski and Pearson, 1990; Ouimet and Tremblay, 1996) and poverty (Arvanites and Asher, 1995; Beckett and Western, 2001), negatively related to the level of AFDC payments (Beckett and Western, 2001), and not significantly related to economic inequality (Arvanites and Asher, 1995, 1998), urbanization (Beckett and Western, 2001; Michalowski and Pearson, 1990), or state revenues (Michalowski and Pearson, 1990). They are higher in the South (Michalowski and Pearson, 1990). Findings with regard to race have been inconsistent. Beckett and Western (2001) find the imprisonment rate to be positively related to the percent black in a state's population, but others (Arvanites and Asher, 1998; Michalowski and Pearson, 1990) do not. Findings with regard to unemployment have also been mixed (Beckett and Western, 2001; Chiricos and Delone, 1992; Galster and Scaturo, 1985; Michalowski and Pearson, 1990).

One limitation to these cross-sectional studies is that they do not explicitly address the question of change. Inferences about change drawn from cross-sectional data can sometimes be problematic. Imagine that a pattern of cross-sectional variation was established at some point in the distant past, and that the processes responsible for bringing about this pattern then cease. All variables then change uniformly over time. In that case, a cross-sectional analysis of data at later times will continue to reproduce the original cross-sectional pattern and provide a misleading impression of the causal relationships at work later.

Panel studies of imprisonment avoid this difficulty by analyzing actual change instead of inferring it from cross-sectional data. The panel studies find change in imprisonment rates to be positively related to the property crime rate (Wallace, 1981), the violent crime rate, the level of imprisonment, and the percent black in the state's population (Carroll and Cornell, 1985), and negatively related to the labor-force participation rate (Wallace, 1981), but not significantly related to the unemployment rate (Carroll and Cornell, 1985; Parker and Horwitz, 1986). These studies span just a few years, none of them more recent than 1981 and, thus, cannot illuminate more recent change. They have been able to explain a far lower percent of the variation than have the cross-sectional analyses. Like the cross-sectional studies, all rely on a highly restricted set of independent variables representing the economic conditions in a state, its sociodemographic makeup, and its crime rate.

Our analysis extends previous work in several ways intended to overcome these limitations. First, we update the data sets employed in earlier studies so that we can consider change in prison populations over a longer time span, namely, the two decades from 1971 to 1991. Data availability would become problematic for earlier decades. Moreover, there are theoretical reasons for restricting our analysis to the years since 1970. After decades in which prison populations rose and fell within fairly narrow limits, the early 1970s initiated an extended period of sustained growth. The forces that kept prison populations from growing out of bounds in earlier decades (Blumstein and Cohen, 1973; Blumstein and Moitra, 1979) stopped operating just after 1970.

We end the study in 1991. The most recent census data are for 1990; and the passage of the 1994 Violent Crime Control and Law Enforcement Act providing federal subsidies for the construction of state prisons partly relieves states of the financial constraints that may have slowed prison expansion in earlier years (Adams, 1996). To obtain the subsidies, states must adopt "truth in sentencing" laws requiring inmates convicted of serious violent felonies to serve at least 85% of their sentences, a measure that will increase sentence lengths in many states. By restricting ourselves to change between 1971 and 1991, we confine our study to a phase of American prison history with its distinct dynamic. Second, we extend the theoretical scope of the explanation of differences in state punitiveness to permit us to state cultural and political influences on imprisonment. Third, we examine actual change by estimating models in which growth in the imprisonment rate, rather than the imprisonment rate itself, is the dependent variable.

THEORIZING IMPRISONMENT RATES

We formulate and estimate models in which each state's imprisonment rate is a response to conditions in that state. We assume that personal victimization and knowledge of others' victimization can generate public pressure to deal with crime. Independently of this pressure, state managers may adopt crime-control policies because they believe it would be desirable to do so. This pressure and these policy initiatives should be responsive to a state's crime patterns. We thus expect institutional responses to law violations to be determined at least in part by the volume of crime in that state, but only in part. We expect a state's responses to be conditioned by its ability to finance their cost, and by its political culture. The anxieties and fears that lead residents and politicians to support the expanded use of imprisonment can be heightened or moderated by factors other than crime.

Building on the work of earlier researchers, we have selected a set of explanatory variables derived from several theoretical perspectives; previous research has found some to be important determinants of prison populations, whereas others have not been considered before. This catholicity is theoretically appropriate, because imprisonment rates are produced by decisions made by different agencies and actors (legislatures, governors, police, prosecutors, judges and juries, and parole boards) with different agendas, constituencies, incentives, and constraints. A monocausal approach might narrow our investigation prematurely.

The first set of variables we consider are measures of the magnitude of the problem that the prisons are nominally built to manage: serious violations of the criminal law. The others represent factors that may constrain or influence the use of imprisonment as a response to crime. We consider four classes of such variables: fiscal constraints that limit the capacity of a state to build and operate prisons; cultural factors governing a state's response to crime; features of state politics that encourage the pursuit of particular policies, as well as those policies themselves; and the presence of threats other than crime to which a state may respond with greater or lesser punitiveness when it punishes criminals.

CRIME RATES

If imprisonment is a strategy for coping with crime, one would expect states with more crime to make more extensive use of imprisonment. We expect imprisonment to be more strongly related to violent crime than to property crime because violent crimes are considered more serious than are nonviolent crimes of acquisition. Defendants convicted of violent crimes are more likely to be sentenced to prison terms than are those convicted of stealing. Nevertheless, substantial numbers of prisoners are serving sentences for property offenses. In 1990, for example, 25% of state prisoners were serving sentences for nonviolent property offenses (Snell, 1995:11). We thus consider the violent crime rate and the property crime rate as two measures of the "problem" to which the prison is supposedly a response.

The past quarter-century has seen substantial public alarm about the sale and use of illegal drugs (Beckett, 1997; Ben-Yehuda, 1990; Reinarman, 1993; Reinarman and Levine, 1989, 1997). During this period, governmental policy toward drug use has relied heavily on punitive sanctions. As a result, the number of prisoners committed for drug-related offenses has grown to the point that, in 1990, just under a third of commitments to prison nationally were for drug-related offenses. Indeed, more commitments were for drug offenses than for violent offenses (Maguire et al., 1993:632). These circumstances have led many researchers (e.g., Blumstein and Beck, 1999; Zimring and Hawkins, 1995) to argue that drug policy is playing a large role in prison population growth.

Drug law violations are expected to influence imprisonment rates because publicity about arrests contributes to public perceptions about the seriousness of crime as a social problem and thus influences public punitiveness. Drug arrestees also represent a caseload burden: If convicted, many drug arrestees will be sentenced to a term of imprisonment. We expect the influence of narcotics arrests to be larger in 1990, when the "War on Drugs" was in full swing, than in earlier decades.

We next turn to factors that may be expected to modify a state's use of imprisonment in response to crime and illegal drug use.

FISCAL CONSTRAINT

Prison construction and maintenance are expensive. Costs of prison construction have been estimated at $23,000 to $54,000 per bed, and operating costs from $9,500 to $39,000 per prisoner each year (Cory and Gettinger, 1984; Irwin and Austin, 1994:144; Loeb, 1978; McDonald and Bernstein,

1980). State governments encounter many demands on the public purse. Voters want roads and parks to be built and maintained, children to be schooled, welfare checks to be distributed, and criminals to be put away. Funds spent on prison construction and operation cannot be spent on other public goods. Very likely, no state could afford everything its citizens want, but a wealthy state can accommodate demands for public spending more easily. Less affluent states may have to restrict spending on criminal justice in order to repair potholes, plant trees, pay teachers, and shelter the homeless. For this reason, we predict a positive relationship between imprisonment rates and a state's capacity to tax its citizens and business enterprises.

PERCEIVED THREAT

Students of penality have argued that imprisonment can be a response to anxiety-provoking conditions other than crime. In particular, it may be targeted at "the dangerous classes"—populations perceived as threatening because of their economic circumstances, race, or ethnicity, independently of their involvement in crime. Marxists have argued that prisons discourage unemployed and marginal workers from rebelling or supporting themselves by stealing. Moreover, when unemployment is high, employers will value potential laborers less and be more willing to see them deprived of their liberty (Myers and Sabol, 1987a, 1987b; Rusche and Kirchheimer, 1939; Speiglman, 1977). Other analyses have suggested that judges' sentencing decisions may be influenced by anxiety over public order. When unemployment levels rise, judges may become frightened about threats from unemployed workers and therefore sentence more punitively (Adamson, 1984; Greenberg, 1977). Or judges may believe that unemployed defendants pose an elevated risk of returning to crime, and therefore sentence them to prison more readily (Box, 1987; Spohn and Holleran, 2000). In some states (e.g., North Carolina and Washington), sentencing guidelines explicitly authorize sentence reductions for defendants who are employed (National Council on Crime and Delinquency, 1996). Moreover, Link and Shover (1986) find the adoption of more punitive state sentencing provisions to be positively related to unemployment. These considerations lead to the prediction that imprisonment rates should be positively related to unemployment, even when crime rates are controlled.

Michalowski and Carlson (1999) argue that in different "social stages of accumulation," official unemployment statistics will be a more or less accurate measure of the size of a threatening population, and unemployment will have different social meanings. They predict that the relationship between unemployment and imprisonment will be positive in the years 1974–1979, and negative between 1980 and 1992 and find empirical confirmation for this prediction in national time-series data. We test this prediction with our panel data.

Much research on imprisonment has taken the unemployment rate as a measure of the size of the population whose labor is not being employed productively, or as an indicator of the presence of a menacing population. The unemployment rate, however, is an imperfect measure of the size of a "dangerous class." Some of the most disadvantaged jobless are not counted in the unemployment statistics. Many of the unemployed have savings and good prospects for future employment. Some are unemployed voluntarily while seeking better jobs, and they are not likely to be perceived as threatening. We introduce the percentage of families below the poverty line as an alternative measure of a population that might be seen as having little to lose and who must, therefore, be dealt with through imprisonment.

The numerical overrepresentation of blacks in prison is high (Donziger, 1996; Mauer, 1990; Miller, 1996; Sabol, 1989; Tonry, 1995). Even though blacks make up about 12% of the population, slightly more than half of all new court commitments to prison are now black (Maguire and Pastore, 1996:553), a rate that is approximately 6.5 times as high as that of whites. This disproportion has been attributed to high levels of black involvement in crime (Blumstein, 1983; Carroll and Doubert, 1983; Willbanks, 1985), discriminatory criminal justice decision-making (Donziger, 1996; Leadership Conference on Civil Rights and Leadership Conference Education Fund, 2000; Mann, 1993; Miller, 1996; Tonry, 1995), and to whites' perceptions of blacks as threats (Blalock, 1957, 1967; Brown and Fuguitt, 1972; Frisbie and Neibert, 1976).

By looking at the effect of a state's racial composition on the prison population controlling for crime rates, we should be able to clarify the relationship between race and imprisonment. We also consider the possibility that in the period we consider, the social meaning attached to being black has changed. In the aftermath of the civil rights movement, blacks are more integrated into major institutions of American life (schools, work settings) than in the past. Though integration could reduce a sense of difference that lies behind fear and prejudice, the increased social contacts between blacks and whites could also lead to heightened white fears of blacks. In addition, white resentment over affirmative action could also lead to increased hostility toward blacks.

If whites view blacks as a threat, it is possible that other minority groups would also be seen as dangerous. From early on in American history, low-income white ethnic immigrants to the United States were perceived as threats to public order and safety. In recent years, Hispanics have also been the subject of prejudice and hostility, and they are overrepresented among arrestees and in prison populations.[2] It is possible that white fears of, or hostility toward, Hispanics or Latinos, who are often stereotyped as illegal immigrants, criminals, drug users, and sellers (Castro, 1998), could lead to higher levels of imprisonment. We therefore included percent Hispanic in our set of explanatory variables.

CULTURAL INFLUENCES

Public opinion may influence governmental decisions about many issues, including punishment. Legislators and governors may take pressures to be tough or lenient on crime into account in drafting criminal statutes and in planning prison construction; prosecutors and judges may do so in decisions about defendants. We expect public opinion about crime and criminal justice issues to be integrated into larger constellations of attitude and belief about a range of issues. These configurations have been variously linked with regional subcultures, urbanism, religious convictions, and social and political philosophies and outlooks.

There are reasons to think that Southern states will have especially high imprisonment rates. Southerners are more likely to spank their children (Zielinski, 1995). Corporal punishment of children may legitimate the use of force in frustrating circumstances later in life (Straus and Donnelly, 1994:9). Spanking may also engender feelings of anger, hostility, and aggression that will, later in life, find an outlet in political authoritarianism and support for harsh punishment (Greven, 1991:196–204). The South's greater use of the death penalty[3] may also lead one to expect that imprisonment rates will be higher in the South. We argue, however, that when appropriate characteristics of the South are taken into account (its higher levels of poverty, the religious and political convictions of its residents), that region will not have any independent significance. Moreover, the culture of the South has changed greatly over the past several decades. Our analysis will consider such possible changes.

Social-structural theories of social control suggest that urbanized polities will make greater use of formal methods of control, such as courts and prisons, to make up for deficiencies in informal social control. The anonymity and heterogeneity of large urban populations linked by impersonal market transactions supposedly impair informal social control, leading to the compensatory strengthening of governmental control (Black, 1976: 107; Horwitz, 1990; Spitzer and Scull, 1977). Rural regions, on the other hand, are presumed to require less vigorous formal social control because

2. In 1991, 20.2% of state prison admissions were Hispanics of all races (Perkins 1994:9), compared with 9% of U.S. residents in 1990 (Bureau of the Census, 1992:22).

3. Between 1977 and 1995, 80.5% of the 313 prisoners executed were put to death in the thirteen states we classify as the South (Bureau of Justice Statistics, 1996:10).

they can rely on personal ties based on kinship and multiplex patterns of informal association. On this basis, one would expect imprisonment rates to be higher in states whose populations are highly urbanized. On the other hand, urban criminal courts may face especially heavy caseloads, necessitating more generous concessions in plea bargaining to induce guilty pleas. This should slow prison growth. Moreover, urban populations, exposed as they are to greater cultural diversity, should be more tolerant of rule-breakers and, thus, less punitive (Stephan and McMullin, 1982; Wilson, 1985).

A recent study of cross-national variation in imprisonment rates (Greenberg, 1999) suggests that imprisonment rates are lower in countries where political arrangements reflect the principle that the major sectors of society are intrinsic to its make-up and well-being; the interests of all sectors are acknowledged and taken into account in public policy. These arrangements, then, reflect an inclusive stance toward members of the polity. On a scale of inclusion-exclusion, imprisonment is situated far toward the exclusion pole. Prison inmates do not circulate freely in society; their liberties are restricted in numerous ways; they are subjected to involuntary material deprivation; they lose certain political rights; and in many circles they are stigmatized upon release. Welfare subsidies, on the other hand, are inclusionary; they permit recipients to live relatively unconstrained lives in their communities, albeit at a low standard of living. They do not entail loss of political rights. Welfare and imprisonment both deal largely with low-income populations, and thus, from the point of view of social control, the inclusionary and exclusionary strategies correspond to placative and coercive strategies for dealing with the poor.

Historically, welfare benefits were instituted as alternatives to penal institutions for poor and marginalized populations (Garland, 1985; Sutton, 1987, 1990). Jock Young (1999) has argued that in recent decades, the conditions of "late modernity" have shifted social policies toward the exclusionary in a number of ways, including higher levels of imprisonment. If imprisonment indeed reflects an exclusionary stance toward those who have broken the law, consistency suggests that it should be used with greater reluctance in those states that are relatively generous toward the poor by providing greater welfare benefits, and that cuts in welfare should be accompanied by increases in imprisonment.[4] Cross-national data support this contention (Sutton, 2000). Beckett and Western (2001), who argue similarly, contend that in recent years, the relationship between imprisonment and welfare has become stronger, as ideologically driven

4. Recent news stories have proposed exactly such a linkage. The recent, very sharp increases in Idaho's prison population, for example, have been linked to its equal sharp reductions in welfare spending (Egan, 1998).

conservatives have explicitly linked the curtailment of welfare with crime control policy. We test this prediction.

Where the gap in wealth and income between rich and poor is higher, the social distance between the classes will be larger, and the well-off are expected to be less concerned about the well-being of the poor. Cross-nationally, there is a strong positive relationship between economic inequality and imprisonment (Greenberg, 1999). We expect the same relationship among the states.

The variables discussed thus far all pertain to state policies or to characteristics of a state's population. Although some of the variables may be related to ideology or its consequences (e.g., ethnicity, poverty level, welfare spending), they do not measure ideology directly. Here, we introduce several direct measures of ideology. We expect conservatives to be more punitive than moderates or liberals. Nowadays, the terms "liberal" and "conservative" are defined by stands taken on a number of issues, including crime control. Almost by definition, liberals advocate egalitarian social reforms to prevent crime, and favor rehabilitative strategies, alternatives to incarceration, and due process protections for defendants in court (Langworthy and Whitehead, 1986; Rosch, 1985; Taylor et al, 1979). Conservatives, on the other hand, tend to favor punitive sanctions. However, the extent to which public opinion actually influences levels of imprisonment is not known. To assess this influence, we introduce a measure of political conservatism in a state's population.

Religious beliefs have long been linked to punishment philosophies and practices. In the contemporary United States, conservative or fundamentalist Protestantism tends to be associated with a "black-and-white" punitive morality based on a voluntaristic understanding of human behavior (Curry, 1996; Grasmick and McGill, 1994; Grasmick et. al., 1992; Warr, 1989). After decades of political quiescence and withdrawal, fundamentalists in the 1960s began to be involved in local, state, and national politics. Following the election of evangelical Jimmy Carter to the presidency in 1976, they became a major political force (Guth, 1996; Wilcox, 1992:11–16). Conservative Christian groups began using television broadcasts and mass mailings to promote conservative political agendas. We expect states with more fundamentalists to adopt more punitive penal policies, as politicians cater to this mobilized segment of their constituencies.

POLITICAL FACTORS

Political scientists and sociologists have called attention to the importance of characteristics of state political arrangements as determinants of a variety of public policy outcomes (Skocpol, 1980; Skocpol and Amenta, 1986). For several decades, crime control policies have figured in political partisanship. Ever since the Presidential election of 1964, Republican candidates for public office have criticized their Democratic opponents for being "soft on crime" and have called for harsher punishment (Finckenauer, 1978). National imprisonment rates have grown faster during Republican presidencies (Jacobs and Helms, 1996). We examine the influence of office-holders' party affiliation at the state level. We focus on the governor because it is the governor who prepares budgets, making decisions about prison construction that should ultimately impact on prison populations. It is also the governor who appoints parole board members. Davey (1998:47–82) presents case studies of states in which governors advocating tougher crime control measures were elected and took steps that resulted in large increases in the state's prison population. Most were Republican. However, Davey does nothing to test this idea in his statistical analysis.

We are skeptical of Davey's emphasis on the Republican Party. The Democratic Party has done little to defend liberal positions on crime and criminal justice (Beckett and Sasson, 2000:54–55). Although some Republican presidential candidates made crime an important issue in their campaigns, conservative Southern Democrats have also backed strong crime control measures (Finckenauer, 1978). When the Republicans tacked a "tough" crime bill onto an emergency spending bill shortly before the Presidential election of 1984, the Democrats, not wanting to be attacked for leniency, came back with a more rigorous bill, including provisions for mandatory minimum sentences for first-time cocaine users (American Civil Liberties Union, 1993). The largest expansion in prison capacity in the history of New York took place during the governorship of liberal Democrat Mario Cuomo, at a cost of $7 billion (Schlosser, 1998). Democratic Governor Ann Richards presided over the largest prison expansion in Texas history (Austin and Irwin, 2000:228–229). The current governor of California, Gray Davis, a Democrat, has backed the death penalty for 14-year-olds, and an end to early release from prison for good behavior (Nieves, 2000).

We also introduce a measure for party competition. In a democratic political system, politicians who want to win competitive elections have a powerful incentive to adopt policies that are responsive to public opinion (Buchanan and Tullock, 1962; Downs, 1957; Peltzman, 1984). There is evidence that they do (Burstein, 1998; Wright et al., 1987, 1993). Theorists of welfare policy have argued that intense party competition induces candidates for public office to attract votes by promising benefits to voters. Protection from crime can be considered a benefit, and politicians may be more prone to offer it when faced with vigorous competition from rival candidates. Where the voting public is worried about crime and feels angry and punitive toward criminals, politicians of both parties may have to endorse harsh penal measures. Surveys showing large majorities of the population saying that the courts are too lenient[5] lead us to expect this to occur. Elevated rises in national prison populations during Presidential election years (Jacobs and Helms, 1996) may stem from competition for votes.

A number of policy analysts have attributed growth in prison populations to determinate sentencing legislation that severely restricts judicial discretion to impose a low sentence and eliminates release on parole for prison inmates (Blumstein, 1993; Casper, 1984; Joyce, 1992; Rothman, 1993). Although the recent wave of "three strikes" legislation postdates the years of our study, ten states adopted fixed sentencing legislation ending release on parole between the mid-1970s and mid-1980s (Marvell and Moody, 1996). Because the adoption of determinate sentencing legislation was often accompanied by "get tough" rhetoric, one might expect that states with determinate sentencing legislation will have higher prison populations and experience more rapid growth in these rates.

During the two decades of our study, federal courts issued orders limiting prison overcrowding in a number of states. In some instances, the court orders applied only to individual prisons; in others, to the entire state prison system. Because an order applying to the entire system should be more effective in limiting prison population growth, we introduce a dummy variable that contrasts states whose entire systems came under court order (coded 1) with those that had no order, or whose orders did not apply to the entire state (coded 0). As Levitt (1996) notes, a state may try to limit growth in prison population during the long period of litigation prior to the issuance of a court order in the hope of avoiding an unfavorable decision, or of minimizing its scope. We therefore expect this variable to curb growth in prison populations even before the date at which the court order was issued.

In this discussion, we have made little distinction between the explanation of levels of imprisonment and the explanation of changes in those levels. Any variable that contributes to change will bring about differences in levels if they are not already present. The reverse, however, is not true, because a static pattern may reflect earlier dynamics that no longer operate. We use the same set of independent variables to predict levels in static models and change in dynamic models.

DATA

We measure the imprisonment rate as the total numbers of prisoners in

5. Between 1980 and 1991, the percent of the population thinking the courts too lenient ranged from 79% to 86% (Maguire and Pastore, 1994:194–195).

a state's jurisdiction serving sentences of a year or more per 100,000 population. Prisoners sentenced in one state but serving sentences in another because of overcrowding are attributed to the state that did the sentencing. Likewise, prisoners serving sentences of a year or more in a local jail because of prison overcrowding are counted. Our concern is with the numbers sentenced in each state, not with the state or the institution where the sentences are served. To allow for the time needed to convict and sentence arrestees, prison populations are measured a year after the other variables (with one exception, discussed in the next paragraph), i.e., for the years 1971, 1981, and 1991. As mean sentence lengths in the years of our study have been in the range of two to three years (Blumstein and Beck, 1999; Koppel, 1984; Langan, 1991), few prisoners serving a sentence in any given year will still be serving that sentence ten years later. Consequently, the choice of waves spaced ten years apart ensures that observations at different times will be almost fully independent of one another.

We measure a state's financial resources by the state's revenues per capita, in each case for 1969, 1979, and 1989; this lags the prison population by two years, to allow time for the budget process. We measure economic inequality by the Gini coefficient and welfare by the per capita expenditures, defined as need-based assistance to the needy, including cash assistance and payments to private vendors for services, but not including expenditures by public agencies such as hospitals. Crime rates are numbers of violent and property offenses reported to the police per 100,000 population, for the years 1970, 1980, and 1990. Classification of offenses follows FBI definitions: homicide, rape, aggravated assault, and robbery are defined as violent; burglary, larceny, and motor vehicle theft are defined as property crimes.

The racial composition of a state is measured by the percent of the state's population consisting of black males. Region is dummy-coded 1 if a state is in the South, and 0 otherwise.[6] Urbanization is defined as the percent of a state's population residing in Standard Metropolitan Statistical Areas (SMSAs), as defined by the U.S. Office of Management and Budget. Welfare payments per capita are adjusted for inflation on the basis of the consumer price index.[7]

In the absence of data for the political affiliations of state prosecutors and judges, we examine the impact of the political affiliation of the governor in office in each decade year. Our measure of party competition is based on the percentage of the vote received by a winning candidate in

6. Following Michalowski and Pearson (1990), we classified Alabama, Arkansas, Florida, Georgia, Kentucky, Louisiana, Maryland, Mississippi, North Carolina, South Carolina, Tennessee, Texas, and Virginia as Southern.

7. We are indebted to Beckett and Western (2001) for the procedure of adjusting for inflation in this way.

congressional districts, the winning candidate's margin of victory, whether the seat was safe, and whether it was contested. Our measure aggregates the index to the state level (Holbrook and Van Dunk, 1993).

To determine the percentages of each state's population that is liberal, moderate, or conservative, Wright et al. (1985) pooled data from 51 CBS News-*New York Times* polls taken from 1974 to 1982, obtaining a total sample of over 76,000 respondents, a number large enough to permit the computation of a reasonably precise estimate of conservatism for each of the 48 contiguous states.[8] In contrast to most of the other variables in our analysis, for which we have repeated measures, we have only a single measure of political conservatism. Because we expect this variable to be highly autocorrelated over the 20 years of our study, this should not be a serious limitation.[9]

Researchers have debated how religious fundamentalism should be defined and measured. We measure fundamentalism by the percentage of a state's population that belongs to a Christian denomination classified by Heatwole (1978) as adhering to a literal interpretation of the Bible.[10] States are dummy-coded 1 if they had determinate-sentencing legislation in effect on January 1 of the census year. The dates on which such laws took effect are found in Marvell and Moody (1996). States with court orders limiting growth in prison population are listed in Levitt (1996).

Values of our party competitiveness variable are missing for Louisiana. Preliminary analyses showed this variable to be unrelated to imprisonment rates in any year. To avoid the loss of this state, this variable was dropped from further analysis. The published imprisonment rate for Vermont in 1971 includes a sizable number of misdemeanants, and the arrest rate for narcotics offenses in Vermont in 1980 is also missing. We therefore dropped Vermont from the analysis. Data for political conservatism are unavailable for Hawaii and Alaska; so we imputed the missing values for these two states on the basis of the state's congressional roll call votes for the years 1964–1977, a procedure that has been used in political science research (Holbrook-Provow and Poe, 1987).

Means and standard deviations for all the variables in our analysis are

8. Wright, et al. (1985) give estimates for their unweighted sample and for a sample that is weighted to compensate for the underrepresentation of certain groups in their sample. We use the unweighted figures, which they suggest provide a better representation of the voting population in each state.

9. We replicated our analysis with four other measures of state political ideology (Holbrook-Provow and Poe, 1987). All are strongly correlated and yield very similar results in our regressions. We report on the analyses based on the survey data.

10. Similar results were obtained when using the percentage of a state's population belonging to "traditionalist" denominations, as ascertained in a 1980 survey (Morgan and Watson, 1991).

displayed in Table 1, and sources are cited in the Appendix when not given in this section of the paper.

Table 1. Means and Standard Deviations of Variables ($N = 49$)

Variable	1970 Mean	S.D.	1980 Mean	S.D.	1990 Mean	S.D.
BLACKPCT	4.34	4.41	4.62	4.41	4.56	4.29
CTORDER	0.24	0.43	0.24	0.43	0.22	0.42
FAMPOV	11.66	5.25	9.68	2.91	9.96	3.56
GINI	.36	.025	.360	.018	.395	.022
GOVPARTY	0.41	0.50	0.43	0.50	0.47	0.50
LATINO	3.39	5.32	4.26	6.66	5.47	7.57
NARCRATE	163.64	122.03	240.54	86.46	319.47	179.23
PCR	2088.80	773.50	5020.05	1242.35	4672.36	1089.46
POLCON	33.15	4.13	33.15	4.13	33.15	4.13
PRISON	78.23	34.01	131.16	55.46	259.98	102.89
REGION	0.24	0.43	0.24	0.43	0.24	0.43
RELIGFUN	10.93	9.91	11.53	10.73	11.19	10.49
SENLAW	0	0	0.12	0.33	0.20	0.41
STREV	355.98	105.72	609.80	249.33	743.56	346.19
UNEMP	4.85	1.38	6.85	1.63	5.36	1.12
URBAN	62.29	23.11	62.17	22.37	67.54	21.26
VCR	261.37	147.22	454.83	223.63	542.39	280.74
WELFARE	44.99	21.17	88.41	33.36	97.85	38.36

METHODS AND RESULTS

To assess the influence of the independent variables on imprisonment rates, we estimated a number of models. To establish a baseline for change, we first examined cross-sectional variation in imprisonment rates; then we considered change in these rates. We began by estimating separate cross-sectional regressions for the 1971, 1981, and 1991 rates. However, with 49 cases and close to 20 variables whose relevance is dictated by theory, the ratio of cases to variables is much lower than the recommended minimum of 5 to 10 (Kleinbaum et al., 1988:318). Under these circumstances, standard errors of estimates are high. Correlations of substantial magnitude among the independent variables further inflate standard errors of estimates. As a result, coefficients of moderate magnitude fail to achieve statistical significance. We deal with these problems by pooling the three waves of our data. This procedure reduces multicollinearity for some variables and increases the precision of our estimates by increasing the ratio of cases to variables.

To take into account possible trends in the imprisonment rate that are common to all states and not accounted for by the variables in the model, we added "fixed effects" by creating dummy variables for the years 1981 and 1991. These dummies allow the constant term in the regression to vary by year. In addition, we added fixed effects for each state to control for stable characteristics of states not represented by the variables in our model.

Our initial models have 19 predictors: percent black male (BLACKPCT), political conservatism (POLCON), percent of families below the poverty line (FAMPOV), economic inequality (GINI), party of the governor (GOVPARTY), percent Hispanic (LATINO), arrest rate for narcotics offenses (NARCRATE), court order (CTORDER), region (REGION), religious fundamentalism (RELIGFUN), determinate sentencing law (SENLAW), state revenue (STREV), unemployment rate (UNEMP), urbanization (URBAN), property crime rate (PCR), violent crime rate (VCR), welfare spending (WELFARE), and dummies for 1981 (YR1981) and 1991 (YR1991). The variable FAMPOV made a trivial and insignificant contribution in all individuals and in the pooled models, but was highly collinear with other variables in the model; so we dropped it from the analysis. Estimation was carried out in STATA.

For reasons that we have given in our theoretical discussion, some models incorporate interactions between specified variables (unemployment, welfare, percent black, region, and narcotics arrests) and the time dummies. The other coefficients are assumed to be approximately constant over time. To ascertain that it was permissible to pool the three waves of our data, we carried out a global Chow test for possible year-variable interactions (Baltagi, 1995:28–29) for those coefficients we assumed to be constant over time. The test was consistent with time invariance ($p = .48$). When the theoretically specified interactions were included in the test, the hypothesis of no time-variable interactions was strongly rejected ($p = .0002$).

Studies of city police force size have found the effect of a city's racial composition to be curvilinear. The relationship between these two variables is positive, but weaker where the percent black in a city is larger. Researchers have theorized these findings by suggesting that whites perceive blacks to be a threat; but where blacks are a higher percentage of the population, they more effectively oppose expanding the police force (Carroll and Jackson, 1982; Heinz et al., 1983; Jackson, 1992; Jackson and Carroll, 1987; Liska et al., 1981). The same pattern might be expected for the effect of race on imprisonment. We tested for curvilinearity and found it to be present to a significant degree. At higher levels of percent black, the influence of percent black on prison populations, although always positive, was weaker. Exploration of different functional dependencies suggested that *BLACKPCT* raised to the power 1/3 provides the best fit to the data. We call this variable *BLACK^1/3*.

Because we are not interested in generalizing beyond the states in our data set to a larger population, it would be tempting to limit our analysis to the fixed-effects model. However, fixed-effect models cannot estimate the effects of predictors that are constant over time. We have several such predictors. In addition, fixed-effects models would use up many degrees of freedom in estimating the coefficients for the state dummies. It would, therefore, be preferable to carry out our analysis using random-effects models, if this is appropriate. A Wu-Hausman test (Baltagi, 1995:68; Greene, 1997:632–634; Hausman, 1978; Johnston and DiNardo, 1997:403–404; Wu, 1973, 1974) was consistent with the absence of any systematic differences between a fixed-effects model and a random-effects model, and an F-test for the joint contribution of the state fixed-effects showed them not to make a significant contribution collectively. On this basis, we treat state effects as random. Because we do not wish to generalize beyond the years we have chosen for our analysis, we treat time effects as fixed. The Breusch-Pagan Lagrange multiplier test (Breusch and Pagan, 1980; Greene, 1997:628–629) shows that the residuals for a given state in different years are consistent with independence. Although these tests can be performed in either order, we have done them in the most common sequence—going from the more complicated model to the simpler (Maddala, 1987, 1994:250). The Cook and Weisberg (1982) test for heteroscedasticity indicated that it was present in our data. We therefore carried out an ordinary least-squares (OLS) estimation of the models, correcting for heteroscedasticity with White's (1980) heteroscedasticity-consistent standard errors.[11]

We estimated models in which the dependent variable was the raw imprisonment rate, and in which it was the natural log of the imprisonment rate. Kolmogorov-Smirnov tests showed the residuals from both models to be consistent with normalcy, but those for models in which the dependent variable was logged were somewhat skewed. This was not true when the dependent variable was the unlogged variable. Most parameter estimates for the two models were similar. We report the estimates for the unlogged model in Table 2.

11. This method of estimation implicitly assumes that crime rates influence imprisonment rates, but are not influenced by them. If imprisonment reduces crime, our estimates understate the influence of crime rates on imprisonment. To avoid possible simultaneity bias stemming from the possible influence of imprisonment on crime rates, we reestimated Model 1 (defined below) using two-stage least squares, taking the violent crime rate and property crime rate lagged by ten years as instruments for the contemporaneous crime rates. Parameter estimates were, on the whole, similar to those reported here.

Table 2. Pooled Regression of *PRISON* on Independent Variables (N = 147)

	Model 1		Model 2		Model 3	
Variable	b	t	b	t	b	t
Constant	−235.806	−1.81	−139.947	−1.06	−31.842	−.27
VCR	.118	3.89***	.104	3.50***	.085	2.78*
PCR	.006	1.02	.009	1.54	.014	2.18*
NARCRATE	.110	3.18**	−.003	−.10	−.017	−.43
STREV	.054	3.47***	.054	3.87***	.066	3.48***
UNEMP	5.30	2.28*	6.499	2.64**	−.309	−.11
GINI (×10^{-3})	.222	.72	−.006	−.02	−.247	−.85
BLACK^1/3	42.189	3.54***	42.40	3.35***	13.692	1.09
LATINO	−1.736	−2.05#	−1.335	−1.54	−1.205	−1.49
REGION	−19.475	−1.23	−15.656	−1.05	19.525	1.27
URBAN	−.044	−.17	−.058	−.24	−.154	−.59
WELFARE	−.632	−3.13**	−.611	−3.49***	.019	.09
POLCON	2.911	1.99*	2.764	2.09*	3.100	2.66**
RELIGFUN	1.066	1.48	1.294	1.77*	1.496	2.34*
GOVPARTY	−.717	−.10	−.283	−.04	2.120	.34
SENLAW	−28.76	−2.36#	−30.000	−2.56#	−22.928	−2.15#
CTORDER	−3.415	−.30	−4.454	−.41	−11.225	−1.24
YR1981	8.24	.46	9.802	.55	−49.331	−1.44
YR1991	125.287	6.27###	83.441	4.19###	−68.82	−1.33
BLACK80	—		—		27.976	2.03*
BLACK90	—		—		83.946	4.12***
NARC90	—		.197	3.67***	.182	2.84**
REGION80	—		—		2.020	.10
REGION90	—		—		−99.549	−3.49##
UNEMP80	—		—		3.388	.97
UNEMP90	—		—		23.117	3.11**
WELFARE80	—		—		−.361	−1.45
WELFARE90	—		—		−.989	−3.10**
R^2	.866		.870		.911	

*Significant in a one-tailed test at the .05 level
**Significant in a one-tailed test at the .01 level
***Significant in a one-tailed test at the .001 level
#Significant in a two-tailed at the .05 level
##Significant in a two-tailed test at the .01 level
###Significant in a two-tailed test at the .001 level

Model 1, which omits the year-variable interactions, explains 86.6% of the variance, indicating that the model is highly successful in accounting for state variation in levels of imprisonment. Model 2 adds the interaction of narcotics arrests with the 1991 dummy, and Model 3 adds eight additional variable-year interactions. For each model, we show the unstandardized regression coefficients and the value of the test statistic t for each estimate. Standardized coefficients will vary with wave and can be computed from the standard deviations in Table 1. The unstandardized coefficients indicate the amount by which the imprisonment rate per 100,000 changes when the independent variable changes by one unit. For most of our variables, theory predicts the direction of the effect we expect, and so we use one-tailed significance tests. Where the direction of the predicted effect is not clearly specified by theory, we use two-tailed tests.

We begin by discussing the estimates for Model 1. Consistent with public choice theory, states with high violent crime rates have higher levels of imprisonment. An increase in the violent crime rate of 1 per 100,000 is associated with an increase of .12 per 100,000 in the imprisonment rate, whereas the increase associated with the property crime rate is smaller and not statistically significant. An increase in the narcotics arrest rate of 1 per 100,000 increases the imprisonment rate by about .11 per 100,000.

As expected, states with higher revenues have higher prison populations.[12] Although economic inequality and urbanization are unrelated to imprisonment, there are more people in prison in states with higher unemployment rates and where there is a higher percentage of blacks in the population. Other things being equal, an increase in the unemployment rate of 5% corresponds to an imprisonment rate that is higher by about 16.5 per 100,000. A state with a population that is 10% black will have an imprisonment rate higher than that of a state that has no blacks by $42.19(10)^{1/3} = 91$ per 100,000, a substantial amount. The presence of Latinos, however, does not raise imprisonment rates. There are no significant differences between states in the South and those in other parts of the country. Although imprisonment rates tend to be higher in the South (zero-order correlation), this is because the South differs from other regions in ways that our model takes into account; for example, it has more conservatives.

Several measures of a state's political culture are related to its imprisonment rate. States that are more generous with welfare payments had lower prison populations.[13] An increase of $30 per person in welfare spending is associated with an imprisonment rate that is smaller by about 19 per 100,000. Prison populations were higher in states where a higher percentage of the population is conservative, and where more people believe in a literal interpretation of the Bible. The latter effect is not statistically significant, but becomes significant when the welfare payment variable is

12. We repeated the analysis with a standard political science measure of a state's financial resources—the state capacity index with an index of a state's capacity to tax (Berry and Fording, 1997)—and obtained similar results. Because the index is normed separately for each year, it is less appropriate than is our measure for an analysis that pools data for different years.

13. We reestimated our model using the size of monthly AFDC payments per family (the measure of welfare used by Beckett and Western, 2001) and obtained similar results.

dropped from the model. Welfare generosity is a consequence of a state's religious composition: States with more fundamentalists have lower welfare payment levels. The party of the state's governor was essentially irrelevant. Consistent with earlier research, prison populations in states with determinate sentencing legislation were smaller than those that are not, by about 29 per 100,000.

Finally, the large coefficient for 1991 indicates the presence of an appreciable national upward trend associated with the year 1991, common to all states and not explained by our analysis, which focuses on differences among states. Political analysts have argued that Presidents Reagan and Bush presided over a *Kulturkampf* against the values and lifestyles associated with the liberatory social movements of the 1960s. This struggle rallied opposition to racial and gender equality, anti-militarism, drug use, and liberal welfare and criminal justice policies (Baggins, 1998; Beckett and Sasson, 2000), while promoting neoliberal economic policies favorable to the wealthy. Prison expansion was part of this larger agenda. National mass media exposure to the perspectives associated with this campaign generated public pressures, inducing state governments across the country to adopt expansionist prison policies. This would show up in our analysis as a trend variable representing effects not associated with the conditions in any given state. Notwithstanding the correlations among some of the independent variables, all coefficients of appreciable magnitude achieve significance. Multicollinearity is not a serious problem for this model.

The estimates for Model 2, which adds an interaction term allowing the coefficient for narcotics arrest to differ in 1990 from that in earlier years, shows the impact of the War on Drugs. Although the term representing narcotics arrests in 1970 and 1980 is small and not significant, the effect for 1990 is both large and significant. In addition, the coefficient for religious fundamentalism is now significantly positive. The other estimates are similar to those in Model 1. The variance inflation factors in this model are only slightly larger than are those in Model 1, and they do not pose a serious problem.

Model 3 tests for additional variable-year interactions involving race, region, unemployment, and welfare. The estimates show the effect of race to be increasing dramatically over time. As predicted by Beckett and Western, the negative effect of welfare payments is larger in 1991 than in earlier decades. The coefficient for the unemployment-1991 interaction is positive, seemingly in contradiction with the negative estimate obtained by Michalowski and Carlson (1999). The contradiction, however, is illusory. Our estimate refers to differences among the states in imprisonment rates, whereas theirs is for national imprisonment rates. If the national level of unemployment affects the imprisonment rates of all states equally, our estimation procedure would not detect it; its effect would be absorbed into the coefficients for the year dummies. Unfortunately, multicollinearity is much higher in Model 3 than in Models 1 and 2. Variance-inflation factors for most of the interaction terms exceed 20 because they share a great deal of variance with the 1991 dummy. Consequently, parameter estimates for the interaction terms are more uncertain than are the those for Models 1 and 2.

With the cross-sectional results as a baseline, we proceeded to estimate a set of models in which the dependent variable is the change in the imprisonment rate, $y_t - y_{t-1}$. The independent variables are the same as those used in the cross-sectional analysis, as well as change in those variables. We began by estimating models with lagged imprisonment rates included among the predictors, so that the models took the form $y_t - y_{t-1} = a + b_1 y_{t-1} + b_2 x_{t-1} + b_3 (x_t - x_{t-1}) + \ldots + e_t$. They were, therefore, the most general two-wave linear panel models. When the coefficient b_1 in such an equation is negative, it represents a self-correction mechanism through which states with unusually high imprisonment rates experience slower rates of growth, whereas states with unusually low rates experience higher rates of growth.

A Wu-Hausman test verified that coefficients associated with fixed-effect and random-effects models were not significantly different from one another, but the Breusch-Pagan test indicated that in the random-effects model, residuals for a given state at different times were not independent. We therefore estimated a fixed-effects model and estimated it using OLS, but modified the computation of the White heteroscedasticity-consistent standard errors to allow arbitrary relationships over time among the residuals. By taking change as the dependent variable, we lost one wave of data, leaving us with an effective sample size of 98. This smaller sample size, together with the larger number of independent variables in our model, limited our ability to examine variable-year interactions. We were, however, able to test for the impact of the War on Drugs by testing for the temporal specificity of the coefficient representing the impact of change in narcotics arrests on change in imprisonment rates.

The intercept in these models is consistent with zero, indicating that once the predictors in the model are taken into account, there is no unexplained tendency for state prison populations to rise or fall. The coefficients for the lagged imprisonment rate are small and not statistically significant, consistent with the absence of any self-correcting process in relation to prison populations. The coefficient for the dummy variable representing the 1981–1991 wave is also small and statistically insignificant. To improve the precision of our estimates, these variables were therefore dropped from the analysis. The resulting estimates are displayed in Table 3. Variables whose names begin with a D represent changes; e.g., DNARCRATE is change in the narcotics arrest rate. Table 3 displays the coefficients for models without, and with, an interaction term involving narcotics arrests and decade (Models A and B, respectively).

Table 3. Pooled Regression of Change in Imprisonment Rates (N = 98)

	Model A		Model B	
Variable	b	t	b	t
Constant	–169.776	–.98	–68.097	–.72
VCR	.061	1.38	.064	1.55*
PCR	.008	1.14	.006	.84
NARCRATE	.068	1.01	.031	.50
STREV	–.000	–.01	.011	.38
UNEMP	6.97	1.88**	7.049	1.90**
GINI ($\times 10^{-3}$)	.087	.21	–27.588	–.07
BLACK^1/3	41.66	2.81***	35.264	2.57***
LATINO	–.38	–.29	–.412	–.30
REGION	–32.54	–2.09##	–29.656	–1.82#
URBAN	–.005	–.01	.070	.16
WELFARE	–.162	–.83	–.211	–1.08
POLCON	3.121	2.11**	3.174	2.13**
RELIGFUN	–.445	–.60	.023	.03
GOVPARTY	–6.940	–.62	–8.498	–.76
SENLAW	–2.718	–.14	5.962	.27
CTORDER	10.090	.69	9.826	.74
DVCR	.017	.33	.012	.24
DPCR	–.011	–1.34	–.010	–1.09
DNARCRATE	.065	1.55*	–.027	–.28
DNARC (1981–91)	—	—	.142	1.23
DSTREV	.065	2.21**	.056	1.89**
DUNEMP	3.902	.96	4.384	1.07
DGINI ($\times 10^{-3}$)	–.251	–.45	–.303	–.54
DBLACK1/3	52.979	4.82***	45.274	4.18****
DLATINO	–3.329	–.69	–2.92	–.63
DURBAN	.965	.47	1.083	.54
DWELFARE	–.450	–1.77**	–.469	–1.79**
DRELIGFUN	4.275	1.21	5.241	1.54
DGOVPARTY	–8.628	–.99	–9.796	–1.10
DSENLAW	–26.274	–1.73#	–29.213	–1.87#
R^2	.690		.698	

*Significant in a one-tailed test at the .10 level
**Significant in a one-tailed test at the .05 level
***Significant in a one-tailed test at the .01 level
****Significant in a one-tailed test at the .001 level
#Significant in a two-tailed test at the .10 level
##Significant in a two-tailed at the .05 level

Multicollinearity is no more severe in these models than in the models reported in Table 2. However, the larger number of independent variables and the smaller sample size lead to larger standard errors. To reduce the probability of failing to reject the null hypothesis for nonvanishing coefficients of moderate magnitude, we interpret coefficients that are significant at the .10 level. Our discussion is based on the estimates for Model B. We see that the lagged violent crime rate contributed to prison population growth, lending support to the argument that sustained high levels of crime have contributed to prison population growth (Garland, 2001; Greenberg, 1999; Young, 1999). However, changes in crime rates did not lead to increases in imprisonment rates.

Increases in narcotics arrests during the 1980–1990 decade boosted imprisonment rates, undoubtedly reflecting the increased probability of a commitment to prison following an arrest between 1980 and 1990 from 2 per 100 to 10 per 100 (Blumstein and Beck, 1999). Although this increase, a product of the so-called War on Drugs, clearly contributed to prison expansion, its contribution to that expansion is often exaggerated. Between 1981 and 1991, state prison populations rose from 333,251 to 728,605, i.e., by 118.6%. Excluding drug offenders, the increase was from 311,551 to 573,405, i.e., 84% (Snell, 1995:53). In the absence of drug offenders, the increases in the numbers of non-drug offenders might well have been larger, because more cells would have been available for other categories of offenders. That imprisonment rates increased greatly for all categories of offenders suggests that the War on Drugs was part of a wider turn toward more stringent crime control policies, rather than a distinct offense-specific phenomenon. Still, its numerical contribution to prison expansion has been appreciable.

Other variables that contributed to variation in imprisonment levels also contributed to its growth. In states where there were more conservatives, imprisonment rates were not only higher, but also grew more rapidly. Growth rates were not higher in states where there are more religious fundamentalists, but were higher in states where the number of fundamentalists increased. This is particularly noteworthy in that where religious fundamentalists have mobilized politically, they have concentrated on issues of gender, sexuality, and public education, not on crime. The processes that led to growth in fundamentalism in certain states may have been accompanied by larger cultural changes supportive of increased imprisonment, even when this was not the specific focus of political mobilization. If cultural differences are associated with the South, they did not contribute to high rates of imprisonment growth; quite the contrary, growth rates were significantly slower in the South than elsewhere, so that by 1991, regional disparities in imprisonment rates were substantially smaller than in 1971. In other words, in recent years regions outside the South have been catching up to the South in imprisonment.

Prisons expanded faster in states where revenues increased and welfare payments declined. Contrary to popular opinion, the adoption of determinate sentencing legislation did not increase imprisonment rates; it moderately reduced them. The adoption of these laws may have helped to placate a punitive public, reducing pressure on state officials to impose harsh sentences. Austin et. al. (1999a, 1999b) suggest that these laws were carefully crafted to be largely symbolic and, in many states, had little effect because prosecutors and judges took steps to minimize their impact.

Some of the most striking findings concern state economic and demographic characteristics. Unemployment was associated with higher rates of prison population growth, as was change in unemployment. Economic inequality was not. Growth in imprisonment rates was also related to the size of the black population and its increase. It cannot be stressed too strongly that the coefficients for unemployment and race are direct effects, with crime rates controlled, and so they cannot be explained away by claims that crime rates are higher where there is more unemployment or where more blacks live.

Consistent with much research showing that party control of state government has little or no impact on state policy and is unrelated to the liberalism or conservatism of the state's voters (Erikson et al., 1989), the political party of a state's governor failed to make a significant contribution to prison populations or their growth. It appears that the political incentives for an expansive prison policy transcend party affiliations. States governed by Democrats responded to the crime issue no differently from states governed by Republicans.

DISCUSSION

Sociological analyses of the history of penalty have taken as their premise that institutionalized punishment practices are not entirely determined by the functional necessity of preventing crimes (Garland, 1990; Rusche and Kirchheimer, 1939). Our findings confirm the validity of this approach for the study of prison populations even across a relatively modest time span, while refuting the claim some have made that prison population growth is entirely unrelated to criminality. Dan O'Brien, Assistant Commissioner of Corrections in Minnesota, for example, asserted in 1996 that "there is no evidence of a relationship between the incarceration rate and violent crime" (quoted in Olson, 1999:1). This statement is false. Although growth in crime was not a major cause of higher prison populations, imprisonment rates have been higher, and have grown faster, in states with higher levels of victimizing crime, especially violent crime. If it is the long-term impact of persistent high crime levels that makes for punitive public attitudes, then it is not surprising to find prison populations continuing to rise even after some years of declining crime rates, as they have been in the last half of the 1990s.

Growth in prison populations has already dropped substantially in response to the downward trend in violent and property crime, now in its eighth year. Whereas the average annual growth rate in state prison populations between 1990 and midyear 1999 was 5.7%, between midyear 1999 and midyear 2000, it was only 1.5%, the lowest growth rate in 29 years. In 11 states, they fell (Beck and Karberg, 2001).

In New York, prison admissions began falling several years ago, though, because of the lengthening of sentences, prison populations continued to climb—although much less rapidly than was expected (Pérez-Peña, 1998). Over the course of the year 2000, however, continuing drops in crime, along with shorter sentences and more lenient parole policies, finally led the prison population to drop by 3% (Rohde, 2001). Further drops may be in the works. New York's Republican governor George Pataki, who in past years has supported increased penalties, has now called for penalty reductions for narcotics offenses, explaining that drops in crime made it possible to reconsider the state's sentencing provisions (Pérez-Peña, 2001). Between mid-1999 and mid-2000, for the first time in more than two decades, prison populations in California dropped (by a very small amount) (Beck and Karberg, 2001; Terry, 2000). In the short run, the California drop is likely to accelerate, because new legislation providing for the diversion of first- and second-time drug offenders goes into effect in July 2001 (Butterfield, 2001). However, this drop may be neutralized in the long-run by the draconian terms of California's Three Strikes legislation extending sentence lengths by large amounts for repeat offenders (Zimring et al., 2001).

With state revenues falling as the economy slows, state governments will be forced to make tougher budgetary decisions than in much of the past decade. Our model suggests that reduced state revenues should reduce prison growth rates. Declining crime rates may enable state officials to cut imprisonment even more in response to falling revenues than they could otherwise. Television news programs have begun to devote less time to crime stories (Finder, 1998), which should reduce public anxieties. With new prison construction under way, and stringent sentencing laws going into effect, it may take some time for diminishing public fears of crime, and concerns about their high costs, to translate into more lenient sentencing provisions and reduced prison populations. On the other hand, if unemployment rises substantially, it will tend to counteract these downward pressures.

Our results are equally consistent with the presence and absence of racial discrimination. A state whose criminal justice system treats black suspects and defendants more harshly might have higher prison populations as a result, but not necessarily. If such a state had especially low overall imprisonment rates, discrimination would not necessarily create a relationship between percent black and the state's imprisonment rate. Conversely, a positive relationship between percent black in a state and the state's imprisonment rate could occur in the absence of racial discrimination.

Our results are consistent with the "racial threat" hypothesis. Blacks—black males in particular—appear to have become "symbolic assailants" whose presence in a city evokes fear of crime independently of the actual level of crime.[14] Survey research on perceived risk of victimization confirms that members of the public at large tend to see blacks as potential threats (Chiricos et al., 1997; Covington and Taylor, 1991; Moeller, 1989; Skogan, 1995; Sniderman and Piazza, 1993:19–34). There is evidence that criminal justice officials are at times influenced by stereotypes of blacks as dangerous (Daly, 1994; Greenberg, 2001; Mann, 1993; Spohn and Halloran, 2000; Steffensmeier et al., 1998; Swigert and Farrell, 1976). This perception could be the source of the association we find between race and imprisonment. That the presence of Latinos is not associated with imprisonment rate growth indicates that it is not minorities in general, but blacks in particular, who are perceived as threatening. Our results also point to unemployment as a separate, distinct source of threat or anxiety.

Analyzing black mobility patterns and the emergence of economic stratification among black Americans, William Julius Wilson (1980:144) has argued that:

> [a]lthough racial oppression . . . was a salient and important feature during the preindustrial and the industrial periods of race relations in the United States, the problems of subordination for certain segments of the black population are more directly associated with economic class in the modern industrial world.

As the significance of race in American life has declined, Wilson suggests, "class has become more important . . . in determining black life-chances" (p. 150). Whatever the validity of Wilson's claims in relation to economic well-being, we find no evidence that race is declining in significance when it comes to the determination of prison populations. Our results suggest that its significance may be increasing.

We think that welfare is important to imprisonment not because it directly restrains legislators, prosecutors, and judges; rather, we see the comparative leniency in high-welfare states as reflecting a more general policy of avoiding excessively harsh treatment of the poor, who make up the bulk of criminal court defendants. As argued earlier, imprisonment

14. The phrase is Skolnick's (1966).

excludes convicted persons from full participation in society. This exclusion is, of course, a matter of degree, and historically relative. Penal confinement was introduced as a substitute for execution and deportation, which entailed permanent exclusion. The rehabilitative program that accompanied the rise of the prison was an incorporative strategy. The decline in recent years of the rehabilitative ideal and of efforts to prevent crime through egalitarian social change represents a partial abandonment of that strategy. Much more than 30 years ago, the social meanings, practices, and consequences associated with imprisonment involved exclusion, not incorporation (Greenberg, 1999; Vaughan, 2000; Young, 1999).

We believe that our work has vindicated the theoretically catholic approach we adopted. We confirmed earlier work indicating that imprisonment rates are responsive to crime rates, to a state's racial composition, and to its economic circumstances. At the same time, we have demonstrated the necessity of expanding the framework for theorizing imprisonment by showing that a state's religious and political culture represent a context for penological decision making that cannot be neglected, and that punishment policy is part of a larger constellation of policies united by a consistent logic. Our work also demonstrates the methodological gain that comes from examining change empirically.

We conclude by noting three limitations to our work. We have established a relationship between growth in state imprisonment rates and a number of characteristics of those states, but we have not determined the contributions different stages of criminal justice processing make to the outcome. Blumstein and Beck (1999) have done so with national data, but differences among the states need to be examined. In addition, we cannot determine the extent to which policies adopted by state government officials reflect their views and agendas, and the extent to which they are accommodating pressures from their constituencies. We have construed certain indicators and findings as measures of public opinion about imprisonment and its effects, but we lack direct measures of opinion. These limitations imply priorities for future research on imprisonment rates.

Finally, although our findings regarding a state's racial composition are consistent with the existence of racial discrimination on the part of criminal justice officials, they are equally consistent with nondiscriminatory decisions that are more punitive for white and black defendants alike in states where the percent black is higher. Indeed, Carroll and Cornell (1985) found that between 1970 and 1980, white prison population growth, not just black, was positively related to the percent black in a state's population. Questions of discrimination and of possible racial differences in prison population expansion are important and should be pursued.

REFERENCES

Adams, Kenneth
1996 The bull market in corrections. The Prison Journal 76:461–467.

Adamson, Christopher
1984 Toward a Marxian penology: Captive criminal population as economic threats and resources. Social Problems 31:435–458.

American Civil Liberties Union
1993 Comments of the American Civil Liberties Union to the United States Sentencing Commission Regarding Disparity in Penalty Between Crack and Powder Cocaine. www.aclu.org/congress/html.

Arvanites, Thomas M. and Martin A. Asher
1995 The direct and indirect effects of socioeconomic variables on state imprisonment rates. Criminal Justice Policy Review 7:27–53.
1998 State and county incarceration rates: The direct and indirect effects of race and inequality. The American Journal of Economics and Sociology 57:207–222.

Austin, James, John Clark, Patricia Hardyman, and D. Alan Henry
1999a Three Strikes and You're Out: The Implementation and Impact of Strike Laws. Washington, D.C.: U.S. National Institute of Justice.
1999b The impact of "three strikes and you're out." Punishment and Society 1:131–162.

Austin, James and John Irwin
2001 It's About Time: America's Imprisonment Binge. 3d ed. Belmont, Calif.: Wadsworth.

Baggins, David Sadofsky
1998 Drug Hate and the Corruption of American Justice. Westport, Conn.: Praeger.

Baltagi, Badi H.
1995 Econometric Analysis of Panel Data. New York: Wiley.

Beck, Alan J. and Jennifer C. Karberg
2001 Prison and Jail Inmates at Midyear 2000. Washington, D.C.: U.S. Department of Justice, Bureau of Justice Statistics.

Beckett, Katharine
1997 Making Crime Pay: Law and Order in Contemporary American Politics. New York: Oxford University Press.

Beckett, Katharine and Theodore Sasson
2000 The Politics of Injustice: Crime and Punishment in America. Thousand Oaks, Calif.: Pine Forge.

Beckett, Katharine and Bruce Western
2001 Governing social marginality: Welfare, incarceration, and the transformation of state policy. Punishment and Society 3:43–59.

Ben-Yehuda, Nachman
1990 The Politics and Morality of Deviance: Moral Panics, Drug Abuse, Deviant Science, and Reverse Stigmatization. Albany: State University of New York Press.

Berry, William D. and Richard C. Fording
1997 Measuring state tax capacity and effort. Social Science Quarterly 78:158–166.

Biles, David
1979 Crime and the use of prisons. Federal Probation 43(2):39–43.

Black, Donald
1976 The Behavior of Law. New York: Academic Press.

Blalock, Hubert M., Jr.
1957 Percent nonwhite and racial discrimination in the South. American Sociological Review 22:677–682.
1967 Toward a Theory of Minority Group Relations. New York: Wiley.

Blumstein, Alfred
1983 On the racial disproportionality of the United States prison population. Journal of Criminal Law and Criminology 73:1259–1281.
1993 Stability of punishment: What happened and what next? In Thomas G. Blomberg and Stanley Cohen (eds.), Punishment and Social Control: Essays in Honor of Sheldon L. Messinger. New York: Aldine de Gruyter.

Blumstein, Alfred and Allen J. Beck
1999 Population growth in U.S. prison populations, 1980–1996. In Michael H. Tonry and Joan Petersilia (eds.), Crime and Justice: A Review of Research. Vol. 26. Chicago: University of Chicago Press.

Blumstein, Alfred and Jacqueline Cohen
1973 A theory of the stability of punishment. Journal of Criminal law and Criminology 64:198–207.

Blumstein, Alfred and Soumo Moitra
1979 An analysis of the time series of the imprisonment rate in the states of the United States: A further test of the stability of punishment process. Journal of Criminal Law and Criminology 70:376–390.

Box, Stephen
1987 Recession, Crime and Punishment. Totawa, N.J.: Barnes and Noble.

Breusch, Trevor S. and Adrian R. Pagan
1980 The Lagrange multiplier test and its applications to model specification in econometrics. Review of Economic Studies 47:239–253.

Brown, David L. and Glenn V. Fuguitt
1972 Recent nonwhite and racial disparity in nonmetropolitan cities in the South. Social Science Quarterly 53:573–582.

Buchanan, James M. and Gordon Tullock
1962 The Calculus of Consent. Ann Arbor: University of Michigan Press.

Bureau of the Census
1992 Statistical Abstracts of the United States—1992. Washington, D.C.: U.S. Government Printing Office.

Bureau of Justice Statistics
1996 Capital Punishment 1995. Bulletin NCJ-162043 Washington, D.C.: U.S. Department of Justice.

Burstein, Paul
1998 Bringing the public back in: Should sociologists consider the impact of public opinion on public policy? Social Forces 77:27–62.

Butterfield, Fox
2001 California lacks resources for law on drug offenders, officials say. New York Times, 12 February:A16.

Cahalan, Margaret Werner and Lee Anne Parsons
1986 Historical Corrections Statistics in the United States, 1850–1984. Washington, D.C.: U.S. Department of Justice, Bureau of Justice Statistics.

Carroll, Leo and Claire P. Cornell
1985 Racial composition, sentencing reforms, and rates of incarceration, 1970–1980. Justice Quarterly 2:475–490.

Carroll, Leo and Mary Beth Doubet
1983 U.S. social structure and imprisonment: A comment. Criminology 21:449–456.

Carroll, Leo and Pamela Irving Jackson
1982 Minority composition, inequality and the growth of municipal police forces, 1960–1971. Sociological Focus 15:326–346.

Casper, Jonathan D.
1984 Determinate sentencing and prison crowding in Illinois. Illinois Law Review 1984:231–252.

Castro, Diego O.
1998 "Hot blood and easy virtue": Mass media and the making of racist Latino/a stereotypes. In Coramae Richey Mann and Marjorie S. Zatz (eds.), Images of Color, Images of Crime. Los Angeles: Roxbury.

Chiricos, Theodore G. and Miriam Delone
1992 Labor surplus and punishment: A review and assessment of theory and evidence. Social Problems 39:421–446.

Chiricos, Ted, Michael Hogan, and Marc Gertz
1997 Racial composition of neighborhood and fear of crime. Criminology 35:107–129.

Cook, R. Dennis and Sanford Weisberg
1982 Residuals and Influence in Regression. New York: Chapman and Hall.

Cory, Bruce and Stephen Gettinger
1984 Time to Build? The Realities of Prison Construction. New York: Edna McConnell Clark Foundation.

Covington, Jeannette and Ralph B. Taylor
1991 Fear of crime in urban residential neighborhoods: implications of between- and within-neighborhood sources for current models. The Sociological Quarterly 32:231–249.

Curry, Theodore R.
1996 Conservative Protestantism and the perceived wrongfulness of crimes: A research note. Criminology 34:453–464.

Daly, Kathleen
1994 Gender, Crime, and Punishment. New Haven, Conn.: Yale University Press.

Davey, Joseph Dillon
1998 The Politics of Prison Expansion: Winning Elections by Waging War on Crime. Westport, Conn.: Praeger.

Donziger, Steve R.
1996 The Real War on Crime: The Report of the National Criminal Justice Commission. New York: HarperPerrenial.

Downs, Anthony
1957 An Economic Theory of Democracy. New York: Harper and Row.

Egan, Timothy
1998 As Idaho booms, prisons fill and spending on poor lags. New York Times, 16 April:A1, A16.

Erikson, Robert S., Gerald C. Wright, Jr., and John P. McIver
1989 Political parties, public opinion, and state policy in the United States. American Political Science Review 83:729–749.

Federal Bureau of Investigation
1991 Crime in the United States—1990. Washington, D.C.: U.S. Government Printing Office.

Finckenauer, James O.
1978 Crime as a national political issue: 1967–76. Crime and Delinquency 24:13–27.

Finder, Alan
1998 As the city grows safer, crime loosens its grip on the news. New York Times, 6 September:L35.

Frisbie, W. Parker and Lisa Neidert
1976 Inequality and relative size of minority populations: a comparative analysis. American Journal of Sociology 82:1007–1030.

Galster, George A. and Laure A. Scaturo
1985 The U.S. criminal justice system: Unemployment and the severity of punishment. Journal of Research in Crime and Delinquency 22:163–189.

Garland, David
1985 Punishment and Welfare: A History of Penal Strategies. Brookfield, Vt.: Gower.
1990 Punishment and Social Theory. Chicago, Ill.: University of Chicago Press.
2001 The Culture of Control: Crime and Social Order in Late Modernity. Chicago, Ill.: University of Chicago Press.

Grasmick, Harold G. and Anne McGill
1994 Religion, attribution style, and punitiveness toward juvenile offenders. Criminology 32:23–46.

Grasmick, Harold G., Elizabeth Davenport, Mitchell B. Chamlin, and Robert J. Bursik, Jr.
1992 Protestant fundamentalism and the retributive doctrine of punishment. Criminology 30:21–45.

Greenberg, David F.
1977 The dynamics of oscillatory punishment processes. Journal of Criminal Law and Criminology 68:643–655.

1999 Punishment, division of labor, and social solidarity. In William S. Laufer and Freda Adler (eds.), The Criminology of Criminal Law: Advances in Criminological Theory. Vol. 8. New Brunswick, N.J.: Transaction.

2001 Unconscious racism and law enforcement. In Darnell F. Hawkins, Samuel L. Myers, Jr., and Randolph N. Stone (eds.), Crime Control and Social Justice: The Delicate Balance. New York: Greenwood Press.

Greene, William H.
1997 Econometric Analysis. 3d ed. New York: Prentice-Hall.

Greven, Philip
1991 Spare the Rod: The Religious Roots of Punishment and the Psychological Impact of Physical Abuse. New York: Alfred A. Knopf.

Guth, James L.
1996 The politics of the Christian right. In John C. Green, James L. Guth, Corwin E. Smidt, and Lyman A. Klellstadt (eds.), Religion and the Culture Wars: Dispatches from the Front. Lanham, Md.: Rowman and Littlefield.

Hausman, J. A.
1978 Specification tests in econometrics. Econometrica 46:1251–1271.

Heatwole, Charles A.
1978 The Bible Belt: A problem in regional definition. Journal of Geography 77:50–55.

Heinz, Anne, Herbert Jacob, and R. L. Lineberry
1983 Crime in City Politics. New York: Longman.

Holbrook, Thomas and Emily Van Dunk
1993 Electoral competition in the American states. American Political Science Review 87:955–962.

Holbrook-Provow, Thomas M. and Steven C. Poe
1987 Measuring state political ideology. American Politics Quarterly 15:399–416.

Horwitz, Allan V.
1990 The Logic of Social Control. New York: Plenum.

Irwin, John and James Austin
1994 It's About Time: America's Imprisonment Binge. Belmont, Calif.: Wadsworth.
1998 Fanning the flames of fear. Crime and Delinquency 44:32–48.

Jackson, Pamela Irving
1992 Minority group threat, social context, and policy. In Allen E. Liska (ed.), Social Threat and Social Control. Albany: State University of New York Press.

Jackson, Pamela Irving, and Leo Carroll
1987 Race and the war on crime: The sociopolitical determinants of municipal police expenditures in 90 non-Southern United States cities. American Sociological Review 46:290–305.

Jacobs, David and Ronald E. Helms
1996 Toward a political model of incarceration: A time-series examination of multiple explanations for prison admission rates. American Journal of Sociology 102:323–357.

Johnston, Jack and John DiNardo
1997 Econometric Methods. 4th ed. New York: McGraw-Hill.

Joyce, Nola M.
1992 A view of the future: The effect of policy on prison population growth. Crime and Delinquency 38:357–369.

Kleinbaum, David G., Lawrence J. Kuiper, and Keith G. Muller
1988 Applied Regression Analysis and Other Multivariate Methods. Belmont, Calif.: Duxberry.

Koppel, Herbert
1984 Time Served in Prison. Special Report. Washington, D.C.: U.S. Department of Justice, Bureau of Justice Statistics.

Langan, Patrick A.
1991 America's soaring prison population. Science 251:1568–1573.

Langworthy, Robert H. and John T. Whitehead
1986 Liberalism and fear as explanations of punitiveness. Criminology 24:575–591.

Leadership Conference on Civil Rights and Leadership Conference Education Fund
2000 Justice on Trial: Racial Disparities in the American Criminal Justice System. www.civilrights.org/images/justice.pdf.

Levitt, Steven D.
1996 The effect of prison population size on crime rates: Evidence from prison overcrowding litigation. Quarterly Journal of Economics 111:319–351.

Link, Christopher and Neal Shover
1986 The origins of criminal sentencing reforms. Justice Quarterly 3:329–342.

Liska, Allen E., Joseph V. Laurence, and Michael Benson
1981 Perspectives on the legal order: The capacity for social control. American Journal of Sociology 87:413–426.

Loeb, Carl M., Jr.
1978 The cost of jailing in New York City. Crime and Delinquency 24:446–452.

Maddala, G. S.
1987 Recent developments in the econometrics of panel data analysis. Transportation Research—A. 21A:303–326.
1994 Econometric Methods and Applications. Vol. 1. Brookfield, Vt.: Edward Elgar.

Maguire, Kathleen and Ann L. Pastore (eds.)
1994 Sourcebook of Criminal Justice Statistics—1993. Washington, D.C: U.S. Government Printing Office.

Maguire, Kathleen and Ann L. Pastore (eds.)
1996 Sourcebook of Criminal Justice Statistics—1995. Washington, D.C.: U.S. Government Printing Office.

Maguire, Kathleen, Ann L. Pastore, and Timothy Flanagan (eds.)
1993 Sourcebook of Criminal Justice Statistics—1992. U.S. Department of Justice, Bureau of Justice Statistics. Washington, D.C.: U.S. Government Printing Office.

Mann, Coramae Richey
1993 Unequal Justice: A Question of Color. Bloomington: Indiana University Press.

Marvell, Thomas B. and Carlisle E. Moody
1996 Determinate sentencing and abolishing parole: The long-term impacts on prisons and crime. Criminology 34:107–128.

Mauer, Marc
1990 Young Black Men and the Criminal Justice System: A Growing National Problem. Washington, D.C.: The Sentencing Project.

McDonald, Douglas and Betty J. Bernstein
1980 The Price of Punishment: Public Spending for Corrections in New York. Boulder, Colo.: Westview.

Michalowski, Raymond J. and Susan M. Carlson
1999 Unemployment, imprisonment, and social structures of accumulation: Historical contingency in the Rusche-Kirchheimer hypothesis. Criminology 37:217–250.

Michalowski, Raymond J. and Michael A. Pearson
1990 Punishment and social structure at the state level: A cross-sectional comparison of 1970 and 1980. Journal of Research in Crime and Delinquency 27:52–78.

Miller, Jerome G.
1996 Search and Destroy: African-American Males in the Criminal Justice System. New York: Cambridge University Press.

Moeller, Gertrude L.
1989 Fear of criminal victimization: the effect of neighborhood racial composition. Sociological Inquiry 59:208–211.

Morgan, David R. and Sheilah S. Watson
1991 Political culture, political system characteristics, and public policies among the American States. Publius: The Journal of Federalism 21:31–48.

Myers, Samuel and William Sabol
1987a Business cycle and racial disparities in punishment. Contemporary Policy Issues 5:46–58.
1987b Unemployment and racial differences in imprisonment. Review of Black Political Economy 16:189–209.

National Council on Crime and Delinquency
1996 National Assessment of Structured Sentencing. Washington, D.C.: U.S. Department of Justice.

Nieves, Evelyn
2000 California's governor plays tough on crime. New York Times, 23 May:A16.

Olson, Joel
1999 Gardens of the law: The role of prisons in capitalist society. www.prison activist.org/crisis/gardens-of-law.html.

Ouimet, Marc and Pierre Tremblay
1996 A normative theory of the relationship between crime rates and imprisonment rates: An analysis of the penal behavior of U.S. states from 1972 to 1992. Journal of Research in Crime and Delinquency 33:109–125.

Parker, Robert Nash and Allan V. Horwitz
1986 Unemployment, crime, and imprisonment: A panel approach. Criminology 24:751–774.

Peltzman, Sam
1984 Constituent interest and congressional voting. Journal of Law and Economics 27:181–210.

Pérez-Peña, Richard
1998 Governor's inmate estimates were too high, memo says. New York Times, 28 January: B2.
2001 Pataki presents his plan to ease state drug laws. New York Times, 18 January: A1, B5.

Perkins, Craig
1994 National Corrections Reporting Program, 1991. NCJ-145861. Washington, D.C.: U.S. Department of Justice, Bureau of Justice Statistics.

Reinarman, Craig
1993 The social construction of drug scares. In Patricia A. Adler and Peter Adler (eds.), Constructions of Deviance: Social Power, Context and Interaction. Belmont, Calif.: Wadsworth.

Reinarman, Craig and Harry G. Levine
1989 Crack attack: Politics and media in America's latest drug scare. In Joel Best (ed.), Images of Issues: Typifying Contemporary Social Problems. New York: Aldine de Gruyter.
1997 Crack in America: Demon Drugs and Social Justice. Berkeley: University of California Press.

Rohde, David
2001 After long climb, prison population falls in New York. New York Times, 2 February: A1, B5.

Rosch, Joel
1985 Crime as an issue in American politics. In Erika S. Fairchild and Vincent J. Webb (eds.), The Politics of Crime and Criminal Justice. Beverly Hills, Calif.: Sage.

Rothman, David
1993 More of the same: American criminal justice policies in the 1990s. In Thomas G. Blomberg and Stanley Cohen (eds.), Punishment and Social Control: Essays in Honor of Sheldon L. Messinger. New York: Aldine de Gruyter.

Rusche, Georg and Otto Kirchheimer
1939 Punishment and Social Structure. New York: Columbia University Press.

Sabol, William J.
1989 Racially disproportionate prison populations in the United States. Contemporary Crises 13:405–432.

Schlosser, Eric
1998 The prison-industrial complex. Atlantic Monthly (December):51–77.

Skocpol, Theda
1980 Political responses to economic crisis: Neo-Marxist theories of the state and the case of the New Deal. Politics and Society 19:155–201.

Skocpol, Theda and Edwin Amenta
1986 States and social policies. Annual Review of Sociology 12:131–157.

Skogan, Wesley G.
1995 Crime and the racial fears of white Americans. The Annals of the American Academy of Political and Social Science 539:59–71.

Skolnick, Jerome H.
1966 Justice Without Trial: Law Enforcement in a Democratic Society. New York: Wiley.

Snell, Tracy L.
1995 Correctional Populations in the United States, 1993. Washington, D.C.: U.S. Department of Justice, Bureau of Justice Statistics.

Sniderman, Paul M. and Thomas Piazza
1993 The Scar of Race. Washington, D.C.: Howard University Press.

Speiglman, Richard
1977 Prison drugs, psychiatry, and the state. In David F. Greenberg (ed.), Corrections and Punishment. Beverly Hills, Calif.: Sage.

Spitzer, Steven and Andrew T. Scull
1977 Privatization and capitalist development. Social Problems 25:18–29.

Spohn, Cassia and David Holleran
2000 The imprisonment penalty paid by young, unemployed Black and Hispanic male offenders. Criminology 38:281–306.

Steffensmeier, Darrell, Jeffery Ulmer, and John Kramer
1998 The interaction of race, gender, and age in criminal sentencing: The punishment of being young, black, and male. Criminology 36:763–793.

Stephan, G. Edward and Douglas R. McMullin
1982 Tolerance of sexual nonconformity. American Sociological Review 46:411–415.

Straus, Murray A. and Denise A. Donnelly
1994 Beating the Devil Out of Them: Corporal Punishment in American Families. New York: Lexington.

Sutton, John R.
1987 Doing time: Dynamics of imprisonment in the Reformist State. American Sociological Review 52:612–630.
1990 Bureaucrats and entrepreneurs: Institutional responses to deviant children in the United States, 1890–1920s. American Journal of Sociology 95:1367–1400.
2000 Imprisonment and social classification in five common-law democracies, 1955–1985. American Journal of Sociology 106:350–386.

Swigert, Victoria Lynn and Ronald A. Farrell
1976 Murder, Inequality and the Law: Differential Treatment in the Legal Process. Lexington, Mass.: Lexington.

Taylor, Douglas C., Kim Lane Scheppele, and Arthur L. Stinchcombe
1979 Salience of crime and support for harsher criminal sanctions. Social Problems 26:413–424.

Terry, Don
2000 California's prison population declines for the first time in more than two decades. New York Times, 6 July: A18.

Tonry, Michael
1995 Malign Neglect—Race, Crime and Punishment in America. New York: Oxford University Press.

Vaughan, Barry
2000 Punishment and conditional citizenship. Punishment and Society 2:23–39.

Wallace, Don
1981 The political economy of incarceration trends in late U.S. capitalism: 1971–1977. Insurgent Sociologist 10:59–66.

Warr, Mark
1989 What is the perceived seriousness of crimes? Criminology 27:795–821.

White, Halbert
1980 A heteroscedastic-consistent covariance matrix and a direct test for heteroscedasticity. Econometrica 48:421–448.

Wilcox, Clyde
1992 God's Warriors: The Christian Right in Twentieth-Century America. Baltimore, Md.: The Johns Hopkins University Press.

Willbanks, William
1985 The Myth of a Racist Criminal Justice System. Belmont, Calif.: Brooks/Cole.

Wilson, Thomas C.
1985 Urbanism and tolerance. American Sociological Review 50:117–123.

Wilson, William Julius
1980 The Declining Significance of Race: Blacks and Changing American Institutions. 2d ed. Chicago, Ill.: University of Chicago Press.

Wright, Gerald C., Robert S. Erikson, and John P. McIver
1985 Measuring state partisanship and ideology with survey data. Journal of Politics 47:469–489.
1987 Public opinion and policy liberalism in the American states. American Journal of Political Science 31:980–1001.
1993 Statehouse Democracy: Public Opinion and Policy in the American States. New York: Cambridge University Press.

Wu, De-Min
1973 Alternative tests of independence between stochastic regressors and disturbances. Econometrica 41:733–750.
1974 Alternative tests of independence between stochastic regressors and disturbances: Finite sample results. Econometrica 42:529–546.

Young, Jock
1999 The Exclusionary Society. London: Sage.

Zielinski, Kristin
1995 Study finds regional, racial patterns in sparing kids the rod. The Cavalier, (16 February).

Zimring, Franklin and Gordon Hawkins
1995 Incapacitation: Penal Confinement and the Restraint of Crime. New York: Oxford University Press.

Zimring, Franklin, Gordon Hawkins, and Sam Kamin
2001 Punishment and Democracy: Three Strikes and You're Out in California. New York: Oxford University Press.

David F. Greenberg is Professor of Sociology at New York University. His current research interests focus on racism in law enforcement, time series analyses of crime rates, factor analysis methodology, the administration of the death penalty, and Babylonian and Sumerian trial procedures.

Valerie West is a doctoral candidate in sociology at New York University. Her current work focuses on capital punishment and the review of capital cases. She is co-author, with James Liebman, Jeffrey Fagan and Jonathan Lloyd, of *Capital Attrition: Error Rates in Capital Cases, 1973–1995* in the *Texas Law Review*, and a technical report, *A Broken System: Error Rates in Capital Cases, 1973–1995*, with James Liebman and Jeffrey Fagan.

Appendix: Data Sources

Data for the variables BLACKPCT, FAMPOV, UNEMP, and URBAN come from the annual volumes of the U.S. Bureau of the Census, *Statistical Abstracts of the United States*. The percentage of a state's population that was Hispanic in 1970 comes from the U.S. Bureau of the Census's 1973 publication, *Census of Population: 1970.* Subject *Reports. Final Report PC(2)-1C. Persons of Spanish Origin*; for subsequent decades, from *Statistical Abstracts*. Gini coefficients were supplied by the U.S. Bureau of the Census. Crime rates were taken from the FBI's *Crime in the United States* (1991). Unpublished arrest figures for narcotics offenses in 1970, 1980, and 1990 were made available to us by the FBI. Imprisonment rates are taken from the annual editions of the *Sourcebook for Criminal Justice*. Governors' political party affiliations are given in *The World Almanac and Book of Facts*. State revenue and welfare payments come from the U.S. Bureau of the Census's *State Government Finances, Series GF-69 No. 3* and *GF-70 No. 3*. Data for religious fundamentalism come from the 1971, 1981, and 1991 volumes of *Churches and Church Membership in the United States*.

[13]
Siting the Death Penalty Internationally

We examine sources of variation in possession and use of the death penalty using data drawn from 193 nations in order to test theories of punishment. We find the death penalty to be rooted in a country's legal and political systems, and to be influenced by its religious traditions. A country's level of economic development, its educational attainment, and its religious composition shape its political institutions and practices, indirectly affecting its use of the death penalty. The article concludes by discussing likely future trends.

INTRODUCTION

The countries of the world vary greatly in their use of the death penalty. Some prohibit it; others allow it but rarely or never use it. The People's Republic of China, on the other hand, executes more than three thousand people a year.[1] Yet, little is known about the reasons for these differences. Our goal is to explain them.

David F. Greenberg is Professor of Sociology at New York University.

Valerie West is Assistant Professor of Law and Police Science at John Jay College.

Direct correspondence to the first author at dg4@nyu.edu. We are grateful to Slawomir Redo, James Galbraith, Robert Barro, Michael Ross, Maria Stylianidou, Margaret Lewis, and Jaw-perng Wang for assistance with data acquisition; to Margaret Lewis for a translation from Chinese; and to Mikaela Arthur, Vanessa Barker, Aaron Beim, Christian Boulanger, Michela Bowman, Stephanos Bibas, Neil Caren, Vivek Chibber, Theodore Christianson, Deborah Denno, Thomas Ertmann, David Garland, Evi Girling, Maria Los, Gerald Marwell, Dario Melossi, Rene Römkens, Joachim Savelsberg, Mildred Schwartz, Franklin Zimring, and the anonymous referees for helpful questions, comments, and suggestions. Earlier versions of this article were presented at the annual meetings of the American Sociological Association in Anaheim, California and the Law and Society Association in Budapest, Hungary, both in 2001.

1. Amnesty International, China: Annual Report, 2004. http://www.amnestyusa.org/countries/china (accessed November 24, 2007).

Our inquiry addresses what has long been a central question for both political philosophy and practical politics: how can one establish a government that will protect citizens from private predation, including violence, without putting citizens in jeopardy of violence at the hands of the state? In many countries, strategies for protecting citizens from state violence have included the establishment of due process in criminal trials, bans on judicial torture, and limits on the severity of criminal penalties. Starting in the second half of the eighteenth century, some governments went further by doing away with the death penalty altogether.

Prior to this most recent phase in penal history, our inquiry would have been unproductive. In the historic past, all countries had capital punishment, though they used it to varying degrees. It was taken for granted and provoked little controversy; executing criminals was a traditional practice that was not thought to need special justification. In the past few decades, however, many countries have stopped executing criminals, generally after a long period of declining use.[2] Countries that retain it now do so as a conscious choice. It becomes of particular interest, then, to understand why some countries make this choice, while others do not.

THEORIZING THE DEATH PENALTY

Theoretical analyses of punishment provide conceptual resources for our enterprise. Until recently, much theorizing about penality has taken place within two distinct, though sometimes overlapping, theoretical frameworks. The first sees state punishment practices as responses to threatening social conditions, including crime. The second conceives of punishment as a strategy deployed by an advantaged sector of society against a subordinate class or stratum.

In the past two decades, theorists have criticized both perspectives as simplistic and reductionist because they envision punishment as a mechanical, knee-jerk reflex in response to worrisome conditions. Yet countries facing similar conditions do not always respond similarly. Newer theoretical efforts

2. The European abolition of capital punishment came as the culmination of a long-term decline in numbers of executions, the adoption of efforts to speed death and to make it less painful, the abandonment of public executions, and the substitution of secondary punishments such as transportation and imprisonment (Garland 2005). This process lies beyond the scope of our investigation. Among the contributing factors would appear to be a long-term decline in the levels of interpersonal violence (Eisner 2003; Greenberg 2003); the consolidation of state authority, reducing the insecurity of rulers and the public; the capacity of growing economies to use labor productively; and popular opposition to excessive or disproportionate punishment. Only after executions became rare did they become shocking enough to stimulate campaigns for abolition. The removal of the slaughtering of food animals from public view may have further led the public to become sensitized to killing.

argue that responses to crime or to a perceived social threat are conditioned by a nation's culture and its political system (Garland 1990, 2001; Melossi 2001; Savelsberg 1994; Simon 2001; Greenberg and West 2001; Sutton 2004).

Much of this work concerns imprisonment rather than capital punishment; however, several authors extend this approach to capital punishment by attributing America's retention of the death penalty even after Europe abolished it to its distinctive culture and political system (Poveda 2000; Steiker 2002; Zimring 2003). These works, however, do not aim to explain all cross-national differences. That is our task.

In our analyses, we will draw on the older body of theory, as well as on insights gleaned from the newer analyses. Because earlier studies of penality have elaborated on the reasons for thinking that the severity of a state's punishments for criminal law violations are responsive to its serious crime rate, unemployment, poverty, economic inequality, and the presence of minority groups perceived to be dangerous, we will discuss these influences only briefly, while offering a more extended discussion of political and cultural influences on punishment.

Social Threat

Reicher (2003) has recently argued that governments are especially likely to resort to capital punishment when they feel threatened. On this basis, the death penalty is expected to be more likely when any of several sources of social threat are present. One of these is crime—when homicide rates are high, the public will be more fearful, and may be more likely to demand that criminals be punished with death. While the evidence that homicide rates explain variation in imprisonment rates is mixed (Greenberg 1999; Greenberg and West 2001; Ruddell 2005), we will be able to determine whether it explains variation in the use of the death penalty.[3]

A body of research indicates that a significant fraction of the white American population feels threatened by the presence of nonwhites in their community and responds to this threat by generously allocating resources to law enforcement (Jackson 1992; Chiricos, Hogan, and Geertz 1997; Alesina, Baqir, and Easterly 1999; Tonry 1999; Beckett and Western 2001; Greenberg and West 2001; Quillian and Pager 2001). Racial, ethnic, and linguistic differences may elicit similar responses.

Lawmakers and judges may consider the unemployed and impoverished as discontented and potentially volatile (Spitzer 1975); countries that are unable to put the idle to work may try to control them with death if they

3. Because most prisoners are serving sentences for crimes other than homicide, homicides may have a stronger impact on death sentences than on imprisonment.

get out of line. When economic conditions are adverse, judges, state policy makers, and the general public may be especially prone to regard law breakers as especially worthy of execution (Greenberg 1977; Box 1987; Chiricos and DeLone 1992; Poveda 2000; Beckett and Western 2001; Greenberg and West 2001).

Governments may also feel threatened by civil unrest or militant political opposition. Incumbent officeholders may want the death penalty, not to deter ordinary homicides or other crimes, but to secure their ability to stay in office and to govern effectively.

Political Influences

Political institutions and practices can influence a country's punishment policies in several ways. We consider the degree to which a country grants political and civil rights to its citizens, the type of legal system it has, the ideological orientation of its government, the size of its population, and its ethnic and linguistic diversity (these last two are not political institutions or practices, but they are structural characteristics that may have political implications).

In the twentieth century, the number of executions taking place under Fascist and Communist dictatorships greatly exceeded the number in the Western democracies (Zimring 2003, 18). We argue that this is because governments responsive to the well-being of the people do not need to torture and kill on a large scale to maintain order or stay in office. Dictatorships lack the checks and balances that inhibit governments from killing the opposition. Undemocratic rulers may pursue political agendas that lack popular support, and turn to violence to compel compliance with unpopular measures. Typically, democracies establish limits on the exercise of government power to protect citizens from its excesses.

In a pioneering study of the relationship between the death penalty and a country's political arrangements, Killias (1986) found in a sample of forty-three nations, whose incomes in 1977 were at least $1,000 per capita and whose populations were at least one million, that nondemocratic governments were more likely than democratic ones to have capital punishment, consistent with our reasoning. However, Killias did not control for other possible influences on capital punishment, making it difficult to be confident that the relationship is not spurious.

Apart from the extent of democracy in a country, the political ideologies espoused by its political leadership may influence its punishment practices. One of the current issues that tends to distinguish different political camps is crime control. Those on the right typically understand crime in individual terms, as the result of a rational choice, or as the product of a personal defect. This individualist understanding of crime meshes well with the conservatives' individualistic understandings of labor market outcomes as the product of inborn traits and personal virtues such as hard work, discipline, and the foresight to acquire human capital. Deterrence, incapacitation, cutbacks in welfare, and the strengthening of conventional families and traditional morality are the conservatives' preferred strategies for preventing and avenging crime (Scheingold 1984; Beckett 1997; Poveda 2000).

Those on the left understand crime to be the product of social inequality and unfair disadvantage. This structural understanding of crime is congruent with the left's understanding of labor market outcomes as shaped by institutionalized advantage and disadvantage. Reflecting these understandings, liberal preferences for crime control policies entail prevention through social reform, especially the reduction of social inequality and discrimination, the rehabilitation of offenders, and gun control (Wilson 1983; Beckett and Sassoon 2000; Gest 2001).

Consistent with these expectations, the United States' imprisonment rates are relatively high and have grown more rapidly in states in which the population is especially conservative (Greenberg and West 2001). In a sample of fifteen affluent democracies, dominance of the cabinet by liberal parties has been associated with lower imprisonment rates (Sutton 2004). In the United Kingdom, conservatives were more strongly opposed to abolition of the death penalty than those with other political leanings (Christoph 1962, 44, 55, 120). As early as 1923, the British Labor Party took a stand against capital punishment, and it was under a Labor government that Britain abolished capital punishment in 1965 (Potter 1993, 202). In Austria, abolition followed the entry of Socialists into the governing coalition, and it took place in France after the election of a Labor government (Zimring 2003, 22–23). We consequently expect leftist governments to be less likely than others to have and use the death penalty.

Jacobs and Kleban (2003) reason that in small states, politicians will be more readily influenced by public preferences, which they assume to be punitive. They assess the relationship between population size and punishment by carrying out a pooled time-series cross-sectional analysis of imprisonment rates for a small sample of nations, finding a negative relationship between population size and the imprisonment rate. The random-effects estimation procedure Jacobs and Kliban use, however, is vulnerable to bias stemming from unmeasured sources of heterogeneity. The matter deserves further attention.

The use of the death penalty may also be influenced by protections for defendants built into the criminal law. The major legal systems of the world developed in different historical contexts and differ in the extent to which they incorporate concerns for the protection of defendants. Historians of law observe that English common law developed in connection with the gentry's efforts to limit royal power and so adopted measures to protect the rights of individuals (Sommerville 1986, 121–27). Weiner (1987) argues that

England exported its political culture of limited government to the Third World. It might then be inferred that common-law countries throughout the world would be less likely to use the death penalty.

Civil law developed in continental Europe as a tool of royal bureaucratic administration, and it has been characterized as giving less emphasis to individual rights (David and Brierley 1978; Sommerville 1986, 121–27; Cantor 1997; La Porta et al. 1999). Consequently, civil-law systems should be more accepting than common-law systems of the instrumental use of capital punishment on behalf of the state's instrumental goals. It is not clear, however, that the historical distinctions between the common law and civil law are as important as they once were. Many civil-law nations now enjoy the same political rights and civil liberties as the common-law countries.

Moreover, to protect property, eighteenth-century England condemned even petty thieves to death (Linebaugh 1991; McGowen 2007). England was not unique in this respect; in eighteenth-century France, most larcenies were capital offenses (Weisser 1979, 138). However, England was slower than other countries to limit the offenses for which death sentences could be imposed, and its execution rate was higher than in continental Europe (Christoph 1962, 14). Evidently, common law did not limit executions in the historic past. Given the ambiguity of theoretical reasoning, we make no prediction as to the effect of common law or civil law.

The implications of Socialism for capital punishment are unclear. The social-structural understandings of crime causation for which the Left has an affinity might lead us to expect Socialist governments to abolish capital punishment. Karl Marx (1981) himself wrote in opposition to the death penalty. The social-democratic parties of Western Europe advocated its abolition (Radzinowic 1999), as did many Bolsheviks in Russia (Janković 1984; Scobell 1991). Religiously based moralistic thinking about crime has sometimes led to support for the death penalty by those who want the state to carry out a deity's will that the wicked be put to death. The Marxist critique of religion should reduce moral zealotry in the enforcement of the law. Because the various Communist parties have been explicitly hostile to religion, we might expect the countries they control to abandon capital punishment.

On the other hand, the Socialist embrace of social engineering might lead to the use of extreme sanctions, unrestrained by religiously based beliefs that human life is sacred. Socialists have often rejected the ideology of individualism which, according to Durkheim (1973), has contributed to the historical trend toward reduced punishment severity. Moreover, the conditions under which "really existing Socialism" was established in Russia were not favorable to the abolition of capital punishment. The social tensions created by rapid industrialization—a necessity for a nation surrounded by hostile powers—might have been difficult to contain without exceptionally harsh punishment. In addition, the Communist insistence on maintaining a monopoly of political power would tend to push any political opposition to extreme measures, perhaps in turn encouraging ruthless punishment. Finally, the totalitarian regime did not tolerate any religious or political opposition that might have nurtured and disseminated ideologies—such as natural law philosophy—calling for limits on the use of state power to accomplish political goals. For these reasons we predict that Socialist nations will have capital punishment and use it.

Religion and Law

The legal systems of the major religions vary in the ways they deal with the death penalty. Some (e.g., the canon law of the Roman Catholic Church) do not mandate capital punishment. Others do, but they are not applied anywhere in the world (e.g., Jewish, Hindu, and Zoroastrian law); still others do not have law codes (Buddhism). Islamic law calls for death for some infractions, there are countries in which Islamic law is used in the courts, and Islamic scripture lacks the "turn the other cheek" tradition of Christian pacifism. Indeed, the Koran explicitly articulates the principle of *al-nafsa bi'l-nafs*—life for life (Kamali 2002, 84). Islamic law designates certain categories of offenses for which judges do not have the discretion to mitigate designated penalties—for some crimes (such as apostasy and adultery), death is mandatory. The entire Koran is understood to be the word of Allah; its provisions could not be rejected without undermining the claim of the entire body of law to be legitimate. Leading Egyptian Islamist Muhammad al-Ghazali contended that legislative abolition of capital punishment was unacceptable because it would "violate the Islamic text, which says that killers must be executed" (quoted in Pipes 2000). Islam also lacks a doctrine of separation of church and state that would limit the influence of religious teachings on criminal legislation; consequently, countries governed by Islamic law should be more likely than others to have the death penalty and to use it.

Even when a scriptural passage cannot be repudiated explicitly, it can be effectively nullified or restricted in application to the point where it is neutralized, through the process of interpretation. In the past, debates about the interpretation of the passages in the Koran did take place, however, according to Khaled Abou El Fadl:

> One thing is quite clear in the contemporary Islamic tradition, all of this discourse, and all of this debate doesn't exist anymore, in the sense that you do not hear any serious discussion, either at the level of Muslim nations, or at the level of Muslim private jurists and scholars, talking about this issue in any serious way. (El Fadl 2003)

Where procedural protections are operative, we would expect them to influence the number of death sentences imposed and executions carried out, without necessarily having an effect on the presence of the death penalty as a possible sanction. The existence of such protections in Islamic law does not alter our expectation that countries whose legal systems are based on Islamic law will be more likely than other countries to have the death penalty.

Though many national legal systems are influenced in their substantive provisions by the laws of religions, other than Islam we know of no instance in which the penalty provisions of a nation's criminal law are explicitly based on the laws of religion. Consequently we do not have to make predictions for legal systems based, for example, on Christian or Hindu law. (We return to an in-depth discussion of religion in the section titled "Religious Influences.")

Societal Influences

Several theorists have argued that penal policies may fruitfully be considered part of a broader array of strategies that governments adopt for managing the poor (Foucault 1975; Garland 1985; Beckett and Western 2001). Under ordinary circumstances, the bulk of criminal court defendants come from the low-income strata of society. In some countries, welfare subsidies provide life support to low-income populations, thereby reducing incentives for crime and political protest or rebellion. If kindness to the poor motivates generous welfare policies, one would expect it to motivate leniency toward criminals as well, leading to a negative relationship between welfare generosity and punishment severity. There is evidence of this. In American history, the elimination of poor-houses for dependent citizens was closely tied to the expansion of reformatories, jails, and prisons (Sutton 1987, 1990). In recent decades, imprisonment rates and their rates of growth have been lower in those U.S. states that are especially generous with welfare payments to the poor (Beckett and Western 2001; Greenberg and West 2001). Moreover, in five common-law countries, welfare spending between 1955 and 1985 was inversely related to imprisonment rates (Sutton 2000).

In the modern world, capital punishment is administered as part of a criminal justice system that sentences most convicted defendants to sentences other than death—for example, fines, probation, or imprisonment. Countries that are more likely to be punitive in general, we argue, are more likely to use capital punishment. To adjust for the general punitiveness of a country, we control for its imprisonment rate.

Increased social differentiation and higher levels of economic inequality can be expected to reduce interpersonal trust among strangers. Those who are disadvantaged in a stratified social order are likely to resent those who are better off, and those who are advantaged may fear the resentment of those who are not (Brockner and Siegel 1996). Lack of trust in others may increase public willingness to rely on harsh punishment to secure safety

(Knack and Keefer 1997; Alesina and La Ferrara 2002; Uslaner 2002), and economic stratification also may reduce empathy between members of classes or strata. Because the death penalty primarily affects the poor, nations that are more solicitous of the well-being of the poor should be less likely to have and use the death penalty.

Ethnic diversity is another form of social differentiation that may have relevance for punishment policy because it reduces social participation and trust (Alessina and La Ferrara 2000; Glaeser et al. 2000; Putnam 2007). Individuals are less likely to help those they consider to be unlike themselves in some important way (Bar-Tal 1976, 78; Gaertner and Dovidio 1977; McCarty 1993), and ethnic identification can lead individuals to value the welfare of members of their own group and devalue the well-being of other groups (Tajfel et al. 1971). In the United States, cities, metropolitan areas, and counties with higher levels of ethnic diversity tend to spend less on public goods, such as education and roads, and more on police (Cutler, Elmendorf, and Zeckhauser 1993; Alesina, Baqir, and Easterly 1999; Easterly and Levine 1997; Goldin and Katz 1999). Nations with greater ethnic diversity tend to spend less on redistributive welfare payments (McCarty 1993). Evidently, people are less likely to favor subsidies to groups other than their own and are more likely to respond to them punitively. We conclude that ethnically diverse societies should be more likely to have capital punishment.

Cultural Influences

Cultures define the seriousness of criminal offenses and provide the values that shape crime policies. Decision makers may adopt policies that realize their own values, or they may accommodate the values of their constituents, or do both. In complex political systems, it may be impossible to implement a public policy that realizes any one person's values fully. Subcultural differences among different groups within a country may need to be accommodated. Cost considerations and competing demands on resources may limit the ability of the state to carry out policies. Nevertheless, values can be relevant to policy making. Where governments take the values and policy preferences of their populations into account, we would expect a people's culture to influence a government's use of the death penalty.

Religious Influences

Though direct measures of the values of the citizens of many countries are not available, we have indicators of several important social sources of values. Values may originate in, or be part of, political philosophies (e.g., libertarianism or welfare-statism), or be rooted in religion. A religion may influence attitudes toward capital punishment through specific teachings relating to life and death, and by conveying broader world views and prescriptions for action that shape the ways its adherents think about capital punishment. Thus, the *New Testament* counsels against repaying violence with violence, while the scriptures of other religions offer no such advice, and may even call for the use of violence against sinners.

The major religions of the world have taken somewhat distinctive positions on capital punishment, and in some cases those positions have changed historically. Christianity presents an inconsistent historical legacy in relation to capital punishment. In the one passage in the *New Testament* in which Jesus addresses the issue of capital punishment—the execution of a woman for adultery—he denies the moral authority of the executioners to carry out the execution (John 8:3–11). His injunctions to turn the other cheek and to forgive one's enemies (Matthew 5:38–45, 6:15; Luke 23:34) can be seen as inconsistent with capital punishment. Yet, though some leaders of the early Church understood Christianity to prohibit the taking of any human life, and flatly condemned the death penalty, others endorsed the state's right to execute in social defense. After Christianity became the official religion of the Roman Empire, the Church leadership became more accepting of the death penalty (Compagnoni 1978; Megivern 1997). Taken at face value, Paul's contention that the "ruler" is "the minister of God, a revenger to execute wrath upon him that doth evil" (Romans 13:1–7) seems to legitimate any punishment that the ruler imposes.

Throughout most of its history, the Roman Catholic Church did not oppose capital punishment. Indeed, it was endorsed by the Church's most influential theologists (Augustine and Thomas Aquinas), in papal bulls, catechisms, and officially approved works of theology (Roos 1957; Savey-Cassard 1961; Megivern 1997, 141, 170–74; Dulles 2005). Only in the past few decades has the Church come to oppose capital punishment. To the extent that Roman Catholics take direction on this issue from Church teachings, the greater the representation of Catholics in a country, the less likely the death penalty will be found.

Protestant Christianity is often thought to allow greater scope for the exercise of individual conscience than Roman Catholicism, whose teachings emphasize the social embeddedness of human life and the collective responsibilities of a community's members for one another (Weber 1930; Schuck 1991; Greeley 2000, 123–24). This valorization of the individual might lead Protestants to oppose capital punishment in order to preserve sacrosanct individual human lives. Yet in Germany, the Protestant (or Evangelic) Church and its affiliated political party, the German Nationalists, supported capital punishment. After 1890, the strongest opposition came from the antireligious Social Democrats and Communists, on political grounds (Evans 1996). Moreover, Melossi (2001) has argued that Roman Catholicism, based on forgiveness, may lead to more lax punishment than the Calvinist denominations of Protestantism, with their doctrines of predestination. However, the historical record of the Roman Catholic Church makes us skeptical of Melossi's argument.

In the United States, major Protestant denominations, including Episcopalians, Lutherans, Methodists, Presbyterians, and the United Church of Christ, have taken stands against capital punishment. However, evangelical, Pentecostal, and fundamentalist Protestant denominations have supported it (Bedau 1997). On the basis of biblical authority, the Southern Baptist Convention—America's largest Protestant denomination—voted overwhelmingly in June 2000 in favor of a resolution affirming the use of capital punishment "by civil magistrates . . . for those guilty of murder or treasonous acts that result in death" (Banks 2000, 1). Given this diversity of opinion, and Melossi's argument as to Catholic leniency, we do not expect the presence of Protestants in a country to influence its probability of having capital punishment. It is possible that individual denominations do so, but we do not explore differences among the Protestant denominations here.

Protestantism and Roman Catholicism are not the only varieties of Christianity. None of the Orthodox churches has ever called for abolition. A recent statement adopted by the Sacred Bishop's Council of the Russian Orthodox Church left capital punishment for society to determine on the basis of the need to protect life.[4] This reluctance to take a decisive stand for or against capital punishment is what might be expected from religious bodies that are organized nationally and consequently do not have the international resources that have enabled the Roman Catholic Church to stand up to the state in some countries. Appointments and finances of the Orthodox Churches are often under state control, resulting in a "caesaropapist" relationship between church and state that prevents the churches from openly opposing the state. Moreover, the emphasis on doctrine and ritual in the Eastern churches has encouraged the quietest of responses to social issues (Stepan 2000, 2001). Under this circumstance, we predict that Orthodoxy is irrelevant to a country's death penalty policy. The Orthodox churches will go along with whatever the state wants.

The Anglican/Episcopalian Churches have some features that resemble Roman Catholicism, but their nonrecognition of the papacy is shared with Protestantism. The thirty-seventh of the Thirty-Nine Articles of Faith adopted by the Church of England in 1563, and by the English Parliament in 1571, provides that "the Laws of the Realm may punish Christian men with death, for heinous and grievous offences" (Gattrell 1994, 373). Significantly, the text does not *require* capital punishment; it merely allows the state to impose it. This Article remains in effect today.

4. See "The Social Basis of the Social Concept of the Russian Orthodox Church." http://incommunion.org/articles/resources/the-orthodox-church/introduction (accessed November 14, 2007).

Until the 1960s, Anglican bishops and theologians gave strong backing to capital punishment, which they saw as a necessary deterrent, a merciful encouragement to contrition for those facing execution, and a fulfillment of biblical commandments (Potter 1993; O'Donovan 1998). Consistent with this consensus, the nineteenth-century Anglican Church did not support abolition. From the early nineteenth century on, both sides of the controversy introduced religious arguments having to do with mercy, forgiveness, and retribution. However, most of the arguments focused on instrumental considerations. In the post-World War II years, members of the Church of England were less likely than adherents of other religions to support abolition (Christoph 1862, 119–20). Only in the final stages of the abolition campaign did Anglican clergy join the abolitionist camp (Tuttle 1961; Potter 1993; Block and Hostettler 1997; Bailey 2000).

As with the Roman Catholic Church, hundreds of years of tradition gave way to change in response to social and culture changes following World War II. By the 1960s, a number of leading figures in the Church of England, including both archbishops and bishops, favored abolition, but the Church itself did not take a stand, and at least one bishop dissented (Block and Hostettler 1997, 224–26). This reticence is what might be expected from a religious body "tied too closely to the state to give the necessary moral lead to the country" (Potter 1993, 206).

In the United States and in Australia, the Episcopalian Church revised the Thirty-Seventh Article by deleting all reference to specific forms of punishment. In the United States, it took a stand against capital punishment in 1958, and again in 1979.[5] Given its minimal involvement in death penalty controversies in England, and the diverse doctrines held by Episcopalian Churches elsewhere, we do not expect Anglicism to have any systematic effects on capital punishment.

As we have already observed, Islamic law explicitly endorses capital punishment. Moreover, Islamic political culture has not favored the separation of church and state. Mohammed was not only a prophet but a military and political leader. In Islamic culture, states are legitimated through their pursuit of justice as defined by Islam, not by their ability to achieve secular goals such as fulfillment of the popular will (Gardet 1954; Binder 1964; Kedourie 1966; Esposito and De Long-Bas 2003). According to Kedourie:

> The notion of popular sovereignty as the foundation of governmental legitimacy, the idea of representation, or elections, of popular suffrage, of political institutions being regulated by laws laid down by a parliamentary assembly, of these laws being guarded and upheld by an

5. See http://www.soci.niu.edu/~critcrim/dp/redir/relcalls.txt (accessed November 25, 2007).

> independent judiciary, the ideas of the secularity of the state, of society being composed of a multitude of self-activating groups and associations—all of these are profoundly alien to the Muslim political tradition. (1994, 5–6)

Indeed, there is nothing in Islam to compare to Jesus's instruction to "Render unto Caesar the things which are Caesar's, and unto God the things which are God's" (Matthew 22:21).

Though recent decades have seen the appearance of secular states in countries where a majority of the population is Muslim, Islam itself has never accepted the bifurcation of life into mutually exclusive realms of the secular and the spiritual (Lewis 1974; Jansen 1979, 17; Taylor 1988; ibn Warraq 1995). Islamist thinkers have insisted that democracy is incompatible with Islam because democracy would permit the adoption of laws that are incompatible with Islam (Pipes 2000). If this is so, countries in which Muslims are a majority may lack the tolerance of difference and the will to compromise that are, arguably, essential cultural requisites to a thriving, stable democracy that protects political and civil rights (Choueiri 1996). Though conservative or fundamentalist political movements pursuing religious goals can be found in various parts of the world and associated with several religions (e.g., Christianity, Hinduism), only the Islamist goal of restoring the caliphate seeks to bring about a particular form of government.

In addition, the theological developments that have had an enormous impact on modern Judaism and Christianity, such as the historicizing of scripture and the abandonment of the belief that it is the literal word of God, have had far less impact on Islam. In a number of predominantly Muslim societies, the recent resurgence of a politicized Islam has been marked by the widespread adoption of conventions regarding clothing and body presentation that mark the wearer as Muslim (women wearing the *chador* or *hijab*, men wearing beards), the proliferation of religious schools, and popular support for the adoption of religiously based law by the state (Stork and Beinem 1997; Haddad and Esposito 1987). As a result, Islam permeates the public life of many of the predominantly Muslim countries to a much greater extent than other religions do in other parts of the world (Adams 1986). In two-thirds of the nations in which a majority of the population is Muslim, Islam is the state religion. This is a higher percentage than for countries in which the majority population is Roman Catholic, Protestant, Anglican, Orthodox, Hindu, or Buddhist.[6] Cross-national surveys show that attendance at houses of worship and beliefs in a number of religious doctrines increases with the percentage of the population that is Muslim (Barro and McCleary 2005). Some Muslim religious leaders issue *fatwas*—edicts authorizing private

6. We use the data on state religions provided by Barro and McCleary (2005).

individuals to kill. This practice, not found in any other major religion, suggests that the culture of Islam is more willing than that of other religions to countenance the taking of human life to achieve religiously sanctioned collective goals. The influence of Islam on state penal practices may, therefore, be greater than the influence of Christian teachings in predominantly Christian nations.

In the United Nations General Assembly and in other international forums, the nations whose populations are predominantly Muslim have opposed abolition (as have a number of nations that are not predominantly Muslim), usually on the grounds that it is incompatible with Islamic law (Schabas 2000). So far as we have been able to determine, a declaration supporting abolition adopted in 1995 in Tunis by a joint meeting of the Institute of the Arab Institute for Human Rights and the Citizens and Parliamentarians' League for the Abolition of the Death Penalty is the only instance in which a Muslim organization anywhere in the world ever took an abolitionist position (Schabas 2000). Given the theological support for capital punishment in Islam, and the strength of conviction among its adherents, we expect the presence of Muslims in a country's population to be positively related to its use of the death penalty.

The very early, prestigious Hindu *Laws of Manu* (written roughly two thousand years ago) and the later *Yājñavalkya-smṛti* (Vasu 1909) charge the king with responsibility for administering criminal justice, and specify a schedule of penalties for various offenses that includes death for some crimes (Buehler 1886; Vasu 1909). Hindu jurisprudence generally has taken the legitimacy of capital punishment for granted (Gupta 1986).

Though opposition to the death penalty is recorded in Hindu sources as early as the *Mahabarata* (ch. 257 of the *Santipavara*), and though a few Hindu rulers refrained from imposing it, it was used by many (Gupta 1986, 21–22). Capital punishment being consistent with Hindu tradition, death sentences failed to provoke opposition when imposed by colonial rulers. In recent years some opposition to capital punishment has emerged in India, but popular support for it remains strong. In the debates over its retention, arguments on both sides of the question have focused primarily on utilitarian considerations, with minimal reference to religion (Gupta 1986; Schreiber 1996).

Several factors weaken the significance of the endorsement of capital punishment in the *Laws of Manu*. The separation of social function between the Brahmin (priestly) and *kshatriya* (warrior) castes makes penal law a secular matter (Lingat 1973, 64). Compared to the clergy in some religions, Hindu holy men are weakly organized, they are not politically influential; there is no canonical body of scripture or liturgy that is common to all Hindus, Hinduism does not have the monolithic organizational structure of Roman Catholicism or the Church of England, and the Hindu view of worldly experience as ultimately unreal or illusory diminishes the religious significance of government policy on any issue (Smith 1963, 27–41).

All these factors interfere with the formulation of a distinctly Hindu position on questions of criminal punishment and with effective mobilization on its behalf. Belief in the law of karma in connection with reincarnation may minimize social pressure on the government to chastise the wicked. If wrong-doers go unpunished in this life, the principle of karma says they will pay the price in the next life. Consistent with the lack of a clear Hindu position on penal policy, India adopted the British penal code at its Independence rather than trying to develop a distinctly Hindu penalty scheme. In more recent years, Hindu revivalism has focused on issues other than penal sanctions. For these reasons, we predict that Hinduism will not have any significant effect on whether a country has the death penalty.

The first of the Five Precepts of Buddhism—the most basic formulation of Buddhist morality—calls for the avoidance of intentionally killing any living thing (Rahula 1974, 80; Harvey 1990, 207). Capital punishment is manifestly inconsistent with this principle, and popular Buddhist literature extols kings who forgive murderers, while underscoring the counterproductiveness of killing in revenge (Lewis 2003). The current (Fourteenth) Dalai Lama has spoken in opposition to the death penalty (Gyatso 1998); yet contemporary countries where Buddhism has been influential have capital punishment (Alarid and Wang 2001). Indeed, this has also been true in the historic past in countries where Buddhist influence has been strong (Riasanovsky 1965; Krueger 1972; Jagchid and Hyer 1979; Nguyen and Tai 1987; French 1995, 324). However, in some of those countries, other religious traditions (e.g., Taoism and Confucianism in China) and political philosophies (Communism in the People's Republic of China) have been more important. In others, adherence to Buddhism appears to be superficial, so that its ethical principles are ignored in the formation of government policy.

With its emphasis on individual enlightenment and its belief, shared with Hinduism, that the mundane world of experience is illusory, Buddhists, even where numerically well represented in a country's population, do not mobilize to make pacifism a state policy. The Five Precepts are not commanded by a god, to break them is not to commit a sin, and violations of the precepts do not occasion a call for punishment. The precepts are simply principles of ethical living. Faced with the practical problems of ruling a country, a Buddhist ruler might well elect to ignore them and can do so without fear of suffering divine sanctions. On the other hand, in the absence of instrumental reasons for carrying out executions, a ruler could refrain without feeling it imperative to punish the wicked and without encountering religiously based public pressure to avenge the violation of a god's commandments. Under these circumstances, Buddhist precepts may not carry weight when it comes to the formulation of criminal justice policy.

Greeley (2000) has argued that American lay Catholics have developed a culture that is independent of the clergy and of the official doctrine and teachings of the institutional church. This may be true of other faiths as well. As a result, followers of a religion may hold distinctive views on policy questions even when their religion does not take an official stand on those questions. This possibility has implications for the influence of religion on policy issues. Even a secular state may be influenced by the religiously based culture of a population. For this reason, it is not clear that the influence of Catholicism, Protestantism, or Islam will be less in countries where the legal system separates church and state.

Educational Influences

The level of education in a country may also influence its death penalty policy. Where education entails more than the uncritical inculcation of religious doctrine, it can foster thinking in utilitarian terms, independently of traditional teachings. Rising levels of education in the Western world over the past few hundred years have been accompanied by a reduced role of religion in social life (McLeod and Ustorf 2003), as well as lessened rigor in religious doctrines. Because a substantial body of written texts questions the efficacy of capital punishment as a method for preventing crime, instrumental thinking may lead to support for abolition of the death penalty. Consistent with this reasoning, American survey research indicates that those with higher levels of education are less likely to believe that executions deter murder (Pastore and Maguire 2000, 137).

Beyond fostering utilitarian abolitionism, education may alter the moral sensibilities of a nation in such a way that it can no longer stomach executions. Possibly the historical trend to abolish the death penalty, to carry out executions in private, and to adopt methods of execution thought to be painless, stems in part from changes in sensibility brought about by the growth of mass education. In the United States, support for the death penalty declines with education, especially at the highest levels[7] (Borg 1997; Pastore and Maguire 2000, 136). However, the upward trend in American educational attainment over the last fifty years has not been matched by a corresponding downward trend in support for the death penalty. As a result, it is uncertain what sort of influence cross-national differences in education will have on capital punishment.

Economic Influences

In Weberian terms, the more advanced economies should be associated with greater use of instrumental rationality and the weakening of religious

7. Using data from the General Social Survey for the years 1974–1993, we verified that the relationship persists when controlling for respondents' age, sex, religious affiliation, attendance at religious services, and income; it is true for blacks and whites. The data can be downloaded from http://www.icpsr.umich.edu (accessed December 14, 2007).

beliefs. Nations with greater involvement in the world economy should see an increase in their citizens' exposure to cultural differences, fostering acceptance of cultural relativism. This acceptance should, in turn, weaken harsh and inflexible moral standards, undercutting support for capital punishment. Durkheim (1933, 1973) argued that economic development takes place through an increase in the division of labor, which, by weakening the collective conscience, reduces punitiveness, and, as a result, capital punishment is gradually replaced by imprisonment.

On the other hand, in conditions of economic stress, such as might occur during a depression, ethnocentricity might lead to intolerance of diversity and deviance (Greenberg and Humphries 1980; Inglehart and Baker 2000)—and hence greater support for the death penalty. Foucault's (1975) analysis of historical trends in French punishment might suggest that modernization will be accompanied by a shift from tortuous penalties that destroy the body until death to those that attempt to refashion the psychological make-up of the law violator through regimens of discipline and therapy. Thus, this perspective, too, suggests that economic development should be associated with the abolition of capital punishment.

One theoretical perspective leads to an opposite prediction. Marxist theory asserts that economic growth is accompanied by increases in the organic composition of capital, intensified exploitation, and the growth of an unemployable "surplus population" that must be restrained from rebellion by the threat or use of state violence (Quinney 1977, 132). This perspective would associate high levels of economic development with the death penalty.

Military Influences

A country involved in a hot or cold war is likely to have a political culture that depicts the enemy as an implacable foe and endorses killing as necessary for defense or to achieve other political goals. Soldiers will be portrayed as heroes for slaughtering the foe. The logic by which an enemy is constituted as unredeemably wicked and is targeted for death is easily extended to those considered to be internal enemies, such as criminals. We might anticipate that militaristic countries will be more likely to use capital punishment as part of a "war on crime."

DATA AND METHODS

To examine the relationship between capital punishment and the explanatory variables that have figured in our theoretical discussion, we have assembled a data set containing information on the death penalty for 197 countries in the year 2000 and a set of explanatory variables measured as close to 2000 as possible. These are all the countries for which Amnesty International provides up-to-date information as to their death penalty status.[8] We exclude four political entities (East Timor, Hong Kong, Macau, and Palestinian Authority) that did not enjoy full political sovereignty in 2000. However, we see no reason to exclude small or less affluent countries, as Killias did (1986). Doing so would restrict our ability to determine the influence of a country's size and wealth on its death penalty policy. Our sample, then, consists of 193 nations.

In choosing to analyze data for almost every nation, we adopt a research strategy quite different from that taken in recent cross-national comparisons. Taking Western Europe, which is now entirely abolitionist, as a primary point of comparison, this literature sees the United States as exceptional and seeks to explain its distinctiveness in terms of American political institutions and culture without explaining abolition in Europe (Poveda 2000; Steiker 2002; Zimring 2003). This strategy leaves the impression that abolition is a logical, almost automatic step in a history of penal progress, hardly needing explanation. Yet the United States does not look unusual when compared with economically developed countries outside of Western Europe, such as Japan, which executes (Garland 2005), and other former British colonies that have retained the death penalty.

Because the number of countries in Europe is small, restriction of comparisons to that continent precludes the adoption of multivariate statistical analyses and forecloses the possibility of learning anything about other regions of the world. We have chosen to assemble data for the largest possible number of countries, so as to have a wider basis for comparison, and to permit the quantitative testing of theoretical expectations. Moreover, our approach makes no assumptions about the normalcy, inevitability, or desirability of abolition.

Operationalization of Variables

We measure use of the death penalty with a four-point scale, scored so that if, at the end of the year 2000,

- a country did not have the death penalty for any offense, it is scored 0 (seventy-three countries).
- if it did not have the death penalty for "ordinary offences" (i.e., regular criminal law violations) but had it for special offenses such as war crimes, it is scored 1 (fourteen countries).
- if a country had the death penalty but did not use it, it is scored 2 (twenty countries);
- but if it used the death penalty, it is scored 3 (eighty-six countries).

8. See Amnesty International, "The Death Penalty: List of Abolitionist and Retentionist Countries 1 January 2007." http://www.amnesty.org (accessed November 25, 2007).

Extrajudicial slayings are disregarded in the scoring. Although it would be desirable to examine the frequency with which nations that have the death penalty use it, reliable data on the annual number of death sentences and executions is unavailable for most nations, including some of those that use it most extensively.

We measure threats by the homicide rate per 100,000 people, as well as by the ethnic and linguistic diversity of the population. Because other kinds of crime might increase support for capital punishment, it would be desirable to have a more encompassing measure of illegality. However, the problem of noncomparable definitions of offenses in different countries and the absence of published crime rates for many nations make this unfeasible. Homicide definitions, on the other hand, are quite similar among the nations of the world (Barclay and Tavares 2003, 3).

Several different sources of information on the homicide rates of different countries are available. We have examined tabulations in the U.N. Demographic Yearbooks for 1998 and 1999; the World Health Organization's Web site, which lists homicide rates for countries in various recent years; the United Nations' Global Report on Crime and Justice, which reports homicide rates based on the first five United Nations Surveys of Crime Trends and Operations of Criminal Justice Systems carried out between 1974 and 1993 (Newman 1999, 312–14), the Sixth and Seventh United Nations Surveys covering the period 1995–1997 and 1998–2000, respectively;[9] and the *World Christian Encyclopedia* (Barrett, Kurian, and Johnson 2001).

Chon (2001) provides a thorough assessment of these sources, and concludes that rates in the U.N. Demographic Yearbooks are the most accurate. Wherever possible we have taken homicide rates from this source. When figures were not available from it, we used the U.N. surveys, choosing the closest year to 2000 for which data were available.[10] Regrettably, homicide rates for many of the nations in our sample are not listed in any of these surveys; quite a few countries seem not to have the administrative capacity to produce reliable homicide rates or do not want to publicize them. The correlation between the homicide rates obtained from the sources we use and those from the World Health Organization is 0.85, demonstrating that this variable is highly reliable. To reduce skewing, we work with the natural logarithm of the quantity (1 plus the homicide rate).

9. U.N. Demographic Yearbook 1998 (485–507) (http://unstats.un.org/unsd/demographic/products/dyb/dybsets/1998%20DYB.pdf); U.N. Demographic Yearbook 1999 (479–505) (http://unstats.un.org/unsd/demographic/products/dyb/dybsets/1999%20DYB.pdf); World Health organization (http://www.int/whosis/statistics); Sixth United Nations Survey 1995–1997 (http://www.unchim.org/Statistics/WCTS/WCTS6.html); Seventh United Nations Survey 1998–2000 (http://www.unodc.org/ONODC/en/data-and-analysis/Seventh-UnitedNations-Survey-on-Crime-Trends-and-the-Operations-of -Criminal-Justice-Systems.html) (all accessed November 25, 2007).

10. The homicide rate for Taiwan is taken from Criminal Investigation Bureau (2000, 49); for Cyprus, from Statistical Service of Cyprus (2000).

The concept of ethnic diversity is ambiguous because of imprecision as to what an ethnic group is. The phrase designates peoples who may be differentiated on the basis of race, language, culture, religion, or tribe (see Rex and Mason 1986; Alesino et al. 2002; Kheng 2001; Caselli and Coleman II 2002.) We explore two measures of ethnic diversity. Our first measure is the largest ethnic group's percentage of the population, taken from the U.S. Central Intelligence Agency's (CIA) *World Factbook 2000*.[11] The social threat hypothesis is that the smaller this percentage, the more likely a country is to have the death penalty—it is in that circumstance that the largest group will feel most insecure.

We also use the Ethnic Fractionalization Index (EFI), the complement of the Herfindahl-Hirschman Index (HHI). EFI is the probability that members of a randomly selected pair of individuals belong to different groups. Where a country is inhabited by just one ethnic group, the index is zero; where every inhabitant belongs to a distinct group, it is 1. This index takes fuller account of a country's diversity than our first measure. Alesina et al. (2002) and Kheng (2001) have each computed values of this index for a large number of nations and regions of the world using a number of different data sources. The correlation between the Alesina et al. index and the Kheng index is .835, but the correlations between these two indices and percent majority ethnic group are, respectively, –.3855 and –.3507. These last two indices are obviously measuring a different dimension of diversity than the first. We assess the effect of a country's linguistic diversity with the similarly defined Ethnolinguistic Fractionalization Index. This index can range from 0 to 1 and averages five components, as defined by La Porta et al. (1999), but we use the more recent data set assembled by Alesina et al. (2002) for this measure.

We use the World Bank scale of political stability (Kaufmann, Kraay, and Zoido-Lobatón 1999) to measure threat from civil unrest. The scale is composed of items measuring the risk of social unrest, major urban riots, major insurgency or rebellion, military coups, political terrorism, political assassination, civil war, war with other countries, and unconstitutional government changes for the year 2000. The scale is scored so that high scores represent countries whose political systems have been more stable. For eight nations, a score on this scale is missing, so we imputed it by regressing the political stability score on five other scales computed by the World Bank, measuring government effectiveness, the regulatory burden on business, control of corruption, the rule of law, and popular voice and accountability.

11. The CIA *World Factbooks* (2000–2006) are available for downloading but not browsing, at http://www.cia.gov/library/publications/the-world-factbook (accessed December 14, 2007).

As noted above, another version of the social threat hypothesis designates the unemployed as a potentially threatening population (Chiricos and DeLone 1992). Our measure of unemployment comes from the CIA *World Factbook 2000*. We explore several indicators of economic inequality: Gini coefficients for income, and the ratio of income received by the highest 20 percent to the income received by the lowest 20 percent of the population, are taken from the World Bank (2001, 282–83). Theil coefficients for sectoral inequality were computed by Hyunsub Kum of the University of Texas Inequality Project from the UNIDO 2000 release.[12] Finally, we measure a nation's level of economic development by the natural logarithm of its Gross National Product (GNP) per capita in 1999, as expressed by its purchasing power parity in U.S. dollars.[13]

To assess the role of religion, we include variables for the percentages in a population that are Catholic, Protestant, Anglican, Orthodox Christian, Muslim, Hindu, and Buddhist. The omitted reference category consists of all others. This includes Jains, Zoroastrians, Taoists, Bahais, Jews, practitioners of Shintoism, ethnoreligionists, and atheists. The diversity of this category precludes the formulation of any prediction as to the effect that membership in this category might have on the death penalty. Membership figures are taken from the *World Christian Encyclopedia* (Barrett, Kurian, and Johnson 2001). Its figures correlate very highly with those in the CIA's *World Factbook 2000* and the U.S. State Department's Annual Report on International Religious Freedom for the year 2000.[14]

As the governments of many countries do not collect information on religious affiliation, the figures should be considered rough estimates. Because we make no prediction about the effects of membership in our reference category, we cannot make any predictions about the effects of differences in religious composition relative to the reference category. However, we can test the proposition that Catholicism reduces the likelihood of capital punishment relative to Protestantism by comparing the coefficients for these two variables.

We measure educational attainment by the percent literate in the adult population using the CIA's *World Factbook 2000*.

We measure militarism by dividing military spending in 1999 by the Gross Domestic Product (GDP); the original data are taken from Turner (2001). When missing from Turner, they are taken from the CIA's *World Factbook 1999*.[15] To reduce skewing, we take the natural log of the quantity {1 + [(military spending)/GNP]}.

---

12. UNIDO 2000 information was taken from http://utip.gov.utexas.edu (accessed May 31, 2001), but the site is no longer available.

13. GNP information is available at http://www.cia.gov/library/publications/index.html (accessed November 25, 2007).

14. U.S. State Department's report. http://www.state.gov/www/global/human_rights/arf/irt.rpt (accessed November 25, 2007).

15. U.S. Central Intelligence Agency 1999 Factbook. http://www.umsl.edu/services/gov/docs/wofact99/51.htm (accessed December 14, 2007).

The extent of political rights in a nation in 1999–2000 is measured with a seven-point scale constructed by country experts at Freedom House (1999, 547–53). The scale rates political systems on the basis of the ability of the population to choose government officials through fair electoral procedures, to organize an effective opposition, and to form competitive political parties. It also considers freedom from domination by the military, foreign powers or particular parties, oligarchies or elites, and protections for cultural, ethnic, religious, or other minority groups. This scale is very highly correlated with several other indices of political rights (Bollen 1980; Inkeles 1990; Jaggers and Gurr 1995) and is widely used in comparative research.

In some analyses we also use the Freedom House ratings of civil liberties, based on freedom of expression and belief, freedom of association and organization, the rule of law (understood as involving an independent judiciary, equal treatment under the law, civilian control of police, protection from political terror and unjustified imprisonment, exile, or torture), personal autonomy, economic rights (including security of private property and the right to operate privately owned businesses), gender equality, freedom of choice of marriage partners, and size of family. Where scores for 1999–2000 were unavailable, we used scores for the most recent date for which they were available. A high score indicates that a country has relatively *few* political or civil rights.

Comparable figures for welfare expenditures for a large sample of nations are not to be had. As a substitute, we take the life expectancy, which can be considered a measure of the health and well-being of the masses of the country. With level of economic development controlled, it may reflect official commitment of personnel and material resources (e.g., clinics, hospitals, medical personnel, sanitation measures, famine relief) to the lower strata of society, who tend to have the shortest life expectancy.

We adopt Newman's (1999, 290–92) classification of legal systems as common law, civil law, Socialist law, Islamic law (in whole or in part), and other (a category that includes mixed systems so long as Islamic law is not part of the mix). We created dummy variables for the major legal systems (1 if common law, 0 otherwise; 1 if civil law, 0 otherwise; 1 if Socialist law, 0 otherwise; and 1 if Islamic law, 0 otherwise). In our statistical analysis, "other" is the reference category.

Following Neumayer (forthcoming), we measure the political ideology of the executive branch of government on a three-point scale, scored so that right-wing = 0, center = 1, and left-wing = 2. We averaged the scores for 1998, 1999, and 2000 in the Database of Political Institutions (Beck et al. 2001; Keefer 2002). These ratings were made by the World Bank on the basis of party names and stands on various issues, with particular attention to government control over the economy. The ratings have their limitations. The United States receives the same classification (left-wing) for the years under the Clinton administration, as Cuba does under Castro and North

Korea does under Kim Il Sung II. We improve on this measure by reclassifying the Socialist countries as missing, so that the classification only applies to the non-Socialist countries. The classification remains a very crude one, but we know of none better. The World Bank did not develop a comparable scale for the legislative branch of government.

We take imprisonment rates per 100,000 from the Web site of the International Centre for Prison Studies, King's College London.[16]

Procedures

We carry out our analysis by estimating statistical models for the explanation of a country's death penalty status. In these models, country conditions, such as its homicide rate, its levels of education and economic development, and its religious composition impact the death penalty status both directly and indirectly through their influence on the level of political rights.[17] A detailed discussion and justification of the model are provided below.

FINDINGS

Political Analyses

We first discuss direct influences on the death penalty, and then consider indirect influences by estimating models for political rights.

Death Penalty—Direct Influences

As our four-point scale for death penalty usage is an ordinal variable, we began by estimating the effects of our independent variables with an ordinal logistic regression. However, we encountered statistical difficulties stemming from the small number of countries that either retain the death

16. See http://www.kcl.ac.uk/depta/rel/icpsworldbrief (accessed March 2007).

17. For purposes of these analyses, we assume that the relationship between economic conditions and political rights primarily reflects the effect of economic conditions on political rights rather than the reverse. This assumption receives support from the research of Przeworski et al. (2000, 136–37, 178–79), who conclude, on the basis of a cross-national panel analysis, that the level of economic development does not influence the establishment of democracies. However, democracies have better chances of surviving when they emerge in countries with higher levels of economic development. Democracies, they find, have similar rates of growth as dictatorships. Other research (Sturm and de Haan 2005) suggests that the short-term effect of democracy on economic growth is at best modest, though the long-term indirect effects may be appreciable. See also Hristos and Ulubasoglu (2006).

penalty *only* for special crimes (coded 1 on our scale), or that retain it but *never* use it (coded 2). Consequently we aggregated the death penalty categories, classifying (1) total abolitionist and partial abolitionist nations together, and (2) nations that retain the death penalty together, whether or not they use it. This produced a dichotomous dependent variable (abolitionist = 0, retentionist = 1).

When we carried out our analyses with all the theoretically relevant predictors using listwise deletion of countries for which values were missing on any variable, more than half of our countries were eliminated from the analysis. The choice of including these theoretically relevant variables at the expense of a sample that is unrepresentative, or of having a more representative sample of nations with the potential for omitted variable bias, is not a happy one. We proceeded by verifying that almost all of the variables responsible for the difficulty (Gini coefficient or other indicator of income inequality, percent below the poverty line, unemployment, linguistic diversity, homicide rate) did not make a statistically significant contribution to the outcome in the sample for which complete data were available, so we deleted them with a clear conscience. The coefficient for percent in majority ethnicity was also not significant, and its use led to the loss of thirty-seven countries, which we deemed unacceptably large. The coefficient for the Alesina et al. Index of Ethnic Fractionalization also failed to achieve significance, and its use led to the loss of eight countries. The Kheng index did not contribute significantly either, and led to the loss of just one country (The Maldives). Results for other variables were similar whether or not we included this variable. In light of its theoretical interest, we report our results with the Kheng index included. The inclusion of the imprisonment rate led to the loss of eight countries. Results for all other predicators were essentially the same whether or not this variable was included, so we included it.

With our new dependent variable, we estimated binary logistic regressions. We alternately used the Freedom House Index of Political Rights (FHPR) and the Freedom House Index of Civil Liberties (FHCL) as predictors (the two variables are too highly correlated for us to use both of them in the same model). At this point, one further computational difficulty arose. Consistent with our prediction, all five countries with Socialist legal systems have the death penalty. Under this circumstance, we could not obtain a numerical estimate of Socialism's effect, and had to drop it from the analysis.

We also estimated the same models with an alternate procedure for dichotomizing the dependent variable, in which nations that have and use the death penalty are contrasted with nations that do not use it. We found the best fit for the models with the first method, with FHPR as a predictor. Estimates for several different model specifications are displayed in Table 1.

It is legitimate to interpret the estimates for a model only if the model is appropriate for the data. The linktest (Pregibon 1980) is one way of ascertaining whether a model is properly specified. Applying this test to Model

TABLE 1.
Binary Logistic Regression of Death Penalty Status on National Characteristics

Independent Variable	Model A b	Model B b	Model C b	Model D b
Constant	.235	−3.244	3.826	4.497
ln(population)	−.069	.061	−.123	−.211
FHPR	.638***	.907***	.741*	.567#
EFI (Kheng)	1.531	2.508#	4.415*	3.654#
Literacy	−.020	−.060*	.009	.009
ln(GDP)	.251	.500	−.498	.163
Life Expectancy	−.019	.025	−.052	−.169
Common Law	2.041**	2.046*	3.209*	4.078**
Civil Law	−.574	−.616	−1.482	.547
Islamic Law	1.404	2.096	—&	—&
% Muslim	−.015	−.034#	.026	.016
% Protestants	−.013	−.032	.025	.027
% Anglicans	−.015	−.023	.010	.039
% Catholics	−.034**	−.042**	−.011	−.004
% Orthodox	−.024	−.036	−.007	.013
% Buddhist	.004	.014	.346#	.463*
% Hindu	−.032	−.055	−.030#	−.029
Imprisonment Rate#	.004	.005#	.005	.006*
ln(mil. spending)	—	−.175#	—	—
Exec. Ideology	—	—	−.790#	—
ln(homicide rate)	—	—	—	.007
Sample Size	184	160	101	116
Model likelihood	126.58	125.39	73.48	92.45
d.f.	17	18	17	17
Model sig	.0000	.0000	.0000	.0000
pseudo-R^2	.499	.571	.545	.579

# $p < .10$; * $p < .05$; ** $p < .01$; *** $p \leq .001$; & Variable dropped because it perfectly predicts outcome.

A in Table 1 (the model with the largest sample size) we find that it is not properly specified. The source of the difficulty is nonlinearity in FHPR, our measure of political rights. To deal with this problem, we created dummy variables for values 2, 3, 4, 5, 6, and 7, keeping 1 as a reference category. Replacing FHPR with the six dummies led to an acceptable linktest. The Hosmer-Lemeshow statistic (another diagnostic tool) computed with ten groups is acceptable in both models. The coefficients for the dummies show that the likelihood of a country having capital punishment increases with its lack of political rights but not linearly. Although this model fits better, conclusions regarding the effects of all variables are essentially the same in the two models, so we show the results for the more parsimonious model, in which FHPR has a linear influence on the logit.

Model A correctly predicts the death penalty status of 85.33 percent of the 184 nations in the analysis (because of missing data, these sets of estimates are based on fewer cases), a substantial improvement over the 54.35 percent correct predictions made by a model relying only on the marginal distribution of the dependent variable. Models B, C, and D add military spending per GNP, executive ideology (political ideology of the executive branch), and the natural log of the homicide rate to the model. With minor exceptions, on which we comment below, estimates are quite consistent across the four models.

The estimates for Model A (and for many models not shown) provide no evidence whatsoever that the death penalty is a response to the social threats we have been able to measure. Ethnic and linguistic diversity do not significantly increase the likelihood that a country has the death penalty, nor does a recent history of political instability. Reicher's (2003) suggestion that threatened states are more likely to use the death penalty may no longer hold. Contemporary states may have alternative, more effective ways of dealing with threats than the eighteenth-century monarchies he studied.

As predicted, countries with higher homicide rates are not significantly more likely to have the death penalty than those with lower rates. However, countries whose imprisonment rates are higher also tend to have the death penalty. Capital punishment is then, in part, a reflection of a more generally punitive stance toward criminals. Yet, controlling for punitiveness, other factors influence whether a country has the death penalty. There is a distinct dimension to capital punishment that is not captured by penal policies in general.

No measure of economic activity significantly predicts the death penalty. Highly developed countries with large GDP per person are as likely to have the death penalty as the less developed countries. Economic inequality—no matter how measured—fails to contribute significantly. Countries with high levels of unemployment are as likely to have the death penalty as those with low levels. The coefficients for the logged population and for life expectancy also fail to achieve statistical significance.

The coefficient for the Freedom House Index of Political Rights is strongly significant. Countries with fewer political rights (higher value of FHPR) are more likely to have the death penalty. The same is true for countries that have fewer civil rights. Where citizens have greater power to shape government policies, and where the different branches of government can balance and check one another, governments tend to punish with greater restraint.

When we discussed the possible effects of a nation's legal system on its use of the death penalty, we considered four distinct legal systems—common law, civil law, Islamic law, and Socialist law. As previously indicated, we could not include *Socialist law* in our estimation because its effect was so consistently and strongly positive. All five of the nations in our sample with Socialist legal systems—China, Cuba, Laos, North Korea, and Vietnam—have and apply the death penalty. Had we been analyzing a comparable set of data for a time when there were more Socialist nations this statement would still be true. All Socialist nations, without exception, have had the death penalty (Scobell 1991; Fijalkowski 2001).

While this might also be said of all non-Socialist nations in the historical past, by 1917, when the first Socialist political system was established, some European nations had already abolished the death penalty. An appreciable number had done so by the time the Communist regimes of Central and Eastern Europe collapsed circa 1989. Among the Communist-led countries (with the exceptions of very brief periods of abolition in the USSR), only the German Democratic Republic ended capital punishment—in 1987, shortly before the regime collapsed. A cynic might construe this step as a hated regime's vain attempt to shore up its legitimacy domestically and internationally. However, the penalty had not been used for some years prior to its abolition, and the State Council abolishing capital punishment may have been accurate in its contention that it was no longer needed—crime rates had dropped and the trials of Nazi leaders were over (Jankovic 1984; Scobell 1991). We consider this pattern to provide strong support for our prediction.

The coefficient for Islamic law is large and positive, but does not achieve statistical significance. It is noteworthy that the zero-order relationship is quite strong. Of the twenty-nine nations in our sample with legal systems based at least in part on Islamic law, twenty-eight have the death penalty on the books, and twenty-four use it. In a logistic regression that includes only Islamic law and no other variables as predictors, its effect is positive and highly significant ($p = .001$). Yet when other factors are taken into account, Islamic law fails to make a significant contribution of its own. This is due to the high standard error of this coefficient (roughly twice as high as for the common-law or civil-law dummies), reflecting the severely skewed distribution of outcomes for this variable. Consequently, our ability to detect a significant effect for this variable when it is present is low. Nevertheless, our best estimate of this effect is consistent with our prediction.

Common-law countries are more likely than countries in the reference category to have the death penalty. Of greater interest, perhaps, is that common-law countries are significantly more likely than civil-law countries to have the death penalty, and indeed, all things being equal, common-law countries are more likely than countries with Islamic legal systems to have the death penalty. Why the common law-civil law difference? Neumayer (forthcoming) suggests that it may reflect the high levels of executions Britain carried out in the eighteenth and nineteenth centuries. Yet this historical past did not prevent Britain for abolishing the death penalty, and doing so before France, which has civil law.

The contemporary difference between common-law and civil-law countries cannot reflect a long-standing difference in the legal systems. Until quite recently, most civil-law countries had the death penalty and used it. Moreover, with the exception of the United States, the older common-law countries (Australia, Canada, Ireland, New Zealand, and United Kingdom) have all abolished the death penalty. The difference, then, reflects a contrast between the former English colonies, on the one hand, and the former colonies of Spain, Portugal, and France, on the other. We speculate that common law, more than civil law, is based on principles of individualism, which tends to favor a more moralistic, and hence more punitive, sanctioning system. Cross-cultural research does, in fact, find evidence that countries that were ever under British rule tend to be more individualistic (Licht, Goldschmidt, and Schwartz 2007). Consistent with our speculation, common-law countries have higher prison populations than civil-law countries (Ruddell 2005).

We next consider the effects of religion. The presence of Catholics significantly reduces the likelihood that a country has the death penalty relative to the heterogeneous reference category. The presence of Muslims in a country does not significantly affect its possession of the death penalty. One might suspect that the failure of percent Muslims to contribute is a result of multicollinearity with Islamic law. However, this is not the case. Though the two variables are positively correlated, the relationship is by no means perfect. Turkey, for example, has a secular state and a legal system based on civil law, not Islamic law. When either one of these variables is deleted from the model, and the estimation is carried out with just the other one as a predictor, the coefficient remains insignificant.

Model B adds military spending divided by Gross National Product to the list of predictors. The sample size drops to 160, but most of the substantive conclusions remain unchanged. Military spending in this model makes a significant contribution in a one-tailed test, but it has the wrong sign. Model C replaces military spending with executive ideology, reducing the sample size to 101. The coefficient for ideology is significantly negative, implying that Left-leaning non-Socialist governments are somewhat less likely to have capital punishment than those in the center, and those in the center are less likely to have it than those on the Right. Findings for the effects of other variables are similar to those for Model A, except that percent Catholic, while still showing a negative effect, is no longer statistically significant, and ethnic fractionalization now makes a positive contribution. The dummy variable for Islamic law drops out of the model because it perfectly predicts the outcome. The conclusions reached from Model D, which includes the logged homicide rate as a predictor, are similar to those in Model C.

The most important discrepancy among the four models has to do with the effect of *percent Catholic*, which is significant in the first two models but not in the last two. The sample sizes for Models C and D are quite a bit smaller than those for Models A and B, leading us to suspect the representativeness of the samples for Models C and D. These estimates may be contaminated by selection bias related to the large number of missing countries.

We can check for this by dropping *executive ideology* from Model C and re-estimating it, not on the full data set, but only on the subsample for which *executive ideology* is not missing. The same procedure can be used for the logged homicide rate in Model D. When this is done, the results for all the other variables are similar to those obtained for Models C and D; however, the variables for the percentages of the population affiliated with different religions do not show the effects they do in the full data set. This indicates that some selection bias is present in the estimates for Models C and D. However, conclusions about the other variables are largely the same in the subsample and in the full data set. We therefore conclude that the political orientation of a government impacts its possession of capital punishment exactly as theorized. This conclusion is consistent with other research on both imprisonment and capital punishment (Sutton 2004; Neumayer forthcoming).

To make sure that our findings are not being skewed by the inclusion of Europe in the sample, we deleted all European countries from the sample and reestimated the models. None of the conclusions summarized above were altered. When a dummy variable for Europe was added to Model A, it had a significant negative coefficient, indicating the presence of a regional effect above and beyond the individual country effects of the model. This may indicate that Europe is distinct from other regions of the world in a manner not captured by the variables represented explicitly in our models. Alternatively, the abolition of capital punishment in some European countries may have facilitated its abolition in neighboring countries. However, the conclusions reached in our previous analyses remain unchanged.

Death Penalty—Indirect Influences

These findings about the effects of our predictor variables refer only to their direct effects, controlling for all the other variables in the models. Without considering their indirect effects, we would have a very misleading impression of the role that some of the predictors play in determining a country's death penalty status. Political rights are not randomly distributed; they are rooted in a nation's social structure and culture. To explore the effects of these factors on penal practices, we must consider not just their direct effects but also the indirect influences they have through their impact on political rights. To examine these indirect effects, we estimated a series of models for political rights. To avoid excessive loss of countries, we began with a base model that included independent variables representing a nation's population size, ethnic diversity, level of economic development (GDP), religious composition, and degree of political stability.

Countries with larger populations might be harder to govern and consequently might tend to have fewer political rights. On the other hand, if large countries are more diverse politically, the differences could lead to the formalization of political rights so as to create a framework that would provide protections and safeguards on which the various factions could rely. The populations of smaller, more homogenous countries might not feel the need to formalize such protections. Ethnic diversity has been thought to impair political trust and hinder coordination, thereby reducing political rights; however, for the reasons just mentioned, diversity could lead to a negotiated political order that protects rights and freedoms.

Wealth may contribute to political rights in a number of ways—it permits investment in education, which, over the long run, may increase public demands for political rights, enable more widespread involvement in politics, and facilitate governing through formal, legal, and rational bureaucracies operating on the basis of checks and balances. Affluent countries can more easily redistribute some of their wealth, reducing discontent and promoting stability. Instability can reduce political rights as governments try to repress political opposition.

That the functioning of a nation's political institutions rests on a cultural foundation has been argued by a number of political scientists (Inglehart 1990; Putnam 1993; Zakaria 2003; Huntington 2004). We examine this issue empirically in relation to the major world religions. As our Index of Political Rights is an ordinal variable, we began by estimating ordinal logistic regressions for FHPR. However, the same computational problems encountered previously arose here as well. We therefore estimated OLS regressions for the natural logarithm of FHPR. In these models, unlike those predicting capital punishment, we do not use legal systems, military spending, executive ideology, or the homicide rate to predict political rights. Political rights are so tightly bound up with the definition of legal system type and the ideology of government leaders that to use them as predictors would be to predict an outcome with part of itself, which would be tautological. We exclude military spending and life expectancy from the predictors of political rights because both are more plausibly consequences of the political system and the way it allocates resources than they are their causes.

After estimating the base model, we added *linguistic diversity*, *Gini coefficient*, *unemployment*, and *ratio of income received by the highest 20 percent to the income received by the lowest 20 percent* to the model. Only the Gini coefficient contributed significantly. The positive coefficient suggests that countries with higher levels of economic inequality tend to have fewer political rights. However, the inclusion of this variable reduces the sample size to 109, and there are indications of sample selection bias. Consequently we must be cautious as to the effect of economic inequality.

Examination of residual plots suggested that curvilinearity in *literacy* was present, and so, after centering this variable, we introduced a quadratic term for it. We carried out an OLS estimation and verified that the residuals were consistent with homoskedasticity. We report the OLS estimates for this model

TABLE 2.
OLS Regression of the Natural Logarithm of Freedom House Political Rights (FHPR) on Independent Variables (N = 190)

Variable	Unstandardized Coefficient	Standard Error	t	sig.
Constant	2.070	.455	4.55	0.000
ln(population)	.0204	.018	1.13	0.259
EFI (kheng)	.0974	.162	0.60	0.549
Literacy	–.0081	.003	–2.45	0.015
Literacy Squared	–.0003	.00008	–3.70	0.000
ln(GDP)	–.1179	.048	–2.44	0.004
% Muslim	.0039	.0018	2.20	0.029
% Protestants	–.0100	.0024	–4.09	0.000
% Anglican	–.0078	.0034	–2.31	0.022
% Catholic	–.0054	.0018	–3.06	0.003
% Orthodox	–.0030	.0026	–1.15	0.251
% Buddhist	.0004	.0025	0.16	0.870
% Hindus	–.0090	.0040	–2.22	0.028
% political stability	–.1865	.0553	–3.37	0.001

R^2 = 0.6475.
Adjusted R^2 = 0.6215.

in Table 2. The model explains a reasonable amount of the variation in political rights (R^2 = 0.6475).

The estimates show that politically stable countries have more political rights, while governments whose very existence is threatened are less likely to accord political rights to their subjects. Economic development significantly increases political rights directly and indirectly through its impact on political stability. The correlation between the natural log of GDP and the political stability index is .665.

Neither the size of a country's population nor its ethnic fractionalization has a significant effect on its political rights. Whatever problems of coordination or reduced solidarity arise from ethnic diversity, they do not seem to bring about reduced political rights. Minorities may insist on political rights and protest until they succeed in getting them. The greater the level of literacy in a country, the more political rights it has, and this effect is more pronounced in countries with especially high levels of literacy. Education presumably increases popular demand for political rights and may make rulers more willing to grant them.

Relative to the heterogeneous reference category for religion, the presence of Muslims significantly reduces political rights.[18] Very similar results

18. Ross (2001) comes to a similar conclusion about the effect of Muslims.

are obtained when, following Fish (2002), we replace the variable *percent Muslim* with a dummy variable equal to 1 when a majority of the population is Muslim and 0 if otherwise. Relative to Protestants, Anglicans, Catholics, Orthodox Christians, and Hindus, Muslims significantly reduce political rights, but the difference between Muslims and Buddhists is not statistically significant, whereas the presence of Christians increases political rights. This is true for all types of Christianity, but the effect is not statistically significant at the .05 level for Orthodox Christians. It is strongest for Protestants, making it tempting to conclude that the emphasis on freedom of conscience in Protestant Christianity and the democratic self-governance of some Protestant denominations carry over to national politics. However, a test for the equality of the coefficients for percent Catholic, percent Protestant, percent Anglican, percent Orthodox, and percent Hindus just fails to achieve statistical significance (p = 0.0505).

That Buddhism fails to influence the level of political rights significantly is consistent with the reduced priority Buddhism gives to worldly concerns. The devaluing of the quotidian world may induce a certain indifference to the form of government. It is not clear why this devaluation in Hinduism does not produce similar results. A similar devaluation can also be found in the *New Testament*, yet, regardless of these scriptural passages,[19] contemporary Christianity appears to increase a country's political rights.

The Question of Spuriousness

As we noted earlier, Islamist thinkers have argued that Islam and democracy are incompatible. For example, political theorists associated with the Muslim Brotherhood in Egypt and Syria have argued that the Islamic state is, by definition, committed to upholding the divine law, not the will of the people (Sivan 1985, 72–76). Some social scientists have also maintained that Islam's theocratic origins, its failure to recognize a separation of church and state, its dogmatism, its tolerance of authoritarianism, and its failure to accept popular sovereignty or political arrangements designed to check governmental power make it inherently antagonistic to a pluralist democracy and political rights (Pipes 1983, 1988; Huntington 1984, 1991; Kedourie 1992; Lewis 1994; ibn Warraq 1995; Choueiri 1996).

We find that there are, in fact, fewer political rights in predominantly Muslim countries. The diversity in political arrangements in the Muslim

19. Jesus remarks, "My kingdom is not of this world" (John 18:36). His advice to "render unto Caesar what is Caesar's and unto God what is God's" (Matthew 22:21), and Peter's injunction to "be subject to every human institution for the Lord's sake, whether to the king as supreme or to governors as sent by him" (1 Peter 2:12–14) seem to urge Christians to accommodate themselves to whatever political system prevails.

countries makes this empirical relationship all the more striking. The fact that political rights are limited in predominantly Muslim countries with secular governments suggests that more is at work than the doctrinal prescriptions of a religion. One possibility lies in the realm of culture—if Islamic culture is unfriendly to political rights, this could explain their absence in predominantly Muslim countries with secular governments.

The contrast between India and Pakistan seems to give support to a cultural explanation of political rights and their absence. The two countries come as close to a controlled experiment as one ever encounters in world affairs. They became independent at the same time from the same colonial power, and both inherited English common law. With the exception of the brief State of Emergency under Indira Gandhi, India has had a vigorous, thriving multiparty democracy with a free press and an independent judiciary ever since it achieved independence. Pakistan, on the other hand, has sustained four military coups, no elected government has ever finished a term (Callard 1968; Weinbaum 1996), and it is currently ruled by a military dictator. These differences may reflect the two countries' different religious compositions. Whereas Muslims are a minority in India, they are an overwhelming majority in Pakistan. However, some analysts of the Muslim world question the existence of an inherent tension between Islam and democracy by contending that there is substantial Muslim support for democracy and political rights (Mernissi 1992; Abed 1995; Hamdi 1996; Esposito and Voll 1996; Krämer 1999).

These doubts raise a question as to whether the relationship is causal or spurious. There are reasons for skepticism regarding causality. Democracy and political rights were established in Europe only in modern times. For centuries, Christian theologians upheld the "divine right of kings" and construed the Bible as saying that subjects had an absolute obligation to obey their rulers (Myers 1982, 270). Yet democracy and political rights did come to Europe, albeit insecurely, as can be witnessed by the fact that when faced with economic and political crises, a number of countries in twentieth-century Europe abandoned both democracy and political rights (Garrard, Tolz, and White 2000; Schulze 1996). Despite these difficult beginnings, democracy and political rights now seem firmly established, at least in Western Europe. Indeed, if the absence of traditions of democracy and political rights completely determined contemporary outcomes, no country in the world would be democratic or have political rights.

Political cultures evolve, sometimes by reinterpreting or repudiating their traditions. In recent years, a number of Muslim countries have taken steps toward greater democracy and political rights (Bahry 1999; Al-Khatib and Al-Abudulla 2001; Esposito and DeLong-Bas 2003; *The Economist* 2004). Moreover, several commentators contend that contemporary authoritarian Islamic governments and social movements draw many of their ideas not from traditional Islamic sources but from twentieth-century European ideologies, such as Fascism and Nazism (Berman 2003; Buruma and Margalit 2004). However, it is precisely because religious and political cultures can change over time that we do not consider this reasoning to be decisive.

Some Muslim political theorists have argued that democracy and Islam are by no means in tension because Muslim doctrines of consultation provide a basis for democracy (Ismael 1995; Esposito and Piscatori 1992; Leca 1995; Esposito and Voll 1996; Abbootalebi 2000). We consider this argument to be part of an internal debate within Islam, which we have no reason to engage. Our interest does not lie in how passages in the Koran could be construed; it is the political culture of Islam as it now exists in the present-day world and the consequences of that "really-existing" Islam that concern us.

More relevant to our inquiry is that some scholars who have considered the Islam-political rights relationship argue that it is spurious. Roy (1994), for example, does not question that Muslim countries lack political rights but contends that this lack is not distinctively Muslim. He considers it to be endemic to the entire Third World. Our results confirm the link between economic underdevelopment and the lack of political rights (see Table 2). However, the relationship between lack of political rights and the percent of a nation's population that is Muslim persists when the level of GDP is controlled.[20] It cannot be the consequence of economic underdevelopment alone.

Huntington (1996, 258–59) adds another dimension to this argument in noting that Muslim countries have much larger military forces than Christian nations. Armed forces operate on the basis of authoritarian command structures and thus provide a template for political organization that is antithetical to democracy and to political rights. Powerful militaries also tend to narrow the scope of functions performed by civilian authorities and to provide the state with the means for political repression of opponents (Rueschemeyer, Stephens, and Stephens 1992, 67–68). We can test this argument by adding military spending to our equation for political rights. It contributes significantly in the predicted direction, but the coefficient for *percent Muslim* remains positive and strongly significant. The Huntington hypothesis fails to account for the negative relationship.

The existence of large petroleum reserves in some of the predominantly Muslim countries has figured in discussions of this issue. A government that can finance a repressive state apparatus (including an army and large police and security forces) by selling oil to other countries reduces its need for tax revenues. Alternately, oil revenues may be able to support a generous welfare

20. The zero-order correlation between FHPR and percent Muslim is .568. Controlling for GDP per capita, it is .562, virtually the same as the zero-order correlation. The correlation between FHPR and GDP per capita is considerably weaker, –.269. Controlling for percent Muslim it is –.277.

state, reducing popular demands for participation in government. A government awash in petro-dollars may not need to stimulate economic growth by modernizing the educational system, a step that might create constituencies supportive of democracy, while internal conflicts over control of oil may destabilize a country, hindering democracy (Crystal 1990; Chaudhry 1997; Karl 1997; Ross 2001).

We tested the petroleum hypothesis by adding the number of barrels of oil a country exported in the year 1998 (the most recent year for which we could obtain data) to the regression.[21] The variance explained increased to 68.4 percent, and the coefficient for *barrels* is statistically significant at the .05 level. Other conclusions remain unchanged; the coefficient for *Muslim* becomes a little larger and remains strongly significant ($p = 0.014$). Though the predominantly Muslim countries have, on average, greater oil reserves than other countries, it is not for this reason alone that they have fewer political rights.

Critics of U.S. foreign policy argue that authoritarian governments in the Muslim world stay in power despite their lack of legitimacy because they are propped up by American financial and military support (Khalidi 2001; Feldman 2003). There is a strong empirical basis for this contention. Transitions away from democratic government in the Third World are positively related to American foreign aid, especially military aid (Muller 1995). In many parts of the world the backing of the U.S. government has kept dictators in power, has prevented democratically chosen political leaders from taking office, and has toppled them when they have assumed office (Blasier 1985; Lowenthal 1991; Chomsky 1973, 1988, 1999; Chomsky and Herman 1979). In the Muslim world, the United States has bolstered authoritarian governments in Jordan, Egypt, Kuwait, Pakistan, Saudi Arabia, and Iran when it was ruled by the Shah (Ali 2002). Yet one can just as easily identify predominantly Muslim nations that do not receive such support and are still lacking in political rights (e.g., Libya, Sudan, Iraq under the late Saddam Hussein, Iran after the Islamic Revolution, Syria, and Afghanistan under Taliban rule).

The long history of American support for governments in non-Muslim countries in Asia and Latin America that do not respect political rights has not prevented a number of them from making substantial progress toward democracy and greater political rights in the last quarter-century (Carothers

21. Data for number of barrels come from Table 3.1 of Energy Information Administration (2002). Barro (1999) and Ross (2001) also found that oil revenues reduced political rights using other measures for dependence on oil revenues. We explored other measures of dependence on oil revenues, including the magnitude of revenues earned from oil exports, revenues divided by Gross Domestic Product (GDP), and OPEC membership. None of these contributed significantly. Revenues from petroleum exports for 1999 were taken from *International Trade Statistics 1999* (United Nations 2000).

2002). Freedom House ratings show much more progress toward political rights in the non-Muslim countries in the past few decades than in the predominantly Muslim countries[22] (Karatnycky 2002); the United States has supported some of these trends. An alternative to a cultural explanation must explain the divergence in trajectories between the Muslim countries and the non-Muslim countries. Analysts who make American intervention central to their argument have not explained adequately why non-Muslim countries have been able to progress so much more in the face of American opposition than Muslim countries.

Focusing in particular on the Middle East, Lust-Okar (2003, 2005) observes that in a number of predominantly Muslim countries dissent from authoritarian rule is divided between a secular or liberal Muslim opposition, on the one hand, and a religious, Islamist opposition, on the other. When opposition to an autocratic regime is divided between factions with divergent long-term goals, coordinated opposition to the incumbent regime becomes difficult to manage. Power holders can discourage mobilization on the part of the secular opposition by pointing to the threat secularists would face were the Islamists to come to power. "Support us," they can say, "if you don't, you'll get them." According to Egyptian sociologist Saad Eddin Ibrahim, President Hosni Mubarak has used exactly this strategy in Egypt to gain support from a middle class that fears the Muslim Brotherhood (Remnick 2004). It is not clear from Lust-Okar's (2003, 2005) analysis why this political circumstance would be present in the Middle East but not in other parts of the Muslim world, where she says it is absent.

Feldman (2003) offers one possible answer to this question by suggesting that in the Middle East, authoritarian rulers can legitimize their exceptional powers by claiming that they are needed to face the threat posed by Israel. We tested Feldman's suggestion by introducing a dummy variable coded 1 if a country was a member of the Arab League, or is Iran or Turkey. It failed to contribute significantly, and conclusions about other variables remained unchanged.

Theoretical arguments can be advanced for and against the proposition that the presence of Muslims in a country reduces its political rights. We have tested a number of the arguments to the effect that the observed relationship is not causal but spurious. None of them holds up empirically. Our inability to rule out as spurious the effect of *percent Muslim* by incorporating into our analysis a number of possible sources of spuriousness requires that the cultural explanation be taken seriously. Provisionally, then, we interpret the relationship as causal.

22. Between 1977 and 2005 political rights scores in the non-Muslim countries improved by 1.58 on a scale of 7—a substantial gain. The countries that were at least 50 percent Roman Catholic improved by 2.17 points. By contrast, the countries whose populations were at least 50 percent Muslim improved by just .20 points.

SUMMARY AND CONCLUDING REFLECTIONS

Summary

We are now in a position to summarize the direct and indirect ways that our variables contribute to death penalty status. In part—but only in part—a country's death penalty status is linked to its general punitiveness toward criminals. Countries that imprison more convicted criminals are also more likely to kill them. Contrary to what might be expected from Jacobs and Kleban's (2003) argument, a country's population has no significant direct or indirect effect on its death penalty status. Nor does its homicide rate. Countries with fewer political rights are more likely to have the death penalty—the latter relationship is illustrated by the recent history of the former members of the Warsaw Pact. Soon after they abandoned Communism and increased their political rights by adopting democratic political systems, many abolished capital punishment. In South Africa, the fall of the apartheid regime was also accompanied by increased political rights and the constitutional abolition of the death penalty. As mentioned above, the more developed economies are more likely to have political rights and, as a result, are less likely to have capital punishment; highly literate countries are less likely to have capital punishment because literacy increases political rights; and leftist governments are less likely to have capital punishment, provided that they are not Socialist. It is these factors that have contributed to the abolition of capital punishment in Europe.

The presence of Catholics in a country directly reduces the chances that it will have the death penalty; no other religion has a significant direct effect. However, countries with many Muslims are more likely to have the death penalty even though the direct effect of Muslims is not significant because their presence is associated with the lack of political rights. Muslims thus influence a country's death penalty status indirectly. Non-Catholic Christians and Hindus reduce the likelihood of a country having capital punishment indirectly through their influence on political rights but have no direct effect once political rights are controlled.

These findings provide substantial support for the recent theoretical developments in the sociology of penalty that inspired this study. All the statistically significant coefficients in our models for death penalty status involve either politics (FHPR, legal system, executive ideology) or culture (religion, literacy). With these variables controlled, none of the variables suggested by social threat or conflict theory contribute significantly. These findings, however, do not allow us to dismiss economic conditions because they serve as a substrate for political freedoms. If we interpret the relationship between economic development and political rights as causal, economic growth brings about greater political freedom, reducing the likelihood that a country will have and use the death penalty. Here, too, though, cultural factors (educational attainment, religious composition) and political stability also prove to be important.

We carried out a parallel analysis for the determinants of the political ideology of a government's executive branch. These efforts were less successful. When *executive ideology* is regressed on the log of the population, ethnic fractionalization, literacy, the log of the GDP, life expectancy, type of legal system, and religious composition, the regression fails to explain a significant amount of variance. Not a single coefficient is significant. It appears that the political ideologies of governments change for transient reasons that are largely unrelated to the social, demographic, political, and legal variables we are considering in this analysis.

In light of these results, we can return to the question we asked at the start of our inquiry: what sorts of countries have the death penalty? No single characteristic neatly distinguishes between abolitionist and nonabolitionist states. Countries without capital punishment tend to have more political rights, more Roman Catholics, and a legal system *not* based on English common law. Yet there are exceptions to these generalizations. Retentionist societies are not all cut from the same cloth, nor are all abolitionist societies.

Past and Future Trends

Seemingly, a cross-sectional study such as ours is ill-equipped to study trends. A country that has capital punishment in a given year may abolish it the next. Indeed, Garland (2005) has observed that a snapshot comparison between the United States and Europe taken at the present time may exaggerate U.S. distinctiveness because transient shocks may be temporarily magnifying their differences. He argues that cultural supports for capital punishment are historically contingent and can change over time. Current U.S. death penalty usages, he observes, must be understood in light of the timing and the particular terms of the U.S. Supreme Court's decision in *Furman v. Georgia* (1972), which struck down all existing capital sentencing statutes. It came after a decade of rising criminal violence and urban riots, widespread hostility toward the Court for ordering school desegregation, and upholding the rights of criminal suspects and defendants. The backlash to this decision led many states to restore the death penalty and to impose it more often than they had before *Furman*—reversing a long-standing decline in American execution rates. Indeed, some observers have remarked that the decline of execution rates in the last few years marks a resumption of that trend, narrowing the difference between the United States and Europe.

If the implication of an argument about contingent historical meanings is that "they can fade almost as quickly as they were formed" (Garland 2005, 361), it is worth considering that the *Furman* decision is now thirty-five years old. The United States continues to sentence substantial numbers of people to death, and to execute some of them.[23] The death penalty, though somewhat restricted judicially and regarded with suspicion because so many death row inmates have been cleared by DNA evidence, still enjoys a great deal of popular support—even if less than in the recent past. Abolition does not appear immanent. Some jolts to a society do not dissipate quickly; they bring about cultural and institutional responses that establish a new social dynamic. We suggest that this has happened to the American criminal justice system in the aftermath of the challenges of the 1960s, with implications for the retention of capital punishment, as well as prison populations, which have risen steadily for thirty-five years with no signs of dropping, even after more than a decade of declining crime rates.

The limitations of cross-sectional data for studying a process that unfolds over time are more significant for a qualitative comparison of one country with a small number of others than for a statistical study of almost two hundred countries. Whereas one country's profile can be distorted briefly for transient reasons, in a larger data set one country does not count for very much. Ephemeral shocks may lead to a single country being misclassified, without seriously distorting estimates of the dominant effects. In our case, the fact that we are able to classify most of the countries in the data set correctly on the basis of a small number of variables characterizing nations' culture and political arrangements points to systemic features as the primary determinants of a country's death penalty status, with omitted variables (stable or transient), not included in our model, playing a relatively minor role.[24]

From a purely statistical point of view, a cross-sectional analysis can yield a relatively accurate, albeit imperfect, picture of a dynamic process unfolding over time, provided that the process is neither just beginning (i.e., when few countries have abolished) nor completed (when all have done so). It is not surprising, then, that many of the conclusions we have reached are similar to those found by Neumayer's (forthcoming) study of abolition as a temporal process.[25]

23. The *Furman* decision could be used to support an argument for historical contingency on the grounds that a more decisive opinion would have ended capital punishment, eliminating the difference between Europe and America. Yet, if this had happened, efforts to amend the Constitution so as to allow capital punishment would have begun. In all likelihood they would have succeeded because of the same public pressures that led thirty-eight of the fifty states to readopt capital punishment after the decision. Had these efforts failed, the appointment of new, more conservative Supreme Court judges might well have reversed the earlier decision. We do not question the importance of historical contingencies to explain short-term phenomena, but America's retention of capital punishment may not be the best example.

24. In this connection, we note that the United States is not an outlier in our analysis. In Model A of Table 1, the predicted probability of a country with the characteristics of the United States having capital punishment is .96. The United States does not appear to require any special theory designed to predict its "exceptionalism."

25. However, by not examining the indirect effects of his predictors, Neumayer (forthcoming) underestimates the role of cultural factors in the abolition of the death penalty.

The Future

Our analysis points to factors that may promote abolition in the future. Of the variables that directly predict capital punishment status, some have changed little over time, and are unlikely to do so in the near future (e.g., religious composition). Left-wing ideology on the part of the executive, associated with abolition, can certainly change, but it is not clear that there is a clearly marked world trend. Left-leaning governments may tend to end capital punishment when they come to power, but their political initiatives are subject to reversal when the political tide shifts in a more conservative direction—except when institutionalized in a manner that makes reversal politically difficult to achieve. Arguably this is the case with European abolition. It would take a political shift of more than ordinary magnitude to restore capital punishment in Europe. A country that did so would lose its membership in the European Union.

Political rights have grown appreciably in a number of countries in the recent past, although the trend has not been a smooth one. Not long ago, it was being argued that the political and economic superiority of democracy had become so clear that it was the wave of the future: authoritarian political philosophies had lost the argument and no longer offered persuasive alternatives to democracy (Fukuyama 1992). To keep up in international economic competition, authoritarian governments would have to become democratic and allow for political and civil rights. Today, optimism that the entire world will quickly adopt Western-style political and legal systems has waned. Authoritarian market systems are displaying vigorous economic growth. In some countries, governments that provide security from predatory crime and civil war, and allow for economic growth, enjoy popular support even in the absence of political rights (Gad 2007).

Our results, along with those of Peerenboom (2004), suggest that increased national wealth promotes political rights, though this conclusion has been challenged by Acemoglu et al. (2005) and Milanovic (2005), who find, on the basis of longitudinal data, that the relationship is not causal but spurious. Notwithstanding the past support Christian denominations have given to authoritarian governments, Christianity is—along with Hinduism—now associated with more political rights; Islam with fewer. However, aggregate change in the World Bank's measures of "voice and accountability" and "rule of law" between 1998 and 2006 is minimal (Kaufmann, Kraay, and Mastruzzi 2007, 19–22, 26), and Freedom House ratings of political and civil rights show little gain in the past decade (Inglehart and Wenzel 2005, 175–80). A further expansion of rights cannot be taken for granted.

Where rights expand, we could see further abolition. However, even where political rights grow, the abolition of capital punishment is by no means a foregone conclusion. Western democracies functioned for long stretches of time without significant opposition to the executions of limited numbers of criminals. Many citizens may conclude that the benefits in public safety and security outweigh the minuscule chances that they themselves will be executed, especially when executions are concentrated in politically weak minority groups.

When there are few executions, abolition would be administratively easy because of the small role that capital punishment in these circumstances plays in the administration of criminal justice. Yet when executions are shielded from public view and are conducted with little publicity, many citizens may be unaware of them, or indifferent, and there will be little vigorous opposition. Japan and India, in precisely this circumstance, may continue to execute small numbers of people indefinitely without arousing mass protest. Though many Americans prefer abolition, few work actively for it.

These considerations, then, make us skeptical about historical projections based on the assumption of a long-term uniform trend toward an abolitionist world, with some countries merely lagging a bit behind the others on the road to total abolition. True, virtually all countries have seen a large reduction in the use of the death penalty. This can be regarded as a genuine, structurally founded trend, and it would take radical political and social changes to reverse. But a decline in executions need not culminate in their elimination. The circumstances that have favored elimination may not ever develop in some countries, and where they do, they may not produce the same outcomes as they have in Western Europe.

REFERENCES

Abed, Shukri. 1995. Islam and Democracy. In *Democracy, War, and Peace in the Middle East*, ed. David Garrnham and Mark Tessler. Bloomington: Indiana University Press.

Abootalebi, Ali R. 1999. Islam, Islamists, and Democracy. *Middle East Review of International Affairs* 3:1–11.

Acemoglu, Daron, Simon Johnson, James A. Robinson, and Pierre Yared. 2005. Income and Democracy. Centre for Economic Policy Research Discussion Paper No. 5274. http://www.cepr.org/pubs/dps/DP5273.asp (accessed November 25, 2007).

Alarid, Leanne Fiftal, and Hsiao-Ming Wang. 2001. Mercy and Punishment: Buddhism and the Death Penalty. *Social Justice* 28:231–47.

Alesina, Alberto, Arnaud Devleeschauer, William Easterly, Sergio Kurlat, and Romain Wacziarg. 2002. Fractionalization. NBER Working Paper 9411. http://www.nber.org (accessed November 25, 2007).

Alesina, Alberto, Reza Baqir, and William Easterly. 1999. Public Goods and Ethnic Divisions. *The Quarterly Journal of Economics* 114:1243–84.

Alesina, Alberto, and Eliana La Ferrara. 1999. Participation in Heterogeneous Communities. *Quarterly Journal of Economics* 115:847–904.

——. 2002. Who Trusts Others? *Journal of Public Economics* 85:207–34.

Al-Khatib, Fawzi, and Sultan M. Al-Abdulla. 2001. The State of Qatar: A Financial and Legal Overview. *Middle East Journal* 8:110–25.

Bahry, Louay. 1999. Elections in Qatar. A Window of Democracy Opens in the Gulf. *Middle East Policy* 6:118–27.

Bailey, Victor. 2000. The Shadow of the Gallows: The Death Penalty and the British Labour Government, 1945–51. *Law and History Review* 18 (2): 305–49.

Banks, Adelle M. 2000. Baptists Say Yes to Death Penalty, No to Women Pastors. *Presbyterian News Service*. http://www.pcusa.org/pcnews/oldnews/2000/02363.htm. (accessed December 15, 2007).

Barclay, Gordon, and Cynthia Tavares. 2003. International Comparisons of Criminal Justice Statistics 2001. *Home Office Bulletin* Issue 12/03. London, UK: Home Office. http://www.csdp.org/research/hosb1203.pdf (accessed November 25, 2007).

Barrett, David B., George T. Kurian, and Todd M. Johnson. 2001. *World Christian Encyclopedia*. 2nd ed. Oxford: Oxford University Press.

Barro, Robert J. 1999. Determinants of Democracy. *Journal of Political Economy* 107:S158–S183.

Barro, Robert J., and Rachel M. McCleary. 2005. Which Countries Have State Religions? *The Quarterly Journal of Economics* 120:1331–71.

Bar-Tal, Daniel. 1976. *Prosocial Behavior: Theory and Research*. New York: John Wiley and Sons.

Beck, Theodore, George Clarke, Alberta Groff, Philip Keefer, and Patrick Walsh. 2001. New Tools in Comparative Political Economy: The Database of Political Institutions. *World Bank Economic Review* 15 (1): 165–76.

Beckett, Katherine. 1997. *Making Crime Pay: Law and Order in Contemporary American Politics*. New York: Oxford University Press.

Beckett, Katherine, and Theodore Sassoon. 2000. *The Politics of Injustice: Crime and Punishment in America*. Thousand Oaks, CA: Pine Forge Press.

Beckett, Katherine, and Bruce Western. 2001. Governing Social Marginality: Welfare, Incarceration, and the Transformation of State Policy. *Punishment & Society* 3:43–60.

Bedau, Hugo, ed. 1997. *The Death Penalty in America: Current Controversies*. New York: Oxford University Press.

Berman, Paul. 2003. *Terror and Liberalism*. New York: Norton.

Binder, Leonard. 1964. *The Ideological Revolution in the Middle East*. New York: John Wiley.

Blasier, Cole. 1985. *The Hovering Giant: U.S. Responses to Revolutionary Change in Latin America*. Revised ed. Pittsburgh, PA: University of Pittsburgh Press.

Block, Brian P., and John Hostettler. 1997. *Hanging in the Balance: A History of the Abolition of Capital Punishment in Britain*. Winchester, UK: Waterside Press.

Bollen, Kenneth A. 1980. Issues in the Comparative Measurement of Political Democracy. *American Sociological Review* 45:370–90.

Borg, Marian J. 1997. The Southern Subculture of Punitiveness? Regional Variation in Support for Capital Punishment. *Journal of Research in Crime and Delinquency* 34:25–45.

Box, Steven. 1987. Recession, Crime, and Punishment. Totowa, NJ: Barnes and Noble.

Brockner, J., and P. Siegel. 1996. Understanding the Interaction Between Procedural and Distributive Justice. In *Trust in Organizations*, ed. Roderick M. Kramer and Tom R. Tyler. Thousand Oaks, CA: Sage.

Buhler, Georg, trans. 1886. *The Laws of Manu*. Vol. 25 of *Sacred Books of the East*. Oxford: Clarendon Press.

Buruma, Ian, and Avishai Margalit. 2004. *Occidentalism: The West in the Eyes of Its Enemies*. New York: Penguin.

Callard, Keith. 1968. *Pakistan, a Political Study*. London: G. Allen and Unwin.

Cantor, Norman F. 1997. *Imagining the Law: Common Law and the Foundations of the American Legal System*. New York: Harper Collins.

Carothers, Thomas. 2002. The End of the Transition Paradigm. *Journal of Democracy* 13 (1): 5–21.

Caselli, Francesco, and Wilbur John Coleman II. 2002. On the Theory of Ethnic Conflict. http://www.wcepr.org/pus/dps/DP56622.asp (accessed November 27, 2007).

Chiricos, Theodore G., and Miriam DeLone. 1992. Labor Surplus and Punishment: A Review and Assessment of Theory and Evidence. *Social Problems* 39:421–46.

Chomsky, Noam. 1973. *For Reasons of State*. New York: Vintage.

——. 1988. *The Culture of Terrorism*. Boston: South End Press.

——. 1999. *Deterring Democracy*. London and New York: Verso.

Chomsky, Noam, and Edward S. Herman. 1979. *The Washington Connection and Third World Fascism*. Boston: South End Press.

Chon, Donsoo. 2001. The Impact of Medical Resources on Criminally Induced Lethality: A Cross-National Assessment. PhD diss., School of Criminology and Criminal Justice, Florida State University.

Choueiri, Y. 1996. The Political Discourse of Contemporary Islamist Movements. In *Islamic Fundamentalism*, ed. Abdel Salem Sidahmed and Anoushiravam Ehteshami. Boulder, CO: Westview Press.

Christoph, James B. 1962. *Capital Punishment and British Politics: The British Movement to Abolish the Death Penalty 1945–1957*. Chicago: University of Chicago Press.

Compagnoni, Francesco. 1978. Capital Punishment and Torture in the Tradition of the Roman Catholic Church. *Concilium* 120:39–53.

Criminal Investigation Bureau. 2000. *1999 Statistics for Criminal Cases in Taiwan and Fujian*. Taipei: Republic of China: National Police Agency.

Crystal, Jill, 1990. *Oil and Politics in the Gulf*. Cambridge: Cambridge University Press.

Cutler, David M., Douglas W. Elmendorf, and Richard J. Zeckhauser. 1993. Demographic Characteristics and the Public Bundle. *Public Finance* 148:178–98.

David, René, and John Brierley. 1978. *Major Legal Systems in the World Today*. New York: Free Press.

Doucouliagos, Hristos, and Mehmet Ulubasoglu. 2006. Democracy and Economic Growth: A Meta-analysis. http://www.international.ucla.edu/cms/files/Doucouliagos.pdf (accessed November 28, 2007).

Dulles, Avery Cardinal. 2005. A Call for Reckoning: Religion and the Death Penalty. In *A Call for Reckoning: Religion and the Death Penalty*, ed. Erik C. Owens, John D. Carlson, and Eric P. Elshtain. Washington, DC: Pew Forum on Religion and Public Life.

Durkheim, Emile. 1933. *The Division of Labor in Society*. Trans. G. Simpson. New York: Macmillan.

——. 1973. Two Laws of Penal Evolution. *Economy & Society* 2:285–308.

Easterly, William, and R. Levine. 1997. Africa's Growth Tragedy: Policies and Ethnic Divisions. *Quarterly Journal of Economics* 112:1203–50.

Eisner, Manuel. 2003. Long-Term Historical Trends in Violent Crime. *Crime and Justice: An Annual Review* 31:83–142.

El Fadl, Khaled Abou. 2003. Islam and the Challenge of Democracy. *Boston Review* (April/May). http://bostonreview.net/BR28.2/abou.html (accessed November 24, 2007).

Energy Information Administration. 2002. *International Energy Annual 2000*. Washington, DC: U.S. Dept. of Energy. http://tonto.eia.doe.gov/FTPROOT/international/021900.pdf (accessed November 14, 2007).

Esposito, John L., with Natana J. De Long-Bas. 2003. Classical Islam. In *God's Rule: The Politics of World Religions*, ed. Jacob Neusner, 131–57. Washington, DC: Georgetown University Press.

Esposito, John L., and James P. Piscatori. 1992. Democratization and Islam. *The Middle East Journal* 45:427–40.

Esposito, John L., and John O. Voll. 1996. *Islam and Democracy*. Vol. 1. New York: Oxford University Press.

Feldman, Noah. 2003. *After Jihad: America and the Struggle for Islamic Democracy*. New York: Farrar, Straus and Giroux.

Fijalkowski, Agata. 2001. The Abolition of the Death Penalty in Central and Eastern Europe. *Tilburg Foreign Law Review* 9:62–83.

Fish, M. Stephen. 2002. Islam and Authoritarianism. *World Politics* 55 (Oct.): 4–37.

Foucault, Michel. 1975. *Surveiller et punir: Naissance de la prison* [Discipline and Punishment: The Birth of the Prison]. Paris: Gallimard.

Freedom House. 2000. *Freedom in the World 2000*. New York: Greenwood Press.

French, Rebecca Redwood. 1995. *The Golden Yoke: The Legal Cosmology of Buddhist Tibet*. Ithaca, NY: Cornell University Press.

Fukuyama, Francis. 1992. *The End of History and the Last Man*. New York: Free Press.

Gad, Azar. 2007. The Return of Authoritarian Great Powers. *Foreign Affairs* 86:59–70.

Gaertner, Samuel F., and John F. Dovidio. 1977. The Subtlety of White Racism, Arousal, and Helping Behavior. *Journal of Personality and Social Psychology* 35:691–707.

Gardet, Louis. 1954. *La cité musulmane: vie sociale et politique* [The Muslim City: Social and Political Life]. Paris: J. Vrin.

Garland, David. 1985. *Punishment and Welfare: A History of Penal Strategies*. Brookfield, VT: Gower.

——. 1990. *Punishment and Modern Society*. Chicago: University of Chicago Press.

——. 2001. *The Culture of Control: Crime and Social Order in Late Modernity*. Chicago: University of Chicago Press.

——. 2005. Capital Punishment and American Culture. *Punishment and Society* 7:347–76.

Garrard, John, Vera Tolz, and Ralph White, eds. 2000. *European Democratization since 1800*. New York: St. Martin's Press.

Gattrell, V. A. C. 1994. *The Hanging Tree: Execution and the English People, 1770–1868*. Oxford: Oxford University Press.

Gest, Ted. 2001. *Crime and Politics: Big Government's Erratic Campaign for Law and Order*. Oxford: Oxford University Press.

Glaeser, Edward L., David I. Laibson, José A. Scheinkman, and Chrstine Soutter. 2000. Measuring Trust. *Quarterly Journal of Economics* 115:811–46.

Goldin, Claudia, and Lawrence F. Katz. 1999. Human Capital and Social Capital: The Rise of Secondary Schooling in America, 1910 to 1940. *Journal of Interdisciplinary History* 29:653–723.

Greeley, Andrew M. 2000. *The Catholic Imagination*. Berkeley: University of California Press.

Greenberg, David F. 1977. The Dynamics of Oscillatory Punishment Processes. *Journal of Criminal Law and Criminology* 68:643–55.

——. 1999. Punishment, Division of Labor, and Social Solidarity. In *The Criminology of Criminal Law*, ed. William S. Laufer and Freda Adler. New Brunswick, NJ: Transaction.

——. 2003. Long-Term Trends in Crimes of Violence. *Criminology* 42:1407–18.

Greenberg, David F., and Drew Humphries. 1980. Social Control and Social Formation: A Marxian Analysis. In vol. 2, *Toward a General Theory of Social Control*, ed. Donald Black, 171–208. New York: Academic Press.

Greenberg, David F., and Valerie West. 2001. State Prison Populations and Their Growth, 1971–1991. *Criminology* 39:615–53.

Gupta, Subhash. 1986. *Capital Punishment in India*. New Delhi, India: Deep and Deep.

Gyatso, Tenzin. 1998. Message Supporting the Moratorium on the Death Penalty. http://www.engaged-zen.org/HHDLMSG.html (accessed November 28, 2007).

Haddad, Yvonne Yazbeck, and John L. Esposito, eds. 1998. *Islam, Gender, and Social Change*. New York: Oxford University Press.

Hamdi, Mohammed Elhachmi. 1996. Islam and Democracy: The Limits of the Western Model. *Journal of Democracy* 7 (April): 81–85.

Harvey, Peter. 1990. *An Introduction to Buddhism: Teaching, History, and Practices*. New York: Cambridge University Press.

Huntington, Samuel P. 1984. Will More Countries Become Democratic? *Political Science Quarterly* 99:193–218.

——. 1991. *The Third Wave: Democratization in the Late Twentieth Century*. Norman: University of Oklahoma Press.

——. 1996. *The Clash of Civilizations and the Remaking of World Order*. New York: Simon and Schuster.

——. 2004. *Who Are We? The Challenges to America's Identity*. New York: Simon and Schuster.

Inglehart, Ronald. 1990. *Culture Shift in Advanced Industrial Society*. Princeton, NJ: Princeton University Press.

Inglehart, Ronald, and Wayne E. Baker. 2000. Modernization, Cultural Change, and the Persistence of Traditional Values. *American Sociological Review* 65:19–51.

Inglehart, Ronald, and Christian Wenzel. 2005. *Modernization, Cultural Change and Democracy: The Human Development Sequence*. New York: Cambridge University Press.

Inkeles, Alex. 1990. Introduction: On Measuring Democracy. *Studies in Comparative International Development* 25 (1): 3–6.

Ismael, Salwa. 1995. Democracy in Contemporary Arab Intellectual Discourse. In vol. 1, *Political Liberalization and Democratization in the Arab World*, ed. Rex Brynen, Bahgat Korany, and Paul Noble, 93–111. Boulder, CO: Lynne Riener.

Jackson, Pamela Irving. 1992. Minority Group Threat, Social Context, and Policy. In *Social Threat and Social Control*, ed. Allen E. Liska. Albany, NY: SUNY Press.

Jacobs, David, and Richard Kleban. 2003. Political Institutions, Minorities, and Punishment: A Pooled Cross-National Analysis of Imprisonment Rates. *Social Forces* 82:725–55.

Jagchid, Sechim, and Paul Hyer. 1979. *Mongolia's Culture and Society*. Boulder, CO: Westview.

Jaggers, Keith, and Ted Robert Gurr. 1995. Tracking Democracy's Third Wave with the Polity III Data. *Journal of Peace Research* 32 (4): 469–82.

Janković, Ivan. 1984. Socialism and the Death Penalty. *Research in Law, Deviance and Social Control* 8:109–37.

Jansen, G. H. 1979. *Political Islam*. New York: Harper and Row.

Kamali, Mohammad Hashim. 2002. *Freedom, Equality and Justice in Islam*. Cambridge, UK: Islamic Texts Society.

Karatnycky, Adrian. 2002. The 2001 Freedom House Survey: Muslim Countries and the Democracy Gap. *Journal of Democracy* 13 (Jan.): 99–112.

Karl, Terry Lynn. 1997. *The Paradox of Plenty: Oil Booms and Petro-States*. Berkeley: University of California Press.

Kaufmann, Daniel, Aart Kraay, and Pablo Zoido-Lobatón. 1999. Governance Matters. Policy Research Working Paper 2196. Washington, DC: World Bank Development Research Group Macroeconomics and Growth and World Bank Institute Governance, Regulation and Finance.

Kaufmann, Daniel, Aart Kraay, and Massimo Mastruzzi. 2007. Governance Matters VI: Governance Indicators for 1996–2006. World Bank Policy Research Working Paper No. 4280. http://www.govindicators.org (accessed November 26. 2007).

Kedourie, Elie. 1966. *Afghani and Abduh: An Essay on Religious Unbelief and Political Activism in Modern Islam*. New York: Humanities Press.

——. 1992. *Democracy and Arab Political Culture*. Washington, DC: Washington Institute for Near East Policy.

Keefer, Philip. 2002. Database of Political Institutions: Changes and Variable Definitions. Development Research Group, World Bank. http://sitesources.worldbank.org/INTRES/Resources/DPI2004_variable-definitions.pdf (accessed November 26, 2007).

Kepe, Gilles. 2002. *Jihad: The Trial of Political Islam*. Cambridge, MA: Harvard University Press.

Khalidi, Rashid. 2001. American Anointed: How the United States Sowed the Whirlwind. *The American Prospect*, Nov. 19, 16–17.

Kheng, Yeoh Kok. 2001. Towards an Index of Ethnic Fractionalization. FEA Working Paper No. 2001-3. http://www.cassey.com/fea2001-3.pdf (accessed November 26, 2007).

Killias, Martin. 1986. Power Concentration, Legitimation Crisis and Penal Severity. In *Punishment and Privilege*, ed. W. Byron Groves and Graeme Newman, 95–117. New York: Harrow and Heston.

Knack, Steven, and Philip Keefer. 1995. Institutions and Economic Performance: Cross-Country Tests Using Alternative Measures. *Economics and Politics* 7 (3): 207–27.

Krämer, Gudrun. 1993. Islamist Notions of Democracy. *Middle East Report* 183:2–8.

Krueger, John R. 1972. New Materials on Oriat Law and History. *Central Asiatic Journal* 16:194–205.

La Porta, Rafael, Florencio Lopez-de-Silanes, Andrei Shleifer, and Robert Vishy. 1999. The Quality of Governance. *Journal of Law, Economics and Organization* 3:222–82.

Leca, Jean. 1995. Democratization in the Arab World: Uncertainty, Vulnerability and Legitimacy: A Tentative Conceptualization and Some Hypotheses. In vol. 1, *Political Liberalization and Democracy in the Arab World*, ed. Rex Brynen, Bahgat Korany, and Paul Noble. Boulder, CO: Lynne Riener.

Lewis, Bernard. 1994. *The Shaping of the Modern Middle East*. Oxford: Oxford University Press.

Lewis, Todd. 2003. Buddhism: The Politics of Compassionate Rule. In *God's Rule: The Politics of World Religions*, ed. Jacob Neusner, 233–56. Washington, DC: Georgetown University Press.

Licht, Amir N., Chanon Goldschmidt, and Shalom H. Schwartz. 2007. Culture Rules: The Foundations of the Rule of Law and Other Norms of Governance. *Journal of Comparative Economics* 35 (4): 659–88.

Linebaugh, Peter. 1991. *The London Hanged*. New York: Penguin.

Lingat, Robert. 1973. *The Classical Law of India*. Berkeley: University of California Press.

Lowenthal, Abraham, ed. 1991. The U.S. and Latin American Democracy: Learning from History. In *Exporting Democracy: The United States and Latin America*, 261–83. Baltimore: Johns Hopkins University Press.

Lust-Okar, Ellen. 2003. Why the Failure of Democratization? Explaining "Middle East Exceptionalism." http://politics.gsas.nyu.edu/docs/IO/4751/lust-okar.pdf (accessed December 15, 2007).

Lust-Okar, Ellen. 2005. *Structuring Conflict in the Arab World*. New York: Cambridge University Press.

Marx, Karl. 1981. On Capital Punishment. In *Crime and Capitalism: Readings in Marxist Criminology*, ed. David F. Greenberg, 55–56. Palo Alto, CA: Mayfield.

McCarty, Theresa A. 1993. Demographic Diversity and the Size of the Public Sector. *KYKLOS* 46:225–40.

McGowen, Randall. 2007. Managing the Gallows: The Bank of England and the Death Penalty, 1979–1821. *Law and History Review* 25:241–82.

McLeod, Hugh, and Werner Ustorf, eds. 2003. *The Decline of Christendom in Western Europe, 1750–2000*. New York: Cambridge University Press.

Megivern, James J. 1997. *The Death Penalty: An Historical and Theological Survey*. New York: Paulist Press.

Melossi, Dario. 2001. The Cultural Embeddedness of Social Control: Reflections on the Comparison of Italian and North-American Cultures Concerning Punishment. *Theoretical Criminology* 5 (4): 402–24.

Mernissi, Fatima. 1992. *Islam and Democracy: Fear of the Modern World*. Reading, MA: Addison-Wesley.

Milanovic, Branko. 2005. Relationship between Income and Emergence of Democracy

Reexamined, 1820–2000: A Non-Parametric Approach. papers.ssrn.com/sol3/paper.cfm?abstract_id=812164 (accessed November 26, 2007).

Muller, Edward N. 1995. Dependent Economic Development, Aid Dependence on the United States, and Democratic Breakdown in the Third World. *International Studies Quarterly* 29:445–69.

Neumayer, Eric. Forthcoming. Death Penalty: The Political Foundations of the Global Trend toward Abolition. *Human Rights Review*.

Newman, Graeme, ed. 1999. *Global Report on Crime and Justice*. New York: Oxford University Press.

Nguyen, Ngoc Hyun, and Ta Van Tai. 1987. *The Lê Code: A Comparative Sino-Vietnamese Legal Study with Historical-Juridical Analysis and Annotations*. Athens: Ohio University Press.

O'Donovan, Oliver. 1988. The Death Penalty in *Evangelium Vitae*. In *Ecumenical Ventures in Ethics: Protestants Engage Pope John Paul II's Moral Encyclicals*, ed. Reinhard Hütter and Theodor Dieter, 219. Grand Rapids, MI: Wm. B. Eerdmans.

Pastore, Ann L., and Kathleen Magiure, eds. 2000. *Sourcebook of Criminal Justice Statistics 1999*. Washington, DC: USGPO (U.S. Dept. of Justice).

Peerenboom, Randall. 2004. Show Me the Money: The Dominance of Wealth in Determining Rights Performance in Asia. *Duke Journal of Comparative and International Law* 15:75–152.

Pipes, Daniel. 1983. *In the Path of God: Islam and Political Power*. New York: Basic.

——. 1988. *Slaves, Soldiers, and Islam: The Genesis of a Military System*. New Haven, CT: Yale University Press.

——. 2000. Are Today's Islamic Movements Compatible with Democracy? *Insight*. http://www.danielpipes.org/article/347 (accessed Decenber 14, 2007).

Potter, Harry. 1993. *Hanging in Judgement: Religion and the Death Penalty in England*. London: SCM Press.

Poveda, Tony G. 2000. American Exceptionalism and the Death Penalty. *Social Justice* 27:252–67.

Pregibon, Daryl. 1980. Goodness of Link Tets for Generalized Linear Models. *Applied Statistics* 29:15–24.

Przeworski, Adam, Michael E. Alvarez, José Antonio Cheibub, and Fernando Limongi. 2000. *Democracy and Development: Political Institutions and Well-Being in the World, 1950–1990*. New York: Cambridge University Press.

Putnam, Robert D. 1993. *Making Democracy Work: Civic Traditions in Modern Italy*. Princeton, NJ: Princeton University Press.

——. 2007. *E Pluribus Unum*: Diversity and Community in the Twenty-First Century: The 2006 Johan Skytte Prize Lecture. *Scandinavian Political Studies* 30:137–74.

Quillian, Lincoln, and Devah Pager. 2001. Black Neighbors, Higher Crime? The Role of Racial Stereotypes in Evaluations of Neighborhood Crime. *American Journal of Sociology* 107:717–67.

Quinney, Richard. 1977. *Class, State and Crime: On the Theory and Practice of Criminal Justice*. New York: David McKay.

Radzinowicz, Leon. 1999. *Adventures in Criminology*. London: Routledge.

Rahula, Walpola. 1974. *What the Buddha Taught*. 2nd ed. New York: Grove Press.

Reicher, Dieter. 2003. *Staat, Schafott und Schuldegefühl: Was Staatsaufbau und Todesstrafe miteinander zu tun haben* [State, Scaffold and Shame Feeling: What State-Building and the Death Penalty Have to Do with One Another]. Opladen, Germany: Leske and Budrich.

Remnick, David. 2004. Letter from Cairo: Going Nowhere. *The New Yorker*, July 12 and 19 (combined issue), 74–83.

Rex, John, and David Mason, eds. 1986. *Theories of Race and Ethnic Relations*. Cambridge: Cambridge University Press.

Riasanovsky, Valentin A. 1965. *Fundamental Principles of Mongol Law*. Bloomington: Indiana University Press.

Rose, Richard. 2002. How Muslims View Democracy: Evidence from Central Asia. *Journal of Democracy* 13 (4): 102–11.

Ross, Michael L. 2001. Does Oil Hinder Democracy? *World Politics* 53 (April): 325–61.

Roy, Olivier. 1994. *The Failure of Political Islam*, trans. Carol Volk. Cambridge, MA: Harvard University Press.

Ruddell, Rick. 2005. Social Disruption, State Priorities, and Minority Threat: A Cross-National Study of Imprisonment. *Punishment & Society* 7 (1): 7–28.

Rueschemeyer, Dietrich, Evelyne Huber Stephens, and John D. Stephens. 1992. *Capitalist Development and Democracy*. Chicago: University of Chicago Press.

Savelsberg, Joachim. 1994. Knowledge, Domination, and Criminal Punishment. *American Journal of Sociology* 99:911–43.

Savey-Cassard, Paul. 1961. L'église catholique et la peine du mort [The Catholic Church and the Death Penalty]. *Revue de Science Criminelle et le Droit Pénal Comparé*, new series 1:773–85.

Schabas, William A. 1997. *The Abolition of the Death Penalty in International Law*. 2nd ed. New York: Cambridge University Press.

——. 2000. Islam and the Death Penalty. *William and Mary Bill of Rights Journal* 9 (1): 223–36.

Scheingold, Stuart A. 1984. *The Politics of Law and Order: Street Crime and Public Policy*. New York: Longman.

Schreiber, Ariane M. 1996. States That Kill: Discretion and the Death Penalty—A Worldwide Perspective. *Cornell International Law Journal* 29:263–327.

Schuck, Michael J. 1991. *That They Be One: The Social Teaching of the Papal Encyclicals, 1740–1989*. Washington, DC: Georgetown University Press.

Schulze, Hagen. 1996. *States, Nations, and Nationalism: From the Middle Ages to the Present*. Cambridge, MA: Blackwell.

Scobell, Andrew. 1991. The Death Penalty under Socialism, 1917–1990: China, the Soviet Union, Cuba, and the German Democratic Republic. *Criminal Justice History* 12:189–234.

Simon, Jonathan. 2001. Fear and Loathing in Late Modernity: Reflections on the Cultural Sources of Mass Imprisonment in the United States. *Punishment & Society* 3:21–34.

Sivan, Emmanuel. 1985. *Radical Islam: Medieval Theology and Modern Politics*. New Haven, CT: Yale University Press.

Smith, Donald Eugene. 1963. *India as a Secular State*. Princeton, NJ: Princeton University Press.

Sommerville, J. P. 1986. *Politics and Ideology in England 1603–1640*. London: Longman.

Spitzer, Steven. 1975. Toward a Marxian Theory of Deviance. *Social Problems* 22:638–51.

Statistical Service of Cyprus. 2000. *Criminal Statistics 1999*. Lefkosia, Cyprus: Government Printing Office.

Steiker, Carol S. 2002. Capital Punishment and American Exceptionalism. *Oregon Law Review* 81:97–130.

Stepan, Alfred. 2000. Religion, Democracy, and the "Twin Tolerations." *Journal of Democracy* 11 (4): 37–57.

——. 2001. *Arguing Comparative Politics*. Oxford: Oxford University Press.

Stork, Joe, and Joel Beinem, eds. 1997. *Political Islam*. Berkeley and Los Angeles: University of California Press.

Sturm, Jan-Egbert, and Jakob de Haan. 2005. Determinants of Long-Term Growth: New Results Applying Robust Estimation and Extreme Bounds Analysis. *Empirical Economics* 30:597–617.

Sutton, John R. 1987. Doing Time: Dynamics of Imprisonment in the Reformist State. *American Sociological Review* 52:612–30.

——. 1990. Bureaucrats and Entrepreneurs: Institutional Responses to Deviant Children in the United States, 1890–1920s. *American Journal of Sociology* 95:1367–1400.

——. 2000. Imprisonment and Social Classification in Five Common-Law Democracies. *American Journal of Sociology* 106:350–86.

——. 2004. The Political Economy of Imprisonment in Affluent Western Democracies, 1960–1990. *American Sociological Review* 69 (April): 151–69.

Tajfel, Henri, M. Billig, R. P. Bundy, and Claude. Flament. 1971. Social Categorization and Intergroup Behavior. *European Journal of Social Psychology* 1:149–78.

Taylor, Alan R. 1988. *The Islamic Question in Middle East Politics*. Boulder, CO: Westview.

The Economist. 2004. Indonesia's Shining Example, July 10, 10.

Tonry, Michael. 1999. Why Are U.S. Incarceration Rates So High? *Crime & Delinquency* 45 (4): 419–37.

Turner, Barry. 2001. *The Statesman's Yearbook 2002: The Politics, Cultures and Economies of the World*. New York: Palgrave.

Tuttle, Elizabeth O. 1961. *The Crusade against Capital Punishment in Great Britain*. London: Stevens and Sons.

United Nations. 2000. *International Trade Statistics Yearbook 1999*. Vol. 1. New York: United Nations Publications.

Uslaner, E. M. 2002. *The Moral Foundations of Trust*. Cambridge: Cambridge University Press.

Vasu, Srisa Chandra. 1909. *Yājñavalkyasmṛti*. Allahabad, India: Pâninî Press.

ibn Warraq. 1995. *Why I Am Not a Muslim*. Buffalo, NY: Prometheus.

Weinbaum, Marvin G. 1999. Civic Culutre and Democracy in Pakistan. *Asian Survey* 36:639–54.

Weiner, Myron. 1987. Empirical Democratic Theory. In *Competitive Elections in Developing Countries*, ed. Myron Weiner and Ergun Özudun. Durham, NC: Duke University Press.

Weisser, Michael. 1979. *Crime and Punishment in Early Modern Europe*. Atlantic Highlands, NJ: Humanities Press.

Wilson, James Q. 1983. *Thinking about Crime*. Rev. ed. New York: Vintage.

World Bank. 2001. *World Development Report 2000/2001*. New York: Oxford University Press.

Zakaria, Fareed. 2003. *The Future of Freedom: Illiberal Democracy at Home and Abroad*. New York: W. W. Norton.

Zimring, Franklin. 2003. *The Contradictions of American Capital Punishment*. New York: Oxford University Press.

CASES CITED

Furman v. Georgia, 408 U.S. 238 (1972).

List of Publications

CRIMINOLOGICAL PUBLICATIONS OF DAVID F. GREENBERG

Books

1. *Struggle for Justice: A Report on Crime and Punishment in America* (co-author) (New York: Hill and Wang, 1971).
2. *Corrections and Punishment* (Beverly Hills: Sage, 1977).
3. *Mathematical Criminology* (Rutgers University Press, 1979).
4. *Crime and Capitalism: Essays in Marxist Criminology* (Palo Alto, Cal.: Mayfield, 1981; 2nd edition, Temple University Press, 1993).
5. *Criminal Careers*, 2 volumes (Aldershot, England: Dartmouth Publishing Company, 1996).
6. *Unlocking America: How and Why to Reduce America's Prison Population* (co-author) (Washington, DC: JFA Institute. 2007).
7. *Building Modern Criminology: Forays and Skirmishes* (Ashgate, 2010).

Journal Articles, Book Chapters

1. 'The Problem of Prisons', (educational pamphlet distributed by the American Friends Service Committee 1970).
2. 'The Prison as a Lawless Agency', *Buffalo Law Review*, **21**, (1972) pp. 799–838 (with Fay Stender).
3. 'Guideposts for Prison Reformers Lost in the Woods of Litigation', pp. 595–607 in Michelle G. Hermann and Marilyn Haft, *Prisoners Rights Sourcebook* (Clark and Boardman Company, 1973).
4. 'A Voucher System for Corrections', *Crime and Delinquency*, **19**, (April, 1973) pp. 212–17 and (October, 1973) pp. 518–19.
5. 'Matthew Davenport Hill: A Study of Class Conflict in Nineteenth-Century British Penal Reform', Introductory Essay to the reprint edition of M.D. Hill's *Suggestions for the Repression of Crime* (Patterson Smith Publishers, 1975; orig. pub. 1853).
6. 'The Incapacitative Effect of Imprisonment: Some Estimates', *Law and Society Review*, **9**, (1975) pp. 541–80.
7. 'Parole Recidivism and the Incapacitative Effect of Imprisonment', pp. 149–72 in Gordon Tullock (ed.), *Frontiers of Economics* (1975. Blacksburg, Va.: University Publications, 1976).
8. 'Problems in Community Corrections', *Issues in Criminology*, **10**, (Spring, 1975) pp. 1–34.

9. 'On One-dimensional Marxist Criminology', Theory and Society, **3**, (1976) pp. 611–21.
10. 'Crime Deterrence Research and Social Policy', pp. 281–96 in Stuart Nagel (ed.), *Modeling the Criminal Justice System* (Sage Publications, 1977).
11. 'Socioeconomic Status and Criminal Sentences: Is There an Association? (Comment on Chiricos and Waldo)', *American Sociological Review*, **42**, (1977) pp. 176–77.
12. 'The Correctional Effects of Corrections: A Survey of Evaluation Studies', in David F. Greenberg (ed.), *Corrections and Punishment* (Sage Publications, 1977), pp. 111–48.
13. 'Delinquency and the Age Structure of Society', *Contemporary Crises: Crime, Law and Social Policy*, **1**.2, (1977) pp. 189–223.
14. 'Recidivism as Radioactive Decay', *Journal of Research in Crime and Delinquency*, **15**, (1978) pp. 124–25.
15. 'The Dynamics of Oscillatory Punishment Processes', *Journal of Criminal Law and Criminology*, **68**, (1977) pp. 643–55.
16. 'A Panel Analysis of Crime Rates and Arrest Rates', *American Sociological Review*, **44**, (1979) pp. 843–50 (with Ronald Kessler and Charles Logan).
17. 'The Cooptation of Fixed Sentencing Reform', *Crime and Delinquency*, **26**, (1980) pp. 206–25 (with Drew Humphries).
18. 'Social Control and Social Formation: A Marxian Analysis', in Donald Black (ed.), *Toward a General Theory of Social Control*, Academic Press, 1980 (with Drew Humphries).
19. 'Penal Sanctions in Poland: A Test of Alternative Models', *Social Problems*, **28**, (1980) pp. 194–204.
20. 'Aggregation Bias in Deterrence Research: An Empirical Analysis', *Journal of Research in Crime and Delinquency*, **18**, (1981) pp. 128–37 (with Ronald C. Kessler).
21. 'The Dialectics of Crime Control', pp. 209–54 in *Crime and Capitalism: Essays in Marxian Crimiology* (Mayfield Publishing Co. 1981; Temple University Press, 1993) (with Drew Humphries).
22. 'Die Dialektik der Kriminalitätskontrolle', in H. Janssen, R. Kaulitzki and R. Michalowski (Hrsg.), *Radikale Kriminologie – Themen und theoretische Positionen der amerikanischen Radical Criminology*. (Bielefeld: AJZ).
23. 'Methodological Issues in Survey Research on the Inhibition of Crime', *Journal of Criminal Law and Criminology*, **72**, (1981) pp. 1094–101.
24. 'The Effect of Arrests on Crime: A Multivariate Panel Analysis', *Social Forces*, **60**, (1982) pp. 771–90 (with Ronald C. Kessler).
25. 'Age and Crime', pp. 30–35 in Sanford Kadish (ed.), *Enyclopedia of Crime and Justice*, (Macmillan, 1983).
26. 'Panel Models in Criminology', pp. 1–17 in James A. Fox (ed.), *Methods in Quantitative Criminology* (Academic Press, 1981) (with Ronald Kessler).
27. 'Model Specification in Dynamic Analyses of Crime Deterrence', pp. 15–32 in John Hagan (ed.), *Deterrence Reconsidered: Methodological Innovations* (Sage Publications, 1982) (with Ronald Kessler).
28. 'Economic Crisis and the Justice Model: A Skeptical View', *Crime and Delinquency*, **28**, (1982) pp. 601–609 (with Drew Humphries).
29. 'Crime', Encyclopedia entry in Tom Bottomore (ed.), *Dictionary of Marxist Thought* (Cambridge, Mass.: Harvard University Press).
30. 'The Effect of Police Employment on Crime', *Criminology*, **21**, (1983) pp. 375–94.

31. 'Reflections on the Justice Model Debate', *Contemporary Crises: Crime, Law and Social Policy*, **7**, (1983) pp. 313–27.
32. 'Social Inequality and Crime Control', *Journal of Criminal Law and Criminology*, **76**, (1985) pp. 684–704 (with Ronald Kessler and Colin Loftin).
33. 'Age, Crime, and Social Explanation', *American Journal of Sociology*, **91**, (1985) pp. 1–21.
34. 'Age-Cohort Analysis of Arrest Rates', *Journal of Quantitative Criminology*, **1**, (1985) pp. 227–41 (with Nancy Larkin).
35. 'Marxist Criminology', pp. 164–207 in Bertell Ollman and Edward Vernoff (eds), *The Left Academy: Marxist Scholarship on American Campuses*, vol. 3 (Praeger, 1986).
36. 'Unemployment and Imprisonment', *Journal of Quantitative Criminology*, **5**, (1989) pp. 187–91.
37. 'Modeling Criminal Careers', *Criminology*, **29**, pp. 17–45 (1991).
38. 'The Cost-Benefit Analysis of Imprisonment', *Social Justice*, **17**, (no.4) pp. 49–75 (1990).
39. 'Comparing Criminal Career Models', *Criminology*, **30**, (1992) pp. 133–47.
40. 'The Gendering of Crime in Marxist Theory', in David F. Greenberg (ed.), *Crime and Capitalism* (2nd ed.), pp. 405–42 (Philadelphia: Temple University Press, 1993).
41. 'Contemporary Criminological Theories and Historical Data: The Case of London Crime', pp. 303–27 in Freda Adler and William S. Laufer (eds) *The Legacy of Anomie Theory: Advances in Theoretical Criminology* vol. 6 (Transaction Books, 1995).
42. 'The Historical Variability of the Age-Crime Relationship', *Journal of Quantitative Criminology*, **10**, (1994) pp. 361–73.
43. 'The Incapacitation of Criminal Opiate Users' (with Nancy J. Larkin), *Crime and Delinquency*, **44**, (1998) pp. 205–28.
44. 'Punishment, Division of Labor, and Social Solidarity', in William S. Laufer and Freda Adler (eds), *The Criminology of Criminal Law: Advances in Criminological Theory*, vol. 8 (1999) pp. 283–362.
45. 'The Weak Strength of Social Control Theory', *Crime and Delinquency*, **45**, (Jan. 1999) pp. 66–81.
46. 'Human Rights Violations and the Prison System', *Souls: A Critical Journal of Black Politics, Culture, and Society,* **2**(1), (Winter, 2000) pp. 70–71.
47. 'The Time Series Analysis of Crime Rates', *Journal of Quantitative Criminology*, **17**, (2001) pp. 291–327. [The entire issue of this journal is a symposium devoted to this paper].
48. 'Criminal Careers', pp. 65–67 in Eugene McLaughlin and John Muncie (eds), *Sage Dictionary of Criminology* (Sage, 2001).
49. '*Novus Ordo Saeclorum?' Punishment and Society,* **3**.1, (2001) pp. 81–93.
50. 'On Theory, Models, Model-Testing and Estimation', *Journal of Quantitative Criminology*, **17**, (2001) pp. 409–22.
51. 'State Prison Populations and Their Growth, 1971–1991', with Valerie West, *Criminology*, **39**, (2001) pp. 615–53. Reprinted in Nora V. Demleitner et al. (eds), *Sentencing Law and Policy* (Aspen Publishers, 2004).
52. 'Striking Out in Democracy', *Punishment and Society*, **4**, (2002) pp. 237–52.
53. 'The Generality of the Self-Control Theory of Crime', (with Robin Tamarelli and Margaret S. Kelley), pp. 49–94 in Elin Waring and David Weisburd (eds), *Crime and*

Social Organization. Advances in Criminological Theory, vol. 10 (New Brunswick, NJ: Transaction Books, 2002).

54. 'Justice and Criminal Justice', pp. 319–54 in Darnell F. Hawkins, Samuel L. Myers, Jr., and Randolph N. Stone (eds), *Crime Control and Social Justice: The Delicate Balance* (Greenwood Press, 2003).
55. 'Long-Term Trends in Crimes of Violence', *Criminology*, **41**.4 (November, 2003) pp. 601–12.
56. 'Criminological Research and Crime Control Policy: Not a Marriage Made in Heaven', *Criminology and Public Policy*, **5**.2 (May, 2006) pp. 203–12.
57. 'Age, Sex and Racial Distributions of Crime', pp. 38–48 in Erich Goode (ed.), *Out of Control: Assessing the General Theory of Crime* (Stanford University Press, 2008).
58. 'Siting the Death Penalty Internationally' (with Valerie West), *Law and Social Inquiry*, **33**(2) (2008) pp. 295–343.
59. 'A Comparison of Methods for Analyzing Criminological Panel Data' (with Julie Phillips), *Journal of Quantitative Criminology*, **24**.1 (March 2008) pp. 51–72.
60. 'More Fictions about Predictions', *Criminal Justice Ethics* (Summer/Fall 2008) pp. 64–81.
61. 'The Effectiveness of an Electronic Security Management System in a Privately-Owned Apartment Complex' (with Jeffrey Roush), Evaluation Review, 33 (Feb. 2009) pp. 3–26.
62. 'Longitudinal Criminology', Journal of Quantitative Criminology (Dec. 2010).

Name Index

For Product Safety Concerns and Information please contact our EU
representative GPSR@taylorandfrancis.com
Taylor & Francis Verlag GmbH, Kaufingerstraße 24, 80331 München, Germany

www.ingramcontent.com/pod-product-compliance
Lightning Source LLC
LaVergne TN
LVHW080802011026
849160LV00015B/1508

* 9 7 8 1 1 3 8 3 7 8 5 4 4 *